COMPILATION OF SELECTED
EMERGENCY MANAGEMENT RELATED LAWS

As amended through the 118th Congress.

Prepared By M. TWINCHEK

2025

Forward

T his Compilation of Selected United States laws related to Federal disaster preparedness, mitigation and response.

The materials included come from publicly available, open source information, prepared for the public by the Office of the Legislative Counsel of the U.S. House of Representatives and the Office of the Law Revision Counsel.

Items listed as a Statute Compilation do not appear in the U.S. Code or that have been classified to a title of the U.S. Code that has not been enacted into positive law. Each Statute Compilation incorporates the amendments made to the underlying statute since it was originally enacted and are current as of the date noted.

This compilation is not an official document and should not be cited as evidence of any law. The official version of Federal law is found in the United States Statutes at Large and in the U.S. Code, the legal effect of which is established in sections 112 and 204, respectively, of title 1, United States Code.

A special thanks is extended to the Office of Law Revision Counsel and the House Office of the Legislative Counsel for providing the U.S. Code and statute compilations; and to the Government Publications Office for hosting and making these available for use to the public. An additional thank you is offered to the staff of the House Committee who were gracious in responding to inquiries and providing background information on the legislation included. Questions and comments may be directed to:

M. Twinchek
Email: mtwinchek@outlook.com

Contents

FOUNDATIONAL EMERGENCY MANAGEMENT LAWS

ROBERT T. STAFFORD DISASTER RELIEF AND EMERGENCY ASSISTANCE ACT

PUBLIC LAW 93–288
AS AMENDED THROUGH P.L. 118–44

ROBERT T. STAFFORD DISASTER RELIEF AND EMERGENCY ASSISTANCE ACT

[Public Law 93–288; Approved May 22, 1974]

[As Amended Through P.L. 118–44, Enacted March 18, 2024]

AN ACT Entitled the Disaster Relief Act Amendments of 1974.

Be it enacted by the Senate and House of Representatives of the United States of America in Congress assembled,

SECTION 1. SHORT TITLE.

This Act may be cited as the "Robert T. Stafford Disaster Relief and Emergency Assistance Act".

[42 U.S.C. 5121 note]

TITLE I—FINDINGS, DECLARATIONS, AND DEFINITIONS

FINDINGS AND DECLARATIONS

SEC. 101. (a) The Congress hereby finds and declares that—

(1) because disasters often cause loss of life, human suffering, loss of income, and property loss and damage; and

(2) because disasters often disrupt the normal functioning of governments and communities, and adversely affect individuals and families with great severity; special measures, designed to assist the efforts of the affected States in expediting the rendering of aid, assistance, and emergency services, and the reconstruction and rehabilitation of devastated areas, are necessary.

(b) It is the intent of the Congress, by this Act, to provide an orderly and continuing means of assistance by the Federal Government to State and local governments in carrying out their responsibilities to alleviate the suffering and damage which result from such disasters by—

(1) revising and broadening the scope of existing disaster relief programs;

(2) encouraging the development of comprehensive disaster preparedness and assistance plans, programs, capabilities, and organizations by the States and by local governments;

(3) achieving greater coordination and responsiveness of disaster preparedness and relief programs;

(4) encouraging individuals, States, and local governments to protect themselves by obtaining insurance coverage to supplement or replace governmental assistance;

(5) encouraging hazard mitigation measures to reduce losses from disasters, including development of land use and construction regulations;

(6) providing Federal assistance programs for both public and private losses sustained in disasters; and

(7) identifying and improving the climate and natural hazard resilience of vulnerable communities.

[42 U.S.C. 5121]

DEFINITIONS

SEC. 102. As used in this Act—

(1) EMERGENCY.— Emergency means any occasion or instance for which, in the determination of the President, Federal assistance is needed to supplement State and local efforts and capabilities to save lives and to protect property and public health and safety, or to lessen or avert the threat of a catastrophe in any part of the United States.

(2) MAJOR DISASTER.— Major disaster means any natural catastrophe (including any hurricane, tornado, storm, high water, winddriven water, tidal wave, tsunami, earthquake, volcanic eruption, landslide, mudslide, snowstorm, or drought), or, regardless of cause, any fire, flood, or explosion, in any part of the United States, which in the determination of the President causes damage of sufficient severity and magnitude to warrant major disaster assistance under this Act to supplement the efforts and available resources of States, local governments, and disaster relief organizations in alleviating the damage, loss, hardship, or suffering caused thereby.

(3) United States means the fifty States, the District of Columbia, Puerto Rico, the Virgin Islands, Guam, American Samoa, and the Commonwealth of the Northern Mariana Islands.

(4) State means any State of the United States, the District of Columbia, Puerto Rico, the Virgin Islands, Guam, American Samoa, and the Commonwealth of the Northern Mariana Islands.

(5) Governor means the chief executive of any State.

(6) INDIAN TRIBAL GOVERNMENT.— The term Indian tribal government means the governing body of any Indian or Alaska Native tribe, band, nation, pueblo, village, or community that the Secretary of the Interior acknowledges to exist as an Indian tribe under the Federally Recognized Indian Tribe List Act of 1994 (25 U.S.C. 479a et seq.).

(7) INDIVIDUAL WITH A DISABILITY.— The term individual with a disability means an individual with a disability as defined in section 3(2) of the Americans with Disabilities Act of 1990 (42 U.S.C. 12102(2)).

(8) LOCAL GOVERNMENT.—The term local government means—

(A) a county, municipality, city, town, township, local public authority, school district, special district, intrastate district, council of governments (regardless of whether the council of governments is incorporated as a nonprofit corporation under State law), regional or interstate government entity, or agency or instrumentality of a local government;

(B) an Indian tribe or authorized tribal organization, or Alaska Native village or organization, that is not an Indian tribal government as defined in paragraph (6); and

(C) a rural community, unincorporated town or village, or other public entity, for which an application for assistance is made by a State or political subdivision of a State.

(9) Federal agency means any department, independent establishment, Government corporation, or other agency of the executive branch of the Federal Government, including the United States Postal Service, but shall not include the American National Red Cross.

(10) PUBLIC FACILITY.— Public facility means the following facilities owned by a State or local government:

(A) Any flood control, navigation, irrigation, reclamation, public power, sewage treatment and collection, water supply and distribution, watershed development, or airport facility.

(B) Any non-Federal-aid street, road, or highway.

(C) Any other public building, structure, or system, including those used for educational, recreational, or cultural purposes.

(D) Any park.

(11) PRIVATE NONPROFIT FACILITY.—

(A) IN GENERAL.— The term private nonprofit facility means private nonprofit educational (without regard to the religious character of the facility), center-based childcare, utility, irrigation, emergency, medical, rehabilitational, and temporary or permanent custodial care facilities (including those for the aged and disabled) and facilities on Indian reservations, as defined by the President.

(B) ADDITIONAL FACILITIES.— In addition to the facilities described in subparagraph (A), the term private nonprofit facility includes any private nonprofit facility that provides essential social services to the general public (including museums, zoos, performing arts facilities, community arts centers, community centers, libraries, homeless shelters, senior citizen centers, rehabilitation facilities, shelter workshops, food banks, broadcasting facilities, houses of worship, and facilities that provide health and safety services of a governmental nature), as defined by the President. No house of worship may be excluded from this definition because leadership or membership in the organization operating the house of worship is limited to persons who share a religious faith or practice.

(12) CHIEF EXECUTIVE.— The term Chief Executive means the person who is the

Chief, Chairman, Governor, President, or similar executive official of an Indian tribal government.

[42 U.S.C. 5122]

SEC. 103. REFERENCES.

Except as otherwise specifically provided, any reference in this Act to State and local, State or local, State, and local, State, or local, or State, local (including plurals) with respect to governments or officials and any reference to a local government in sections 406(d)(3) and 417 is deemed to refer also to Indian tribal governments and officials, as appropriate.

[42 U.S.C. 5123]

TITLE II—DISASTER PREPAREDNESS AND MITIGATION ASSISTANCE

FEDERAL AND STATE DISASTER PREPAREDNESS PROGRAMS

SEC. 201. (a) The President is authorized to establish a program of disaster preparedness that utilizes services of all appropriate agencies and includes—

(1) preparation of disaster preparedness plans for mitigation, warning, emergency operations, rehabilitation, and recovery;

(2) training and exercises;

(3) postdisaster critiques and evaluations;

(4) annual review of programs;

(5) coordination of Federal, State, and local preparedness programs;

(6) application of science and technology;

(7) research.

(b) The President shall provide technical assistance to the States in developing comprehensive plans and practicable programs for preparation against disasters, including hazard reduction, avoidance, and mitigation; for assistance to individuals, businesses, and State and local governments following such disasters; and for recovery of damaged or destroyed public and private facilities.

(c) Upon application by a State, the President is authorized to make grants, not to exceed in the aggregate to such State $250,000, for the development of plans, programs, and capabilities for disaster preparedness and prevention. Such grants shall be applied for within one year from the date of enactment of this Act. Any State desiring financial assistance under this section shall designate or create an agency to plan and administer such a disaster preparedness program, and shall, through such agency, submit a State plan to the President, which shall—

(1) set forth a comprehensive and detailed State program for preparation against and assistance following, emergencies and major disasters, including provisions for assistance to individuals, businesses, and local governments; and

(2) include provisions for appointment and training of appropriate staffs, formulation of necessary regulations and procedures and conduct of required

exercises.

(d)   The President is authorized to make grants not to exceed 50 per centum of the cost of improving, maintaining and updating State disaster assistance plans, including evaluations of natural hazards and development of the programs and actions required to mitigate such hazards, except that no such grant shall exceed $50,000 per annum to any State.

[42 U.S.C. 5131]

DISASTER WARNINGS

SEC. 202.   (a)   The President shall insure that all appropriate Federal agencies are prepared to issue warnings of disasters to State and local officials.

(b)   The President shall direct appropriate Federal agencies to provide technical assistance to State and local governments to insure that timely and effective disaster warning is provided.

(c)   The President is authorized to utilize or to make available to Federal, State, and local agencies the facilities of the civil defense communications system established and maintained pursuant to section 611(c) of this Act or any other Federal communications system for the purpose of providing warning to governmental authorities and the civilian population in areas endangered by disasters.

(d)   The President is authorized to enter into agreements with the officers or agents of any private or commercial communications systems who volunteer the use of their systems on a reimbursable or nonreimbursable basis for the purpose of providing warning to governmental authorities and the civilian population endangered by disasters.

[42 U.S.C. 5132]

SEC. 203. PREDISASTER HAZARD MITIGATION.

(a) DEFINITION OF SMALL IMPOVERISHED COMMUNITY.— In this section, the term small impoverished community means a community of 3,000 or fewer individuals that is economically disadvantaged, as determined by the State in which the community is located and based on criteria established by the President.

(b) ESTABLISHMENT OF PROGRAM.— The President may establish a program to provide technical and financial assistance to States and local governments to assist in the implementation of predisaster hazard mitigation measures that are cost-effective and are designed to reduce injuries, loss of life, and damage and destruction of property, including damage to critical services and facilities under the jurisdiction of the States or local governments.

(c) APPROVAL BY PRESIDENT.— If the President determines that a State or local government has identified natural disaster hazards in areas under its jurisdiction and has demonstrated the ability to form effective public-private natural disaster hazard mitigation partnerships, the President, using amounts in the National Public Infrastructure Predisaster Mitigation Fund established under subsection (i) (referred to in this section as the Fund), may provide technical and financial assistance to the State or local government to be used in accordance with subsection (e).

(d) STATE RECOMMENDATIONS.—

(1) IN GENERAL.—

(A) RECOMMENDATIONS.— The Governor of each State may recommend to the President not fewer than five local governments to receive assistance under this section.

(B) DEADLINE FOR SUBMISSION.— The recommendations under subparagraph (A) shall be submitted to the President not later than October 1, 2001, and each October 1st thereafter or such later date in the year as the President may establish.

(C) CRITERIA.— In making recommendations under subparagraph (A), a Governor shall consider the criteria specified in subsection (g).

(2) USE.—

(A) IN GENERAL.— Except as provided in subparagraph (B), in providing assistance to local governments under this section, the President shall select from local governments recommended by the Governors under this subsection.

(B) EXTRAORDINARY CIRCUMSTANCES.— In providing assistance to local governments under this section, the President may select a local government that has not been recommended by a Governor under this subsection if the President determines that extraordinary circumstances justify the selection and that making the selection will further the purpose of this section.

(3) EFFECT OF FAILURE TO NOMINATE.— If a Governor of a State fails to submit recommendations under this subsection in a timely manner, the President may select, subject to the criteria specified in subsection (g), any local governments of the State to receive assistance under this section.

(e) USES OF TECHNICAL AND FINANCIAL ASSISTANCE.—

(1) IN GENERAL.—Technical and financial assistance provided under this section—

(A) shall be used by States and local governments principally to implement predisaster hazard mitigation measures that are cost-effective and are described in proposals approved by the President under this section; and

(B) may be used—

(i) to support effective public-private natural disaster hazard mitigation partnerships;

(ii) to improve the assessment of a community's vulnerability to natural hazards;

(iii) to establish hazard mitigation priorities, and an appropriate hazard mitigation plan, for a community; or

(iv) to establish and carry out enforcement activities and implement the latest published editions of relevant consensus-based codes, specifications, and standards that incorporate the latest hazard-resistant designs and establish minimum acceptable criteria for the design, construction, and maintenance of residential structures and facilities that may be eligible for assistance under this Act for the purpose of protecting the health, safety, and general welfare of the buildings' users against disasters.

(2) DISSEMINATION.— A State or local government may use not more than 10 percent of the financial assistance received by the State or local government under this section for a fiscal year to fund activities to disseminate information regarding cost-effective mitigation technologies.

(f) ALLOCATION OF FUNDS.—

(1) IN GENERAL.— The President shall award financial assistance under this section on a competitive basis for mitigation activities that are cost effective and in accordance with the criteria in subsection (g).

(2) MINIMUM AND MAXIMUM AMOUNTS.—In providing financial assistance under this section, the President shall ensure that the amount of financial assistance made available to a State (including amounts made available to local governments of the State) for a fiscal year—

(A) is not less than the lesser of—

(i) $575,000; or

(ii) the amount that is equal to 1 percent of the total funds appropriated to carry out this section for the fiscal year; and

(B) does not exceed the amount that is equal to 15 percent of the total funds appropriated to carry out this section for the fiscal year.

(3) REDISTRIBUTION OF UNOBLIGATED AMOUNTS.—The President may—

(A) withdraw amounts of financial assistance made available to a State (including amounts made available to local governments of a State) under this subsection that remain unobligated by the end of the third fiscal year after the fiscal year for which the amounts were allocated; and

(B) in the fiscal year following a fiscal year in which amounts were withdrawn under subparagraph (A), add the amounts to any other amounts available to be awarded on a competitive basis pursuant to paragraph (1).

(g) CRITERIA FOR ASSISTANCE AWARDS.—In determining whether to provide technical and financial assistance to a State or local government under this section, the President shall provide financial assistance only in States that have received a major disaster declaration in the previous 7 years, or to any Indian tribal government located partially or entirely within the boundaries of such States, and take into account—

(1) the extent and nature of the hazards to be mitigated;

(2) the degree of commitment of the State or local government to reduce damages from future natural disasters;

(3) the degree of commitment by the State or local government to support ongoing non-Federal support for the hazard mitigation measures to be carried out using the technical and financial assistance;

(4) the extent to which the hazard mitigation measures to be carried out using the technical and financial assistance contribute to the mitigation goals and priorities established by the State;

(5)   the extent to which the technical and financial assistance is consistent with other assistance provided under this Act;

(6)   the extent to which prioritized, cost-effective mitigation activities that produce meaningful and definable outcomes are clearly identified;

(7)   if the State or local government has submitted a mitigation plan under section 322, the extent to which the activities identified under paragraph (6) are consistent with the mitigation plan;

(8)   the opportunity to fund activities that maximize net benefits to society;

(9)   the extent to which assistance will fund mitigation activities in small impoverished communities;

(10)   the extent to which the State, local, Indian tribal, or territorial government has facilitated the adoption and enforcement of the latest published editions of relevant consensus-based codes, specifications, and standards, including amendments made by State, local, Indian tribal, or territorial governments during the adoption process that incorporate the latest hazard-resistant designs and establish criteria for the design, construction, and maintenance of residential structures and facilities that may be eligible for assistance under this Act for the purpose of protecting the health, safety, and general welfare of the buildings' users against disasters;

(11)   the extent to which the assistance will fund activities that increase the level of resiliency; and

(12)   such other criteria as the President establishes in consultation with State and local governments.

(h) FEDERAL SHARE.—

(1) IN GENERAL.— Financial assistance provided under this section may contribute up to 75 percent of the total cost of mitigation activities approved by the President.

(2) SMALL IMPOVERISHED COMMUNITIES.— Notwithstanding paragraph (1), the President may contribute up to 90 percent of the total cost of a mitigation activity carried out in a small impoverished community.

(i) NATIONAL PUBLIC INFRASTRUCTURE PREDISASTER MITIGATION ASSISTANCE.—

(1) IN GENERAL.— The President may set aside from the Disaster Relief Fund, with respect to each major disaster, an amount equal to 6 percent of the estimated aggregate amount of the grants to be made pursuant to sections 403, 406, 407, 408, 410, 416, and 428 for the major disaster in order to provide technical and financial assistance under this section and such set aside shall be deemed to be related to activities carried out pursuant to major disasters under this Act.

(2) ESTIMATED AGGREGATE AMOUNT.— Not later than 180 days after each major disaster declaration pursuant to this Act, the estimated aggregate amount of grants for purposes of paragraph (1) shall be determined by the President and such estimated amount need not be reduced, increased, or changed due to variations in estimates.

(3) NO REDUCTION IN AMOUNTS.— The amount set aside pursuant to paragraph (1) shall not reduce the amounts otherwise made available for sections 403, 404, 406, 407, 408, 410, 416, and 428 under this Act.

(j) MULTIHAZARD ADVISORY MAPS.—

(1) DEFINITION OF MULTIHAZARD ADVISORY MAP.— In this subsection, the term multihazard advisory map means a map on which hazard data concerning each type of natural disaster is identified simultaneously for the purpose of showing areas of hazard overlap.

(2) DEVELOPMENT OF MAPS.— In consultation with States, local governments, and appropriate Federal agencies, the President shall develop multihazard advisory maps for areas, in not fewer than five States, that are subject to commonly recurring natural hazards (including flooding, hurricanes and severe winds, and seismic events).

(3) USE OF TECHNOLOGY.— In developing multihazard advisory maps under this subsection, the President shall use, to the maximum extent practicable, the most cost-effective and efficient technology available.

(4) USE OF MAPS.—

(A) ADVISORY NATURE.— The multihazard advisory maps shall be considered to be advisory and shall not require the development of any new policy by, or impose any new policy on, any government or private entity.

(B) AVAILABILITY OF MAPS.—The multihazard advisory maps shall be made available to the appropriate State and local governments for the purposes of—

(i) informing the general public about the risks of natural hazards in the areas described in paragraph (2);

(ii) supporting the activities described in subsection (e); and

(iii) other public uses.

(k) REPORT ON FEDERAL AND STATE ADMINISTRATION.— Not later than 18 months after the date of the enactment of this section, the President, in consultation with State and local governments, shall submit to Congress a report evaluating efforts to implement this section and recommending a process for transferring greater authority and responsibility for administering the assistance program established under this section to capable States.

(l) PROHIBITION ON EARMARKS.—

(1) DEFINITION.— In this subsection, the term congressionally directed spending means a statutory provision or report language included primarily at the request of a Senator or a Member, Delegate or Resident Commissioner of the House of Representatives providing, authorizing, or recommending a specific amount of discretionary budget authority, credit authority, or other spending authority for a contract, loan, loan guarantee, grant, loan authority, or other expenditure with or to an entity, or targeted to a specific State, locality, or Congressional district, other than through a statutory or administrative formula-driven or competitive award process.

(2) PROHIBITION.— None of the funds appropriated or otherwise made available to carry out this section may be used for congressionally directed spending.

(3) CERTIFICATION TO CONGRESS.— The Administrator of the Federal Emergency Management Agency shall submit to Congress a certification regarding whether all financial assistance under this section was awarded in accordance with this section.

[42 U.S.C. 5133]

SEC. 204. INTERAGENCY TASK FORCE.

(a) IN GENERAL.— The President shall establish a Federal interagency task force for the purpose of coordinating the implementation of predisaster hazard mitigation programs administered by the Federal Government.

(b) CHAIRPERSON.— The Administrator of the Federal Emergency Management Agency shall serve as the chairperson of the task force.

(c) MEMBERSHIP.—The membership of the task force shall include representatives of—

(1)   relevant Federal agencies;

(2)   State and local government organizations (including Indian tribes); and

(3)   the American Red Cross.

[42 U.S.C. 5134]

SEC. 205. GRANTS TO ENTITIES FOR ESTABLISHMENT OF HAZARD MITIGATION REVOLVING LOAN FUNDS.

(a) GENERAL AUTHORITY.—

(1) IN GENERAL.—The Administrator may enter into agreements with eligible entities to make capitalization grants to such entities for the establishment of hazard mitigation revolving loan funds (referred to in this section as entity loan funds) for providing funding assistance to local governments to carry out eligible projects under this section to reduce disaster risks for homeowners, businesses, nonprofit organizations, and communities in order to decrease—

(A)   the loss of life and property;

(B)   the cost of insurance; and

(C)   Federal disaster payments.

(2) AGREEMENTS.—Any agreement entered into under this section shall require the participating entity to—

(A)   comply with the requirements of this section; and

(B)   use accounting, audit, and fiscal procedures conforming to generally accepted accounting standards.

(b) APPLICATION.—

(1) IN GENERAL.—To be eligible to receive a capitalization grant under this section, an eligible entity shall submit to the Administrator an application that includes the following:

(A)   Project proposals comprised of local government hazard mitigation projects, on the condition that the entity provides public notice not less than 6 weeks prior to the submission of an application.

(B)   An assessment of recurring major disaster vulnerabilities impacting the entity that demonstrates a risk to life and property.

(C)   A description of how the hazard mitigation plan of the entity has or has not taken the vulnerabilities described in subparagraph (B) into account.

(D)   A description about how the projects described in subparagraph (A) could conform with the hazard mitigation plan of the entity and of the unit of local government.

(E)   A proposal of the systematic and regional approach to achieve resilience in a vulnerable area, including impacts to river basins, river corridors, watersheds, estuaries, bays, coastal regions, micro-basins, micro-watersheds, ecosystems, and areas at risk of earthquakes, tsunamis, droughts, severe storms, and wildfires, including the wildland-urban interface.

(2) TECHNICAL ASSISTANCE.— The Administrator shall provide technical assistance to eligible entities for applications under this section.

(c) ENTITY LOAN FUND.—

(1) ESTABLISHMENT OF FUND.— An entity that receives a capitalization grant under this section shall establish an entity loan fund that complies with the requirements of this subsection.

(2) FUND MANAGEMENT.—Except as provided in paragraph (3), entity loan funds shall—

(A)   be administered by the agency responsible for emergency management; and

(B) include only—

(i)   funds provided by a capitalization grant under this section;

(ii)   repayments of loans under this section to the entity loan fund; and

(iii)   interest earned on amounts in the entity loan fund.

(3) ADMINISTRATION.—A participating entity may combine the financial administration of the entity loan fund of such entity with the financial administration of any other revolving fund established by such entity if the Administrator determines that—

(A)   the capitalization grant, entity share, repayments of loans, and interest earned on amounts in the entity loan fund are accounted for separately from other amounts in the revolving fund; and

(B)   the authority to establish assistance priorities and carry out oversight activities remains in the control of the entity agency responsible for emergency management.

(4) ENTITY SHARE OF FUNDS.—

(A) IN GENERAL.— On or before the date on which a participating entity receives a capitalization grant under this section, the entity shall deposit into the entity loan fund of such entity, an amount equal to not less than 10 percent of the amount of the capitalization grant.

(B) REDUCED GRANT.— If, with respect to a capitalization grant under this section, a participating entity deposits in the entity loan fund of the entity an amount that is less than 10 percent of the total amount of the capitalization grant that the participating entity would otherwise receive, the Administrator shall reduce the amount of the capitalization grant received by the entity to the amount that is 10 times the amount so deposited.

(d) APPORTIONMENT.—

(1) IN GENERAL.— Except as otherwise provided by this subsection, the Administrator shall apportion funds made available to carry out this section to entities that have entered into an agreement under subsection (a)(2) in amounts as determined by the Administrator.

(2) RESERVATION OF FUNDS.—The Administrator shall reserve not more than 2.5 percent of the amount made available to carry out this section for the Federal Emergency Management Agency for—

(A) administrative costs incurred in carrying out this section; and

(B) providing technical assistance to participating entities under subsection (b)(2).

(3) PRIORITY.—In the apportionment of capitalization grants under this subsection, the Administrator shall give priority to entity applications under subsection (b) that—

(A) propose projects increasing resilience and reducing risk of harm to natural and built infrastructure;

(B) involve a partnership between two or more eligible entities to carry out a project or similar projects;

(C) take into account regional impacts of hazards on river basins, river corridors, micro-watersheds, macro-watersheds, estuaries, lakes, bays, and coastal regions and areas at risk of earthquakes, tsunamis, droughts, severe storms, and wildfires, including the wildland-urban interface; or

(D) propose projects for the resilience of major economic sectors or critical national infrastructure, including ports, global commodity supply chain assets (located within an entity or within the jurisdiction of local governments and Tribal governments), power and water production and distribution centers, and bridges and waterways essential to interstate commerce.

(e) ENVIRONMENTAL REVIEW OF REVOLVING LOAN FUND PROJECTS.— The Administrator may delegate to a participating entity all of the responsibilities for environmental review, decision making, and action pursuant to the National Environmental Policy Act of 1969 (42 U.S.C. 4321 et seq.), and other applicable Federal environmental laws including the Endangered Species Act of 1973 (16 U.S.C. 1531 et seq.) and the National Historic Preservation Act of 1966 (54 U.S.C. 300101 et seq.) that would apply to the Administrator were the Administrator to undertake projects under this section as Federal projects so long as the participating entity carries out such responsibilities in the same manner and subject to the same requirements as if the Administrator carried out such responsibilities.

(f) USE OF FUNDS.—

(1) TYPES OF ASSISTANCE.—Amounts deposited in an entity loan fund, including loan repayments and interest earned on such amounts, may be used—

(A) to make loans, on the condition that—

(i)   such loans are made at an interest rate of not more than 1 percent;

(ii) annual principal and interest payments will commence not later than 1 year after completion of any project and all loans made under this subparagraph will be fully amortized—

(I)   not later than 20 years after the date on which the project is completed; or

(II)   for projects in a low-income geographic area, not later than 30 years after the date on which the project is completed and not longer than the expected design life of the project;

(iii)   the loan recipient of a loan under this subparagraph establishes a dedicated source of revenue for repayment of the loan;

(iv)   the loan recipient of a loan under this subparagraph has a hazard mitigation plan that has been approved by the Administrator; and

(v)   the entity loan fund will be credited with all payments of principal and interest on all loans made under this subparagraph;

(B)   for mitigation efforts, in addition to mitigation planning under section 322 not to exceed 10 percent of the capitalization grants made to the participating entity in a fiscal year;

(C)   for the reasonable costs of administering the fund and conducting activities under this section, except that such amounts shall not exceed $100,000 per year, 2 percent of the capitalization grants made to the participating entity in a fiscal year, or 1 percent of the value of the entity loan fund, whichever amount is greatest, plus the amount of any fees collected by the entity for such purpose regardless of the source; and

(D)   to earn interest on the entity loan fund.

(2) PROHIBITION ON DETERMINATION THAT LOAN IS A DUPLICATION.— In carrying out this section, the Administrator may not determine that a loan is a duplication of assistance or programs under this Act.

(3) PROJECTS AND ACTIVITIES ELIGIBLE FOR ASSISTANCE.—Except as provided in this subsection, a participating entity may use funds in the entity loan fund to provide financial assistance for projects or activities that mitigate the impacts of natural hazards including—

(A)   drought and prolonged episodes of intense heat;

(B)   severe storms, including hurricanes, tornados, wind storms, cyclones, and severe winter storms;

(C)   wildfires;

(D)   earthquakes;

(E) flooding, including the construction, repair, or replacement of a non-Federal levee or other flood control structure, provided that the Administrator, in consultation with the Army Corps of Engineers (if appropriate), requires an eligible entity to determine that such levee or structure is designed, constructed, and maintained in accordance with sound engineering practices and standards equivalent to the purpose for which such levee or structure is intended;

(F) shoreline erosion;

(G) high water levels; and

(H) storm surges.

(4) ZONING AND LAND USE PLANNING CHANGES.—A participating entity may use not more than 10 percent of a capitalization grant under this section to enable units of local government to implement zoning and land use planning changes focused on—

(A) the development and improvement of zoning and land use codes that incentivize and encourage low-impact development, resilient wildland-urban interface land management and development, natural infrastructure, green stormwater management, conservation areas adjacent to floodplains, implementation of watershed or greenway master plans, and reconnection of floodplains;

(B) the study and creation of agricultural risk compensation districts where there is a desire to remove or set-back levees protecting highly developed agricultural land to mitigate for flooding, allowing agricultural producers to receive compensation for assuming greater flood risk that would alleviate flood exposure to population centers and areas with critical national infrastructure;

(C) the study and creation of land use incentives that reward developers for greater reliance on low impact development stormwater best management practices, exchange density increases for increased open space and improvement of neighborhood catch basins to mitigate urban flooding, reward developers for including and augmenting natural infrastructure adjacent to and around building projects without reliance on increased sprawl, and reward developers for addressing wildfire ignition; and

(D) the study and creation of an erosion response plan that accommodates river, lake, forest, plains, and ocean shoreline retreating or bluff stabilization due to increased flooding and disaster impacts.

(5) ESTABLISHING AND CARRYING OUT BUILDING CODE ENFORCEMENT.— A participating entity may use capitalization grants under this section to enable units of local government to establish and carry out the latest published editions of relevant building codes, specifications, and standards for the purpose of protecting the health, safety, and general welfare of the building's users against disasters and natural hazards.

(6) ADMINISTRATIVE AND TECHNICAL COSTS.—For each fiscal year, a participating entity may use the amount described in paragraph (1)(C) to—

(A) pay the reasonable costs of administering the programs under this section, including the cost of establishing an entity loan fund; and

(B) provide technical assistance to recipients of financial assistance from the entity loan fund, on the condition that such technical assistance does not exceed 5 percent of the capitalization grant made to such entity.

(7) LIMITATION FOR SINGLE PROJECTS.— A participating entity may not provide an amount equal to or more than $5,000,000 to a single hazard mitigation project.

(8) REQUIREMENTS.— For fiscal year 2022 and each fiscal year thereafter, the requirements of subchapter IV of chapter 31 of title 40, United States Code, shall apply to the construction of projects carried out in whole or in part with assistance made available by an entity loan fund authorized by this section.

(g) INTENDED USE PLANS.—

(1) IN GENERAL.— After providing for public comment and review, and consultation with appropriate government agencies of the State or Indian tribal government, Federal agencies, and interest groups, each participating entity shall annually prepare and submit to the Administrator a plan identifying the intended uses of the entity loan fund.

(2) CONTENTS OF PLAN.—An entity intended use plan prepared under paragraph (1) shall include—

(A) the integration of entity planning efforts, including entity hazard mitigation plans and other programs and initiatives relating to mitigation of major disasters carried out by such entity;

(B) an explanation of the mitigation and resiliency benefits the entity intends to achieve by—

(i) reducing future damage and loss associated with hazards;

(ii) reducing the number of severe repetitive loss structures and repetitive loss structures in the entity;

(iii) decreasing the number of insurance claims in the entity from injuries resulting from major disasters or other natural hazards; and

(iv) increasing the rating under the community rating system under section 1315(b) of the National Flood Insurance Act of 1968 (42 U.S.C. 4022(b)) for communities in the entity;

(C) information on the availability of, and application process for, financial assistance from the entity loan fund of such entity;

(D) the criteria and methods established for the distribution of funds;

(E) the amount of financial assistance that the entity anticipates apportioning;

(F) the expected terms of the assistance provided from the entity loan fund; and

(G) a description of the financial status of the entity loan fund, including short-term and long-term goals for the fund.

(h) AUDITS, REPORTS, PUBLICATIONS, AND OVERSIGHT.—

(1) BIENNIAL ENTITY AUDIT AND REPORT.—Beginning not later than the last day of the second fiscal year after the receipt of payments under this section, and biennially thereafter, any participating entity shall—

(A) conduct an audit of the entity loan fund established under subsection (c); and

(B) provide to the Administrator a report including—

(i) the result of any such audit; and

(ii) a review of the effectiveness of the entity loan fund of the entity with respect to meeting the goals and intended benefits described in the intended use plan submitted by the entity under subsection (g).

(2) PUBLICATION.—A participating entity shall publish and periodically update information about all projects receiving funding from the entity loan fund of such entity, including—

(A) the location of the project;

(B) the type and amount of assistance provided from the entity loan fund;

(C) the expected funding schedule; and

(D) the anticipated date of completion of the project.

(3) OVERSIGHT.—

(A) IN GENERAL.— The Administrator shall, at least every 4 years, conduct reviews and audits as may be determined necessary or appropriate by the Administrator to carry out the objectives of this section and determine the effectiveness of the fund in reducing natural hazard risk.

(B) GAO REQUIREMENTS.— A participating entity shall conduct audits under paragraph (1) in accordance with the auditing procedures of the Government Accountability Office, including generally accepted government auditing standards.

(C) RECOMMENDATIONS BY ADMINISTRATOR.— The Administrator may at any time make recommendations for or require specific changes to an entity loan fund in order to improve the effectiveness of the fund.

(i) REGULATIONS OR GUIDANCE.—The Administrator shall issue such regulations or guidance as are necessary to—

(1) ensure that each participating entity uses funds as efficiently as possible;

(2) reduce waste, fraud, and abuse to the maximum extent possible; and

(3) require any party that receives funds directly or indirectly under this section, including a participating entity and a recipient of amounts from an entity loan fund, to use procedures with respect to the management of the funds that conform to generally accepted accounting standards.

(j) WAIVER AUTHORITY.—Until such time as the Administrator issues final regulations to implement this section, the Administrator may—

(1) waive notice and comment rulemaking, if the Administrator determines the waiver is necessary to expeditiously implement this section; and

(2) provide capitalization grants under this section as a pilot program.

(k) LIABILITY PROTECTIONS.— The Agency shall not be liable for any claim based on the exercise or performance of, or the failure to exercise or perform, a discretionary function or duty by the Agency, or an employee of the Agency in carrying out this section.

(l) GAO REPORT.—Not later than 1 year after the date on which the first entity loan fund is established under subsection (c), the Comptroller General of the United States shall submit to the Committee on Homeland Security and Governmental Affairs of the Senate and the Committee on Transportation and Infrastructure of the House of Representatives a report that examines—

(1) the appropriateness of regulations and guidance issued by the Administrator for the program, including any oversight of the program;

(2) a description of the number of the entity loan funds established, the projects funded from such entity loan funds, and the extent to which projects funded by the loan funds adhere to any applicable hazard mitigation plans;

(3) the effectiveness of the entity loan funds to lower disaster related costs; and

(4) recommendations for improving the administration of entity loan funds.

(m) DEFINITIONS.—In this section, the following definitions apply:

(1) ADMINISTRATOR.— The term Administrator means the Administrator of the Federal Emergency Management Agency.

(2) AGENCY.— The term Agency means the Federal Emergency Management Agency.

(3) ELIGIBLE ENTITY.— The term eligible entity means a State or an Indian tribal government that has received a major disaster declaration pursuant to section 401.

(4) HAZARD MITIGATION PLAN.— The term hazard mitigation plan means a mitigation plan submitted under section 322.

(5) LOW-INCOME GEOGRAPHIC AREA.— The term low-income geographic area means an area described in paragraph (1) or (2) of section 301(a) of the Public Works and Economic Development Act of 1965 (42 U.S.C. 3161(a)).

(6) PARTICIPATING ENTITY.— The term participating entity means an eligible entity that has entered into an agreement under this section.

(7) REPETITIVE LOSS STRUCTURE.— The term repetitive loss structure has the meaning given the term in section 1370 of the National Flood Insurance Act of 1968 (42 U.S.C. 4121).

(8) SEVERE REPETITIVE LOSS STRUCTURE.— The term severe repetitive loss structure has the meaning given the term in section 1366(h) of the National Flood Insurance Act of 1968 (42 U.S.C. 4104c(h)).

(9) WILDLAND-URBAN INTERFACE.— The term wildland-urban interface has the meaning given the term in section 101 of the Healthy Forests Restoration Act of 2003 (16 U.S.C. 6511).

(n) AUTHORIZATION OF APPROPRIATIONS.— There are authorized to be appropriated $100,000,000 for each of fiscal years 2022 through 2023 to carry out this section.

[42 U.S.C. 5135]

SEC. 206. NATURAL HAZARD RISK ASSESSMENT.

(a) DEFINITIONS.—In this section:

(1) COMMUNITY DISASTER RESILIENCE ZONE.— The term community disaster resilience zone means a census tract designated by the President under subsection (d)(1).

(2) ELIGIBLE ENTITY.—The term eligible entity means—

(A)   a State;

(B)   an Indian tribal government; or

(C)   a local government.

(b) PRODUCTS.—The President shall continue to maintain a natural hazard assessment program that develops and maintains products that—

(1)   are available to the public; and

(2)   define natural hazard risk across the United States.

(c) FEATURES.—The products maintained under subsection (b) shall, for lands within States and areas under the jurisdiction of Indian tribal governments—

(1)   show the risk of natural hazards; and

(2) include ratings and data for—

(A)   loss exposure, including population equivalence, buildings, and agriculture;

(B)   social vulnerability;

(C)   community resilience; and

(D)   any other element determined by the President.

(d) COMMUNITY DISASTER RESILIENCE ZONES DESIGNATION.—

(1) IN GENERAL.—Not later than 30 days after the date on which the President makes the update and enhancement required under subsection (e)(4), and not less frequently than every 5 years thereafter, the President shall identify and designate community disaster resilience zones, which shall be—

(A)   the 50 census tracts assigned the highest individual hazard risk ratings; and

(B)   subject to paragraph (3), in each State, not less than 1 percent of census tracts that are assigned high individual risk ratings.

(2) RISK RATINGS.—In carrying out paragraph (1), the President shall use census tract risk ratings derived from a product maintained under subsection (b) that—

(A) reflect—

(i) high levels of individual hazard risk ratings based on an assessment of the intersection of—

(I)   loss to population equivalence;

22

(II) building value; and

(III) agriculture value;

(ii) high social vulnerability ratings and low community resilience ratings; and

(iii) any other elements determined by the President; and

(B) reflect the principal natural hazard risks identified for the respective census tracts.

(3) GEOGRAPHIC BALANCE.—In identifying and designating the community disaster resilience zones described in paragraph (1)(B)—

(A) for the purpose of achieving geographic balance, when applicable, the President shall consider making designations in coastal, inland, urban, suburban, and rural areas; and

(B) the President shall include census tracts on Tribal lands located within a State.

(4) DURATION.— The designation of a community disaster resilience zone under paragraph (1) shall be effective for a period of not less than 5 years.

(e) REVIEW AND UPDATE.—Not later than 180 days after the date of enactment of the Community Disaster Resilience Zones Act of 2022, and not less frequently than every 5 years thereafter, the President shall—

(1) with respect to any product that is a natural hazard risk assessment—

(A) review the underlying methodology of the product; and

(B) receive public input on the methodology and data used for the product;

(2) consider including additional data in any product that is a natural hazard risk assessment, such as—

(A) the most recent census tract data;

(B) data from the American Community Survey of the Bureau of the Census, a successor survey, a similar survey, or another data source, including data by census tract on housing characteristics and income;

(C) information relating to development, improvements, and hazard mitigation measures;

(D) data that assesses past and future loss exposure, including analysis on the effects of a changing climate on future loss exposure;

(E) data from the Resilience Analysis and Planning Tool of the Federal Emergency Management Agency; and

(F) other information relevant to prioritizing areas that have—

(i) high risk levels of—

(I) natural hazard loss exposure, including population equivalence, buildings, infrastructure, and agriculture; and

(II) social vulnerability; and

(ii)   low levels of community resilience;

(3)   make publicly available any changes in methodology or data used to inform an update to a product maintained under subsection (b); and

(4)   update and enhance the products maintained under subsection (b), as necessary.

(f) NATURAL HAZARD RISK ASSESSMENT INSIGHTS.—In determining additional data to include in products that are natural hazard risk assessments under subsection (e)(2), the President shall consult with, at a minimum—

(1)   the Administrator of the Federal Emergency Management Agency;

(2)   the Secretary of Agriculture and the Chief of the Forest Service;

(3)   the Secretary of Commerce, the Administrator of the National Oceanic and Atmospheric Administration, the Director of the Bureau of the Census, and the Director of the National Institute of Standards and Technology;

(4)   the Secretary of Defense and the Commanding Officer of the United States Army Corps of Engineers;

(5)   the Administrator of the Environmental Protection Agency;

(6)   the Secretary of the Interior and the Director of the United States Geological Survey;

(7)   the Secretary of Housing and Urban Development; and

(8)   the Director of the Federal Housing Finance Agency.

(g) COMMUNITY DISASTER RESILIENCE ZONE.— With respect to financial assistance provided under section 203(i) to perform a resilience or mitigation project within, or that primarily benefits, a community disaster resilience zone, the President may increase the amount of the Federal share described under section 203(h) to not more than 90 percent of the total cost of the resilience or mitigation project.

(h) RESILIENCE OR MITIGATION PROJECT PLANNING ASSISTANCE.—

(1) IN GENERAL.— The President may provide financial, technical, or other assistance under this title to an eligible entity that plans to perform a resilience or mitigation project within, or that primarily benefits, a community disaster resilience zone.

(2) PURPOSE.— The purpose of assistance provided under paragraph (1) shall be to carry out activities in preparation for a resilience or mitigation project or seek an evaluation and certification under subsection (i)(2) for a resilience or mitigation project before the date on which permanent work of the resilience or mitigation project begins.

(3) APPLICATION.— If required by the President, an eligible entity seeking assistance under paragraph (1) shall submit an application in accordance with subsection (i)(1).

(4) FUNDING.— In providing assistance under paragraph (1), the President may use amounts set aside under section 203(i).

(i) COMMUNITY DISASTER RESILIENCE ZONE PROJECT APPLICATIONS.—

(1) IN GENERAL.— If required by the President or other Federal law, an eligible entity shall submit to the President an application at such time, in such manner, and containing or accompanied by such information as the President may reasonably require.

(2) EVALUATION AND CERTIFICATION.—

(A) IN GENERAL.—Not later than 120 days after the date on which an eligible entity submits an application under paragraph (1), the President shall evaluate the application to determine whether the resilience or mitigation project that the entity plans to perform within, or that primarily benefits, a community disaster resilience zone—

(i) is designed to reduce injuries, loss of life, and damage and destruction of property, such as damage to critical services and facilities; and

(ii) substantially reduces the risk of, or increases resilience to, future damage, hardship, loss, or suffering.

(B) CERTIFICATION.— If the President determines that an application submitted under paragraph (1) meets the criteria described in subparagraph (A), the President shall certify the proposed resilience or mitigation project.

(C) EFFECT OF CERTIFICATION.— The certification of a proposed resilience or mitigation project under subparagraph (B) shall not be construed to exempt the resilience or mitigation project from the requirements of any other law.

(3) PROJECTS CAUSING DISPLACEMENT.—With respect to a resilience or mitigation project certified under paragraph (2)(B) that involves the displacement of a resident from any occupied housing unit, the entity performing the resilience or mitigation project shall—

(A) provide, at the option of the resident, a suitable and habitable housing unit that is, with respect to the housing unit from which the resident is displaced—

(i) of a comparable size;

(ii) located in the same local community or a community with reduced hazard risk; and

(iii) offered under similar costs, conditions, and terms;

(B) ensure that property acquisitions resulting from the displacement and made in connection with the resilience or mitigation project—

(i) are deed restricted in perpetuity to preclude future property uses not relating to mitigation or resilience; and

(ii) are the result of a voluntary decision by the resident; and

(C) plan for robust public participation in the resilience or mitigation project.

[42 U.S.C. 5136]

TITLE III—MAJOR DISASTER AND EMERGENCY ASSISTANCE ADMINISTRATION

SEC. 301. WAIVER OF ADMINISTRATIVE CONDITIONS.

Any Federal agency charged with the administration of a Federal assistance program may, if so requested by the applicant State or local authorities, modify or waive, for a major disaster, such administrative conditions for assistance as would otherwise prevent the giving of assistance under such programs if the inability to meet such conditions is a result of the major disaster.
[42 U.S.C. 5141]

COORDINATING OFFICERS

SEC. 302. (a) Immediately upon his declaration of a major disaster or emergency, the President shall appoint a Federal coordinating officer to operate in the affected area.

(b) In order to effectuate the purposes of this Act, the Federal coordinating officer, within the affected area, shall—

(1) make an initial appraisal of the types of relief most urgently needed;

(2) establish such field offices as he deems necessary and as are authorized by the President;

(3) coordinate the administration of relief, including activities of the State and local governments, the American National Red Cross, the Salvation Army, the Mennonite Disaster Service, and other relief or disaster assistance organizations, which agree to operate under his advise or direction, except that nothing contained in this Act shall limit or in any way affect the responsibilities of the American National Red Cross under the Act of January 5, 1905, as amended (33 Stat. 599); and

(4) take such other action, consistent with authority delegated to him by the President, and consistent with the provisions of this Act, as he may deem necessary to assist local citizens and public officials in promptly obtaining assistance to which they are entitled.

(c) When the President determines assistance under this Act is necessary, he shall request that the Governor of the affected State designate a State coordinating officer for the purpose of coordinating State and local disaster assistance efforts with those of the Federal Government.

(d) Where the area affected by a major disaster or emergency includes parts of more than 1 State, the President, at the discretion of the President, may appoint a single Federal coordinating officer for the entire affected area, and may appoint such deputy Federal coordinating officers to assist the Federal coordinating officer as the President determines appropriate.
[42 U.S.C. 5143]

SEC. 303. EMERGENCY SUPPORT AND RESPONSE TEAMS.[1]

---

[1]

Paragraph (1) of section 633 of Public Law 109–295 provides as follows:

SEC. 633. EMERGENCY RESPONSE TEAMS.

Section 303 of the Robert T. Stafford Disaster Relief and Emergency Assistance Act (42 U.S.C. 5144) is amended—

(1) by striking ^{sec. 303.} and all that follows through The President shall and inserting the following:

"SEC. 303. EMERGENCY SUPPORT AND RESPONSE TEAMS.

"(a) Emergency Support Teams.—The President shall"; and

Such amendment should have struck the centered section heading which precedes Sec. 303. and reads emergency support team and all that follows through The President shall. The amendment was executed to reflect the probable intent of Congress.

(a) EMERGENCY SUPPORT TEAMS.— The President shall form emergency support teams of Federal personnel to be deployed in an area affected by a major disaster or emergency. Such emergency support teams shall assist the Federal coordinating officer in carrying out his responsibilities pursuant to this Act. Upon request of the President, the head of any Federal agency is directed to detail to temporary duty with the emergency support teams on either a reimbursable or nonreimbursable basis, as is determined necessary by the President, such personnel within the administrative jurisdiction of the head of the Federal agency as the President may need or believe to be useful for carrying out the functions of the emergency support teams, each such detail to be without loss of seniority, pay, or other employee status.

(b) EMERGENCY RESPONSE TEAMS.—

(1) ESTABLISHMENT.—In carrying out subsection (a), the President, acting through the Administrator of the Federal Emergency Management Agency, shall establish—

(A) at a minimum 3 national response teams; and

(B) sufficient regional response teams, including Regional Office strike teams under section 507 of the Homeland Security Act of 2002; and

(C) other response teams as may be necessary to meet the incident management responsibilities of the Federal Government.

(2) TARGET CAPABILITY LEVEL.— The Administrator shall ensure that specific target capability levels, as defined pursuant to the guidelines established under section 646(a) of the Post-Katrina Emergency Management Reform Act of 2006, are established for Federal emergency response teams.

(3) PERSONNEL.— The President, acting through the Administrator, shall ensure that the Federal emergency response teams consist of adequate numbers of properly planned, organized, equipped, trained, and exercised personnel to achieve the established target capability levels. Each emergency response team shall work in coordination with State and local officials and onsite personnel associated with a particular incident.

(4) READINESS REPORTING.— The Administrator shall evaluate team readiness on a regular basis and report team readiness levels in the report required under section 652(a) of the Post-Katrina Emergency Management Reform Act of 2006.

[42 U.S.C. 5144]

REIMBURSEMENT

SEC. 304.   Federal agencies may be reimbursed for expenditures under this Act from funds appropriated for the purposes of this Act. Any funds received by Federal agencies

as reimbursement for services or supplies furnished under the authority of this Act shall be deposited to the credit of the appropriation or appropriations currently available for such services or supplies.
[42 U.S.C. 5147]

NONLIABILITY

SEC. 305. The Federal Government shall not be liable for any claim based upon the exercise or performance of or the failure to exercise or perform a discretionary function or duty on the part of a Federal agency or an employee of the Federal Government in carrying out the provisions of this Act.
[42 U.S.C. 5148]

PERFORMANCE OF SERVICES

SEC. 306. (a) In carrying out the purposes of this Act, any Federal agency is authorized to accept and utilize the services or facilities of any State or local government, or of any agency, office, or employee thereof, with the consent of such government.

(b) In performing any services under this Act, any Federal agency is authorized—

(1) to appoint and fix the compensation of such temporary personnel as may be necessary, without regard to the provisions of title 5, United States Code, governing appointments in competitive service;

(2) to employ experts and consultants in accordance with the provisions of section 3109 of such title, without regard to the provisions of chapter 51 and subchapter III of chapter 53 of such title relating to classification and General Schedule pay rates; and

(3) to incur obligations on behalf of the United States by contract or otherwise for the acquisition, rental, or hire of equipment, services, materials, and supplies for shipping, drayage, travel, and communications, and for the supervision and administration of such activities. Such obligations, including obligations arising out of the temporary employment of additional personnel, may be incurred by an agency in such amount as may be made available to it by the President.

(c) The Administrator of the Federal Emergency Management Agency is authorized to appoint temporary personnel, after serving continuously for 3 years, to positions in the Federal Emergency Management Agency in the same manner that competitive service employees with competitive status are considered for transfer, reassignment, or promotion to such positions. An individual appointed under this subsection shall become a career-conditional employee, unless the employee has already completed the service requirements for career tenure.

(d) PERSONNEL PERFORMING SERVICE RESPONDING TO DISASTERS AND EMERGENCIES.—

(1) USERRA EMPLOYMENT AND REEMPLOYMENT RIGHTS.— The protections, rights, benefits, and obligations provided under chapter 43 of title 38, United States Code, shall apply to intermittent personnel appointed pursuant to subsection (b)(1) to perform service to the Federal Emergency Management Agency under sections 401 and 501 or to train for such service.

(2) NOTICE OF ABSENCE FROM POSITION OF EMPLOYMENT.— Preclusion of giving

notice of service by necessity of service under subsection (b)(1) to perform service to the Federal Emergency Management Agency under sections 401 and 501 or to train for such service shall be considered preclusion by military necessity for purposes of section 4312(b) of title 38, United States Code, pertaining to giving notice of absence from a position of employment. A determination of such necessity shall be made by the Administrator and shall not be subject to review in any judicial or administrative proceeding.

[42 U.S.C. 5149]

SEC. 307. USE OF LOCAL FIRMS AND INDIVIDUALS.

(a) CONTRACTS OR AGREEMENTS WITH PRIVATE ENTITIES.—

(1) IN GENERAL.— In the expenditure of Federal funds for debris clearance, distribution of supplies, reconstruction, and other major disaster or emergency assistance activities which may be carried out by contract or agreement with private organizations, firms, or individuals, preference shall be given, to the extent feasible and practicable, to those organizations, firms, and individuals residing or doing business primarily in the area affected by such major disaster or emergency.

(2) CONSTRUCTION.— This subsection shall not be considered to restrict the use of Department of Defense resources under this Act in the provision of assistance in a major disaster.

(3) SPECIFIC GEOGRAPHIC AREA.— In carrying out this section, a contract or agreement may be set aside for award based on a specific geographic area.

(b) IMPLEMENTATION.—

(1) CONTRACTS NOT TO ENTITIES IN AREA.— Any expenditure of Federal funds for debris clearance, distribution of supplies, reconstruction, and other major disaster or emergency assistance activities which may be carried out by contract or agreement with private organizations, firms, or individuals, not awarded to an organization, firm, or individual residing or doing business primarily in the area affected by such major disaster shall be justified in writing in the contract file.

(2) TRANSITION.— Following the declaration of an emergency or major disaster, an agency performing response, relief, and reconstruction activities shall transition work performed under contracts in effect on the date on which the President declares the emergency or major disaster to organizations, firms, and individuals residing or doing business primarily in any area affected by the major disaster or emergency, unless the head of such agency determines that it is not feasible or practicable to do so.

(3) FORMULATION OF REQUIREMENTS.— The head of a Federal agency, as feasible and practicable, shall formulate appropriate requirements to facilitate compliance with this section.

(c) PRIOR CONTRACTS.— Nothing in this section shall be construed to require any Federal agency to breach or renegotiate any contract in effect before the occurrence of a major disaster or emergency.

[42 U.S.C. 5150]

NONDISCRIMINATION IN DISASTER ASSISTANCE

SEC. 308. (a)   The President shall issue, and may alter and amend, such regulations as may be necessary for the guidance of personnel carrying out Federal assistance functions at the site of a major disaster or emergency. Such regulations shall include provisions for insuring that the distribution of supplies, the processing of applications, and other relief and assistance activities shall be accomplished in an equitable and impartial manner, without discrimination on the grounds of race, color, religion, nationality, sex, age, disability, English proficiency, or economic status.

(b)   As a condition of participation in the distribution of assistance or supplies under this Act or of receiving assistance under this Act, governmental bodies and other organizations shall be required to comply with regulations relating to nondiscrimination promulgated by the President, and such other regulations applicable to activities within an area affected by a major disaster or emergency as he deems necessary for the effective coordination of relief efforts.

[42 U.S.C. 5151]

USE AND COORDINATION OF RELIEF ORGANIZATIONS

SEC. 309. (a)   In providing relief and assistance under this Act, the President may utilize, with their consent, the personnel and facilities of the American National Red Cross, the Salvation Army, the Mennonite Disaster Service, long-term recovery groups, domestic hunger relief, and other relief, or disaster assistance organizations, in the distribution of medicine, food, supplies, or other items, and in the restoration, rehabilitation, or reconstruction of community services housing and essential facilities, whenever the President finds that such utilization is necessary.

(b)   The President is authorized to enter into agreements with the American National Red Cross, the Salvation Army, the Mennonite Disaster Service, long-term recovery groups, domestic hunger relief, and other relief, or disaster assistance organizations under which the disaster relief activities of such organizations may be coordinated by the Federal coordinating officer whenever such organizations are engaged in providing relief during and after a major disaster or emergency. Any such agreement shall include provisions assuring that use of Federal facilities, supplies, and services will be in compliance with regulations prohibiting duplication of benefits and guaranteeing nondiscrimination promulgated by the President under this Act, and such other regulation as the President may require.

[42 U.S.C. 5152]

SEC. 310. PRIORITY TO CERTAIN APPLICATIONS FOR PUBLIC FACILITY AND PUBLIC HOUSING ASSISTANCE.

(a) PRIORITY.—In the processing of applications for assistance, priority and immediate consideration shall be given by the head of the appropriate Federal agency, during such period as the President shall prescribe, to applications from public bodies situated in areas affected by major disasters under the following Acts:

(1)   The United States Housing Act of 1937 for the provision of low-income housing.

(2)   Section 702 of the Housing Act of 1954 for assistance in public works planning.

(3)   The Community Development Block Grant Program under title I of the Housing and Community Development Act of 1974.

(4)   Section 306 of the Consolidated Farm and Rural Development Act.

(5)   The Public Works and Economic Development Act of 1965.

(6)   The Appalachian Regional Development Act of 1965.

(7)   The Federal Water Pollution Control Act.

(b) OBLIGATION OF CERTAIN DISCRETIONARY FUNDS.— In the obligation of discretionary funds or funds which are not allocated among the States or political subdivisions of a State, the Secretary of Housing and Urban Development and the Secretary of Commerce shall give priority to applications for projects for major disaster areas.

[42 U.S.C. 5153]

SEC. 311. INSURANCE.

(a) APPLICANTS FOR REPLACEMENT OF DAMAGED FACILITIES.—

(1) COMPLIANCE WITH CERTAIN REGULATIONS.— An applicant for assistance under section 406 of this Act (relating to repair, restoration, and replacement of damaged facilities), section 422 of this Act (relating to simplified procedure) or section 209(c)(2) of the Public Works and Economic Development Act of 1965 (42 U.S.C. 3149(c)(2)) shall comply with regulations prescribed by the President to assure that, with respect to any property to be replaced, restored, repaired, or constructed with such assistance, such types and extent of insurance will be obtained and maintained as may be reasonably available, adequate, and necessary, to protect against future loss to such property.

(2) DETERMINATION.— In making a determination with respect to availability, adequacy, and necessity under paragraph (1), the President shall not require greater types and extent of insurance than are certified to him as reasonable by the appropriate State insurance commissioner responsible for regulation of such insurance.

(b) MAINTENANCE OF INSURANCE.— No applicant for assistance under section 406 of this Act (relating to repair, restoration, and replacement of damaged facilities), section 422 of this Act (relating to simplified procedure), or section 209(c)(2) of the Public Works and Economic Development Act of 1965 (42 U.S.C. 3149(c)(2)) may receive such assistance for any property or part thereof for which the applicant has previously received assistance under this Act unless all insurance required pursuant to this section has been obtained and maintained with respect to such property. The requirements of this subsection may not be waived under section 301.

(c) STATE ACTING AS SELF-INSURER.— A State may elect to act as a self-insurer with respect to any or all of the facilities owned by the State. Such an election, if declared in writing at the time of acceptance of assistance under section 406 or 422 of this Act or section 209(c)(2) of the Public Works and Economic Development Act of 1965 (42 U.S.C. 3149(c)(2)) or subsequently and accompanied by a plan for self-insurance which is satisfactory to the President, shall be deemed compliance with subsection (a). No such self-insurer may receive assistance under section 406 or 422 of this Act for any property or part thereof for which it has previously received assistance under this Act, to the extent that insurance for such property or part thereof would have been reasonably available.

[42 U.S.C. 5154]

SEC. 312. DUPLICATION OF BENEFITS.

(a) GENERAL PROHIBITION.— The President, in consultation with the head of each Federal agency administering any program providing financial assistance to persons, business concerns, or other entities suffering losses as a result of a major disaster or emergency, shall assure that no such person, business concern, or other entity will receive such assistance with respect to any part of such loss as to which he has received financial assistance under any other program or from insurance or any other source.

(b) SPECIAL RULES.—

(1) LIMITATION.— This section shall not prohibit the provision of Federal assistance to a person who is or may be entitled to receive benefits for the same purposes from another source if such person has not received such other benefits by the time of application for Federal assistance and if such person agrees to repay all duplicative assistance to the agency providing the Federal assistance.

(2) PROCEDURES.— The President shall establish such procedures as the President considers necessary to ensure uniformity in preventing duplication of benefits.

(3) EFFECT OF PARTIAL BENEFITS.— Receipt of partial benefits for a major disaster or emergency shall not preclude provision of additional Federal assistance for any part of a loss or need for which benefits have not been provided.

(c) RECOVERY OF DUPLICATIVE BENEFITS.— A person receiving Federal assistance for a major disaster or emergency shall be liable to the United States to the extent that such assistance duplicates benefits available to the person for the same purpose from another source. The agency which provided the duplicative assistance shall collect such duplicative assistance from the recipient in accordance with chapter 37 of title 31, United States Code, relating to debt collection, when the head of such agency considers it to be in the best interest of the Federal Government.

(d) ASSISTANCE NOT INCOME.— Federal major disaster and emergency assistance provided to individuals and families under this Act, and comparable disaster assistance provided by States, local governments, and disaster assistance organizations, shall not be considered as income or a resource when determining eligibility for or benefit levels under federally funded income assistance or resource-tested benefit programs.

[42 U.S.C. 5155]

SEC. 313. STANDARDS AND REVIEWS.

The President shall establish comprehensive standards which shall be used to assess the efficiency and effectiveness of Federal major disaster and emergency assistance programs administered under this Act. The President shall conduct annual reviews of the activities of Federal agencies and State and local governments in major disaster and emergency preparedness and in providing major disaster and emergency assistance in order to assure maximum coordination and effectiveness of

such programs and consistency in policies for reimbursement of States under this Act.
[42 U.S.C. 5156]

SEC. 314. PENALTIES.

(a) MISUSE OF FUNDS.— Any person who knowingly misapplies the proceeds of a loan or other cash benefit obtained under this Act shall be fined an amount equal to one and one-half times the misapplied amount of the proceeds or cash benefit.

(b) CIVIL ENFORCEMENT.— Whenever it appears that any person has violated or is about to violate any provision of this Act, including any civil penalty imposed under this Act, the Attorney General may bring a civil action for such relief as may be appropriate. Such action may be brought in an appropriate United States district court.

(c) REFERRAL TO ATTORNEY GENERAL.— The President shall expeditiously refer to the Attorney General for appropriate action any evidence developed in the performance of functions under this Act that may warrant consideration for criminal prosecution.

(d) CIVIL PENALTY.— Any individual who knowingly violates any order or regulation issued under this Act shall be subject to a civil penalty of not more than $5,000 for each violation.
[42 U.S.C. 5157]

AVAILABILITY OF MATERIALS

SEC. 315.   The President is authorized, at the request of the Governor of an affected State, to provide for a survey of construction materials needed in the area affected by a major disaster on an emergency basis for housing repairs, replacement housing, public facilities repairs and replacement, farming operations, and business enterprises and to take appropriate action to assure the availability and fair distribution of needed materials, including, where possible, the allocation of such materials for a period of not more than one hundred and eighty days after such major disaster. Any allocation program shall be implemented by the President to the extent possible, by working with and through those companies which traditionally supply construction materials in the affected area. For the purposes of this section construction materials shall include building materials and materials required for repairing housing, replacement housing, public facilities repairs and replacement, and for normal farm and business operations.
[42 U.S.C. 5158]

SEC. 316. PROTECTION OF ENVIRONMENT.

An action which is taken or assistance which is provided pursuant to section 402, 403, 406, 407, or 502, including such assistance provided pursuant to the procedures provided for in section 422, which has the effect of restoring a facility substantially to its condition prior to the disaster or emergency, shall not be deemed a major Federal action significantly affecting the quality of the human environment within the meaning of the National Environmental Policy Act of 1969 (83 Stat. 852). Nothing in this section shall alter or affect the applicability of the National Environmental Policy Act of 1969 to other Federal actions taken under this Act or under any other provisions of law.
[42 U.S.C. 5159]

SEC. 317. RECOVERY OF ASSISTANCE.

(a) PARTY LIABLE.— Any person who intentionally causes a condition for which Federal assistance is provided under this Act or under any other Federal law as a result of a declaration of a major disaster or emergency under this Act shall be liable to the United States for the reasonable costs incurred by the United States in responding to such disaster or emergency to the extent that such costs are attributable to the intentional act or omission of such person which caused such condition. Such action for reasonable costs shall be brought in an appropriate United States district court.

(b) RENDERING OF CARE.— A person shall not be liable under this section for costs incurred by the United States as a result of actions taken or omitted by such person in the course of rendering care or assistance in response to a major disaster or emergency.

[42 U.S.C. 5160]

SEC. 318. AUDITS AND INVESTIGATIONS.

(a) IN GENERAL.— Subject to the provisions of chapter 75 of title 31, United States Code, relating to requirements for single audits, the President shall conduct audits and investigations as necessary to assure compliance with this Act, and in connection therewith may question such persons as may be necessary to carry out such audits and investigations.

(b) ACCESS TO RECORDS.— For purposes of audits and investigations under this section, the President and Comptroller General may inspect any books, documents, papers, and records of any person relating to any activity undertaken or funded under this Act.

(c) STATE AND LOCAL AUDITS.— The President may require audits by State and local governments in connection with assistance under this Act when necessary to assure compliance with this Act or related regulations.

[42 U.S.C. 5161]

SEC. 319. ADVANCE OF NON-FEDERAL SHARE.

(a) IN GENERAL.—The President may lend or advance to an eligible applicant or a State the portion of assistance for which the State is responsible under the cost-sharing provisions of this Act in any case in which—

(1) the State is unable to assume its financial responsibility under such cost-sharing provisions—

(A) with respect to concurrent, multiple major disasters in a jurisdiction, or

(B) after incurring extraordinary costs as a result of a particular disaster; and

(2) the damages caused by such disasters or disaster are so overwhelming and severe that it is not possible for the applicant or the State to assume immediately their financial responsibility under this Act.

(b) TERMS OF LOANS AND ADVANCES.—

(1) IN GENERAL.— Any loan or advance under this section shall be repaid to the United States.

(2) INTEREST.— Loans and advances under this section shall bear interest at

a rate determined by the Secretary of the Treasury, taking into consideration the current market yields on outstanding marketable obligations of the United States with remaining periods to maturity comparable to the reimbursement period of the loan or advance.

(c) REGULATIONS.— The President shall issue regulations describing the terms and conditions under which any loan or advance authorized by this section may be made.
[42 U.S.C. 5162]

SEC. 320. LIMITATION ON USE OF SLIDING SCALES.

No geographic area shall be precluded from receiving assistance under this Act solely by virtue of an arithmetic formula or sliding scale based on income or population.
[42 U.S.C. 5163]

SEC. 321. RULES AND REGULATIONS.

The President may prescribe such rules and regulations as may be necessary and proper to carry out the provisions of this Act, and may exercise, either directly or through such Federal agency as the President may designate, any power or authority conferred to the President by this Act.
[42 U.S.C. 5164]

SEC. 322. MITIGATION PLANNING.

(a) REQUIREMENT OF MITIGATION PLAN.— As a condition of receipt of an increased Federal share for hazard mitigation measures under subsection (e), a State, local, or tribal government shall develop and submit for approval to the President a mitigation plan that outlines processes for identifying the natural hazards, risks, and vulnerabilities of the area under the jurisdiction of the government.

(b) LOCAL AND TRIBAL PLANS.—Each mitigation plan developed by a local or tribal government shall—

(1) describe actions to mitigate hazards, risks, and vulnerabilities identified under the plan; and

(2) establish a strategy to implement those actions.

(c) STATE PLANS.—The State process of development of a mitigation plan under this section shall—

(1) identify the natural hazards, risks, and vulnerabilities of areas in the State;

(2) support development of local mitigation plans;

(3) provide for technical assistance to local and tribal governments for mitigation planning; and

(4) identify and prioritize mitigation actions that the State will support, as resources become available.

(d) FUNDING.—

(1) IN GENERAL.— Federal contributions under section 404 may be used to fund the development and updating of mitigation plans under this section.

(2) MAXIMUM FEDERAL CONTRIBUTION.— With respect to any mitigation plan, a

State, local, or tribal government may use an amount of Federal contributions under section 404 not to exceed 7 percent of the amount of such contributions available to the government as of a date determined by the government.

(e) INCREASED FEDERAL SHARE FOR HAZARD MITIGATION MEASURES.—

(1) IN GENERAL.— If, at the time of the declaration of a major disaster or event under section 420, a State has in effect an approved mitigation plan under this section, the President may increase to 20 percent, with respect to the major disaster or event under section 420, the maximum percentage specified in the last sentence of section 404(a).

(2) FACTORS FOR CONSIDERATION.—In determining whether to increase the maximum percentage under paragraph (1), the President shall consider whether the State has established—

(A) eligibility criteria for property acquisition and other types of mitigation measures;

(B) requirements for cost effectiveness that are related to the eligibility criteria;

(C) a system of priorities that is related to the eligibility criteria; and

(D) a process by which an assessment of the effectiveness of a mitigation action may be carried out after the mitigation action is complete.

[42 U.S.C. 5165]

SEC. 323. MINIMUM STANDARDS FOR PUBLIC AND PRIVATE STRUCTURES.

(a) IN GENERAL.—As a condition of receipt of a disaster loan or grant under this Act—

(1) the recipient shall carry out any repair or construction to be financed with the loan or grant in accordance with applicable standards of safety, decency, and sanitation and in conformity with applicable codes, specifications, and standards; and

(2) the President may require safe land use and construction practices, after adequate consultation with appropriate State and local government officials.

(b) EVIDENCE OF COMPLIANCE.— A recipient of a disaster loan or grant under this Act shall provide such evidence of compliance with this section as the President may require by regulation.

[42 U.S.C. 5165a]

SEC. 324. MANAGEMENT COSTS.

(a) DEFINITION OF MANAGEMENT COST.— In this section, the term management cost includes any indirect cost, any direct administrative cost, and any other administrative expense associated with a specific project under a major disaster, emergency, or disaster preparedness or mitigation activity or measure.

(b) ESTABLISHMENT OF MANAGEMENT COST RATES.—

(1) IN GENERAL.— Notwithstanding any other provision of law (including any administrative rule or guidance), the President shall by regulation implement

management cost rates, for grantees and subgrantees, that shall be used to determine contributions under this Act for management costs.

(2) SPECIFIC MANAGEMENT COSTS.—The Administrator of the Federal Emergency Management Agency shall provide the following percentage rates, in addition to the eligible project costs, to cover direct and indirect costs of administering the following programs:

(A) HAZARD MITIGATION.— A grantee under section 404 may be reimbursed not more than 15 percent of the total amount of the grant award under such section of which not more than 10 percent may be used by the grantee and 5 percent by the subgrantee for such costs.

(B) PUBLIC ASSISTANCE.— A grantee under sections 403, 406, 407, and 502 may be reimbursed not more than 12 percent of the total award amount under such sections, of which not more than 7 percent may be used by the grantee and 5 percent by the subgrantee for such costs.

(c) REVIEW.— The President shall review the management cost rates established under subsection (b) not later than 3 years after the date of establishment of the rates and periodically thereafter.

[42 U.S.C. 5165b]

SEC. 325. PUBLIC NOTICE, COMMENT, AND CONSULTATION REQUIREMENTS.

(a) PUBLIC NOTICE AND COMMENT CONCERNING NEW OR MODIFIED POLICIES.—

(1) IN GENERAL.—The President shall provide for public notice and opportunity for comment before adopting any new or modified policy that—

(A) governs implementation of the public assistance program administered by the Federal Emergency Management Agency under this Act; and

(B) could result in a significant reduction of assistance under the program.

(2) APPLICATION.— Any policy adopted under paragraph (1) shall apply only to a major disaster or emergency declared on or after the date on which the policy is adopted.

(b) CONSULTATION CONCERNING INTERIM POLICIES.—

(1) IN GENERAL.—Before adopting any interim policy under the public assistance program to address specific conditions that relate to a major disaster or emergency that has been declared under this Act, the President, to the maximum extent practicable, shall solicit the views and recommendations of grantees and subgrantees with respect to the major disaster or emergency concerning the potential interim policy, if the interim policy is likely—

(A) to result in a significant reduction of assistance to applicants for the assistance with respect to the major disaster or emergency; or

(B) to change the terms of a written agreement to which the Federal Government is a party concerning the declaration of the major disaster or emergency.

(2) NO LEGAL RIGHT OF ACTION.— Nothing in this subsection confers a legal right of action on any party.

(c) PUBLIC ACCESS.— The President shall promote public access to policies governing the implementation of the public assistance program.

[42 U.S.C. 5165c]

SEC. 326. DESIGNATION OF SMALL STATE AND RURAL ADVOCATE.

(a) IN GENERAL.— The President shall designate in the Federal Emergency Management Agency a Small State and Rural Advocate.

(b) RESPONSIBILITIES.— The Small State and Rural Advocate shall be an advocate for the fair treatment of small States and rural communities in the provision of assistance under this Act.

(c) DUTIES.—The Small State and Rural Advocate shall—

(1) participate in the disaster declaration process under section 401 and the emergency declaration process under section 501, to ensure that the needs of rural communities are being addressed;

(2) assist small population States in the preparation of requests for major disaster or emergency declarations;

(3) assist States in the collection and presentation of material in the disaster or emergency declaration request relevant to demonstrate severe localized impacts within the State for a specific incident, including—

(A) the per capita personal income by local area, as calculated by the Bureau of Economic Analysis;

(B) the disaster impacted population profile, as reported by the Bureau of the Census, including—

(i) the percentage of the population for whom poverty status is determined;

(ii) the percentage of the population already receiving Government assistance such as Supplemental Security Income and Supplemental Nutrition Assistance Program benefits;

(iii) the pre-disaster unemployment rate;

(iv) the percentage of the population that is 65 years old and older;

(v) the percentage of the population 18 years old and younger;

(vi) the percentage of the population with a disability;

(vii) the percentage of the population who speak a language other than English and speak English less than very well; and

(viii) any unique considerations regarding American Indian and Alaskan Native Tribal populations raised in the State's request for a major disaster declaration that may not be reflected in the data points referenced in this subparagraph;

(C) the impact to community infrastructure, including—

(i) disruptions to community life-saving and life-sustaining services;

(ii) disruptions or increased demand for essential community services;

and

    (iii)   disruptions to transportation, infrastructure, and utilities; and

    (D)   any other information relevant to demonstrate severe local impacts; and

    (4)   conduct such other activities as the Administrator of the Federal Emergency Management Agency considers appropriate.

[42 U.S.C. 5165d]

SEC. 327. NATIONAL URBAN SEARCH AND RESCUE RESPONSE SYSTEM.

(a) DEFINITIONS.—In this section, the following definitions shall apply:

    (1) ADMINISTRATOR.— The term Administrator means the Administrator of the Federal Emergency Management Agency.

    (2) AGENCY.— The term Agency means the Federal Emergency Management Agency.

    (3) HAZARD.— The term hazard has the meaning given the term in section 602.

    (4) NONEMPLOYEE SYSTEM MEMBER.— The term nonemployee System member means a System member not employed by a sponsoring agency or participating agency.

    (5) PARTICIPATING AGENCY.— The term participating agency means a State or local government, nonprofit organization, or private organization that has executed an agreement with a sponsoring agency to participate in the System.

    (6) SPONSORING AGENCY.— The term sponsoring agency means a State or local government that is the sponsor of a task force designated by the Administrator to participate in the System.

    (7) SYSTEM.— The term System means the National Urban Search and Rescue Response System to be administered under this section.

    (8) SYSTEM MEMBER.— The term System member means an individual who is not a full-time employee of the Federal Government and who serves on a task force or on a System management or other technical team.

    (9) TASK FORCE.— The term task force means an urban search and rescue team designated by the Administrator to participate in the System.

(b) GENERAL AUTHORITY.— Subject to the requirements of this section, the Administrator shall continue to administer the emergency response system known as the National Urban Search and Rescue Response System.

(c) FUNCTIONS.— In administering the System, the Administrator shall provide for a national network of standardized search and rescue resources to assist States and local governments in responding to hazards.

(d) TASK FORCES.—

    (1) DESIGNATION.— The Administrator shall designate task forces to participate in the System. The Administration shall determine the criteria for such participation.

(2) SPONSORING AGENCIES.— Each task force shall have a sponsoring agency. The Administrator shall enter into an agreement with the sponsoring agency with respect to the participation of each task force in the System.

(3) COMPOSITION.—

(A) PARTICIPATING AGENCIES.— A task force may include, at the discretion of the sponsoring agency, one or more participating agencies. The sponsoring agency shall enter into an agreement with each participating agency with respect to the participation of the participating agency on the task force.

(B) OTHER INDIVIDUALS.— A task force may also include, at the discretion of the sponsoring agency, other individuals not otherwise associated with the sponsoring agency or a participating agency. The sponsoring agency of a task force may enter into a separate agreement with each such individual with respect to the participation of the individual on the task force.

(e) MANAGEMENT AND TECHNICAL TEAMS.— The Administrator shall maintain such management teams and other technical teams as the Administrator determines are necessary to administer the System.

(f) APPOINTMENT OF SYSTEM MEMBERS INTO FEDERAL SERVICE.—

(1) IN GENERAL.— The Administrator may appoint a System member into Federal service for a period of service to provide for the participation of the System member in exercises, preincident staging, major disaster and emergency response activities, and training events sponsored or sanctioned by the Administrator.

(2) NONAPPLICABILITY OF CERTAIN CIVIL SERVICE LAWS.— The Administrator may make appointments under paragraph (1) without regard to the provisions of title 5, United States Code, governing appointments in the competitive service.

(3) RELATIONSHIP TO OTHER AUTHORITIES.— The authority of the Administrator to make appointments under this subsection shall not affect any other authority of the Administrator under this Act.

(4) LIMITATION.— A System member who is appointed into Federal service under paragraph (1) shall not be considered an employee of the United States for purposes other than those specifically set forth in this section.

(g) COMPENSATION.—

(1) PAY OF SYSTEM MEMBERS.—Subject to such terms and conditions as the Administrator may impose by regulation, the Administrator shall make payments to the sponsoring agency of a task force—

(A) to reimburse each employer of a System member on the task force for compensation paid by the employer to the System member for any period during which the System member is appointed into Federal service under subsection (f)(1); and

(B) to make payments directly to a nonemployee System member on the task force for any period during which the nonemployee System member is appointed into Federal service under subsection (f)(1).

(2) REIMBURSEMENT FOR EMPLOYEES FILLING POSITIONS OF SYSTEM MEMBERS.—

(A) IN GENERAL.— Subject to such terms and conditions as the Administrator may impose by regulation, the Administrator shall make payments to the sponsoring agency of a task force to be used to reimburse each employer of a System member on the task force for compensation paid by the employer to an employee filling a position normally filled by the System member for any period during which the System member is appointed into Federal service under subsection (f)(1).

(B) LIMITATION.— Costs incurred by an employer shall be eligible for reimbursement under subparagraph (A) only to the extent that the costs are in excess of the costs that would have been incurred by the employer had the System member not been appointed into Federal service under subsection (f)(1).

(3) METHOD OF PAYMENT.— A System member shall not be entitled to pay directly from the Agency for a period during which the System member is appointed into Federal Service under subsection (f)(1).

(h) PERSONAL INJURY, ILLNESS, DISABILITY, OR DEATH.—

(1) IN GENERAL.— A System member who is appointed into Federal service under subsection (f)(1) and who suffers personal injury, illness, disability, or death as a result of a personal injury sustained while acting in the scope of such appointment, shall, for the purposes of subchapter I of chapter 81 of title 5, United States Code, be treated as though the member were an employee (as defined by section 8101 of that title) who had sustained the injury in the performance of duty.

(2) ELECTION OF BENEFITS.—

(A) IN GENERAL.—A System member (or, in the case of the death of the System member, the System member's dependent) who is entitled under paragraph (1) to receive benefits under subchapter I of chapter 81 of title 5, United States Code, by reason of personal injury, illness, disability, or death, and to receive benefits from a State or local government by reason of the same personal injury, illness, disability or death shall elect to—

(i)   receive benefits under such subchapter; or

(ii)   receive benefits from the State or local government.

(B) DEADLINE.— A System member or dependent shall make an election of benefits under subparagraph (A) not later than 1 year after the date of the personal injury, illness, disability, or death that is the reason for the benefits, or until such later date as the Secretary of Labor may allow for reasonable cause shown.

(C) EFFECT OF ELECTION.— An election of benefits made under this paragraph is irrevocable unless otherwise provided by law.

(3) REIMBURSEMENT FOR STATE OR LOCAL BENEFITS.— Subject to such terms and conditions as the Administrator may impose by regulation, if a System member or dependent elects to receive benefits from a State or local government under paragraph (2)(A), the Administrator shall reimburse the State or local government for the value of the benefits.

(4) PUBLIC SAFETY OFFICER CLAIMS.— Nothing in this subsection shall be construed to bar any claim by, or with respect to, any System member who is a public safety officer, as defined in section 1204 of title I of the Omnibus Crime Control and Safe Streets Act of 1968 (42 U.S.C. 3796b), for any benefits authorized under part L of title I of that Act (42 U.S.C. 3796 et seq.).

(i) LIABILITY.— A System member appointed into Federal service under subsection (f)(1), while acting within the scope of the appointment, shall be considered to be an employee of the Federal Government under section 1346(b) of title 28, United States Code, and chapter 171 of that title, relating to tort claims procedure.

(j) EMPLOYMENT AND REEMPLOYMENT RIGHTS.—With respect to a System member who is not a regular full-time employee of a sponsoring agency or participating agency, the following terms and conditions apply:

(1) SERVICE.— Service as a System member shall be considered to be service in the uniformed services for purposes of chapter 43 of title 38, United States Code, relating to employment and reemployment rights of individuals who have performed service in the uniformed services (regardless of whether the individual receives compensation for such participation). All rights and obligations of such persons and procedures for assistance, enforcement, and investigation shall be as provided for in such chapter.

(2) PRECLUSION.— Preclusion of giving notice of service by necessity of appointment under this section shall be considered to be preclusion by military necessity for purposes of section 4312(b) of title 38, United States Code, pertaining to giving notice of absence from a position of employment. A determination of such necessity shall be made by the Administrator and shall not be subject to judicial review.

(k) LICENSES AND PERMITS.— If a System member holds a valid license, certificate, or other permit issued by any State or other governmental jurisdiction evidencing the member's qualifications in any professional, mechanical, or other skill or type of assistance required by the System, the System member is deemed to be performing a Federal activity when rendering aid involving such skill or assistance during a period of appointment into Federal service under subsection (f)(1).

(l) PREPAREDNESS COOPERATIVE AGREEMENTS.—Subject to the availability of appropriations for such purpose, the Administrator shall enter into an annual preparedness cooperative agreement with each sponsoring agency. Amounts made available to a sponsoring agency under such a preparedness cooperative agreement shall be for the following purposes:

(1) Training and exercises, including training and exercises with other Federal, State, and local government response entities.

(2) Acquisition and maintenance of equipment, including interoperable communications and personal protective equipment.

(3) Medical monitoring required for responder safety and health in anticipation of and following a major disaster, emergency, or other hazard, as determined by the Administrator.

(m) RESPONSE COOPERATIVE AGREEMENTS.— The Administrator shall enter into a response cooperative agreement with each sponsoring agency, as appropriate, under which the Administrator agrees to reimburse the sponsoring agency for costs incurred by the sponsoring agency in responding to a major disaster or emergency.

(n) OBLIGATIONS.— The Administrator may incur all necessary obligations consistent with this section in order to ensure the effectiveness of the System.

(o) EQUIPMENT MAINTENANCE AND REPLACEMENT.— Not later than 180 days after the date of enactment of this section, the Administrator shall submit to the appropriate congressional committees (as defined in section 2 of the Homeland Security Act of 2002 (6 U.S.C. 101)) a report on the development of a plan, including implementation steps and timeframes, to finance, maintain, and replace System equipment.

(p) FEDERAL EMPLOYEES.— Nothing in this section shall be construed to mean that a task force may not include Federal employees. In the case of a Federal employee detailed to a task force, the sponsoring agency shall enter into an agreement with the relevant employing Federal agency.

[42 U.S.C. 5165f]

TITLE IV—MAJOR DISASTER ASSISTANCE PROGRAMS

SEC. 401. PROCEDURE FOR DECLARATION.

(a) IN GENERAL.— All requests for a declaration by the President that a major disaster exists shall be made by the Governor of the affected State. Such a request shall be based on a finding that the disaster is of such severity and magnitude that effective response is beyond the capabilities of the State and the affected local governments and that Federal assistance is necessary. As part of such request, and as a prerequisite to major disaster assistance under this Act, the Governor shall take appropriate response action under State law and direct execution of the State's emergency plan. The Governor shall furnish information on the nature and amount of State and local resources which have been or will be committed to alleviating the results of the disaster, and shall certify that, for the current disaster, State and local government obligations and expenditures (of which State commitments must be a significant proportion) will comply with all applicable cost-sharing requirements of this Act. Based on the request of a Governor under this section, the President may declare under this Act that a major disaster or emergency exists.

(b) INDIAN TRIBAL GOVERNMENT REQUESTS.—

(1) IN GENERAL.— The Chief Executive of an affected Indian tribal government may submit a request for a declaration by the President that a major disaster exists consistent with the requirements of subsection (a).

(2) REFERENCES.— In implementing assistance authorized by the President under this Act in response to a request of the Chief Executive of an affected Indian tribal government for a major disaster declaration, any reference in this title or title III (except sections 310 and 326) to a State or the Governor of a State is deemed to refer to an affected Indian tribal government or the Chief Executive of an affected Indian tribal government, as appropriate.

(3) SAVINGS PROVISION.— Nothing in this subsection shall prohibit an Indian tribal government from receiving assistance under this title through a declaration

made by the President at the request of a State under subsection (a) if the President does not make a declaration under this subsection for the same incident.

(c) COST SHARE ADJUSTMENTS FOR INDIAN TRIBAL GOVERNMENTS.—

(1) IN GENERAL.—In providing assistance to an Indian tribal government under this title, the President may waive or adjust any payment of a non-Federal contribution with respect to the assistance if—

(A) the President has the authority to waive or adjust the payment under another provision of this title; and

(B) the President determines that the waiver or adjustment is necessary and appropriate.

(2) CRITERIA FOR MAKING DETERMINATIONS.— The President shall establish criteria for making determinations under paragraph (1)(B).

[42 U.S.C. 5170]

SEC. 402. GENERAL FEDERAL ASSISTANCE.

In any major disaster, the President may—

(1) direct any Federal agency, with or without reimbursement, to utilize its authorities and the resources granted to it under Federal law (including personnel, equipment, supplies, facilities, and managerial, technical, and advisory services) in support of State and local assistance response or recovery efforts, including precautionary evacuations;

(2) coordinate all disaster relief assistance (including voluntary assistance) provided by Federal agencies, private organizations, and State and local governments, including precautionary evacuations and recovery;

(3) provide technical and advisory assistance to affected State and local governments for—

(A) the performance of essential community services;

(B) issuance of warnings of risks and hazards;

(C) public health and safety information, including dissemination of such information;

(D) provision of health and safety measures;

(E) management, control, and reduction of immediate threats to public health and safety; and

(F) recovery activities, including disaster impact assessments and planning;

(4) assist State and local governments in the distribution of medicine, food, and other consumable supplies, and emergency assistance;

(5) provide assistance to State and local governments for building code and floodplain management ordinance administration and enforcement, including inspections for substantial damage compliance; and

(6) provide accelerated Federal assistance and Federal support where necessary

to save lives, prevent human suffering, or mitigate severe damage, which may be provided in the absence of a specific request and in which case the President—

(A) shall, to the fullest extent practicable, promptly notify and coordinate with officials in a State in which such assistance or support is provided; and

(B) shall not, in notifying and coordinating with a State under subparagraph (A), delay or impede the rapid deployment, use, and distribution of critical resources to victims of a major disaster.

[42 U.S.C. 5170a]

SEC. 403. ESSENTIAL ASSISTANCE.

(a) IN GENERAL.—Federal agencies may on the direction of the President, provide assistance essential to meeting immediate threats to life and property resulting from a major disaster, as follows:

(1) FEDERAL RESOURCES, GENERALLY.— Utilizing, lending, or donating to State and local governments Federal equipment, supplies, facilities, personnel, and other resources, other than the extension of credit, for use or distribution by such governments in accordance with the purposes of this Act.

(2) MEDICINE, FOOD, AND OTHER CONSUMABLES.— Distributing or rendering through State and local governments, the American National Red Cross, the Salvation Army, the Mennonite Disaster Service, and other relief and disaster assistance organizations medicine durable medical equipment,,[2] food, and other consumable supplies, and other services and assistance to disaster victims.

---

[2]   So in law. See amendments made by section 689(b) of Public Law 109–295.

---

(3) WORK AND SERVICES TO SAVE LIVES AND PROTECT PROPERTY.—Performing on public or private lands or waters any work or services essential to saving lives and protecting and preserving property or public health and safety, including—

(A) debris removal;

(B) search and rescue, emergency medical care, emergency mass care, emergency shelter, and provision of food, water, medicinedurable medical equipment,,[2] and other essential needs, including movement of supplies or persons;

(C) clearance of roads and construction of temporary bridges necessary to the performance of emergency tasks and essential community services;

(D) provision of temporary facilities for schools and other essential community services;

(E) demolition of unsafe structures which endanger the public;

(F) warning of further risks and hazards;

(G) dissemination of public information and assistance regarding health and safety measures;

(H) provision of technical advice to State and local governments on disaster management and control;

(I) reduction of immediate threats to life, property, and public health and safety; and

(J) provision of rescue, care, shelter, and essential needs—

(i) to individuals with household pets and service animals; and

(ii) to such pets and animals.

(4) CONTRIBUTIONS.— Making contributions to State or local governments or owners or operators of private nonprofit facilities for the purpose of carrying out the provisions of this subsection.

(b) FEDERAL SHARE.— The Federal share of assistance under this section shall be not less than 75 percent of the eligible cost of such assistance.

(c) UTILIZATION OF DOD RESOURCES.—

(1) GENERAL RULE.— During the immediate aftermath of an incident which may ultimately qualify for assistance under this title or title V of this Act, the Governor of the State in which such incident occurred may request the President to direct the Secretary of Defense to utilize the resources of the Department of Defense for the purpose of performing on public and private lands any emergency work which is made necessary by such incident and which is essential for the preservation of life and property. If the President determines that such work is essential for the preservation of life and property, the President shall grant such request to the extent the President determines practicable. Such emergency work may only be carried out for a period not to exceed 10 days.

(2) RULES APPLICABLE TO DEBRIS REMOVAL.— Any removal of debris and wreckage carried out under this subsection shall be subject to section 407(b), relating to unconditional authorization and indemnification for debris removal.

(3) EXPENDITURES OUT OF DISASTER RELIEF FUNDS.— The cost of any assistance provided pursuant to this subsection shall be reimbursed out of funds made available to carry out this Act.

(4) FEDERAL SHARE.— The Federal share of assistance under this subsection shall be not less than 75 percent.

(5) GUIDELINES.— Not later than 180 days after the date of the enactment of the Disaster Relief and Emergency Assistance Amendments of 1988, the President shall issue guidelines for carrying out this subsection. Such guidelines shall consider any likely effect assistance under this subsection will have on the availability of other forms of assistance under this Act.

(6) DEFINITIONS.—For purposes of this section—

(A) DEPARTMENT OF DEFENSE.— The term Department of Defense has the meaning the term department has under section 101 of title 10, United States Code.

(B) EMERGENCY WORK.— The term emergency work includes clearance and removal of debris and wreckage and temporary restoration of essential public facilities and services.

(d) SALARIES AND BENEFITS.—

(1) IN GENERAL.—If the President declares a major disaster or emergency for an area within the jurisdiction of a State, tribal, or local government, the President may reimburse the State, tribal, or local government for costs relating to—

(A) basic pay and benefits for permanent employees of the State, tribal, or local government conducting emergency protective measures under this section, if—

(i) the work is not typically performed by the employees; and

(ii) the type of work may otherwise be carried out by contract or agreement with private organizations, firms, or individuals.;[3] or

---
[3] The grammar at the end of subparagraph (A)(ii) is so in law.

(B) overtime and hazardous duty compensation for permanent employees of the State, tribal, or local government conducting emergency protective measures under this section.

(2) OVERTIME.— The guidelines for reimbursement for costs under paragraph (1) shall ensure that no State, tribal, or local government is denied reimbursement for overtime payments that are required pursuant to the Fair Labor Standards Act of 1938 (29 U.S.C. 201 et seq.).

(3) NO EFFECT ON MUTUAL AID PACTS.— Nothing in this subsection shall affect the ability of the President to reimburse labor force expenses provided pursuant to an authorized mutual aid pact.

[42 U.S.C. 5170b]

SEC. 404. HAZARD MITIGATION.

(a) IN GENERAL.— The President may contribute up to 75 percent of the cost of hazard mitigation measures which the President has determined are cost effective and which substantially reduce the risk of, or increase resilience to, future damage, hardship, loss, or suffering in any area affected by a major disaster, or any area affected by a fire for which assistance was provided under section 420. Such measures shall be identified following the evaluation of natural hazards under section 322 and shall be subject to approval by the President. Subject to section 322, the total of contributions under this section for a major disaster or event under section 420 shall not exceed 15 percent for amounts not more than $2,000,000,000, 10 percent for amounts of more than $2,000,000,000 and not more than $10,000,000,000, and 7.5 percent on amounts of more than $10,000,000,000 and not more than $35,333,000,000 of the estimated aggregate amount of grants to be made (less any associated administrative costs) under this Act with respect to the major disaster or event under section 420.

(b) PROPERTY ACQUISITION AND RELOCATION ASSISTANCE.—

(1) GENERAL AUTHORITY.— In providing hazard mitigation assistance under this section in connection with flooding, the Administrator of the Federal Emergency Management Agency may provide property acquisition and relocation assistance for projects that meet the requirements of paragraph (2).

(2) TERMS AND CONDITIONS.—An acquisition or relocation project shall be eligible to receive assistance pursuant to paragraph (1) only if—

(A)   the applicant for the assistance is otherwise eligible to receive assistance under the hazard mitigation grant program established under subsection (a); and

(B) on or after the date of enactment of this subsection, the applicant for the assistance enters into an agreement with the Administrator that provides assurances that—

(i)   any property acquired, accepted, or from which a structure will be removed pursuant to the project will be dedicated and maintained in perpetuity for a use that is compatible with open space, recreational, or wetlands management practices;

(ii) no new structure will be erected on property acquired, accepted or from which a structure was removed under the acquisition or relocation program other than—

(I)   a public facility that is open on all sides and functionally related to a designated open space;

(II)   a rest room; or

(III)   a structure that the Administrator approves in writing before the commencement of the construction of the structure; and

(iii) after receipt of the assistance, with respect to any property acquired, accepted or from which a structure was removed under the acquisition or relocation program—

(I)   no subsequent application for additional disaster assistance for any purpose will be made by the recipient to any Federal entity; and

(II)   no assistance referred to in subclause (I) will be provided to the applicant by any Federal source.

(3) STATUTORY CONSTRUCTION.— Nothing in this subsection is intended to alter or otherwise affect an agreement for an acquisition or relocation project carried out pursuant to this section that was in effect on the day before the date of enactment of this subsection.

(c) PROGRAM ADMINISTRATION BY STATES.—

(1) IN GENERAL.— A State desiring to administer the hazard mitigation grant program established by this section with respect to hazard mitigation assistance in the State may submit to the President an application for the delegation of the authority to administer the program.

(2) CRITERIA.—The President, in consultation and coordination with States and local governments, shall establish criteria for the approval of applications submitted under paragraph (1). Until such time as the Administrator promulgates regulations to implement this paragraph, the Administrator may waive notice and comment rulemaking, if the Administrator determines doing so is necessary to expeditiously implement this section, and may carry out this section as a pilot program. The criteria shall include, at a minimum—

(A)   the demonstrated ability of the State to manage the grant program under this section;

(B) there being in effect an approved mitigation plan under section 322; and

(C) a demonstrated commitment to mitigation activities.

(3) APPROVAL.— The President shall approve an application submitted under paragraph (1) that meets the criteria established under paragraph (2).

(4) WITHDRAWAL OF APPROVAL.— If, after approving an application of a State submitted under paragraph (1), the President determines that the State is not administering the hazard mitigation grant program established by this section in a manner satisfactory to the President, the President shall withdraw the approval.

(5) AUDITS.— The President shall provide for periodic audits of the hazard mitigation grant programs administered by States under this subsection.

(d) STREAMLINED PROCEDURES.—

(1) IN GENERAL.—For the purpose of providing assistance under this section, the President shall ensure that—

(A) adequate resources are devoted to ensure that applicable environmental reviews under the National Environmental Policy Act of 1969 and historic preservation reviews under the National Historic Preservation Act are completed on an expeditious basis; and

(B) the shortest existing applicable process under the National Environmental Policy Act of 1969 and the National Historic Preservation Act is utilized.

(2) AUTHORITY FOR OTHER EXPEDITED PROCEDURES.— The President may utilize expedited procedures in addition to those required under paragraph (1) for the purpose of providing assistance under this section, such as procedures under the Prototype Programmatic Agreement of the Federal Emergency Management Agency, for the consideration of multiple structures as a group and for an analysis of the cost-effectiveness and fulfillment of cost-share requirements for proposed hazard mitigation measures.

(e) ADVANCE ASSISTANCE.— The President may provide not more than 25 percent of the amount of the estimated cost of hazard mitigation measures to a State grantee eligible for a grant under this section before eligible costs are incurred.

(f) USE OF ASSISTANCE.—Recipients of hazard mitigation assistance provided under this section and section 203 may use the assistance to conduct activities to help reduce the risk of future damage, hardship, loss, or suffering in any area affected by a wildfire or windstorm, such as—

(1) reseeding ground cover with quick-growing or native species;

(2) mulching with straw or chipped wood;

(3) constructing straw, rock, or log dams in small tributaries to prevent flooding;

(4) placing logs and other erosion barriers to catch sediment on hill slopes;

(5)   installing debris traps to modify road and trail drainage mechanisms;

(6)   modifying or removing culverts to allow drainage to flow freely;

(7)   adding drainage dips and constructing emergency spillways to keep roads and bridges from washing out during floods;

(8)   planting grass to prevent the spread of noxious weeds;

(9)   installing warning signs;

(10)   establishing defensible space measures;

(11)   reducing hazardous fuels;

(12) mitigating windstorm and wildfire damage, including—

(A)   replacing or installing electrical transmission or distribution utility pole structures with poles that are resilient to extreme wind, wildfire, and combined ice and wind loadings for the basic wind speeds and ice conditions associated with the relevant location; and

(B)   the installation of fire-resistant wires and infrastructure and the undergrounding of wires;

(13)   removing standing burned trees; and

(14)   replacing water systems that have been burned and have caused contamination.

(g) USE OF ASSISTANCE FOR EARTHQUAKE HAZARDS.—Recipients of hazard mitigation assistance provided under this section and section 203 may use the assistance to conduct activities to help reduce the risk of future damage, hardship, loss, or suffering in any area affected by earthquake hazards, including—

(1)   improvements to regional seismic networks in support of building a capability for earthquake early warning;

(2)   improvements to geodetic networks in support of building a capability for earthquake early warning; and

(3)   improvements to seismometers, Global Positioning System receivers, and associated infrastructure in support of building a capability for earthquake early warning.

[42 U.S.C. 5170c]

FEDERAL FACILITIES

SEC. 405. (a)   The President may authorize any Federal agency to repair, reconstruct, restore, or replace any facility owned by the United States and under the jurisdiction of such agency which is damaged or destroyed by any major disaster if he determines that such repair, reconstruction, restoration, or replacement is of such importance and urgency that it cannot reasonably be deferred pending the enactment of specific authorizing legislation or the making of an appropriation for such purposes, or the obtaining of congressional committee approval.

(b)   In order to carry out the provisions of this section, such repair, reconstruction, restoration, or replacement may be begun notwithstanding a lack or an insufficiency of funds appropriated for such purpose, where such lack or insufficiency can be remedied by the transfer, in accordance with law, of funds appropriated to that agency for another purpose.

(c)   In implementing this section, Federal agencies shall evaluate the natural hazards to which these facilities are exposed and shall take appropriate action to mitigate such hazards, including safe land-use and construction practices, in accordance with standards prescribed by the President.

[42 U.S.C. 5171]

SEC. 406. REPAIR, RESTORATION, AND REPLACEMENT OF DAMAGED FACILITIES.

(a) CONTRIBUTIONS.—

(1) IN GENERAL.—The President may make contributions—

(A)   to a State or local government for the repair, restoration, reconstruction, or replacement of a public facility damaged or destroyed by a major disaster and for associated expenses incurred by the government; and

(B)   subject to paragraph (3), to a person that owns or operates a private nonprofit facility damaged or destroyed by a major disaster for the repair, restoration, reconstruction, or replacement of the facility and for associated expenses incurred by the person.

(2) ASSOCIATED EXPENSES.—For the purposes of this section, associated expenses shall include—

(A)   the costs of mobilizing and employing the National Guard for performance of eligible work;

(B)   the costs of using prison labor to perform eligible work, including wages actually paid, transportation to a worksite, and extraordinary costs of guards, food, and lodging;

(C)   base and overtime wages for the employees and extra hires of a State, local government, or person described in paragraph (1) that perform eligible work, plus fringe benefits on such wages to the extent that such benefits were being paid before the major disaster; and

(D)   base and overtime wages for extra hires to facilitate the implementation and enforcement of adopted building codes for a period of not more than 180 days after the major disaster is declared.

(3) CONDITIONS FOR ASSISTANCE TO PRIVATE NONPROFIT FACILITIES.—

(A) IN GENERAL.—The President may make contributions to a private nonprofit facility under paragraph (1)(B) only if—

(i)   the facility provides critical services (as defined by the President) in the event of a major disaster; or

(ii) the owner or operator of the facility—

(I)   has applied for a disaster loan under section 7(b) of the Small Business Act (15 U.S.C. 636(b)); and

(II)(aa)   has been determined to be ineligible for such a loan; or (bb) has obtained such a loan in the maximum amount for which the Small Business Administration determines the facility is eligible.

(B) DEFINITION OF CRITICAL SERVICES.— In this paragraph, the term critical services includes power, water (including water provided by an irrigation organization or facility), sewer, wastewater treatment, communications (including broadcast and telecommunications), education, and emergency medical care.

(C) RELIGIOUS FACILITIES.— A church, synagogue, mosque, temple, or other house of worship, educational facility, or any other private nonprofit facility, shall be eligible for contributions under paragraph (1)(B), without regard to the religious character of the facility or the primary religious use of the facility. No house of worship, educational facility, or any other private nonprofit facility may be excluded from receiving contributions under paragraph (1)(B) because leadership or membership in the organization operating the house of worship is limited to persons who share a religious faith or practice.

(4) NOTIFICATION TO CONGRESS.—Before making any contribution under this section in an amount greater than $20,000,000, the President shall notify—

(A) the Committee on Environment and Public Works of the Senate;

(B) the Committee on Transportation and Infrastructure of the House of Representatives;

(C) the Committee on Appropriations of the Senate; and

(D) the Committee on Appropriations of the House of Representatives.

(b) FEDERAL SHARE.—

(1) MINIMUM FEDERAL SHARE.— Except as provided in paragraph (2), the Federal share of assistance under this section shall be not less than 75 percent of the eligible cost of repair, restoration, reconstruction, or replacement carried out under this section.

(2) REDUCED FEDERAL SHARE.—The President shall promulgate regulations to reduce the Federal share of assistance under this section to not less than 25 percent in the case of the repair, restoration, reconstruction, or replacement of any eligible public facility or private nonprofit facility following an event associated with a major disaster—

(A) that has been damaged, on more than one occasion within the preceding 10-year period, by the same type of event; and

(B) the owner of which has failed to implement appropriate mitigation measures to address the hazard that caused the damage to the facility.

(3) INCREASED FEDERAL SHARE.—

(A) INCENTIVE MEASURES.—The President may provide incentives to a State or Tribal government to invest in measures that increase readiness for, and resilience from, a major disaster by recognizing such investments through a sliding scale that increases the minimum Federal share to 85 percent. Such

52

measures may include—

(i)   the adoption of a mitigation plan approved under section 322;

(ii)   investments in disaster relief, insurance, and emergency management programs;

(iii)   encouraging the adoption and enforcement of the latest published editions of relevant consensus-based codes, specifications, and standards that incorporate the latest hazard-resistant designs and establish minimum acceptable criteria for the design, construction, and maintenance of residential structures and facilities that may be eligible for assistance under this Act for the purpose of protecting the health, safety, and general welfare of the buildings' users against disasters;

(iv)   facilitating participation in the community rating system; and

(v)   funding mitigation projects or granting tax incentives for projects that reduce risk.

(B) COMPREHENSIVE GUIDANCE.— Not later than 1 year after the date of enactment of this paragraph, the President, acting through the Administrator, shall issue comprehensive guidance to State and Tribal governments regarding the measures and investments, weighted appropriately based on actuarial assessments of eligible actions, that will be recognized for the purpose of increasing the Federal share under this section. Guidance shall ensure that the agency's review of eligible measures and investments does not unduly delay determining the appropriate Federal cost share.

(C) REPORT.— One year after the issuance of the guidance required by subparagraph (B), the Administrator shall submit to the Committee on Transportation and Infrastructure of the House of Representatives and the Committee on Homeland Security and Governmental Affairs of the Senate a report regarding the analysis of the Federal cost shares paid under this section.

(D) SAVINGS CLAUSE.— Nothing in this paragraph prevents the President from increasing the Federal cost share above 85 percent.

(c) LARGE IN-LIEU CONTRIBUTIONS.—

(1) FOR PUBLIC FACILITIES.—

(A) IN GENERAL.— In any case in which a State or local government determines that the public welfare would not best be served by repairing, restoring, reconstructing, or replacing any public facility owned or controlled by the State or local government, the State or local government may elect to receive, in lieu of a contribution under subsection (a)(1)(A), a contribution in an amount equal to the Federal share of the Federal estimate of the cost of repairing, restoring, reconstructing, or replacing the facility and of management expenses.

(B) USE OF FUNDS.—Funds contributed to a State or local government under this paragraph may be used—

(i)   to repair, restore, or expand other selected public facilities;

(ii)   to construct new facilities; or

(iii)   to fund hazard mitigation measures that the State or local government determines to be necessary to meet a need for governmental services and functions in the area affected by the major disaster.

(C) LIMITATIONS.—Funds made available to a State or local government under this paragraph may not be used for—

(i)   any public facility located in a regulatory floodway (as defined in section 59.1 of title 44, Code of Federal Regulations (or a successor regulation)); or

(ii)   any uninsured public facility located in a special flood hazard area identified by the Administrator of the Federal Emergency Management Agency under the National Flood Insurance Act of 1968 (42 U.S.C. 4001 et seq.).

(2) FOR PRIVATE NONPROFIT FACILITIES.—

(A) IN GENERAL.— In any case in which a person that owns or operates a private nonprofit facility determines that the public welfare would not best be served by repairing, restoring, reconstructing, or replacing the facility, the person may elect to receive, in lieu of a contribution under subsection (a)(1)(B), a contribution in an amount equal to the Federal share of the Federal estimate of the cost of repairing, restoring, reconstructing, or replacing the facility and of management expenses.

(B) USE OF FUNDS.—Funds contributed to a person under this paragraph may be used—

(i)   to repair, restore, or expand other selected private nonprofit facilities owned or operated by the person;

(ii)   to construct new private nonprofit facilities to be owned or operated by the person; or

(iii)   to fund hazard mitigation measures that the person determines to be necessary to meet a need for the person's services and functions in the area affected by the major disaster.

(C) LIMITATIONS.—Funds made available to a person under this paragraph may not be used for—

(i)   any private nonprofit facility located in a regulatory floodway (as defined in section 59.1 of title 44, Code of Federal Regulations (or a successor regulation)); or

(ii)   any uninsured private nonprofit facility located in a special flood hazard area identified by the Administrator of the Federal Emergency Management Agency under the National Flood Insurance Act of 1968 (42 U.S.C. 4001 et seq.).

(d) FLOOD INSURANCE.—

(1) REDUCTION OF FEDERAL ASSISTANCE.— If a public facility or private nonprofit facility located in a special flood hazard area identified for more than 1 year by

the Administrator pursuant to the National Flood Insurance Act of 1968 (42 U.S.C. 4001 et seq.) is damaged or destroyed, after the 180th day following the date of the enactment of the Disaster Relief and Emergency Assistance Amendments of 1988, by flooding in a major disaster and such facility is not covered on the date of such flooding by flood insurance, the Federal assistance which would otherwise be available under this section with respect to repair, restoration, reconstruction, and replacement of such facility and associated expenses shall be reduced in accordance with paragraph (2). This section shall not apply to more than one building of a multi-structure educational, law enforcement, correctional, fire, or medical campus, for any major disaster or emergency declared by the President under section 401 or 501, respectively, of the Robert T. Stafford Disaster Relief and Emergency Assistance Act (42 U.S.C. 5170, 5191) on or after January 1, 2016, through December 31, 2018.

(2) AMOUNT OF REDUCTION.—The amount of a reduction in Federal assistance under this section with respect to a facility shall be the lesser of—

(A)   the value of such facility on the date of the flood damage or destruction, or

(B)   the maximum amount of insurance proceeds which would have been payable with respect to such facility if such facility had been covered by flood insurance under the National Flood Insurance Act of 1968 on such date.

(3) EXCEPTION.— Paragraphs (1) and (2) shall not apply to a private nonprofit facility which is not covered by flood insurance solely because of the local government's failure to participate in the flood insurance program established by the National Flood Insurance Act.

(4) DISSEMINATION OF INFORMATION.— The President shall disseminate information regarding the reduction in Federal assistance provided for by this subsection to State and local governments and the owners and operators of private nonprofit facilities who may be affected by such a reduction.

(e) ELIGIBLE COST.—

(1) DETERMINATION.—

(A) IN GENERAL.—For the purposes of this section, for disasters declared on or after August 1, 2017, or a disaster in which a cost estimate has not yet been finalized for a project, or for any project for which the finalized cost estimate is on appeal, the President shall estimate the eligible cost of repairing, restoring, reconstructing, or replacing a public facility or private nonprofit facility—

(i)   on the basis of the design of the facility as the facility existed immediately before the major disaster;

(ii)   in conformity with the latest published editions of relevant consensus-based codes, specifications, and standards that incorporate the latest hazard-resistant designs and establish minimum acceptable criteria for the design, construction, and maintenance of residential structures and facilities that may be eligible for assistance under this Act for the purposes of protecting the health, safety, and general welfare of a facility's users against disasters (including floodplain management and hazard mitigation criteria required by the President or under the Coastal Barrier Resources Act (16

U.S.C. 3501 et seq.)) ; and

(iii)   in a manner that allows the facility to meet the definition of resilient developed pursuant to this subsection.

(B) COST ESTIMATION PROCEDURES.—

(i) IN GENERAL.— Subject to paragraph (2), the President shall use the cost estimation procedures established under paragraph (3) to determine the eligible cost under this subsection.

(ii) APPLICABILITY.— The procedures specified in this paragraph and paragraph (2) shall apply only to projects the eligible cost of which is equal to or greater than the amount specified in section 422.

(C) CONTRIBUTIONS.— Contributions for the eligible cost made under this section may be provided on an actual cost basis or on cost-estimation procedures.

(2) MODIFICATION OF ELIGIBLE COST.—

(A) ACTUAL COST GREATER THAN CEILING PERCENTAGE OF ESTIMATED COST.— In any case in which the actual cost of repairing, restoring, reconstructing, or replacing a facility under this section is greater than the ceiling percentage established under paragraph (3) of the cost estimated under paragraph (1), the President may determine that the eligible cost includes a portion of the actual cost of the repair, restoration, reconstruction, or replacement that exceeds the cost estimated under paragraph (1).

(B) ACTUAL COST LESS THAN ESTIMATED COST.—

(i) GREATER THAN OR EQUAL TO FLOOR PERCENTAGE OF ESTIMATED COST.— In any case in which the actual cost of repairing, restoring, reconstructing, or replacing a facility under this section is less than 100 percent of the cost estimated under paragraph (1), but is greater than or equal to the floor percentage established under paragraph (3) of the cost estimated under paragraph (1), the State or local government or person receiving funds under this section shall use the excess funds to carry out cost-effective activities that reduce the risk of future damage, hardship, or suffering from a major disaster.

(ii) LESS THAN FLOOR PERCENTAGE OF ESTIMATED COST.— In any case in which the actual cost of repairing, restoring, reconstructing, or replacing a facility under this section is less than the floor percentage established under paragraph (3) of the cost estimated under paragraph (1), the State or local government or person receiving assistance under this section shall reimburse the President in the amount of the difference.

(C) NO EFFECT ON APPEALS PROCESS.— Nothing in this paragraph affects any right of appeal under section 423.

(3) EXPERT PANEL.—

(A) ESTABLISHMENT.— Not later than 18 months after the date of the enactment of this paragraph, the President, acting through the Administrator of the Federal Emergency Management Agency, shall establish an expert panel,

56

which shall include representatives from the construction industry and State and local government.

(B) DUTIES.—The expert panel shall develop recommendations concerning—

(i) procedures for estimating the cost of repairing, restoring, reconstructing, or replacing a facility consistent with industry practices; and

(ii) the ceiling and floor percentages referred to in paragraph (2).

(C) REGULATIONS.—Taking into account the recommendations of the expert panel under subparagraph (B), the President shall promulgate regulations that establish—

(i) cost estimation procedures described in subparagraph (B)(i); and

(ii) the ceiling and floor percentages referred to in paragraph (2).

(D) REVIEW BY PRESIDENT.— Not later than 2 years after the date of promulgation of regulations under subparagraph (C) and periodically thereafter, the President shall review the cost estimation procedures and the ceiling and floor percentages established under this paragraph.

(E) REPORT TO CONGRESS.— Not later than 1 year after the date of promulgation of regulations under subparagraph (C), 3 years after that date, and at the end of each 2-year period thereafter, the expert panel shall submit to Congress a report on the appropriateness of the cost estimation procedures.

(4) SPECIAL RULE.— In any case in which the facility being repaired, restored, reconstructed, or replaced under this section was under construction on the date of the major disaster, the cost of repairing, restoring, reconstructing, or replacing the facility shall include, for the purposes of this section, only those costs that, under the contract for the construction, are the owner's responsibility and not the contractor's responsibility.

(5) NEW RULES.—

(A) IN GENERAL.— Not later than 18 months after the date of enactment of this paragraph, the President, acting through the Administrator of the Federal Emergency Management Agency, and in consultation with the heads of relevant Federal departments and agencies, shall issue a final rulemaking that defines the terms resilient and resiliency for purposes of this subsection.

(B) INTERIM GUIDANCE.— Not later than 60 days after the date of enactment of this paragraph, the Administrator shall issue interim guidance to implement this subsection. Such interim guidance shall expire 18 months after the date of enactment of this paragraph or upon issuance of final regulations pursuant to subparagraph (A), whichever occurs first.

(C) GUIDANCE.— Not later than 90 days after the date on which the Administrator issues the final rulemaking under this paragraph, the Administrator shall issue any necessary guidance related to the rulemaking.

(D) REPORT.— Not later than 2 years after the date of enactment of this paragraph, the Administrator shall submit to Congress a report summarizing the regulations and guidance issued pursuant to this paragraph.

[42 U.S.C. 5172]

DEBRIS REMOVAL

SEC. 407. (a) The President, whenever he determines it to be in the public interest, is authorized—

(1)   through the use of Federal departments, agencies, and instrumentalities, to clear debris and wreckage resulting from a major disaster from publicly and privately owned lands and waters; and

(2)   to make grants to any State or local government or owner or operator of a private nonprofit facility for the purpose of removing debris or wreckage resulting from a major disaster from publicly or privately owned lands and waters.

(b)   No authority under this section shall be exercised unless the affected State or local government shall first arrange an unconditional authorization for removal of such debris or wreckage from public and private property, and, in the case of removal of debris or wreckage from private property, shall first agree to indemnify the Federal Government against any claim arising from such removal.

(c) RULES RELATING TO LARGE LOTS.— The President shall issue rules which provide for recognition of differences existing among urban, suburban, and rural lands in implementation of this section so as to facilitate adequate removal of debris and wreckage from large lots.

(d) FEDERAL SHARE.— The Federal share of assistance under this section shall be not less than 75 percent of the eligible cost of debris and wreckage removal carried out under this section.

(e) EXPEDITED PAYMENTS.—

(1) GRANT ASSISTANCE.— In making a grant under subsection (a)(2), the President shall provide not less than 50 percent of the President's initial estimate of the Federal share of assistance as an initial payment in accordance with paragraph (2).

(2) DATE OF PAYMENT.— Not later than 60 days after the date of the estimate described in paragraph (1) and not later than 90 days after the date on which the State or local government or owner or operator of a private nonprofit facility applies for assistance under this section, an initial payment described in paragraph (1) shall be paid.

[42 U.S.C. 5173]

SEC. 408. FEDERAL ASSISTANCE TO INDIVIDUALS AND HOUSEHOLDS.

(a) IN GENERAL.—

(1) PROVISION OF ASSISTANCE.— In accordance with this section, the President, in consultation with the Governor of a State, may provide financial assistance, and, if necessary, direct services, to individuals and households in the State who, as a direct result of a major disaster, have necessary expenses and serious needs in cases in which the individuals and households are unable to meet such expenses or needs through other means.

(2) RELATIONSHIP TO OTHER ASSISTANCE.— Under paragraph (1), an individual or household shall not be denied assistance under paragraph (1), (3), or (4) of subsection (c) solely on the basis that the individual or household has not applied for or received any loan or other financial assistance from the Small Business Administration or any other Federal agency.

(b) HOUSING ASSISTANCE.—

(1) ELIGIBILITY.— The President may provide financial or other assistance under this section to individuals and households to respond to the disaster-related housing needs of individuals and households who are displaced from their predisaster primary residences or whose predisaster primary residences are rendered uninhabitable, or with respect to individuals with disabilities, rendered inaccessible or uninhabitable, as a result of damage caused by a major disaster.

(2) DETERMINATION OF APPROPRIATE TYPES OF ASSISTANCE.—

(A) IN GENERAL.— The President shall determine appropriate types of housing assistance to be provided under this section to individuals and households described in subsection (a)(1) based on considerations of cost effectiveness, convenience to the individuals and households, and such other factors as the President may consider appropriate.

(B) MULTIPLE TYPES OF ASSISTANCE.— One or more types of housing assistance may be made available under this section, based on the suitability and availability of the types of assistance, to meet the needs of individuals and households in the particular disaster situation.

(c) TYPES OF HOUSING ASSISTANCE.—

(1) TEMPORARY HOUSING.—

(A) FINANCIAL ASSISTANCE.—

(i) IN GENERAL.— The President may provide financial assistance to individuals or households to rent alternate housing accommodations, existing rental units, manufactured housing, recreational vehicles, or other readily fabricated dwellings. Such assistance may include the payment of the cost of utilities, excluding telephone service.

(ii) AMOUNT.— The amount of assistance under clause (i) shall be based on the fair market rent for the accommodation provided plus the cost of any transportation, utility hookups, security deposits, or unit installation not provided directly by the President.

(B) DIRECT ASSISTANCE.—

(i) IN GENERAL.— The President may provide temporary housing units, acquired by purchase or lease, directly to individuals or households who, because of a lack of available housing resources, would be unable to make use of the assistance provided under subparagraph (A).

(ii) LEASE AND REPAIR OF RENTAL UNITS FOR TEMPORARY HOUSING.—

(I) IN GENERAL.—The President, to the extent the President determines it would be a cost-effective alternative to other temporary housing options, may—

(aa) enter into lease agreements with owners of multifamily rental property impacted by a major disaster or located in areas covered by a major disaster declaration to house individuals and households eligible for assistance under this section; and

(bb) make repairs or improvements to properties under such lease agreements, to the extent necessary to serve as safe and adequate temporary housing.

(II) IMPROVEMENTS OR REPAIRS.— Under the terms of any lease agreement for property entered into under this subsection, the value of the improvements or repairs shall be deducted from the value of the lease agreement.

(iii) PERIOD OF ASSISTANCE.— The President may not provide direct assistance under clause (i) with respect to a major disaster after the end of the 18-month period beginning on the date of the declaration of the major disaster by the President, except that the President may extend that period if the President determines that due to extraordinary circumstances an extension would be in the public interest.

(iv) COLLECTION OF RENTAL CHARGES.— After the end of the 18-month period referred to in clause (iii), the President may charge fair market rent for each temporary housing unit provided.

(2) REPAIRS.—

(A) IN GENERAL.—The President may provide financial assistance for—

(i) the repair of owner-occupied private residences, utilities, and residential infrastructure (such as a private access route) damaged by a major disaster to a safe and sanitary living or functioning condition; and

(ii) eligible hazard mitigation measures that reduce the likelihood of future damage to such residences, utilities, or infrastructure.

(B) RELATIONSHIP TO OTHER ASSISTANCE.— A recipient of assistance provided under this paragraph shall not be required to show that the assistance can be met through other means, except insurance proceeds.

(3) REPLACEMENT.—

(A) IN GENERAL.— The President may provide financial assistance for the replacement of owner-occupied private residences damaged by a major disaster.

(B) APPLICABILITY OF FLOOD INSURANCE REQUIREMENT.— With respect to assistance provided under this paragraph, the President may not waive any provision of Federal law requiring the purchase of flood insurance as a condition of the receipt of Federal disaster assistance.

(4) PERMANENT HOUSING CONSTRUCTION.—The President may provide financial assistance or direct assistance to individuals or households to construct permanent or semi-permanent housing in insular areas outside the continental United States and

in other locations in cases in which—

(A) no alternative housing resources are available; and

(B) the types of temporary housing assistance described in paragraph (1) are unavailable, infeasible, or not cost-effective.

(d) TERMS AND CONDITIONS RELATING TO HOUSING ASSISTANCE.—

(1) SITES.—

(A) IN GENERAL.—Any readily fabricated dwelling provided under this section shall, whenever practicable, be located on a site that—

(i) is complete with utilities;

(ii) meets the physical accessibility requirements for individuals with disabilities; and

(iii) is provided by the State or local government, by the owner of the site, or by the occupant who was displaced by the major disaster.

(B) SITES PROVIDED BY THE PRESIDENT.— A readily fabricated dwelling may be located on a site provided by the President if the President determines that such a site would be more economical or accessible.

(2) DISPOSAL OF UNITS.—

(A) SALE TO OCCUPANTS.—

(i) IN GENERAL.— Notwithstanding any other provision of law, a temporary housing unit purchased under this section by the President for the purpose of housing disaster victims may be sold directly to the individual or household who is occupying the unit if the individual or household lacks permanent housing.

(ii) SALE PRICE.— A sale of a temporary housing unit under clause (i) shall be at a price that is fair and equitable.

(iii) DEPOSIT OF PROCEEDS.— Notwithstanding any other provision of law, the proceeds of a sale under clause (i) shall be deposited in the appropriate Disaster Relief Fund account.

(iv) HAZARD AND FLOOD INSURANCE.— A sale of a temporary housing unit under clause (i) shall be made on the condition that the individual or household purchasing the housing unit agrees to obtain and maintain hazard and flood insurance on the housing unit.

(v) USE OF GSA SERVICES.— The President may use the services of the General Services Administration to accomplish a sale under clause (i).

(B) OTHER METHODS OF DISPOSAL.—If not disposed of under subparagraph (A), a temporary housing unit purchased under this section by the President for the purpose of housing disaster victims—

(i) may be sold to any person; or

(ii) may be sold, transferred, donated, or otherwise made available directly to a State or other governmental entity or to a voluntary organization for the sole purpose of providing temporary housing to disaster victims in major disasters and emergencies if, as a condition of the sale, transfer, or donation, the State, other governmental agency, or voluntary organization agrees—

(I)   to comply with the nondiscrimination provisions of section 308; and

(II)   to obtain and maintain hazard and flood insurance on the housing unit.

(e) FINANCIAL ASSISTANCE TO ADDRESS OTHER NEEDS.—

(1) MEDICAL, DENTAL, CHILD CARE, AND FUNERAL EXPENSES.— The President, in consultation with the Governor of a State, may provide financial assistance under this section to an individual or household in the State who is adversely affected by a major disaster to meet disaster-related medical, dental, child care, and funeral expenses.

(2) PERSONAL PROPERTY, TRANSPORTATION, AND OTHER EXPENSES.— The President, in consultation with the Governor of a State, may provide financial assistance under this section to an individual or household described in paragraph (1) to address personal property, transportation, and other necessary expenses or serious needs resulting from the major disaster.

(f) STATE ROLE.—

(1) STATE- OR INDIAN TRIBAL GOVERNMENT-ADMINISTERED ASSISTANCE AND OTHER NEEDS ASSISTANCE.—

(A) GRANT TO STATE.— Subject to subsection (g), a Governor may request a grant from the President to provide assistance to individuals and households in the State under subsections (c)(1)(B), (c)(4), and (e) if the President and the State or Indian tribal government comply, as determined by the Administrator, with paragraph (3).

(B) ADMINISTRATIVE COSTS.— A State that receives a grant under subparagraph (A) may expend not more than 5 percent of the amount of the grant for the administrative costs of providing assistance to individuals and households in the State under subsections (c)(1)(B), (c)(4), and (e).

(2) ACCESS TO RECORDS.— In providing assistance to individuals and households under this section, the President shall provide for the substantial and ongoing involvement of the States in which the individuals and households are located, including by providing to the States access to the electronic records of individuals and households receiving assistance under this section in order for the States to make available any additional State and local assistance to the individuals and households.

(3) REQUIREMENTS.—

(A) APPLICATION.— A State or Indian tribal government desiring to provide assistance under subsection (c)(1)(B), (c)(4), or (e) shall submit to the President an application for a grant to provide financial assistance under the program.

(B) CRITERIA.—The President, in consultation and coordination with State and Indian tribal governments, shall establish criteria for the approval of applications submitted under subparagraph (A). The criteria shall include, at a minimum—

(i)   a requirement that the State or Indian tribal government submit a housing strategy under subparagraph (C);

(ii)   the demonstrated ability of the State or Indian tribal government to manage the program under this section;

(iii)   there being in effect a plan approved by the President as to how the State or Indian tribal government will comply with applicable Federal laws and regulations and how the State or Indian tribal government will provide assistance under its plan;

(iv)   a requirement that the State or Indian tribal government comply with rules and regulations established pursuant to subsection (j); and

(v)   a requirement that the President, or the designee of the President, comply with subsection (i).

(C) REQUIREMENT OF HOUSING STRATEGY.—

(i) IN GENERAL.— A State or Indian tribal government submitting an application under this paragraph shall have an approved housing strategy, which shall be developed and submitted to the President for approval.

(ii) REQUIREMENTS.—The housing strategy required under clause (i) shall—

(I)   outline the approach of the State in working with Federal partners, Indian tribal governments, local communities, nongovernmental organizations, and individual disaster survivors to meet disaster-related sheltering and housing needs; and

(II)   include the establishment of an activation plan for a State Disaster Housing Task Force, as outlined in the National Disaster Housing Strategy, to bring together State, tribal, local, Federal, nongovernmental, and private sector expertise to evaluate housing requirements, consider potential solutions, recognize special needs populations, and propose recommendations.

(D) QUALITY ASSURANCE.— Before approving an application submitted under this section, the President, or the designee of the President, shall institute adequate policies, procedures, and internal controls to prevent waste, fraud, abuse, and program mismanagement for this program and for programs under subsections (c)(1)(B), (c)(4), and (e). The President shall monitor and conduct quality assurance activities on a State or Indian tribal government's implementation of programs under subsections (c)(1)(B), (c)(4), and (e). If, after approving an application of a State or Indian tribal government submitted under this paragraph, the President determines that the State or Indian tribal government is not administering the program established by this section in a manner satisfactory to the President, the President shall withdraw the approval.

(E) AUDITS.— The Inspector General of the Department of Homeland Security shall provide for periodic audits of the programs administered by States and Indian tribal governments under this subsection.

(F) APPLICABLE LAWS.— All Federal laws applicable to the management, administration, or contracting of the programs by the Federal Emergency Management Agency under this section shall be applicable to the management, administration, or contracting by a non-Federal entity under this section.

(G) REPORT ON EFFECTIVENESS.—Not later than 18 months after the date of enactment of this paragraph, the Inspector General of the Department of Homeland Security shall submit a report to the Committee on Homeland Security and Governmental Affairs of the Senate and the Committee on Transportation and Infrastructure of the House of Representatives on the State or Indian tribal government's role to provide assistance under this section. The report shall contain an assessment of the effectiveness of the State or Indian tribal government's role in providing assistance under this section, including—

(i) whether the State or Indian tribal government's role helped to improve the general speed of disaster recovery;

(ii) whether the State or Indian tribal government providing assistance under this section had the capacity to administer this section; and

(iii) recommendations for changes to improve the program if the State or Indian tribal government's role to administer the programs should be continued.

(H) REPORT ON INCENTIVES.— Not later than 12 months after the date of enactment of this paragraph, the Administrator of the Federal Emergency Management Agency shall submit a report to the Committee on Homeland Security and Governmental Affairs of the Senate and the Committee on Transportation and Infrastructure of the House of Representatives on a potential incentive structure for awards made under this section to encourage participation by eligible States and Indian tribal governments. In developing this report, the Administrator of the Federal Emergency Management Agency shall consult with State, local, and Indian tribal entities to gain their input on any such incentive structure to encourage participation and shall include this information in the report. This report should address, among other options, potential adjustments to the cost-share requirement and management costs to State and Indian tribal governments.

(I) PROHIBITION.— The President may not condition the provision of Federal assistance under this Act on a State or Indian tribal government requesting a grant under this section.

(J) MISCELLANEOUS.—

(i) NOTICE AND COMMENT.— The Administrator of the Federal Emergency Management Agency may waive notice and comment rulemaking with respect to rules to carry out this section, if the Administrator determines doing so is necessary to expeditiously implement this section, and may carry out this section as a pilot program until such regulations are promulgated.

(ii) FINAL RULE.— Not later than 2 years after the date of enactment of this paragraph, the Administrator of the Federal Emergency Management Agency shall issue final regulations to implement this subsection as amended by the Disaster Recovery Reform Act of 2018.

(iii) WAIVER AND EXPIRATION.— The authority under clause (i) and any pilot program implemented pursuant to such clause shall expire 2 years after the date of enactment of this paragraph or upon issuance of final regulations pursuant to clause (ii), whichever occurs sooner.

(g) COST SHARING.—

(1) FEDERAL SHARE.— Except as provided in paragraph (2), the Federal share of the costs eligible to be paid using assistance provided under this section shall be 100 percent.

(2) FINANCIAL ASSISTANCE TO ADDRESS OTHER NEEDS.—In the case of financial assistance provided under subsection (e)—

(A) the Federal share shall be 75 percent; and

(B) the non-Federal share shall be paid from funds made available by the State.

(h) MAXIMUM AMOUNT OF ASSISTANCE.—

(1) IN GENERAL.— No individual or household shall receive financial assistance greater than $25,000 under this section with respect to a single major disaster, excluding financial assistance to rent alternate housing accommodations under subsection (c)(1)(A)(i) and financial assistance to address other needs under subsection (e).

(2) OTHER NEEDS ASSISTANCE.— The maximum financial assistance any individual or household may receive under subsection (e) shall be equivalent to the amount set forth in paragraph (1) with respect to a single major disaster.

(3) ADJUSTMENT OF LIMIT.— The limit established under paragraphs (1) and (2) shall be adjusted annually to reflect changes in the Consumer Price Index for All Urban Consumers published by the Department of Labor.

(4) EXCLUSION OF NECESSARY EXPENSES FOR INDIVIDUALS WITH DISABILITIES.—

(A) IN GENERAL.— The maximum amount of assistance established under paragraph (1) shall exclude expenses to repair or replace damaged accessibility-related improvements under paragraphs (2), (3), and (4) of subsection (c) for individuals with disabilities.

(B) OTHER NEEDS ASSISTANCE.— The maximum amount of assistance established under paragraph (2) shall exclude expenses to repair or replace accessibility-related personal property under subsection (e)(2) for individuals with disabilities.

(i) VERIFICATION MEASURES.—In carrying out this section, the President shall develop a system, including an electronic database, that shall allow the President, or the designee of the President, to—

(1) verify the identity and address of recipients of assistance under this section to provide reasonable assurance that payments are made only to an individual or household that is eligible for such assistance;

(2) minimize the risk of making duplicative payments or payments for

fraudulent claims under this section;

(3) collect any duplicate payment on a claim under this section, or reduce the amount of subsequent payments to offset the amount of any such duplicate payment;

(4) provide instructions to recipients of assistance under this section regarding the proper use of any such assistance, regardless of how such assistance is distributed; and

(5) conduct an expedited and simplified review and appeal process for an individual or household whose application for assistance under this section is denied.

(j) RULES AND REGULATIONS.— The President shall prescribe rules and regulations to carry out this section, including criteria, standards, and procedures for determining eligibility for assistance.

[42 U.S.C. 5174]

[Sec. 409 repealed by section 104(c)(2) of Public Law 106–390 (114 Stat. 1559).]

UNEMPLOYMENT ASSISTANCE

SEC. 410. (a) The President is authorized to provide to any individual unemployed as a result of a major disaster such benefit assistance as he deems appropriate while such individual is unemployed for the weeks of such unemployment with respect to which the individual is not entitled to any other unemployment compensation (as that term is defined in section 85(b) of the Internal Revenue Code of 1986) or waiting period credit. Such assistance as the President shall provide shall be available to an individual as long as the individual's unemployment caused by the major disaster continues or until the individual is reemployed in a suitable position, but no longer than 26 weeks after the major disaster is declared. Such assistance for a week of unemployment shall not exceed the maximum weekly amount authorized under the unemployment compensation law of the State in which the disaster occurred. The President is directed to provide such assistance through agreements with States which, in his judgment, have an adequate system for administering such assistance through existing State agencies.

(b) REEMPLOYMENT ASSISTANCE.—

(1) STATE ASSISTANCE.— A State shall provide, without reimbursement from any funds provided under this Act, reemployment assistance services under any other law administered by the State to individuals receiving benefits under this section.

(2) FEDERAL ASSISTANCE.— The President may provide reemployment assistance services under other laws to individuals who are unemployed as a result of a major disaster and who reside in a State which does not provide such services.

(c) APPLICATION DEADLINE.—

(1) IN GENERAL.— With respect to a major disaster for which assistance is provided under this section and section 408, the application deadline for an individual seeking assistance under this section shall match the application deadline for individuals and households seeking assistance under section 408.

(2) EXTENSION.—The President may accept an application from an individual

described in paragraph (1) that is submitted after the deadline described in paragraph (1) if—

(A)   the individual has good cause for the late submission; and

(B)   the individual submits the application before the date on which the period during which assistance is provided under this section for the applicable major disaster expires.

[42 U.S.C. 5177]

[Sec. 411 repealed by section 206(c) of Public Law 106–390 (114 Stat. 1571).]

BENEFITS AND DISTRIBUTION

SEC. 412. (a)   Whenever the President determines that, as a result of a major disaster, low-income households are unable to purchase adequate amounts of nutritious food, he is authorized, under such terms and conditions as he may prescribe, to distribute through the Secretary of Agriculture or other appropriate agencies benefit allotments to such households pursuant to the provisions of the Food Stamp Act of 1964[4] (P.L. 91–671; 84 Stat. 2048) and to make surplus commodities available pursuant to the provisions of this Act.

---

[4]   The reference to the Food Stamp Act of 1964 probably should be a reference to the Food Stamp Act of 2008. The global amendment to the Robert T. Stafford Disaster Relief and Emergency Assistance Act made by section 4002(b)(1)(C) and (2)(DD) of Public Law 110–246 to strike Food Stamp Act and insert Food and Nutrition Act of 2008 was not carried out.

(b)   The President, through the Secretary of Agriculture or other appropriate agencies, is authorized to continue to make such benefit allotments and surplus commodities available to such households for so long as he determines necessary, taking into consideration such factors as he deems appropriate, including the consequences of the major disaster on the earning power of the households, to which assistance is made available under this section.

(c)   Nothing in this section shall be construed as amending or otherwise changing the provisions of the Food Stamp Act of 1964[4] except as they relate to the availability of supplemental nutrition assistance program benefits in an area affected by a major disaster.

[42 U.S.C. 5179]

FOOD COMMODITIES

SEC. 413. (a)   The President is authorized and directed to assure that adequate stocks of food will be ready and conveniently available for emergency mass feeding or distribution in any area of the United States which suffers a major disaster or emergency.

(b)   The Secretary of Agriculture shall utilize funds appropriated under section 32 of the Act of August 24, 1935 (7 U.S.C. 612c), to purchase food commodities necessary to provide adequate supplies for use in any area of the United States in the event of a major disaster or emergency in such area.

[42 U.S.C. 5180]

RELOCATION ASSISTANCE

SEC. 414. Notwithstanding any other provision of law, no person otherwise eligible for any kind of replacement housing payment under the Uniform Relocation Assistance and Real Property Acquisition Policies Act of 1970 (P.L. 91–646) shall be denied such eligibility as a result of his being unable, because of a major disaster as determined by the President, to meet the occupancy requirements set by such Act.
[42 U.S.C. 5181]

LEGAL SERVICES

SEC. 415. Whenever the President determines that low-income individuals are unable to secure legal services adequate to meet their needs as a consequence of a major disaster, consistent with the goals of the programs authorized by this Act, the President shall assure that such programs are conducted with the advice and assistance of appropriate Federal agencies and State and local bar associations.
[42 U.S.C. 5182]

CRISIS COUNSELING ASSISTANCE AND TRAINING

SEC. 416. [42 U.S.C. 5183]

(a) IN GENERAL.— The President is authorized to provide professional counseling services, including financial assistance to State or local agencies or private mental health organizations to provide such services or training of disaster workers, to victims of major disasters in order to relieve mental health problems caused or aggravated by such major disaster or its aftermath.

(b) TRAINING.— Each State, local agency, or private mental health organization providing professional counseling services described in subsection (a) shall ensure that, any individual providing professional counseling services to victims of a major disaster as authorized under subsection (a), including individuals working for nonprofit partners and recovery organizations, is appropriately trained to address impacts from major disasters in communities, and to individuals, with socio-economically disadvantaged backgrounds.

COMMUNITY DISASTER LOANS

SEC. 417. (a) IN GENERAL.— The President is authorized to make loans to any local government which may suffer a substantial loss of tax and other revenues as a result of a major disaster, and has demonstrated a need for financial assistance in order to perform its governmental functions.

(b) AMOUNT.—The amount of any such loan shall be based on need, shall not exceed—

(1) 25 percent of the annual operating budget of that local government for the fiscal year in which the major disaster occurs, and shall not exceed $5,000,000; or

(2) if the loss of tax and other revenues of the local government as a result of the major disaster is at least 75 percent of the annual operating budget of that local government for the fiscal year in which the major disaster occurs, 50 percent of the annual operating budget of that local government for the fiscal year in which the major disaster occurs, and shall not exceed $5,000,000.

(c) Repayment.—

(1) Cancellation.— Repayment of all or any part of such loan to the extent that revenues of the local government during the three full fiscal year period following the major disaster are insufficient to meet the operating budget of the local government, including additional disaster-related expenses of a municipal operation character shall be cancelled.

(2) Condition on continuing eligibility.— A local government shall not be eligible for further assistance under this section during any period in which the local government is in arrears with respect to a required repayment of a loan under this section.

(d) Effect on Other Assistance.— Any loans made under this section shall not reduce or otherwise affect any grants or other assistance under this Act.

[42 U.S.C. 5184]

EMERGENCY COMMUNICATIONS

Sec. 418. The President is authorized during, or in anticipation of, an emergency or major disaster to establish temporary communications systems and to make such communications available to State and local government officials and other persons as he deems appropriate.

[42 U.S.C. 5185]

EMERGENCY PUBLIC TRANSPORTATION

Sec. 419. The President is authorized to provide temporary public transportation service in an area affected by a major disaster to meet emergency needs and to provide transportation to governmental offices, supply centers, stores, post offices, schools, major employment centers, and such other places as may be necessary in order to enable the community to resume its normal pattern of life as soon as possible.

[42 U.S.C. 5186]

SEC. 420. FIRE MANAGEMENT ASSISTANCE.

(a) In General.— The President is authorized to provide assistance, including grants, equipment, supplies, and personnel, to any State or local government for the mitigation, management, and control of any fire on public or private forest land or grassland that threatens such destruction as would constitute a major disaster.

(b) Coordination With State and Tribal Departments of Forestry.— In providing assistance under this section, the President shall coordinate with State and tribal departments of forestry.

(c) Essential Assistance.— In providing assistance under this section, the President may use the authority provided under section 403.

(d) Hazard Mitigation Assistance.— Whether or not a major disaster is declared, the President may provide hazard mitigation assistance in accordance with section 404 in any area affected by a fire for which assistance was provided under this section.

(e) Rules and Regulations.— The President shall prescribe such rules and regulations as are necessary to carry out this section.

[42 U.S.C. 5187]

TIMBER SALE CONTRACTS

SEC. 421. (a)   Where an existing timber sale contract between the Secretary of Agriculture or the Secretary of the Interior and a timber purchaser does not provide relief from major physical change not due to negligence of the purchaser prior to approval of construction of any section of specified road or of any other specified development facility and, as a result of a major disaster, a major physical change results in additional construction work in connection with such road or facility by such purchaser with an estimated cost, as determined by the appropriate Secretary, (1) of more than $1,000 for sales under one million board feet, (2) of more than $1 per thousand board feet for sales of one to three million board feet, or (3) of more than $3,000 for sales over three million board feet, such increased construction cost shall be borne by the United States.

(b)   If the appropriate Secretary determines that damages are so great that restoration, reconstruction, or construction is not practical under the cost-sharing arrangement authorized by subsection (a) of this section, he may allow cancellation of a contract entered into by his Department not withstanding contrary provisions therein.

(c)   The Secretary of Agriculture is authorized to reduce to seven days the minimum period of advance public notice required by the first section of the Act of June 4, 1897 (16 U.S.C. 476), in connection with the sale of timber from national forests, whenever the Secretary determines that (1) the sale of such timber will assist in the construction of any area of a State damaged by a major disaster, (2) the sale of such timber will assist in sustaining the economy of such area, or (3) the sale of such timer is necessary to salvage the value of timber damaged in such major disaster or to protect undamaged timber.

(d)   The President, when he determines it to be in the public interest, is authorized to make grants to any State or local government for the purpose of removing from privately owned lands timber damaged as a result of a major disaster, and such State or local government is authorized upon application, to make payments out of such grants to any person for reimbursement of expenses actually incurred by such person in the removal of damaged timber, not to exceed the amount that such expenses exceed the salvage value of such timber.

[42 U.S.C. 5188]

SEC. 422. SIMPLIFIED PROCEDURE.

(a) IN GENERAL.—If the Federal estimate of the cost of—

(1)   repairing, restoring, reconstructing, or replacing under section 406 any damaged or destroyed public facility or private nonprofit facility,

(2)   emergency assistance under section 403 or 502, or

(3)   debris removed under section 407,

is less than $1,000,000 (or, if the Administrator has established a threshold under subsection (b), the amount established under subsection (b)), the President (on application of the State or local government or the owner or operator of the private nonprofit facility) may make the contribution to such State or local government or owner or operator under section 403, 406, 407, or 502, as the case may be, on the basis of such Federal estimate. Such $1,000,000 amount or, if applicable, the amount established under subsection (b), shall be adjusted annually to reflect changes in the

Consumer Price Index for All Urban Consumers published by the Department of Labor.

(b) THRESHOLD.—

(1) REPORT.—Not later than 1 year after the date of enactment of this subsection, the President, acting through the Administrator of the Federal Emergency Management Agency (in this section referred to as the Administrator), shall—

(A) complete an analysis to determine whether an increase in the threshold for eligibility under subsection (a) is appropriate, which shall include consideration of cost-effectiveness, speed of recovery, capacity of grantees, past performance, and accountability measures; and

(B) submit to the Committee on Transportation and Infrastructure of the House of Representatives and the Committee on Homeland Security and Governmental Affairs of the Senate a report regarding the analysis conducted under subparagraph (A).

(2) AMOUNT.—After the Administrator submits the report required under paragraph (1), the President shall direct the Administrator to—

(A) immediately establish a threshold for eligibility under this section in an appropriate amount, without regard to chapter 5 of title 5, United States Code; and

(B) adjust the threshold annually to reflect changes in the Consumer Price Index for all Urban Consumers published by the Department of Labor.

(3) REVIEW AND REPORT.— Not later than 3 years after the date on which the Administrator establishes a threshold under paragraph (2), and every 3 years thereafter, the President, acting through the Administrator, shall review the threshold for eligibility under this section and submit to the Committee on Transportation and Infrastructure of the House of Representatives and the Committee on Homeland Security and Governmental Affairs of the Senate a report regarding such review, including any recommendations developed pursuant to such review.

[42 U.S.C. 5189]

SEC. 423. APPEALS OF ASSISTANCE DECISIONS.

(a) RIGHT OF APPEAL.— Any decision regarding eligibility for, from, or amount of assistance under this title may be appealed within 60 days after the date on which the applicant for such assistance is notified of the award or denial of award of such assistance.

(b) PERIOD FOR DECISION.— A decision regarding an appeal under subsection (a) shall be rendered within 90 days after the date on which the Federal official designated to administer such appeals receives notice of such appeal.

(c) RULES.— The President shall issue rules which provide for the fair and impartial consideration of appeals under this section.

(d) RIGHT OF ARBITRATION.—

(1) IN GENERAL.— Notwithstanding this section, an applicant for assistance under this title may request arbitration to dispute the eligibility for assistance or repayment of assistance provided for a dispute of more than $500,000 for any

disaster that occurred after January 1, 2016. Such arbitration shall be conducted by the Civilian Board of Contract Appeals and the decision of such Board shall be binding.

(2) REVIEW.— The Civilian Board of Contract Appeals shall consider from the applicant all original and additional documentation, testimony, or other such evidence supporting the applicant's position at any time during arbitration.

(3) RURAL AREAS.— For an applicant for assistance in a rural area under this title, the assistance amount eligible for arbitration pursuant to this subsection shall be $100,000.

(4) RURAL AREA DEFINED.— For the purposes of this subsection, the term rural area means an area with a population of less than 200,000 outside an urbanized area.

(5) ELIGIBILITY.—To participate in arbitration under this subsection, an applicant—

(A) shall submit the dispute to the arbitration process established under the authority granted under section 601 of Public Law 111–5; and

(B) may submit a request for arbitration after the completion of the first appeal under subsection (a) at any time before the Administrator of the Federal Emergency Management Agency has issued a final agency determination or 180 days after the Administrator's receipt of the appeal if the Administrator has not provided the applicant with a final determination on the appeal. The applicant's request shall contain documentation from the administrative record for the first appeal and may contain additional documentation supporting the applicant's position.

[42 U.S.C. 5189a]

SEC. 424. DATE OF ELIGIBILITY; EXPENSES INCURRED BEFORE DATE OF DISASTER.

Eligibility for Federal assistance under this title shall begin on the date of the occurrence of the event which results in a declaration by the President that a major disaster exists; except that reasonable expenses which are incurred in anticipation of and immediately preceding such event may be eligible for Federal assistance under this Act.

[42 U.S.C. 5189b]

SEC. 425. TRANSPORTATION ASSISTANCE TO INDIVIDUALS AND HOUSEHOLDS.

The President may provide transportation assistance to relocate individuals displaced from their predisaster primary residences as a result of an incident declared under this Act or otherwise transported from their predisaster primary residences under section 403(a)(3) or 502, to and from alternative locations for short or long-term accommodation or to return an individual or household to their predisaster primary residence or alternative location, as determined necessary by the President.

[42 U.S.C. 5189c]

SEC. 426. CASE MANAGEMENT SERVICES.

[42 U.S.C. 5189d]

(a) IN GENERAL.— The President may provide case management services, including financial assistance, to State or local government agencies or qualified private organizations to provide such services, to victims of major disasters to identify and address unmet needs.

(b) TRAINING.— Each State, local government agency, or qualified private organization providing professional counseling services described in subsection (a) shall ensure that any individual providing case management services to victims of a major disaster as authorized under subsection (a), including individuals working for nonprofit partners and recovery organizations, is appropriately trained to address impacts from major disasters in communities, and to individuals, with socio-economically disadvantaged backgrounds.

SEC. 427. ESSENTIAL SERVICE PROVIDERS.

(a) DEFINITION.—In this section, the term essential service provider means an entity that—

(1)(A) provides—

(i)   wireline or mobile telephone service, Internet access service, radio or television broadcasting, cable service, or direct broadcast satellite service;

(ii)   electrical power;

(iii)   natural gas;

(iv)   water and sewer services; or

(v)   any other essential service, as determined by the President; or

(B)[5]   is a tower owner or operator;

---

[5]   Margin of subparagraph (B) is so in law.

---

(2) is—

(A)   a municipal entity;

(B)   a nonprofit entity; or

(C)   a private, for profit entity; and

(3)   is contributing to efforts to respond to an emergency or major disaster.

(b) AUTHORIZATION FOR ACCESSIBILITY.—Unless exceptional circumstances apply, in an emergency or major disaster, the head of a Federal agency, to the greatest extent practicable, shall not—

(1)   deny or impede access to the disaster site to an essential service provider whose access is necessary to restore and repair an essential service; or

(2)   impede the restoration or repair of the services described in subsection (a)(1).

(c) IMPLEMENTATION.— In implementing this section, the head of a Federal agency shall follow all applicable Federal laws, regulations, and policies.

[42 U.S.C. 5189e]

SEC. 428. PUBLIC ASSISTANCE PROGRAM ALTERNATIVE PROCEDURES.

(a) APPROVAL OF PROJECTS.— The President, acting through the Administrator of the Federal Emergency Management Agency, may approve projects under the alternative procedures adopted under this section for any major disaster or emergency declared on or after the date of enactment of this section[6]. The Administrator may also apply the alternate procedures adopted under this section to a major disaster or emergency declared before enactment of this Act[6] for which construction has not begun as of the date of enactment of this Act[6].

---

[6] The date of enactment of P.L. 113–2 is January 29, 2013.

(b) ADOPTION.— The Administrator, in coordination with States, tribal and local governments, and owners or operators of private nonprofit facilities, may adopt alternative procedures to administer assistance provided under sections 403(a)(3)(A), 406, 407, and 502(a)(5).

(c) GOALS OF PROCEDURES.—The alternative procedures adopted under subsection (a) shall further the goals of—

(1) reducing the costs to the Federal Government of providing such assistance;

(2) increasing flexibility in the administration of such assistance;

(3) expediting the provision of such assistance to a State, tribal or local government, or owner or operator of a private nonprofit facility; and

(4) providing financial incentives and disincentives for a State, tribal or local government, or owner or operator of a private nonprofit facility for the timely and cost-effective completion of projects with such assistance.

(d) PARTICIPATION.—

(1) IN GENERAL.— Participation in the alternative procedures adopted under this section shall be at the election of a State, tribal or local government, or owner or operator of a private nonprofit facility consistent with procedures determined by the Administrator.

(2) NO CONDITIONS.— The President may not condition the provision of Federal assistance under this Act on the election by a State, local, or Indian tribal government, or owner or operator of a private nonprofit facility to participate in the alternative procedures adopted under this section.

(e) MINIMUM PROCEDURES.—The alternative procedures adopted under this section shall include the following:

(1) For repair, restoration, and replacement of damaged facilities under section 406—

(A) making grants on the basis of fixed estimates, if the State, tribal or local government, or owner or operator of the private nonprofit facility agrees to be responsible for any actual costs that exceed the estimate;

(B) providing an option for a State, tribal or local government, or owner or operator of a private nonprofit facility to elect to receive an in-lieu contribution, without reduction, on the basis of estimates of—

(i)   the cost of repair, restoration, reconstruction, or replacement of a public facility owned or controlled by the State, tribal or local government or owner or operator of a private nonprofit facility; and

(ii) management expenses;

(C) consolidating, to the extent determined appropriate by the Administrator, the facilities of a State, tribal or local government, or owner or operator of a private nonprofit facility as a single project based upon the estimates adopted under the procedures;

(D) if the actual costs of a project completed under the procedures are less than the estimated costs thereof, the Administrator may permit a grantee or subgrantee to use all or part of the excess funds for—

(i) cost-effective activities that reduce the risk of future damage, hardship, or suffering from a major disaster; and

(ii) other activities to improve future Public Assistance operations or planning;

(E) in determining eligible costs under section 406, the Administrator shall make available, at an applicant's request and where the Administrator or the certified cost estimate prepared by the applicant's professionally licensed engineers has estimated an eligible Federal share for a project of at least $5,000,000, an independent expert panel to validate the estimated eligible cost consistent with applicable regulations and policies implementing this section;

(F) in determining eligible costs under section 406, the Administrator shall, at the applicant's request, consider properly conducted and certified cost estimates prepared by professionally licensed engineers (mutually agreed upon by the Administrator and the applicant), to the extent that such estimates comply with applicable regulations, policy, and guidance; and

(G) once certified by a professionally licensed engineer and accepted by the Administrator, the estimates on which grants made pursuant to this section are based shall be presumed to be reasonable and eligible costs, as long as there is no evidence of fraud.

(2) For debris removal under sections 403(a)(3)(A), 407, and 502(a)(5)—

(A) making grants on the basis of fixed estimates to provide financial incentives and disincentives for the timely or cost-effective completion if the State, tribal or local government, or owner or operator of the private nonprofit facility agrees to be responsible to pay for any actual costs that exceed the estimate;

(B) using a sliding scale for determining the Federal share for removal of debris and wreckage based on the time it takes to complete debris and wreckage removal;

(C) allowing use of program income from recycled debris without offset to the grant amount;

(D) reimbursing base and overtime wages for employees and extra hires of a State, tribal or local government, or owner or operator of a private nonprofit facility performing or administering debris and wreckage removal;

(E)   providing incentives to a State or tribal or local government to have a debris management plan approved by the Administrator and have pre-qualified 1 or more debris and wreckage removal contractors before the date of declaration of the major disaster; and

(F)   if the actual costs of projects under subparagraph (A) are less than the estimated costs of the project, the Administrator may permit a grantee or subgrantee to use all or part of the excess funds for—

(i)   debris management planning;

(ii)   acquisition of debris management equipment for current or future use; and

(iii)   other activities to improve future debris removal operations, as determined by the Administrator.

(f) WAIVER AUTHORITY.—Until such time as the Administrator promulgates regulations to implement this section, the Administrator may—

(1)   waive notice and comment rulemaking, if the Administrator determines the waiver is necessary to expeditiously implement this section; and

(2)   carry out the alternative procedures under this section as a pilot program.

(g) OVERTIME PAYMENTS.— The guidelines for reimbursement for costs under subsection (e)(2)(D) shall ensure that no State or local government is denied reimbursement for overtime payments that are required pursuant to the Fair Labor Standards Act of 1938 (29 U.S.C. 201 et seq.).

(h) REPORT.—

(1) IN GENERAL.— Not earlier than 3 years, and not later than 5 years, after the date of enactment of this section, the Inspector General of the Department of Homeland Security shall submit to the Committee on Homeland Security and Governmental Affairs of the Senate and the Committee on Transportation and Infrastructure of the House of Representatives a report on the alternative procedures for the repair, restoration, and replacement of damaged facilities under section 406 authorized under this section.

(2) CONTENTS.—The report shall contain an assessment of the effectiveness of the alternative procedures, including—

(A)   whether the alternative procedures helped to improve the general speed of disaster recovery;

(B)   the accuracy of the estimates relied upon;

(C)   whether the financial incentives and disincentives were effective;

(D)   whether the alternative procedures were cost effective;

(E)   whether the independent expert panel described in subsection (e)(1)(E) was effective; and

(F)   recommendations for whether the alternative procedures should be continued and any recommendations for changes to the alternative procedures.

[42 U.S.C. 5189f]

SEC. 429. UNIFIED FEDERAL REVIEW.

(a) IN GENERAL.— Not later than 18 months after the date of enactment of this section, and in consultation with the Council on Environmental Quality and the Advisory Council on Historic Preservation, the President shall establish an expedited and unified interagency review process to ensure compliance with environmental and historic requirements under Federal law relating to disaster recovery projects, in order to expedite the recovery process, consistent with applicable law.

(b) CONTENTS.— The review process established under this section shall include mechanisms to expeditiously address delays that may occur during the recovery from a major disaster and be updated, as appropriate, consistent with applicable law.
[42 U.S.C. 5189g]

SEC. 430. [42 U.S.C. 5189h] AGENCY ACCOUNTABILITY.

(a) PUBLIC ASSISTANCE.—Not later than 5 days after an award of a public assistance grant is made under section 406 that is in excess of $1,000,000, the Administrator of the Federal Emergency Management Agency shall publish on the website of the Federal Emergency Management Agency the specifics of each such grant award, including—

(1)   identifying the Federal Emergency Management Agency Region;

(2)   the disaster or emergency declaration number;

(3)   the State, county, and applicant name;

(4)   if the applicant is a private nonprofit organization;

(5)   the damage category code;

(6)   the amount of the Federal share obligated; and

(7)   the date of the award.

(b) MISSION ASSIGNMENTS.—

(1) IN GENERAL.—Not later than 5 days after the issuance of a mission assignment or mission assignment task order, the Administrator of the Federal Emergency Management Agency shall publish on the website of the Federal Emergency Management Agency any mission assignment or mission assignment task order to another Federal department or agency regarding a major disaster in excess of $1,000,000, including—

(A)   the name of the impacted State or Indian Tribe;

(B)   the disaster declaration for such State or Indian Tribe;

(C)   the assigned agency;

(D)   the assistance requested;

(E)   a description of the disaster;

(F)   the total cost estimate;

(G)   the amount obligated;

(H)   the State or Indian tribal government cost share, if applicable;

(I)   the authority under which the mission assignment or mission assignment task order was directed; and

(J)   if applicable, the date a State or Indian Tribe requested the mission assignment.

(2) RECORDING CHANGES.— Not later than 10 days after the last day of each month until a mission assignment or mission assignment task order described in paragraph (1) is completed and closed out, the Administrator of the Federal Emergency Management Agency shall update any changes to the total cost estimate and the amount obligated.

(c) DISASTER RELIEF MONTHLY REPORT.—Not later than 10 days after the first day of each month, the Administrator of the Federal Emergency Management Agency shall publish on the website of the Federal Emergency Management Agency reports, including a specific description of the methodology and the source data used in developing such reports, including—

(1) an estimate of the amounts for the fiscal year covered by the President's most recent budget pursuant to section 1105(a) of title 31, United States Code, including—

(A)   the unobligated balance of funds to be carried over from the prior fiscal year to the budget year;

(B)   the unobligated balance of funds to be carried over from the budget year to the budget year plus 1;

(C)   the amount of obligations for noncatastrophic events for the budget year;

(D)   the amount of obligations for the budget year for catastrophic events delineated by event and by State;

(E)   the total amount that has been previously obligated or will be required for catastrophic events delineated by event and by State for all prior years, the current fiscal year, the budget year, and each fiscal year thereafter;

(F)   the amount of previously obligated funds that will be recovered for the budget year;

(G)   the amount that will be required for obligations for emergencies, as described in section 102(1), major disasters, as described in section 102(2), fire management assistance grants, as described in section 420, surge activities, and disaster readiness and support activities; and

(H)   the amount required for activities not covered under section 251(b)(2)(D)(iii) of the Balanced Budget and Emergency Deficit Control Act of 1985 (2 U.S.C. 901(b)(2)(D)(iii)); and

(2) an estimate or actual amounts, if available, of the following for the current fiscal year, which shall be submitted not later than the fifth day of each month, published by the Administrator of the Federal Emergency Management Agency on the website of the Federal Emergency Management Agency not later than the fifth day of each month:

(A)   A summary of the amount of appropriations made available by source, the transfers executed, the previously allocated funds recovered, and the commitments, allocations, and obligations made.

(B) A table of disaster relief activity delineated by month, including—

(i) the beginning and ending balances;

(ii) the total obligations to include amounts obligated for fire assistance, emergencies, surge, and disaster support activities;

(iii) the obligations for catastrophic events delineated by event and by State; and

(iv) the amount of previously obligated funds that are recovered.

(C) A summary of allocations, obligations, and expenditures for catastrophic events delineated by event.

(D) The cost of the following categories of spending:

(i) Public assistance.

(ii) Individual assistance.

(iii) Mitigation.

(iv) Administrative.

(v) Operations.

(vi) Any other relevant category (including emergency measures and disaster resources) delineated by disaster.

(E) The date on which funds appropriated will be exhausted.

(d) CONTRACTS.—

(1) INFORMATION.—Not later than 10 days after the first day of each month, the Administrator of the Federal Emergency Management Agency shall publish on the website of the Federal Emergency Management Agency the specifics of each contract in excess of $1,000,000 that the Federal Emergency Management Agency enters into, including—

(A) the name of the party;

(B) the date the contract was awarded;

(C) the amount and scope of the contract;

(D) if the contract was awarded through a competitive bidding process;

(E) if no competitive bidding process was used, the reason why competitive bidding was not used; and

(F) the authority used to bypass the competitive bidding process.

The information shall be delineated by disaster, if applicable, and specify the damage category code, if applicable.

(2) REPORT.—Not later than 10 days after the last day of the fiscal year, the Administrator of the Federal Emergency Management Agency shall provide a report to the appropriate committees of Congress summarizing the following information for the preceding fiscal year:

(A)   The number of contracts awarded without competitive bidding.

(B)   The reasons why a competitive bidding process was not used.

(C)   The total amount of contracts awarded with no competitive bidding.

(D)   The damage category codes, if applicable, for contracts awarded without competitive bidding.

(e) COLLECTION OF PUBLIC ASSISTANCE RECIPIENT AND SUBRECIPIENT CONTRACTS.—

(1) IN GENERAL.—Not later than 180 days after the date of enactment of this subsection, the Administrator of the Federal Emergency Management Agency shall initiate and maintain an effort to collect and store information, prior to the project closeout phase on any contract entered into by a public assistance recipient or subrecipient that through the base award, available options, or any subsequent modifications has an estimated value of more than $1,000,000 and is funded through section 324, 403, 404, 406, 407, 428, or 502, including—

(A)   the disaster number, project worksheet number, and the category of work associated with each contract;

(B)   the name of each party;

(C)   the date the contract was awarded;

(D)   the amount of the contract;

(E)   the scope of the contract;

(F)   the period of performance for the contract; and

(G)   whether the contract was awarded through a competitive bidding process.

(2) AVAILABILITY OF INFORMATION COLLECTED.— The Administrator of the Federal Emergency Management Agency shall make the information collected and stored under paragraph (1) available to the Inspector General of the Department of Homeland Security, the Government Accountability Office, and appropriate committees of Congress, upon request.

(3) REPORT.— Not later than 365 days after the date of enactment of this subsection, the Administrator of the Federal Emergency Management Agency shall submit a report to the Committee on Homeland Security and Governmental Affairs of the Senate and the Committee on Transportation and Infrastructure of the House of Representatives on the efforts of the Federal Emergency Management Agency to collect the information described in paragraph (1).

TITLE V—EMERGENCY ASSISTANCE PROGRAMS

SEC. 501. PROCEDURE FOR DECLARATION.

(a) REQUEST AND DECLARATION.— All requests for a declaration by the President that an emergency exists shall be made by the Governor of the affected State. Such a request shall be based on a finding that the situation is of such severity and magnitude that effective response is beyond the capabilities of the State and the affected local governments and that Federal assistance is necessary. As a part of such request, and as a

---

prerequisite to emergency assistance under this Act, the Governor shall take appropriate action under State law and direct execution of the State's emergency plan. The Governor shall furnish information describing the State and local efforts and resources which have been or will be used to alleviate the emergency, and will define the type and extent of Federal aid required. Based upon such Governor's request, the President may declare that an emergency exists.

(b) CERTAIN EMERGENCIES INVOLVING FEDERAL PRIMARY RESPONSIBILITY.— The President may exercise any authority vested in him by section 502 or section 503 with respect to an emergency when he determines that an emergency exists for which the primary responsibility for response rests with the United States because the emergency involves a subject area for which, under the Constitution or laws of the United States, the United States exercises exclusive or preeminent responsibility and authority. In determining whether or not such an emergency exists, the President shall consult the Governor of any affected State, if practicable. The President's determination may be made without regard to subsection (a).

(c) INDIAN TRIBAL GOVERNMENT REQUESTS.—

(1) IN GENERAL.— The Chief Executive of an affected Indian tribal government may submit a request for a declaration by the President that an emergency exists consistent with the requirements of subsection (a).

(2) REFERENCES.— In implementing assistance authorized by the President under this title in response to a request of the Chief Executive of an affected Indian tribal government for an emergency declaration, any reference in this title or title III (except sections 310 and 326) to a State or the Governor of a State is deemed to refer to an affected Indian tribal government or the Chief Executive of an affected Indian tribal government, as appropriate.

(3) SAVINGS PROVISION.— Nothing in this subsection shall prohibit an Indian tribal government from receiving assistance under this title through a declaration made by the President at the request of a State under subsection (a) if the President does not make a declaration under this subsection for the same incident.

[42 U.S.C. 5191]

SEC. 502. FEDERAL EMERGENCY ASSISTANCE.

(a) SPECIFIED.—In any emergency, the President may—

(1) direct any Federal agency, with or without reimbursement, to utilize its authorities and the resources granted to it under Federal law (including personnel, equipment, supplies, facilities, and managerial, technical and advisory services) in support of State and local emergency assistance efforts to save lives, protect property and public health and safety, and lessen or avert the threat of a catastrophe, including precautionary evacuations;

(2) coordinate all disaster relief assistance (including voluntary assistance) provided by Federal agencies, private organizations, and State and local governments;

(3) provide technical and advisory assistance to affected State and local governments for—

(A)   the performance of essential community services;

(B)   issuance of warnings of risks or hazards;

(C)   public health and safety information, including dissemination of such information;

(D)   provision of health and safety measures; and

(E)   management, control, and reduction of immediate threats to public health and safety;

(4)   provide emergency assistance through Federal agencies;

(5)   remove debris in accordance with the terms and conditions of section 407;

(6)   provide assistance in accordance with section 408 and section 416;

(7)   assist State and local governments in the distribution of medicine, food, and other consumable supplies, and emergency assistance; and

(8) provide accelerated Federal assistance and Federal support where necessary to save lives, prevent human suffering, or mitigate severe damage, which may be provided in the absence of a specific request and in which case the President—

(A)   shall, to the fullest extent practicable, promptly notify and coordinate with a State in which such assistance or support is provided; and

(B)   shall not, in notifying and coordinating with a State under subparagraph (A), delay or impede the rapid deployment, use, and distribution of critical resources to victims of an emergency.

(b) GENERAL.— Whenever the Federal assistance provided under subsection (a) with respect to an emergency is inadequate, the President may also provide assistance with respect to efforts to save lives, protect property and public health and safety, and lessen or avert the threat of a catastrophe, including precautionary evacuations.

(c) GUIDELINES.— The President shall promulgate and maintain guidelines to assist Governors in requesting the declaration of an emergency in advance of a natural or man-made disaster (including for the purpose of seeking assistance with special needs and other evacuation efforts) under this section by defining the types of assistance available to affected States and the circumstances under which such requests are likely to be approved.
[42 U.S.C. 5192]

SEC. 503. AMOUNT OF ASSISTANCE.

(a) FEDERAL SHARE.— The Federal share for assistance provided under this title shall be equal to not less than 75 percent of the eligible costs.

(b) LIMIT ON AMOUNT OF ASSISTANCE.—

(1) IN GENERAL.— Except as provided in paragraph (2), total assistance provided under this title for a single emergency shall not exceed $5,000,000.

(2) ADDITIONAL ASSISTANCE.—The limitation described in paragraph (1) may be exceeded when the President determines that—

(A)   continued emergency assistance is immediately required;

(B)   there is a continuing and immediate risk to lives, property, public health or safety; and

(C)   necessary assistance will not otherwise be provided on a timely basis.

(3) REPORT.— Whenever the limitation described in paragraph (1) is exceeded, the President shall report to the Congress on the nature and extent of emergency assistance requirements and shall propose additional legislation if necessary.

[42 U.S.C. 5193]

TITLE VI—EMERGENCY PREPAREDNESS

SEC. 601. DECLARATION OF POLICY.

The purpose of this title is to provide a system of emergency preparedness for the protection of life and property in the United States from hazards and to vest responsibility for emergency preparedness jointly in the Federal Government and the States and their political subdivisions. The Congress recognizes that the organizational structure established jointly by the Federal Government and the States and their political subdivisions for emergency preparedness purposes can be effectively utilized to provide relief and assistance to people in areas of the United States struck by a hazard. The Federal Government shall provide necessary direction, coordination, and guidance, and shall provide necessary assistance, as authorized in this title so that a comprehensive emergency preparedness system exists for all hazards.

[42 U.S.C. 5195]

SEC. 602. DEFINITIONS.

(a) DEFINITIONS.—For purposes of this title only:

(1) HAZARD.—The term hazard means an emergency or disaster resulting from—

(A)   a natural disaster; or

(B)   an accidental or man-caused event.

(2) NATURAL DISASTER.— The term natural disaster means any hurricane, tornado, storm, flood, high water, wind-driven water, tidal wave, tsunami, earthquake, volcanic eruption, landslide, mudslide, snowstorm, drought, fire, or other catastrophe in any part of the United States which causes, or which may cause, substantial damage or injury to civilian property or persons.

(3) EMERGENCY PREPAREDNESS.—The term emergency preparedness means all those activities and measures designed or undertaken to prepare for or minimize the effects of a hazard upon the civilian population, to deal with the immediate emergency conditions which would be created by the hazard, and to effectuate emergency repairs to, or the emergency restoration of, vital utilities and facilities destroyed or damaged by the hazard. Such term includes the following:

(A)   Measures to be undertaken in preparation for anticipated hazards (including the establishment of appropriate organizations, operational plans, and supporting agreements, the recruitment and training of personnel, the conduct of research, the procurement and stockpiling of necessary materials and supplies,

83

the provision of suitable warning systems, the construction or preparation of shelters, shelter areas, and control centers, and, when appropriate, the non-military evacuation of the civilian population).

(B) Measures to be undertaken during a hazard (including the enforcement of passive defense regulations prescribed by duly established military or civil authorities, the evacuation of personnel to shelter areas, the control of traffic and panic, and the control and use of lighting and civil communications).

(C) Measures to be undertaken following a hazard (including activities for fire fighting, rescue, emergency medical, health and sanitation services, monitoring for specific dangers of special weapons, unexploded bomb reconnaissance, essential debris clearance, emergency welfare measures, and immediately essential emergency repair or restoration of damaged vital facilities).

(4) ORGANIZATIONAL EQUIPMENT.— The term organizational equipment means equipment determined by the Administrator to be necessary to an emergency preparedness organization, as distinguished from personal equipment, and of such a type or nature as to require it to be financed in whole or in part by the Federal Government. Such term does not include those items which the local community normally uses in combating local disasters, except when required in unusual quantities dictated by the requirements of the emergency preparedness plans.

(5) MATERIALS.— The term materials includes raw materials, supplies, medicines, equipment, component parts and technical information and processes necessary for emergency preparedness.

(6) FACILITIES.— The term facilities, except as otherwise provided in this title, includes buildings, shelters, utilities, and land.

(7) ADMINISTRATOR.— The term Administrator means the Administrator of the Federal Emergency Management Agency.

(8) NEIGHBORING COUNTRIES.— The term neighboring countries includes Canada and Mexico.

(9) UNITED STATES AND STATES.— The terms United States and States includes[7] the several States, the District of Columbia, and territories and possessions of the United States.

---

[7] The word includes in subsections (a)(9) and (b) probably should read include.

---

(10) STATE.— The term State includes interstate emergency preparedness authorities established under section 611(h).

(b) CROSS REFERENCE.— The terms national defense and defense, as used in the Defense Production Act of 1950 (50 U.S.C. App. 2061 et seq.), includes[7] emergency preparedness activities conducted pursuant to this title.
[42 U.S.C. 5195a]

SEC. 603. ADMINISTRATION OF TITLE.

This title shall be carried out by the Administrator of the Federal Emergency Management Agency.

[42 U.S.C. 5195b]

Subtitle A—Powers and Duties

SEC. 611. DETAILED FUNCTIONS OF ADMINISTRATION.

(a) In General.— In order to carry out the policy described in section 601, the Administrator shall have the authorities provided in this section.

(b) Federal Emergency Response Plans and Programs.— The Administrator may prepare Federal response plans and programs for the emergency preparedness of the United States and sponsor and direct such plans and programs. To prepare such plans and programs and coordinate such plans and programs with State efforts, the Administrator may request such reports on State plans and operations for emergency preparedness as may be necessary to keep the President, Congress, and the States advised of the status of emergency preparedness in the United States.

(c) Delegation of Emergency Preparedness Responsibilities.— With the approval of the President, the Administrator may delegate to other departments and agencies of the Federal Government appropriate emergency preparedness responsibilities and review and coordinate the emergency preparedness activities of the departments and agencies with each other and with the activities of the States and neighboring countries.

(d) Communications and Warnings.— The Administrator may make appropriate provision for necessary emergency preparedness communications and for dissemination of warnings to the civilian population of a hazard.

(e) Emergency Preparedness Measures.—The Administrator may study and develop emergency preparedness measures designed to afford adequate protection of life and property, including—

(1) research and studies as to the best methods of treating the effects of hazards;

(2) developing shelter designs and materials for protective covering or construction;

(3) developing equipment or facilities and effecting the standardization thereof to meet emergency preparedness requirements; and

(4) plans that take into account the needs of individuals with pets and service animals prior to, during, and following a major disaster or emergency.

(f) Training Programs.—(1) The Administrator may—

(A) conduct or arrange, by contract or otherwise, for training programs for the instruction of emergency preparedness officials and other persons in the organization, operation, and techniques of emergency preparedness;

(B) conduct or operate schools or including the payment of travel expenses, in accordance with subchapter I of chapter 57 of title 5, United States Code, and the Standardized Government Travel Regulations, and per diem allowances, in lieu of subsistence for trainees in attendance or the furnishing of subsistence and quarters for trainees and instructors on terms prescribed by the Administrator; and

(C)   provide instructors and training aids as necessary.

(2)   The terms prescribed by the Administrator for the payment of travel expenses and per diem allowances authorized by this subsection shall include a provision that such payment shall not exceed one-half of the total cost of such expenses.

(3)   The Administrator may lease real property required for the purpose of carrying out this subsection, but may not acquire fee title to property unless specifically authorized by law.

(g) PUBLIC DISSEMINATION OF EMERGENCY PREPAREDNESS INFORMATION.— The Administrator may publicly disseminate appropriate emergency preparedness information by all appropriate means.

(h) EMERGENCY PREPAREDNESS COMPACTS.—(1) The Administrator shall establish a program supporting the development of emergency preparedness compacts for acts of terrorism, disasters, and emergencies throughout the Nation, by—

(A)   identifying and cataloging existing emergency preparedness compacts for acts of terrorism, disasters, and emergencies at the State and local levels of government;

(B)   disseminating to State and local governments examples of best practices in the development of emergency preparedness compacts and models of existing emergency preparedness compacts, including agreements involving interstate jurisdictions; and

(C)   completing an inventory of Federal response capabilities for acts of terrorism, disasters, and emergencies, making such inventory available to appropriate Federal, State, and local government officials, and ensuring that such inventory is as current and accurate as practicable.

(2) The Administrator may—

(A)   assist and encourage the States to negotiate and enter into interstate emergency preparedness compacts;

(B)   review the terms and conditions of such proposed compacts in order to assist, to the extent feasible, in obtaining uniformity between such compacts and consistency with Federal emergency response plans and programs;

(C)   assist and coordinate the activities under such compacts; and

(D)   aid and assist in encouraging reciprocal emergency preparedness legislation by the States which will permit the furnishing of mutual aid for emergency preparedness purposes in the event of a hazard which cannot be adequately met or controlled by a State or political subdivision thereof threatened with or experiencing a hazard.

(3)   A copy of each interstate emergency preparedness compact shall be transmitted promptly to the Senate and the House of Representatives. The consent of Congress is deemed to be granted to each such compact upon the expiration of the 60-day period beginning on the date on which the compact is transmitted to Congress.

(4) Nothing in this subsection shall be construed as preventing Congress from disapproving, or withdrawing at any time its consent to, any interstate emergency preparedness compact.

(i) MATERIALS AND FACILITIES.—(1) The Administrator may procure by condemnation or otherwise, construct, lease, transport, store, maintain, renovate or distribute materials and facilities for emergency preparedness, with the right to take immediate possession thereof.

(2) Facilities acquired by purchase, donation, or other means of transfer may be occupied, used, and improved for the purposes of this title before the approval of title by the Attorney General as required by section 355 of the Revised Statutes (40 U.S.C. 255).

(3) The Administrator may lease real property required for the purpose of carrying out the provisions of this subsection, but shall not acquire fee title to property unless specifically authorized by law.

(4) The Administrator may procure and maintain under this subsection radiological, chemical, bacteriological, and biological agent monitoring and decontamination devices and distribute such devices by loan or grant to the States for emergency preparedness purposes, under such terms and conditions as the Administrator shall prescribe.

(j) FINANCIAL CONTRIBUTIONS.—(1) The Administrator may make financial contributions, on the basis of programs or projects approved by the Administrator, to the States for emergency preparedness purposes, including the procurement, construction, leasing, or renovating of materials and facilities. Such contributions shall be made on such terms or conditions as the Administrator shall prescribe, including the method of purchase, the quantity, quality, or specifications of the materials or facilities, and such other factors or care or treatment to assure the uniformity, availability, and good condition of such materials or facilities.

(2) The Administrator may make financial contributions, on the basis of programs or projects approved by the Administrator, to the States and local authorities for animal emergency preparedness purposes, including the procurement, construction, leasing, or renovating of emergency shelter facilities and materials that will accommodate people with pets and service animals.

(3) No contribution may be made under this subsection for the procurement of land or for the purchase of personal equipment for State or local emergency preparedness workers.

(4) The amounts authorized to be contributed by the Administrator to each State for organizational equipment shall be equally matched by such State from any source it determines is consistent with its laws.

(5) Financial contributions to the States for shelters and other protective facilities shall be determined by taking the amount of funds appropriated or available to the Administrator for such facilities in each fiscal year and apportioning such funds among the States in the ratio which the urban population of the critical target areas (as determined by the Administrator) in each State, at the time of the determination, bears to the total urban population of the critical target areas of all of

the States.

(6)   The amounts authorized to be contributed by the Administrator to each State for such shelters and protective facilities shall be equally matched by such State from any source it determines is consistent with its laws and, if not matched within a reasonable time, the Administrator may reallocate such amounts to other States under the formula described in paragraph (4). The value of any land contributed by any State or political subdivision thereof shall be excluded from the computation of the State share under this subsection.

(7)   The amounts paid to any State under this subsection shall be expended solely in carrying out the purposes set forth herein and in accordance with State emergency preparedness programs or projects approved by the Administrator. The Administrator shall make no contribution toward the cost of any program or project for the procurement, construction, or leasing of any facility which (A) is intended for use, in whole or in part, for any purpose other than emergency preparedness, and (B) is of such kind that upon completion it will, in the judgment of the Administrator, be capable of producing sufficient revenue to provide reasonable assurance of the retirement or repayment of such cost; except that (subject to the preceding provisions of this subsection) the Administrator may make a contribution to any State toward that portion of the cost of the construction, reconstruction, or enlargement of any facility which the Administrator determines to be directly attributable to the incorporation in such facility of any feature of construction or design not necessary for the principal intended purpose thereof but which is, in the judgment of the Administrator necessary for the use of such facility for emergency preparedness purposes.

(8)   The Administrator shall submit to Congress a report, at least annually, regarding all contributions made pursuant to this subsection.

(9)   All laborers and mechanics employed by contractors or subcontractors in the performance of construction work financed with the assistance of any contribution of Federal funds made by the Administrator under this subsection shall be paid wages at rates not less than those prevailing on similar construction in the locality as determined by the Secretary of Labor in accordance with the Act of March 3, 1931 (commonly known as the Davis-Bacon Act (40 U.S.C. 276a–276a–5)), and every such employee shall receive compensation at a rate not less than one and ½ times the basic rate of pay of the employee for all hours worked in any workweek in excess of eight hours in any workday or 40 hours in the workweek, as the case may be. The Administrator shall make no contribution of Federal funds without first obtaining adequate assurance that these labor standards will be maintained upon the construction work. The Secretary of Labor shall have, with respect to the labor standards specified in this subsection, the authority and functions set forth in Reorganization Plan Numbered 14 of 1950 (5 U.S.C. App.) and section 2 of the Act of June 13, 1934 (40 U.S.C. 276(c)).

(k) SALE OR DISPOSAL OF CERTAIN MATERIALS AND FACILITIES.— The Administrator may arrange for the sale or disposal of materials and facilities found by the Administrator to be unnecessary or unsuitable for emergency preparedness purposes in the same manner as provided for excess property under the Federal Property and Administrative Services Act of 1949 (40 U.S.C. 471 et seq.). Any funds received as

proceeds from the sale or other disposition of such materials and facilities shall be deposited into the Treasury as miscellaneous receipts.
[42 U.S.C. 5196]

SEC. 612. MUTUAL AID PACTS BETWEEN STATES AND NEIGHBORING COUNTRIES.

The Administrator shall give all practicable assistance to States in arranging, through the Department of State, mutual emergency preparedness aid between the States and neighboring countries.
[42 U.S.C. 5196a]

SEC. 613. CONTRIBUTIONS FOR PERSONNEL AND ADMINISTRATIVE EXPENSES.

(a) GENERAL AUTHORITY.— To further assist in carrying out the purposes of this title, the Administrator may make financial contributions to the States (including interstate emergency preparedness authorities established pursuant to section 611(h)) for necessary and essential State and local emergency preparedness personnel and administrative expenses, on the basis of approved plans (which shall be consistent with the Federal emergency response plans for emergency preparedness) for the emergency preparedness of the States. The financial contributions to the States under this section may not exceed one-half of the total cost of such necessary and essential State and local emergency preparedness personnel and administrative expenses.

(b) PLAN REQUIREMENTS.—A plan submitted under this section shall—

(1)   provide, pursuant to State law, that the plan shall be in effect in all political subdivisions of the State and be mandatory on them and be administered or supervised by a single State agency;

(2)   provide that the State shall share the financial assistance with that provided by the Federal Government under this section from any source determined by it to be consistent with State law;

(3)   provide for the development of State and local emergency preparedness operational plans, including a catastrophic incident annex, pursuant to standards approved by the Administrator;

(4)   provide for the employment of a full-time emergency preparedness director, or deputy director, by the State;

(5)   provide that the State shall make such reports in such form and content as the Administrator may require;

(6)   make available to duly authorized representatives of the Administrator and the Comptroller General, books, records, and papers necessary to conduct audits for the purposes of this section; and

(7)   include a plan for providing information to the public in a coordinated manner.

(c) CATASTROPHIC INCIDENT ANNEX.—

(1) CONSISTENCY.—A catastrophic incident annex submitted under subsection (b)(3) shall be—

(A)   modeled after the catastrophic incident annex of the National Response Plan; and

(B) consistent with the national preparedness goal established under section 643 of the Post-Katrina Emergency Management Reform Act of 2006, the National Incident Management System, the National Response Plan, and other related plans and strategies.

(2) CONSULTATION.— In developing a catastrophic incident annex submitted under subsection (b)(3), a State shall consult with and seek appropriate comments from local governments, emergency response providers, locally governed multijurisdictional councils of government, and regional planning commissions.

(d) TERMS AND CONDITIONS.— The Administrator shall establish such other terms and conditions as the Administrator considers necessary and proper to carry out this section.

(e) APPLICATION OF OTHER PROVISIONS.— In carrying out this section, the provisions of section[8] 611(h) and 621(h) shall apply.

---

[8] So in law. The word section in subsection (e) probably should read sections.

(f) ALLOCATION OF FUNDS.— For each fiscal year concerned, the Administrator shall allocate to each State, in accordance with regulations and the total sum appropriated under this title, amounts to be made available to the States for the purposes of this section. Regulations governing allocations to the States under this subsection shall give due regard to (1) the criticality of the areas which may be affected by hazards with respect to the development of the total emergency preparedness readiness of the United States, (2) the relative state of development of emergency preparedness readiness of the State, (3) population, and (4) such other factors as the Administrator shall prescribe. The Administrator may reallocate the excess of any allocation not used by a State in a plan submitted under this section. Amounts paid to any State or political subdivision under this section shall be expended solely for the purposes set forth in this section.

(g) STANDARDS FOR STATE AND LOCAL EMERGENCY PREPAREDNESS OPERATIONAL PLANS.— In approving standards for State and local emergency preparedness operational plans pursuant to subsection (b)(3), the Administrator shall ensure that such plans take into account the needs of individuals with household pets and service animals prior to, during, and following a major disaster or emergency.

(h) SUBMISSION OF PLAN.— If a State fails to submit a plan for approval as required by this section within 60 days after the Administrator notifies the States of the allocations under this section, the Administrator may reallocate such funds, or portions thereof, among the other States in such amounts as, in the judgment of the Administrator, will best assure the adequate development of the emergency preparedness capability of the United States.

(h)[9] ANNUAL REPORTS.— The Administrator shall report annually to the Congress all contributions made pursuant to this section.

---

[9] So in law. Two subsections (h) have been enacted.

[42 U.S.C. 5196b]

SEC. 614. GRANTS FOR CONSTRUCTION OF EMERGENCY OPERATIONS CENTERS.

(a) GRANTS.— The Administrator of the Federal Emergency Management Agency may make grants to States and Indian tribal governments under this title for equipping, upgrading, and constructing State, local, and Tribal emergency operations centers.

(b) FEDERAL SHARE.— Notwithstanding any other provision of this title, the Federal share of the cost of an activity carried out using amounts from grants made under this section shall not exceed 75 percent.

[42 U.S.C. 5196c]

SEC. 615. USE OF FUNDS TO PREPARE FOR AND RESPOND TO HAZARDS.

Funds made available to the States under this title may be used by the States for the purposes of preparing for hazards and providing emergency assistance in response to hazards. Regulations prescribed to carry out this section shall authorize the use of emergency preparedness personnel, materials, and facilities supported in whole or in part through contributions under this title for emergency preparedness activities and measures related to hazards.

[42 U.S.C. 5196d]

SEC. 616. DISASTER RELATED INFORMATION SERVICES.

(a) IN GENERAL.—Consistent with section 308(a), the Administrator of[10] Federal Emergency Management Agency shall—

---

[10] So in law. Probably should read of the Federal.

---

(1) identify, in coordination with State and local governments, population groups with limited English proficiency and take into account such groups in planning for an emergency or major disaster;

(2) ensure that information made available to individuals affected by a major disaster or emergency is made available in formats that can be understood by—

(A) population groups identified under paragraph (1); and

(B) individuals with disabilities or other special needs; and

(3) develop and maintain an informational clearinghouse of model language assistance programs and best practices for State and local governments in providing services related to a major disaster or emergency.

(b) GROUP SIZE.— For purposes of subsection (a), the Administrator of Federal Emergency Management Agency shall define the size of a population group.

[42 U.S.C. 5196f]

Subtitle B—GENERAL PROVISIONS

SEC. 621. ADMINISTRATIVE AUTHORITY.

(a) IN GENERAL.— For the purpose of carrying out the powers and duties assigned to the Administrator under this title, the Administrator may exercise the administrative authorities provided under this section.

(b) ADVISORY PERSONNEL.—(1) The Administrator may employ not more than 100 part-time or temporary advisory personnel (including not to exceed 25 subjects of the

United Kingdom or citizens of Canada) as the Administrator considers to be necessary in carrying out the provisions of this title.

(2)   Persons holding other offices or positions under the United States for which they receive compensation, while serving as advisory personnel, shall receive no additional compensation for such service. Other part-time or temporary advisory personnel so employed may serve without compensation or may receive compensation at a rate not to exceed $180 for each day of service, plus authorized subsistence and travel, as determined by the Administrator.

(c) SERVICES OF OTHER AGENCY PERSONNEL AND VOLUNTEERS.—The Administrator may—

(1)   use the services of Federal agencies and, with the consent of any State or local government, accept and use the services of State and local agencies;

(2)   establish and use such regional and other offices as may be necessary; and

(3)   use such voluntary and uncompensated services by individuals or organizations as may from time to time be needed.

(d) GIFTS.— Notwithstanding any other provision of law, the Administrator may accept gifts of supplies, equipment, and facilities and may use or distribute such gifts for emergency preparedness purposes in accordance with the provisions of this title.

(e) REIMBURSEMENT.— The Administrator may reimburse any Federal agency for any of its expenditures or for compensation of its personnel and use or consumption of its materials and facilities under this title to the extent funds are available.

(f) PRINTING.— The Administrator may purchase such printing, binding, and blank-book work from public, commercial, or private printing establishments or binderies as the Administrator considers necessary upon orders placed by the Public Printer or upon waivers issued in accordance with section 504 of title 44, United States Code.

(g) RULES AND REGULATIONS.— The Administrator may prescribe such rules and regulations as may be necessary and proper to carry out any of the provisions of this title and perform any of the powers and duties provided by this title. The Administrator may perform any of the powers and duties provided by this title through or with the aid of such officials of the Federal Emergency Management Agency as the Administrator may designate.

(h) FAILURE TO EXPEND CONTRIBUTIONS CORRECTLY.—(1)   When, after reasonable notice and opportunity for hearing to the State or other person involved, the Administrator finds that there is a failure to expend funds in accordance with the regulations, terms, and conditions established under this title for approved emergency preparedness plans, programs, or projects, the Administrator may notify such State or person that further payments will not be made to the State or person from appropriations under this title (or from funds otherwise available for the purposes of this title for any approved plan, program, or project with respect to which there is such failure to comply) until the Administrator is satisfied that there will no longer be any such failure.

(2)   Until so satisfied, the Administrator shall either withhold the payment of any financial contribution to such State or person or limit payments to those programs or projects with respect to which there is substantial compliance with the regulations, terms, and conditions governing plans, programs, or projects hereunder.

(3) As used in this subsection, the term person means the political subdivision of any State or combination or group thereof or any person, corporation, association, or other entity of any nature whatsoever, including instrumentalities of States and political subdivisions.

[42 U.S.C. 5197]

SEC. 622. SECURITY REGULATIONS.

(a) ESTABLISHMENT.— The Administrator shall establish such security requirements and safeguards, including restrictions with respect to access to information and property as the Administrator considers necessary.

(b) LIMITATIONS ON EMPLOYEE ACCESS TO INFORMATION.— No employee of the Federal Emergency Management Agency shall be permitted to have access to information or property with respect to which access restrictions have been established under this section, until it shall have been determined that no information is contained in the files of the Federal Bureau of Investigation or any other investigative agency of the Government indicating that such employee is of questionable loyalty or reliability for security purposes, or if any such information is so disclosed, until the Federal Bureau of Investigation shall have conducted a full field investigation concerning such person and a report thereon shall have been evaluated in writing by the Administrator.

(c) NATIONAL SECURITY POSITIONS.— No employee of the Federal Emergency Management Agency shall occupy any position determined by the Administrator to be of critical importance from the standpoint of national security until a full field investigation concerning such employee shall have been conducted by the Director of the Office of Personnel Management and a report thereon shall have been evaluated in writing by the Administrator of the Federal Emergency Management Agency. In the event such full field investigation by the Director of the Office of Personnel Management develops any data reflecting that such applicant for a position of critical importance is of questionable loyalty or reliability for security purposes, or if the Administrator of the Federal Emergency Management Agency for any other reason considers it to be advisable, such investigation shall be discontinued and a report thereon shall be referred to the Administrator of the Federal Emergency Management Agency for evaluation in writing. Thereafter, the Administrator of the Federal Emergency Management Agency may refer the matter to the Federal Bureau of Investigation for the conduct of a full field investigation by such Bureau. The result of such latter investigation by such Bureau shall be furnished to the Administrator of the Federal Emergency Management Agency for action.

(d) EMPLOYEE OATHS.— Each Federal employee of the Federal Emergency Management Agency acting under the authority of this title, except the subjects of the United Kingdom and citizens of Canada specified in section 621(b), shall execute the loyalty oath or appointment affidavits prescribed by the Director of the Office of Personnel Management. Each person other than a Federal employee who is appointed to serve in a State or local organization for emergency preparedness shall before entering upon duties, take an oath in writing before a person authorized to administer oaths, which oath shall be substantially as follows:

I, —————, do solemnly swear (or affirm) that I will support and defend the Constitution of the United States against all enemies, foreign and domestic;

that I will bear true faith and allegiance to the same; that I take this obligation freely, without any mental reservation or purpose of evasion; and that I will well and faithfully discharge the duties upon which I am about to enter.

And I do further swear (or affirm) that I do not advocate, nor am I a member or an affiliate of any organization, group, or combination of persons that advocates the overthrow of the Government of the United States by force or violence; and that during such time as I am a member of ———— (name of emergency preparedness organization), I will not advocate nor become a member or an affiliate of any organization, group, or combination of persons that advocates the overthrow of the Government of the United States by force or violence."

After appointment and qualification for office, the director of emergency preparedness of any State, and any subordinate emergency preparedness officer within such State designated by the director in writing, shall be qualified to administer any such oath within such State under such regulations as the director shall prescribe. Any person who shall be found guilty of having falsely taken such oath shall be punished as provided in section 1621 of title 18, United States Code."

[42 U.S.C. 5197a]

SEC. 623. USE OF EXISTING FACILITIES.

In performing duties under this title, the Administrator—

(1) shall cooperate with the various departments and agencies of the Federal Government;

(2) shall use, to the maximum extent, the existing facilities and resources of the Federal Government and, with their consent, the facilities and resources of the States and political subdivisions thereof, and of other organizations and agencies; and

(3) shall refrain from engaging in any form of activity which would duplicate or parallel activity of any other Federal department or agency unless the Administrator, with the written approval of the President, shall determine that such duplication is necessary to accomplish the purposes of this title.

[42 U.S.C. 5197b]

SEC. 624. ANNUAL REPORT TO CONGRESS.

The Administrator shall annually submit a written report to the President and Congress covering expenditures, contributions, work, and accomplishments of the Federal Emergency Management Agency pursuant to this title, accompanied by such recommendations as the Administrator considers appropriate.

[42 U.S.C. 5197c]

SEC. 625. APPLICABILITY OF TITLE.

The provisions of this title shall be applicable to the United States, its States, Territories and possessions, and the District of Columbia, and their political subdivisions.

[42 U.S.C. 5197d]

SEC. 626. AUTHORIZATION OF APPROPRIATIONS AND TRANSFERS OF FUNDS.

(a) AUTHORIZATION OF APPROPRIATIONS.— There are authorized to be appropriated such sums as may be necessary to carry out the provisions of this title.

(b) Transfer Authority.— Funds made available for the purposes of this title may be allocated or transferred for any of the purposes of this title, with the approval of the Director of the Office of Management and Budget, to any agency or government corporation designated to assist in carrying out this title. Each such allocation or transfer shall be reported in full detail to the Congress within 30 days after such allocation or transfer.

[42 U.S.C. 5197e]

SEC. 627. RELATION TO ATOMIC ENERGY ACT OF 1954.

Nothing in this title shall be construed to alter or modify the provisions of the Atomic Energy Act of 1954 (42 U.S.C. 2011 et seq.).

[42 U.S.C. 5197f]

SEC. 628. FEDERAL BUREAU OF INVESTIGATION.

Nothing in this title shall be construed to authorize investigations of espionage, sabotage, or subversive acts by any persons other than personnel of the Federal Bureau of Investigation.

[42 U.S.C. 5197g]

SEC. 629. MINORITY EMERGENCY PREPAREDNESS DEMONSTRATION PROGRAM.

(a) In General.— The Administrator shall establish a minority emergency preparedness demonstration program to research and promote the capacity of minority communities to provide data, information, and awareness education by providing grants to or executing contracts or cooperative agreements with eligible nonprofit organizations to establish and conduct such programs.

(b) Activities Supported.—An eligible nonprofit organization may use a grant, contract, or cooperative agreement awarded under this section—

(1) to conduct research into the status of emergency preparedness and disaster response awareness in African American and Hispanic households located in urban, suburban, and rural communities, particularly in those States and regions most impacted by natural and manmade disasters and emergencies; and

(2) to develop and promote awareness of emergency preparedness education programs within minority communities, including development and preparation of culturally competent educational and awareness materials that can be used to disseminate information to minority organizations and institutions.

(c) Eligible Organizations.— A nonprofit organization is eligible to be awarded a grant, contract, or cooperative agreement under this section with respect to a program if the organization is a nonprofit organization that is described in section 501(c)(3) of the Internal Revenue Code of 1986 (26 U.S.C. 501(c)(3)) and exempt from tax under section 501(a) of such Code, whose primary mission is to provide services to communities predominately populated by minority citizens, and that can demonstrate a partnership with a minority-owned business enterprise or minority business located in a HUBZone (as defined in section 3(p) of the Small Business Act (15 U.S.C. 632(p))) with respect to the program.

(d) Use of Funds.—A recipient of a grant, contract, or cooperative agreement awarded under this section may only use the proceeds of the grant, contract, or agreement to—

(1)   acquire expert professional services necessary to conduct research in communities predominately populated by minority citizens, with a primary emphasis on African American and Hispanic communities;

(2)   develop and prepare informational materials to promote awareness among minority communities about emergency preparedness and how to protect their households and communities in advance of disasters;

(3)   establish consortia with minority national organizations, minority institutions of higher education, and faith-based institutions to disseminate information about emergency preparedness to minority communities; and

(4)   implement a joint project with a minority serving institution, including a part B institution (as defined in section 322(2) of the Higher Education Act of 1965 (20 U.S.C. 1061(2))), an institution described in subparagraph (A), (B), or (C) of section 326[11] of that Act (20 U.S.C. 1063b(e)(1)(A), (B), or (C)), and a Hispanic-serving institution (as defined in section 502(a)(5) of that Act (20 U.S.C. 1101a(a)(5))).

---

[11]   So in law. Should read section 326(e)(1).

(e) APPLICATION AND REVIEW PROCEDURE.— To be eligible to receive a grant, contract, or cooperative agreement under this section, an organization must submit an application to the Administrator at such time, in such manner, and accompanied by such information as the Administrator may reasonably require. The Administrator shall establish a procedure by which to accept such applications.

(f) AUTHORIZATION OF APPROPRIATION.— There is authorized to be appropriated to carry out this section $1,500,000 for fiscal year 2002 and such funds as may be necessary for fiscal years 2003 through 2007. Such sums shall remain available until expended.

[42 U.S.C. 5197h]

TITLE VII—MISCELLANEOUS

AUTHORITY TO PRESCRIBE RULES AND ACCEPT GIFTS

SEC. 701. (a)(1)   The President may prescribe such rules and regulations as may be necessary and proper to carry out any of the provisions of this Act, and he may exercise any power or authority conferred on him by any section of this Act either directly or through such Federal agency or agencies as he may designate.

(2) DEADLINE FOR PAYMENT OF ASSISTANCE.— Rules and regulations authorized by paragraph (1) shall provide that payment of any assistance under this Act to a State shall be completed within 60 days after the date of approval of such assistance.

(b)   In furtherance of the purposes of this Act, the President or his delegate may accept and use bequests, gifts, or donations of service, money, or property, real, personal, or mixed, tangible, or intangible. All sums received under this subsection shall be deposited in a separate fund on the books of the Treasury and shall be available for expenditure upon the certification of the President or his delegate. At the request of the President or his delegate, the Secretary of the Treasury may invest and reinvest excess monies in the fund. Such investments shall be in public debt securities with maturities suitable for the needs of the fund and shall bear interest at rates determined by the Secretary of the Treasury, taking into consideration current market yields on outstanding marketable obligations of the United States of comparable maturities. The interest on such investments shall be credited to, and form a part of, the fund.

[42 U.S.C. 5201]

SEC. 702. [Amended various other Acts] .

REPEAL OF EXISTING LAW

SEC. 703. The Disaster Relief Act of 1970, as amended (84 Stat. 1744), is hereby repealed, except sections 231, 233, 234, 235, 236, 237, 301, 302, 303, and 304. Notwithstanding such repeal the provisions of the Disaster Relief Act of 1970 shall continue in effect with respect to any major disaster declared prior to the enactment of this Act.

PRIOR ALLOCATION OF FUNDS

SEC. 704. Funds heretofore appropriated and available under Public Laws 91–606, as amended, and 92–385 shall continue to be available for the purpose of providing assistance under those Acts as well as for the purposes of this Act.

SEC. 705. DISASTER GRANT CLOSEOUT PROCEDURES.

(a) STATUTE OF LIMITATIONS.—

(1) IN GENERAL.— Notwithstanding section 3716(e) of title 31, United States Code, and except as provided in paragraph (2), no administrative action to recover any payment made to a State or local government for disaster or emergency assistance under this Act shall be initiated in any forum after the date that is 3 years after the date of transmission of the final expenditure report for project completion as certified by the grantee.

(2) FRAUD EXCEPTION.— The limitation under paragraph (1) shall apply unless there is evidence of civil or criminal fraud.

(b) REBUTTAL OF PRESUMPTION OF RECORD MAINTENANCE.—

(1) IN GENERAL.— In any dispute arising under this section after the date that is 3 years after the date of transmission of the final expenditure report for project completion as certified by the grantee, there shall be a presumption that accounting records were maintained that adequately identify the source and application of funds provided for financially assisted activities.

(2) AFFIRMATIVE EVIDENCE.— The presumption described in paragraph (1) may be rebutted only on production of affirmative evidence that the State or local government did not maintain documentation described in that paragraph.

(3) INABILITY TO PRODUCE DOCUMENTATION.— The inability of the Federal, State, or local government to produce source documentation supporting expenditure reports later than 3 years after the date of transmission of the final expenditure report

for project completion as certified by the grantee shall not constitute evidence to rebut the presumption described in paragraph (1).

(4) RIGHT OF ACCESS.— The period during which the Federal, State, or local government has the right to access source documentation shall not be limited to the required 3-year retention period referred to in paragraph (3), but shall last as long as the records are maintained.

(c) BINDING NATURE OF GRANT REQUIREMENTS.—A State or local government shall not be liable for reimbursement or any other penalty for any payment made under this Act if—

(1)   the payment was authorized by an approved agreement specifying the costs;

(2)   the costs were reasonable; and

(3)   the purpose of the grant was accomplished.

(d) FACILITATING CLOSEOUT.—

(1) INCENTIVES.— The Administrator of the Federal Emergency Management Agency may develop incentives and penalties that encourage State, local, or Indian tribal governments to close out expenditures and activities on a timely basis related to disaster or emergency assistance.

(2) AGENCY REQUIREMENTS.— The Federal Emergency Management Agency shall, consistent with applicable regulations and required procedures, meet its responsibilities to improve closeout practices and reduce the time to close disaster program awards.

[42 U.S.C. 5205]

SEC. 706. FIREARMS POLICIES.

(a) PROHIBITION ON CONFISCATION OF FIREARMS.—No officer or employee of the United States (including any member of the uniformed services), or person operating pursuant to or under color of Federal law, or receiving Federal funds, or under control of any Federal official, or providing services to such an officer, employee, or other person, while acting in support of relief from a major disaster or emergency, may—

(1)   temporarily or permanently seize, or authorize seizure of, any firearm the possession of which is not prohibited under Federal, State, or local law, other than for forfeiture in compliance with Federal law or as evidence in a criminal investigation;

(2)   require registration of any firearm for which registration is not required by Federal, State, or local law;

(3)   prohibit possession of any firearm, or promulgate any rule, regulation, or order prohibiting possession of any firearm, in any place or by any person where such possession is not otherwise prohibited by Federal, State, or local law; or

(4)   prohibit the carrying of firearms by any person otherwise authorized to carry firearms under Federal, State, or local law, solely because such person is operating under the direction, control, or supervision of a Federal agency in support of relief from the major disaster or emergency.

(b) LIMITATION.— Nothing in this section shall be construed to prohibit any person in subsection (a) from requiring the temporary surrender of a firearm as a condition for entry into any mode of transportation used for rescue or evacuation during a major disaster or emergency, provided that such temporarily surrendered firearm is returned at the completion of such rescue or evacuation.

(c) PRIVATE RIGHTS OF ACTION.—

(1) IN GENERAL.— Any individual aggrieved by a violation of this section may seek relief in an action at law, suit in equity, or other proper proceeding for redress against any person who subjects such individual, or causes such individual to be subjected, to the deprivation of any of the rights, privileges, or immunities secured by this section.

(2) REMEDIES.— In addition to any existing remedy in law or equity, under any law, an individual aggrieved by the seizure or confiscation of a firearm in violation of this section may bring an action for return of such firearm in the United States district court in the district in which that individual resides or in which such firearm may be found.

(3) ATTORNEY FEES.— In any action or proceeding to enforce this section, the court shall award the prevailing party, other than the United States, a reasonable attorney's fee as part of the costs.

[42 U.S.C. 5207]

★

42 U.S.C. Ch. 68–Disaster Relief

TITLE 42—THE PUBLIC HEALTH AND WELFARE

* * * * * * *

CHAPTER 68—DISASTER RELIEF

* * * * * * *

SUBCHAPTER V—MISCELLANEOUS

* * * * * * *

§5204. INSULAR AREAS DISASTER SURVIVAL AND RECOVERY; DEFINITIONS

As used in sections 5204 to 5204c of this title—

(1) the term "insular area" means any of the following: American Samoa, the Federated States of Micronesia, Guam, the Marshall Islands, the Northern Mariana Islands, the Trust Territory of the Pacific Islands, and the Virgin Islands;

(2) the term "disaster" means a declaration of a major disaster by the President after September 1, 1989, pursuant to section 5170 of this title; and

(3) the term "Secretary" means the Secretary of the Interior.

(Pub. L. 102–247, title II, §201, Feb. 24, 1992, 106 Stat. 37.)

§5204A. AUTHORIZATION OF APPROPRIATIONS FOR INSULAR AREAS

There are hereby authorized to be appropriated to the Secretary such sums as may be necessary to—

(1) reconstruct essential public facilities damaged by disasters in the insular areas that occurred prior to February 24, 1992; and

(2) enhance the survivability of essential public facilities in the event of disasters in the insular areas,

except that with respect to the disaster declared by the President in the case of Hurricane Hugo, September 1989, amounts for any fiscal year shall not exceed 25 percent of the estimated aggregate amount of grants to be made under sections 5170b and 5172 of this title for such disaster. Such sums shall remain available until expended.

(Pub. L. 102–247, title II, §202, Feb. 24, 1992, 106 Stat. 37.)

§5204B. TECHNICAL ASSISTANCE FOR INSULAR AREAS

(a) Upon the declaration by the President of a disaster in an insular area, the President,

103

acting through the Administrator of the Federal Emergency Management Agency, shall assess, in cooperation with the Secretary and chief executive of such insular area, the capability of the insular government to respond to the disaster, including the capability to assess damage; coordinate activities with Federal agencies, particularly the Federal Emergency Management Agency; develop recovery plans, including recommendations for enhancing the survivability of essential infrastructure; negotiate and manage reconstruction contracts; and prevent the misuse of funds. If the President finds that the insular government lacks any of these or other capabilities essential to the recovery effort, then the President shall provide technical assistance to the insular area which the President deems necessary for the recovery effort.

(b) One year following the declaration by the President of a disaster in an insular area, the Secretary, in consultation with the Administrator of the Federal Emergency Management Agency, shall submit to the Senate Committee on Energy and Natural Resources and the House Committee on Natural Resources a report on the status of the recovery effort, including an audit of Federal funds expended in the recovery effort and recommendations on how to improve public health and safety, survivability of infrastructure, recovery efforts, and effective use of funds in the event of future disasters.

(Pub. L. 102–247, title II, §203, Feb. 24, 1992, 106 Stat. 37; Pub. L. 103–437, §15(p), Nov. 2, 1994, 108 Stat. 4594; Pub. L. 109–295, title VI, §612(c), Oct. 4, 2006, 120 Stat. 1410.)

§5204C. HAZARD MITIGATION FOR INSULAR AREAS

The total of contributions under the last sentence of section 5170c of this title for the insular areas shall not exceed 10 percent of the estimated aggregate amounts of grants to be made under sections 5170b, 5172, 5173, 5174, and 5178 [1] of this title for any disaster: *Provided*, That the President shall require a 50 percent local match for assistance in excess of 10 percent of the estimated aggregate amount of grants to be made under section 5172 of this title for any disaster.

(Pub. L. 102–247, title II, §204, Feb. 24, 1992, 106 Stat. 38.)

DISASTER MITIGATION ACT OF 2000

PUBLIC LAW 106–390
AS AMENDED THROUGH PUB. L. 117–81

DISASTER MITIGATION ACT OF 2000

[(Public Law 106–390)]

[As Amended Through P.L. 117–81, Enacted December 27, 2021]

AN ACT To amend the Robert T. Stafford Disaster Relief and Emergency Assistance Act to authorize a program for predisaster mitigation, to streamline the administration of disaster relief, to control the Federal costs of disaster assistance, and for other purposes.

Be it enacted by the Senate and House of Representatives of the United States of America in Congress assembled,

SECTION 1. SHORT TITLE; TABLE OF CONTENTS.

(a) [**42 U.S.C. 5121 note**] SHORT TITLE.— This Act may be cited as the " Disaster Mitigation Act of 2000 ".

TITLE III—MISCELLANEOUS

* * * * * * *

SEC. 306. [42 U.S.C. 5206] BUY AMERICAN.

(a) COMPLIANCE WITH BUY AMERICAN ACT.— No funds authorized to be appropriated under this Act or any amendment made by this Act may be expended by an entity unless the entity, in expending the funds, complies with the Buy American Act (41 U.S.C. 10a et seq.).

(b) DEBARMENT OF PERSONS CONVICTED OF FRAUDULENT USE OF MADE IN AMERICA LABELS.—

(1) IN GENERAL.— If the Director of the Federal Emergency Management Agency determines that a person has been convicted of intentionally affixing a label bearing a Made in America inscription to any product sold in or shipped to the United States that is not made in America, the Director shall determine, not later than 90 days after determining that the person has been so convicted, whether the person should be debarred from contracting under the Robert T. Stafford Disaster Relief and Emergency Assistance Act (42 U.S.C. 5121 et seq.).

(2) DEFINITION OF DEBAR.— In this subsection, the term debar has the meaning given the term in section 4654(c) of title 10, United States Code.

★

POST-KATRINA EMERGENCY MANAGEMENT REFORM ACT OF 2006

PUBLIC LAW 109–295
AS AMENDED THROUGH PUB. L. 116–64

POST-KATRINA EMERGENCY MANAGEMENT REFORM ACT OF 2006

(Title VI of the Department of Homeland Security Appropriations Act, 2007)

[(Public Law 109–295)]

[As Amended Through P.L. 116–64, Enacted October 9, 2019]

AN ACT Making appropriations for the Department of Homeland Security for the fiscal year ending September 30, 2007, and for other purposes.

Be it enacted by the Senate and House of Representatives of the United States of America in Congress assembled,

* * * * * * *

TITLE VI—NATIONAL EMERGENCY MANAGEMENT

SEC. 601. [6 U.S.C. 701 note] SHORT TITLE.

This title may be cited as the "Post-Katrina Emergency Management Reform Act of 2006".

SEC. 602. DEFINITIONS.

In this title—

(1) the term Administrator means the Administrator of the Agency;

(2) the term Agency means the Federal Emergency Management Agency;

(3) the term appropriate committees of Congress means——

(A) the Committee on Homeland Security and Governmental Affairs of the Senate; and

(B) those committees of the House of Representatives that the Speaker of the House of Representatives determines appropriate;

(4) the term catastrophic incident means any natural disaster, act of terrorism, or other man-made disaster that results in extraordinary levels of casualties or damage or disruption severely affecting the population (including mass evacuations), infrastructure, environment, economy, national morale, or government functions in an area;

(5) the term Department means the Department of Homeland Security;

(6)   the terms emergency and major disaster have the meanings given the terms in section 102 of the Robert T. Stafford Disaster Relief and Emergency Assistance Act (42 U.S.C. 5122);

(7)   the term emergency management means the governmental function that coordinates and integrates all activities necessary to build, sustain, and improve the capability to prepare for, protect against, respond to, recover from, or mitigate against threatened or actual natural disasters, acts of terrorism, or other man-made disasters;

(8)   the term emergency response provider has the meaning given the term in section 2 of the Homeland Security Act of 2002 (6 U.S.C. 101), as amended by this Act;

(9)   the term Federal coordinating officer means a Federal coordinating officer as described in section 302 of the Robert T. Stafford Disaster Relief and Emergency Assistance Act (42 U.S.C. 5143);

(10)   the term individual with a disability has the meaning given the term in section 3 of the Americans with Disabilities Act of 1990 (42 U.S.C. 12102);

(11)   the terms local government and State have the meaning given the terms in section 2 of the Homeland Security Act of 2002 (6 U.S.C. 101);

(12)   the term National Incident Management System means a system to enable effective, efficient, and collaborative incident management;

(13)   the term National Response Plan means the National Response Plan or any successor plan prepared under section 502(a)(6) of the Homeland Security Act of 2002 (as amended by this Act);

(14)   the term Secretary means the Secretary of Homeland Security;

(15)   the term surge capacity means the ability to rapidly and substantially increase the provision of search and rescue capabilities, food, water, medicine, shelter and housing, medical care, evacuation capacity, staffing (including disaster assistance employees), and other resources necessary to save lives and protect property during a catastrophic incident; and

(16)   the term tribal government means the government of an Indian tribe or authorized tribal organization, or in Alaska a Native village or Alaska Regional Native Corporation.

* * * * * * *

Subtitle C—COMPREHENSIVE PREPAREDNESS SYSTEM

CHAPTER 1—NATIONAL PREPAREDNESS SYSTEM

* * * * * * *

SEC. 648. [6 U.S.C. 748] TRAINING AND EXERCISES.

(a) NATIONAL TRAINING PROGRAM.—

(1) IN GENERAL.— Beginning not later than 180 days after the date of enactment of this Act, the Administrator, in coordination with the heads of appropriate Federal agencies, the National Council on Disability, and the National Advisory Council, shall carry out a national training program to implement the national preparedness goal, National Incident Management System, National Response Plan, and other related plans and strategies.

(2) TRAINING PARTNERS.—In developing and implementing the national training program, the Administrator shall—

(A) work with government training facilities, academic institutions, private organizations, and other entities that provide specialized, state-of-the-art training for emergency managers or emergency response providers; and

(B) utilize, as appropriate, training courses provided by community colleges, State and local public safety academies, State and private universities, and other facilities.

(b) NATIONAL EXERCISE PROGRAM.—

(1) IN GENERAL.— Beginning not later than 180 days after the date of enactment of this Act, the Administrator, in coordination with the heads of appropriate Federal agencies, the National Council on Disability, and the National Advisory Council, shall carry out a national exercise program to test and evaluate the national preparedness goal, National Incident Management System, National Response Plan, and other related plans and strategies.

(2) REQUIREMENTS.—The national exercise program—

(A) shall be—

(i) as realistic as practicable, based on current risk assessments, including credible and emerging threats, vulnerabilities, and consequences, and designed to stress the national preparedness system;

(ii) designed, as practicable, to simulate the partial or complete incapacitation of a State, local, or tribal government;

(iii) carried out, as appropriate, with a minimum degree of notice to involved parties regarding the timing and details of such exercises, consistent with safety considerations;

(iv) designed to provide for the systematic evaluation of readiness and enhance operational understanding of the incident command system and relevant mutual aid agreements;

(v) designed to address the unique requirements of populations with special needs, including the elderly; and

(vi) designed to promptly develop after-action reports and plans for quickly incorporating lessons learned into future operations; and

(B) shall include a selection of model exercises that State, local, and tribal governments can readily adapt for use and provide assistance to State, local, and tribal governments with the design, implementation, and evaluation of exercises (whether a model exercise program or an exercise designed locally) that—

(i)   conform to the requirements under subparagraph (A);

(ii)   are consistent with any applicable State, local, or tribal strategy or plan; and

(iii)   provide for systematic evaluation of readiness.

(3) NATIONAL LEVEL EXERCISES.—The Administrator shall periodically, but not less than biennially, perform national exercises for the following purposes:

(A)   To test and evaluate the capability of Federal, State, local, and tribal governments to detect, disrupt, and prevent threatened or actual catastrophic acts of terrorism, especially those involving weapons of mass destruction.

(B)   To test and evaluate the readiness of Federal, State, local, and tribal governments to respond and recover in a coordinated and unified manner to catastrophic incidents.

SEC. 650. [6 U.S.C. 750] REMEDIAL ACTION MANAGEMENT PROGRAM.

The Administrator, in coordination with the National Council on Disability and the National Advisory Council, shall establish a remedial action management program to—

(1)   analyze training, exercises, and real-world events to identify and disseminate lessons learned and best practices;

(2)   generate and disseminate, as appropriate, after action reports to participants in exercises and real-world events; and

(3)   conduct remedial action tracking and long-term trend analysis.

* * * * * * *

SEC. 653. [6 U.S.C. 753] FEDERAL PREPAREDNESS.

(a) AGENCY RESPONSIBILITY.—In support of the national preparedness system, the President shall ensure that each Federal agency with responsibilities under the National Response Plan—

(1)   has the operational capability to meet the national preparedness goal, including—

(A)   the personnel to make and communicate decisions;

(B)   organizational structures that are assigned, trained, and exercised for the missions of the agency;

(C)   sufficient physical resources; and

(D)   the command, control, and communication channels to make, monitor, and communicate decisions;

(2)   complies with the National Incident Management System, including credentialing of personnel and typing of resources likely needed to respond to a natural disaster, act of terrorism, or other man-made disaster in accordance with section 510 of the Homeland Security Act of 2002 (6 U.S.C. 320);

(3)   develops, trains, and exercises rosters of response personnel to be deployed when the agency is called upon to support a Federal response;

(4)   develops deliberate operational plans and the corresponding capabilities, including crisis planning, to respond effectively to natural disasters, acts of terrorism, and other man-made disasters in support of the National Response Plan to ensure a coordinated Federal response; and

(5)   regularly updates, verifies the accuracy of, and provides to the Administrator the information in the inventory required under section 651.

(b) OPERATIONAL PLANS.—An operations plan developed under subsection (a)(4) shall meet the following requirements:

(1)   The operations plan shall be coordinated under a unified system with a common terminology, approach, and framework.

(2)   The operations plan shall be developed, in coordination with State, local, and tribal government officials, to address both regional and national risks.

(3) The operations plan shall contain, as appropriate, the following elements:

(A)   Concepts of operations.

(B)   Critical tasks and responsibilities.

(C)   Detailed resource and personnel requirements, together with sourcing requirements.

(D)   Specific provisions for the rapid integration of the resources and personnel of the agency into the overall response.

(4) The operations plan shall address, as appropriate, the following matters:

(A) Support of State, local, and tribal governments in conducting mass evacuations, including—

(i)   transportation and relocation;

(ii)   short- and long-term sheltering and accommodation;

(iii)   provisions for populations with special needs, keeping families together, and expeditious location of missing children; and

(iv)   policies and provisions for pets.

(B)   The preparedness and deployment of public health and medical resources, including resources to address the needs of evacuees and populations with special needs.

(C)   The coordination of interagency search and rescue operations, including land, water, and airborne search and rescue operations.

(D)   The roles and responsibilities of the Senior Federal Law Enforcement Official with respect to other law enforcement entities.

(E)   The protection of critical infrastructure.

(F)   The coordination of maritime salvage efforts among relevant agencies.

(G)   The coordination of Department of Defense and National Guard support of civilian authorities.

(H)   To the extent practicable, the utilization of Department of Defense,

National Air and Space Administration, National Oceanic and Atmospheric Administration, and commercial aircraft and satellite remotely sensed imagery.

(I)   The coordination and integration of support from the private sector and nongovernmental organizations.

(J)   The safe disposal of debris, including hazardous materials, and, when practicable, the recycling of debris.

(K)   The identification of the required surge capacity.

(L)   Specific provisions for the recovery of affected geographic areas.

(c) MISSION ASSIGNMENTS.— To expedite the provision of assistance under the National Response Plan, the President shall ensure that the Administrator, in coordination with Federal agencies with responsibilities under the National Response Plan, develops prescripted mission assignments, including logistics, communications, mass care, health services, and public safety.

(d) CERTIFICATION.— The President shall certify to the Committee on Homeland Security and Governmental Affairs of the Senate and the Committee on Homeland Security and the Committee on Transportation and Infrastructure of the House of Representatives on an annual basis that each Federal agency with responsibilities under the National Response Plan complies with subsections (a) and (b).

(e) CONSTRUCTION.—Nothing in this section shall be construed to limit the authority of the Secretary of Defense with regard to—

(1)   the command, control, training, planning, equipment, exercises, or employment of Department of Defense forces; or

(2)   the allocation of Department of Defense resources.

* * * * * * *

CHAPTER 2—ADDITIONAL PREPAREDNESS

SEC. 661. [6 U.S.C. 761] EMERGENCY MANAGEMENT ASSISTANCE COMPACT GRANTS.

(a) IN GENERAL.— The Administrator may make grants to administer the Emergency Management Assistance Compact consented to by the Joint Resolution entitled Joint Resolution granting the consent of Congress to the Emergency Management Assistance Compact (Public Law 104-321; 110 Stat. 3877).

(b) USES.—A grant under this section shall be used—

(1)   to carry out recommendations identified in the Emergency Management Assistance Compact after-action reports for the 2004 and 2005 hurricane season;

(2)   to administer compact operations on behalf of all member States and territories;

(3)   to continue coordination with the Agency and appropriate Federal agencies;

(4)   to continue coordination with State, local, and tribal government entities and their respective national organizations; and

(5)   to assist State and local governments, emergency response providers, and organizations representing such providers with credentialing emergency response providers and the typing of emergency response resources.

(c) COORDINATION.— The Administrator shall consult with the Administrator of the Emergency Management Assistance Compact to ensure effective coordination of efforts in responding to requests for assistance.

(d) AUTHORIZATION.— There is authorized to be appropriated to carry out this section $4,000,000 for each of fiscal years 2018 through 2022. Such sums shall remain available until expended.

SEC. 662. [6 U.S.C. 762] EMERGENCY MANAGEMENT PERFORMANCE GRANTS PROGRAM

(a) DEFINITIONS.—In this section—

(1)   the term program means the emergency management performance grants program described in subsection (b); and

(2)   the term State has the meaning given that term in section 102 of the Robert T. Stafford Disaster Relief and Emergency Assistance Act (42 U.S.C. 5122).

(b) IN GENERAL.— The Administrator of the Federal Emergency Management Agency shall continue implementation of an emergency management performance grants program, to make grants to States to assist State, local, and tribal governments in preparing for all hazards, as authorized by the Robert T. Stafford Disaster Relief and Emergency Assistance Act (42 U.S.C. 5121 et seq.).

(c) FEDERAL SHARE.— Except as otherwise specifically provided by title VI of the Robert T. Stafford Disaster Relief and Emergency Assistance Act (42 U.S.C. 5121 et seq.), the Federal share of the cost of an activity carried out using funds made available under the program shall not exceed 50 percent.

(d) APPORTIONMENT.—For fiscal year 2008, and each fiscal year thereafter, the Administrator shall apportion the amounts appropriated to carry out the program among the States as follows:

(1) BASELINE AMOUNT.— The Administrator shall first apportion 0.25 percent of such amounts to each of American Samoa, the Commonwealth of the Northern Mariana Islands, Guam, and the Virgin Islands and 0.75 percent of such amounts to each of the remaining States.

(2) REMAINDER.—The Administrator shall apportion the remainder of such amounts in the ratio that—

(A)   the population of each State; bears to

(B)   the population of all States.

(e) CONSISTENCY IN ALLOCATION.— Notwithstanding subsection (d), in any fiscal year before fiscal year 2013 in which the appropriation for grants under this section is equal to or greater than the appropriation for emergency management performance grants in fiscal year 2007, no State shall receive an amount under this section for that fiscal year less than the amount that State received in fiscal year 2007.

(f) AUTHORIZATION OF APPROPRIATIONS.— There is authorized to be appropriated to carry out the program, for each of fiscal years 2018 through 2022, $950,000,000.

* * * * * *

Subtitle G—AUTHORIZATION OF APPROPRIATIONS

SEC. 699. [6 U.S.C. 811] AUTHORIZATION OF APPROPRIATIONS.

There are authorized to be appropriated to carry out this title and the amendments made by this title for the administration and operations of the Agency—

(1) for fiscal year 2008, an amount equal to the amount appropriated for fiscal year 2007 for administration and operations of the Agency, multiplied by 1.1;

(2) for fiscal year 2009, an amount equal to the amount described in paragraph (1), multiplied by 1.1; and

(3) for fiscal year 2010, an amount equal to the amount described in paragraph (2), multiplied by 1.1.

★

SANDY RECOVERY IMPROVEMENT ACT OF 2013

PUBLIC LAW 113–2
AS AMENDED THROUGH PUB. L. 114–301

SANDY RECOVERY IMPROVEMENT ACT OF 2013

(Division B of the Disaster Relief Appropriations Act, 2013)

[(Public Law 113-2)]

[As Amended Through P.L. 114-301, Enacted December 16, 2016]

AN ACT Making supplemental appropriations for the fiscal year ending September 30, 2013, to improve and streamline disaster assistance for Hurricane Sandy, and for other purposes.

Be it enacted by the Senate and House of Representatives of the United States of America in Congress assembled,

That the following sums are appropriated, out of any money in the Treasury not otherwise appropriated, for the fiscal year ending September 30, 2013, and for other purposes, namely:

* * * * * * *

DIVISION B—SANDY RECOVERY IMPROVEMENT ACT OF 2013

SEC. 1101. SHORT TITLE; TABLE OF CONTENTS.

(a) [42 U.S.C. 5121 note] SHORT TITLE.— This division may be cited as the "Sandy Recovery Improvement Act of 2013".

(b) TABLE OF CONTENTS.— The table of contents for this division is as follows:

Sec. 1111.   Recommendations for reducing costs of future disasters.

* * * * * * *

SEC. 1104. HAZARD MITIGATION.

(a) STREAMLINED PROCEDURES; ADVANCE ASSISTANCE.— Section 404 of the Robert T. Stafford Disaster Relief and Emergency Assistance Act (42 U.S.C. 5170c) is amended by adding at the end the following:

"(d) STREAMLINED PROCEDURES.

"(1) IN GENERAL. For the purpose of providing assistance under this section, the President shall ensure that—

"(A)   adequate resources are devoted to ensure that applicable environmental reviews under the National Environmental Policy Act of 1969 and historic preservation reviews under the National Historic Preservation Act are completed on an expeditious basis; and

"(B)   the shortest existing applicable process under the National Environmental Policy Act of 1969 and the National Historic Preservation Act is utilized.

"(2) AUTHORITY FOR OTHER EXPEDITED PROCEDURES.   The President may utilize expedited procedures in addition to those required under paragraph (1) for the purpose of providing assistance under this section, such as procedures under the Prototype Programmatic Agreement of the Federal Emergency Management Agency, for the consideration of multiple structures as a group and for an analysis of the cost-effectiveness and fulfillment of cost-share requirements for proposed hazard mitigation measures.

"(e) ADVANCE ASSISTANCE.   The President may provide not more than 25 percent of the amount of the estimated cost of hazard mitigation measures to a State grantee eligible for a grant under this section before eligible costs are incurred.".

(b) ESTABLISHMENT OF CRITERIA RELATING TO ADMINISTRATION OF HAZARD MITIGATION ASSISTANCE BY STATES.— Section 404(c)(2) of the Robert T. Stafford Disaster Relief and Emergency Assistance Act (42 U.S.C. 5170c(c)(2)) is amended by inserting after applications submitted under paragraph (1). the following: Until such time as the Administrator promulgates regulations to implement this paragraph, the Administrator may waive notice and comment rulemaking, if the Administrator determines doing so is necessary to expeditiously implement this section, and may carry out this section as a pilot program..

(c) [42 U.S.C. 5170c note] APPLICABILITY.—The authority under the amendments made by this section shall apply to—

(1)   any major disaster or emergency declared under the Robert T. Stafford Disaster Relief and Emergency Assistance Act (42 U.S.C. 5121 et seq.) on or after the date of enactment of this division; and

(2)   a major disaster or emergency declared under that Act before the date of enactment of this division for which the period for processing requests for assistance

has not ended as of the date of enactment of this division.

SEC. 1105. DISPUTE RESOLUTION PILOT PROGRAM.

(a) [42 U.S.C. 5189a note] DEFINITIONS.—In this section, the following definitions apply:

(1) ADMINISTRATOR.— The term Administrator means the Administrator of the Federal Emergency Management Agency.

(2) ELIGIBLE ASSISTANCE.—The term eligible assistance means assistance—

(A) under section 403, 406, or 407 of the Robert T. Stafford Disaster Relief and Emergency Assistance Act (42 U.S.C. 5170b, 5172, 5173);

(B) for which the legitimate amount in dispute is not less than $1,000,000, which sum the Administrator shall adjust annually to reflect changes in the Consumer Price Index for all Urban Consumers published by the Department of Labor;

(C) for which the applicant has a non-Federal share; and

(D) for which the applicant has received a decision on a first appeal.

(b) PROCEDURES.—

(1) IN GENERAL.— Not later than 180 days after the date of enactment of this section, and in order to facilitate an efficient recovery from major disasters, the Administrator shall establish procedures under which an applicant may request the use of alternative dispute resolution, including arbitration by an independent review panel, to resolve disputes relating to eligible assistance.

(2) BINDING EFFECT.— A decision by an independent review panel under this section shall be binding upon the parties to the dispute.

(3) CONSIDERATIONS.—The procedures established under this section shall—

(A) allow a party of a dispute relating to eligible assistance to request an independent review panel for the review;

(B) require a party requesting an independent review panel as described in subparagraph (A) to agree to forgo rights to any further appeal of the dispute relating to any eligible assistance;

(C) require that the sponsor of an independent review panel for any alternative dispute resolution under this section be—

(i) an individual or entity unaffiliated with the dispute (which may include a Federal agency, an administrative law judge, or a reemployed annuitant who was an employee of the Federal Government) selected by the Administrator; and

(ii) responsible for identifying and maintaining an adequate number of independent experts qualified to review and resolve disputes under this section;

(D) require an independent review panel to—

(i) resolve any remaining disputed issue in accordance with all applicable laws, regulations, and Agency interpretations of those laws through its published policies and guidance;

(ii)   consider only evidence contained in the administrative record, as it existed at the time at which the Agency made its initial decision;

(iii)   only set aside a decision of the Agency found to be arbitrary, capricious, an abuse of discretion, or otherwise not in accordance with law; and

(iv)   in the case of a finding of material fact adverse to the claimant made on first appeal, only set aside or reverse such finding if the finding is clearly erroneous;

(E)   require an independent review panel to expeditiously issue a written decision for any alternative dispute resolution under this section; and

(F)   direct that if an independent review panel for any alternative dispute resolution under this section determines that the basis upon which a party submits a request for alternative dispute resolution is frivolous, the independent review panel shall direct the party to pay the reasonable costs to the Federal Emergency Management Agency relating to the review by the independent review panel. Any funds received by the Federal Emergency Management Agency under the authority of this section shall be deposited to the credit of the appropriation or appropriations available for the eligible assistance in dispute on the date on which the funds are received.

(c) SUNSET.— A request for review by an independent review panel under this section may not be made after December 31, 2015.

* * * * * * *

SEC. 1109. [42 U.S.C. 5170 note] INDIVIDUAL ASSISTANCE FACTORS.

In order to provide more objective criteria for evaluating the need for assistance to individuals, to clarify the threshold for eligibility and to speed a declaration of a major disaster or emergency under the Robert T. Stafford Disaster Relief and Emergency Assistance Act (42 U.S.C. 5121 et seq.), not later than 1 year after the date of enactment of this division, the Administrator of the Federal Emergency Management Agency, in cooperation with representatives of State, tribal, and local emergency management agencies, shall review, update, and revise through rulemaking the factors considered under section 206.48 of title 44, Code of Federal Regulations (including section 206.48(b)(2) of such title relating to trauma and the specific conditions or losses that contribute to trauma), to measure the severity, magnitude, and impact of a disaster.

SEC. 1110. TRIBAL REQUESTS FOR A MAJOR DISASTER OR EMERGENCY DECLARATION UNDER THE STAFFORD ACT.

(a) MAJOR DISASTER REQUESTS.—Section 401 of the Robert T. Stafford Disaster Relief and Emergency Assistance Act (42 U.S.C. 5170) is amended—

(1)   by striking All requests for a declaration and inserting (a) In General.—All requests for a declaration; and

(2)   by adding at the end the following:

SEC. 1110. [42 U.S.C. 5170 note] INDIVIDUAL ASSISTANCE FACTORS.

Sandy Recovery Improvement Act of 2013

"(b) INDIAN TRIBAL GOVERNMENT REQUESTS.

"(1) IN GENERAL. The Chief Executive of an affected Indian tribal government may submit a request for a declaration by the President that a major disaster exists consistent with the requirements of subsection (a).

"(2) REFERENCES. In implementing assistance authorized by the President under this Act in response to a request of the Chief Executive of an affected Indian tribal government for a major disaster declaration, any reference in this title or title III (except sections 310 and 326) to a State or the Governor of a State is deemed to refer to an affected Indian tribal government or the Chief Executive of an affected Indian tribal government, as appropriate.

"(3) SAVINGS PROVISION. Nothing in this subsection shall prohibit an Indian tribal government from receiving assistance under this title through a declaration made by the President at the request of a State under subsection (a) if the President does not make a declaration under this subsection for the same incident.

"(c) COST SHARE ADJUSTMENTS FOR INDIAN TRIBAL GOVERNMENTS.

"(1) IN GENERAL. In providing assistance to an Indian tribal government under this title, the President may waive or adjust any payment of a non-Federal contribution with respect to the assistance if—

"(A) the President has the authority to waive or adjust the payment under another provision of this title; and

"(B) the President determines that the waiver or adjustment is necessary and appropriate.

"(2) CRITERIA FOR MAKING DETERMINATIONS. The President shall establish criteria for making determinations under paragraph (1)(B).".

(b) EMERGENCY REQUESTS.— Section 501 of the Robert T. Stafford Disaster Relief and Emergency Assistance Act (42 U.S.C. 5191) is amended by adding at the end the following:

"(c) INDIAN TRIBAL GOVERNMENT REQUESTS.

"(1) IN GENERAL. The Chief Executive of an affected Indian tribal government may submit a request for a declaration by the President that an emergency exists consistent with the requirements of subsection (a).

"(2) REFERENCES. In implementing assistance authorized by the President under this title in response to a request of the Chief Executive of an affected Indian tribal government for an emergency declaration, any reference in this title or title III (except sections 310 and 326) to a State or the Governor of a State is deemed to refer to an affected Indian tribal government or the Chief Executive of an affected Indian tribal government, as appropriate.

"(3) SAVINGS PROVISION. Nothing in this subsection shall prohibit an Indian tribal government from receiving assistance under this title through a declaration made by the President at the request of a State under subsection (a) if the President does not make a declaration under this subsection for the same incident.".

(c) DEFINITIONS.—Section 102 of the Robert T. Stafford Disaster Relief and Emergency Assistance Act (42 U.S.C. 5122) is amended—

(1) in paragraph (7)(B) by striking ; and and inserting , that is not an Indian tribal government as defined in paragraph (6); and;

(2) by redesignating paragraphs (6) through (10) as paragraphs (7) through (11), respectively;

(3) by inserting after paragraph (5) the following:

"(6) INDIAN TRIBAL GOVERNMENT. The term 'Indian tribal government' means the governing body of any Indian or Alaska Native tribe, band, nation, pueblo, village, or community that the Secretary of the Interior acknowledges to exist as an Indian tribe under the Federally Recognized Indian Tribe List Act of 1994 (25 U.S.C. 479a et seq.)."; and

(4) by adding at the end the following:

"(12) CHIEF EXECUTIVE. The term 'Chief Executive' means the person who is the Chief, Chairman, Governor, President, or similar executive official of an Indian tribal government.".

(d) REFERENCES.— Title I of the Robert T. Stafford Disaster Relief and Emergency Assistance Act (42 U.S.C. 5121 et seq.) is amended by adding after section 102 the following:

"SEC. 103. [42 U.S.C. 5123] REFERENCES

"Except as otherwise specifically provided, any reference in this Act to 'State and local', 'State or local', 'State, and local', 'State, or local', or 'State, local' (including plurals) with respect to governments or officials and any reference to a 'local government' in sections 406(d)(3) and 417 is deemed to refer also to Indian tribal governments and officials, as appropriate.".

(e) [42 U.S.C. 5122 note] REGULATIONS.—

(1) ISSUANCE.— The President shall issue regulations to carry out the amendments made by this section.

(2) FACTORS.— In issuing the regulations, the President shall consider the unique conditions that affect the general welfare of Indian tribal governments.

SEC. 1111. RECOMMENDATIONS FOR REDUCING COSTS OF FUTURE DISASTERS.

(a) REPORT TO CONGRESS.— Not later than 180 days after the date of enactment of this division, the Administrator of the Federal Emergency Management Agency shall submit to Congress recommendations for the development of a national strategy for reducing future costs, loss of life, and injuries associated with extreme disaster events in vulnerable areas of the United States.

(b) NATIONAL STRATEGY.—The national strategy should—

(1) respect the constitutional role and responsibilities of Federal, State, and local governments and the private sector;

(2) consider the vulnerability of the United States to damage from flooding,

severe weather events, and other hazards;

(3)   analyze gaps and duplication of emergency preparedness, response, recovery, and mitigation measures provided by Federal, State, and local entities; and

(4)   include recommendations on how to improve the resiliency of local communities and States for the purpose of lowering future costs of disaster response and recovery.

★

CONSOLIDATED AND FURTHER CONTINUING APPROPRIATIONS ACT, 2013

PUBLIC LAW 113–6
AS AMENDED THROUGH PUB. L. 117–286

CONSOLIDATED AND FURTHER CONTINUING APPROPRIATIONS ACT, 2013

[(Public Law 113–6)]

[As Amended Through P.L. 117–286, Enacted December 27, 2022]

AN ACT Making consolidated appropriations and further continuing appropriations for the fiscal year ending September 30, 2013, and for other purposes.

Be it enacted by the Senate and House of Representatives of the United States of America in Congress assembled,

SHORT TITLE

SECTION 1. This Act may be cited as the "Consolidated and Further Continuing Appropriations Act, 2013".

* * * * * * *

Title III—RURAL DEVELOPMENT PROGRAMS

* * * * * * *

Division D—DEPARTMENT OF HOMELAND SECURITY APPROPRIATIONS ACT, 2013

* * * * * * *

FEDERAL EMERGENCY MANAGEMENT AGENCY

* * * * * * *

DISASTER RELIEF FUND (INCLUDING TRANSFER OF FUNDS)

* * * * * * *

Provided, That the Administrator of the Federal Emergency Management Agency shall submit an expenditure plan to the Committees on Appropriations of the Senate and the House of Representatives detailing the use of the funds made available in this or any other Act for disaster readiness and support not later than 60 days after the date of enactment of this Act: Provided further, That the Administrator of the Federal Emergency Management

Agency shall submit to such Committees a quarterly report detailing obligations against the expenditure plan and a justification for any changes from the initial plan:

★

SELECTED PROVISIONS OF THE CONSOLIDATED APPROPRIATIONS ACT, 2016

PUBLIC LAW 114–113
AS AMENDED THROUGH PUB. L. 119–4

CONSOLIDATED APPROPRIATIONS ACT, 2016

[(Public Law 114–113)]

[As Amended Through P.L. 119–4, Enacted March 15, 2025]

AN ACT Making appropriations for military construction, the Department of Veterans Affairs, and related agencies for the fiscal year ending September 30, 2016, and for other purposes.

Be it enacted by the Senate and House of Representatives of the United States of America in Congress assembled,

SECTION 1. SHORT TITLE.
This Act may be cited as the "Consolidated Appropriations Act, 2016".

* * * * * * *

Division E—FINANCIAL SERVICES AND GENERAL GOVERNMENT APPROPRIATIONS ACT, 2016

* * * * * * *

Title VII—GENERAL PROVISIONS—GOVERNMENT-WIDE

DEPARTMENTS, AGENCIES, AND CORPORATIONS

(INCLUDING TRANSFER OF FUNDS)

* * * * * * *

SEC. 750.

(a) None of the funds made available under this or any other Act may be used to—

(1) implement, administer, carry out, modify, revise, or enforce Executive Order 13690, entitled Establishing a Federal Flood Risk Management Standard and a Process for Further Soliciting and Considering Stakeholder Input (issued January 30, 2015), other than for—

(A) acquiring, managing, or disposing of Federal lands and facilities;

(B) providing federally undertaken, financed, or assisted construction or improvements; or

(C) conducting Federal activities or programs affecting land use, including water and related land resources planning, regulating, and licensing activities;

(2) implement Executive Order 13690 in a manner that modifies the non-grant components of the National Flood Insurance Program; or

(3) apply Executive Order 13690 or the Federal Flood Risk Management Standard by any component of the Department of Defense, including the Army Corps of Engineers in a way that changes the floodplain considered when determining whether or not to issue a Department of the Army permit under section 404 of the Clean Water Act or section 10 of the Rivers and Harbors Act.

(b) Subsection (a) of this section shall not be in effect during the period beginning on October 1, 2016 and ending on September 30, 2017.

* * * * * * *

Division F—DEPARTMENT OF HOMELAND SECURITY APPROPRIATIONS ACT, 2016

* * * * * * *

Title V—GENERAL PROVISIONS

(INCLUDING TRANSFERS AND RESCISSIONS OF FUNDS)

* * * * * * *

SEC. 519. None of the funds provided by this or previous appropriations Acts shall be used to fund any position designated as a Principal Federal Official (or the successor thereto) for any Robert T. Stafford Disaster Relief and Emergency Assistance Act (42 U.S.C. 5121 et seq.) declared disasters or emergencies unless—

(1) the responsibilities of the Principal Federal Official do not include operational functions related to incident management, including coordination of operations, and are consistent with the requirements of section 509(c) and sections 503(c)(3) and 503(c)(4)(A) of the Homeland Security Act of 2002 (6 U.S.C. 319(c), 313(c)(3), and 313(c)(4)(A)) and section 302 of the Robert T. Stafford Disaster Relief and Assistance Act (42 U.S.C. 5143);

(2) not later than 10 business days after the latter of the date on which the Secretary of Homeland Security appoints the Principal Federal Official and the date on which the President issues a declaration under section 401 or section 501 of the Robert T. Stafford Disaster Relief and Emergency Assistance Act (42 U.S.C. 5170 and 5191, respectively), the Secretary of Homeland Security shall submit a notification of the appointment of the Principal Federal Official and a description of the responsibilities of such Official and how such responsibilities are consistent with paragraph (1) to the Committees on Appropriations of the Senate and the House of Representatives, the Committee on Homeland Security and Governmental Affairs of the Senate, and

the Committee on Transportation and Infrastructure of the House of Representatives; and

(3)   not later than 60 days after the date of enactment of this Act, the Secretary shall provide a report specifying timeframes and milestones regarding the update of operations, planning and policy documents, and training and exercise protocols, to ensure consistency with paragraph (1) of this section.

* * * * * * *

SEC. 520. None of the funds provided or otherwise made available in this Act shall be available to carry out section 872 of the Homeland Security Act of 2002 (6 U.S.C. 452) unless explicitly authorized by Congress.

* * * * * * *

SEC. 548. None of the funds provided in this or any other Act may be obligated to implement the National Preparedness Grant Program or any other successor grant programs unless explicitly authorized by Congress.

★

SELECT PROVISIONS OF THE ADDITIONAL SUPPLEMENTAL APPROPRIATIONS FOR DISASTER RELIEF REQUIREMENTS ACT OF 2017

PUBLIC LAW 106–390
AS AMENDED THROUGH PUB. L. 117–81

ADDITIONAL SUPPLEMENTAL APPROPRIATIONS FOR DISASTER RELIEF REQUIREMENTS ACT OF 2017

[(Public Law 115–72)]

[As Amended Through P.L. 115–123, Enacted February 9, 2018]

AN ACT Making additional supplemental appropriations for disaster relief requirements for the fiscal year ending September 30, 2018, and for other purposes.

Be it enacted by the Senate and House of Representatives of the United States of America in Congress assembled,

SECTION 1. SHORT TITLE.

This Act may be cited as the "Additional Supplemental Appropriations for Disaster Relief Requirements Act, 2017".

Division A—ADDITIONAL SUPPLEMENTAL APPROPRIATIONS FOR DISASTER RELIEF REQUIREMENTS ACT OF 2017

The following sums are hereby appropriated, out of any money in the Treasury not otherwise appropriated, and out of applicable corporate or other revenues, receipts, and funds, for the several departments, agencies, corporations, and other organizational units of Government for fiscal year 2018, and for other purposes, namely:

Title I—DEPARTMENT OF HOMELAND SECURITY

FEDERAL EMERGENCY MANAGEMENT AGENCY

DISASTER RELIEF FUND (INCLUDING TRANSFERS OF FUNDS)

For an additional amount for Disaster Relief Fund for major disasters declared pursuant to the Robert T. Stafford Disaster Relief and Emergency Assistance Act (42 U.S.C. 5121 et seq.), $18,670,000,000, to remain available until expended, of which $10,000,000 shall be transferred to the Department of Homeland Security Office of Inspector General for audits and investigations related to disasters: Provided, That the Administrator of the Federal Emergency Management Agency shall publish on the Agency's website not later than 5 days after an award of a public assistance grant under section 406 of the Robert T. Stafford Disaster Relief and Emergency

Assistance Act (42 U.S.C. 5172) that is in excess of $1,000,000, the specifics of each such grant award: Provided further, That for any mission assignment or mission assignment task order to another Federal department or agency regarding a major disaster in excess of $1,000,000, not later than 5 days after the issuance of such mission assignment or mission assignment task order, the Administrator shall publish on the Agency's website the following: the name of the impacted State, the disaster declaration for such State, the assigned agency, the assistance requested, a description of the disaster, the total cost estimate, and the amount obligated: Provided further, That not later than 10 days after the last day of each month until a mission assignment or mission assignment task order described in the preceding proviso is completed and closed out, the Administrator shall update any changes to the total cost estimate and the amount obligated: Provided further, That for a disaster declaration related to Hurricane Harvey, Hurricane Irma, or Hurricane Maria, the Administrator shall submit to the Committees on Appropriations of the House of Representatives and the Senate, not later than 5 days after the first day of each month beginning after the date of enactment of this Act, and shall publish on the Agency's website, not later than 10 days after the first day of each such month, an estimate or actual amount, if available, for the current fiscal year of the cost of the following categories of spending: public assistance, individual assistance, operations, mitigation, administrative, and any other relevant category (including emergency measures and disaster resources): Provided further, That not later than 10 days after the first day of each month, the Administrator shall publish on the Agency's website the report (referred to as the Disaster Relief Monthly Report) as required by Public Law 114-4.

Of the amounts provided in this division for the Disaster Relief Fund, up to $4,900,000,000 may be transferred to the Disaster Assistance Direct Loan Program Account for the cost of direct loans as authorized under section 417 of the Robert T. Stafford Disaster Relief and Emergency Assistance Act (42 U.S.C. 5184) to be used to assist local governments in providing essential services as a result of Hurricanes Harvey, Irma, or Maria: Provided further, That such amounts may subsidize gross obligations for the principal amount of direct loans not to exceed $4,900,000,000 under section 417 of the Stafford Act: Provided further, That notwithstanding section 417 of the Stafford Act, a territory or possession, and instrumentalities and local governments thereof, of the United States shall be deemed to be a local government for purposes of this paragraph: Provided further, That notwithstanding section 417(b) of the Stafford Act, the amount of any such loan issued to a territory or possession, and instrumentalities and local governments thereof, may be based on the projected loss of tax and other revenues and on projected cash outlays not previously budgeted for a period not to exceed 365 days from the date of the major disaster, and may exceed $5,000,000: Provided further, That notwithstanding any other provision of law or the constitution of a territory or possession that limits the issuance of debt, a territory or possession, and instrumentalities and local governments thereof, may each receive more than one loan with repayment provisions and other terms specific to the type of lost tax and other revenues and on projected unbudgeted cash outlays for which the loan is provided: Provided further, That notwithstanding section 417(c)(1) of the Stafford Act, loans to a territory or possession, and instrumentalities and local governments thereof, may be cancelled in whole or in part only at the discretion of the Secretary of Homeland Security in consultation with the Secretary of the Treasury: *Provided further*, That notwithstanding any other provision of law, the Secretary of Homeland Security, in consultation with the Secretary of the Treasury, shall determine the terms, conditions, eligible uses, and timing and amount of Federal disbursements of loans issued to a territory or possession, and instrumentalities and local governments thereof: *Provided further*, That such costs, including the cost of modifying such loans, shall be as defined in section 502 of the Congressional Budget Act of 1974 (2 U.S.C. 661a): *Provided further*, That FEMA may transfer up to 1.5 percent of the amount under this paragraph to the Disaster Assistance Direct Loan Program Account for administrative expenses to carry out under this paragraph the direct loan program, as authorized by section 417 of the Stafford Act: *Provided further*, That of the amount provided under this paragraph for transfer, up to $150,000,000 may be transferred to the Disaster Assistance Direct Loan Program Account for the cost to lend a territory or possession of the United States that portion of assistance for which the territory or possession is responsible under the cost-sharing provisions of the major disaster declaration for Hurricanes Irma or Maria, as authorized under section 319 of the Robert T. Stafford Disaster Relief and Emergency Assistance Act (42 U.S.C. 5162): *Provided further*, That of the amount provided under this paragraph for transfer, up to $1,000,000 may be transferred to the Disaster Assistance Direct Loan Program Account for administrative expenses to carry out the Advance of Non-Federal Share program, as authorized by section 319 of the Stafford Act.

The amount provided under this heading is designated by the Congress as being for an emergency requirement pursuant to section 251(b)(2)(A)(i) of the Balanced Budget and Emergency Deficit Control Act of 1985.

Title II— DEPARTMENT OF AGRICULTURE

FOREST SERVICE

WILDLAND FIRE MANAGEMENT (INCLUDING TRANSFER OF FUNDS)

For an additional amount for Wildland Fire Management, $184,500,000, to remain available through September 30, 2021, for urgent wildland fire suppression operations: *Provided*, That such funds shall be solely available to be transferred to and merged with other appropriations accounts from which funds were previously transferred for wildland fire suppression in fiscal year 2017 to fully repay those amounts: *Provided further*, That such amount is designated by the Congress as being for an emergency requirement pursuant to section 251(b)(2)(A)(i) of the Balanced Budget and Emergency Deficit Control Act of 1985.

FLAME WILDFIRE SUPPRESSION RESERVE FUND (INCLUDING TRANSFER OF FUNDS)

For an additional amount for FLAME Wildfire Suppression Reserve Fund, $342,000,000, to remain available through September 30, 2021, for necessary expenses for large wildland fire suppression operations of the Department of Agriculture and as a reserve fund for suppression and Federal emergency response activities: *Provided*, That notwithstanding the FLAME Act of 2009 (43 U.S.C.

1748a(e)), such funds shall be solely available to be transferred to and merged with other appropriations accounts from which funds were previously transferred for wildland fire suppression in fiscal year 2017 to fully repay those amounts: Provided further, That such amount is designated by the Congress as being for an emergency requirement pursuant to section 251(b)(2)(A)(i) of the Balanced Budget and Emergency Deficit Control Act of 1985.

DEPARTMENT OF THE INTERIOR

DEPARTMENT-WIDE PROGRAMS

WILDLAND FIRE MANAGEMENT (INCLUDING TRANSFER OF FUNDS)

For an additional amount for Wildland Fire Management, $50,000,000, to remain available until expended, for urgent wildland fire suppression activities and funds necessary to repay any transfers needed for these costs: Provided, That such funds may be available to be transferred to and merged with other appropriations accounts to fully repay amounts previously transferred for wildland fire suppression: Provided further, That such amount is designated by the Congress as being for an emergency requirement pursuant to section 251(b)(2)(A)(i) of the Balanced Budget and Emergency Deficit Control Act of 1985.

Title III—GENERAL PROVISIONS

SEC. 301. Each amount appropriated or made available by this division is in addition to amounts otherwise appropriated for the fiscal year involved.

SEC. 302. No part of any appropriation contained in this division shall remain available for obligation beyond the current fiscal year unless expressly so provided herein.

SEC. 303. The terms and conditions applicable to the funds provided in this division, including those provided by this title, shall also apply to the funds made available in division B of Public Law 115-56.

SEC. 304. Each amount designated in this division by the Congress as being for an emergency requirement pursuant to section 251(b)(2)(A)(i) of the Balanced Budget and Emergency Deficit Control Act of 1985 shall be available only if the President subsequently so designates all such amounts and transmits such designations to the Congress.

SEC. 305. (a) Not later than March 31, 2018, in accordance with criteria to be established by the Director of the Office of Management and Budget (referred to in this section as OMB), each Federal agency shall submit to OMB, the Government Accountability Office, the respective Inspector General of each agency, and the Committees on Appropriations of the House of Representatives and the Senate internal control plans for funds provided by this division and division B of Public Law 115-56.

(b) All programs and activities expending more than $10,000,000 of funds provided by this division and division B of Public Law 115–56 in any one fiscal year shall be deemed to be susceptible to significant improper payments for purposes of the Improper Payments Information Act of 2002 (31 U.S.C. 3321 note), notwithstanding section 2(a) of such Act.

(c) Funds for grants provided by this division or division B of Public Law 115-56 shall be expended by the grantees within the 24-month period following the agency's obligation of funds for the grant, unless, in accordance with guidance to be issued by the Director of OMB, the Director waives this requirement for a particular grant program and submits a written justification for such waiver to the Committees on Appropriations of the House of Representatives and the Senate. In the case of such grants, the agency shall include a term in the grant that requires the grantee to return to the agency any funds not expended within the 24-month period.

SEC. 306. (a) The first proviso under the heading Department of Housing and Urban Development—Community Planning and Development—Community Development Fund in division B of Public Law 115-56 is amended by striking State or unit of general local government and inserting State, unit of general local government, or Indian tribe (as such term is defined in section 102 of the Housing and Community Development Act of 1974 (42 U.S.C. 5302)).

(b) Amounts repurposed pursuant to subsection (a) that were previously designated by the Congress as an emergency requirement pursuant to the Balanced Budget and Emergency Deficit Control Act of 1985 are designated by the Congress as being for an emergency requirement pursuant to section 251(b)(2)(A)(i) of such Act.

* * * * * * *

SEC. 308. (a) Notwithstanding sections 1309, 1310, and 1310a of the National Flood Insurance Act of 1968 (42 U.S.C. 4016-4017a) and section 15(e) of the Federal Flood Insurance Act of 1956 (42 U.S.C. 2414(e)), and any borrowing agreement entered into between the Department of the Treasury and the Federal Emergency Management Agency, of the indebtedness of the Administrator under any notes or other obligations issued pursuant to section 1309(a) of the National Flood Insurance Act of 1968 (42 U.S.C. 4016(a)) and section 15(e) of the Federal Insurance Act of 1956 (42 U.S.C. 2414(e)) that is outstanding as of the date of the enactment of this Act, an amount of $16,000,000,000 is hereby cancelled. To the extent of the amount cancelled, the Administrator and the National Flood Insurance Fund are relieved of all liability to the Secretary of the Treasury under any such notes or other obligations, including for any interest due under such notes and any other fees and charges payable in connection with such notes, and the total amount of notes and obligations issued by the Administrator pursuant to such sections shall be considered to be reduced by such amount for the purposes of the limitation on such total amount under such section 1309(a).

(b) The amount of the indebtedness cancelled under subsection (a) may be treated as public debt of the United States.

(c)(1) This section is designated as an emergency requirement pursuant to section 4(g) of the Statutory Pay-As-You-Go Act of 2010 (2 U.S.C. 933(g)).

(2) The amount provided in this section is designated by the Congress as being for an emergency requirement pursuant to section 251(b)(2)(A)(i) of the Balanced

Budget and Emergency Deficit Control Act of 1985.

SEC. 309. Notwithstanding section 19(a)(2)(B) of the Food and Nutrition Act of 2008 (7 U.S.C. 2028), not to exceed $1,270,000,000 of funds made available for the contingency reserve under the heading Supplemental Nutrition Assistance Program of division A of Public Law 114-113 shall be available for the Secretary to provide a grant to the Commonwealth of Puerto Rico for disaster nutrition assistance in response to the Presidentially declared major disasters and emergencies: *Provided*, That funds made available to Puerto Rico under this section shall remain available for obligation by the Commonwealth until September 30, 2019, and shall be in addition to funds otherwise made available: *Provided further*, That such amount is designated by the Congress as being for an emergency requirement pursuant to section 251(b)(2)(A)(i) of the Balanced Budget and Emergency Deficit Control Act of 1985.

SEC. 310. Notwithstanding section 2208(l)(3) of title 10, United States Code, during fiscal year 2018, the dollar limitation on advance billing of a customer of a working-capital fund in such section shall not apply with respect to the advance billing of the Federal Emergency Management Agency. In the preceding sentence, the term advance billing has the meaning given the term in section 2208(l)(4) of title 10, United States Code.

This division may be cited as the "Additional Supplemental Appropriations for Disaster Relief Requirements Act of 2017".

★

HAZARD-SPECIFIC LAWS
FLOODS

NATIONAL FLOOD INSURANCE ACT OF 1968
TITLE XIII OF THE HOUSING AND URBAN DEVELOPMENT ACT OF 1968

PUBLIC LAW 99–448
AS AMENDED THROUGH PUB. L. 117–328

NATIONAL FLOOD INSURANCE ACT OF 1968

(Title XIII of the Housing and Urban Development Act of 1968)

[Public Law 90–448; 82 Stat. 572; 42 U.S.C. 4001 et seq.]

[As Amended Through P.L. 117–328, Enacted December 29, 2022]

TITLE XIII—NATIONAL FLOOD INSURANCE

SHORT TITLE

SEC. 1301. [42 U.S.C. 4001 note] This title may be cited as the "National Flood Insurance Act of 1968".

FINDINGS AND DECLARATION OF PURPOSE

SEC. 1302. [42 U.S.C. 4001] (a) The Congress finds that (1) from time to time flood disasters have created personal hardships and economic distress which have required unforeseen disaster relief measures and have placed an increasing burden on the Nation's resources; (2) despite the installation of preventive and protective works and the adoption of other public programs designed to reduce losses caused by flood damage, these methods have not been sufficient to protect adequately against growing exposure to future flood losses; (3) as a matter of national policy, a reasonable method of sharing the risk of flood losses is through a program a flood insurance which can complement and encourage preventive and protective measures; and (4) if such a program is initiated and carried out gradually, it can be expanded as knowledge is gained and experience is appraised, thus eventually making flood insurance coverage available on reasonable terms and conditions to persons who have need for such protection.

(b) The Congress also finds that (1) many factors have made it uneconomic for the private insurance industry alone to make flood insurance available to those in need of such protection on reasonable terms and conditions; but (2) a program of flood insurance with large-scale participation of the Federal Government and carried out to the maximum extent practicable by the private insurance industry is feasible and can be initiated.

(c) The Congress further finds that (1) a program of flood insurance can promote the public interest by providing appropriate protection against the perils of flood losses and encouraging sound land use by minimizing exposure of property to flood losses; and (2) the objectives of a flood insurance program should be integrally related to a unified national program for flood plain management and, to this end, it is the sense of Congress

151

that within two years following the effective date of this title the President should transmit to the Congress for its consideration any further proposals necessary for such a unified program, including proposals for the allocation of costs among beneficiaries of flood protection.

(d)   It is therefore the purpose of this title to (1) authorize a flood insurance program by means of which flood insurance, over a period of time, can be made available on a nationwide basis through the cooperative efforts of the Federal Government and the private insurance industry, and (2) provide flexibility in the program so that such flood insurance may be based on workable methods of pooling risks, minimizing costs, and distributing burdens equitably among those who will be protected by flood insurance and the general public.

(e)   It is the further purpose of this title to (1) encourage State and local governments to make appropriate land use adjustments to constrict the development of land which is exposed to flood damage and minimize damage caused by flood losses, (2) guide the development of proposed future construction, where practicable, away from locations which are threatened by flood hazards, (3) encourage lending and credit institutions, as a matter of national policy, to assist in furthering the objectives of the flood insurance program, (4) assure that any Federal assistance provided under the program will be related closely to all flood-related programs and activities of the Federal Government, and (5) authorize continuing studies of flood hazards in order to provide for a constant reappraisal of the flood insurance and its effect on land use requirements.

(f)   The Congress also finds that (1) the damage and loss which results from mudslides is related in cause and similar in effect to that which results directly from storms, deluges, overflowing waters, and other forms of flooding, and (2) the problems involved in providing protection against this damage and loss, and the possibilities for making such protection available through a Federal or federally sponsored program, are similar to those which exist in connection with efforts to provide protection against damage and loss caused by such other forms of flooding. It is therefore the further purpose of this title to make available, by means of the methods, procedures, and instrumentalities which are otherwise established or available under this title for purposes of the flood insurance program, protection against damage and loss resulting from mudslides that are caused by accumulations of water on or under the ground.

AMENDMENTS TO THE FEDERAL FLOOD INSURANCE ACT OF 1956

SEC. 1303. (a)   The second sentence of section 15(e) of the Federal Flood Insurance Act of 1956 (79 Stat. 1078) is amended—

* * * * * * *

CHAPTER I—THE NATIONAL FLOOD INSURANCE PROGRAM

BASIC AUTHORITY

SEC. 1304. [42 U.S.C. 4011] (a)   To carry out the purposes of this title, the Administrator of the Federal Emergency Management Agency is authorized to establish and carry out a national flood insurance program which will enable interested persons to purchase insurance against loss resulting from physical damage to or loss of real property or personal property related thereto arising from any flood occurring in the United States.

(b) ADDITIONAL COVERAGE FOR COMPLIANCE WITH LAND USE AND CONTROL MEASURES.—The national flood insurance program established pursuant to subsection (a) shall enable the purchase of insurance to cover the cost of implementing measures that are consistent with land use and control measures established by the community under section 1361 for—

(1)   properties that are repetitive loss structures;

(2)   properties that are substantially damaged structures;

(3)   properties that have sustained flood damage on multiple occasions, if the Administrator determines that it is cost-effective and in the best interests of the National Flood Insurance Fund to require compliance with the land use and control measures.[1]

---

[1]   Section 105(a)(3) of the Bunning-Bereuter-Blumenauer Flood Insurance Reform Act of 2004 (Pub. L. 108–264; 118 Stat. 723) provides that this paragraph is amended 'by striking compliance with land use and control measures. and inserting the implementation of such measures; and ''. The amendment could not be executed because the matter to be struck does not appear.

---

(4) properties for which an offer of mitigation assistance is made under—

(A)   section 1366 (Flood Mitigation Assistance Program);

(B)   the Hazard Mitigation Grant Program authorized under section 404 of the Robert T. Stafford Disaster Assistance and Emergency Relief Act (42 U.S.C. 5170c);

(C)   the Predisaster Hazard Mitigation Program under section 203 of the Robert T. Stafford Disaster Assistance and Emergency Relief Act (42 U.S.C. 5133); and

(D)   any programs authorized or for which funds are appropriated to address any unmet needs or for which supplemental funds are made available.

The Administrator shall impose a surcharge on each insured of not more than $75 per policy to provide cost of compliance coverage in accordance with the provisions of this subsection.

(c) In carrying out the flood insurance program the Administrator shall, to the maxmium extent practicable, encourage and arrange for—

(1)   appropriate financial participation and risk sharing in the program by insurance companies and other insurers, and

(2)   other appropriate participation on other than a risk-sharing basis, by insurance companies and other insurers, insurance agents and brokers, and insurance adjustment organizations, in accordance with the provisions of chapter II.

SCOPE OF PROGRAM AND PRIORITIES

SEC. 1305. [42 U.S.C. 4012] (a)   In carrying out the flood insurance program the Administrator shall afford a priority to making flood insurance available to cover residential properties which are designed for the occupancy of from one to four families, church properties, and business properties which are owned or leased and operated by small business concerns.

(b) If on the basis of—

(1) studies and investigations undertaken and carried out and information received or exchanged under section 1307, and

(2) such other information as may be necessary, the Administrator determines that it would be feasible to extend the flood insurance program to cover other properties, he may take such action under this title as from time to time may be necessary in order to make flood insurance available to cover, on such basis as may be feasible, any types and classes of—

(A) other residential properties not described in subsection (a) or (d)[2],

---

[2] Section 100204 of Public Law 112–141 inserts language after properties in subsection (b)(2)(A). Subparagraph (A) is not a subdivision of paragraph (2), but was carried out to subsection (b)(A) to reflect the probable intent of Congress.

(B) other business properties,

(C) agricultural properties,

(D) properties occupied by private nonprofit organizations, and

(E) properties owned by State and local governments and agencies thereof, and any such extensions of the program to any types and classes of these properties shall from time to time be prescribed in regulations.

(c) The Administrator shall make flood insurance available in only those States or areas (or subdivisions thereof) which he has determined have—

(1) evidenced a positive interest in securing flood insurance coverage under the flood insurance program, and

(2) given satisfactory assurance that by December 31, 1971, adequate land use and control measures will have been adopted for the State or area (or subdivision) which are consistent with the comprehensive critiera for land management and use developed under section 1361, and that the application and enforcement of such measures will commence as soon as technical information on floodways and on controlling flood elevations is available.

(d) AVAILABILITY OF INSURANCE FOR MULTIFAMILY PROPERTIES.—

(1) IN GENERAL.— The Administrator shall make flood insurance available to cover residential properties of 5 or more residences. Notwithstanding any other provision of law, the maximum coverage amount that the Administrator may make available under this subsection to such residential properties shall be equal to the coverage amount made available to commercial properties.

(2) RULE OF CONSTRUCTION.— Nothing in this subsection shall be construed to limit the ability of individuals residing in residential properties of 5 or more residences to obtain insurance for the contents and personal articles located in such residences.

NATURE AND LIMITATION OF INSURANCE COVERAGE

154

SEC. 1306. [42 U.S.C. 4013] (a) The Administrator shall from time to time, after consultation with the advisory committee authorized under section 1318, appropriate representatives of the pool formed or otherwise created under section 1331, and appropriate representatives of the insurance authorities of the respective States, provide by regulation for general terms and conditions of insurability which shall be applicable to properties eligible for flood insurance coverage under section 1305, including—

(1) the types, classes, and locations of any such properties which shall be eligible for flood insurance;

(2) the nature and limits of loss or damage in any areas (or subdivisions thereof) which may be covered by such insurance;

(3) the classification, limitation, and rejection of any risks which may be advisable;

(4) appropriate minimum premiums;

(5) appropriate loss-deductibles; and

(6) any other terms and conditions relating to insurance coverage or exclusion which may be necessary to carry out the purposes of this title.

(b) In addition to any other terms and conditions under subsection (a), such regulations shall provide that—

(1) any flood insurance coverage based on chargeable premium rates under section 1308 which are less than the estimated premium rates under section 1307(a)(1) shall not exceed—

(A) in the case of residential properties—

(i) $35,000 aggregate liability for any single-family dwelling, and $100,000 for any residential structure containing more than one dwelling unit,

(ii) $10,000 aggregate liability per dwelling unit for any contents related to such unit, and

(iii) in the States of Alaska and Hawaii, and in the Virgin Islands and Guam, the limits provided in clause (i) of this sentence shall be: $50,000 aggregate liability for any single-family dwelling, and $150,000 for any residential structure containing more than one dwelling unit;

(B) in the case of business properties which are owned or leased and operated by small business concerns, an aggregate liability with respect to any single structure, including any contents thereof related to premises of small business occupants (as term is defined by the Administrator), which shall be equal to (i) $100,000 plus (ii) $100,000 multiplied by the number of such occupants and shall be allocated among such occupants (or among the occupant or occupants and the owner) under regulations prescribed by the Administrator; except that the aggregate liability for the structure itself may in no case exceed $100,000; and

(C) in the case of church properties which may become eligible for flood insurance under section 1305—

(i) $100,000 aggregate liability for any single structure, and

(ii) $100,000 aggregate liability per unit for any contents related to such unit; and

(2)   in the case of any residential building designed for the occupancy of from 1 to 4 families for which the risk premium rate is determined in accordance with the provisions of section 1307(a)(1), additional flood insurance in excess of the limits specified in clause (i) of subparagraph (A) of paragraph (1) shall be made available, with respect to any single such building, up to an aggregate liability (including such limits specified in paragraph (1)(A)(i)) of $250,000;

(3)   in the case of any residential property for which the risk premium rate is determined in accordance with the provisions of section 1307(a)(1), additional flood insurance in excess of the limits specified in clause (ii) of subparagraph (A) of paragraph (1) shall be made available to every insured upon renewal and every applicant for insurance so as to enable any such insured or applicant to receive coverage up to a total amount (including such limits specified in paragraph (1)(A)(ii)) of $100,000;

(4)   in the case of any nonresidential building, including a church, for which the risk premium rate is determined in accordance with the provisions of section 1307(a)(1), additional flood insurance in excess of the limits specified in subparagraphs (B) and (C) of paragraph (1) shall be made available with respect to any single such building, up to an aggregate liability (including such limits specified in subparagraph (B) or (C) of paragraph (1), as applicable) of $500,000, and coverage shall be made available up to a total of $500,000 aggregate liability for contents owned by the building owner and $500,000 aggregate liability for each unit within the building for contents owned by the tenant; and

(5)   any flood insurance coverage which may be made available in excess of the limits specified in subparagraph (A), (B), or (C) of paragraph (1), shall be based only on chargeable premium rates under section 1308 which are not less than the estimated premium rates under section 1307(a)(1), and the amount of such excess coverage shall not in any case exceed an amount equal to the applicable limit so specified (or allocated) under paragraph (1)(C), (2), (3), or (4), as applicable.

(c)[3] EFFECTIVE DATE OF POLICIES.—

---

[3]

Section 552(a) of the Riegle Community Development and Regulatory Improvement Act of 1994, Pub. L. 103–325, approved September 23, 1994, repealed this subsection, as previously in effect. Section 579(a) of such Act then added this subsection as it appears in this compilation. As in effect before such Act, this subsection authorized the Director to pay claims under flood insurance contracts for demolition and relocation of properties that were subject to imminent collapse or subsidence because of erosion. Such section 552 provides as follows:

``SEC. 552. TERMINATION OF EROSION-THREATENED STRUCTURES PROGRAM.

``(a) In General.—Section 1306 of the National Flood Insurance Act of 1968 (42 U.S.C. 4013) is amended by striking subsection (c).

``(b) Transition Phase.—Notwithstanding subsection (a), during the 1-year period beginning on the date of enactment of this Act, the Director of the Federal Emergency Management Agency may pay amounts under flood insurance contracts for demolition or relocation of structures as provided in section 1306(c) of the National Flood Insurance Act of 1968 (as in effect immediately before the enactment of this Act).

``(c) Savings Provision.—Notwithstanding subsection (a), the Director shall take any action necessary to make payments under flood insurance contracts pursuant to any commitments made before the expiration of the period referred to in subsection (b) pursuant to the authority under section 1306(c) of the National Flood Insurance Act of 1968 or subsection (b).

``(d) Repeal of Findings Provision.—Section 1302 of the National Flood Insurance Act of 1968 (42 U.S.C. 4001) is amended by striking subsection (g).''.

(1) WAITING PERIOD.— Except as provided in paragraph (2), coverage under a new contract for flood insurance coverage under this title entered into after the date of enactment of the Riegle Community Development and Regulatory Improvement Act of 1994,[4] and any modification to coverage under an existing flood insurance contract made after such date, shall become effective upon the expiration of the 30-day period beginning on the date that all obligations for such coverage (including completion of the application and payment of any initial premiums owed) are satisfactorily completed.

[4]   September 23, 1994.

(2) EXCEPTION.—The provisions of paragraph (1) shall not apply to—

(A) the initial purchase of flood insurance coverage under this title when the purchase of insurance is in connection with the making, increasing, extension, or renewal of a loan;

(B) the initial purchase of flood insurance coverage pursuant to a revision or updating of floodplain areas or flood-risk zones under section 1360(f), if such purchase occurs during the 1-year period beginning upon publication of notice of the revision or updating under section 1360(h); or

(C) the initial purchase of flood insurance coverage for private property if—

(i) the Administrator determines that the property is affected by flooding on Federal land that is a result of, or is exacerbated by, post-wildfire conditions, after consultation with an authorized employee of the Federal agency that has jurisdiction of the land on which the wildfire that caused the post-wildfire conditions occurred; and

(ii) the flood insurance coverage was purchased not later than 60 days after the fire containment date, as determined by the appropriate Federal employee, relating to the wildfire that caused the post-wildfire conditions described in clause (i).

(d) OPTIONAL HIGH-DEDUCTIBLE POLICIES FOR RESIDENTIAL PROPERTIES.—

(1) AVAILABILITY.— In the case of residential properties, the Administrator shall make flood insurance coverage available, at the option of the insured, that provides for a loss-deductible for damage to the covered property in various amounts, up to and including $10,000.

(2) DISCLOSURE.—

(A) FORM.— The Administrator shall provide the information described in subparagraph (B) clearly and conspicuously on the application form for flood insurance coverage or on a separate form, segregated from all unrelated information and other required disclosures.

(B) INFORMATION.—The information described in this subparagraph is—

(i) information sufficient to inform the applicant of the availability of the coverage option required by paragraph (1) to applicants for flood insurance coverage; and

(ii) a statement explaining the effect of a loss-deductible and that, in the event of an insured loss, the insured is responsible out-of-pocket for losses to the extent of the deductible selected.

ESTIMATES OF PREMIUM RATES

SEC. 1307. [42 U.S.C. 4014] (a) The Administrator is authorized to undertake and carry out such studies and investigations and receive or exchange such information as may be necessary to estimate, and shall from time to time estimate, on an area, subdivision, or other appropriate basis—

(1) the risk premium rates for flood insurance which—

(A) based on consideration of—

(i) the risk involved and accepted actuarial principles; and

(ii) the flood mitigation activities that an owner or lessee has undertaken on a property, including differences in the risk involved due to land use measures, floodproofing, flood forecasting, and similar measures, and

(B) including—

(i) the applicable operating costs and allowances set forth in the schedules prescribed under section 1311 and reflected in such rates,

(ii) any administrative expenses (or portion of such expenses) of carrying out the flood insurance program which, in his discretion, should properly be reflected in such rates,

(iii) any remaining administrative expenses incurred in carrying out the flood insurance and floodplain management programs (including the costs of mapping activities under section 1360) not included under clause (ii), which shall be recovered by a fee charged to policyholders and such fee shall not be subject to any agents' commissions, company expense allowances, or State or local premium taxes,[5] and

---

[5] The Departments of Veterans Affairs and Housing and Urban Development, and Independent Agencies Appropriations Act, 2003 (Division K of the Consolidated Appropriations Resolution, 2003; Pub. L. 108–7; 117 Stat. 517) provides [t]hat beginning in fiscal year 2003 and thereafter, fees authorized in 42 U.S.C. 4014(a)(1)(B)(iii) shall be collected only if provided in advance in appropriation acts.

(iv) all costs, as prescribed by principles and standards of practice in

ratemaking adopted by the American Academy of Actuaries and the Casualty Actuarial Society, including—

(I) an estimate of the expected value of future costs,

(II) all costs associated with the transfer of risk, and

(III) the costs associated with an individual risk transfer with respect to risk classes, as defined by the Administrator,

would be required in order to make such insurance available on an actuarial basis for any types and classes of properties for which insurance coverage is available under section 1305(a) (or is recommended to the Congress under section 1305(b));

(2) the rates, if less than the rates estimated under paragraph (1), which would be reasonable, would encourage prospective insureds to purchase flood insurance, and would be consistent with the purposes of this title, and which, together with a fee charged to policyholders that shall not be not subject to any agents' commission, company expenses allowances, or State or local premium taxes, shall include any administrative expenses incurred in carrying out the flood insurance and floodplain management programs (including the costs of mapping activities under section 1360), except that the Administrator shall not estimate rates under this paragraph for—

(A) any residential property which is not the primary residence of an individual;

(B) any severe repetitive loss property;

(C) any property that has incurred flood-related damage in which the cumulative amounts of payments under this title equaled or exceeded the fair market value of such property;

(D) any business property; or

(E) any property which on or after the date of enactment of the Biggert-Waters Flood Insurance Reform Act of 2012 has experienced or sustained—

(i) substantial damage exceeding 50 percent of the fair market value of such property; or

(ii) substantial improvement exceeding 50 percent of the fair market value of such property; and

(3) the extent, if any, to which federally assisted or other flood protection measures initiated after the date of the enactment of this title[6] affect such rates.

---

[6]   August 1, 1968.

(b)   In carrying out subsection (a), the Administrator shall, to the maximum extent feasible and on a reimbursable basis, utilize the services of the Department of the Army, the Department of the Interior, The Department of Agriculture, the Department of Commerce, and the Tennessee Valley Authority, and, as appropriate, other Federal departments or agencies, and for such purposes may enter into agreements or other appropriate arrangements with any persons.

(c)   The Administrator shall give priority to conducting studies and investigations and making estimates under this section in those States or areas (or subdivisions thereof) which he has determined have evidenced a positive interest in securing flood insurance coverage under the flood insurance program.

(d) Notwithstanding any other provision of law, any structure existing on the date of enactment of the Flood Disaster Protection Act of 1973[7] and located within Avoyelles, Evangeline, Rapides, or Saint Landry Parish in the State of Louisiana, which the Administrator determines is subject to additional flood hazards as a result of the construction or operation of the Atchafalaya Basin Levee System, shall be eligible for flood insurance under this title (if and to the extent it is eligible for such insurance under the other provisions of this title) at premium rates that shall not exceed those which would be applicable if such additional hazards did not exist.

---

[7]   December 31, 1973.

(e) Notwithstanding any other provision of law, any community that has made adequate progress, acceptable to the Administrator, on the construction or reconstruction of a flood protection system which will afford flood protection for the one-hundred-year frequency flood as determined by the Administrator, shall be eligible for flood insurance under this title (if and to the extent it is eligible for such insurance under the other provisions of this title) at premium rates not exceeding those which would be applicable under this section if such flood protection system had been completed. The Administrator shall find that adequate progress on the construction or reconstruction of a flood protection system, based on the present value of the completed flood protection system, has been made only if: (1) 100 percent of the cost of the system has been authorized; (2) at least 60 percent of the cost of the system has been appropriated; (3) at least 50 percent of the cost of the system has been expended; and (4) the system is at least 50 percent completed.Notwithstanding any other provision of law, in determining whether a community has made adequate progress on the construction, reconstruction, or improvement of a flood protection system, the Administrator shall consider all sources of funding, including Federal, State, and local funds.

(f) Notwithstanding any other provision of law, this subsection shall apply to riverine and coastal levees that are located in a community which has been determined by the Administrator of the Federal Emergency Management Agency to be in the process of restoring flood protection afforded by a flood protection system that had been previously accredited on a Flood Insurance Rate Map as providing 100-year frequency flood protection but no longer does so, and shall apply without regard to the level of Federal funding of or participation in the construction, reconstruction, or improvement of the flood protection system. Except as provided in this subsection, in such a community, flood insurance shall be made available to those properties impacted by the disaccreditation of the flood protection system at premium rates that do not exceed those which would be applicable to any property located in an area of special flood hazard, the construction of which was started prior to the effective date of the initial Flood Insurance Rate Map published by the Administrator for the community in which such property is located. A revised Flood Insurance Rate Map shall be prepared for the community to delineate as Zone AR the areas of special flood hazard that result from the disaccreditation of the flood protection system. A community will be considered to be in the process of restoration if—

(1) the flood protection system has been deemed restorable by a Federal agency in consultation with the local project sponsor;

(2) a minimum level of flood protection is still provided to the community by the disaccredited system; and

(3) restoration of the flood protection system is scheduled to occur within a designated time period and in accordance with a progress plan negotiated between the community and the Federal Emergency Management Agency. Communities that the Administrator of the Federal Emergency Management Agency determines to meet the criteria set forth in paragraphs (1) and (2) as of January 1, 1992, shall not be subject to revised Flood Insurance Rate Maps that contravene the intent of this subsection. Such communities shall remain eligible for C zone rates for properties located in zone AR for any policy written prior to promulgation of final regulations for this section. Floodplain management criteria for such communities shall not require the elevation of improvements to existing structures and shall not exceed 3 feet above existing grade for new construction, provided the base flood elevation based on the disaccredited flood control system does not exceed five feet above existing grade, or the remaining new construction in such communities is limited to infill sites, rehabilitation of existing structures, or redevelopment of previously developed areas.

The Administrator of the Federal Emergency Management Agency shall develop and promulgate regulations to implement this subsection, including minimum floodplain management criteria, within 24 months after the date of enactment of this subsection.[8]

---

[8]   The date of enactment was October 28, 1992.

(g) No Extension of Subsidy to New Policies or Lapsed Policies.—The Administrator shall not provide flood insurance to prospective insureds at rates less than those estimated under subsection (a)(1), as required by paragraph (2) of that subsection, for—

(1) any policy under the flood insurance program that has lapsed in coverage,,[9] unless the decision of the policy holder to permit a lapse in flood insurance coverage was as a result of the property covered by the policy no longer being required to retain such coverage; or

---

[9]   Two commas so in law. See amendment made by section 3(a)(1)(B) of Public Law 113–89.

---

(2) any prospective insured who refuses to accept any offer for mitigation assistance by the Administrator (including an offer to relocate), including an offer of mitigation assistance—

(A) following a major disaster, as defined in section 102 of the Robert T. Stafford Disaster Relief and Emergency Assistance Act (42 U.S.C. 5122); or

(B) in connection with—

(i) a repetitive loss property; or

(ii) a severe repetitive loss property.

(h) Definition.—In this section, the term severe repetitive loss property has the following meaning:

(1) SINGLE-FAMILY PROPERTIES.—In the case of a property consisting of 1 to 4 residences, such term means a property that—

(A)   is covered under a contract for flood insurance made available under this title; and

(B) has incurred flood-related damage—

(i)   for which 4 or more separate claims payments have been made under flood insurance coverage under this chapter, with the amount of each such claim exceeding $5,000, and with the cumulative amount of such claims payments exceeding $20,000; or

(ii)   for which at least 2 separate claims payments have been made under such coverage, with the cumulative amount of such claims exceeding the value of the property.

(2) MULTIFAMILY PROPERTIES.—   In the case of a property consisting of 5 or more residences, such term shall have such meaning as the Director[10] shall by regulation provide.

---

[10]   So in law. Probably should read Administrator. See amendments made by sections 100205(b)(1)(B) and 100238(b)(1) of Public Law 112–141.

ESTABLISHMENT OF CHARGEABLE PREMIUM RATES

SEC. 1308. [42 U.S.C. 4015] (a) On the basis of estimates made under section 1307 and such other information as may be necessary, the Administrator shall from time to time prescribe, after providing notice—

(1)   chargeable premium rates for any types and classes of properties for which insurance coverage shall be available under section 1305 (at less than the estimated risk premium rates under section 1307(a)(1), where necessary), and

(2)   the terms and conditions under which, and the areas (including subdivisions thereof) within which such rates shall apply.

(b) Such rates shall, insofar as practicable, be—

(1)   based on a consideration of the respective risks involved, including differences in risks due to land use measures, flood-proofing, flood forecasting, and similar measures;

(2)   adequate, on the basis of accepted actuarial principles, to provide reserves for anticipated losses, or if less than such amount consistent with the objective of making flood insurance available where necessary at reasonable rates so as to encourage prospective insureds to purchase such insurance and with the purposes of this title;

(3)   adequate, together with the fee under paragraph (1)(B)(iii) or (2) of section 1307(a), to provide for any administrative expenses of the flood insurance and floodplain management programs (including the costs of mapping activities under section 1360);

(4)   stated so as to reflect the basis for such rates, including the differences (if any) between the estimated risk premium rates under section 1307(a)(1) and the

estimated rates under section 1307(a)(2); and

(5)   adequate, on the basis of accepted actuarial principles, to cover the average historical loss year obligations incurred by the National Flood Insurance Fund.

(c) ACTUARIAL RATE PROPERTIES.—Subject only to the limitations provided under paragraphs (1) and (2), the chargeable rate shall not be less than the applicable estimated risk premium rate for such area (or subdivision thereof) under section 1307(a)(1) with respect to the following properties:

(1)   POST-FIRM PROPERTIES.— Any property the construction or substantial improvement of which the Administrator determines has been started after December 31, 1974, or started after the effective date of the initial rate map published by the Administrator under paragraph (2) of section 1360 for the area in which such property is located, whichever is later, except that the chargeable rate for properties under this paragraph shall be subject to the limitation under subsection (e).

(2) CERTAIN LEASED COASTAL AND RIVER PROPERTIES.— Any property leased from the Federal Government (including residential and nonresidential properties) that the Administrator determines is located on the river-facing side of any dike, levee, or other riverine flood control structure, or seaward of any seawall or other coastal flood control structure.

(d)   With respect to any chargeable premium rate prescribed under this section, a sum equal to the portion of the rate that covers any administrative expenses of carrying out the flood insurance and floodplain management programs which have been estimated under paragraphs (1)(B)(ii) and (1)(B)(iii) of section 1307(a) or paragraph (2) of such section (including the fees under such paragraphs), shall be paid to the Administrator. The Administrator shall deposit the sum in the National Flood Insurance Fund established under section 1310.

(e) ANNUAL LIMITATION ON PREMIUM INCREASES.—Except with respect to properties described under paragraph (2) of subsection (c), and notwithstanding any other provision of this title—

(1) the chargeable risk premium rate for flood insurance under this title for any property may not be increased by more than 18 percent each year, except—

(A)   as provided in paragraph (4);

(B)   in the case of property identified under section 1307(g); or

(C) in the case of a property that—

(i)   is located in a community that has experienced a rating downgrade under the community rating system program carried out under section 1315(b);

(ii) is covered by a policy with respect to which the policyholder has—

(I)   decreased the amount of the deductible; or

(II)   increased the amount of coverage; or

(iii)   was misrated;

(2)   the chargeable risk premium rates for flood insurance under this title for

any properties initially rated under section 1307(a)(2) within any single risk classification, excluding properties for which the chargeable risk premium rate is not less than the applicable estimated risk premium rate under section 1307(a)(1), shall be increased by an amount that results in an average of such rate increases for properties within the risk classification during any 12-month period of not less than 5 percent of the average of the risk premium rates for such properties within the risk classification upon the commencement of such 12-month period;

(3) the chargeable risk premium rates for flood insurance under this title for any properties within any single risk classification may not be increased by an amount that would result in the average of such rate increases for properties within the risk classification during any 12-month period exceeding 15 percent of the average of the risk premium rates for properties within the risk classification upon the commencement of such 12-month period; and

(4) the chargeable risk premium rates for flood insurance under this title for any properties described in subparagraphs (A) through (E) of section 1307(a)(2) shall be increased by 25 percent each year, until the average risk premium rate for such properties is equal to the average of the risk premium rates for properties described under paragraph (3).

(f) ADJUSTMENT OF PREMIUM.— Notwithstanding any other provision of law, if the Administrator determines that the holder of a flood insurance policy issued under this Act is paying a lower premium than is required under this section due to an error in the flood plain determination, the Administrator may only prospectively charge the higher premium rate.

(g) FREQUENCY OF PREMIUM COLLECTION.— With respect to any chargeable premium rate prescribed under this section, the Administrator shall provide policyholders that are not required to escrow their premiums and fees for flood insurance as set forth under section 102 of the Flood Disaster Protection Act of 1973 (42 U.S.C. 4012a) with the option of paying their premiums annually or monthly.

(h) RULE OF CONSTRUCTION.—For purposes of this section, the calculation of an average historical loss year—

(1) includes catastrophic loss years; and

(2) shall be computed in accordance with generally accepted actuarial principles.

(i) RATES FOR PROPERTIES NEWLY MAPPED INTO AREAS WITH SPECIAL FLOOD HAZARDS.—Notwithstanding subsection (f), the premium rate for flood insurance under this title that is purchased on or after the date of the enactment of this subsection—

(1) on a property located in an area not previously designated as having special flood hazards and that, pursuant to any issuance, revision, updating, or other change in a flood insurance map, becomes designated as such an area; and

(2) where such flood insurance premium rate is calculated under subsection (a)(1) of section 1307 (42 U.S.C. 4014(a)(1)),

shall for the first policy year be the preferred risk premium for the property and upon renewal shall be calculated in accordance with subsection (e) of this section until the rate reaches the rate calculated under subsection (a)(1) of section 1307.

(j) PREMIUMS AND REPORTS.— In setting premium risk rates, in addition to striving to achieve the objectives of this title the Administrator shall also strive to minimize the number of policies with annual premiums that exceed one percent of the total coverage provided by the policy. For any policies premiums that exceed this one percent threshold, the Administrator shall report such exceptions to the Committee on Financial Services of the House of Representatives and the Committee on Banking, Housing, and Urban Affairs of the Senate.

(k) CONSIDERATION OF MITIGATION METHODS.— In calculating the risk premium rate charged for flood insurance for a property under this section, the Administrator shall take into account the implementation of any mitigation method identified by the Administrator in the guidance issued under section 1361(d) (42 U.S.C. 4102(d)).

(l) CLEAR COMMUNICATIONS.— The Administrator shall clearly communicate full flood risk determinations to individual property owners regardless of whether their premium rates are full actuarial rates.

(m) PROTECTION OF SMALL BUSINESSES, NON-PROFITS, HOUSES OF WORSHIP, AND RESIDENCES.—

(1) REPORT.—Not later than 18 months after the date of the enactment of this section and semiannually thereafter, the Administrator shall monitor and report to Committee on Financial Services of the House Representatives and the Committee on Banking, Housing, and Urban Affairs of the Senate, the Administrator's assessment of the impact, if any, of the rate increases required under subparagraphs (A) and (D) of section 1307(a)(2) and the surcharges required under section 1308A on the affordability of flood insurance for—

(A)   small businesses with less than 100 employees;

(B)   non-profit entities;

(C)   houses of worship; and

(D)   residences with a value equal to or less than 25 percent of the median home value of properties in the State in which the property is located.

(2) RECOMMENDATIONS.— If the Administrator determines that the rate increases or surcharges described in paragraph (1) are having a detrimental effect on affordability, including resulting in lapsed policies, late payments, or other criteria related to affordability as identified by the Administrator, for any of the properties identified in subparagraphs (A) through (D) of such paragraph, the Administrator shall, not later than 3 months after making such a determination, make such recommendations as the Administrator considers appropriate to improve affordability to the Committee on Financial Services of the House of Representatives and the Committee on Banking, Housing, and Urban Affairs of the Senate.

SEC. 1308A. [42 U.S.C. 4015a] PREMIUM SURCHARGE.

(a) IMPOSITION AND COLLECTION.— The Administrator shall impose and collect an annual surcharge, in the amount provided in subsection (b), on all policies for flood insurance coverage under the National Flood Insurance Program that are newly issued or renewed after the date of the enactment of this section. Such surcharge shall be in addition to the surcharge under section 1304(b) and any other assessments and surcharges applied to such coverage.

(b) AMOUNT.—The amount of the surcharge under subsection (a) shall be—

(1) $25, except as provided in paragraph (2); and

(2) $250, in the case of a policy for any property that is—

(A) a non-residential property; or

(B) a residential property that is not the primary residence of an individual.

(c) TERMINATION.— Subsections (a) and (b) shall cease to apply on the date on which the chargeable risk premium rate for flood insurance under this title for each property covered by flood insurance under this title, other than properties for which premiums are calculated under subsection (e) or (f) of section 1307 or section 1336 of this Act (42 U.S.C. 4014, 4056) or under section 100230 of the Biggert-Waters Flood Insurance Reform Act of 2012 (42 U.S.C. 4014 note), is not less than the applicable estimated risk premium rate under section 1307(a)(1) for such property.

FINANCING

SEC. 1309. [42 U.S.C. 4016] (a)   All authority which was vested in the Housing and Home Finance Administrator by virtue of section 15(e) of the Federal Flood Insurance Act of 1956[11] (70 Stat. 1084) (pertaining to the issue of notes or other obligations or the Secretary of the Treasury), as amended by subsections (a) and (b) of section 1303 of this Act, shall be available to the Administrator for the purpose of carrying out the flood insurance program under this title; except that the total amount of notes and obligations which may be issued by the Administrator pursuant to such authority (1) without the approval of the President, may not exceed $500,000,000, and (2) with the approval of the President, may not exceed $1,500,000,000 through the date specified in section 1319, and $1,000,000,000 thereafter; except that, through September 30, 2023, clause (2) of this sentence shall be applied by substituting $30,425,000,000 for $1,500,000,000. The Administrator shall report to the Committee on Banking, Finance and Urban Affairs of the House of Representatives and the Committee on Banking, Housing, and Urban Affairs of the Senate at any time when he requests the approval of the President in accordance with the preceding sentence.

---

[11] Such section is set forth, *post*, in this compilation.

(b)   Any funds borrowed by the Administrator under this authority shall, from time to time, be deposited in the National Flood Insurance Fund established under section 1310.

(c)   Upon the exercise of the authority established under subsection (a), the Administrator shall transmit a schedule for repayment of such amounts to—

(1)   the Secretary of the Treasury;

(2)   the Committee on Banking, Housing, and Urban Affairs of the Senate; and

(3)   the Committee on Financial Services of the House of Representatives.

(d) In connection with any funds borrowed by the Administrator under the authority established in subsection (a), the Administrator, beginning 6 months after the date on which such funds are borrowed, and continuing every 6 months thereafter until such borrowed funds are fully repaid, shall submit a report on the progress of such repayment to—

(1) the Secretary of the Treasury;

(2) the Committee on Banking, Housing, and Urban Affairs of the Senate; and

(3) the Committee on Financial Services of the House of Representatives.

NATIONAL FLOOD INSURANCE FUND

SEC. 1310. [42 U.S.C. 4017] (a) To carry out the flood insurance program authorized by this title, the Administrator shall establish in the Treasury of the United States a National Flood Insurance Fund (hereinafter referred to as the fund) which shall be an account separate from any other accounts or funds available to the Administrator and shall be available as described in subsection (f), without fiscal year limitation (except as otherwise provided in this section)—

(1) for making such payments as may, from time to time, be required under section 1334;

(2) to pay reinsurance claims under the excess loss reinsurance coverage provided under section 1335;

(3) to repay to the Secretary of the Treasury such sums as may be borrowed from him (together with interest) in accordance with the authority provided in section 1309;

(4) to the extent approved in appropriations Acts, to pay any administrative expenses of the flood insurance and floodplain management programs (including the costs of mapping activities under section 1360);

(5) for the purposes specified in subsection (d) under the conditions provided therein;

(6) for carrying out the program under section 1315(b);

(7) for transfers to the National Flood Mitigation Fund, but only to the extent provided in section 1367(b)(1); and

(8) for carrying out section 1363(f).

(b) The fund shall be credited with—

(1) such funds borrowed in accordance with the authority provided in section 1309 as may from time to time be deposited in the fund;

(2) premiums, fees, or other charges which may be paid or collected in connection with the excess loss reinsurance coverage provided under section 1335;

(3) such amounts as may be advanced to the fund from appropriations in order to maintain the fund in an operative condition adequate to meet its liabilities;

(4) interest which may be earned on investments of the fund pursuant to subsection (c);

(5) such sums as are required to be paid to the Administrator under section 1308(d); and

(6) receipts from any other operations under this title (including premiums under the conditions specified in subsection (d), and salvage proceeds, if any, resulting from reinsurance coverage).

(c) If, after—

(1) all outstanding obligations of the fund have been liquidated, and

(2) any outstanding amounts which may have been advanced to the fund from appropriations authorized under section 1376(a)(2)(B) have been credited to the appropriation from which advanced, with interest accrued at the rate, prescribed under section 15(e) of the Federal Flood Insurance Act of 1956, as in effect immediately prior to the enactment of this title,

the Administrator determines that the moneys of the fund are in excess of current needs, he may request the investment of such amounts as he deems advisable by the Secretary of the Treasury in obligations issued or guaranteed by the United States.

(d) In the event the Administrator makes a determination in accordance with the provisions of section 1340 that operation of the flood insurance program, in whole or in part, should be carried out through the facilities of the Federal Government, the fund shall be available for all purposes incident thereto, including—

(1) cost incurred in the adjustment and payment of any claims for losses, and

(2) payment of applicable operating costs set forth in the schedules prescribed under section 1311,

for so long as the program is so carried out, and in such event any premiums paid shall be deposited by the Administrator to the credit of the fund.

(e) An annual business-type budget for the fund shall be prepared, transmitted to the Congress, considered, and enacted in the manner prescribed by sections 9103 and 9104 of title 31, United States Code, for wholly-owned Government corporations.

(f) The Fund shall be available, with respect to any fiscal year beginning on or after October 1, 1981, only to the extent approved in appropriation Acts; except that the fund shall be available for the purpose described in subsection (d)(1) without such approval.

SEC. 1310A. [42 U.S.C. 4017A] RESERVE FUND.

(a) ESTABLISHMENT OF RESERVE FUND.—In carrying out the flood insurance program authorized by this chapter, the Administrator shall establish in the Treasury of the United States a National Flood Insurance Reserve Fund (in this section referred to as the Reserve Fund) which shall—

(1) be an account separate from any other accounts or funds available to the Administrator; and

(2) be available for meeting the expected future obligations of the flood insurance program, including—

(A) the payment of claims;

(B) claims adjustment expenses; and

(C) the repayment of amounts outstanding under any note or other obligation issued by the Administrator under section 1309(a).

(b) RESERVE RATIO.—Subject to the phase-in requirements under subsection (d), the

Reserve Fund shall maintain a balance equal to—

    (1) 1 percent of the sum of the total potential loss exposure of all outstanding flood insurance policies in force in the prior fiscal year; or

    (2) such higher percentage as the Administrator determines to be appropriate, taking into consideration any circumstance that may raise a significant risk of substantial future losses to the Reserve Fund.

  (c) MAINTENANCE OF RESERVE RATIO.—

    (1) IN GENERAL.—The Administrator shall have the authority to establish, increase, or decrease the amount of aggregate annual insurance premiums to be collected for any fiscal year necessary—

      (A) to maintain the reserve ratio required under subsection (b); and

      (B) to achieve such reserve ratio, if the actual balance of such reserve is below the amount required under subsection (b).

    (2) CONSIDERATIONS.—In exercising the authority granted under paragraph (1), the Administrator shall consider—

      (A) the expected operating expenses of the Reserve Fund;

      (B) the insurance loss expenditures under the flood insurance program;

      (C) any investment income generated under the flood insurance program; and

      (D) any other factor that the Administrator determines appropriate.

    (3) LIMITATIONS.—

      (A) RATES.— In exercising the authority granted under paragraph (1), the Administrator shall be subject to all other provisions of this Act, including any provisions relating to chargeable premium rates or annual increases of such rates.

      (B) USE OF ADDITIONAL ANNUAL INSURANCE PREMIUMS.— Notwithstanding any other provision of law or any agreement entered into by the Administrator, the Administrator shall ensure that all amounts attributable to the establishment or increase of annual insurance premiums under paragraph (1) are transferred to the Administrator for deposit into the Reserve Fund, to be available for meeting the expected future obligations of the flood insurance program as described in subsection (a)(2).

    (4) DEPOSIT OF PREMIUM SURCHARGES.— The Administrator shall deposit in the Reserve Fund any surcharges collected pursuant to section 1308A.

  (d) PHASE-IN REQUIREMENTS.—The phase-in requirements under this subsection are as follows:

    (1) IN GENERAL.— Beginning in fiscal year 2013 and not ending until the fiscal year in which the ratio required under subsection (b) is achieved, in each such fiscal year the Administrator shall place in the Reserve Fund an amount equal to not less than 7.5 percent of the reserve ratio required under subsection (b).

    (2) AMOUNT SATISFIED.— As soon as the ratio required under subsection (b) is

achieved, and except as provided in paragraph (3), the Administrator shall not be required to set aside any amounts for the Reserve Fund.

(3) EXCEPTION.— If at any time after the ratio required under subsection (b) is achieved, the Reserve Fund falls below the required ratio under subsection (b), the Administrator shall place in the Reserve Fund for that fiscal year an amount equal to not less than 7.5 percent of the reserve ratio required under subsection (b).

(e) LIMITATION ON RESERVE RATIO.—In any given fiscal year, if the Administrator determines that the reserve ratio required under subsection (b) cannot be achieved, the Administrator shall submit, on a calendar quarterly basis, a report to Congress that—

(1)   describes and details the specific concerns of the Administrator regarding the consequences of the reserve ratio not being achieved;

(2)   demonstrates how such consequences would harm the long-term financial soundness of the flood insurance program; and

(3)   indicates the maximum attainable reserve ratio for that particular fiscal year.

(f) INVESTMENT.— The Secretary of the Treasury shall invest such amounts of the Reserve Fund as the Secretary determines advisable in obligations issued or guaranteed by the United States.

OPERATING COSTS AND ALLOWANCES

SEC. 1311. [42 U.S.C. 4018] (a) The Administrator shall from time to time negotiate with appropriate representatives of the insurance industry for the purpose of establishing—

(1)   a current schedule of operating costs applicable both to risk-sharing insurance companies and other insurers and to insurance companies and other insurers, insurance agents and brokers, and insurance adjustment organizations participating on other than a risk-sharing basis, and

(2)   a current schedule of operating allowances applicable to risk-sharing insurance companies and other insurers,
which may be payable in accordance with the provisions of chapter II, and such schedules shall from time to time be prescribed in regulations.

(b) For purposes of subsection (a)—

(1) the term operating costs shall (without limiting such term) include—

(A)   expense reimbursements covering the direct, actual and necessary expenses incurred in connection with selling and servicing flood insurance coverage;

(B)   reasonable compensation payable for selling and servicing flood insurance coverage, or commissions or service fees paid to producers;

(C)   loss adjustment expenses; and

(D)   other direct, actual, and necessary expenses which the Administrator finds are incurred in connection with selling or servicing flood insurance coverage; and

(2)   the term operating allowances shall (without limiting such term) include

amounts for profit and contingencies which the Administrator finds reasonable and necessary to carry out the purposes of this title.

PAYMENT OF CLAIMS

SEC. 1312. [42 U.S.C. 4019] (a) IN GENERAL.— The Administrator is authorized to prescribe regulations establishing the general method or methods by which proved and approved claims for losses may be adjusted and paid for any damage to or loss of property which is covered by flood insurance made available under the provisions of this title.

(b) MINIMUM ANNUAL DEDUCTIBLE.—

(1) PRE-FIRM PROPERTIES.—For any structure which is covered by flood insurance under this title, and on which construction or substantial improvement occurred on or before December 31, 1974, or before the effective date of an initial flood insurance rate map published by the Administrator under section 1360 for the area in which such structure is located, the minimum annual deductible for damage to such structure shall be—

(A) $1,500, if the flood insurance coverage for such structure covers loss of, or physical damage to, such structure in an amount equal to or less than $100,000; and

(B) $2,000, if the flood insurance coverage for such structure covers loss of, or physical damage to, such structure in an amount greater than $100,000.

(2) POST-FIRM PROPERTIES.—For any structure which is covered by flood insurance under this title, and on which construction or substantial improvement occurred after December 31, 1974, or after the effective date of an initial flood insurance rate map published by the Administrator under section 1360 for the area in which such structure is located, the minimum annual deductible for damage to such structure shall be—

(A) $1,000, if the flood insurance coverage for such structure covers loss of, or physical damage to, such structure in an amount equal to or less than $100,000; and

(B) $1,250, if the flood insurance coverage for such structure covers loss of, or physical damage to, such structure in an amount greater than $100,000.

(c) PAYMENT OF CLAIMS TO CONDOMINIUM OWNERS.— The Administrator may not deny payment for any damage to or loss of property which is covered by flood insurance to condominium owners who purchased such flood insurance separate and apart from the flood insurance purchased by the condominium association in which such owner is a member, based solely, or in any part, on the flood insurance coverage of the condominium association or others on the overall property owned by the condominium association.

DISSEMINATION OF FLOOD INSURANCE INFORMATION

SEC. 1313. [42 U.S.C. 4020] The Administrator shall from time to time take such action as may be necessary in order to make information and data available to the public, and to any State or local agency or official, with regard to—

(1)   the flood insurance program, its coverage and objectives, and

(2)   estimated and chargeable flood insurance premium rates, including the basis for and differences between such rates in accordance with the provisions of section 1308.

SEC. 1314. [42 U.S.C. 4021] PARTICIPATION IN STATE DISASTER CLAIMS MEDIATION PROGRAMS.

(a) REQUIREMENT TO PARTICIPATE.— In the case of the occurrence of a major disaster, as defined in section 102 of the Robert T. Stafford Disaster Relief and Emergency Assistance Act (42 U.S.C. 5122), that may have resulted in flood damage covered under the national flood insurance program established under this title and other personal lines residential property insurance coverage offered by a State regulated insurer, upon a request made by the insurance commissioner of a State (or such other official responsible for regulating the business of insurance in the State) for the participation of representatives of the Administrator in a program sponsored by such State for nonbinding mediation of insurance claims resulting from a major disaster, the Administrator shall cause representatives of the national flood insurance program to participate in such a State program where claims under the national flood insurance program are involved to expedite settlement of flood damage claims resulting from such disaster.

(b) EXTENT OF PARTICIPATION.—In satisfying the requirements of subsection (a), the Administrator shall require that each representative of the Administrator—

(1)   be certified for purposes of the national flood insurance program to settle claims against such program resulting from such disaster in amounts up to the limits of policies under such program;

(2)   attend State-sponsored mediation meetings regarding flood insurance claims resulting from such disaster at such times and places as may be arranged by the State;

(3)   participate in good-faith negotiations toward the settlement of such claims with policyholders of coverage made available under the national flood insurance program; and

(4)   finalize the settlement of such claims on behalf of the national flood insurance program with such policyholders.

(c) COORDINATION.— Representatives of the Administrator shall at all times coordinate their activities with insurance officials of the State and representatives of insurers for the purposes of consolidating and expediting settlement of claims under the national flood insurance program resulting from such disaster.

(d) QUALIFICATIONS OF MEDIATORS.—Each State mediator participating in State-sponsored mediation under this section shall be—

(1)(A)   a member in good standing of the State bar in the State in which the mediation is to occur with at least 2 years of practical experience; and

(B)   an active member of such bar for at least 1 year prior to the year in which such mediator's participation is sought; or

(2)   a retired trial judge from any United States jurisdiction who was a member

in good standing of the bar in the State in which the judge presided for at least 5 years prior to the year in which such mediator's participation is sought.

(e) Mediation Proceedings and Documents Privileged.— As a condition of participation, all statements made and documents produced pursuant to State-sponsored mediation involving representatives of the Administrator shall be deemed privileged and confidential settlement negotiations made in anticipation of litigation.

(f) Liability, Rights, or Obligations Not Affected.—Participation in State-sponsored mediation, as described in this section does not—

(1) affect or expand the liability of any party in contract or in tort; or

(2) affect the rights or obligations of the parties, as established—

(A) in any regulation issued by the Administrator, including any regulation relating to a standard flood insurance policy;

(B) under this title; and

(C) under any other provision of Federal law.

(g) Exclusive Federal Jurisdiction.— Participation in State-sponsored mediation shall not alter, change, or modify the original exclusive jurisdiction of United States courts, as set forth in this title.

(h) Cost Limitation.— Nothing in this section shall be construed to require the Administrator or a representative of the Administrator to pay additional mediation fees relating to flood insurance claims associated with a State-sponsored mediation program in which such representative of the Administrator participates.

(i) Exception.—In the case of the occurrence of a major disaster that results in flood damage claims under the national flood insurance program and that does not result in any loss covered by a personal lines residential property insurance policy—

(1) this section shall not apply; and

(2) the provisions of the standard flood insurance policy under the national flood insurance program and the appeals process established under section 205 of the Bunning-Bereuter-Blumenauer Flood Insurance Reform Act of 2004 (42 U.S.C. 4011 note) and the regulations issued pursuant to such section shall apply exclusively.

(j) Representatives of the Administrator.— For purposes of this section, the term representatives of the Administrator means representatives of the national flood insurance program who participate in the appeals process established under section 205 of the Bunning-Bereuter-Blumenauer Flood Insurance Reform Act of 2004 (42 U.S.C. 4011 note).

STATE AND LOCAL LAND USE CONTROLS

Sec. 1315. [42 U.S.C. 4022] (a) Requirement for Participation in Flood Insurance Program.—

(1) In general.— After December 31, 1971, no new flood insurance coverage shall be provided under this title in any area (or subdivision thereof) unless an appropriate public body shall have adopted adequate land use and control measures (with effective enforcement provisions) which the Administrator finds are consistent

with the comprehensive criteria for land management and use under section 1361.

(2) AGRICULTURAL STRUCTURES.—

(A) ACTIVITY RESTRICTIONS.—Notwithstanding any other provision of law, the adequate land use and control measures required to be adopted in an area (or subdivision thereof) pursuant to paragraph (1) may provide, at the discretion of the appropriate State or local authority, for the repair and restoration to predamaged conditions of an agricultural structure that—

(i) is a repetitive loss structure; or

(ii) has incurred flood-related damage to the extent that the cost of restoring the structure to its predamaged condition would equal or exceed 50 percent of the market value of the structure before the damage occurred.

(B) PREMIUM RATES AND COVERAGE.— To the extent applicable, an agricultural structure repaired or restored pursuant to subparagraph (A) shall pay chargeable premium rates established under section 1308 at the estimated risk premium rates under section 1307(a)(1). If resources are available, the Administrator shall provide technical assistance and counseling, upon request of the owner of the structure, regarding wet flood-proofing and other flood damage reduction measures for agricultural structures. The Administrator shall not be required to make flood insurance coverage available for such an agricultural structure unless the structure is wet flood-proofed through permanent or contingent measures applied to the structure or its contents that prevent or provide resistance to damage from flooding by allowing flood waters to pass through the structure, as determined by the Administrator.

(C) PROHIBITION ON DISASTER RELIEF.— Notwithstanding any other provision of law, any agricultural structure repaired or restored pursuant to subparagraph (A) shall not be eligible for disaster relief assistance under any program administered by the Administrator or any other Federal agency.

(D) DEFINITIONS.—For purposes of this paragraph—

(i) the term agricultural structure means any structure used exclusively in connection with the production, harvesting, storage, raising, or drying of agricultural commodities; and

(ii) the term agricultural commodities means agricultural commodities and livestock.

(b) COMMUNITY RATING SYSTEM AND INCENTIVES FOR COMMUNITY FLOODPLAIN MANAGEMENT.—

(1) AUTHORITY AND GOALS.—The Administrator shall carry out a community rating system program, under which communities participate voluntarily—

(A) to provide incentives for measures that reduce the risk of flood or erosion damage that exceed the criteria set forth in section 1361 and evaluate such measures;

(B) to encourage adoption of more effective measures that protect natural and beneficial floodplain functions;

(C)   to encourage floodplain and erosion management; and

(D)   to promote the reduction of Federal flood insurance losses.

(2) INCENTIVES.— The program shall provide incentives in the form of credits on premium rates for flood insurance coverage in communities that the Administrator determines have adopted and enforced measures that reduce the risk of flood and erosion damage that exceed the criteria set forth in section 1361. In providing incentives under this paragraph, the Administrator may provide for credits to flood insurance premium rates in communities that the Administrator determines have implemented measures that protect natural and beneficial floodplain functions.

(3) CREDITS.— The credits on premium rates for flood insurance coverage shall be based on the estimated reduction in flood and erosion damage risks resulting from the measures adopted by the community under this program. If a community has received mitigation assistance under section 1366, the credits shall be phased in a manner, determined by the Administrator, to recover the amount of such assistance provided for the community.

(4) REPORTS.— Not later than 2 years after the date of enactment of the Riegle Community Development and Regulatory Improvement Act of 1994[12] and not less than every 2 years thereafter, the Administrator shall submit a report to the Congress regarding the program under this subsection. Each report shall include an analysis of the cost-effectiveness of the program, any other accomplishments or shortcomings of the program, and any recommendations of the Administrator for legislation regarding the program.

---

[12]   The date of enactment was September 23, 1994.

PROPERTIES IN VIOLATION OF STATE AND LOCAL LAW

SEC. 1316. [42 U.S.C. 4023]   No new flood insurance coverage shall be provided under this title for any property which the Administrator finds has been declared by a duly constituted State or local zoning authority, or other authorized public body, to be in violation of State or local laws, regulations or ordinances which are intended to discourage or otherwise restrict land development or occupancy in flood-prone areas.

COORDINATION WITH OTHER PROGRAMS

SEC. 1317. [42 U.S.C. 4024]   In carrying out this title, the Administrator shall consult with other departments and agencies of the Federal Government, and with interstate, State, and local agencies having responsibilities for flood control, flood forecasting, or flood damage prevention, in order to assure that the programs of such agencies and the flood insurance program authorized under this title are mutually consistent.

ADVISORY COMMITTEE

SEC. 1318. [42 U.S.C. 4025] (a)   The Administrator shall appoint a flood insurance advisory committee without regard to the provisions of title 5, United States Code, governing appointments in the competitive service, and such committee shall advise the Administrator in the preparation of any regulations prescribed in accordance with this title and with respect to policy matters arising in the administration of this title, and shall perform such other responsibilities as the Administrator may, from time to time, assign to such committee.

(b) Such committee shall consist of not more than fifteen persons and such persons shall be selected from among representatives of—

(1)   the insurance industry,

(2)   State and local governments,

(3)   lending institutions,

(4)   the homebuilding industry, and

(5)   the general public.

(c)   Members of the committee shall, while attending conferences or meetings thereof, be entitled to receive compensation at a rate fixed by the Administrator but not exceeding $100 per day, including traveltime, and while so serving away from their homes or regular places of business they may be allowed travel expenses, including per diem in lieu of subsistence, as is authorized under section 5703 of title 5, United States Code, for persons in the Government service employed intermittently.

PROGRAM EXPIRATION

SEC. 1319. [42 U.S.C. 4026]   No new contract for flood insurance under this title shall be entered into after September 30, 2023.

REPORT TO THE PRESIDENT

SEC. 1320. [42 U.S.C. 4027] (a) IN GENERAL.— The Administrator shall biennially submit a report of operations under this title to the President for submission to the Congress.

(b) EFFECTS OF FLOOD INSURANCE PROGRAM.— The Administrator shall include, as part of the biennial report submitted under subsection (a), a chapter reporting on the effects on the flood insurance program observed through implementation of requirements under the Riegle Community Development and Regulatory Improvement Act of 1994.

JOHN H. CHAFEE COASTAL BARRIER RESOURCES SYSTEM

SEC. 1321. [42 U.S.C. 4028] (a)   No new flood insurance coverage may be provided under this title on or after October 1, 1983, for any new construction or substantial improvements of structures located on any coastal barrier within the John H. Chafee Coastal Barrier Resources System established by section 4 of the John H. Chafee Coastal Barrier Resources Act. A federally insured financial institution may make loans secured by structures which are not eligible for flood insurance by reason of this section.

(b)   No new flood insurance coverage may be provided under this title after the expiration of the 1-year period beginning on the date of the enactment of the Coastal Barrier Improvement Act of 1990[13] for any new construction or substantial improvements of structures located in any area identified and depicted on the maps referred to in section 4(a) of the Coastal Barrier Resources Act as an area that is (1) not within the John H. Chafee Coastal Barrier Resources System and (2) is in an otherwise protected area. Notwithstanding the preceding sentence, new flood insurance coverage may be provided for structures in such protected areas that are used in a manner consistent with the purpose for which the area is protected.

---

[13] The date of enactment was November 16, 1990.

COLORADO RIVER FLOODWAY

SEC. 1322. [42 U.S.C. 4029] (a) Owners of existing National Flood Insurance Act[32] policies with respect to structures located within the Floodway established under section 5 of the Colorado River Floodway Protection Act shall have the right to renew and transfer such policies. Owners of existing structures located within said Floodway on the date of enactment of the Colorado River Floodway Protection Act[14/ref> who have not acquired National Flood Insurance Act policies shall have the right to acquire policies with respect to such structures for six months after the Secretary of the Interior files the Floodway maps required by section 5(b)(2) of the Colorado River Floodway Protection Act and to renew and transfer such policies.

---

[14] So in law. Probably should refer to this Act.

---

[33] October 8, 1986.

(b) No new flood insurance coverage may be provided under this title on or after a date six months after the enactment of the Colorado River Floodway Protection Act[15] for any new construction or substantial improvements of structures located within the Colorado River Floodway established by section 5 of the Colorado River Floodway Protection Act. New construction includes all structures that are not insurable prior to that date.

---

[15] The date of enactment was October 8, 1986.

(c) The Secretary of the Interior may by rule after notice and comment pursuant to 5 U.S.C. 553 establish temporary Floodway boundaries to be in effect until the maps required by section 5(b)(2) of the Colorado River Floodway Protection Act are filed, for the purpose of enforcing subsections (b) and (d) of this section.

(d) A regulated lending institution or Federal agency lender may make loans secured by structures which are not eligible for flood insurance by reason of this section: *Provided,* That prior to making such a loan, such institution determines that the loans or structures securing the loan are within the Floodway.

[Section 1323 was repealed by section 100225(b) of Public Law 112–141.]

TREATMENT OF CERTAIN PAYMENTS

SEC. 1324. [42 U.S.C. 4031] Assistance provided under a program under this title for flood mitigation activities (including any assistance provided under the mitigation pilot program under section 1361A, any assistance provided under the mitigation assistance program under section 1366, and any funding provided under section 1323) with respect to a property shall not be considered income or a resource of the owner of the property when determining eligibility for or benefit levels under any income assistance or resource-tested program that is funded in whole or in part by an agency of the United States or by appropriated funds of the United States.

SEC. 1325. [42 U.S.C. 4032] TREATMENT OF SWIMMING POOL ENCLOSURES OUTSIDE OF HURRICANE SEASON.

(a) IN GENERAL.—Notwithstanding any other provision of law, including the adequate land use and control measures developed pursuant to section 1361 and applicable to non-one- and two-family structures located within coastal areas, as identified by the Administrator, the following may be permitted:

(1) Nonsupporting breakaway walls in the space below the lowest elevated floor of a building, if the space is used solely for a swimming pool between November 30 and June 1 of any year, in an area designated as Zone V on a flood insurance rate map.

(2) Openings in walls in the space below the lowest elevated floor of a building, if the space is used solely for a swimming pool between November 30 and June 1 of any year, in an area designated as Zone A on a flood insurance rate map.

(b) RULE OF CONSTRUCTION.— Nothing in subsection (a) shall be construed to alter the terms and conditions of eligibility and insurability of coverage for a building under the standard flood insurance policy under the national flood insurance program.

CHAPTER II—ORGANIZATION AND ADMINISTRATION OF THE FLOOD INSURANCE PROGRAM

ORGANIZATION AND ADMINISTRATION

SEC. 1330. [42 U.S.C. 4041] Following such consultation with representatives of the insurance industry as may be necessary, the Administrator shall implement the flood insurance program authorized under chapter I in accordance with the provisions of part A of this chapter and, if a determination is made by him under section 1340, under part B of this chapter.

Part A—INDUSTRY PROGRAM WITH FEDERAL FINANCIAL ASSISTANCE

INDUSTRY FLOOD INSURANCE POOL

SEC. 1331. [42 U.S.C. 4051] (a) The Administrator is authorized to encourage and otherwise assist any insurance companies and other insurers which meet the requirements prescribed under subsection (b) to form, associate, or otherwise join together in a pool—

(1) in order to provide the floor insurance coverage authorized under chapter I; and

(2) for the purpose of assuming, including as reinsurance of coverage provided by the flood insurance program, on such terms and conditions as may be agreed upon, such financial responsibility as will enable such companies and other insurers, with the Federal financial and other assistance available under this title, to assure a reasonable proportion of responsibility for the adjustment and payment of claims for losses under the flood insurance program.

(b)   In order to promote the effective administration of the flood insurance program under this part, and to assure that the objectives of this title are furthered, the Administrator is authorized to prescribe appropriate requirements for insurance companies and other insurers participating in such pool including, but not limited to, minimum requirements for capital or surplus or assets.

AGREEMENTS WITH FLOOD INSURANCE POOL

SEC. 1332. [42 U.S.C. 4052] (a)   The Administrator is authorized to enter into such agreements with the pool formed or otherwise created under this part as he deems necessary to carry out the purposes of this title.

(b) Such agreements shall specify—

(1)   the terms and conditions under which risk capital will be available for the adjustment and payments of claims,

(2)   the terms and conditions under which the pool (and the companies and other insurers participating therein) shall participate in premiums received and profits or losses realized or sustained,

(3)   the maximum amount of profit, established by the Administrator and set forth in the schedules prescribed under section 1311, which may be realized by such pool (and the companies and other insurers participating therein),

(4)   the terms and conditions under which operating costs and allowances set forth in the schedules prescribed under section 1311 may be paid, and

(5)   the terms and conditions under which premium equalization payments under section 1334 will be made and reinsurance claims under section 1335 will be paid.

(c) In addition, such agreements shall contain such provisions as the Administrator finds necessary to assure that—

(1)   no insurance company or other insurer which meets the requirements prescribed under section 1331(b), and which has indicated an intention to participate in the flood insurance program on a risk-sharing basis, will be excluded from participating in the pool,

(2)   the insurance companies and other insurers participating in the pool will take whatever action may be necessary to provide continuity of flood insurance coverage or reinsurance by the pool, and

(3)   any insurance companies and other insurers, insurance agents and brokers and insurance adjustment organizations will be permitted to cooperated with the pool as fiscal agents or otherwise, on other than a risk-sharing basis, to the maximum extent practicable.

ADJUSTMENT AND PAYMENT OF CLAIMS AND JUDICIAL REVIEW

SEC. 1333. [42 U.S.C. 4053]   The insurance companies and other insurers which form, associate, or otherwise join together in the pool under this part may adjust and pay all claims for proved and approved losses covered by flood insurance in accordance with the provisions of this title and, upon the disallowance by any such company or other insurer of any such claim, or upon the refusal of the claimant to accept the amount allowed upon any such claim, the claimant, within one year after the date of mailing of notice of disallowance or partial disallowance of the claim, may institute an action on such claim against such company or other insurer in the United States district court for the district in which the insured property or the major part thereof shall have been situated, and original exclusive jurisdiction is hereby conferred upon such court to hear and determine such action without regard to the amount in controversy.

PREMIUM EQUALIZATION PAYMENTS

SEC. 1334. [42 U.S.C. 4054] (a)   The Administrator, on such terms and conditions as he may from time to time prescribe, shall make periodic payments to the pool formed or otherwise created under section 1331, in recognition of such reductions in chargeable premium rates under section 1308 below estimated premium rates under section 1307(a)(1) as are required in order to make flood insurance available on reasonable terms and conditions.

(b)   Designated periods under this section and the methods for determining the sum of premiums paid or payable during such periods shall be established by the Administrator.

REINSURANCE COVERAGE

SEC. 1335. [42 U.S.C. 4055] (a)[16]

---

[16]   So in law.

---

(1) IN GENERAL.— The Administrator is authorized to take such action as may be necessary in order to make available, to the pool formed or otherwise created under section 1331, reinsurance for losses (due to claims for proved and approved losses covered by flood insurance) which are in excess of losses assumed by such pool in accordance with the excess loss agreement entered into under subsection (c).

(2) PRIVATE REINSURANCE.— The Administrator is authorized to secure reinsurance of coverage provided by the flood insurance program from the private market at rates and on terms determined by the Administrator to be reasonable and appropriate, in an amount sufficient to maintain the ability of the program to pay claims.

(b)   Such reinsurance shall be made available pursuant to contract, agreement, or any other arrangement, in consideration of such payment of a premium, fee, or other charge as the Administrator finds necessary to cover anticipated losses and other costs of providing such reinsurance.

(c)   The Administrator is authorized to negotiate an excess loss agreement, from time to time, under which the amount of flood insurance retained by the pool, after ceding reinsurance, shall be adequate to further the purposes of this title, consistent with the objective of maintaining appropriate financial participation and risk sharing to the maximum extent practicable on the part of participating insurance companies and other insurers.

(d)   All reinsurance claims for losses in excess of losses assumed by the pool shall be submitted on a portfolio basis by such pool in accordance with terms and conditions established by the Administrator.

EMERGENCY IMPLEMENTATION OF PROGRAM

SEC. 1336. [42 U.S.C. 4056] (a)   Notwithstanding any other provisions of this title, for the purpose of providing flood insurance coverage at the earliest possible time, the Administrator shall carry out the flood insurance program authorized under chapter I during the period ending on the date specified in section 1319, in accordance with the provisions of this part and the other provision of this title insofar as they relate to this part but subject to the modifications made by or under subsection (b).

(b) In carrying out the flood insurance program pursuant to subsection (a), the Administrator—

(1)   shall provide insurance coverage without regard to any estimated risk premium rates which would otherwise be determined under section 1307; and

(2)   shall utilize the provisions and procedures contained in or prescribed by this part (other than section 1334) and sections 1345 and 1346 to such extent and in such manner as he may consider necessary or appropriate to carry out the purpose of this section.

SEC. 1337. [42 U.S.C. 4057] ALTERNATIVE LOSS ALLOCATION SYSTEM FOR INDETERMINATE CLAIMS.

(a) DEFINITIONS.—In this section:

(1) ADMINISTRATOR.— The term Administrator means the Administrator of the Federal Emergency Management Agency.

(2) COASTAL FORMULA.— The term COASTAL Formula means the formula established under subsection (b).

(3) COASTAL STATE.— The term coastal State has the meaning given the term coastal state in section 304 of the Coastal Zone Management Act of 1972 (16 U.S.C. 1453), except that the term shall not apply with respect to a State or territory that has an operational wind and flood loss allocation system.

(4) INDETERMINATE LOSS.—

(A) IN GENERAL.— The term indeterminate loss means, as determined by an insurance claims adjuster certified under the national flood insurance program and in consultation with an engineer as appropriate, a loss resulting from physical damage to, or loss of, property located in any coastal State arising from the combined perils of flood and wind associated with a named storm.

(B) REQUIREMENTS.—An insurance claims adjuster certified under the national flood insurance program shall only determine that a loss is an indeterminate loss if the claims adjuster determines that—

(i)   no material remnant of physical buildings or man-made structures remain except building foundations for the specific property for which the claim is made; and

(ii)   there is insufficient or no tangible evidence created, yielded, or otherwise left behind of the specific property for which the claim is made as a result of the named storm.

(5) NAMED STORM.— The term named storm means any organized weather

system with a defined surface circulation and maximum sustained winds of not less than 39 miles per hour which the National Hurricane Center of the United States National Weather Service names as a tropical storm or a hurricane.

(6) POST-STORM ASSESSMENT.— The term post-storm assessment means the post-storm assessment developed under section 12312(b) of the Omnibus Public Land Management Act of 2009.

(7) STATE.— The term State means a State of the United States, the District of Columbia, the Commonwealth of Puerto Rico, and any other territory or possession of the United States.

(8) SECRETARY.— The term Secretary means the Secretary of Homeland Security.

(9) STANDARD INSURANCE POLICY.— The term standard insurance policy means any insurance policy issued under the national flood insurance program that covers loss or damage to property resulting from water peril.

(10) PROPERTY.— The term property means real or personal property that is insured under a standard insurance policy for loss or damage to structure or contents.

(11) UNDER SECRETARY.— The term Under Secretary means the Under Secretary of Commerce for Oceans and Atmosphere, in the Under Secretary's capacity as Administrator of the National Oceanic and Atmospheric Administration.

(b) ESTABLISHMENT OF FLOOD LOSS ALLOCATION FORMULA FOR INDETERMINATE CLAIMS.—

(1) IN GENERAL.— Not later than 180 days after the date on which the protocol is established under section 12312(c)(1) of the Omnibus Public Land Management Act of 2009, the Secretary, acting through the Administrator and in consultation with the Under Secretary, shall publish for comment in the Federal Register a standard formula to determine and allocate wind losses and flood losses for claims involving indeterminate losses.

(2) CONTENTS.—The standard formula established under paragraph (1) shall—

(A) incorporate data available from the Coastal Wind and Water Event Database established under section 12312(f) of the Omnibus Public Land Management Act of 2009;

(B) use relevant data provided on the National Flood Insurance Program Elevation Certificate, or other data or information used to determine a property's current risk of flood, as determined by the Administrator, for each indeterminate loss for which the formula is used;

(C) consider any sufficient and credible evidence, approved by the Administrator, of the pre-event condition of a specific property, including the findings of any policyholder or insurance claims adjuster in connection with the indeterminate loss to that specific property;

(D) include other measures, as the Administrator considers appropriate, required to determine and allocate by mathematical formula the property damage caused by flood or storm surge associated with a named storm; and

(E) subject to paragraph (3), for each indeterminate loss, use the post-storm assessment to allocate water damage (flood or storm surge) associated with a named storm.

(3) DEGREE OF ACCURACY REQUIRED.— The standard formula established under paragraph (1) shall specify that the Administrator may only use the post-storm assessment for purposes of the formula if the Under Secretary certifies that the post-storm assessment has a degree of accuracy of not less than 90 percent in connection with the specific indeterminate loss for which the assessment and formula are used.

(c) AUTHORIZED USE OF POST-STORM ASSESSMENT AND COASTAL FORMULA.—

(1) IN GENERAL.—Subject to paragraph (3), the Administrator may use the post-storm assessment and the COASTAL Formula to—

(A) review flood loss payments for indeterminate losses, including as part of the quality assurance reinspection program of the Federal Emergency Management Agency for claims under the national flood insurance program and any other process approved by the Administrator to review and validate payments under the national flood insurance program for indeterminate losses following a named storm; and

(B) assist the national flood insurance program to—

(i) properly cover qualified flood loss for claims for indeterminate losses; and

(ii) avoid paying for any loss or damage to property caused by any peril (including wind), other than flood or storm surge, that is not covered under a standard policy under the national flood insurance program.

(2) FEDERAL DISASTER DECLARATION.— Subject to paragraph (3), in order to expedite claims and reduce costs to the national flood insurance program, following any major disaster declared by the President under section 401 of the Robert T. Stafford Disaster Relief and Emergency Assistance Act (42 U.S.C. 5170) relating to a named storm in a coastal State, the Administrator may use the COASTAL Formula to determine and pay for any flood loss covered under a standard insurance policy under the national flood insurance program, if the loss is an indeterminate loss.

(3) NATIONAL ACADEMY OF SCIENCES EVALUATION.—

(A) EVALUATION REQUIRED.—

(i) EVALUATION.—Upon publication of the COASTAL Formula in the Federal Register as required by subsection (b)(1), and each time the Administrator modifies the COASTAL Formula, the National Academy of Sciences shall—

(I) evaluate the expected financial impact on the national flood insurance program of the use of the COASTAL Formula as so established or modified; and

(II) evaluate the validity of the scientific assumptions upon which the formula is based and determine whether the COASTAL formula can achieve a degree of accuracy of not less than 90 percent in allocating flood losses for indeterminate losses.

(ii) REPORT.— The National Academy of Sciences shall submit a report containing the results of each evaluation under clause (i) to the Administrator, the Committee on Banking, Housing, and Urban Affairs and the Committee on Commerce, Science, and Transportation of the Senate, and the Committee on Financial Services and the Committee on Science, Space, and Technology of the House of Representatives.

(B) EFFECTIVE DATE AND APPLICABILITY.—

(i) EFFECTIVE DATE.— Paragraphs (1) and (2) of this subsection shall not take effect unless the report under subparagraph (A) relating to the establishment of the COASTAL Formula concludes that the use of the COASTAL Formula for purposes of paragraph (1) and (2) would not have an adverse financial impact on the national flood insurance program and that the COASTAL Formula is based on valid scientific assumptions that would allow a degree of accuracy of not less than 90 percent to be achieved in allocating flood losses for indeterminate losses.

(ii) EFFECT OF MODIFICATIONS.— Unless the report under subparagraph (A) relating to a modification of the COASTAL Formula concludes that the use of the COASTAL Formula, as so modified, for purposes of paragraphs (1) and (2) would not have an adverse financial impact on the national flood insurance program and that the COASTAL Formula is based on valid scientific assumptions that would allow a degree of accuracy of not less than 90 percent to be achieved in allocating flood losses for indeterminate losses the Administrator may not use the COASTAL Formula, as so modified, for purposes of paragraphs (1) and (2).

(C) FUNDING.— Notwithstanding section 1310 of the National Flood Insurance Act of 1968 (42 U.S.C. 4017), there shall be available to the Administrator from the National Flood Insurance Fund, of amounts not otherwise obligated, not more than $750,000 to carry out this paragraph.

(d) DISCLOSURE OF COASTAL FORMULA.—Not later than 30 days after the date on which a post-storm assessment is submitted to the Secretary under section 12312(b)(2)(E) of the Omnibus Public Land Management Act of 2009, for each indeterminate loss for which the COASTAL Formula is used pursuant to subsection (c)(2), the Administrator shall disclose to the policyholder that makes a claim relating to the indeterminate loss—

(1) that the Administrator used the COASTAL Formula with respect to the indeterminate loss; and

(2) a summary of the results of the use of the COASTAL Formula.

(e) CONSULTATION.—In carrying out subsections (b) and (c), the Secretary shall consult with—

(1) the Under Secretary for Oceans and Atmosphere;

(2) the Director of the National Institute of Standards and Technology;

(3) the Chief of Engineers of the Corps of Engineers;

(4) the Director of the United States Geological Survey;

(5) the Office of the Federal Coordinator for Meteorology;

(6) State insurance regulators of coastal States; and

(7) such public, private, and academic sector entities as the Secretary considers appropriate for purposes of carrying out such subsections.

(f) RECORDKEEPING.— Each consideration and measure the Administrator determines necessary to carry out subsection (b) may be required, with advanced approval of the Administrator, to be provided for on the National Flood Insurance Program Elevation Certificate, or maintained otherwise on record if approved by the Administrator, for any property that qualifies for the COASTAL Formula under subsection (c).

(g) CIVIL PENALTY.—

(1) IN GENERAL.— If an insurance claims adjuster knowingly and willfully makes a false or inaccurate determination relating to an indeterminate loss, the Administrator may, after notice and opportunity for hearing, impose on the insurance claims adjuster a civil penalty of not more than $1,000.

(2) DEPOSIT.— Notwithstanding section 3302 of title 31, United States Code, or any other law relating to the crediting of money, the Administrator shall deposit in the National Flood Insurance Fund any amounts received under this subsection, which shall remain available until expended and be available to the Administrator for purposes authorized for the National Flood Insurance Fund without further appropriation.

(h) RULE OF CONSTRUCTION.— Nothing in this subsection shall be construed to require the Administrator to make any payment under the national flood insurance program, or an insurance company that issues a standard flood insurance policy under the national flood insurance program to make any payment, for an indeterminate loss based upon post-storm assessment, the COASTAL Formula, or any other loss allocation or post-storm assessment arising under the laws or ordinances of any State.

(i) APPLICABILITY.— Subsection (c) shall apply with respect to an indeterminate loss associated with a named storm that occurs 60 days after publication of the COASTAL Formula in the Federal Register as required by subsection (b)(1).

(j) RULE OF CONSTRUCTION.— Nothing in this subsection shall be construed to negate, set aside, or void any policy limit, including any loss limitation, set forth in a standard insurance policy.

(k) RULE OF CONSTRUCTION.— Nothing in this section shall be construed to create a cause of action under this Act.

Part B—GOVERNMENT PROGRAM WITH INDUSTRY ASSISTANCE

FEDERAL OPERATION OF THE PROGRAM

SEC. 1340. [42 U.S.C. 4071] (a) If at any time, after consultation with representatives of the insurance industry, the Administrator determines that operation of the flood insurance program as provided under part A cannot be carried out, or that such operation, in itself, would be assisted materially by the Federal Government's assumption, in whole or in part, of the operational responsibility for flood insurance under this title (on a temporary or other basis) he shall promptly undertake any necessary arrangements to carry out the program of flood insurance authorized under chapter I through the facilities of the Federal Government, utilizing, for purposes of providing flood insurance coverage, either—

(1)   insurance companies and other insurers, insurance agents and brokers, and insurance adjustment organizations, as fiscal agents of the United States,

(2)   such other officers and employees of any executive agency (as defined in section 105 of title 5 of the United States Code) as the Administrator and the head of any such agency may from time to time, agree upon, on a reimbursement or other basis, or

(3)   both the alternative specified in paragraphs (1) and (2).

(b) Upon making the determination referred to in subsection (a), the Administrator shall make a report to the Congress and, at the same time, to the private insurance companies participating in the National Flood Insurance Program pursuant to section 1310 of this Act. Such report shall—

(1)   state the reason for such determinations,

(2)   be supported by pertinent findings,

(3)   indicate the extent to which it is anticipated that the insurance industry will be utilized in providing flood insurance coverage under the program, and

(4)   contain such recommendations as the Administrator deems advisable.

The Administrator shall not implement the program of flood insurance authorized under chapter I through the facilities of the Federal Government until 9 months after the date of submission of the report under this subsection unless it would be impossible to continue to effectively carry out the National Flood Insurance Program operations during this time.

ADJUSTMENT AND PAYMENT OF CLAIMS AND JUDICIAL REVIEW

SEC. 1341. [42 U.S.C. 4072]   In the event the program is carried out as provided in section 1340, the Administrator shall be authorized to adjust and make payment of any claims for proved and approved losses covered by flood insurance, and upon the disallowance by the Administrator of any such claims, or upon the refusal of the claimant to accept the amount allowed upon any such claim, the claimant, within one year after the date of mailing of notice of disallowance or partial disallowance by the Administrator, may institute an action against the Administrator on such claim in the United States district court for the district in which the insured property or the major part thereof shall have been situated, and original exclusive jurisdiction is hereby conferred upon such court to hear and determine such action without regard to the amount in controversy.

Part C—PROVISIONS OF GENERAL APPLICABILITY

SERVICES BY INSURANCE INDUSTRY

SEC. 1345. [42 U.S.C. 4081] (a)   In administering the flood insurance program under this chapter, the Administrator is authorized to enter into any contracts, agreements, or other appropriate arrangements which may, from time to time, be necessary for the purpose of utilizing, on such terms and conditions as may be agreed upon, the facilities and services of any insurance companies or other insurers, insurance agents and brokers, or insurance adjustment organizations; and such contracts, agreements, or arrangements may include provision for payment of applicable operating costs and allowances for such facilities and services as set forth in the schedules prescribed under section 1311.

(b) Any such contracts, agreements, or other arrangements may be entered into without regard to the provisions of section 3709 of the Revised Statutes (41 U.S.C. 5) or any other provisions of law requiring competitive bidding and without regard to the provisions of chapter 10 of title 5, United States Code.

(c) The Administrator of the Federal Emergency Management Agency shall hold any agent or broker selling or undertaking to sell flood insurance under this title harmless from any judgment for damages against such agent or broker as a result of any court action by a policyholder or applicant arising out of an error or omission on the part of the Federal Emergency Management Agency, and shall provide any such agent or broker with indemnification, including court costs and reasonable attorney fees, arising out of and caused by an error or omission on the part of the Federal Emergency Management Agency and its contractors. The Administrator of the Federal Emergency Management Agency may not hold harmless or indemnify an agent or broker for his or her error or omission.

(d) FEMA AUTHORITY ON TRANSFER OF POLICIES.— Notwithstanding any other provision of this title, the Administrator may, at the discretion of the Administrator, refuse to accept the transfer of the administration of policies for coverage under the flood insurance program under this title that are written and administered by any insurance company or other insurer, or any insurance agent or broker.

(e) RISK TRANSFER.— The Administrator may secure reinsurance of coverage provided by the flood insurance program from the private reinsurance and capital markets at rates and on terms determined by the Administrator to be reasonable and appropriate, in an amount sufficient to maintain the ability of the program to pay claims.

USE OF INSURANCE POOL, COMPANIES, OR OTHER PRIVATE ORGANIZATIONS FOR CERTAIN PAYMENTS

SEC. 1346. [42 U.S.C. 4082] (a) In order to provide for maximum efficency in the administration of the flood insurance program and in order to facilitate the expeditious payment of any Federal funds under such program, the Administrator may enter into contracts with a pool formed or otherwise created under section 1331, or any insurance company or other private organization, for the purpose of securing reinsurance of insurance coverage provided by the program or for the purpose of securing performance by such pool, company, or organization of any or all of the following responsibilities:

(1) Estimating and later determining any amounts of payments to be made.

(2) Receiving from the Administrator, disbursing, and accounting for funds in making such payments.

(3) Making such audits of the records of any insurance company or other insurer, insurance agent or broker, or insurance adjustment organization as may be necessary to assure that proper payments are made.

(4)   Placing reinsurance coverage on insurance provided by such program.

(5)   Otherwise assisting in such manner as the contract may provide to further the purposes of this title.

(b)   Any contract with the pool or an insurance company or other private organization under this section may contain such terms and conditions at the Administrator finds necessary or appropriate for carrying out responsibilities under subsection (a), and may provide for payment of any costs which the Administrator determines are incidental to carrying out such responsibilities which are covered by the contract.

(c)   Any contract entered into under subsection (a) may be entered into without regard to section 3709 of the Revised Statutes (41 U.S.C. 5) or any other provision of law requiring competitive bidding.

(d)   No contract may be entered into under this section unless the Administrator finds that the pool, company, or organization will perform its obligations under the contract efficiently and effectively, and will meet such requirements as to financial responsibility, legal authority, and other matters as he finds pertinent.

(e)(1)   Any such contract may require the pool, company, or organization or any of its officers or employees certifying payments or disbursing funds pursuant to the contract, or otherwise participating in carrying out the contract, to give surety bond to the United States in such amount as the Administrator may deem appropriate.

(2)   No individual designated pursuant to a contract under this section to certify payments shall, in the absence of gross negligence or intend to defraud the United States, be liable with respect to any payment certified by him under this section.

(3)   No officer disbursing funds shall in the absence of gross negligence or intent to defraud the United States, be liable with respect to any payment by him under this section if it was based upon a voucher signed by an individual designated to certify payments as provided in paragraph (2) of this subsection.

(f)   Any contract entered into under this section shall be for a term of one year, and may be made automatically renewable from term to term in the absence of notice by either party of an intention to terminate at the end of the current term; except that the Administrator may terminate any such contract at any time (after reasonable notice to the pool, company, or organization involved) if he finds that the pool, company, or organization has failed substantially to carry out the contract, or is carrying out the contract in a manner inconsistent with the efficient and effective administration of the flood insurance program authorized under this title.

SETTLEMENT AND ARBITRATION

Sec. 1347. [42 U.S.C. 4083] (a)   The Administrator is authorized to make final settlement of any claims or demands which may arise as a result of any financial transactions which he is authorized to carry out under this chapter, and may, to assist him in making any such settlement, refer any disputes relating to such claims or demands to arbitration, with the consent of the parties concerned.

(b)   Such arbitration shall be advisory in nature, and any award, decision, or recommendation which may be made shall become final only upon the approval of the

Administrator.

RECORDS AND AUDITS

SEC. 1348. [42 U.S.C. 4084] (a)   The flood insurance pool formed or otherwise created under part A of this chapter, and any insurance company or other private organization executing any contract, agreement, or other appropriate arrangement with the Administrator under part B of this chapter or this part, shall keep such records as the Administrator shall prescribe, including records which fully disclose the total costs of the program undertaken or the services being rendered, and such other records as will facilitate an effective audit.

(b)   The Administrator and the Comptroller General of the United States, or any of their duly authorized representatives, shall have access for the purpose of audit and examination to any books, documents, papers, and records of the pool and any such insurance company or other private organization that are pertinent to the costs of the program undertaken or the services being rendered.

CHAPTER III—COORDINATION OF FLOOD INSURANCE WITH LAND-MANAGEMENT PROGRAMS IN FLOOD-PRONE AREAS

IDENTIFICATION OF FLOOD-PRONE AREAS

SEC. 1360. [42 U.S.C. 4101] (a) The Administrator is authorized to consult with, receive information from, and enter into any agreements or other arrangements with the Secretaries of the Army, the Interior, Agriculture, and Commerce, the Tennessee Valley Authority, and the heads of other Federal departments or agencies, on a reimbursement basis, or with the head of any State or local agency, or enter into contracts with any persons or private firms, in order that he may—

(1)   identify and publish information with respect to all flood plain areas, including coastal areas located in the United States, which have special flood hazards, within five years following the date of the enactment of this Act,[17] and

---

[17]   The date of enactment was August 1, 1968.

---

(2)   establish or update flood-risk zone data in all such areas, and make estimates with respect to the rates of probable flood caused loss for the various flood risk zones for each of these areas until the date specified in section 1319.

(b)   The Administrator is directed to accelerate the identification of risk zones within flood-prone and mudslide-prone areas, as provided by subsection (a)(2) of this section, in order to make known the degree of hazard within each such zone at the earliest possible date. To accomplish this objective, the Administrator is authorized, without regard to subsections (a) and (b) of section 3324 of title 31, United States Code, and section 3709 of the Revised Statutes (41 U.S.C. 5), to make grants, provide technical assistance, and enter into contracts, cooperative agreements, or other transactions, on such terms as he may deem appropriate, or consent to modifications thereof, and to make advance or progress payments in connection therewith.

(c)   The Secretary of Defense (through the Army Corps of Engineers), the Secretary of the Interior (through the United States Geological Survey), the Secretary of

189

Agriculture (through the Soil Conservation Service), the Secretary of Commerce (through the National Oceanic and Atmospheric Administration), the head of the Tennessee Valley Authority, and the heads of all other Federal agencies engaged in the identification or delineation of flood-risk zones within the several States shall, in consultation with the Administrator, give the highest practicable priority in the allocation of available manpower and other available resources to the identification and mapping of flood hazard areas and flood-risk zones, in order to assist the Administrator to meet the deadline established by this section.

(d)   The Administrator shall, not later than September 30, 1984, submit to the Congress a plan for bringing all communities containing flood-risk zones into full program status by September 30, 1987.

(e) REVIEW OF FLOOD MAPS.— Once during each 5-year period (the 1st such period beginning on the date of enactment of the Riegle Community Development and Regulatory Improvement Act of 1994[18]) or more often as the Administrator determines necessary, the Administrator shall assess the need to revise and update all floodplain areas and flood risk zones identified, delineated, or established under this section, based on an analysis of all natural hazards affecting flood risks.

---

[18]   The date of enactment was September 23, 1994.

(f) UPDATING FLOOD MAPS.—The Administrator shall revise and update any floodplain areas and flood-risk zones—

(1)   upon the determination of the Administrator, according to the assessment under subsection (e), that revision and updating are necessary for the areas and zones; or

(2)   upon the request from any State or local government stating that specific floodplain areas or flood-risk zones in the State or locality need revision or updating, if sufficient technical data justifying the request is submitted and the unit of government making the request agrees to provide funds in an amount determined by the Administrator.

(g) AVAILABILITY OF FLOOD MAPS.— To promote compliance with the requirements of this title, the Administrator shall make flood insurance rate maps and related information available free of charge to the Federal entities for lending regulation, Federal agency lenders, State agencies directly responsible for coordinating the national flood insurance program, and appropriate representatives of communities participating in the national flood insurance program, and at a reasonable cost to all other persons. Any receipts resulting from this subsection shall be deposited in the National Flood Insurance Fund, pursuant to section 1310(b)(6).

(h) NOTIFICATION OF FLOOD MAP CHANGES.— The Administrator shall cause notice to be published in the Federal Register (or shall provide notice by another comparable method) of any change to flood insurance map panels and any change to flood insurance map panels issued in the form of a letter of map amendment or a letter of map revision. Such notice shall be published or otherwise provided not later than 30 days after the map change or revision becomes effective. Notice by any method other than publication in the Federal Register shall include all pertinent information, provide for regular and frequent distribution, and be at least as accessible to map users as notice in the Federal

Register. All notices under this subsection shall include information on how to obtain copies of the changes or revisions.

(i) COMPENDIA OF FLOOD MAP CHANGES.— Every 6 months, the Administrator shall publish separately in their entirety within a compendium, all changes and revisions to flood insurance map panels and all letters of map amendment and letters of map revision for which notice was published in the Federal Register or otherwise provided during the preceding 6 months. The Administrator shall make such compendia available, free of charge, to Federal entities for lending regulation, Federal agency lenders, and States and communities participating in the national flood insurance program pursuant to section 1310 and at cost to all other parties. Any receipts resulting from this subsection shall be deposited in the National Flood Insurance Fund, pursuant to section 1310(b)(6).

(j) PROVISION OF INFORMATION.— In the implementation of revisions to and updates of flood insurance rate maps, the Administrator shall share information, to the extent appropriate, with the Under Secretary of Commerce for Oceans and Atmosphere and representatives from State coastal zone management programs.

CRITERIA FOR LAND MANAGEMENT AND USE

SEC. 1361. [42 U.S.C. 4102] (a)   The Administrator is authorized to carry out studies and investigations, utilizing to the maximum extent practicable the existing facilities and services of other Federal departments or agencies, and State and local governmental agencies, and any other organizations, with respect to the adequacy of State and local measures in flood-prone areas as to land management and use, flood control, flood zoning, and flood damage prevention, and may enter into any contracts, agreements or other appropriate arrangements to carry out such authority.

(b)   Such studies and investigations shall include, but not be limited to, laws, regulations or ordinances relating to encroachments and obstructions on stream channels and floodways, the orderly development and use of flood plains of rivers or streams, floodway encroachment lines, and flood plain zoning, building codes, building permits, and subdivision or other building restrictions.

(c) On the basis of such studies and investigations, and such other information as he deems necessary, the Administrator shall from time to time develop comprehensive critera designed to encourage, where necessary, the adoption of adequate State and local measures which, to the maximum extent feasible, will—

(1)   construct the development of land which is exposed to flood damage where appropriate,

(2)   guide the development of proposed construction away from locations which are threatened by flood hazards,

(3)   assist in reducing damage caused by floods, and

(4)   otherwise improve the long-range land management and use of flood prone areas,

and he shall work closely with and provide any necessary technical assistance to State, interstate, and local governmental agencies, to encourage the application of such criteria and the adoption and enforcement of such measures.

(d) FLOOD MITIGATION METHODS FOR BUILDINGS.—The Administrator shall establish guidelines for property owners that—

(1) provide alternative methods of mitigation, other than building elevation, to reduce flood risk to residential buildings that cannot be elevated due to their structural characteristics, including—

(A) types of building materials; and

(B) types of floodproofing; and

(2) inform property owners about how the implementation of mitigation methods described in paragraph (1) may affect risk premium rates for flood insurance coverage under the National Flood Insurance Program.

[Section 1361A was repealed by section 100225(c) of Public Law 112–141.]

PURCHASE OF CERTAIN INSURED PROPERTIES

SEC. 1362. [Repealed.19]

19

Section 551(a) of the Riegle Community Development and Regulatory Improvement Act of 1994, Pub. L. 103–325, approved September 23, 1994, repealed this section, which provided authority for the Director to purchase property insured under the national flood insurance program that had incurred significant flood damage and to make loans for elevating certain properties. Such section 551 provides as follows:

''SEC. 551. REPEAL OF FLOODED PROPERTY PURCHASE AND LOAN PROGRAM.

''(a) Repeal.—Section 1362 of the National Flood Insurance Act of 1968 (42 U.S.C. 4103) is hereby repealed.

''(b) Transition Phase.—Notwithstanding subsection (a), during the 1-year period beginning on the date of enactment of this Act, the Director of the Federal Emergency Management Agency may enter into loan and purchase commitments as provided under section 1362 of the National Flood Insurance Act of 1968 (as in effect immediately before the enactment of this Act).

''(c) Savings Provision.—Notwithstanding subsection (a), the Director shall take any action necessary to comply with any purchase or loan commitment entered into before the expiration of the period referred to in subsection (b) pursuant to authority under section 1362 of the National Flood Insurance Act of 1968 or subsection (b).''.

APPEALS

SEC. 1363. [42 U.S.C. 4104] (a) In establishing projected flood elevations and designating areas having special flood hazards for land use purposes with respect to any community pursuant to section 1361, the Administrator shall first propose such determinations and designations by publication for comment in the Federal Register, by direct notification to the chief executive officer of the community, and by publication in a prominent local newspaper.

(b) The Administrator shall publish notification of flood elevation determinations and designations of areas having special flood hazards in a prominent local newspaper at least twice during the ten-day period following notification to the local government. During the ninety-day period following the second publication, any owner or lessee of real property within the community who believes his property rights to be adversely affected by the Administrator's proposed determination may appeal such determination to the local government. The sole grounds for appeal shall be the possession of knowledge or information indicating that (1) the elevations being proposed by the Administrator with respect to an identified area having special flood hazards are scientifically or technically incorrect, or (2) the designation of an identified special flood hazard area is scientifically or technically incorrect.

(c) Appeals by private persons shall be made to the chief executive officer of the community, or to such agency as he shall publicly designate, and shall set forth the data that tend to negate or contradict the Administrator's finding in such form as the chief executive officer may specify. The community shall review and consolidate all such appeals and issue a written opinion stating whether the evidence presented is sufficient to justify an appeal on behalf of such persions by the community in its own name. Whether or not the community decides to appeal the Administrator's determination, copies of individual appeals shall be sent to the Administrator as they are received by the community, and the community's appeal or a copy of its decision not to appeal shall be filed with the Administrator not later than ninety days after the date of the second newspaper publication of the Administrator's notification.

(d) In the event the Administrator does not receive an appeal from the community within the ninety days provided he shall consolidate and review on their own merits, in accordance with the procedures set forth in subsection (e), the appeals filed within the community by private persons and shall make such modifications of his proposed determinations as may be appropriate, taking into account the written opinion, if any, issued by the community in not supporting such appeals. The Administrator's decision shall be in written form, and copies thereof shall be sent both to the chief executive officer of the community and to each individual appellant.

(e) Upon appeal by any community, as provided by this section, the Administrator shall review and take fully into account any technical or scientific data submitted by the community that tend to negate or contradict the information upon which his proposed determination is based. The Administrator shall resolve such appeal by consultation with officials of the local government involved, by administrative hearing, or by submission of the conflicting data to the Scientific Resolution Panel provided for in section 1363A. Until the conflict in data is resolved, and the Administrator makes a final determination on the basis of his findings in the Federal Register, and so notifies the governing body of the community, flood insurance previously available within the community shall continue to be available, and no person shall be denied the right to purchase such insurance at chargeable rates. The Administrator shall make his determination within a reasonable time. The community shall be given a reasonable time after the Administrator's final determination in which to adopt local land use and control measures consistent with the Administrator's determination. The reports and other information used by the Administrator in making his final determination shall be made available for public inspection and shall be admissible in a court of law in the event the community seeks judicial review as provided by this section.

(f) REIMBURSEMENT OF CERTAIN EXPENSES.— When, incident to any appeal under subsection (b) or (c) of this section, the owner or lessee of real property or the community, as the case may be, or, in the case of an appeal that is resolved by submission of conflicting data to the Scientific Resolution Panel provided for in section

1363A, the community, incurs expense in connection with the services of surveyors, engineers, or similar services, but not including legal services, in the effecting of an appeal based on a scientific or technical error on the part of the Federal Emergency Management Agency, which is successful in whole or part, the Administrator shall reimburse such individual or community to an extent measured by the ratio of the successful portion of the appeal as compared to the entire appeal and applying such ratio to the reasonable value of all such services, but no reimbursement shall be made by the Administrator in respect to any fee or expense payment, the payment of which was agreed to be contingent upon the result of the appeal. The Administrator may use such amounts from the National Flood Insurance Fund established under section 1310 as may be necessary to carry out this subsection. The Administrator shall promulgate regulations to carry out this subsection.

(g)   Except as provided in section 1363A, any appellant aggrieved by any final determination of the Administrator upon administrative appeal, as provided by this section, may appeal such determination to the United States district court for the district within which the community is located not more than sixty days after receipt of notice of such determination. The scope of review by the court shall be as provided by chapter 7 of title 5, United States Code. During the pendency of any such litigation, all final determinations of the Administrator shall be effective for the purposes of this title unless stayed by the court for good cause shown.

SEC. 1363A. [42 U.S.C. 4104–1] SCIENTIFIC RESOLUTION PANEL.

(a) AVAILABILITY.—

(1) IN GENERAL.—Pursuant to the authority provided under section 1363(e), the Administrator shall make available an independent review panel, to be known as the Scientific Resolution Panel, to any community—

(A) that has—

(i)   filed a timely map appeal in accordance with section 1363;

(ii)   completed 60 days of consultation with the Federal Emergency Management Agency on the appeal; and

(iii)   not allowed more than 120 days, or such longer period as may be provided by the Administrator by waiver, to pass since the end of the appeal period; or

(B)   that has received an unsatisfactory ruling under the map revision process established pursuant to section 1360(f).

(2) APPEALS BY OWNERS AND LESSEES.—If a community and an owner or lessee of real property within the community appeal a proposed determination of a flood elevation under section 1363(b), upon the request of the community—

(A)   the owner or lessee shall submit scientific and technical data relating to the appeals to the Scientific Resolution Panel; and

(B)   the Scientific Resolution Panel shall make a determination with respect to the appeals in accordance with subsection (c).

(3) DEFINITION.—For purposes of paragraph (1)(B), an unsatisfactory ruling

means that a community—

(A)   received a revised Flood Insurance Rate Map from the Federal Emergency Management Agency, via a Letter of Final Determination, after September 30, 2008, and prior to the date of enactment of this section;

(B)   has subsequently applied for a Letter of Map Revision or Physical Map Revision with the Federal Emergency Management Agency; and

(C)   has received an unfavorable ruling on their request for a map revision.

(b) MEMBERSHIP.— The Scientific Resolution Panel made available under subsection (a) shall consist of 5 members with expertise that relates to the creation and study of flood hazard maps and flood insurance. The Scientific Resolution Panel may include representatives from Federal agencies not involved in the mapping study in question and from other impartial experts. Employees of the Federal Emergency Management Agency may not serve on the Scientific Resolution Panel.

(c) DETERMINATION.—

(1) IN GENERAL.— Following deliberations, and not later than 90 days after its formation, the Scientific Resolution Panel shall issue a determination of resolution of the dispute. Such determination shall set forth recommendations for the base flood elevation determination or the designation of an area having special flood hazards that shall be reflected in the Flood Insurance Rate Maps.

(2) BASIS.—The determination of the Scientific Resolution Panel shall be based on—

(A)   data previously provided to the Administrator by the community, and, in the case of a dispute submitted under subsection (a)(2), an owner or lessee of real property in the community; and

(B)   data provided by the Administrator.

(3) NO ALTERNATIVE DETERMINATIONS PERMISSIBLE.—The Scientific Resolution Panel—

(A) shall provide a determination of resolution of a dispute that—

(i)   is either in favor of the Administrator or in favor of the community on each distinct element of the dispute; or

(ii)   in the case of a dispute submitted under subsection (a)(2), is in favor of the Administrator, in favor of the community, or in favor of the owner or lessee of real property in the community on each distinct element of the dispute; and

(B)   may not offer as a resolution any other alternative determination.

(4) EFFECT OF DETERMINATION.—

(A) BINDING.—The recommendations of the Scientific Resolution Panel shall be binding on all appellants and not subject to further judicial review unless the Administrator determines that implementing the determination of the panel would—

(i)   pose a significant threat due to failure to identify a substantial risk of special flood hazards; or

    (ii)   violate applicable law.

    (B) WRITTEN JUSTIFICATION NOT TO ENFORCE.— If the Administrator elects not to implement the determination of the Scientific Resolution Panel pursuant to subparagraph (A), then not later than 60 days after the issuance of the determination, the Administrator shall issue a written justification explaining such election.

    (C) APPEAL OF DETERMINATION NOT TO ENFORCE.— If the Administrator elects not to implement the determination of the Scientific Resolution Panel pursuant to subparagraph (A), the community may appeal the determination of the Administrator as provided for under section 1363(g).

(d) MAPS USED FOR INSURANCE AND MANDATORY PURCHASE REQUIREMENTS.—With respect to any community that has a dispute that is being considered by the Scientific Resolution Panel formed pursuant to this subsection, the Federal Emergency Management Agency shall ensure that for each such community that—

    (1)   the Flood Insurance Rate Map described in the most recently issued Letter of Final Determination shall be in force and effect with respect to such community; and

    (2)   flood insurance shall continue to be made available to the property owners and residents of the participating community.

NOTICE REQUIREMENTS

SEC. 1364. [42 U.S.C. 4104a] (a) NOTIFICATION OF SPECIAL FLOOD HAZARDS.—

    (1) REGULATED LENDING INSTITUTIONS.— Each Federal entity for lending regulation (after consultation and coordination with the Financial Institutions Examination Council) shall by regulation require regulated lending institutions, as a condition of making, increasing, extending, or renewing any loan secured by improved real estate or a mobile home that the regulated lending institution determines is located or is to be located in an area that has been identified by the Administrator under this title or the Flood Disaster Protection Act of 1973 as an area having special flood hazards, to notify the purchaser or lessee (or obtain satisfactory assurances that the seller or lessor has notified the purchaser or lessee) and the servicer of the loan of such special flood hazards, in writing, a reasonable period in advance of the signing of the purchase agreement, lease, or other documents involved in the transaction. The regulations shall also require that the regulated lending institution retain a record of the receipt of the notices by the purchaser or lessee and the servicer.

    (2) FEDERAL AGENCY LENDERS.— Each Federal agency lender shall by regulation require notification in the manner provided under paragraph (1) with respect to any loan that is made by the Federal agency lender and secured by improved real estate or a mobile home located or to be located in an area that has been identified by the Administrator under this title or the Flood Disaster Protection Act of 1973 as an area having special flood hazards. Any regulations issued under this paragraph shall be consistent with and substantially identical to the regulations issued under paragraph

196

(1).

(3) CONTENTS OF NOTICE.—Written notification required under this subsection shall include—

(A) a warning, in a form to be established by the Administrator, stating that the building on the improved real estate securing the loan is located, or the mobile home securing the loan is or is to be located, in an area having special flood hazards;

(B) a description of the flood insurance purchase requirements under section 102(b) of the Flood Disaster Protection Act of 1973;

(C) a statement that flood insurance coverage may be purchased under the national flood insurance program and is also available from private insurers, as required under section 102(b)(6) of the Flood Disaster Protection Act of 1973 (42 U.S.C. 4012a(b)(6)); and

(D) any other information that the Administrator considers necessary to carry out the purposes of the national flood insurance program.

(b) NOTIFICATION OF CHANGE OF SERVICER.—

(1) LENDING INSTITUTIONS.— Each Federal entity for lending regulation (after consultation and coordination with the Financial Institutions Examination Council) shall by regulation require regulated lending institutions, in connection with the making, increasing, extending, renewing, selling, or transferring any loan described in subsection (a)(1), to notify the Administrator (or the designee of the Administrator) in writing during the term of the loan of the servicer of the loan. Such institutions shall also notify the Administrator (or such designee) of any change in the servicer of the loan, not later than 60 days after the effective date of such change. The regulations under this subsection shall provide that upon any change in the servicing of a loan, the duty to provide notification under this subsection shall transfer to the transferee servicer of the loan.

(2) FEDERAL AGENCY LENDERS.— Each Federal agency lender shall by regulation provide for notification in the manner provided under paragraph (1) with respect to any loan described in subsection (a)(1) that is made by the Federal agency lender. Any regulations issued under this paragraph shall be consistent with and substantially identical to the regulations issued under paragraph (1) of this subsection.

(c) NOTIFICATION OF EXPIRATION OF INSURANCE.— The Administrator (or the designee of the Administrator) shall, not less than 45 days before the expiration of any contract for flood insurance under this title, issue notice of such expiration by first class mail to the owner of the property covered by the contract, the servicer of any loan secured by the property covered by the contract, and (if known to the Administrator) the owner of the loan.

STANDARD HAZARD DETERMINATION FORMS

SEC. 1365. [42 U.S.C. 4104b] (a) DEVELOPMENT.— The Administrator, in consultation with representatives of the mortgage and lending industry, the Federal entities for lending regulation, the Federal agency lenders, and any other appropriate individuals, shall develop a standard form for determining, in the case of a loan secured by improved real estate or a mobile home, whether the building or mobile home is located in an area identified by the Administrator as an area having special flood hazards and in which flood insurance under this title is available. The form shall be established by regulations issued not later than 270 days after the date of enactment of the Riegle Community Development and Regulatory Improvement Act of 1994.[20]

---

[20] The date of enactment was September 23, 1994.

(b) DESIGN AND CONTENTS.—

(1) PURPOSE.— The form under subsection (a) shall be designed to facilitate compliance with the flood insurance purchase requirements of this title.

(2) CONTENTS.— The form shall require identification of the type of flood-risk zone in which the building or mobile home is located, the complete map and panel numbers for the improved real estate or property on which the mobile home is located, the community identification number and community participation status (for purposes of the national flood insurance program) of the community in which the improved real estate or such property is located, and the date of the map used for the determination, with respect to flood hazard information on file with the Administrator. If the building or mobile home is not located in an area having special flood hazards the form shall require a statement to such effect and shall indicate the complete map and panel numbers of the improved real estate or property on which the mobile home is located. If the complete map and panel numbers are not available because the building or mobile home is not located in a community that is participating in the national flood insurance program or because no map exists for the relevant area, the form shall require a statement to such effect. The form shall provide for inclusion or attachment of any relevant documents indicating revisions or amendments to maps.

(c) REQUIRED USE.— The Federal entities for lending regulation shall by regulation require the use of the form under this section by regulated lending institutions. Each Federal agency lender shall by regulation provide for the use of the form with respect to any loan made by such Federal agency lender. The Federal National Mortgage Association and the Federal Home Loan Mortgage Corporation and the Government National Mortgage Association shall require the use of the form with respect to any loan purchased by such entities. A lender or other person may comply with the requirement under this subsection by using the form in a printed, computerized, or electronic manner.

(d) GUARANTEES REGARDING INFORMATION.— In providing information regarding special flood hazards on the form developed under this section, any lender (or other person required to use the form) who makes, increases, extends, or renews a loan secured by improved real estate or a mobile home may provide for the acquisition or determination of such information to be made by a person other than such lender (or other person), only to the extent such person guarantees the accuracy of the information.

(e) RELIANCE ON PREVIOUS DETERMINATION.—Any person increasing, extending, renewing, or purchasing a loan secured by improved real estate or a mobile home may rely on a previous determination of whether the building or mobile home is located in an area having special flood hazards (and shall not be liable for any error in such previous determination), if the previous determination was made not more than 7 years before the date of the transaction and the basis for the previous determination has been set forth on a form under this section, unless—

(1) map revisions or updates pursuant to section 1360(f) after such previous determination have resulted in the building or mobile home being located in an area having special flood hazards; or

(2) the person contacts the Administrator to determine when the most recent map revisions or updates affecting such property occurred and such revisions and updates have occurred after such previous determination.

(f) EFFECTIVE DATE.— The regulations under this section requiring use of the form established pursuant to this section shall be issued together with the regulations required under subsection (a) and shall take effect upon the expiration of the 180-day period beginning on such issuance.

MITIGATION ASSISTANCE

SEC. 1366. [42 U.S.C. 4104c] (a) AUTHORITY.—The Administrator shall carry out a program to provide financial assistance to States and communities, using amounts made available from the National Flood Mitigation Fund under section 1367, for planning and carrying out activities designed to reduce the risk of flood damage to structures covered under contracts for flood insurance under this title. Such financial assistance shall be made available—

(1) to States and communities in the form of grants under this section for carrying out mitigation activities;

(2) to States and communities in the form of grants under this section for carrying out mitigation activities that reduce flood damage to severe repetitive loss structures; and

(3) to property owners in the form of direct grants under this section for carrying out mitigation activities that reduce flood damage to individual structures for which 2 or more claim payments for losses have been made under flood insurance coverage under this title if the Administrator, after consultation with the State and community, determines that neither the State nor community in which such a structure is located has the capacity to manage such grants.

(b) ELIGIBILITY FOR MITIGATION ASSISTANCE.— To be eligible to receive financial assistance under this section for mitigation activities, a State or community shall develop, and have approved by the Administrator, a flood risk mitigation plan (in this section referred to as a mitigation plan), that describes the mitigation activities to be carried out with assistance provided under this section, is consistent with the criteria established by the Administrator under section 1361, provides for reduction of flood losses to structures for which contracts for flood insurance are available under this title, and may be included in a multihazard mitigation plan. The mitigation plan shall be consistent with a comprehensive strategy for mitigation activities for the area affected by the mitigation plan, that has been adopted by the State or community following a public hearing.

(c) ELIGIBLE MITIGATION ACTIVITIES.—

(1) REQUIREMENT OF CONSISTENCY WITH APPROVED MITIGATION
PLAN.— Amounts provided under this section may be used only for mitigation
activities that are consistent with mitigation plans that are approved by the
Administrator and identified under paragraph (4). The Administrator shall provide
assistance under this section to the extent amounts are available in the National
Flood Mitigation Fund pursuant to appropriation Acts, subject only to the absence
of approvable mitigation plans.

(2) REQUIREMENTS OF TECHNICAL FEASIBILITY, COST EFFECTIVENESS, AND INTEREST
OF NATIONAL FLOOD INSURANCE FUND.—

(A) IN GENERAL.—The Administrator may approve only mitigation activities
that the Administrator determines—

(i)   are technically feasible and cost-effective; or

(ii)   will eliminate future payments from the National Flood Insurance
Fund for severe repetitive loss structures through an acquisition or relocation
activity.

(B) CONSIDERATIONS.— In making a determination under subparagraph (A),
the Administrator shall take into consideration recognized ancillary benefits.

(3) ELIGIBLE ACTIVITIES.—Eligible activities under a mitigation plan may
include—

(A)   demolition or relocation of any structure located on land that is along
the shore of a lake or other body of water and is certified by an appropriate State
or local land use authority to be subject to imminent collapse or subsidence as a
result of erosion or flooding;

(B)   elevation, relocation, demolition, or floodproofing of structures
(including public structures) located in areas having special flood hazards or
other areas of flood risk;

(C)   acquisition by States and communities of properties (including public
properties) located in areas having special flood hazards or other areas of flood
risk and properties substantially damaged by flood, for public use, as the
Administrator determines is consistent with sound land management and use in
such area;

(D)   elevation, relocation, or floodproofing of utilities (including equipment
that serves structures);

(E)   minor physical mitigation efforts that do not duplicate the flood
prevention activities of other Federal agencies and that lessen the frequency
or severity of flooding and decrease predicted flood damages, which shall not
include major flood control projects such as dikes, levees, seawalls, groins, and
jetties unless the Administrator specifically determines in approving a mitigation
plan that such activities are the most cost-effective mitigation activities for the
National Flood Mitigation Fund;

(F)   the development or update of mitigation plans by a State or community
which meet the planning criteria established by the Administrator, except that the

amount from grants under this section that may be used under this subparagraph may not exceed $50,000 for any mitigation plan of a State or $25,000 for any mitigation plan of a community;

(G)   the provision of technical assistance by States to communities and individuals to conduct eligible mitigation activities;

(H)   other activities that the Administrator considers appropriate and specifies in regulation;

(I)   other mitigation activities not described in subparagraphs (A) through (G) or the regulations issued under subparagraph (H), that are described in the mitigation plan of a State or community; and

(J)   without regard to the requirements under paragraphs (1) and (2) of subsection (d), and if the State applied for and was awarded at least $1,000,000 in grants available under this section in the prior fiscal year, technical assistance to communities to identify eligible activities, to develop grant applications, and to implement grants awarded under this section, not to exceed $50,000 to any 1 State in any fiscal year.

(4) ELIGIBILITY OF DEMOLITION AND REBUILDING OF PROPERTIES.— The Administrator shall consider as an eligible activity the demolition and rebuilding of properties to at least base flood elevation or greater, if required by the Administrator or if required by any State regulation or local ordinance, and in accordance with criteria established by the Administrator.

(d) MATCHING REQUIREMENT.—The Administrator may provide grants for eligible mitigation activities as follows:

(1) SEVERE REPETITIVE LOSS STRUCTURES.—In the case of mitigation activities to severe repetitive loss structures, in an amount up to—

(A)   100 percent of all eligible costs, if the activities are approved under subsection (c)(2)(A)(i); or

(A)[21]   the expected savings to the National Flood Insurance Fund from expected avoided damages through acquisition or relocation activities, if the activities are approved under subsection (c)(2)(A)(ii).

---

[21]   So in law. Probably should be redesignated as (B).

---

(2) REPETITIVE LOSS STRUCTURES.— In the case of mitigation activities to repetitive loss structures, in an amount up to 90 percent of all eligible costs.

(3) OTHER MITIGATION ACTIVITIES.— In the case of all other mitigation activities, in an amount up to 75 percent of all eligible costs

(e) RECAPTURE.—

(1) NONCOMPLIANCE WITH PLAN.— If the Administrator determines that a State or community that has received mitigation assistance under this section has not carried out the mitigation activities as set forth in the mitigation plan, the Administrator shall recapture any unexpended amounts and deposit the amounts in the National Flood Mitigation Fund under section 1367.

(2) FAILURE TO PROVIDE MATCHING FUNDS.— If the Administrator determines that a State or community that has received mitigation assistance under this section has not provided matching funds in the amount required under subsection (d), the Administrator shall recapture any unexpended amounts of mitigation assistance exceeding the amount of such matching funds actually provided and deposit the amounts in the National Flood Mitigation Fund under section 1367.

(f) REPORTS.— Not later than 1 year after the date of enactment of the Biggert-Waters Flood Insurance Reform Act of 2012[22] and biennially thereafter, the Administrator shall submit a report to the Congress describing the status of mitigation activities carried out with assistance provided under this section.

---

[22] The date of enactment was July 6, 2012.

(g) FAILURE TO MAKE GRANT AWARD WITHIN 5 YEARS.— For any application for a grant under this section for which the Administrator fails to make a grant award within 5 years of the date of the application, the grant application shall be considered to be denied and any funding amounts allocated for such grant applications shall remain in the National Flood Mitigation Fund under section 1367 of this title and shall be made available for grants under this section.

(h) DEFINITIONS.—For purposes of this section, the following definitions shall apply:

(1) COMMUNITY.—The term community means—

(A) a political subdivision that—

(i) has zoning and building code jurisdiction over a particular area having special flood hazards; and

(ii) is participating in the national flood insurance program; or

(B) a political subdivision of a State, or other authority, that is designated by political subdivisions, all of which meet the requirements of subparagraph (A), to administer grants for mitigation activities for such political subdivisions.

(2) REPETITIVE LOSS STRUCTURE.— The term repetitive loss structure has the meaning given such term in section 1370.

(3) SEVERE REPETITIVE LOSS STRUCTURE.—The term severe repetitive loss structure means a structure that—

(A) is covered under a contract for flood insurance made available under this title; and

(B) has incurred flood-related damage—

(i) for which 4 or more separate claims payments have been made under flood insurance coverage under this title, with the amount of each such claim exceeding $5,000, and with the cumulative amount of such claims payments exceeding $20,000; or

(ii) for which at least 2 separate claims payments have been made under such coverage, with the cumulative amount of such claims exceeding the value of the insured structure.

NATIONAL FLOOD MITIGATION FUND

SEC. 1367. [42 U.S.C. 4104d] (a) ESTABLISHMENT AND AVAILABILITY.— The Administrator shall establish in the Treasury of the United States a fund to be known as the National Flood Mitigation Fund, which shall be credited with amounts described in subsection (b) and shall be available, to the extent provided in appropriation Acts, for providing assistance under section 1366.

(b) CREDITS.—The National Flood Mitigation Fund shall be credited with—

(1) in each fiscal year, amounts from the National Flood Insurance Fund not to exceed $90,000,000 and to remain available until expended, of which—

(A) not more than $40,000,000 shall be available pursuant to subsection (a) of this section for assistance described in section 1366(a)(1);

(B) not more than $40,000,000 shall be available pursuant to subsection (a) of this section for assistance described in section 1366(a)(2); and

(C) not more than $10,000,000 shall be available pursuant to subsection (a) of this section for assistance described in section 1366(a)(3);

(2) any penalties collected under section 102(f) of the Flood Disaster Protection Act of 1973; and

(3) any amounts recaptured under section 1366(e).

(c) ADMINISTRATIVE EXPENSES.— The Administrator may use not more than 5 percent of amounts made available under subsection (b) to cover salaries, expenses, and other administrative costs incurred by the Administrator to make grants and provide assistance under section 1366.

(d) PROHIBITION ON OFFSETTING COLLECTIONS.— Notwithstanding any other provision of this title, amounts made available pursuant to this section shall not be subject to offsetting collections through premium rates for flood insurance coverage under this title.

(e) CONTINUED AVAILABILITY AND REALLOCATION.— Any amounts made available pursuant to subparagraph (A), (B), or (C) of subsection (b)(1) that are not used in any fiscal year shall continue to be available for the purposes specified in the subparagraph of subsection (b)(1) pursuant to which such amounts were made available, unless the Administrator determines that reallocation of such unused amounts to meet demonstrated need for other mitigation activities under section 1366 is in the best interest of the National Flood Insurance Fund.

(f) INVESTMENT.— If the Administrator determines that the amounts in the National Flood Mitigation Fund are in excess of amounts needed under subsection (a), the Administrator may invest any excess amounts the Administrator determines advisable in interest-bearing obligations issued or guaranteed by the United States.

(g) REPORT.— The Administrator shall submit a report to the Congress not later than the expiration of the 1-year period beginning on the date of enactment of this Act[23] and not less than once during each successive 2-year period thereafter. The report shall describe the status of the Fund and any activities carried out with amounts from the Fund.

CHAPTER IV—APPROPRIATIONS AND MISCELLANEOUS PROVISIONS

DEFINITIONS

SEC. 1370. [42 U.S.C. 4121] (a) As used in this title—

(1)   the term flood shall have such meaning as may be prescribed in regulations of the Administrator, and may include inundation from rising waters or from the overflow of streams, rivers, or other bodies of water, or from tidal surges, abnormally high tidal water, tidal waves, tsunamis, hurricanes, or other severe storms or deluge;

(2)   the terms United States (when used in a geographic sense) and State includes the several States, the District of Columbia, the territories and possessions, the Commonwealth of Puerto Rico, and the Trust Territory of the Pacific Islands;

(3)   the terms insurance company, other insurer and insurance agent or broker include any organization or person that is authorized to engage in the business of insurance under the laws of any State, subject to the reporting requirements of the Securities Exchange Act of 1934 pursuant to section 13(a) or 15(d) of such Act (15 U.S.C. 78m(a) and 78o(d)), or authorized by the Administrator to assume reinsurance on risks insured by the flood insurance program;

(4)   the term insurance adjustment organization includes any organizations and persons engaged in the business of adjusting loss claims arising under insurance policies issued by any insurance company or other insurer;

(5)   the term person includes any individual or group of individuals, corporation, partnership, association, or any other organized group of persons, including State and local governments and agencies thereof;

(6)   the term Administrator means the Administrator of the Federal Emergency Management Agency;

(7) the term repetitive loss structure means a structure covered by a contract for flood insurance that—

(A)   has incurred flood-related damage on 2 occasions, in which the cost of repair, on the average, equaled or exceeded 25 percent of the value of the structure at the time of each such flood event; and

(B)   at the time of the second incidence of flood-related damage, the contract for flood insurance contains increased cost of compliance coverage.[24]

[24]   So in law.

(8)   the term Federal agency lender means a Federal agency that makes direct loans secured by improved real estate or a mobile home, to the extent such agency acts in such capacity;

(9)   the term Federal entity for lending regulation means the Board of Governors of the Federal Reserve System, the Federal Deposit Insurance Corporation, the Comptroller of the Currency, the National Credit Union Administration, and the Farm Credit Administration, and with respect to a particular regulated lending institution means the entity primarily responsible for the supervision of the institution;

(10)   the term improved real estate means real estate upon which a building is located;

(11)   the term lender means a regulated lending institution or Federal agency lender;

(12) the term natural and beneficial floodplain functions means—

(A)   the functions associated with the natural or relatively undisturbed floodplain that (i) moderate flooding, retain flood waters, reduce erosion and sedimentation, and mitigate the effect of waves and storm surge from storms, and (ii) reduce flood related damage; and

(B)   ancillary beneficial functions, including maintenance of water quality and recharge of ground water, that reduce flood related damage;

(13)   the term regulated lending institution means any bank, savings and loan association, credit union, farm credit bank, Federal land bank association, production credit association, or similar institution subject to the supervision of a Federal entity for lending regulation;

(14)   the term servicer means the person responsible for receiving any scheduled periodic payments from a borrower pursuant to the terms of a loan, including amounts for taxes, insurance premiums, and other charges with respect to the property securing the loan, and making the payments of principal and interest and such other payments with respect to the amounts received from the borrower as may be required pursuant to the terms of the loan; and

(15)   the term substantially damaged structure means a structure covered by a contract for flood insurance that has incurred damage for which the cost of repair exceeds an amount specified in any regulation promulgated by the Administrator, or by a community ordinance, whichever is lower.

(b)   The term flood shall also include inundation from mudslides which are proximately caused by accumulations of water on or under the ground; and all of the provisions of this title shall apply with respect to such mudslides in the same manner and to the same extent as with respect to floods described in subsection (a)(1), subject to and in accordance with such regulations, modifying the provisions of this title (including the provisions relating to land management and use) to the extent necessary to insure that they can be effectively so applied, as the Administrator may prescribe to achieve (with respect to such mudslides) the purposes of this title and the objectives of the program.

(c)   The term flood shall also include the collapse or subsidence of land along the shore of a lake or other body of water as a result of erosion or undermining caused by waves or currents of water exceeding anticipated cyclical levels, and all of the provisions of this title shall apply with respect to such collapse or subsidence in the same manner and to the same extent as with respect to floods described in subsection (a)(1), subject to and in accordance with such regulations, modifying the provisions of this title (including the provisions relating to land management and use) to the extent necessary to insure that they can be effectively so applied, as the Administrator may prescribe to achieve (with respect to such collapse or subsidence) the purposes of this title and the objectives of the program.

STUDIES OF OTHER NATURAL DISASTERS

SEC. 1371. [42 U.S.C. 4122] (a)   The Administrator is authorized to undertake such studies as may be necessary for the purpose of determining the extent to which insurance protection against earthquakes or any other natural disaster perils, other than flood, is not available from public or private sources, and the feasibility of such insurance protection being made available.

(b)   Studies under this section shall be carried out, to the maximum extent practicable, with the cooperation of other Federal departments and agencies and State and local agencies, and the Administrator is authorized to consult with, receive information from, and enter into any necessary agreements or other arrangements with such other Federal departments and agencies (on a reimbursement basis) and such State and local agencies.

PAYMENTS

SEC. 1372. [42 U.S.C. 4123]   Any payments under this title may be made (after necessary adjustment on account of previously made underpayments or overpayments) in advance or by way of reimbursement, and in such installments and on such conditions, as the Administrator may determine.

GOVERNMENT CORPORATION CONTROL ACT

SEC. 1373. [42 U.S.C. 4124]   The provisions of chapter 91 of title 31, United States Code, shall apply to the program authorized under this title to the same extent as they apply to wholly owned Government corporations.

FINALITY OF CERTAIN TRANSACTIONS

SEC. 1374. [42 U.S.C. 4125] Notwithstanding the provisions of any other law—

(1)   Any financial transaction authorized to be carried out under this title, and

(2)   any payment authorized to be made or to be received in connection with any such financial transaction,

shall be final and conclusive upon all officers of the Government.

ADMINISTRATIVE EXPENSES

SEC. 1375. [42 U.S.C. 4126]   Any administrative expenses which may be sustained by the Federal Government in carrying out the flood insurance and floodplain management programs authorized under this title may be paid with amounts from the National Flood Insurance Fund (as provided under section 1310(a)(4)), subject to approval in appropriations Acts.

APPROPRIATIONS

SEC. 1376. [42 U.S.C. 4127] (a) There are hereby authorized to be appropriated such sums as may from time to time be necessary to carry out this title, including sums—

(1) to cover administrative expenses authorized under section 1375;

(2) to reimburse the National Flood Insurance Fund established under section 1310 for—

(A) premium equalization payments under section 1334 which have been made from such fund; and

(B) reinsurance claims paid under the excess loss reinsurance coverage provided under section 1335; and

(3) to make such other payments as may be necessary to carry out the purposes of this title.

(b) All such funds shall be available without fiscal year limitation.

(c) There are authorized to be appropriated such sums as may be necessary through the date specified in section 1319, for studies under this title.

EFFECTIVE DATE

SEC. 1377. [42 U.S.C. 4001 note] This title shall take effect one hundred and twenty days following the date of its enactment,25 except that the Administrator on the basis of a finding that conditions exist necessitating the prescribing of an additional period, may prescribe a later effective date which in no event shall be more than one hundred and eighty days following such date of enactment.

---

25   The date of enactment was August 1, 1968.

★

BIGGERT-WATERS FLOOD INSURANCE REFORM ACT OF 2012

PUBLIC LAW 112–141
AS AMENDED THROUGH PUB. L. 117–58

[(Public Law 112–141)]

[As Amended Through P.L. 117–58, Enacted November 15, 2021]

AN ACT Moving Ahead for Progress in the 21st Century Act

Be it enacted by the Senate and House of Representatives of the United States of America in Congress assembled,

* * * * * * *

DIVISION F—MISCELLANEOUS

* * * * * * *

TITLE II—FLOOD INSURANCE

Subtitle A—Flood Insurance Reform and Modernization

SEC. 100201. [42 U.S.C. 4001 note] SHORT TITLE.

This subtitle may be cited as the "Biggert-Waters Flood Insurance Reform Act of 2012".

SEC. 100202. [42 U.S.C. 4004] DEFINITIONS.

(a) In General.—In this subtitle, the following definitions shall apply:

(1) 100-YEAR FLOODPLAIN.— The term 100-year floodplain means that area which is subject to inundation from a flood having a 1-percent chance of being equaled or exceeded in any given year.

(2) 500-YEAR FLOODPLAIN.— The term 500-year floodplain means that area which is subject to inundation from a flood having a 0.2-percent chance of being equaled or exceeded in any given year.

(3) Administrator.— The term Administrator means the Administrator of the Federal Emergency Management Agency.

(4) National flood insurance program.— The term National Flood Insurance Program means the program established under the National Flood Insurance Act of 1968 (42 U.S.C. 4011 et seq.).

(5) WRITE YOUR OWN.— The term Write Your Own means the cooperative undertaking between the insurance industry and the Federal Insurance Administration which allows participating property and casualty insurance companies to write and service standard flood insurance policies.

(b) COMMON TERMINOLOGY.— Except as otherwise provided in this subtitle, any terms used in this subtitle shall have the meaning given to such terms under section 1370 of the National Flood Insurance Act of 1968 (42 U.S.C. 4121).

* * * * * * *

SEC. 100205. REFORM OF PREMIUM RATE STRUCTURE.

(a) TO EXCLUDE CERTAIN PROPERTIES FROM RECEIVING SUBSIDIZED PREMIUM RATES.—

(1) IN GENERAL.—Section 1307 of the National Flood Insurance Act of 1968 (42 U.S.C. 4014) is amended—

(A) in subsection (a)(2), by striking for any residential property which is not the primary residence of an individual; and and inserting the following:"for—

"(A) any residential property which is not the primary residence of an individual;

"(B) any severe repetitive loss property;

"(C) any property that has incurred flood-related damage in which the cumulative amounts of payments under this title equaled or exceeded the fair market value of such property;

"(D) any business property; or

"(E) any property which on or after the date of enactment of the Biggert-Waters Flood Insurance Reform Act of 2012 has experienced or sustained—

"(i) substantial damage exceeding 50 percent of the fair market value of such property; or

"(ii) substantial improvement exceeding 30 percent of the fair market value of such property; and"; and

(B) by adding at the end the following:

"(g) NO EXTENSION OF SUBSIDY TO NEW POLICIES OR LAPSED POLICIES. The Administrator shall not provide flood insurance to prospective insureds at rates less than those estimated under subsection (a)(1), as required by paragraph (2) of that subsection, for—

"(1) any property not insured by the flood insurance program as of the date of enactment of the Biggert-Waters Flood Insurance Reform Act of 2012;

"(2)   any property purchased after the date of enactment of the Biggert-Waters Flood Insurance Reform Act of 2012;

"(3)   any policy under the flood insurance program that has lapsed in coverage, as a result of the deliberate choice of the holder of such policy; or

"(4) any prospective insured who refuses to accept any offer for mitigation assistance by the Administrator (including an offer to relocate), including an offer of mitigation assistance—

"(A)   following a major disaster, as defined in section 102 of the Robert T. Stafford Disaster Relief and Emergency Assistance Act (42 U.S.C. 5122); or

"(B) in connection with—

"(i)   a repetitive loss property; or

"(ii)   a severe repetitive loss property.

"(h) Definition. In this section, the term 'severe repetitive loss property' has the following meaning:

"(1) Single-family properties. In the case of a property consisting of 1 to 4 residences, such term means a property that—

"(A)   is covered under a contract for flood insurance made available under this title; and

"(B) has incurred flood-related damage—

"(i)   for which 4 or more separate claims payments have been made under flood insurance coverage under this chapter, with the amount of each such claim exceeding $5,000, and with the cumulative amount of such claims payments exceeding $20,000; or

"(ii)   for which at least 2 separate claims payments have been made under such coverage, with the cumulative amount of such claims exceeding the value of the property.

"(2) Multifamily properties.   In the case of a property consisting of 5 or more residences, such term shall have such meaning as the Director shall by regulation provide.".

(2) [42 U.S.C. 4014 note] Effective date.— The amendments made by paragraph (1) shall become effective 90 days after the date of enactment of this Act.

(b) Estimates of Premium Rates.—Section 1307(a)(1)(B) of the National Flood Insurance Act of 1968 (42 U.S.C. 4014(a)(1)(B)) is amended—

(1)   in clause (ii), by striking and at the end;

(2)   in clause (iii), by adding and at the end; and

(3)   by inserting after clause (iii) the following:

"(iv) all costs, as prescribed by principles and standards of practice in ratemaking adopted by the American Academy of Actuaries and the Casualty Actuarial Society, including—

"(I)   an estimate of the expected value of future costs,

"(II)   all costs associated with the transfer of risk, and

"(III)   the costs associated with an individual risk transfer with respect to risk classes, as defined by the Administrator,".

(c) INCREASE IN ANNUAL LIMITATION ON PREMIUM INCREASES.—Section 1308(e) of the National Flood Insurance Act of 1968 (42 U.S.C. 4015(e)) is amended—

(1) in the matter preceding paragraph (1)—

(A)   by striking or (3); and

(B)   by inserting any properties after under this title for;

(2) in paragraph (1)—

(A)   by striking any properties within any single and inserting within any single; and

(B)   by striking 10 percent and inserting 20 percent; and

(3)   by striking paragraph (2) and inserting the following:

"(2)   described in subparagraphs (A) through (E) of section 1307(a)(2) shall be increased by 25 percent each year, until the average risk premium rate for such properties is equal to the average of the risk premium rates for properties described under paragraph (1).".

(d)   PREMIUM PAYMENT FLEXIBILITY FOR NEW AND EXISTING POLICYHOLDERS.— Section 1308 of the National Flood Insurance Act of 1968 (42 U.S.C. 4015) is amended by adding at the end the following:

"(g) FREQUENCY OF PREMIUM COLLECTION.   With respect to any chargeable premium rate prescribed under this section, the Administrator shall provide policyholders that are not required to escrow their premiums and fees for flood insurance as set forth under section 102 of the Flood Disaster Protection Act of 1973 (42 U.S.C. 4012a) with the option of paying their premiums either annually or in more frequent installments.".

(e) [42 U.S.C. 4015 note] RULE OF CONSTRUCTION.— Nothing in this section or the amendments made by this section may be construed to affect the requirement under section 2(c) of the Act entitled An Act to extend the National Flood Insurance Program, and for other purposes, approved May 31, 2012 (Public Law 112-123), that the first increase in chargeable risk premium rates for residential properties which are not the primary residence of an individual take effect on July 1, 2012.

* * * * * * *

SEC. 100213. REPAYMENT PLAN FOR BORROWING AUTHORITY.

* * * * * * *

C. 100215. [42 U.S.C. 4101a] TECHNICAL
APPING ADVISORY COUNCIL.

Biggert-Waters Flood Insurance Reform Act of
2012

(b) REPORT.— Not later than the expiration of the 6-month period beginning on the date of enactment of this Act, the Administrator shall submit a report to the Congress setting forth options for repaying within 10 years all amounts, including any amounts previously borrowed but not yet repaid, owed pursuant to clause (2) of subsection (a) of section 1309 of the National Flood Insurance Act of 1968 (42 U.S.C. 4016(a)(2)).

* * * * * * *

SEC. 100215. [42 U.S.C. 4101a] TECHNICAL MAPPING ADVISORY COUNCIL.

(a) ESTABLISHMENT.— There is established a council to be known as the Technical Mapping Advisory Council (in this section referred to as the Council).

(b) MEMBERSHIP.—

(1) IN GENERAL.—The Council shall consist of—

(A) the Administrator (or the designee thereof);

(B) the Secretary of the Interior (or the designee thereof);

(C) the Secretary of Agriculture (or the designee thereof);

(D) the Under Secretary of Commerce for Oceans and Atmosphere (or the designee thereof); and

(E) 16 additional members appointed by the Administrator or the designee of the Administrator, who shall be—

(i) a member of a recognized professional surveying association or organization;

(ii) a member of a recognized professional mapping association or organization;

(iii) a member of a recognized professional engineering association or organization;

(iv) a member of a recognized professional association or organization representing flood hazard determination firms;

(v) a representative of the United States Geological Survey;

(vi) a representative of a recognized professional association or organization representing State geographic information;

(vii) a representative of State national flood insurance coordination offices;

(viii) a representative of the Corps of Engineers;

(ix) a member of a recognized regional flood and storm water management organization;

(x) 2 representatives of different State government agencies that have entered into cooperating technical partnerships with the Administrator and have demonstrated the capability to produce flood insurance rate maps;

(xi) 2 representatives of different local government agencies that have entered into cooperating technical partnerships with the Administrator and have demonstrated the capability to produce flood insurance maps;

(xii)   a member of a recognized floodplain management association or organization;

(xiii)   a member of a recognized risk management association or organization; and

(xiv)   a State mitigation officer.

(2) QUALIFICATIONS.— Members of the Council shall be appointed based on their demonstrated knowledge and competence regarding surveying, cartography, remote sensing, geographic information systems, or the technical aspects of preparing and using flood insurance rate maps. In appointing members under paragraph (1)(E), the Administrator shall, to the maximum extent practicable, ensure that the membership of the Council has a balance of Federal, State, local, tribal, and private members, and includes geographic diversity, including representation from areas with coastline on the Gulf of Mexico and other States containing areas identified by the Administrator as at high risk for flooding or as areas having special flood hazards.

(c) DUTIES.—The Council shall—

(1) recommend to the Administrator how to improve in a cost-effective manner the—

(A)   accuracy, general quality, ease of use, and distribution and dissemination of flood insurance rate maps and risk data; and

(B)   performance metrics and milestones required to effectively and efficiently map flood risk areas in the United States;

(2) recommend to the Administrator mapping standards and guidelines for—

(A)   flood insurance rate maps; and

(B)   data accuracy, data quality, data currency, and data eligibility;

(3)   recommend to the Administrator how to maintain, on an ongoing basis, flood insurance rate maps and flood risk identification;

(4)   recommend procedures for delegating mapping activities to State and local mapping partners;

(5) recommend to the Administrator and other Federal agencies participating in the Council—

(A)   methods for improving interagency and intergovernmental coordination on flood mapping and flood risk determination; and

(B)   a funding strategy to leverage and coordinate budgets and expenditures across Federal agencies; and

(6) submit an annual report to the Administrator that contains—

(A)   a description of the activities of the Council;

(B)   an evaluation of the status and performance of flood insurance rate maps and mapping activities to revise and update flood insurance rate maps, as required under section 100216; and

(C) a summary of recommendations made by the Council to the Administrator.

(d) FUTURE CONDITIONS RISK ASSESSMENT AND MODELING REPORT.—

(1) IN GENERAL.—The Council shall consult with scientists and technical experts, other Federal agencies, States, and local communities to—

(A) develop recommendations on how to—

(i) ensure that flood insurance rate maps incorporate the best available climate science to assess flood risks; and

(ii) ensure that the Federal Emergency Management Agency uses the best available methodology to consider the impact of—

(I) the rise in the sea level; and

(II) future development on flood risk; and

(B) not later than 1 year after the date of enactment of this Act, prepare written recommendations in a future conditions risk assessment and modeling report and to submit such recommendations to the Administrator.

(2) RESPONSIBILITY OF THE ADMINISTRATOR.— The Administrator, as part of the ongoing program to review and update National Flood Insurance Program rate maps under section 100216, shall incorporate any future risk assessment submitted under paragraph (1)(B) in any such revision or update.

(e) CHAIRPERSON.— The members of the Council shall elect 1 member to serve as the chairperson of the Council (in this section referred to as the Chairperson).

(f) COORDINATION.— To ensure that the Council's recommendations are consistent, to the maximum extent practicable, with national digital spatial data collection and management standards, the Chairperson shall consult with the Chairperson of the Federal Geographic Data Committee (established pursuant to Office of Management and Budget Circular A-16).

(g) COMPENSATION.— Members of the Council shall receive no additional compensation by reason of their service on the Council.

(h) MEETINGS AND ACTIONS.—

(1) IN GENERAL.— The Council shall meet not less frequently than twice each year at the request of the Chairperson or a majority of its members, and may take action by a vote of the majority of the members.

(2) INITIAL MEETING.— The Administrator, or a person designated by the Administrator, shall request and coordinate the initial meeting of the Council.

(i) OFFICERS.— The Chairperson may appoint officers to assist in carrying out the duties of the Council under subsection (c).

(j) STAFF.—

(1) STAFF OF FEMA.— Upon the request of the Chairperson, the Administrator may detail, on a nonreimbursable basis, personnel of the Federal Emergency Management Agency to assist the Council in carrying out its duties.

(2) STAFF OF OTHER FEDERAL AGENCIES.— Upon request of the Chairperson,

any other Federal agency that is a member of the Council may detail, on a nonreimbursable basis, personnel to assist the Council in carrying out its duties.

(k) POWERS.— In carrying out this section, the Council may hold hearings, receive evidence and assistance, provide information, and conduct research, as it considers appropriate.

(l) REPORT TO CONGRESS.—The Administrator, on an annual basis, shall report to the Committee on Banking, Housing, and Urban Affairs of the Senate, the Committee on Financial Services of the House of Representatives, and the Office of Management and Budget on the—

(1) recommendations made by the Council;

(2) actions taken by the Federal Emergency Management Agency to address such recommendations to improve flood insurance rate maps and flood risk data; and

(3) any recommendations made by the Council that have been deferred or not acted upon, together with an explanatory statement.

SEC. 100216. [42 U.S.C. 4101b] NATIONAL FLOOD MAPPING PROGRAM.

(a) REVIEWING, UPDATING, AND MAINTAINING MAPS.— The Administrator, in coordination with the Technical Mapping Advisory Council established under section 100215, shall establish an ongoing program under which the Administrator shall review, update, and maintain National Flood Insurance Program rate maps in accordance with this section.

(b) MAPPING.—

(1) IN GENERAL.—In carrying out the program established under subsection (a), the Administrator shall—

(A) identify, review, update, maintain, and publish National Flood Insurance Program rate maps with respect to—

(i) all populated areas and areas of possible population growth located within the 100-year floodplain;

(ii) all populated areas and areas of possible population growth located within the 500-year floodplain;

(iii) areas of residual risk, including areas that are protected by levees, dams, and other flood control structures;

(iv) areas that could be inundated as a result of the failure of a levee, dam, or other flood control structure;

(v) areas that are protected by non-structural flood mitigation features; and

(vi) the level of protection provided by flood control structures and by non-structural flood mitigation features;

(B) establish or update flood-risk zone data in all such areas, and make estimates with respect to the rates of probable flood caused loss for the various flood risk zones for each such area; and

(C)   use, in identifying, reviewing, updating, maintaining, or publishing any National Flood Insurance Program rate map required under this section or under the National Flood Insurance Act of 1968 (42 U.S.C. 4011 et seq.), the most accurate topography and elevation data available.

(2) MAPPING ELEMENTS.—Each map updated under this section shall—

(A)   assess the accuracy of current ground elevation data used for hydrologic and hydraulic modeling of flooding sources and mapping of the flood hazard and wherever necessary acquire new ground elevation data utilizing the most up-to-date geospatial technologies in accordance with guidelines and specifications of the Federal Emergency Management Agency; and

(B) develop National Flood Insurance Program flood data on a watershed basis—

(i)   to provide the most technically effective and efficient studies and hydrologic and hydraulic modeling; and

(ii)   to eliminate, to the maximum extent possible, discrepancies in base flood elevations between adjacent political subdivisions.

(3) OTHER INCLUSIONS.—In updating maps under this section, the Administrator shall include—

(A) any relevant information on coastal inundation from—

(i)   an applicable inundation map of the Corps of Engineers; and

(ii)   data of the National Oceanic and Atmospheric Administration relating to storm surge modeling;

(B)   any relevant information of the United States Geological Survey on stream flows, watershed characteristics, and topography that is useful in the identification of flood hazard areas, as determined by the Administrator;

(C)   any relevant information on land subsidence, coastal erosion areas, changing lake levels, and other flood-related hazards;

(D)   any relevant information or data of the National Oceanic and Atmospheric Administration and the United States Geological Survey relating to the best available science regarding future changes in sea levels, precipitation, and intensity of hurricanes; and

(E)   any other relevant information as may be recommended by the Technical Mapping Advisory Committee.

(c) STANDARDS.—In updating and maintaining maps under this section, the Administrator shall—

(1) establish standards to—

(A) ensure that maps are adequate for—

(i)   flood risk determinations; and

(ii)   use by State and local governments in managing development to reduce the risk of flooding; and

(B)   facilitate identification and use of consistent methods of data collection and analysis by the Administrator, in conjunction with State and local governments, in developing maps for communities with similar flood risks, as determined by the Administrator; and

(2) publish maps in a format that is—

(A) digital geospatial data compliant;

(B) compliant with the open publishing and data exchange standards established by the Open Geospatial Consortium; and

(C) aligned with official data defined by the National Geodetic Survey.

(d) COMMUNICATION AND OUTREACH.—

(1) IN GENERAL.—The Administrator shall—

(A) before commencement of any mapping or map updating process, notify each community affected of the model or models that the Administrator plans to use in such process and provide an explanation of why such model or models are appropriate;

(B) provide each community affected a 30-day period beginning upon notification under subparagraph (A) to consult with the Administrator regarding the appropriateness, with respect to such community, of the mapping model or models to be used; provided that consultation by a community pursuant to this subparagraph shall not waive or otherwise affect any right of the community to appeal any flood hazard determinations;

(C) upon completion of the first Independent Data Submission, transmit a copy of such Submission to the affected community, provide the affected community a 30-day period during which the community may provide data to Administrator that can be used to supplement or modify the existing data, and incorporate any data that is consistent with prevailing engineering principles;

(D) work with States, local communities, and property owners to identify areas and features described in subsection (b)(1)(A)(v);

(E) work to enhance communication and outreach to States, local communities, and property owners about the effects—

(i) of any potential changes to National Flood Insurance Program rate maps that may result from the mapping program required under this section; and

(ii) that any such changes may have on flood insurance purchase requirements;

(F) engage with local communities to enhance communication and outreach to the residents of such communities, including tenants (with regard to contents insurance), on the matters described under subparagraph (E); and

(G) not less than 30 days before issuance of any preliminary map, notify the Senators for each State affected and each Member of the House of Representatives for each congressional district affected by the preliminary map in writing of—

(i) the estimated schedule for—

(I)   community meetings regarding the preliminary map;

(II)   publication of notices regarding the preliminary map in local newspapers; and

(III)   the commencement of the appeals process regarding the map; and

(ii)   the estimated number of homes and businesses that will be affected by changes contained in the preliminary map, including how many structures will be that were not previously located in an area having special flood hazards will be located within such an area under the preliminary map; and

(H)   upon the issuance of any proposed map and any notice of an opportunity to make an appeal relating to the proposed map, notify the Senators for each State affected each Member of the House of Representatives for each congressional district affected by the proposed map of any action taken by the Administrator with respect to the proposed map or an appeal relating to the proposed map.

(2) REQUIRED ACTIVITIES.—The communication and outreach activities required under paragraph (1) shall include—

(A)   notifying property owners when their properties become included in, or when they are excluded from, an area covered by the mandatory flood insurance purchase requirement under section 102 of the Flood Disaster Protection Act of 1973 (42 U.S.C. 4012a);

(B)   educating property owners regarding the flood risk and reduction of this risk in their community, including the continued flood risks to areas that are no longer subject to the flood insurance mandatory purchase requirement;

(C)   educating property owners regarding the benefits and costs of maintaining or acquiring flood insurance, including, where applicable, lower-cost preferred risk policies under the National Flood Insurance Act of 1968 (42 U.S.C. 4011 et seq.) for such properties and the contents of such properties;

(D)   educating property owners about flood map revisions and the process available to such owners to appeal proposed changes in flood elevations through their community, including by notifying local radio and television stations; and

(E)   encouraging property owners to maintain or acquire flood insurance coverage.

(e) COMMUNITY REMAPPING REQUEST.— Upon the adoption by the Administrator of any recommendation by the Technical Mapping Advisory Council for reviewing, updating, or maintaining National Flood Insurance Program rate maps in accordance with this section, a community that believes that its flood insurance rates in effect prior to adoption would be affected by the adoption of such recommendation may submit a request for an update of its rate maps, which may be considered at the Administrator's sole discretion. The Administrator shall establish a protocol for the evaluation of such community map update requests.

(f) AUTHORIZATION OF APPROPRIATIONS.— There is authorized to be appropriated to the Administrator to carry out this section $400,000,000 for each of fiscal years 2013 through 2017.

* * * * * * *

SEC. 100220. [42 U.S.C. 4101c] COORDINATION.

(a) INTERAGENCY BUDGET CROSSCUT AND COORDINATION REPORT.—

(1) IN GENERAL.— The Secretary of Homeland Security, the Administrator, the Director of the Office of Management and Budget, and the heads of each Federal department or agency carrying out activities under sections 100215 and 100216 shall work together to ensure that flood risk determination data and geospatial data are shared among Federal agencies in order to coordinate the efforts of the Nation to reduce its vulnerability to flooding hazards.

(2) REPORT.—Not later than 30 days after the submission of the budget of the United States Government by the President to Congress, the Director of the Office of Management and Budget, in coordination with the Federal Emergency Management Agency, the United States Geological Survey, the National Oceanic and Atmospheric Administration, the Corps of Engineers, and other Federal agencies, as appropriate, shall submit to the appropriate authorizing and appropriating committees of the Senate and the House of Representatives an interagency budget crosscut and coordination report, certified by the Secretary or head of each such agency, that—

(A)   contains an interagency budget crosscut report that displays relevant sections of the budget proposed for each of the Federal agencies working on flood risk determination data and digital elevation models, including any planned interagency or intra-agency transfers; and

(B)   describes how the efforts aligned with such sections complement one another.

(b) DUTIES OF THE ADMINISTRATOR.—In carrying out sections 100215 and 100216, the Administrator shall—

(1)   participate, pursuant to section 216 of the E-Government Act of 2002 (44 U.S.C. 3501 note), in the establishment of such standards and common protocols as are necessary to assure the interoperability of geospatial data for all users of such information;

(2)   coordinate with, seek assistance and cooperation of, and provide a liaison to the Federal Geographic Data Committee pursuant to the Office of Management and Budget Circular A-16 and Executive Order 12906 (43 U.S.C. 1457 note; relating to the National Spatial Data Infrastructure) for the implementation of and compliance with such standards;

(3)   integrate with, leverage, and coordinate funding of, to the maximum extent practicable, the current flood mapping activities of each unit of State and local government;

(4)   integrate with, leverage, and coordinate, to the maximum extent practicable, the current geospatial activities of other Federal agencies and units of State and local government; and

(5) develop a funding strategy to leverage and coordinate budgets and expenditures, and to maintain or establish joint funding and other agreement mechanisms with other Federal agencies and units of State and local government to share in the collection and utilization of geospatial data among all governmental users.

SEC. 100221. INTERAGENCY COORDINATION STUDY.

(a) In General.—The Administrator shall enter into a contract with the National Academy of Public Administration to conduct a study on how the Federal Emergency Management Agency—

(1) should improve interagency and intergovernmental coordination on flood mapping, including a funding strategy to leverage and coordinate budgets and expenditures; and

(2) can establish joint funding mechanisms with other Federal agencies and units of State and local government to share the collection and utilization of data among all governmental users.

(b) Timing.—A contract entered into under subsection (a) shall require that, not later than 180 days after the date of enactment of this subtitle, the National Academy of Public Administration shall report the findings of the study required under subsection (a) to—

(1) the Committee on Banking, Housing, and Urban Affairs of the Senate;

(2) the Committee on Financial Services of the House of Representatives;

(3) the Committee on Appropriations of the Senate; and

(4) the Committee on Appropriations of the House of Representatives.

* * * * * * *

SEC. 100224. [42 U.S.C. 4081 note] OVERSIGHT AND EXPENSE REIMBURSEMENTS OF INSURANCE COMPANIES.

(a) Submission of Biennial Reports.—

(1) To the administrator.— Not later than 20 days after the date of enactment of this Act, each property and casualty insurance company participating in the Write Your Own program shall submit to the Administrator any biennial report required by the Federal Emergency Management Agency to be prepared in the prior 5 years by such company.

(2) To gao.— Not later than 10 days after the submission of the biennial reports under paragraph (1), the Administrator shall submit all such reports to the Comptroller General of the United States.

(3) Notice to congress of failure to comply.— The Administrator shall notify and report to the Committee on Banking, Housing, and Urban Affairs of the Senate and the Committee on Financial Services of the House of Representatives on any property and casualty insurance company participating in the Write Your Own program that failed to submit its biennial reports as required under paragraph (1).

(4) FAILURE TO COMPLY.— A property and casualty insurance company participating in the Write Your Own program which fails to comply with the reporting requirement under this subsection or the requirement under section 62.23(j)(1) of title 44, Code of Federal Regulations (relating to biennial audit of the flood insurance financial statements) shall be subject to a civil penalty in an amount of not more than $1,000 per day for each day that the company remains in noncompliance with either such requirement.

(b) METHODOLOGY TO DETERMINE REIMBURSED EXPENSES.—Not later than 180 days after the date of enactment of this Act, the Administrator shall develop a methodology for determining the appropriate amounts that property and casualty insurance companies participating in the Write Your Own program should be reimbursed for selling, writing, and servicing flood insurance policies and adjusting flood insurance claims on behalf of the National Flood Insurance Program. The methodology shall be developed using actual expense data for the flood insurance line and can be derived from—

(1)   flood insurance expense data produced by the property and casualty insurance companies;

(2)   flood insurance expense data collected by the National Association of Insurance Commissioners; or

(3)   a combination of the methodologies described in paragraphs (1) and (2).

(c) SUBMISSION OF EXPENSE REPORTS.— To develop the methodology established under subsection (b), the Administrator may require each property and casualty insurance company participating in the Write Your Own program to submit a report to the Administrator, in a format determined by the Administrator and within 60 days of the request, that details the expense levels of each such company for selling, writing, and servicing standard flood insurance policies and adjusting and servicing claims.

(d) FEMA RULEMAKING ON REIMBURSEMENT OF EXPENSES UNDER THE WRITE YOUR OWN PROGRAM.— Not later than 12 months after the date of enactment of this Act, the Administrator shall issue a rule to formulate revised expense reimbursements to property and casualty insurance companies participating in the Write Your Own program for their expenses (including their operating and administrative expenses for adjustment of claims) in selling, writing, and servicing standard flood insurance policies, including how such companies shall be reimbursed in both catastrophic and noncatastrophic years. Such reimbursements shall be structured to ensure reimbursements track the actual expenses, including standard business costs and operating expenses, of such companies as closely as practicably possible.

(e) REPORT OF THE ADMINISTRATOR.—Not later than 60 days after the effective date of the final rule issued pursuant to subsection (d), the Administrator shall submit to the Committee on Banking, Housing, and Urban Affairs of the Senate and the Committee on Financial Services of the House of Representatives a report containing—

(1)   the specific rationale and purposes of such rule;

(2)   the reasons for the adoption of the policies contained in such rule; and

(3)   the degree to which such rule accurately represents the true operating costs and expenses of property and casualty insurance companies participating in the Write Your Own program.

(f) GAO STUDY AND REPORT ON EXPENSES OF WRITE YOUR OWN PROGRAM.—

(1) STUDY.—Not later than 180 days after the effective date of the final rule issued pursuant to subsection (d), the Comptroller General of the United States shall—

(A)   conduct a study on the efficacy, adequacy, and sufficiency of the final rules issued pursuant to subsection (d); and

(B)   report to the Committee on Banking, Housing, and Urban Affairs of the Senate and the Committee on Financial Services of the House of Representatives on the findings of the study conducted under subparagraph (A).

(2) GAO AUTHORITY.—In conducting the study and report required under paragraph (1), the Comptroller General—

(A)   may use any previous findings, studies, or reports that the Comptroller General previously completed on the Write Your Own program;

(B) shall determine if—

(i)   the final rule issued pursuant to subsection (d) allows the Federal Emergency Management Agency to access adequate information regarding the actual expenses of property and casualty insurance companies participating in the Write Your Own program; and

(ii)   the actual reimbursements paid out under the final rule issued pursuant to subsection (d) accurately reflect the expenses reported by property and casualty insurance companies participating in the Write Your Own program, including the standard business costs and operating expenses of such companies; and

(C)   shall analyze the effect of the final rule issued pursuant to subsection (d) on the level of participation of property and casualty insurers in the Write Your Own program.

* * * * * * *

SEC. 100226. [42 U.S.C. 4101 note] FLOOD PROTECTION STRUCTURE ACCREDITATION TASK FORCE.

(a) DEFINITIONS.—In this section—

(1)   the term flood protection structure accreditation requirements means the requirements established under section 65.10 of title 44, Code of Federal Regulations, for levee systems to be recognized on maps created for purposes of the National Flood Insurance Program;

(2)   the term National Committee on Levee Safety means the Committee on Levee Safety established under section 9003 of the National Levee Safety Act of 2007 (33 U.S.C. 3302); and

(3)   the term task force means the Flood Protection Structure Accreditation Task Force established under subsection (b).

(b) ESTABLISHMENT.—

(1) IN GENERAL.— The Administrator and the Secretary of the Army, acting

through the Chief of Engineers, in cooperation with the National Committee on Levee Safety, shall jointly establish a Flood Protection Structure Accreditation Task Force.

(2) DUTIES.—

(A) DEVELOPING PROCESS.—The task force shall develop a process to better align the information and data collected by or for the Corps of Engineers under the Inspection of Completed Works Program with the flood protection structure accreditation requirements so that—

(i) information and data collected for either purpose can be used interchangeably; and

(ii) information and data collected by or for the Corps of Engineers under the Inspection of Completed Works Program is sufficient to satisfy the flood protection structure accreditation requirements.

(B) GATHERING RECOMMENDATIONS.— The task force shall gather, and consider in the process developed under subparagraph (A), recommendations from interested persons in each region relating to the information, data, and accreditation requirements described in subparagraph (A).

(3) CONSIDERATIONS.—In developing the process under paragraph (2), the task force shall consider changes to—

(A) the information and data collected by or for the Corps of Engineers under the Inspection of Completed Works Program; and

(B) the flood protection structure accreditation requirements.

(4) RULE OF CONSTRUCTION.— Nothing in this section shall be construed to require a reduction in the level of public safety and flood control provided by accredited levees, as determined by the Administrator for purposes of this section.

(c) IMPLEMENTATION.— The Administrator and the Secretary of the Army, acting through the Chief of Engineers, shall implement the process developed by the task force under subsection (b) not later than 1 year after the date of enactment of this Act and shall complete the process under subsection (b) not later than 2 years after the date of enactment of this Act.

(d) REPORTS.—The Administrator and the Secretary of the Army, acting through the Chief of Engineers, in cooperation with the National Committee on Levee Safety, shall jointly submit to the Committee on Banking, Housing, and Urban Affairs and the Committee on Environment and Public Works of the Senate and the Committee on Financial Services, the Committee on Transportation and Infrastructure, and the Committee on Natural Resources of the House of Representatives reports concerning the activities of the task force and the implementation of the process developed by the task force under subsection (b), including—

(1) an interim report, not later than 180 days after the date of enactment of this Act; and

(2) a final report, not later than 1 year after the date of enactment of this Act.

(e) TERMINATION.— The task force shall terminate on the date of submission of the report under subsection (d)(2).

;C. 100227. [42 U.S.C. 4011 note] FLOOD IN
ROGRESS DETERMINATIONS.

Biggert-Waters Flood Insurance Reform Act of
2012

SEC. 100227. [42 U.S.C. 4011 note] FLOOD IN PROGRESS DETERMINATIONS.

(a) REPORT.—

(1) REVIEW.—The Administrator shall review—

(A) the processes and procedures for determining that a flood event has commenced or is in progress for purposes of flood insurance coverage made available under the National Flood Insurance Program;

(B) the processes and procedures for providing public notification that such a flood event has commenced or is in progress;

(C) the processes and procedures regarding the timing of public notification of flood insurance requirements and availability; and

(D) the effects and implications that weather conditions, including rainfall, snowfall, projected snowmelt, existing water levels, and other conditions, have on the determination that a flood event has commenced or is in progress.

(2) REPORT.—Not later than 6 months after the date of enactment of this Act, the Administrator shall submit a report to Congress that describes—

(A) the results and conclusions of the review under paragraph (1); and

(B) any actions taken, or proposed actions to be taken, by the Administrator to provide for more precise and technical processes and procedures for determining that a flood event has commenced or is in progress.

(b) EFFECTIVE DATE OF POLICIES COVERING PROPERTIES AFFECTED BY FLOODING OF THE MISSOURI RIVER IN 2011.—

(1) ELIGIBLE COVERAGE.— For purposes of this subsection, the term eligible coverage means coverage under a new contract for flood insurance coverage under the National Flood Insurance Program, or a modification to coverage under an existing flood insurance contract, for property damaged by the flooding of the Missouri River that commenced on June 1, 2011, that was purchased or made during the period beginning May 1, 2011, and ending June 6, 2011.

(2) EFFECTIVE DATES.—Notwithstanding section 1306(c) of the National Flood Insurance Act of 1968 (42 U.S.C. 4013(c)), or any other provision of law, any eligible coverage shall—

(A) be deemed to take effect on the date that is 30 days after the date on which all obligations for the eligible coverage (including completion of the application and payment of any initial premiums owed) are satisfactorily completed; and

(B) cover damage to property occurring after the effective date described in subparagraph (A) that resulted from the flooding of the Missouri River that commenced on June 1, 2011, if the property did not suffer damage or loss as a result of such flooding before the effective date described in subparagraph (A).

(c) TIMELY NOTIFICATION.— Not later than 90 days after the date on which the Administrator submits the report required under subsection (a)(2), the Administrator shall, taking into consideration the results of the review under subsection (a)(1)(B), develop procedures for providing timely notification, to the extent practicable, to policyholders who have purchased flood insurance coverage under the National Flood Insurance Program within 30 days of a determination of a flood in progress and who may be affected by the flood of the determination and how the determination may affect their coverage.

* * * * * * *

SEC. 100229. LOCAL DATA REQUIREMENT.

(a) IN GENERAL.—Notwithstanding any other provision of this subtitle, no area or community participating in the National Flood Insurance Program that is or includes a community that is identified by the Administrator as Community Identification Number 360467 and impacted by the Jamaica Bay flooding source or identified by the Administrator as Community Identification Number 360495 may be or become designated as an area having special flood hazards for purposes of the National Flood Insurance Program, unless the designation is made on the basis of—

(1) flood hazard analyses of hydrologic, hydraulic, or coastal flood hazards that have been properly calibrated and validated, and are specific and directly relevant to the geographic area being studied; and

(2) ground elevation information of sufficient accuracy and precision to meet the guidelines of the Administration for accuracy at the 95 percent confidence level.

(b) REMAPPING.—

(1) REMAPPING REQUIRED.—If the Administrator determines that an area described in subsection (a) has been designated as an area of special flood hazard on the basis of information that does not comply with the requirements under subsection (a), the Administrator shall revise and update any National Flood Insurance Program rate map for the area—

(A) using information that complies with the requirements under subsection (a); and

(B) in accordance with the procedures established under section 1363 of the National Flood Insurance Act of 1968 (42 U.S.C. 4104) for flood elevation determinations.

(2) INTERIM PERIOD.—A National Flood Insurance Program rate map in effect on the date of enactment of this Act for an area for which the Administrator has made a determination under paragraph (1) shall continue in effect with respect to the area during the period—

(A) beginning on the date of enactment of this Act; and

(B) ending on the date on which the Administrator determines that the requirements under section 1363 of the National Flood Insurance Act of 1968 (42 U.S.C. 4104) for flood elevation determinations have been met with respect to a revision and update under paragraph (1) of a National Flood Insurance Program rate map for the area.

(3) DEADLINE.— The Administrator shall issue a preliminary National Flood Insurance Program rate map resulting from a revision and update required under paragraph (1) not later than 1 year after the date of enactment of this Act.

(4) RISK PREMIUM RATE CLARIFICATION.—

(A) IN GENERAL.—If a revision and update required under paragraph (1) results in a reduction in the risk premium rate for a property in an area for which the Administrator has made a determination under paragraph (1), the Administrator shall—

(i) calculate the difference between the reduced risk premium rate and the risk premium rate paid by a policyholder with respect to the property during the period—

(I) beginning on the date on which the National Flood Insurance Program rate map in effect for the area on the date of enactment of this Act took effect; and

(II) ending on the date on which the revised or updated National Flood Insurance Program rate map takes effect; and

(ii) reimburse the policyholder an amount equal to such difference.

(B) FUNDING.— Notwithstanding section 1310 of the National Flood Insurance Act of 1968 (42 U.S.C. 4017), there shall be available to the Administrator from premiums deposited in the National Flood Insurance Fund pursuant to subsection (d) of such section 1310, of amounts not otherwise obligated, the amount necessary to carry out this paragraph.

(c) TERMINATION.—

(1) IN GENERAL.— Except as provided in paragraph (2), this section shall cease to have effect on the effective date of a National Flood Insurance Program rate map revised and updated under subsection (b)(1).

(2) REIMBURSEMENTS.— Subsection (b)(4) shall cease to have effect on the date on which the Administrator has made all reimbursements required under subsection (b)(4).

SEC. 100230. [42 U.S.C. 4014 note] ELIGIBILITY FOR FLOOD INSURANCE FOR PERSONS RESIDING IN COMMUNITIES THAT HAVE MADE ADEQUATE PROGRESS ON THE RECONSTRUCTION OR IMPROVEMENT OF A FLOOD PROTECTION SYSTEM.

(a) ELIGIBILITY FOR FLOOD INSURANCE COVERAGE.—

(1) IN GENERAL.—Notwithstanding any other provision of law (including section 1307(e) of the National Flood Insurance Act of 1968 (42 U.S.C. 4014(e))), a person residing in a community that the Administrator determines has made adequate progress on the reconstruction or improvement of a flood protection system that will afford flood protection for a 100-year floodplain (without regard to the level of Federal funding of or participation in the construction, reconstruction, or improvement), shall be eligible for flood insurance coverage under the National Flood Insurance Program—

(A) if the person resides in a community that is a participant in the National Flood Insurance Program; and

(B) at a risk premium rate that does not exceed the risk premium rate that would be chargeable if the flood protection system had been completed.

(2) ADEQUATE PROGRESS.—

(A) RECONSTRUCTION OR IMPROVEMENT.—For purposes of paragraph (1), the Administrator shall determine that a community has made adequate progress on the reconstruction or improvement of a flood protection system if—

(i)   100 percent of the project cost has been authorized;

(ii)   not less than 60 percent of the project cost has been secured or appropriated;

(iii)   not less than 50 percent of the flood protection system has been assessed as being without deficiencies; and

(iv)   the reconstruction or improvement has a project schedule that does not exceed 5 years, beginning on the date on which the reconstruction or construction of the improvement commences.

(B) CONSIDERATIONS.— In determining whether a flood protection system has been assessed as being without deficiencies, the Administrator shall consider the requirements under section 65.10 of chapter 44, Code of Federal Regulations, or any successor thereto.

(C) DATE OF COMMENCEMENT.— For purposes of subparagraph (A)(iv) of this paragraph and subsection (b)(2)(B), the date of commencement of the reconstruction or improvement of a flood protection system that is undergoing reconstruction or improvement on the date of enactment of this Act shall be deemed to be the date on which the owner of the flood protection system submits a request under paragraph (3).

(3) REQUEST FOR DETERMINATION.— The owner of a flood protection system that is undergoing reconstruction or improvement on the date of enactment of this Act may submit to the Administrator a request for a determination under paragraph (2) that the community in which the flood protection system is located has made adequate progress on the reconstruction or improvement of the flood protection system.

(4) RULE OF CONSTRUCTION.— Nothing in this subsection shall be construed to prohibit the Administrator from making a determination under paragraph (2) for any community in which a flood protection system is not undergoing reconstruction or improvement on the date of enactment of this Act.

(b) TERMINATION OF ELIGIBILITY.—

(1) ADEQUATE CONTINUING PROGRESS.—The Administrator shall issue rules to establish a method of determining whether a community has made adequate continuing progress on the reconstruction or improvement of a flood protection system that includes—

(A) a requirement that the Administrator shall—

(i) consult with the owner of the flood protection system—

(I)   6 months after the date of a determination under subsection (a);

(II)   18 months after the date of a determination under subsection (a); and

(III)   36 months after the date of a determination under subsection (a); and

(ii)   after each consultation under clause (i), determine whether the reconstruction or improvement is reasonably likely to be completed in accordance with the project schedule described in subsection (a)(2)(A)(iv); and

(B) a requirement that, if the Administrator makes a determination under subparagraph (A)(ii) that reconstruction or improvement is not reasonably likely to be completed in accordance with the project schedule, the Administrator shall—

(i)   not later than 30 days after the date of the determination, notify the owner of the flood protection system of the determination and provide the rationale and evidence for the determination; and

(ii)   provide the owner of the flood protection system the opportunity to appeal the determination.

(2) TERMINATION.—The Administrator shall terminate the eligibility for flood insurance coverage under subsection (a) for persons residing in a community with respect to which the Administrator made a determination under subsection (a) if—

(A)   the Administrator determines that the community has not made adequate continuing progress; or

(B)   on the date that is 5 years after the date on which the reconstruction or construction of the improvement commences, the project has not been completed.

(3) WAIVER.—A person whose eligibility would otherwise be terminated under paragraph (2)(B) shall continue to be eligible to purchase flood insurance coverage described in subsection (a) if the Administrator determines—

(A)   the community has made adequate continuing progress on the reconstruction or improvement of a flood protection system; and

(B)   there is a reasonable expectation that the reconstruction or improvement of the flood protection system will be completed not later than 1 year after the date of the determination under this paragraph.

(4) RISK PREMIUM RATE.— If the Administrator terminates the eligibility of persons residing in a community to purchase flood insurance coverage described in subsection (a), the Administrator shall establish an appropriate risk premium rate for flood insurance coverage under the National Flood Insurance Program for persons residing in the community that purchased flood insurance coverage before the date on which the termination of eligibility takes effect, taking into consideration the then-current state of the flood protection system.

(c) ADDITIONAL AUTHORITY.—

(1) ADDITIONAL AUTHORITY.—Notwithstanding subsection (a), in exceptional and exigent circumstances, the Administrator may, in the Administrator's sole discretion, determine that a person residing in a community, which is a participant in the National Flood Insurance Program, that has begun reconstruction or

improvement of a flood protection system that will afford flood protection for a 100-year floodplain (without regard to the level of Federal funding of or participation in the reconstruction or improvement) shall be eligible for flood insurance coverage under the National Flood Insurance Program at a risk premium rate that does not exceed the risk premium rate that would be chargeable if the flood protection system had been completed, provided—

(A)   the community makes a written request for the determination setting forth the exceptional and exigent circumstances, including why the community cannot meet the criteria for adequate progress set forth in under subsection (a)(2)(A) and why immediate relief is necessary;

(B)   the Administrator submits a written report setting forth findings of the exceptional and exigent circumstances on which the Administrator based an affirmative determination to the Committee on Banking, Housing, and Urban Affairs of the Senate, and the Committee on Financial Services of the House of Representatives not later than 15 days before making the determination; and

(C)   the eligibility for flood insurance coverage at a risk premium rate determined under this subsection terminates no later than 1 year after the date on which the Administrator makes the determination.

(2) LIMITATION.— Upon termination of eligibility under paragraph (1)(C), a community may submit another request pursuant to paragraph (1)(A). The Administrator may make no more than two determinations under paragraph (1) with respect to persons residing within any single requesting community.

(3) TERMINATION.— The authority provided under paragraphs (1) and (2) shall terminate two years after the enactment of this Act.

SEC. 100231. STUDIES AND REPORTS.

(a) REPORT ON IMPROVING THE NATIONAL FLOOD INSURANCE PROGRAM.—Not later than 1 year after the date of enactment of this Act, the Comptroller General of the United States shall conduct a study and submit a report to the Committee on Banking, Housing, and Urban Affairs of the Senate and the Committee on Financial Services of the House of Representatives, on—

(1) the number of flood insurance policy holders currently insuring—

(A) a residential structure up to the maximum available coverage amount, as established in section 61.6 of title 44, Code of Federal Regulations, of—

(i) $250,000 for the structure; and

(ii) $100,000 for the contents of such structure; or

(B)   a commercial structure up to the maximum available coverage amount, as established in section 61.6 of title 44, Code of Federal Regulations, of $500,000;

(2)   the increased losses the National Flood Insurance Program would have sustained during the 2004 and 2005 hurricane season if the National Flood Insurance Program had insured all policyholders up to the maximum conforming loan limit for fiscal year 2006 of $417,000, as established under section 302(b)(2) of the Federal

National Mortgage Association Charter Act (12 U.S.C. 1717(b)(2));

(3) the availability in the private marketplace of flood insurance coverage in amounts that exceed the current limits of coverage amounts established in section 61.6 of title 44, Code of Federal Regulations; and

(4) what effect, if any—

(A) raising the current limits of coverage amounts established in section 61.6 of title 44, Code of Federal Regulations, would have on the ability of private insurers to continue providing flood insurance coverage; and

(B) reducing the current limits of coverage amounts established in section 61.6 of title 44, Code of Federal Regulations, would have on the ability of private insurers to provide sufficient flood insurance coverage to effectively replace the current level of flood insurance coverage being provided under the National Flood Insurance Program.

(b) [42 U.S.C. 4027a] REPORT OF THE ADMINISTRATOR ON ACTIVITIES UNDER THE NATIONAL FLOOD INSURANCE PROGRAM.—

(1) IN GENERAL.— The Administrator shall, on an annual basis, submit a full report on the operations, activities, budget, receipts, and expenditures of the National Flood Insurance Program for the preceding 12-month period to the Committee on Banking, Housing, and Urban Affairs of the Senate and the Committee on Financial Services of the House of Representatives.

(2) TIMING.— Each report required under paragraph (1) shall be submitted to the committees described in paragraph (1) not later than 3 months following the end of each fiscal year.

(3) CONTENTS.—Each report required under paragraph (1) shall include—

(A) the current financial condition and income statement of the National Flood Insurance Fund established under section 1310 of the National Flood Insurance Act of 1968 (42 U.S.C. 4017), including—

(i) premiums paid into such Fund;

(ii) policy claims against such Fund; and

(iii) expenses in administering such Fund;

(B) the number and face value of all policies issued under the National Flood Insurance Program that are in force;

(C) a description and summary of the losses attributable to repetitive loss structures;

(D) a description and summary of all losses incurred by the National Flood Insurance Program due to—

(i) hurricane related damage; and

(ii) nonhurricane related damage;

(E) the amounts made available by the Administrator for mitigation assistance under section 1366(c)(4) of the National Flood Insurance Act of 1968 (42 U.S.C. 4104c(c)(4)), as so redesignated by this Act, for the purchase of properties substantially damaged by flood for that fiscal year, and the actual number of flood damaged properties purchased and the total cost expended to purchase such properties;

(F) the estimate of the Administrator as to the average historical loss year, and the basis for that estimate;

(G) the estimate of the Administrator as to the maximum amount of claims that the National Flood Insurance Program would have to expend in the event of a catastrophic year;

(H) the average—

(i) amount of insurance carried per flood insurance policy;

(ii) premium per flood insurance policy; and

(iii) loss per flood insurance policy; and

(I) the number of claims involving damages in excess of the maximum amount of flood insurance available under the National Flood Insurance Program and the sum of the amount of all damages in excess of such amount.

(c) GAO STUDY ON PRE-FIRM STRUCTURES.—Not later than 1 year after the date of enactment of this Act, the Comptroller General of the United States shall conduct a study and submit a report to the Committee on Banking, Housing, and Urban Affairs of the Senate and the Committee on Financial Services of the House of Representatives, on the—

(1) composition of the remaining pre-FIRM structures that are explicitly receiving discounted premium rates under section 1307 of the National Flood Insurance Act of 1968 (42 U.S.C. 4014), including the historical basis for the receipt of such subsidy and the extent to which pre-FIRM structures are currently owned by the same owners of the property at the time of the original National Flood Insurance Program rate map;

(2) number and fair market value of such structures;

(3) respective income level of the owners of such structures;

(4) number of times each such structure has been sold since 1968, including specific dates, sales price, and any other information the Secretary determines appropriate;

(5) total losses incurred by such structures since the establishment of the National Flood Insurance Program compared to the total losses incurred by all structures that are charged a nondiscounted premium rate;

(6) total cost of foregone premiums since the establishment of the National Flood Insurance Program, as a result of the subsidies provided to such structures;

(7) annual cost as a result of the subsidies provided to such structures;

(8) the premium income collected and the losses incurred by the National Flood Insurance Program as a result of such explicitly subsidized structures compared to the premium income collected and the losses incurred by such Program as a result of structures that are charged a nondiscounted premium rate, on a State-by-State basis; and

(9)   the options for eliminating the subsidy to such structures.

(d) GAO REVIEW OF FEMA CONTRACTORS.—The Comptroller General of the United States, in conjunction with the Office of the Inspector General of the Department of Homeland Security, shall—

(1)   conduct a review of the 3 largest contractors the Administrator uses in administering the National Flood Insurance Program; and

(2)   not later than 18 months after the date of enactment of this Act, submit a report on the findings of such review to the Administrator, the Committee on Banking, Housing, and Urban Affairs of the Senate, and the Committee on Financial Services of the House of Representatives.

(e) STUDY AND REPORT ON GRADUATED RISK.—

(1) STUDY.—

(A) STUDY REQUIRED.— The Administrator shall enter into a contract under which the National Academy of Sciences shall conduct a study exploring methods for understanding graduated risk behind levees and the associated land development, insurance, and risk communication dimensions.

(B) CONTENTS OF STUDY.—The study under this paragraph shall—

(i)   research, review, and recommend current best practices for estimating direct annualized flood losses behind levees for residential and commercial structures;

(ii)   rank each best practice recommended under clause (i) based on the best value, balancing cost, scientific integrity, and the inherent uncertainties associated with all aspects of the loss estimate, including geotechnical engineering, flood frequency estimates, economic value, and direct damages;

(iii)   research, review, and identify current best floodplain management and land use practices behind levees that effectively balance social, economic, and environmental considerations as part of an overall flood risk management strategy;

(iv)   identify areas in which the best floodplain management and land use practices described in clause (iii) have proven effective and recommend methods and processes by which such practices could be applied more broadly across the United States, given the variety of different flood risks, State and local legal frameworks, and evolving judicial opinions;

(v)   research, review, and identify a variety of flood insurance pricing options for flood hazards behind levees that are actuarially sound and based on the flood risk data developed using the 3 best practices recommended under clause (i) that have the best value as determined under clause (ii);

(vi)   evaluate and recommend methods to reduce insurance costs through creative arrangements between insureds and insurers while keeping a clear accounting of how much financial risk is being borne by various parties such that the entire risk is accounted for, including establishment of explicit limits on disaster aid or other assistance in the event of a flood; and

(vii) taking into consideration the recommendations under clauses (i) through (iii), recommend approaches to communicate the associated risks to community officials, homeowners, and other residents of communities.

(2) REPORT.— The contract under paragraph (1)(A) shall provide that not later than 12 months after the date of enactment of this Act, the National Academy of Sciences shall submit to the Committee on Banking, Housing, and Urban Affairs of the Senate and the Committee on Financial Services and the Committee on Science, Space, and Technology of the House of Representatives a report on the study under paragraph (1) that includes the information and recommendations required under paragraph (1).

SEC. 100232. REINSURANCE.

(a) FEMA AND GAO REPORTS ON PRIVATIZATION.—Not later than 18 months after the date of enactment of this Act, the Administrator and the Comptroller General of the United States shall each—

(1) conduct a separate study to assess a broad range of options, methods, and strategies for privatizing the National Flood Insurance Program; and

(2) submit a report to the Committee on Financial Services of the House of Representatives and the Committee on Banking, Housing, and Urban Affairs of the Senate with recommendations for the best manner to accomplish the privatization described in paragraph (1).

(b) PRIVATE RISK-MANAGEMENT INITIATIVES.— The Administrator may carry out such private risk-management initiatives as are otherwise authorized under applicable law, as the Administrator considers appropriate to determine the capacity of private insurers, reinsurers, and financial markets to assist communities, on a voluntary basis only, in managing the full range of financial risks associated with flooding.

(c) REINSURANCE ASSESSMENT.—

(1) PRIVATE MARKET PRICING ASSESSMENT.—Not later than 12 months after the date of enactment of this Act, the Administrator shall submit to Congress a report that—

(A) assesses the capacity of the private reinsurance, capital, and financial markets to assist communities, on a voluntary basis, in managing the full range of financial risks associated with flooding by requesting proposals to assume a portion of the insurance risk of the National Flood Insurance Program;

(B) describes any responses to the request for proposals under subparagraph (A);

(C) assesses whether the rates and terms contained in any proposals received by the Administrator are—

(i) reasonable and appropriate; and

(ii) in an amount sufficient to maintain the ability of the National Flood Insurance Program to pay claims;

(D) describes the extent to which carrying out the proposals received by the Administrator would minimize the likelihood that the Administrator would use the borrowing authority under section 1309 of the National Flood Insurance Act of 1968 (42 U.S.C. 4016);

(E) describes fluctuations in historical reinsurance rates; and

(F) includes an economic cost-benefit analysis of the impact on the National Flood Insurance Program if the Administrator were to exercise the authority under section 1335(a)(2) of the National Flood Insurance Act of 1968 (42 U.S.C. 4055(a)(2)), as added by this section, to secure reinsurance of coverage provided by the National Flood Insurance Program from the private market.

(2) PROTOCOL FOR RELEASE OF DATA.— The Administrator shall develop a protocol, including adequate privacy protections, to provide for the release of data sufficient to conduct the assessment required under paragraph (1).

* * * * * * *

(e) [42 U.S.C. 4027b] ASSESSMENT OF CLAIMS-PAYING ABILITY.—

(1) ASSESSMENT.—

(A) ASSESSMENT REQUIRED.—

(i) IN GENERAL.— Not later than September 30 of each year, the Administrator shall conduct an assessment of the ability of the National Flood Insurance Program to pay claims.

(ii) PRIVATE MARKET REINSURANCE.— The assessment under this paragraph for any year in which the Administrator exercises the authority under section 1335(a)(2) of the National Flood Insurance Act of 1968 (42 U.S.C. 4055(a)(2)), as added by this section, to secure reinsurance of coverage provided by the National Flood Insurance Program from the private market shall include information relating the use of private sector reinsurance and reinsurance equivalents by the Administrator, whether or not the Administrator used the borrowing authority under section 1309 of the National Flood Insurance Act of 1968 (42 U.S.C. 4016).

(iii) FIRST ASSESSMENT.— The Administrator shall conduct the first assessment required under this paragraph not later than September 30, 2012.

(B) CONSIDERATIONS.— In conducting an assessment under subparagraph (A), the Administrator shall take into consideration regional concentrations of coverage written by the National Flood Insurance Program, peak flood zones, and relevant mitigation measures.

(2) ANNUAL REPORT OF THE ADMINISTRATOR OF ACTIVITIES UNDER THE NATIONAL FLOOD INSURANCE PROGRAM.—The Administrator shall—

(A) include the results of each assessment in the report required under section 100231(b); and

(B) not later than 30 days after the date on which the Administrator completes an assessment required under paragraph (1), make the results of the assessment available to the public.

SEC. 100233. GAO STUDY ON BUSINESS INTERRUPTION AND ADDITIONAL LIVING

EXPENSES COVERAGES.

(a) STUDY.—The Comptroller General of the United States shall conduct a study concerning—

(1) the availability of additional living expenses and business interruption coverage in the private marketplace for flood insurance;

(2) the feasibility of allowing the National Flood Insurance Program to offer such coverage at the option of the consumer;

(3) the estimated cost to consumers if the National Flood Insurance Program priced such optional coverage at true actuarial rates;

(4) the impact such optional coverage would have on consumer participation in the National Flood Insurance Program; and

(5) the fiscal impact such optional coverage would have upon the National Flood Insurance Fund if such optional coverage were included in the National Flood Insurance Program, as described in paragraph (2), at the price described in paragraph (3).

(b) REPORT.— Not later than 1 year after the date of enactment of this Act, the Comptroller General shall submit to the Committee on Banking, Housing, and Urban Affairs of the Senate and the Committee on Financial Services of the House of Representatives a report containing the results of the study under subsection (a).

SEC. 100234. [42 U.S.C. 4013a] POLICY DISCLOSURES.

(a) IN GENERAL.— Notwithstanding any other provision of law, in addition to any other disclosures that may be required, each policy under the National Flood Insurance Program shall state all conditions, exclusions, and other limitations pertaining to coverage under the subject policy, regardless of the underlying insurance product, in plain English, in boldface type, and in a font size that is twice the size of the text of the body of the policy.

(b) VIOLATIONS.— The Administrator may impose a civil penalty of not more than $50,000 on any person that fails to comply with subsection (a).

SEC. 100235. REPORT ON INCLUSION OF BUILDING CODES IN FLOODPLAIN MANAGEMENT CRITERIA.

Not later than 6 months after the date of enactment of this Act, the Administrator of the Federal Emergency Management Agency shall conduct a study and submit a report to the Committee on Banking, Housing, and Urban Affairs of the Senate and the Committee on Financial Services of the House of Representatives regarding the impact, effectiveness, and feasibility of amending section 1361 of the National Flood Insurance Act of 1968 (42 U.S.C. 4102) to include widely used and nationally recognized building codes as part of the floodplain management criteria developed under such section, and shall determine—

(1) the regulatory, financial, and economic impacts of such a building code requirement on homeowners, States and local communities, local land use policies, and the Federal Emergency Management Agency;

(2) the resources required of State and local communities to administer and enforce

such a building code requirement;

(3) the effectiveness of such a building code requirement in reducing flood-related damage to buildings and contents;

(4) the impact of such a building code requirement on the actuarial soundness of the National Flood Insurance Program;

(5) the effectiveness of nationally recognized codes in allowing innovative materials and systems for flood-resistant construction;

(6) the feasibility and effectiveness of providing an incentive in lower premium rates for flood insurance coverage under such Act for structures meeting whichever of such widely used and nationally recognized building codes or any applicable local building codes provides greater protection from flood damage;

(7) the impact of such a building code requirement on rural communities with different building code challenges than urban communities; and

(8) the impact of such a building code requirement on Indian reservations.

SEC. 100236. STUDY OF PARTICIPATION AND AFFORDABILITY FOR CERTAIN POLICYHOLDERS.

(a) FEMA STUDY.—The Administrator shall conduct a study of—

(1) methods to encourage and maintain participation in the National Flood Insurance Program;

(2) methods to educate consumers about the National Flood Insurance Program and the flood risk associated with their property;

(3) methods for establishing an affordability framework for the National Flood Insurance Program, including methods to aid individuals to afford risk-based premiums under the National Flood Insurance Program through targeted assistance rather than generally subsidized rates, including means-tested vouchers;

(4) the implications for the National Flood Insurance Program and the Federal budget of using each such method;

(5) options for maintaining affordability if annual premiums for flood insurance coverage were to increase to an amount greater than 2 percent of the liability coverage amount under the policy, including options for enhanced mitigation assistance and means-tested assistance;

(6) the effects that the establishment of catastrophe savings accounts would have regarding long-term affordability of flood insurance coverage; and

(7) options for modifying the surcharge under 1308A, including based on homeowner income, property value or risk of loss.

(b) NATIONAL ACADEMY OF SCIENCES ECONOMIC ANALYSIS.— To inform the Administrator in the conduct of the study under subsection (a), the Administrator shall enter into a contract under which the National Academy of Sciences, in consultation with the Comptroller General of the United States, shall conduct and submit to the Administrator an economic analysis of the costs and benefits to the Federal Government of a flood insurance program with full risk-based premiums, combined with means-tested Federal assistance to aid individuals who cannot afford coverage, through an insurance voucher program. The analysis shall compare the costs of a program of risk-based rates and means-tested assistance to the current system of subsidized flood insurance rates and federally funded disaster relief for people without coverage.

(c) REPORT.— Not later than 270 days after the date of enactment of this Act, the Administrator shall submit to the Committee on Banking, Housing, and Urban Affairs of the Senate and the Committee on Financial Services of the House of Representatives a report that contains the results of the study and analysis under this section.

(d) FUNDING.— Notwithstanding section 1310 of the National Flood Insurance Act of 1968 (42 U.S.C. 4017), there shall be available to the Administrator from the National Flood Insurance Fund, of amounts not otherwise obligated, not more than $2,500,000 to carry out this section.

SEC. 100237. STUDY AND REPORT CONCERNING THE PARTICIPATION OF INDIAN TRIBES AND MEMBERS OF INDIAN TRIBES IN THE NATIONAL FLOOD INSURANCE PROGRAM.

(a) DEFINITION.— In this section, the term Indian tribe has the meaning given that term in section 4 of the Indian Self-Determination and Education Assistance Act (25 U.S.C. 450b).

(b) FINDINGS.— Congress finds that participation by Indian tribes in the National Flood Insurance Program is low. Only 45 of 565 Indian tribes participate in the National Flood Insurance Program.

(c) STUDY.—The Comptroller General of the United States, in coordination and consultation with Indian tribes and members of Indian tribes throughout the United States, shall carry out a study that examines—

(1) the factors contributing to the current rates of participation by Indian tribes and members of Indian tribes in the National Flood Insurance Program; and

(2) methods of encouraging participation by Indian tribes and members of Indian tribes in the National Flood Insurance Program.

(d) REPORT.—Not later than 6 months after the date of enactment of this Act, the Comptroller General shall submit to Congress a report that—

(1) contains the results of the study carried out under subsection (c);

(2) describes the steps that the Administrator should take to increase awareness and encourage participation by Indian tribes and members of Indian tribes in the National Flood Insurance Program; and

(3) identifies any legislative changes that would encourage participation by Indian tribes and members of Indian tribes in the National Flood Insurance Program.

* * * * * * *

SEC. 100240. LEVEES CONSTRUCTED ON CERTAIN PROPERTIES.

(a) DEFINITION.—In this section, the term covered hazard mitigation land means land that—

(1) was acquired and deed restricted under section 1366 of the National Flood

Insurance Act of 1968 (42 U.S.C. 4104c) during the period beginning on January 1, 1999, and ending December 31, 2011;

(2) is located at—

(A) 1029 Oak Street, Fargo, North Dakota;

(B) 27 South Terrace, Fargo, North Dakota;

(C) 1033 Oak Street, Fargo, North Dakota;

(D) 308 Schnell Drive, Oxbow, North Dakota; or

(E) 306 Schnell Drive, Oxbow, North Dakota; and

(3) is located in a community that—

(A) is participating in the National Flood Insurance Program on the date on which a State, local, or tribal government submits an application requesting to construct a permanent flood risk reduction levee under subsection (b); and

(B) certifies to the Administrator and the Chief of Engineers that the community will continue to participate in the National Flood Insurance Program.

(b) AUTHORITY.—Notwithstanding any other prohibition on construction on property acquired with funding from the Federal Emergency Management Agency for conversion to open space purposes, the Administrator shall allow the construction of a permanent flood risk reduction levee by a State, local, or tribal government on covered hazard mitigation land if—

(1) the Administrator and the Chief of Engineers make a determination that—

(A) construction of the proposed permanent flood risk reduction levee would more effectively mitigate against flooding risk than an open floodplain or other flood risk reduction measures;

(B) the proposed permanent flood risk reduction levee complies with Federal, State, and local requirements, including mitigation of adverse impacts and implementation of floodplain management requirements, which shall include an evaluation of whether the construction, operation, and maintenance of the proposed levee—

(i) would continue to meet best available industry standards and practices;

(ii) would be the most cost-effective measure to protect against the assessed flood risk; and

(iii) minimizes future costs to the Federal Government;

(C) the State, local, or tribal government seeking to construct the proposed permanent flood risk reduction levee has provided an adequate maintenance plan that documents the procedures the State, local, or tribal government will use to ensure that the stability, height, and overall integrity of the proposed levee and the structure and systems of the proposed levee are maintained, including—

(i) specifying the maintenance activities to be performed;

(ii) specifying the frequency with which maintenance activities will be performed;

(iii) specifying the person responsible for performing each maintenance activity (by name or title);

(iv) detailing the plan for financing the maintenance of the levee; and

(v) documenting the ability of the State, local, or tribal government to finance the maintenance of the levee; and

(2) before the commencement of construction, the State, local, or tribal government provides to the Administrator an amount—

(A) equal to the Federal share of all project costs previously provided by the Administrator under the applicable program for each deed restricted parcel of the covered hazard mitigation land, which the Administrator shall deposit in the National Flood Insurance Fund; and

(B) that does not include any Federal funds.

(c) MAINTENANCE CERTIFICATION.—

(1) IN GENERAL.— A State, local, or tribal government that constructs a permanent flood risk reduction levee under subsection (b) shall submit to the Administrator and the Chief of Engineers an annual certification indicating whether the State, local, or tribal government is in compliance with the maintenance plan provided under subsection (b)(1)(C).

(2) REVIEW.— The Chief of Engineers shall review each certification submitted under paragraph (1) and determine whether the State, local, or tribal government has complied with the maintenance plan.

* * * * * * *

SEC. 100243. CDBG ELIGIBILITY FOR FLOOD INSURANCE OUTREACH ACTIVITIES AND COMMUNITY BUILDING CODE ADMINISTRATION GRANTS.

* * * * * * *

(b) SUNSET.—Effective on the date that is 2 years after the date of enactment of this Act, section 105(a) of the Housing and Community Development Act of 1974 (42 U.S.C. 5305(a)) is amended—

(1) in paragraph (25), as so redesignated by subsection (a) of this subsection, by adding and at the end;

(2) in paragraph (26), as so redesignated by subsection (a) of this subsection, by striking the semicolon at the end and inserting a period; and

(3) by striking paragraphs (27) and (28), as added by subsection (a) of this subsection.

* * * * * * *

SEC. 100247. FIO STUDY ON RISKS, HAZARDS, AND INSURANCE.

(a) IN GENERAL.— Not later than 1 year after the date of enactment of this Act, the Director of the Federal Insurance Office shall conduct a study and submit to the Committee on Banking, Housing, and Urban Affairs of the Senate and the Committee on Financial Services of the House of Representatives a report providing an assessment of the current state of the market for natural catastrophe insurance in the United States.

(b) FACTORS.—The study and report required under subsection (a) shall assess—

(1)   the current condition of, as well as the outlook for, the availability and affordability of insurance for natural catastrophe perils in all regions of the United States;

(2)   the current ability of States, communities, and individuals to mitigate their natural catastrophe risks, including the affordability and feasibility of such mitigation activities;

(3)   the current state of catastrophic insurance and reinsurance markets and the current approaches in providing insurance protection to different sectors of the population of the United States;

(4)   the current financial condition of State residual markets and catastrophe funds in high-risk regions, including the likelihood of insolvency following a natural catastrophe, the concentration of risks within such funds, the reliance on post-event assessments and State funding, and the adequacy of rates; and

(5)   the current role of the Federal Government and State and local governments in providing incentives for feasible risk mitigation efforts and the cost of providing post-natural catastrophe aid in the absence of insurance.

(c) ADDITIONAL FACTORS.— The study and report required under subsection (a) shall also contain an assessment of current approaches to insuring natural catastrophe risks in the United States and such other information as the Director of the Federal Insurance Office determines necessary or appropriate.

(d) CONSULTATION.— In carrying out the study and report under subsection (a), the Director of the Federal Insurance Office shall consult with the National Academy of Sciences, State insurance regulators, consumer organizations, representatives of the insurance and reinsurance industry, policyholders, and other organizations and experts, as appropriate.

SEC. 100248. FLOOD PROTECTION IMPROVEMENTS CONSTRUCTED ON CERTAIN PROPERTIES.

(a) DEFINITION.—In this section, the term covered hazard mitigation land means land that—

(1)   was acquired and deed restricted under section 1366 of the National Flood Insurance Act of 1968 (42 U.S.C. 4104c) during the period beginning on March 1, 2008, and ending on December 31, 2008;

(2)   is located at—

(A)   809 East Main Cross Street, Findlay, Ohio, 45840;

(B)   801 East Main Cross Street, Findlay, Ohio, 45840;

(C)   725 East Main Cross Street, Findlay, Ohio, 45840; or

(D)   631 East Main Cross Street, Findlay, Ohio, 45840; and

(3) is located in a community that—

(A)   is participating in the National Flood Insurance Program on the date on which a State, local, or tribal government submits an application requesting to construct a flood protection improvement under subsection (b); and

(B)   certifies to the Administrator and the Chief of Engineers that the community will continue to participate in the National Flood Insurance Program.

(b) AUTHORITY.—Notwithstanding any other prohibition on construction on property acquired with funding from the Federal Emergency Management Agency for conversion to open space purposes, the Administrator shall allow the construction of a flood protection improvement by a State, local, or tribal government on covered hazard mitigation land if—

(1) the Administrator and the Chief of Engineers make a determination that—

(A)   construction of the proposed flood protection improvement would more effectively mitigate against flooding risk than an open floodplain or other flood risk reduction measures;

(B) the proposed flood protection improvement complies with Federal, State, and local requirements, including mitigation of adverse impacts and implementation of floodplain management requirements, which shall include an evaluation of whether the construction, operation, and maintenance of the proposed flood protection improvement—

(i)   would continue to meet best available industry standards and practices;

(ii)   would be the most cost-effective measure to protect against the assessed flood risk; and

(iii)   minimizes future costs to the Federal Government;

(C) the State, local, or tribal government seeking to construct the flood protection improvement has provided an adequate maintenance plan that documents the procedures the State, local, or tribal government will use to ensure that the stability, height, and overall integrity of the proposed flood protection improvement and the structure and systems of the proposed flood protection improvement are maintained, including—

(i)   specifying the maintenance activities to be performed;

(ii)   specifying the frequency with which maintenance activities will be performed;

(iii)   specifying the person responsible for performing each maintenance activity (by name or title);

(iv)   detailing the plan for financing the maintenance of the flood protection improvement; and

(v)   documenting the ability of the State, local, or tribal government to finance the maintenance of the flood protection improvement; and

(2) before the commencement of construction, the State, local, or tribal government provides to the Administrator an amount—

(A) equal to the Federal share of all project costs previously provided by the Administrator under the applicable program for each deed restricted parcel of the covered hazard mitigation land, which the Administrator shall deposit in the National Flood Insurance Fund; and

(B) that does not include any Federal funds.

(c) MAINTENANCE CERTIFICATION.—

(1) IN GENERAL.— A State, local, or tribal government that constructs a flood protection improvement under subsection (b) shall submit to the Administrator and the Chief of Engineers an annual certification indicating whether the State, local, or tribal government is in compliance with the maintenance plan provided under subsection (b)(1)(C).

(2) REVIEW.— The Chief of Engineers shall review each certification submitted under paragraph (1) and determine whether the State, local, or tribal government has complied with the maintenance plan.

SEC. 100249. [42 U.S.C. 4130] NO CAUSE OF ACTION.

No cause of action shall exist and no claim may be brought against the United States for violation of any notification requirement imposed upon the United States by this subtitle or any amendment made by this subtitle.

★

HOMEOWNER FLOOD INSURANCE
AFFORDABILITY ACT OF 2014

PUBLIC LAW 113–89

HOMEOWNER FLOOD INSURANCE AFFORDABILITY ACT OF 2014

[(Public Law 113–89)]

[This law has not been amended]

AN ACT To delay the implementation of certain provisions of the Biggert-Waters Flood Insurance Reform Act of 2012, and for other purposes.

Be it enacted by the Senate and House of Representatives of the United States of America in Congress assembled,

SECTION 1. SHORT TITLE AND TABLE OF CONTENTS.

(a) [42 U.S.C. 4001 note] SHORT TITLE.— This Act may be cited as the "Homeowner Flood Insurance Affordability Act of 2014".

(b) TABLE OF CONTENTS.— The table of contents for this Act is as follows:

SEC. 2. [42 U.S.C. 4005] DEFINITIONS.

For purposes of this title, the following definitions shall apply:

(1) ADMINISTRATOR.— The term Administrator means the Administrator of the Federal Emergency Management Agency.

(2) NATIONAL FLOOD INSURANCE PROGRAM.— The term National Flood Insurance Program means the program established under the National Flood Insurance Act of 1968 (42 U.S.C. 4001 et seq.).

SEC. 3. [42 U.S.C. 4014 note] REPEAL OF CERTAIN RATE INCREASES.

(a) REPEAL.—

(1) IN GENERAL.—Section 1307(g) of the National Flood Insurance Act of 1968 (42 U.S.C. 4014(g)) is amended—

(A) by striking paragraphs (1) and (2);

(B) in paragraph (3), by striking as a result of the deliberate choice of the holder of such policy and inserting , unless the decision of the policy holder to permit a lapse in flood insurance coverage was as a result of the property covered by the policy no longer being required to retain such coverage; and

(C) by redesignating paragraphs (3) and (4) as paragraphs (1) and (2), respectively.

(2) EFFECTIVE DATE.— The Administrator shall make available such rate tables, as necessary to implement the amendments made by paragraph (1) as if it were enacted as part of the Biggert-Waters Flood Insurance Reform Act of 2012 (Public Law 112-141; 126 Stat. 957).

(3) IMPLEMENTATION, COORDINATION, AND GUIDANCE.—

(A) FACILITATION OF TIMELY REFUNDS.— To ensure the participation of Write Your Own companies (as such term is defined in section 100202(a) of the Biggert-Waters Flood Insurance Reform Act of 2012 (42 U.S.C. 4004(a)), the Administrator and the Federal Emergency Management Agency shall consult with Write Your Own companies throughout the development of guidance and rate tables necessary to implement the provisions of and the amendments made by this Act.

(B) IMPLEMENTATION AND GUIDANCE.— The Administrator shall issue final guidance and rate tables necessary to implement the provisions of and the amendments made by this Act not later than eight months following the date of the enactment of this Act. Write Your Own companies, in coordination with the Federal Emergency Management Agency, shall have not less than six months but not more than eight months following the issuance of such final guidance and rate tables to implement the changes required by such final guidance and rate tables.

(4) REFUND OF EXCESS PREMIUM CHARGES COLLECTED.— The Administrator shall refund directly to insureds any premiums for flood insurance coverage under the National Flood Insurance Program collected in excess of the rates required under the provisions of and amendments made by this section. To allow for necessary and appropriate implementation of such provisions and amendments, any premium changes necessary to implement such provisions and amendments, including any such premium refund due to policy holders, which shall be paid directly by the National Flood Insurance Program, shall not be charged or paid to policyholders by the National Flood Insurance Program until after the Administrator issues guidance and makes available such rate tables to implement the provisions of and amendments made by this Act.

(b) ASSUMPTION OF POLICIES AT EXISTING PREMIUM RATES.— The Administrator shall provide that the purchaser of a property that, as of the date of such purchase, is covered under an existing flood insurance policy under this title may assume such existing policy and coverage for the remainder of the term of the policy at the chargeable premium rates under such existing policy. Such rates shall continue with respect to such property until the implementation of subsection (a).

SEC. 4. RESTORATION OF GRANDFATHERED RATES.

(a) IN GENERAL.—Section 1308 of the National Flood Insurance Act of 1968 (42 U.S.C. 4015) is amended—

(1) by striking subsection (h); and

(2) by redesignating subsection (i) as subsection (h).

(b) [42 U.S.C. 4015 note] EFFECTIVE DATE.— The amendments made by subsection (a) shall take effect as if enacted as part of the Biggert-Waters Flood Insurance Reform Act of 2012 (Public Law 112-141; 126 Stat. 957).

* * * * * * *

SEC. 9. DRAFT AFFORDABILITY FRAMEWORK.

(a) IN GENERAL.— The Administrator shall prepare a draft affordability framework that proposes to address, via programmatic and regulatory changes, the issues of affordability of flood insurance sold under the National Flood Insurance Program, including issues identified in the affordability study required under section 100236 of the Bigger-Waters Flood Insurance Reform Act of 2012 (Public Law 112-141; 126 Stat. 957).

(b) CRITERIA.—In carrying out the requirements under subsection (a), the Administrator shall consider the following criteria:

(1) Accurate communication to consumers of the flood risk associated with their properties.

(2) Targeted assistance to flood insurance policy holders based on their financial ability to continue to participate in the National Flood Insurance Program.

(3)   Individual or community actions to mitigate the risk of flood or lower the cost of flood insurance.

(4)   The impact of increases in risk premium rates on participation in the National Flood Insurance Program.

(5)   The impact flood insurance rate map updates have on the affordability of flood insurance.

(c) DEADLINE FOR SUBMISSION.— Not later than 18 months after the date on which the Administrator submits the affordability study referred to in subsection (a), the Administrator shall submit to the full Committee on Banking, Housing, and Urban Affairs and the full Committee on Appropriations of the Senate and the full Committee on Financial Services and the full Committee on Appropriations of the House of Representatives the draft affordability framework required under subsection (a).

(d) INTERAGENCY AGREEMENTS.—The Administrator may enter into an agreement with another Federal agency to—

(1)   complete the affordability study referred to in subsection (a); or

(2)   prepare the draft affordability framework required under subsection (a).

(e) RULE OF CONSTRUCTION.— Nothing in this section shall be construed to provide the Administrator with the authority to provide assistance to homeowners based on affordability that was not available prior to the enactment of the Biggert-Waters Flood Insurance Reform Act of 2012 (Public Law 112-141; 126 Stat. 916).

* * * * * * *

SEC. 11. MONTHLY INSTALLMENT PAYMENT FOR PREMIUMS.

(a) IN GENERAL.— Subsection (g) of section 1308 of the National Flood Insurance Act of 1968 (42 U.S.C. 4015(g)) is amended by striking either annually or in more frequent installments and inserting annually or monthly.

(b) [42 U.S.C. 4015 note] IMPLEMENTATION.— The Administrator shall implement the requirement under section 1308(g) of the National Flood Insurance Act of 1968, as amended by subsection (a), not later than the expiration of the 18-month period beginning on the date of the enactment of this Act.

* * * * * * *

SEC. 16. AFFORDABILITY STUDY AND REPORT.

(a) STUDY ISSUES.—Subsection (a) of section 100236 of the Biggert-Waters Flood Insurance Reform Act of 2012 (Public Law 112-141; 126 Stat. 957) is amended—

(1)   in paragraph (3), by striking and at the end;

(2)   in paragraph (4), by striking the period at the end and inserting a semicolon; and

(3)   by adding at the end the following new paragraphs:

"(5)   options for maintaining affordability if annual premiums for flood insurance coverage were to increase to an amount greater than 2 percent of the liability coverage amount under the policy, including options for enhanced mitigation assistance and means-tested assistance;

"(6) the effects that the establishment of catastrophe savings accounts would have regarding long-term affordability of flood insurance coverage; and

"(7) options for modifying the surcharge under 1308A, including based on homeowner income, property value or risk of loss.".

(b) TIMING OF SUBMISSION.— Notwithstanding the deadline under section 100236(c) of the Biggert-Waters Flood Insurance Reform Act of 2012 (Public Law 112-141; 126 Stat. 957), not later than 18 months after the date of enactment of this Act, the Administrator shall submit to the full Committee on Banking, Housing, and Urban Affairs and the full Committee on Appropriations of the Senate and the full Committee on Financial Services and the full Committee on Appropriations of the House of Representatives the affordability study and report required under such section 100236.

(c) AFFORDABILITY STUDY FUNDING.— Section 100236(d) of the Biggert-Waters Flood Insurance Reform Act of 2012 (Public Law 112-141; 126 Stat. 957) is amended by striking $750,000 and inserting $2,500,000.

SEC. 17. [42 U.S.C. 4101d] FLOOD INSURANCE RATE MAP CERTIFICATION.

The Administrator shall implement a flood mapping program for the National Flood Insurance Program, only after review by the Technical Mapping Advisory Council, that, when applied, results in technically credible flood hazard data in all areas where Flood Insurance Rate Maps are prepared or updated, shall certify in writing to the Congress when such a program has been implemented, and shall provide to the Congress the Technical Mapping Advisory Council review report.

* * * * * * *

SEC. 21. [42 U.S.C. 4012a note] TREATMENT OF FLOODPROOFED RESIDENTIAL BASEMENTS.

The Administrator shall continue to extend exceptions and variances for floodproofed basements consistent with section 60.6 of title 44, Code of Federal Regulations, which are effective April 3, 2009; and section 60.3 of such title, which are effective April 3, 2009.

SEC. 22. [42 U.S.C. 4101e] EXEMPTION FROM FEES FOR CERTAIN MAP CHANGE REQUESTS.

Notwithstanding any other provision of law, a requester shall be exempt from submitting a review or processing fee for a request for a flood insurance rate map change based on a habitat restoration project that is funded in whole or in part with Federal or State funds, including dam removal, culvert redesign or installation, or the installation of fish passage.

SEC. 23. STUDY OF VOLUNTARY COMMUNITY-BASED FLOOD INSURANCE OPTIONS.

(a) STUDY.—

(1) STUDY REQUIRED.— The Administrator shall conduct a study to assess

options, methods, and strategies for making available voluntary community-based flood insurance policies through the National Flood Insurance Program.

(2) CONSIDERATIONS.—The study conducted under paragraph (1) shall—

(A) take into consideration and analyze how voluntary community-based flood insurance policies—

(i) would affect communities having varying economic bases, geographic locations, flood hazard characteristics or classifications, and flood management approaches; and

(ii) could satisfy the applicable requirements under section 102 of the Flood Disaster Protection Act of 1973 (42 U.S.C. 4012a); and

(B) evaluate the advisability of making available voluntary community-based flood insurance policies to communities, subdivisions of communities, and areas of residual risk.

(3) CONSULTATION.— In conducting the study required under paragraph (1), the Administrator may consult with the Comptroller General of the United States, as the Administrator determines is appropriate.

(b) REPORT BY THE ADMINISTRATOR.—

(1) REPORT REQUIRED.— Not later than 18 months after the date of enactment of this Act, the Administrator shall submit to the Committee on Banking, Housing, and Urban Affairs of the Senate and the Committee on Financial Services of the House of Representatives a report that contains the results and conclusions of the study conducted under subsection (a).

(2) CONTENTS.—The report submitted under paragraph (1) shall include recommendations for—

(A) the best manner to incorporate voluntary community-based flood insurance policies into the National Flood Insurance Program; and

(B) a strategy to implement voluntary community-based flood insurance policies that would encourage communities to undertake flood mitigation activities, including the construction, reconstruction, or improvement of levees, dams, or other flood control structures.

(c) REPORT BY COMPTROLLER GENERAL.—Not later than 6 months after the date on which the Administrator submits the report required under subsection (b), the Comptroller General of the United States shall—

(1) review the report submitted by the Administrator; and

(2) submit to the Committee on Banking, Housing, and Urban Affairs of the Senate and the Committee on Financial Services of the House of Representatives a report that contains—

(A) an analysis of the report submitted by the Administrator;

(B) any comments or recommendations of the Comptroller General relating to the report submitted by the Administrator; and

(C) any other recommendations of the Comptroller General relating to community-based flood insurance policies.

SEC. 24. [42 U.S.C. 4033] DESIGNATION OF FLOOD INSURANCE ADVOCATE.

(a) IN GENERAL.— The Administrator shall designate a Flood Insurance Advocate to advocate for the fair treatment of policy holders under the National Flood Insurance Program and property owners in the mapping of flood hazards, the identification of risks from flood, and the implementation of measures to minimize the risk of flood.

(b) DUTIES AND RESPONSIBILITIES.—The duties and responsibilities of the Flood Insurance Advocate designated under subsection (a) shall be to—

(1) educate property owners and policyholders under the National Flood Insurance Program on—

(A) individual flood risks;

(B) flood mitigation;

(C) measures to reduce flood insurance rates through effective mitigation;

(D) the flood insurance rate map review and amendment process; and

(E) any changes in the flood insurance program as a result of any newly enacted laws (including this Act);

(2) assist policy holders under the National Flood Insurance Program and property owners to understand the procedural requirements related to appealing preliminary flood insurance rate maps and implementing measures to mitigate evolving flood risks;

(3) assist in the development of regional capacity to respond to individual constituent concerns about flood insurance rate map amendments and revisions;

(4) coordinate outreach and education with local officials and community leaders in areas impacted by proposed flood insurance rate map amendments and revisions; and

(5) aid potential policy holders under the National Flood Insurance Program in obtaining and verifying accurate and reliable flood insurance rate information when purchasing or renewing a flood insurance policy.

SEC. 25. EXCEPTIONS TO ESCROW REQUIREMENT FOR FLOOD INSURANCE PAYMENTS.

(a) IN GENERAL.—Section 102(d)(1) of the Flood Disaster Protection Act of 1973 (42 U.S.C. 4012a(d)(1)) is amended—

(1) in subparagraph (A), in the second sentence, by striking subparagraph (C) and inserting subparagraph (B); and

(2) in subparagraph (B)—

(A) in clause (ii), by redesignating subclauses (I) and (II) as items (aa) and (bb), respectively, and adjusting the margins accordingly;

(B) by redesignating clauses (i) and (ii) as subclauses (I) and (II), respectively, and adjusting the margins accordingly;

(C) in the matter preceding subclause (I), as redesignated by subparagraph

(B), by striking (A) or (B), if— and inserting the following:"(A)   —

"(i)   if—";

(D)   by striking the period at the end and inserting ; or; and

(E)   by adding at the end the following:

"(ii) in the case of a loan that—

"(I)   is in a junior or subordinate position to a senior lien secured by the same residential improved real estate or mobile home for which flood insurance is being provided at the time of the origination of the loan;

"(II) is secured by residential improved real estate or a mobile home that is part of a condominium, cooperative, or other project development, if the residential improved real estate or mobile home is covered by a flood insurance policy that—

"(aa)   meets the requirements that the regulated lending institution is required to enforce under subsection (b)(1);

"(bb)   is provided by the condominium association, cooperative, homeowners association, or other applicable group; and

"(cc)   the premium for which is paid by the condominium association, cooperative, homeowners association, or other applicable group as a common expense;

"(III)   is secured by residential improved real estate or a mobile home that is used as collateral for a business purpose;

"(IV)   is a home equity line of credit;

"(V)   is a nonperforming loan; or

"(VI)   has a term of not longer than 12 months.".

(b) [42 U.S.C. 4012a note] APPLICABILITY.—

(1) IN GENERAL.—

(A) REQUIRED APPLICATION.—   The amendments to section 102(d)(1) of the Flood Disaster Protection Act of 1973 (42 U.S.C. 4012a(d)(1)) made by section 100209(a) of the Biggert-Waters Flood Insurance Reform Act of 2012 (Public Law 112-141; 126 Stat. 920) and by subsection (a) of this section shall apply to any loan that is originated, refinanced, increased, extended, or renewed on or after January 1, 2016.

(B) OPTIONAL APPLICATION.—

(i) DEFINITIONS.—In this subparagraph—

(I)   the terms Federal entity for lending regulation, improved real estate, regulated lending institution, and servicer have the meanings given the terms in section 3 of the Flood Disaster Protection Act of 1973 (42 U.S.C. 4003);

(II) the term outstanding loan means a loan that—

(aa)   is outstanding as of January 1, 2016;

(bb) is not subject to the requirement to escrow premiums and fees for flood insurance under section 102(d)(1) of the Flood Disaster Protection Act of 1973 (42 U.S.C. 4012a(d)(1)) as in effect on July 5, 2012; and

(cc) would, if the loan had been originated, refinanced, increased, extended, or renewed on or after January 1, 2016, be subject to the requirements under section 102(d)(1)(A) of the Flood Disaster Protection Act of 1973, as amended; and

(III) the term section 102(d)(1)(A) of the Flood Disaster Protection Act of 1973, as amended means section 102(d)(1)(A) of the Flood Disaster Protection Act of 1973 (42 U.S.C. 4012a(d)(1)(A)), as amended by—

(aa) section 100209(a) of the Biggert-Waters Flood Insurance Reform Act of 2012 (Public Law 112-141; 126 Stat. 920); and

(bb) subsection (a) of this section.

(ii) OPTION TO ESCROW FLOOD INSURANCE PAYMENTS.— Each Federal entity for lending regulation (after consultation and coordination with the Federal Financial Institutions Examination Council) shall, by regulation, direct that each regulated lending institution or servicer of an outstanding loan shall offer and make available to a borrower the option to have the borrower's payment of premiums and fees for flood insurance under the National Flood Insurance Act of 1968 (42 U.S.C. 4001 et seq.), including the escrow of such payments, be treated in the same manner provided under section 102(d)(1)(A) of the Flood Disaster Protection Act of 1973, as amended.

(2) [42 U.S.C. 4012a note] REPEAL OF 2-YEAR DELAY ON APPLICABILITY.— Subsection (b) of section 100209 of the Biggert-Waters Flood Insurance Reform Act of 2012 (Public Law 112-141; 126 Stat. 920) is repealed.

(3) [42 U.S.C. 4012a note] RULE OF CONSTRUCTION.— Nothing in this section or the amendments made by this section shall be construed to supersede, during the period beginning on July 6, 2012 and ending on December 31, 2015, the requirements under section 102(d)(1) of the Flood Disaster Protection Act of 1973 (42 U.S.C. 4012a(d)(1)), as in effect on July 5, 2012.

SEC. 26. FLOOD MITIGATION METHODS FOR BUILDINGS.

(a) GUIDELINES.—

(1) IN GENERAL.— Section 1361 of the National Flood Insurance Act of 1968 (42 U.S.C. 4102) is amended by adding at the end the following new subsection:

"(d) FLOOD MITIGATION METHODS FOR BUILDINGS. The Administrator shall establish guidelines for property owners that—

"(1) provide alternative methods of mitigation, other than building elevation, to reduce flood risk to residential buildings that cannot be elevated due to their structural characteristics, including—

"(A)   types of building materials; and

"(B)   types of floodproofing; and

"(2)   inform property owners about how the implementation of mitigation methods described in paragraph (1) may affect risk premium rates for flood insurance coverage under the National Flood Insurance Program.".

(2) [42 U.S.C. 4102 note] ISSUANCE.— The Administrator shall issue the guidelines required under section 1361(d) of the National Flood Insurance Act of 1968 (42 U.S.C. 4102(d)), as added by the amendment made by paragraph (1) of this subsection, not later than the expiration of the 1-year period beginning on the date of the enactment of this Act.

(b) CALCULATION OF RISK PREMIUM RATES.— Section 1308 of the National Flood Insurance Act of 1968 (42 U.S.C. 4015), as amended by the preceding provisions of this Act, is further amended by adding at the end the following new subsection:

"(k) CONSIDERATION OF MITIGATION METHODS.   In calculating the risk premium rate charged for flood insurance for a property under this section, the Administrator shall take into account the implementation of any mitigation method identified by the Administrator in the guidance issued under section 1361(d) (42 U.S.C. 4102(d)).".

* * * * * * *

SEC. 31. DISCLOSURE.

(a) [42 U.S.C. 4014 note] CHANGES IN RATES RESULTING FROM THIS ACT.— Not later than the date that is 6 months before the date on which any change in risk premium rates for flood insurance coverage under the National Flood Insurance Program resulting from this Act or any amendment made by this Act is implemented, the Administrator shall make publicly available the rate tables and underwriting guidelines that provide the basis for the change.

(b) REPORT ON POLICY AND CLAIMS DATA.—

(1) IN GENERAL.—Not later than 90 days after the date of enactment of this Act, the Administrator shall submit to the Congress a report on the feasibility of—

(A)   releasing property-level policy and claims data for flood insurance coverage under the National Flood Insurance Program; and

(B)   establishing guidelines for releasing property-level policy and claims data for flood insurance coverage under the National Flood Insurance Program in accordance with section 552a of title 5, United States Code (commonly known as the Privacy Act of 1974).

(2) CONTENTS.—The report submitted under paragraph (1) shall include—

(A)   an analysis and assessment of how releasing property-level policy and claims data for flood insurance coverage under the National Flood Insurance Program will aid policy holders and insurers to understand how the Administration determines actuarial premium rates and assesses flood risks; and

(B)   recommendations for protecting personal information in accordance with section 552a of title 5, United States Code (commonly known as the Privacy Act of 1974).

★

HAZARD-SPECIFIC LAWS
EARTHQUAKES

EARTHQUAKE HAZARDS REDUCTION ACT OF 1977

PUBLIC LAW 95–124
AS AMENDED THROUGH PUB. L. 117–286

EARTHQUAKE HAZARDS REDUCTION ACT OF 1977

[Pub. L. 95–124; Approved Oct. 7, 1977; 91 Stat. 1098]

[As Amended Through P.L. 117–286, Enacted December 27, 2022]

AN ACT To reduce the hazards of earthquakes, and for other purposes.

Be it enacted by the Senate and House of Representatives of the United States of America in Congress assembled,

SECTION 1. [42 U.S.C. 7701 note] SHORT TITLE.

That this Act may be cited as the "Earthquake Hazards Reduction Act of 1977".

SEC. 2. FINDINGS.

The Congress finds and declares the following:

(1) All 50 States, and the Commonwealth of Puerto Rico,[1] are vulnerable to the hazards of earthquakes, and at least 39 of them are subject to major or moderate seismic risk, including Alaska, California, Hawaii, Illinois, Massachusetts, Missouri, Montana, Nevada, New Jersey, New York, Oregon, South Carolina Tennessee,,[2] Utah, and Washington. A large portion of the population of the United States lives in areas vulnerable to earthquake hazards.

---

[1] Section 2(a)(1)(A) in Public Law 115-307 amends paragraph (1) by inserting , and the Commonwealth of Puerto Rico, after States. Such amendment did not specify the occurrence of the word States; however, such amendment was carried out to the first occurrence to reflect the probable intent of Congress.

---

[2] Double commas are so in law. See the amendment made by section 2(a)(1)(C) in Public Law 115-307.

---

(2) Earthquakes have caused, and can cause in the future, enormous loss of life, injury, destruction of property, and economic and social disruption. With respect to future earthquakes, such loss, destruction, and disruption can be substantially reduced through the development and implementation of earthquake hazards reduction measures, including (A) improved design and construction methods and practices, (B) land-use controls and redevelopment, (C) early-warning systems, (D) coordinated emergency preparedness plans, and (E) public education and involvement programs.

(3) An expertly staffed and adequately financed earthquake hazards reduction

program, based on Federal, State, local, and private research, planning, decisionmaking, and contributions would reduce the risk of such loss, destruction, and disruption in seismic areas by an amount far greater than the cost of such program.

(4)   A well-funded seismological research program could provide the scientific understanding needed to fully implement an effective earthquake early warning system.

(5)   The geological study of active faults and features can reveal how recently and how frequently major earthquakes have occurred on those faults and how much risk they pose. Such long-term seismic risk assessments are needed in virtually every aspect of earthquake hazards management, whether emergency planning, public regulation, detailed building design, insurance rating, or investment decision.

(6)   The vulnerability of buildings, lifeline infrastructure, public works, and industrial and emergency facilities can be reduced through proper earthquake resistant design and construction practices. The economy and efficacy of such procedures can be substantially increased through research and development.

(7)   Programs and practices of departments and agencies of the United States are important to the communities they serve; some functions, such as emergency communications and national defense, and lifeline infrastructure, such as dams, bridges, and public works, must remain in service during and after an earthquake. Federally owned, operated, and influenced structures and lifeline infrastructure should serve as models for how to reduce and minimize hazards to the community.

(8)   The implementation of earthquake hazards reduction measures would, as an added benefit, also reduce the risk of loss, destruction, and disruption from other natural hazards and man-made hazards, including hurricanes, tornadoes, accidents, explosions, landslides, building and structural cave-ins, and fires.

(9)   Reduction of loss, destruction, and disruption from earthquakes will depend on the actions of individuals, and organizations in the private sector and governmental units at Federal, State, and local levels. The current capability to transfer knowledge and information to these sectors is insufficient. Improved mechanisms are needed to translate existing information and research findings into reasonable and usable specifications, criteria, and practices so that individuals, organizations, and governmental units may make informed decisions and take appropriate actions.

(10)   Severe earthquakes are a worldwide problem. Since damaging earthquakes occur infrequently in any one nation, international cooperation is desirable for mutual learning from limited experiences.

(11)   An effective Federal program in earthquake hazard reduction will require input from and review by persons outside the Federal Government expert in the sciences of earthquake hazards reduction and in the practical application of earthquake hazards reduction measures.

(12)   The built environment has generally been constructed and maintained to meet the needs of the users under normal conditions. When earthquakes occur, the built environment is generally designed to prevent severe injuries or loss of human life

and is not expected to remain operational or able to recover under any specified schedule.

(13)   The National Research Council published a study on reducing hazards and risks associated with earthquakes based on the goals and objectives for achieving national earthquake resilience described in the strategic plan entitled Strategic Plan for the National Earthquake Hazards Reduction Program. The study and an accompanying report called for work in 18 tasks focused on research, preparedness, and mitigation and annual funding of approximately $300,000,000 per year for 20 years.

[42 U.S.C. 7701]

SEC. 3. PURPOSE.

It is the purpose of the Congress in this Act to reduce the risks of life and property from future earthquakes and increase the resilience of communities in the United States through the establishment and maintenance of an effective earthquake hazards reduction program. The objectives of such program shall include—

(1)   the education of the public, including State and local officials, as to earthquake phenomena, the identification of locations and structures which are especially susceptible to earthquake damage, ways to reduce the adverse consequences of an earthquake to individuals and the communities, and related matters;

(2)   the development of technologically and economically feasible design and construction methods and procedures to make new and existing structures, in areas of seismic risk, earthquake resistant, giving priority to the development of such methods and procedures for power generating plants, dams, hospitals, schools, public utilities and other lifeline infrastructure, public safety structures, high occupancy buildings, and other structures which are especially needed to facilitate community-wide post-earthquake recovery and in times of disaster;

(3)   the implementation to the greatest extent practicable, in all areas of high or moderate seismic risk, of a system (including personnel, technology, and procedures) for identifying, evaluating, and accurately characterizing seismic hazards;

(4)   the development, publication, and promotion, in conjunction with State and local officials and professional organizations, of model building and planning codes and other means to encourage consideration of information about seismic risk in making decisions about land-use policy and construction activity;

(5)   the development, in areas of seismic risk, of improved understanding of, and capability with respect to, earthquake-related issues, including methods of mitigating the risks from earthquakes, planning to prevent such risks, disseminating warnings of earthquakes, organization emergency services, and planning for re-occupancy, recovery, reconstruction, and redevelopment after an earthquake;

(6)   the development of ways to increase the use of existing scientific and engineering knowledge to mitigate earthquake hazards; and

(7)   the development of ways to assure the availability of affordable earthquake insurance.

267

[42 U.S.C. 7702]

SEC. 4. DEFINITIONS.

As used in this Act, unless the context otherwise requires:

(1)　The term includes and variants thereof should be read as if the phrase but is not limited to were also set forth.

(2)　The term Program means the National Earthquake Hazards Reduction Program established under section 5.

(3)　The term seismic and variants thereof mean having to do with, or caused by earthquakes.

(4)　The term State means each of the States of the United States, the District of Columbia, the Commonwealth of Puerto Rico, the Virgin Islands, Guam, American Samoa, the commonwealth of the Mariana Islands, and any other territory or possession of th United States.

(5)　The term United States means, when used in geographical sense, all of the States as defined in section 4(4).

(6)　The term lifeline infrastructure means public works and utilities, including transportation facilities and infrastructure, oil and gas pipelines, electrical power and communication facilities and infrastructure, and water supply and sewage treatment facilities.

(7)　The term Program agencies means the Federal Emergency Management Agency, the United States Geological Survey, the National Science Foundation, and the National Institute of Standards and Technology.

(8)　The term Interagency Coordinating Committee means the Interagency Coordinating Committee on Earthquake Hazards Reduction established under section 5(a).

(9)　The term Advisory Committee means the Advisory Committee established under section 5(a)(5).

(10)　The term community resilience means the ability of a community to prepare and plan for, absorb, recover from, and more successfully adapt to adverse seismic events.

[42 U.S.C. 7703]

SEC. 5. NATIONAL EARTHQUAKE HAZARDS REDUCTION PROGRAM.

(a) ESTABLISHMENT.—

(1) IN GENERAL.— There is established the National Earthquake Hazards Reduction Program.

(2) PROGRAM ACTIVITIES.—The activities of the Program shall be designed to—

(A)　develop effective measures for earthquake hazards reduction;

(B)　promote the adoption of earthquake hazards reduction measures by Federal, State, and local governments, national standards and model code organizations, architects and engineers, building owners, and others with a role in planning and constructing buildings, structures, and lifeline infrastructure through—

(i)   grants, contracts, cooperative agreements, and technical assistance;

(ii)   development of standards, guidelines, and voluntary consensus codes for earthquake hazards reduction for buildings, structures, and lifeline infrastructure;

(iii)   development and maintenance of a repository of information, including technical data, on seismic risk, community resilience, and hazards reduction; and

(iv)   publishing a systematic set of maps of active faults and folds, liquefaction susceptibility, susceptibility for earthquake induced landslides, and other seismically induced hazards; and

(C)   improve the understanding of earthquakes and their effects on communities, buildings, structures, and lifeline infrastructure, through interdisciplinary research that involves engineering, natural sciences, and social, economic, and decisions sciences; and

(D)   continue the development of the Advanced National Seismic System, including earthquake early warning capabilities and the Global Seismographic Network.

(3) INTERAGENCY COORDINATING COMMITTEE ON EARTHQUAKE HAZARDS REDUCTION.—

(A) IN GENERAL.— There is established an Interagency Coordinating Committee on Earthquake Hazards Reduction chaired by the Director of the National Institute of Standards and Technology (referred to in this subsection as the Director).

(B) MEMBERSHIP.—In addition to the Director, the committee shall be composed of—

(i)   the Administrator of the Federal Emergency Management Agency;

(ii)   the Director of the United States Geological Survey;

(iii)   the Director of the National Science Foundation;

(iv)   the Director of the Office of Science and Technology Policy; and

(v)   the Director of the Office of Management and Budget.

(C) MEETINGS.— The Committee shall meet not less frequently than once each year at the call of the Director.

(D) DUTIES.—

(i) GENERAL DUTY.— The Interagency Coordinating Committee shall oversee the planning, management, and coordination of the Program.

(ii) SPECIFIC DUTIES.—The duties of the Interagency Coordinating Committee include the following:

(I) Developing, not later than 6 months after the date of the enactment of the National Earthquake Hazards Reduction Program Reauthorization Act of 2004 and updating periodically—

> (aa)　a strategic plan that establishes goals and priorities for the Program activities described under subsection (a)(2); and

> (bb)　a detailed management plan to implement such strategic plan.

(II)　Developing a coordinated interagency budget for the Program that will ensure appropriate balance among the Program activities described under subsection (a)(2), and, in accordance with the plans developed under subclause (I), submitting such budget to the Director of the Office of Management and Budget at the time designated by the Director for agencies to submit biennial budgets.

(III)　Developing interagency memorandums of understanding with any relevant Federal agencies on data sharing and resource commitment in the event of an earthquake disaster.

(IV)　Coordinating with the Interagency Coordinating Committee on Windstorm Impact Reduction and other natural hazards coordination committees as the Director determines appropriate to share data and best practices.

(V)　Coordinating with the Administrator of the National Aeronautics and Space Administration and the Administrator of the National Oceanic and Atmospheric Administration on data sharing and resource allocation to ensure judicious use of Government resources and the free-flowing exchange of information related to earthquakes.

(VI)　Coordinating with the Secretary of Agriculture and the Secretary of the Interior on the use of public lands for earthquake monitoring and research stations, and related data collection.

(VII)　Coordinating with the Secretary of Transportation and the Secretary of Housing and Urban Development on the effects of earthquakes on transportation and housing stocks.

(iii) ASSISTANCE FROM SECRETARY OF AGRICULTURE AND SECRETARY OF THE INTERIOR.— To the extent practicable, the Secretary of Agriculture and the Secretary of the Interior shall expedite any request for a permit to use public land under clause (ii)(VI).

(4) BIENNIAL REPORT.—

(A) IN GENERAL.—Not less frequently than once every two years, the Interagency Coordinating Committee shall submit to the Committee on Commerce, Science, and Transportation, the Committee on Energy and Natural Resources, and the Committee on Homeland Security and Governmental Affairs of the Senate and the Committee on Science, Space, and Technology, the Committee on Energy and Commerce, the Committee on Natural Resources, and the Committee on Homeland Security of the House of Representatives a report on the Program. Such report shall include—

(i) the Program budget for the current fiscal year for each agency that participates in the Program, and for each major goal established for the Program activities under paragraph (3)(D)(i)(I)[3];

---

[3] Clause (i) of paragraph (3)(D), as amended by section 3(b)(3) of Public Law 115–307, does not contain subclauses.

(ii) the proposed Program budget for the next fiscal year for each agency that participates in the Program, and for each major goal established for the Program activities under paragraph (3)(D)(i)(I)[3];

(iii) a description of the activities and results of the Program during the previous year, including an assessment of the effectiveness of the Program in furthering the goals established in the strategic plan under paragraph (3)(D)(i)(I)[3];

(iv) a description of the extent to which the Program has incorporated the recommendations of the Advisory Committee;

(v) a description of activities, including budgets for the current fiscal year and proposed budgets for the next fiscal year, that are carried out by Program agencies and contribute to the Program, but are not included in the Program;

(vi) a description of the activities, including budgets for the current fiscal year and proposed budgets for the following fiscal year, related to the grant program carried out under subsection (b)(2)(A)(i); and

(vii) a statement regarding whether the Administrator of the Federal Emergency Management Agency has lowered or waived the cost share requirement for assistance provided under subsection (b)(2)(A)(i).

(B) SUPPORT FOR PREPARATION OF REPORT.— Each head of a Program agency shall submit to the Director of the National Institute of Standards and Technology such information as the Director may request for the preparation of a report under subparagraph (A) not later than 90 days after the date on which the Director requests such information.

(5) ADVISORY COMMITTEE.—

(A) IN GENERAL.— The Director shall establish an Advisory Committee on Earthquake Hazards Reduction of at least 11 members, none of whom may be an employee (as defined in subparagraphs (A) through (F) of section 7342(a)(1) of title 5, United States Code, including representatives of research and academic institutions, industry standards development organizations, State and local government, and financial communities who are qualified to provide advice on earthquake hazards reduction and represent all related scientific, architectural, and engineering disciplines. The recommendations of the Advisory Committee shall be considered by Federal agencies in implementing the Program.

(B) ASSESSMENT.—The Advisory Committee shall assess—

(i) trends and developments in the science and engineering of earthquake hazards reduction;

(ii)   effectiveness of the Program in carrying out the activities under (a)(2);

(iii)   the need to revise the Program; and

(iv)   the management, coordination, implementation, and activities of the Program.

(C) REPORT.— Not later than 1 year after the date of enactment of the National Earthquake Hazards Reduction Program Reauthorization Act of 2004 and at least once every 2 years thereafter, the Advisory Committee shall report to the Director on its findings of the assessment carried out under subparagraph (B) and its recommendations for ways to improve the Program. In developing recommendations, the Committee shall consider the recommendations of the United States Geological Survey Scientific Earthquake Studies Advisory Committee.

(D) APPLICATION OF CHAPTER 10 OF TITLE 5, UNITED STATES CODE.— Section 1013 of title 5, United States Code, shall not apply to the Advisory Committee.

(b) RESPONSIBILITIES OF PROGRAM AGENCIES.—

(1) LEAD AGENCY.—The National Institute of Standards and Technology shall have the primary responsibility for planning and coordinating the Program. In carrying out this paragraph, the Director of the Institute shall—

(A)   ensure that the Program includes the necessary steps to promote the implementation of earthquake hazard reduction measures by Federal, State, and local governments, national standards and model building code organizations, architects and engineers, and others with a role in planning and constructing[4] buildings and lifeline infrastructure;

---

[4]   Section 3(c)(1)(A) of Public Law 115-307 amends section 5(b)(1)(A) by striking and constructing[,] and inserting constructing, evaluating, and retrofitting. The amendment could not be carried out due to the inclusion of a comma following constructing in the stricken matter.

(B)   support the development of performance-based seismic engineering tools, and work with appropriate groups to promote the commercial application of such tools, through earthquake-related building codes, standards, and construction practices;

(C)   request the assistance of Federal agencies other than the Program agencies, as necessary to assist in carrying out this Act; and

(D)   work with the Federal Emergency Management Agency, the National Science Foundation[5], and the United States Geological Survey, to develop a comprehensive plan for earthquake engineering research to provide new and effectively use existing testing facilities and laboratories (existing at the time of the development of the plan), upgrade facilities and equipment as needed, and integrate new, innovative testing approaches to the research infrastructure in a systematic manner.

---

[5]   The amendment made by section 103(2)(A)(v) of Public Law 108–360 (118 Stat. 1671) to strike National Science Foundation, the National Institute[s] of Standards and Technology and

insert Federal Emergency Management Agency, the National Science Foundation, was executed by striking National Science Foundation, the National Institute of Standards and Technology in the matter to be struck to reflect the probable intent of Congress.

(2) DEPARTMENT OF HOMELAND SECURITY; FEDERAL EMERGENCY MANAGEMENT AGENCY.—

(A) PROGRAM RESPONSIBILITIES.—The Administrator of the Federal Emergency Management Agency—

(i) shall operate a program of grants and assistance to enable States to develop mitigation, preparedness, and response plans, purchase necessary instrumentation, prepare inventories and conduct seismic safety inspections of critical structures and lifeline infrastructure, update building, land use planning, and zoning codes and ordinances to enhance seismic safety, increase earthquake awareness and education, and provide assistance to multi-State groups for such purposes;

(ii) shall support the implementation of a comprehensive earthquake education, outreach, and public awareness program, including development of materials and their wide dissemination to all appropriate audiences and support public access to locality-specific information that may assist the public in preparing for, mitigating against, responding to and recovering from earthquakes and related disasters;

(iii) shall, in conjunction with the Director of the National Institute of Standards and Technology, other Federal agencies, and private sector groups, use research results to support the preparation, maintenance, and wide dissemination of seismic resistant design guidance and related information on building codes, standards, and practices for new and existing buildings, structures, and lifeline infrastructure, aid in the development of performance-based design guidelines and methodologies, and support model codes that are cost effective and affordable in order to promote better practices within the design and construction industry and reduce losses from earthquakes;

(iv) shall enter into cooperative agreements or contracts with States and local jurisdictions and other Federal agencies to establish demonstration projects on earthquake hazard mitigation, to link earthquake research and mitigation efforts with emergency management programs, or to prepare educational materials for national distribution; and

(v) shall support the Director of the National Institute of Standards and Technology in the completion of programmatic goals.

(B) STATE ASSISTANCE PROGRAM CRITERIA.—In order to qualify for assistance under subparagraph (A)(i), a State must—

(i) demonstrate that the assistance will result in enhanced seismic safety in the State;

(ii) provide 25 percent of the costs of the activities for which assistance is being given, except that the Administrator may lower or waive the cost-share requirement for these activities for a small impoverished community,

273

as defined in section 203 of the Disaster Relief Act of 1974 (42 U.S.C. 5133(a)); and

(iii)   meet such other requirements as the Administrator shall prescribe.

(3) UNITED STATES GEOLOGICAL SURVEY.—The United States Geological Survey shall report on significant domestic and international earthquakes and conduct research and other activities necessary to characterize and identify earthquake hazards, assess earthquake risks, monitor seismic activity, and improve earthquake forecasts. In carrying out this paragraph, the Director of the United States Geological Survey shall—

(A)   conduct a systematic assessment of the seismic risks in each region of the Nation prone to earthquakes, including, where appropriate, the establishment and operation of intensive monitoring projects on hazardous faults, seismic microzonation studies in urban and other developed areas where earthquake risk is determined to be significant, and engineering seismology studies;

(B)   work with officials of State and local governments to ensure that they are knowledgeable about the specific seismic risks in their areas;

(C)   develop standard procedures, in consultation with the Administrator of the Federal Emergency Management Agency and the Director of the National Institute of Standards and Technology, for issuing earthquake alerts and early warnings;

(D)   issue when necessary and feasible, and notify the Administrator of the Federal Emergency Management Agency, the Director of the National Institute of Standards and Technology, and State and local officials, an alert and an earthquake warning;

(E) operate, including the National Earthquake Information Center, a forum for the international exchange of earthquake information which shall—

(i)   promote the exchange of information on earthquake research and earthquake preparedness between the United States and other nations;

(ii)   maintain a library containing selected reports, research papers, and data produced through the Program;

(iii)   answer requests from other nations for information on United States earthquake research and earthquake preparedness programs; and

(iv)   direct foreign requests to the agency involved in the Program which is best able to respond to the request;

(F)   operate a National Seismic System;

(G)   support regional seismic networks, which shall complement the National Seismic Network; and

(H)   work with the National Science Foundation, the Federal Emergency Management Agency, and the National Institute of Standards and Technology to develop a comprehensive plan for earthquake engineering research to effectively use existing testing facilities and laboratories (in existence at the time of the development of the plan), upgrade facilities and equipment as needed, and integrate new, innovative testing approaches to the research infrastructure in a systematic manner.

(I)　work with other Program agencies to coordinate Program activities with similar earthquake hazards reduction efforts in other countries, to ensure that the Program benefits from relevant information and advances in those countries;

(J)　maintain suitable seismic hazard maps and data in support of building codes for structures and lifeline infrastructure, including additional maps needed for performance-based design approaches; and

(K)　support the Director of the National Institute of Standards and Technology in the completion of programmatic goals.

(4) NATIONAL SCIENCE FOUNDATION.—

(A) IN GENERAL.—The National Science Foundation shall be responsible for funding research on earth sciences to improve the understanding of the causes and behavior of earthquakes, on earthquake engineering, and on human response to earthquakes. In carrying out this paragraph, the Director of the National Science Foundation shall—

(i)　encourage prompt dissemination of significant findings, sharing of data, samples, physical collections, and other supporting materials, and development of intellectual property so research results can be used by appropriate organizations to mitigate earthquake damage;

(ii)　in addition to supporting individual investigators, support university research consortia, State agencies, State geological surveys, and centers for research in geosciences and in earthquake engineering;

(iii)　work closely with the United States Geological Survey to support applied science in the production of a systematic series of earthquake-related geologic hazard maps, and to identify geographic regions of national concern that should be the focus of targeted solicitations for earthquake-related research proposals;

(iv)　support research that improves the safety and performance of buildings, structures, and lifeline systems using experimental and computational facilities;

(v)　emphasize, in earthquake engineering research, development of economically feasible methods to retrofit existing buildings and to protect lifeline infrastructure to mitigate earthquake damage;

(vi)　support research that studies the political, economic, and social factors that influence the implementation of hazard reduction measures;

(vii)　include to the maximum extent practicable diverse institutions, including Historically Black Colleges and Universities and those serving large proportions of Hispanics, Native Americans, Asian-Pacific Americans, and other underrepresented populations;

(viii)　develop, in conjunction with the Federal Emergency Management Agency, the National Institute of Standards and Technology, and the United States Geological Survey, a comprehensive plan for earthquake engineering

275

research to effectively use existing testing facilities and laboratories (in existence at the time of the development of the plan), upgrade facilities and equipment as needed, and integrate new, innovative testing approaches to the research infrastructure in a systematic manner; and

(ix)   support the Director of the National Institute of Standards and Technology in the completion of programmatic goals.

(B) IDENTIFICATION OF FUNDING.—The National Science Foundation shall—

(i)   to the extent practicable, note in any notice of Program funding or other funding possibilities under the Program that the funds are part of the Program;

(ii)   to the extent practicable, track the awarding of Federal funds through the Program; and

(iii)   not less frequently than once every 2 years, submit to the director of the Program a report specifying the amount of Federal funds awarded to conduct research that enhances the understanding of earthquake science.

(5) NATIONAL INSTITUTE OF STANDARDS AND TECHNOLOGY.—In addition to the lead agency responsibilities described under paragraph (1), the National Institute of Standards and Technology shall be responsible for carrying out research and development to improve community resilience through building codes and standards and practices for structures and lifeline infrastructure. In carrying out this paragraph, the Director of the National Institute of Standards and Technology shall—

(A)   work closely with national standards and model building code organizations, in conjunction with the Agency, to promote the implementation of research results;

(B)   promote better building practices among architects and engineers;

(C)   work closely with national standards organizations to develop seismic safety standards and practices for new and existing lifeline infrastructure;

(D)[6]   support the development and commercial application of cost effective and affordable performance-based seismic engineering by providing technical support for seismic engineering practices and related building code, standards, and practices development; and

---

[6]   Margin so in law.

(E)   work with the National Science Foundation, the Federal Emergency Management Agency, and the United States Geological Survey to develop a comprehensive plan for earthquake engineering research to effectively use existing testing facilities and laboratories (in existence at the time of the development of the plan), upgrade facilities and equipment as needed, and integrate new, innovative testing approaches to the research infrastructure in a systematic manner.

(c) BUDGET COORDINATION.—

(1) GUIDANCE.— The Interagency Coordinating Committee shall each year

provide guidance to the other Program agencies concerning the preparation of requests for appropriations for activities related to the Program, and shall prepare, in conjunction with the other Program agencies, an annual Program budget to be submitted to the Office of Management and Budget.

(2) REPORTS.—Each Program agency shall include with its annual request for appropriations submitted to the Office of Management and Budget a report that—

(A) identifies each element of the proposed Program activities of the agency;

(B) specifies how each of these activities contributes to the Program; and

(C) states the portion of its request for appropriations allocated to each element of the Program.

[42 U.S.C. 7704]

[Sec. 6. Repealed by section 4 of P.L. 105–47, 111 Stat. 1164] [Sec. 7. Repealed by section 4 of P.L. 105–47, 111 Stat. 1164]

SEC. 8. SEISMIC STANDARDS.

(a) ASSESSMENT AND RECOMMENDATIONS.— Not later than December 1, 2019, the Director of the National Institute of Standards and Technology and the Administrator of the Federal Emergency Management Agency shall jointly convene a committee of experts from Federal agencies, nongovernmental organizations, private sector entities, disaster management professional associations, engineering professional associations, and professional construction and homebuilding industry associations, to assess and recommend options for improving the built environment and critical infrastructure to reflect performance goals stated in terms of post-earthquake reoccupancy and functional recovery time.

(b) REPORT TO CONGRESS.— Not later than June 30, 2020, the committee convened under paragraph (1) shall submit to the Committee on Commerce, Science, and Transportation, the Committee on Energy and Natural Resources, and the Committee on Homeland Security and Governmental Affairs of the Senate and the Committee on Science, Space, and Technology, the Committee on Natural Resources, and the Committee on Homeland Security of the House of Representatives a report on recommended options for improving the built environment and critical infrastructure to reflect performance goals stated in terms of post-earthquake reoccupancy and functional recovery time.

[42 U.S.C. 7705b]

SEC. 9. ACCEPTANCE OF GIFTS.

(a) AUTHORITY.— In furtherance of the purposes of this Act, the Administrator of the Federal Emergency Management Agency may accept and use bequests, gifts, or donations of services, money, or property, notwithstanding section 3679 of the Revised Statutes (31 U.S.C. 1342).

(b) CRITERIA.— The Administrator of the Federal Emergency Management Agency shall establish by regulation criteria for determining whether to accept bequests, gifts, or donations of services, money, or property. Such criteria shall take into consideration whether the acceptance of the bequest, gift, or donation would reflect unfavorably on the Director's ability to carry out his responsibilities in a fair and objective manner, or would compromise the integrity of, or the appearance of the integrity of, the Program or any official involved in administering the Program.

[42 U.S.C. 7705c]

[Sec. 10. Repealed by section 203 of P.L. 106–503 (114 Stat. 2305).]

SEC. 11. POST-EARTHQUAKE INVESTIGATIONS PROGRAM.

There is established within the United States Geological Survey a post-earthquake investigations program, the purpose of which is to investigate major earthquakes, so as to learn lessons which can be applied to reduce the loss of lives and property in future earthquakes. The United States Geological Survey, in consultation with each Program agency, shall organize investigations to study the implications of the earthquake in the areas of responsibility of each Program agency. The investigations shall begin as rapidly as possible and may be conducted by grantees and contractors. The Program agencies shall ensure that the results of investigations are disseminated widely. The Director of the Survey is authorized to utilize earthquake expertise from the Agency, the National Science Foundation, the National Institute of Standards and Technology, other Federal agencies, and private contractors, on a reimbursable basis, in the conduct of such earthquake investigations. At a minimum, investigations under this section shall include—

(1)   analysis by the National Science Foundation and the United States Geological Survey of the causes of the earthquake and the nature of the resulting ground motion;

(2)   analysis by the National Science Foundation and the National Institute of Standards and Technology of the behavior of structures and lifeline infrastructure, both those that were damaged and those that were undamaged; and

(3)   analysis by each of the Program agencies of the effectiveness of the earthquake hazards mitigation programs and actions relating to its area of responsibility under the Program, and how those programs and actions could be strengthened.

[42 U.S.C. 7705e]

SEC. 12. AUTHORIZATION OF APPROPRIATIONS.

(a)(1) GENERAL.— There are authorized to be appropriated to the President to carry out the provisions of section 5 and 6 of this Act (in addition to any authorizations for similar purposes included in other Acts and the authorizations set forth in subsections (b) and (c) of this section), not to exceed $1,000,000 for the fiscal year ending September 30, 1978, not to exceed $2,000,000 for the fiscal year ending September 30, 1979, and not to exceed $2,000,000 for the fiscal year ending September 30, 1980.

(2) There are authorized to be appropriated to the Director to carry out the provisions of sections 5 and 6 of this Act for the fiscal year ending September 30, 1981—

(A) $1,000,000 for continuation of the Interagency Committee on Seismic Safety in Construction and the Building Seismic Safety Council programs,

(B) $1,500,000 for plans and preparedness for earthquake disasters,

278

(C) $500,000 for prediction response planning,

(D) $600,000 for architectural and engineering planning and practice programs,

(E) $1,000,000 for development and application of a public education program,

(F) $3,000,000 for use by the National Science Foundation in addition to the amount authorized to be appropriated under subsection (c), which amount includes $2,400,000 for earthquake policy research and $600,000 for the strong ground motion element of the siting program, and

(G) $1,000,000 for use by the Center for Building Technology, National Bureau of Standards in addition to the amount authorized to be appropriated under subsection (d) for earthquake activities in the Center.

(3) There are authorized to be appropriated to the Director for the fiscal year ending September 30, 1982, $2,000,000 to carry out the provisions of section 5 and 6 of this Act.

(4) There are authorized to be appropriated to the Director, to carry out the provisions of section 5 and 6 of this Act, $1,281,000 for the fiscal year ending September 30, 1983.

(5) There are authorized to be appropriated to the Director, to carry out the provisions of section 5 and 6 of this Act, for the fiscal year ending September 30, 1984, $3,705,000 and for the fiscal year ending September 30, 1985, $6,096,000.

(6) There are authorized to be appropriated to the Director, to carry out the provisions of section 5 and 6 of this Act, for the fiscal year ending September 30, 1986, $5,596,000, and for the fiscal year ending September 30, 1987, $5,848,000.

(7) There are authorized to be appropriated to the Director of the Agency, to carry out this Act, $5,778,000 for the fiscal year ending September 30, 1988, $5,788,000 for the fiscal year ending September 30, 1989, $8,798,000 for the fiscal year ending September 30, 1990, $14,750,000 for the fiscal year ending September 30, 1991, $19,000,000 for the fiscal year ending September 30, 1992, $22,000,000 for the fiscal year ending September 30, 1993, $25,000,000 for the fiscal year ending September 30, 1995, $25,750,000 for the fiscal year ending September 30, 1996, $20,900,000 for the fiscal year ending September 30, 1998, $21,500,000 for the fiscal year ending September 30, 1999; $19,861,000 for the fiscal year ending September 30, 2001, of which $450,000 is for National Earthquake Hazard Reduction Program-eligible efforts of an established multi-state consortium to reduce the unacceptable threat of earthquake damages in the New Madrid seismic region through efforts to enhance preparedness, response, recovery, and mitigation; $20,705,000 for the fiscal year ending September 30, 2002; and $21,585,000 for the fiscal year ending September 30, 2003.

(8)[7] There are authorized to be appropriated to the Federal Emergency Management Agency for carrying out this title—

---

[7] Margin so in law.

    (A) $21,000,000 for fiscal year 2005,

    (B) $21,630,000 for fiscal year 2006,

    (C) $22,280,000 for fiscal year 2007,

    (D) $22,950,000 for fiscal year 2008,

    (E) $23,640,000 for fiscal year 2009,

    (F) $8,758,000 for fiscal year 2019,

    (G) $8,758,000 for fiscal year 2020,

    (H) $8,758,000 for fiscal year 2021,

    (I) $8,758,000 for fiscal year 2022, and

    (J) $8,758,000 for fiscal year 2023,

of which not less than 10 percent of available program funds actually appropriated shall be made available each such fiscal year for supporting the development of performance-based, cost-effective, and affordable design guidelines and methodologies in codes for buildings, structures, and lifeline infrastructure.

    (b) GEOLOGICAL SURVEY.—(1) There are authorized to be appropriated to the Secretary of the Interior for purposes for carrying out, through the Director of the United States Geological Survey, the responsibilities that may be assigned to the Director under this Act not to exceed $27,500,000 for the fiscal year ending September 30, 1978; not to exceed $35,000,000 for the fiscal year ending September 30, 1979; not to exceed $40,000,000 for the fiscal year ending September 30, 1980; $32,484,000 for the fiscal year ending September 30, 1981; $34,425,000 for the fiscal year ending September 30, 1982; $31,843,000 for the fiscal year ending September 30, 1983; $35,524,000 for the fiscal year ending September 30, 1984; $37,300,200 for the fiscal year ending September 30, 1985[8] $35,578,000 for the fiscal year ending September 30, 1986; $37,179,000 for the fiscal year ending September 30, 1987; $38,540,000 for the fiscal year ending September 30, 1988; $41,819,000 for the fiscal year ending September 30, 1989; $55,283,000 for the fiscal year ending September 30, 1990, of which $8,000,000 shall be for earthquake investigations under section 11; $50,000,000 for the fiscal year ending September 30, 1991; $54,500,000 for the fiscal year ending September 30, 1992; $62,500,000 for the fiscal year ending September 30, 1993; $49,200,000 for the fiscal year ending September 30, 1995; $50,676,000 for the fiscal year ending September 30, 1996; $52,565,000 for the fiscal year ending September 30, 1998, of which $3,800,000 shall be used for the Global Seismic Network operated by the Agency; and $54,052,000 for the fiscal year ending September 30, 1999, of which $3,800,000 shall be used for the Global Seismic Network operated by the Agency. There are authorized to be appropriated to the Secretary of the Interior for purposes of carrying out, through the Director of the United States Geological Survey, the responsibilities that may be assigned to the Director under this Act $48,360,000 for fiscal year 2001, of which $3,500,000 is for the Global Seismic Network and $100,000 is for the Scientific Earthquake Studies Advisory Committee established under section 210 of the Earthquake Hazards Reduction Authorization Act of 2000; $50,415,000 for fiscal year 2002, of which $3,600,000 is for the Global Seismic Network and $100,000 is for the Scientific Earthquake Studies Advisory Committee; and $52,558,000 for fiscal year 2003, of which $3,700,000 is for the Global Seismic Network and $100,000 is for the Scientific Earthquake Studies Advisory Committee. Of the amounts authorized to be appropriated under this paragraph9, at least—

---

8   So in law. Probably should have a semicolon.

---

9   The amendment made by section 104(a)(3) of Public Law 108–360 (118 Stat. 1674) to strike ```subsection' in the last sentence and inserting `paragraph'" was executed by striking and inserting such words in the last sentence of subsection (b) to reflect the probable intent of Congress.``National Science Foundation, the National Institute[s] of Standards and Technology" and insert ``Federal Emergency Management Agency, the National Science Foundation", was executed by striking ``National Science Foundation, the National Institute of Standards and Technology" in the matter to be struck to reflect the probable intent of Congress.

(A) $8,000,000 of the amount authorized to be appropriated for the fiscal year ending September 30, 1998;

(B) $8,250,000 of the amount authorized for the fiscal year ending September 30, 1999;

(C) $9,000,000 of the amount authorized to be appropriated for fiscal year 2001;

(D) $9,250,000 of the amount authorized to be appropriated for fiscal year 2002; and

(E) $9,500,000 of the amount authorized to be appropriated for fiscal year 2003,

shall be used for carrying out a competitive, peer-reviewed program under which the Director, in close coordination with and as a complement to related activities of the United States Geological Survey, awards grants to, or enters into cooperative agreements with, State and local governments and persons or entities from the academic community and the private sector.

(2) There are authorized to be appropriated to the United States Geological Survey for carrying out this title—

(A) $77,000,000 for fiscal year 2005, of which not less than $30,000,000 shall be made available for completion of the Advanced National Seismic System established under section 13;

(B) $84,410,000 for fiscal year 2006, of which not less than $36,000,000 shall be made available for completion of the Advanced National Seismic System established under section 13;

(C) $85,860,000 for fiscal year 2007, of which not less than $36,000,000 shall be made available for completion of the Advanced National Seismic System established under section 13;

(D) $87,360,000 for fiscal year 2008, of which not less than $36,000,000 shall be made available for completion of the Advanced National Seismic System established under section 13;

(E) $88,900,000 for fiscal year 2009, of which not less than $36,000,000 shall be made available for completion of the Advanced National Seismic System established under section 13;

(F) $83,403,000 for fiscal year 2019, of which not less than $30,000,000 shall be made available for completion of the Advanced National Seismic System established under section 7707 of this title;

(G) $83,403,000 for fiscal year 2020, of which not less than $30,000,000 shall be made available for completion of the Advanced National Seismic System established under section 7707 of this title;

(H) $83,403,000 for fiscal year 2021, of which not less than $30,000,000 shall be made available for completion of the Advanced National Seismic System established under section 7707 of this title;

(I) $83,403,000 for fiscal year 2022, of which not less than $30,000,000 shall be made available for completion of the Advanced National Seismic System established under section 7707 of this title; and

(J) $83,403,000 for fiscal year 2023, of which not less than $30,000,000 shall be made available for completion of the Advanced National Seismic System established under section 7707 of this title.

(c) NATIONAL SCIENCE FOUNDATION.—(1)   To enable the Foundation to carry out responsibilities that may be assigned to it under this Act, there are authorized to be appropriated to the Foundation not to exceed $27,500,000 for the fiscal year ending September 30, 1978; not to exceed $35,000,000 for the fiscal year ending September 30, 1979; not to exceed $40,000,000 for the first year ending September 30, 1980; $26,600,000 for the fiscal year ending September 30, 1981; $27,150,000 for the fiscal year ending September 30 1982; $25,000,000 for the fiscal year ending September 30, 1983; $25,800,000 for the fiscal year ending September 30, 1984; $28,665,000 for the fiscal year ending September 30, 1985[10] $27,760,000 for the fiscal year ending September 30, 1986; $29,009,000 for the fiscal year ending September 30, 1987; $28,235,000 for the fiscal year ending September 30, 1988; $31,634,000 for the fiscal year ending September 30, 1989;[11] $38,454,000 for the fiscal year ending September 30, 1990. Of the amounts authorized for Engineering under section 101(d)(1)(B) of the National Science Foundation Authorization Act of 1988, $24,000,000 is authorized for carrying out this Act for the fiscal year ending September 30, 1991, and of the amounts authorized for Geosciences under section 101(d)(1)(D) of the National Science Foundation Authorization Act of 1988, $13,000,000 is authorized for carrying out this Act for the fiscal year ending September 30, 1991. Of the amounts authorized for Research and Related Activities under section 101(e)(1) of the National Science Foundation Authorization Act of 1988, $29,000,000 is authorized for engineering research under this Act, and $14,750,000 is authorized for geosciences research under this Act, for the fiscal year ending September 30, 1992. Of the amounts authorized for Research and Related Activities under section 101(f)(1) of the National Science Foundation Authorization Act of 1988, $34,500,000 is authorized for engineering research under this Act, and $17,500,000 is authorized for geosciences research under this Act, for the fiscal year ending September 30, 1993. There are authorized to be appropriated, out of funds otherwise authorized to be appropriated to the National Science Foundation: (1) $16,200,000 for engineering research and $10,900,000 for geosciences research for the fiscal year ending September 30, 1995, (2) $16,686,000 for engineering research and $11,227,000 for geosciences research for the fiscal year ending September 30, 1996, (3) $18,450,000 for engineering research and $11,920,000 for geosciences research for the fiscal year ending September 30, 1998, (4) $19,000,000 for engineering research and $12,280,000 for geosciences research for the fiscal year ending September 30, 1999. There are authorized to be appropriated to the National Science Foundation $19,000,000 for engineering research and $11,900,000 for geosciences research for fiscal year 2001; $19,808,000 for engineering research and $12,406,000 for geosciences research for fiscal year 2002; and $20,650,000 for engineering research and $12,933,000 for geosciences research for fiscal year 2003.

---

[10]   So in law. Probably should have a semicolon.

---

[11]   So in law. Probably should have and.

---

(2) There are authorized to be appropriated to the National Science Foundation for carrying out this title—

    (A) $38,000,000 for fiscal year 2005;

    (B) $39,140,000 for fiscal year 2006;

    (C) $40,310,000 for fiscal year 2007;

    (D) $41,520,000 for fiscal year 2008;

    (E) $42,770,000 for fiscal year 2009;

    (F) $54,000,000 for fiscal year 2019,

    (G) $54,000,000 for fiscal year 2020,

    (H) $54,000,000 for fiscal year 2021,

    (I) $54,000,000 for fiscal year 2022, and

    (J) $54,000,000 for fiscal year 2023.

(d) NATIONAL INSTITUTE OF STANDARDS AND TECHNOLOGY[12].—(1) To enable the National Institute of Standards and Technology to carry out responsibilities that may be assigned to it under this Act, there are authorized to be appropriated $425,000 for the fiscal year ending September 30, 1981; $425,000 for the fiscal year ending September 30, 1982; $475,000 for the fiscal year ending September 30, 1983; $475,000 for the fiscal year ending September 30, 1984; $498,750 for the fiscal year ending September 30, 1985[13] $499,000 for the fiscal year ending September 30, 1986; $521,000 for the fiscal year ending September 30, 1987; $525,000 for the fiscal year ending September 30, 1988; $525,000 for the fiscal year ending September 30, 1989; $2,525,000 for the fiscal year ending September 30, 1990; $1,000,000 for the fiscal year ending September 30, 1991; $3,000,000 for the fiscal year ending September 30, 1992; and $4,750,000 for the fiscal year ending September 30, 1993. There are authorized to be appropriated, out of funds otherwise authorized to be appropriated to the National Institute of Standards and Technology, $1,900,000 for the fiscal year ending September 30, 1995, $1,957,000 for the fiscal year ending September 30, 1996, $2,000,000 for the fiscal year ending September 30, 1998, $2,060,000 for the fiscal year ending September 30, 1999, $2,332,000 for fiscal year 2001, $2,431,000 for fiscal year 2002, and $2,534,300 for fiscal year 2003.

---

[12]   Section 12(4)(A) of P.L. 101–614, 104 Stat. 3240, amended the heading of subsection (d). The

amendment probably used the wrong size type.

[13]   So in law. Probably should have a semicolon.

(2) There are authorized to be appropriated to the National Institute of Standards and Technology for carrying out this title—

(A) $10,000,000 for fiscal year 2005,

(B) $11,000,000 for fiscal year 2006,

(C) $12,100,000 for fiscal year 2007,

(D) $13,310,000 for fiscal year 2008,

(E) $14,640,000 for fiscal year 2009,

(F) $5,900,000 for fiscal year 2019,

(G) $5,900,000 for fiscal year 2020,

(H) $5,900,000 for fiscal year 2021,

(I) $5,900,000 for fiscal year 2022, and

(J) $5,900,000 for fiscal year 2023.

of which $2,000,000 shall be made available each such fiscal year for supporting the development of performance-based, cost-effective, and affordable codes for buildings, structures, and lifeline infrastructure.

[42 U.S.C. 7706]

SEC. 13. ADVANCED NATIONAL SEISMIC SYSTEM.

(a) ESTABLISHMENT.— The Director of the United States Geological Survey shall establish and operate an Advanced National Seismic System. The purpose of such system shall be to organize, modernize, standardize, and stabilize the national, regional, and urban seismic monitoring systems in the United States, including sensors, recorders, and data analysis centers, into a coordinated system that will measure and record the full range of frequencies and amplitudes exhibited by seismic waves, in order to enhance earthquake research and warning capabilities.

(b) MANAGEMENT PLAN.— Not later than 90 days after the date of the enactment of the Earthquake Hazards Reduction Authorization Act of 2000, the Director of the United States Geological Survey shall transmit to the Congress a 5-year management plan for establishing and operating the Advanced National Seismic System. The plan shall include annual cost estimates for both modernization and operation, milestones, standards, and performance goals, as well as plans for securing the participation of all existing networks in the Advanced National Seismic System and for establishing new, or enhancing existing, partnerships to leverage resources.

[42 U.S.C. 7707]

SEC. 14. NETWORK FOR EARTHQUAKE ENGINEERING SIMULATION.

(a) ESTABLISHMENT.— The Director of the National Science Foundation shall establish the George E. Brown, Jr. Network for Earthquake Engineering Simulation that will upgrade, link, and integrate a system of geographically distributed experimental facilities for earthquake engineering testing of full-sized structures and their components and partial-scale physical models. The system shall be integrated through networking software so that integrated models and databases can be used to create model-based simulation, and the components of the system shall be interconnected with a computer network and allow for remote access, information sharing, and collaborative research.

(b) AUTHORIZATION OF APPROPRIATIONS.—In addition to amounts appropriated under section 12(c), there are authorized to be appropriated to the National Science Foundation for the George E. Brown, Jr. Network for Earthquake Engineering Simulation—

(1) $28,200,000 for fiscal year 2001;

(2) $24,400,000 for fiscal year 2002;

(3) $4,500,000 for fiscal year 2003;

(4) $17,000,000 for fiscal year 2004;

(5) $20,000,000 for fiscal year 2005, all of which shall be available for operations and maintenance;

(6) $20,400,000 for fiscal year 2006, all of which shall be available for operations and maintenance;

(7) $20,870,000 for fiscal year 2007, all of which shall be available for operations and maintenance;

(8) $21,390,000 for fiscal year 2008, all of which shall be available for operations and maintenance; and

(9) $21,930,000 for fiscal year 2009, all of which shall be available for operations and maintenance.

[42 U.S.C. 7708]

★

NATIONAL EARTHQUAKE HAZARDS REDUCTION PROGRAM REAUTHORIZATION ACT OF 2018

PUBLIC LAW 115–307

NATIONAL EARTHQUAKE HAZARDS REDUCTION PROGRAM REAUTHORIZATION ACT OF 2018

[(Public Law 115–307)]

[This law has not been amended]

AN ACT To reauthorize and amend the National Earthquake Hazards Reduction Program, and for other purposes.

Be it enacted by the Senate and House of Representatives of the United States of America in Congress assembled,

SECTION 1. [42 U.S.C. 7701 note] SHORT TITLE.

This Act may be cited as the "National Earthquake Hazards Reduction Program Reauthorization Act of 2018".

* * * * * * *

SEC. 3. MODIFICATION OF NATIONAL EARTHQUAKE HAZARDS REDUCTION PROGRAM.

* * * * * * *

(b) AMENDMENTS RELATING TO INTERAGENCY COORDINATING COMMITTEE ON EARTHQUAKE HAZARDS REDUCTION.—

* * * * * * *

(4) REDUCTION IN FREQUENCY OF REPORTING BY INTERAGENCY COORDINATING COMMITTEE ON EARTHQUAKE HAZARDS REDUCTION.—

(A) IN GENERAL.—Subsection (a)(4) of such section is amended—

(i) in the paragraph heading, by striking Annual and inserting Biennial;

(ii) by redesignating subparagraphs (A) through (F) as clauses (i) through (vi), respectively, and adjusting the indentation of the margin of such clauses, as so redesignated, two ems to the right;

(iii) in clause (v), as so redesignated, by striking ; and and inserting a semicolon;

(iv) in clause (vi), as so redesignated, by striking the period at the end and inserting ; and;

(v) by inserting after clause (vi), as so redesignated, the following:

"(vii) a statement regarding whether the Administrator of the Federal Emergency Management Agency has lowered or waived the cost share requirement for assistance provided under subsection (b)(2)(A)(i).";

(vi) in the matter preceding clause (i), as so redesignated, by striking The Interagency and all that follows through Senate and inserting the following:

"(A) IN GENERAL.— Not less frequently than once every two years, the Interagency Coordinating Committee shall submit to the Committee on Commerce, Science, and Transportation, the Committee on Energy and Natural Resources, and the Committee on Homeland Security and Governmental Affairs of the Senate and the Committee on Science, Space, and Technology, the Committee on Energy and Commerce, the Committee on Natural Resources, and the Committee on Homeland Security of the House of Representatives a report on the Program"; and

(vii) by adding at the end the following:

"(B) SUPPORT FOR PREPARATION OF REPORT.— Each head of a Program agency shall submit to the Director of the National Institute of Standards and Technology such information as the Director .may request for the preparation of a report under subparagraph (A) not later than 90 days after the date on which the Director requests such information."

* * * * * * *

(c) MODIFICATION OF RESPONSIBILITIES OF NATIONAL INSTITUTE OF STANDARDS AND TECHNOLOGY.—Subsection (b) of such section is amended—

(1) in paragraph (1)—

(A) in subparagraph (A), by striking and constructing, and inserting constructing, evaluating, and retrofitting; and

(B) in subparagraph (D), by inserting provide new and after research to; and

(2) in paragraph (5), in the matter preceding subparagraph (A), in the first sentence, by inserting community resilience through after improve.

(d) MODIFICATION OF RESPONSIBILITIES OF FEDERAL EMERGENCY MANAGEMENT AGENCY.— Paragraph (2) of subsection (b) of such section is amended to read as follows:

"(2) DEPARTMENT OF HOMELAND SECURITY; FEDERAL EMERGENCY MANAGEMENT AGENCY.—

"(A) PROGRAM RESPONSIBILITIES.—The Administrator of the Federal Emergency Management Agency—

"(i) shall operate a program of grants and assistance to enable States to develop mitigation, preparedness, and response plans, purchase necessary instrumentation, prepare inventories and conduct seismic safety inspections of critical structures and lifeline infrastructure, update building, land use planning, and zoning codes and ordinances to enhance seismic safety, increase earthquake awareness and education, and provide assistance to multi-State groups for such purposes;

"(ii)   shall support the implementation of a comprehensive earthquake education, outreach, and public awareness program, including development of materials and their wide dissemination to all appropriate audiences and support public access to locality-specific information that may assist the public in preparing for, mitigating against, responding to and recovering from earthquakes and related disasters;

"(iii)   shall, in conjunction with the Director of the National Institute of Standards and Technology, other Federal agencies, and private sector groups, use research results to support the preparation, maintenance, and wide dissemination of seismic resistant design guidance and related information on building codes, standards, and practices for new and existing buildings, structures, and lifeline infrastructure, aid in the development of performance-based design guidelines and methodologies, and support model codes that are cost effective and affordable in order to promote better practices within the design and construction industry and reduce losses from earthquakes;

"(iv)   shall enter into cooperative agreements or contracts with States and local jurisdictions and other Federal agencies to establish demonstration projects on earthquake hazard mitigation, to link earthquake research and mitigation efforts with emergency management programs, or to prepare educational materials for national distribution; and

"(v)   shall support the Director of the National Institute of Standards and Technology in the completion of programmatic goals.

"(B) STATE ASSISTANCE PROGRAM CRITERIA.—In order to qualify for assistance under subparagraph (A)(i), a State must—

"(i)   demonstrate that the assistance will result in enhanced seismic safety in the State;

"(ii)   provide 25 percent of the costs of the activities for which assistance is being given, except that the Administrator may lower or waive the cost-share requirement for these activities for a small impoverished community, as defined in section 203 of the Disaster Relief Act of 1974 (42 U.S.C. 5133(a)); and

"(iii)   meet such other requirements as the Administrator shall prescribe.".

(e)   MODIFICATION OF RESPONSIBILITIES OF UNITED STATES GEOLOGICAL SURVEY.—Subsection (b)(3) of such section is amended—

(1) in the matter preceding subparagraph (A), in the first sentence—

(A)   by inserting report on significant domestic and international earthquakes and after Survey shall; and

(B)   by striking predictions. and inserting forecasts.;

(2) in subparagraph (C), by striking predictions, including aftershock advisories and inserting alerts and early warnings;

(3) by striking subparagraph (D) and inserting the following:

"(D) issue when necessary and feasible, and notify the Administrator of the Federal Emergency Management Agency, the Director of the National Institute of Standards and Technology, and State and local officials, an alert and an earthquake warning;";

(4) in subparagraph (E), in the matter preceding clause (i), by striking using and inserting including;

(5) in subparagraph (I), by striking ; and and inserting a semicolon;

(6) in subparagraph (J)—

(A) by inserting and data after hazard maps; and

(B) by striking the period at the end and inserting ; and; and

(7) by adding at the end the following:

"(K) support the Director of the National Institute of Standards and Technology in the completion of programmatic goals.".

(f) MODIFICATION OF RESPONSIBILITIES OF NATIONAL SCIENCE FOUNDATION.—Subsection (b)(4) of such section is amended—

(1) in subparagraph (B), by inserting , State agencies, State geological surveys, after consortia;

(2) in subparagraph (C), by inserting to support applied science in the production of a systematic series of earthquake-related geologic hazard maps, and after Survey;

(3) in subparagraph (D), by striking large-scale experimental and computational facilities of the George E. Brown Jr. Network for Earthquake Engineering Simulation and other institutions engaged in research and the implementation of the National Earthquake Hazards Reduction Program and inserting experimental and computational facilities;

(4) in subparagraph (G), by striking ; and and inserting a semicolon;

(5) in subparagraph (H), by striking the period at the end and inserting ; and;

(6) by adding at the end the following:

"(I) support the Director of the National Institute of Standards and Technology in the completion of programmatic goals.";

(7) by redesignating subparagraphs (A) through (I) as clauses (i) through (ix), respectively, and indenting such clauses accordingly;

(8) in the matter before clause (i), as redesignated by paragraph (7), in the first sentence, by striking The National Science Foundation and inserting the following:

"(A) IN GENERAL.— The National Science Foundation"; and

(9) by adding at the end the following:

"(B) IDENTIFICATION OF FUNDING.—The National Science Foundation shall—

"(i) to the extent practicable, note in any notice of Program funding or other funding possibilities under the Program that the funds are part of the Program;

"(ii) to the extent practicable, track the awarding of Federal funds through the Program; and

"(iii) not less frequently than once every 2 years, submit to the director of the Program a report specifying the amount of Federal funds awarded to conduct research that enhances the understanding of earthquake science.".

SEC. 4. REVIEW OF THE NATIONAL EARTHQUAKE HAZARD REDUCTION PROGRAM.

(a) IN GENERAL.— As soon as practicable, but not later than such date as is necessary for the Comptroller General of the United States to submit the report required by subsection (c) in accordance with such subsection, the Comptroller General shall complete a review of Federal earthquake hazard risk reduction efforts.

(b) ELEMENTS.—The review conducted under subsection (a) shall include the following:

(1) A comprehensive assessment of—

(A) the extent to which the United States Geological Survey has identified the risks and hazards to the United States posed by earthquakes, including risks and hazards resulting from tsunamis and landslides that are generated by earthquakes;

(B) the efforts of the Federal Emergency Management Agency and the National Institute of Standards and Technology to improve the resilience of the United States to earthquakes and to identify important gaps in the resilience of the United States to earthquakes;

(C) the progress made by the National Institute of Standards and Technology and the Interagency Coordinating Committee (as defined in section 4 the Earthquake Hazards Reduction Act of 1977 of the Earthquake Hazards Reduction Act of 1977 (42 U.S.C. 7703)) to coordinate effectively the budget and activities of the Program agencies (as defined in such section 4) in advancing the plans and goals of the Program (as defined in such section 4) and how coordination among the Program agencies may be improved;

(D) the extent to which the results of research in earthquake risk and hazards reduction supported by the National Science Foundation during the 40 years of the Program has been effectively disseminated to Federal, State, local, and private sector stakeholders; and

(E) the extent to which the research done during the 40 years of the Program has been applied to both public and private earthquake risk and hazards reduction.

(2) Recommendations to improve the Program and the resiliency of the United States to earthquake risks.

(c) REPORT.— As soon as practicable, but not later than 3 years after the date of the enactment of this Act, the Comptroller General shall submit to the Committee on Commerce, Science, and Transportation, the Committee on Energy and Natural Resources, and the Committee on Homeland Security and Governmental Affairs of the Senate and the Committee on Science, Space, and Technology, the Committee on Natural Resources, and the Committee on Homeland Security of the House of Representatives a report on the findings of the Comptroller General with respect to the review completed under subsection (a).

* * * * * * *

SEC. 6. MANAGEMENT PLAN FOR ADVANCED NATIONAL SEISMIC SYSTEM.

(a) PLAN REQUIRED.— Not later than 1 year after the date of the enactment of this Act, the United States Geological Survey shall submit to Congress a 5-year management plan for the continued operation of the Advanced National Seismic System.

(b) ELEMENTS.—The plan required by subsection (a) shall include the following:

(1) Strategies to continue the development of an earthquake early warning system.

(2) A mechanism for securing the participation of State and regional level earthquake monitoring entities, including those defunded by the Advanced National Seismic System in the last five years.

(3) A plan to encourage and support the integration of geodetic and geospatial data products into earthquake monitoring in regions experiencing large earthquakes.

(4) A plan to identify and evaluate existing data sets available across commercial, civil, and defense entities to determine if there are additional data sources to inform the development and deployment of the Advanced National Seismic System and an earthquake early warning system.

(5) A plan to ensure that there is an active, geographically diverse, management and advisory structure for the Advanced National Seismic System.

★

HAZARD-SPECIFIC LAWS
DAMS

NATIONAL DAM SAFETY PROGRAM ACT

PUBLIC LAW 92–367
AS AMENDED THROUGH PUB. L. 118–272

NATIONAL DAM SAFETY PROGRAM ACT

[Public Law 92-367]

[As Amended Through P.L. 118–272, Enacted January 4, 2025]

AN ACT To authorize the Secretary of the Army to undertake a national program of inspection of dams.

Be it enacted by the Senate and House of Representatives of the United States of America in Congress assembled,

SECTION 1. SHORT TITLE.

This Act may be cited as the "National Dam Safety Program Act".
[33 U.S.C. 467 nt]

SEC. 2. DEFINITIONS.

In this Act, the following definitions apply:

(1) ADMINISTRATOR.— The term Administrator means the Administrator of the Federal Emergency Management Agency.

(2) BOARD.— The term Board means a National Dam Safety Review Board established under section 8(f).

(3) DAM.—The term dam —

(A) means any artificial barrier that has the ability to impound water, wastewater, or any liquid-borne material, for the purpose of storage or control of water, that—

(i) is 25 feet or more in height from—

(I) the natural bed of the stream channel or watercourse measured at the downstream toe of the barrier; or

(II) if the barrier is not across a stream channel or watercourse, from the lowest elevation of the outside limit of the barrier;
to the maximum water storage elevation; or

(ii) has an impounding capacity for maximum storage elevation of 50 acre-feet or more; but

(B) does not include—

(i) a levee; or

(ii) a barrier described in subparagraph (A) that—

(I)   is 6 feet or less in height regardless of storage capacity; or

(II)   has a storage capacity at the maximum water storage elevation that is 15 acre-feet or less regardless of height;

unless the barrier, because of the location of the barrier or another physical characteristic of the barrier, is likely to pose a significant threat to human life or property if the barrier fails (as determined by the Administrator).

(4) ELIGIBLE HIGH HAZARD POTENTIAL DAM.—

(A) IN GENERAL.—The term eligible high hazard potential dam means a non-Federal dam that—

(i)   is located in a State with a State dam safety program;

(ii)   is classified as high hazard potential by the State dam safety agency in the State in which the dam is located;

(iii) has an emergency action plan that—

(I)   is approved by the relevant State dam safety agency; or

(II)   is in conformance with State law and pending approval by the relevant State dam safety agency;

(iv)   fails to meet minimum dam safety standards of the State in which the dam is located, as determined by the State; and

(v)   poses an unacceptable risk to the public, as determined by the Administrator, in consultation with the Board.

(B) EXCLUSION.—The term eligible high hazard potential dam does not include—

(i)   a licensed hydroelectric dam under a hydropower project with an authorized installed capacity of greater than 1.5 megawatts; or

(ii)   a dam built under the authority of the Secretary of Agriculture.

(5) FEDERAL AGENCY.— The term Federal agency means a Federal agency that designs, finances, constructs, owns, operates, maintains, or regulates the construction, operation, or maintenance of a dam.

(6) FEDERAL GUIDELINES FOR DAM SAFETY.— The term Federal Guidelines for Dam Safety means the FEMA publication, numbered 93 and dated June 1979, that defines management practices for dam safety at all Federal agencies.

(7) FEMA.— The term FEMA means the Federal Emergency Management Agency.

(8) HAZARD REDUCTION.— The term hazard reduction means the reduction in the potential consequences to life and property of dam failure.

(9) ICODS.— The term ICODS means the Interagency Committee on Dam Safety established by section 7.

(10) ELIGIBLE SUBRECIPIENT.—The term eligible subrecipient , in the case of a project receiving assistance under section 8A, includes—

(A)   a governmental organization; and

(B)   a nonprofit organization.

(11) PROGRAM.— The term Program means the national dam safety program established under section 8.

(12) REHABILITATION.— The term rehabilitation means the repair, replacement, reconstruction, or removal of a dam that is carried out to meet applicable State dam safety and security standards.

(13) STATE.— The term State means each of the several States of the United States, the District of Columbia, the Commonwealth of Puerto Rico, the Virgin Islands, Guam, American Samoa, the Commonwealth of the Northern Mariana Islands, and any other territory or possession of the United States.

(14) STATE DAM SAFETY AGENCY.— The term State dam safety agency means a State agency that has regulatory authority over the safety of non-Federal dams.

(15) STATE DAM SAFETY PROGRAM.— The term State dam safety program means a State dam safety program approved and assisted under section 8(e).

(16) UNDERSERVED COMMUNITY.— The term underserved community means a community with a population of less than 50,000 that has a median household income of less than 80 percent of the statewide median household income.

(17) UNITED STATES.— The term United States , when used in a geographical sense, means all of the States.

[33 U.S.C. 467]

SEC. 3. INSPECTION OF DAMS.

(a) IN GENERAL.— As soon as practicable, the Secretary of the Army, acting through the Chief of Engineers, shall carry out a national program of inspection of dams for the purpose of protecting human life and property. All dams in the United States shall be inspected by the Secretary except (1) dams under the jurisdiction of the Bureau of Reclamation, the Tennessee Valley Authority, or the International Boundary and Water Commission, (2) dams which have been constructed pursuant to licenses issued under the authority of the Federal Power Act, (3) dams which have been inspected within the twelve-month period immediately prior to the enactment of this Act by a State agency and which the Governor of such State requests be excluded from inspection, and (4) dams which the Secretary of the Army determines do not pose any threat to human life or property. The Secretary may inspect dams which have been licensed under the Federal Power Act upon request of the Federal Power Commission and dams under the jurisdiction of the International Boundary and Water Commission upon request of such Commission.

(b) STATE PARTICIPATION.—On request of a State dam safety agency, with respect to any dam the failure of which would affect the State, the head of a Federal agency shall—

(1)   provide information to the State dam safety agency on the construction, operation, maintenance, condition, or provisions for emergency operations of the dam; or

(2)   allow any official of the State dam safety agency to participate in the Federal

inspection of the dam.
[33 U.S.C. 467a]

SEC. 4. INVESTIGATION REPORTS TO GOVERNORS.

As soon as practicable after inspection of a dam, the Secretary shall notify the Governor of the State in which such dam is located the results of such investigation. In any case in which any hazardous conditions are found during an inspection, upon request by the owner, the Secretary, acting through the Chief of Engineers, may perform detailed engineering studies to determine the structural integrity of the dam, subject to reimbursement of such expense by the owner of such dam. The Secretary shall immediately notify the Governor of any hazardous conditions found during an inspection. The Secretary shall provide advice to the Governor, upon request, relating to timely remedial measures necessary to mitigate or obviate any hazardous conditions found during an inspection.
[33 U.S.C. 467b]

SEC. 5. DETERMINATION OF DANGER TO HUMAN LIFE AND PROPERTY.

For the purpose of determining whether a dam (including the waters impounded by such dam) constitutes a danger to human life or property, the Secretary shall take into consideration the possibility that the dam might be endangered by overtopping, seepage, settlement, erosion, sediment, cracking, earth movement, earthquakes, failure of bulkheads, flashboard, gates on conduits, or other conditions which exist or which might occur in any area in the vicinity of the dam.
[33 U.S.C. 467c]

SEC. 6. NATIONAL INVENTORY OF DAMS AND LOW-HEAD DAMS.

(a) IN GENERAL.— The Secretary of the Army shall maintain and update information on the inventory of dams and low-head dams in the United States.

(b) DAMS.— The inventory maintained under subsection (a) shall include any available information assessing each dam based on inspections completed by a Federal agency, a State dam safety agency, or a Tribal government.

(c) LOW-HEAD DAMS.—The inventory maintained under subsection (a) shall include—

(1)   the location, ownership, description, current use, condition, height, and length of each low-head dam;

(2)   any information on public safety conditions at each low-head dam; and

(3)   any other relevant information concerning low-head dams.

(d) DATA.—In carrying out this section, the Secretary shall—

(1)   coordinate with Federal and State agencies, Tribal governments, and other relevant entities; and

(2)   use data provided to the Secretary by those agencies and entities.

(e) PUBLIC AVAILABILITY.—The Secretary shall make the inventory maintained under subsection (a) publicly available (including on a publicly available website), including—

(1)   public safety information on the dangers of low-head dams; and

(2)   a directory of financial and technical assistance resources available to reduce safety hazards and fish passage barriers at low-head dams.

(f) CLARIFICATION.— Nothing in this section provides authority to the Secretary to carry out an activity, with respect to a low-head dam, that is not explicitly authorized under this section.

(g) LOW-HEAD DAM DEFINED.— In this section, the term low-head dam means a river-wide artificial barrier that generally spans a stream channel, blocking the waterway and creating a backup of water behind the barrier, with a drop off over the wall of not less than 6 inches and not more than 25 feet. [33 U.S.C. 467d]

SEC. 7. INTERAGENCY COMMITTEE ON DAM SAFETY.

(a) ESTABLISHMENT.—There is established an Interagency Committee on Dam Safety—

(1)   comprised of a representative of each of the Department of Agriculture, the Department of Defense, the Department of Energy, the Department of the Interior, the Department of Labor, FEMA, the Federal Energy Regulatory Commission, the Nuclear Regulatory Commission, the Tennessee Valley Authority, and the United States Section of the International Boundary Commission; and

(2)   chaired by the Administrator.

(b) DUTIES.— ICODS shall encourage the establishment and maintenance of effective Federal programs, policies, and guidelines intended to enhance dam safety for the protection of human life and property through coordination and information exchange among Federal agencies concerning implementation of the Federal Guidelines for Dam Safety.

[33 U.S.C. 467e]

SEC. 8. NATIONAL DAM SAFETY PROGRAM.

(a) IN GENERAL.—The Administrator, in consultation with ICODS and State dam safety agencies, and the Board shall establish and maintain, in accordance with this section, a coordinated national dam safety program. The Program shall—

(1)   be administered by FEMA to achieve the objectives set forth in subsection (c);

(2)   involve, to the extent appropriate, each Federal agency; and

(3)   include—

(A)   each of the components described in subsection (d);

(B)   the strategic plan described in subsection (b); and

(C)   assistance for State dam safety programs described in subsection (e).

(b) DUTIES.—The Administrator shall prepare a strategic plan—

(1)   to establish goals, priorities, performance measures, and target dates toward effectively administering this Act in order to improve the safety of dams in the United States; and

(2)   to the extent feasible, to establish cooperation and coordination with, and

assistance to, interested governmental entities in all States.

(c) OBJECTIVES.—The objectives of the Program are to—

(1) ensure that new and existing dams are safe through the development of technologically and economically feasible programs and procedures for national dam safety hazard reduction;

(2) encourage acceptable engineering policies and procedures to be used for dam site investigation, design, construction, operation and maintenance, and emergency preparedness;

(3) encourage the establishment and implementation of effective dam safety programs in each State based on State standards;

(4) develop and implement a comprehensive dam safety hazard education and public awareness initiative to assist the public in preparing for, mitigating, responding to, and recovering from dam incidents;

(5) develop technical assistance materials for Federal and non-Federal dam safety programs;

(6) develop mechanisms with which to provide Federal technical assistance for dam safety to the non-Federal sector; and

(7) develop technical assistance materials, seminars, and guidelines to improve security for dams in the United States.

(d) COMPONENTS.—

(1) IN GENERAL.—The Program shall consist of—

(A) a Federal element and a non-Federal element; and

(B) leadership activity, technical assistance activity, and public awareness activity.

(2) ELEMENTS.—

(A) FEDERAL.— The Federal element shall incorporate the activities and practices carried out by Federal agencies under section 7 to implement the Federal Guidelines for Dam Safety.

(B) NON-FEDERAL.—The non-Federal element shall consist of—

(i) the activities and practices carried out by States, local governments, and the private sector to safely build, regulate, operate, and maintain dams; and

(ii) Federal activities that foster State efforts to develop and implement effective programs for the safety of dams.

(3) FUNCTIONAL ACTIVITIES.—

(A) LEADERSHIP.— The leadership activity shall be the responsibility of FEMA and shall be exercised by chairing the Board to coordinate national efforts to improve the safety of the dams in the United States.

(B) TECHNICAL ASSISTANCE.— The technical assistance activity shall consist of the transfer of knowledge and technical information among the Federal and non-Federal elements described in paragraph (2).

(C) PUBLIC AWARENESS.— The public awareness activity shall provide for the education of the public, including State and local officials, in the hazards of dam failure, methods of reducing the adverse consequences of dam failure, and related matters.

(e) ASSISTANCE FOR STATE DAM SAFETY PROGRAMS.—

(1) IN GENERAL.— To encourage the establishment and maintenance of effective State programs intended to ensure dam safety, to protect human life and property, and to improve State dam safety programs, the Administrator shall provide assistance with amounts made available under section 13 to assist States in establishing, maintaining, and improving dam safety programs in accordance with the criteria specified in paragraph (2).

(2) CRITERIA AND BUDGETING REQUIREMENT.—For a State to be eligible for assistance under this subsection, a State dam safety program must be working toward meeting the following criteria and budgeting requirement:

(A) CRITERIA.—A State dam safety program must be authorized by State legislation to include, at a minimum—

(i) the authority to review and approve plans and specifications to construct, enlarge, modify, remove, and abandon dams;

(ii) the authority to perform periodic inspections during dam construction to ensure compliance with approved plans and specifications;

(iii) a requirement that, on completion of dam construction, State approval must be given before operation of the dam;

(iv) the authority to require or perform periodic evaluations of all dams and reservoirs to determine the extent of the threat to human life and property in case of failure;

(v)(I) the authority to require or perform the inspection, at least once every 5 years, of all dams and reservoirs that would pose a significant threat to human life and property in case of failure to determine the continued safety of the dams and reservoirs; and

(II) a procedure for more detailed and frequent safety inspections;

(vi) a requirement that all inspections be performed under the supervision of a State-registered professional engineer with related experience in dam design and construction;

(vii) the authority to issue notices, when appropriate, to require owners of dams to perform necessary maintenance or remedial work, install and monitor instrumentation, improve security, revise operating procedures, or take other actions, including breaching dams when necessary;

(viii) regulations for carrying out the legislation of the State described in this subparagraph;

(ix) provision for necessary funds—

(I) to ensure timely repairs or other changes to, or removal of, a dam in order to protect human life and property; and

(II)   if the owner of the dam does not take action described in subclause (I), to take appropriate action as expeditiously as practicable;

(x)   a system of emergency procedures to be used if a dam fails or if the failure of a dam is imminent; and

(xi) an identification of—

(I)   each dam the failure of which could be reasonably expected to endanger human life;

(II)   the maximum area that could be flooded if the dam failed; and

(III)   necessary public facilities that would be affected by the flooding.

(B) BUDGETING REQUIREMENT.— For a State to be eligible for assistance under this subsection, State appropriations must be budgeted to carry out the legislation of the State under subparagraph (A).

(3) WORK PLANS.— The Administrator shall enter into a agreement with each State receiving assistance under paragraph (2) to develop a work plan necessary for the State dam safety program to reach a level of program performance specified in the agreement.

(4) MAINTENANCE OF EFFORT.— Assistance may not be provided to a State under this subsection for a fiscal year unless the State enters into such agreement with the Administrator as the Administrator requires to ensure that the State will maintain the aggregate expenditures of the State from all other sources for programs to ensure dam safety for the protection of human life and property at or above a level equal to the average annual level of such expenditures for the 2 fiscal years preceding the fiscal year.

(5) APPROVAL OF PROGRAMS.—

(A) SUBMISSION.— For a State to be eligible for assistance under this subsection, a plan for a State dam safety program shall be submitted to the Administrator for approval.

(B) APPROVAL.— A State dam safety program shall be deemed to be approved 120 days after the date of receipt by the Administrator unless the Administrator determines within the 120-day period that the State dam safety program fails to meet the requirements of paragraphs (1) through (3).

(C) NOTIFICATION OF DISAPPROVAL.— If the Administrator determines that a State dam safety program does not meet the requirements for approval, the Administrator shall immediately notify the State in writing and provide the reasons for the determination and the changes that are necessary for the plan to be approved.

(6) REVIEW OF STATE DAM SAFETY PROGRAMS.— Using the expertise of the Board, the Administrator shall periodically review State dam safety programs. If the Board finds that a State dam safety program has proven inadequate to reasonably protect human life and property and the Administrator concurs, the Administrator shall

revoke approval of the State dam safety program, and withhold assistance under this subsection, until the State dam safety program again meets the requirements for approval.

(f) BOARD.—

(1) ESTABLISHMENT.— The Administrator shall establish an advisory board to be known as the National Dam Safety Review Board to monitor the safety of dams in the United States, to monitor State implementation of this section, and to advise the Administrator on national dam safety policy.

(2) AUTHORITY.— The Board may use the expertise of Federal agencies and enter into contracts for necessary studies to carry out this section.

(3) VOTING MEMBERSHIP.—The Board shall consist of 11 voting members selected by the Administrator for expertise in dam safety, of whom—

(A)   1 member shall represent the Department of Agriculture;

(B)   1 member shall represent the Department of Defense;

(C)   1 member shall represent the Department of the Interior;

(D)   1 member shall represent FEMA;

(E)   1 member shall represent the Federal Energy Regulatory Commission;

(F)   5 members shall be selected by the Administrator from among State dam safety officials; and

(G)   1 member shall be selected by the Administrator to represent the private sector.

(4) NONVOTING MEMBERSHIP.— The Administrator, in consultation with the Board, may invite a representative of the National Laboratories of the Department of Energy and may invite representatives from Federal or State agencies, representatives from nongovernmental organizations, or dam safety experts, as needed, to participate in meetings of the Board.

(5) DUTIES.—

(A) IN GENERAL.— The Board shall encourage the establishment and maintenance of effective programs, policies, and guidelines to enhance dam safety for the protection of human life and property throughout the United States.

(B) COORDINATION AND INFORMATION EXCHANGE AMONG AGENCIES.— In carrying out subparagraph (A), the Board shall encourage coordination and information exchange among Federal and State dam safety agencies that share common problems and responsibilities for dam safety, including planning, design, construction, operation, emergency action planning, inspections, maintenance, regulation or licensing, technical or financial assistance, research, and data management.

(6) WORK GROUPS.— The Administrator may establish work groups under the Board to assist the Board in accomplishing its goals. The work groups shall consist of members of the Board and other individuals selected by the Administrator.

(7) COMPENSATION OF MEMBERS.—

(A) FEDERAL EMPLOYEES.— Each member of the Board who is an officer or employee of the United States shall serve without compensation in addition to compensation received for the services of the member as an officer or employee of the United States.

(B) OTHER MEMBERS.— Each member of the Board who is not an officer or employee of the United States shall serve without compensation.

(8) TRAVEL EXPENSES.—

(A) REPRESENTATIVES OF FEDERAL AGENCIES.— To the extent amounts are made available in advance in appropriations Acts, each member of the Board who represents a Federal agency shall be reimbursed of appropriations for travel expenses by his or her agency, including per diem in lieu of subsistence, at rates authorized for an employee of an agency under subchapter I of chapter 57 of title 5, United States Code, while away from the home or regular place of business of the member in the performance of services for the Board.

(B) OTHER INDIVIDUALS.— To the extent amounts are made available in advance in appropriations Acts, each member of the Board who represents a State agency, the member of the Board who represents the private sector, and each member of a work group created under paragraph (1) shall be reimbursed for travel expenses by FEMA, including per diem in lieu of subsistence, at rates authorized for an employee of an agency under subchapter I of chapter 57 of title 5, United States Code, while away from home or regular place of business of the member in performance of services for the Board.

(9) APPLICABILITY OF CHAPTER 10 OF TITLE 5, UNITED STATES CODE.— Chapter 10 of title 5, United States Code, shall not apply to the Board.

[33 U.S.C. 467f]

SEC. 8A. REHABILITATION OF HIGH HAZARD POTENTIAL DAMS.

(a) ESTABLISHMENT OF PROGRAM.— The Administrator shall establish, within FEMA, a program to provide technical, planning, design, and construction assistance in the form of grants to States with dam safety programs for rehabilitation of eligible high hazard potential dams.

(b) ELIGIBLE ACTIVITIES.—A grant awarded under this section to a State may be used by the State to award grants to eligible subrecipients for—

(1) repair;

(2) removal; or

(3) any other structural or nonstructural measures to rehabilitate an eligible high hazard potential dam.

(c) AWARD OF GRANTS.—

(1) APPLICATION.—

(A) IN GENERAL.— A State interested in receiving a grant under this section may submit to the Administrator an application for the grant.

(B) REQUIREMENTS.— An application submitted to the Administrator under this section shall be submitted at such time, be in such form, and contain such information as the Administrator may prescribe by regulation.

(2) GRANT.—

(A) IN GENERAL.— The Administrator may make a grant in accordance with this section for rehabilitation of eligible high hazard potential dams to a State that submits an application for the grant in accordance with the regulations prescribed by the Administrator.

(B) GRANT AGREEMENT.— The Administrator shall enter into a grant agreement with the State to establish the terms of the grant and the projects for which the grant is awarded, including the amount of the grant.

(C) GRANT ASSURANCE.— As part of a grant agreement under subparagraph (B), the Administrator shall require that each eligible subrecipient to which the State awards a grant under this section provides an assurance from the dam owner, with respect to the dam to be rehabilitated, that the dam owner will carry out a plan for maintenance of the dam during the expected life of the dam.

(D) LIMITATION.—A State may not award a grant to an eligible subrecipient under this section that exceeds, for any 1 dam, the lesser of—

(i)   12.5 percent of the total amount of funds made available to carry out this section; or

(ii) $7,500,000.

(d) REQUIREMENTS.—

(1) APPROVAL.— A grant awarded under this section to an eligible subrecipient for a project shall be approved by the relevant State dam safety agency.

(2) ELIGIBLE SUBRECIPIENT REQUIREMENTS.—To receive a grant under this section, an eligible subrecipient shall, with respect to the dam to be rehabilitated by the eligible subrecipient—

(A)   demonstrate that the community in which the dam is located participates in, and complies with, all applicable Federal flood insurance programs, including demonstrating that such community is participating in the National Flood Insurance Program, and is not on probation, suspended, or withdrawn from such Program;

(B)   beginning not later than 2 years after the date on which the Administrator publishes criteria for hazard mitigation plans under paragraph (3), demonstrate that the Tribal or local government with jurisdiction over the area in which the dam is located has in place a hazard mitigation plan that—

(i)   includes all dam risks; and

(ii)   complies with the Disaster Mitigation Act of 2000 (Public Law 106–390; 114 Stat. 1552);

(C)   for a project not including removal, obtain a commitment from the dam owner to provide operation and maintenance of the project for the expected life of the dam following completion of rehabilitation;

(D) comply with such minimum eligibility requirements as the Administrator may establish to ensure that each owner and operator of a dam under a participating State dam safety program and that receives assistance under this section—

(i) acts in accordance with the State dam safety program; and

(ii) carries out activities relating to the public in the area around the dam in accordance with the hazard mitigation plan described in subparagraph (B); and

(E) comply with section 611(j)(9) of the Robert T. Stafford Disaster Relief and Emergency Assistance Act (42 U.S.C. 5196(j)(9)) (as in effect on the date of enactment of this section) with respect to projects receiving assistance under this section in the same manner as recipients are required to comply in order to receive financial contributions from the Administrator for emergency preparedness purposes.

(3) HAZARD MITIGATION PLAN CRITERIA.— Not later than 1 year after the date of enactment of this paragraph, the Administrator, in consultation with the Board, shall publish criteria for hazard mitigation plans required under paragraph (2)(B).

(e) FLOODPLAIN MANAGEMENT PLANS.—

(1) IN GENERAL.—As a condition of receipt of assistance under this section, an eligible subrecipient shall demonstrate that a floodplain management plan to reduce the impacts of future flood events from a controlled or uncontrolled release from the dam or management of water levels in the area impacted by the dam—

(A) for a removal—

(i) is in place; and

(ii) identifies areas that would be impacted by the removal of the dam and includes a communication and outreach plan for the project and the impact of the project on the affected communities; or

(B) for a project not including removal—

(i) is in place; or

(ii) will be—

(I) developed not later than 2 years after the date of execution of a project agreement for assistance under this section; and

(II) implemented not later than 2 years after the date of completion of construction of the project.

(2) REQUIREMENT.— In the case of a plan for a removal, the Administrator may not impose any additional requirements or conditions other than the requirements in paragraph (1)(A).

(3) INCLUSIONS.—A plan under paragraph (1)(B) shall address—

(A) potential measures, practices, and policies to reduce loss of life, injuries, damage to property and facilities, public expenditures, and other adverse impacts of flooding in the area protected or impacted by the dam;

(B) plans for flood fighting and evacuation; and

(C) public education and awareness of flood risks.

(4) PLAN CRITERIA AND TECHNICAL SUPPORT.— The Administrator, in consultation with the Board, shall provide criteria, and may provide technical support, for the development and implementation of floodplain management plans prepared under this subsection.

(f) PRIORITY SYSTEM.— The Administrator, in consultation with the Board, shall develop a risk-based priority system for use in identifying eligible high hazard potential dams for which grants may be made under this section.

(g) FUNDING.—

(1) COST SHARING.—

(A) IN GENERAL.— Except as provided in subparagraph (C), any assistance provided under this section for a project shall be subject to a non-Federal cost-sharing requirement of not less than 35 percent.

(B) IN-KIND CONTRIBUTIONS.— The non-Federal share under subparagraph (A) may be provided in the form of in-kind contributions.

(C) UNDERSERVED COMMUNITIES.— Subparagraph (A) shall not apply to a project carried out by or for the benefit of an underserved community.

(2) ALLOCATION OF FUNDS.—The total amount of funds made available to carry out this section for each fiscal year shall be distributed as follows:

(A) EQUAL DISTRIBUTION.— ⅓ shall be distributed equally among the States in which the projects for which applications are submitted under subsection (c)(1) are located.

(B) NEED-BASED.— ⅔ shall be distributed among the States in which the projects for which applications are submitted under subsection (c)(1) are located based on the proportion that—

(i) the number of eligible high hazard potential dams in the State; bears to

(ii) the number of eligible high hazard potential dams in all such States.

(h) USE OF FUNDS.—None of the funds provided in the form of a grant or otherwise made available under this section shall be used—

(1) to rehabilitate a Federal dam;

(2) to perform routine operation or maintenance of a dam;

(3) to modify a dam to produce hydroelectric power;

(4) to increase water supply storage capacity; or

(5) to make any other modification to a dam that does not also improve the safety of the dam.

(i) CONTRACTUAL REQUIREMENTS.—

(1) IN GENERAL.—Subject to paragraph (2), as a condition on the receipt of a grant under this section of an amount greater than $1,000,000, an eligible subrecipient

that receives the grant shall require that each contract and subcontract for program management, construction management, planning studies, feasibility studies, architectural services, preliminary engineering, design, engineering, surveying, mapping, and related services entered into using funds from the grant be awarded in the same manner as a contract for architectural and engineering services is awarded under—

(A)   chapter 11 of title 40, United States Code; or

(B)   an equivalent qualifications-based requirement prescribed by the relevant State.

(2) No PROPRIETARY INTEREST.— A contract awarded in accordance with paragraph (1) shall not be considered to confer a proprietary interest upon the United States.

(j) AUTHORIZATION OF APPROPRIATIONS.—There are authorized to be appropriated to carry out this section—

(1) $10,000,000 for fiscal years 2017 and 2018;

(2) $25,000,000 for fiscal year 2019;

(3) $40,000,000 for fiscal year 2020; and

(4) $60,000,000 for each of fiscal years 2021 through 2026.

[33 U.S.C. 467f–2]

SEC. 9. RESEARCH.

(a) IN GENERAL.—The Administrator, in cooperation with the Board, shall carry out a program of technical and archival research to develop and support—

(1)   improved techniques, historical experience, and equipment for rapid and effective dam construction, rehabilitation, and inspection;

(2)   devices for the continued monitoring of the safety of dams;

(3)   development and maintenance of information resources systems needed to support managing the safety of dams; and

(4)   initiatives to guide the formulation of effective public policy and advance improvements in dam safety engineering, security, and management.

(b) CONSULTATION.— The Administrator shall provide for State participation in research under subsection (a) and periodically advise all States and Congress of the results of the research.

[33 U.S.C. 467g]

SEC. 10. DAM SAFETY TRAINING.

At the request of any State that has or intends to develop a State dam safety program, the Administrator shall provide training for State dam safety staff and inspectors.

[33 U.S.C. 467g–1]

SEC. 11. PUBLIC AWARENESS AND OUTREACH FOR DAM SAFETY.

The Administrator, in consultation with other Federal agencies, State and local governments, dam owners, the emergency management community, the private sector, nongovernmental organizations and associations, institutions of higher education, and any other appropriate entities shall, subject to the availability of appropriations, carry out a nationwide public awareness and outreach initiative to assist the public in preparing for, mitigating, responding to, and recovering from dam incidents.

[33 U.S.C. 467g–2]

SEC. 12. REPORTS.

Not later than 90 days after the end of each odd-numbered fiscal year, the Administrator shall submit a report to Congress that—

(1) describes the status of the Program;

(2) describes the progress achieved by Federal agencies during the 2 preceding fiscal years in implementing the Federal Guidelines for Dam Safety;

(3) describes the progress achieved in dam safety by States participating in the Program; and

(4) includes any recommendations for legislative and other action that the Administrator considers necessary.

[33 U.S.C. 467h]

SEC. 13. STATUTORY CONSTRUCTION.

Nothing in this Act and no action or failure to act under this Act shall—

(1) create any liability in the United States or its officers or employees for the recovery of damages caused by such action or failure to act;

(2) relieve an owner or operator of a dam of the legal duties, obligations, or liabilities incident to the ownership or operation of the dam; or

(3) preempt any other Federal or State law.

[33 U.S.C. 467i]

SEC. 14. AUTHORIZATION OF APPROPRIATIONS.

(a) NATIONAL DAM SAFETY PROGRAM.—

(1) ANNUAL AMOUNTS.— There are authorized to be appropriated to FEMA to carry out sections 7, 8, and 12 (in addition to any amounts made available for similar purposes included in any other Act and amounts made available under subsections (b) through (e)), $9,200,000 for each of fiscal years 2019 through 2028, to remain available until expended.

(2) ALLOCATION.—

(A) IN GENERAL.—Subject to subparagraphs (B) and (C), for each fiscal year, amounts made available under this subsection to carry out section 8 shall be allocated among the States as follows:

(i) One-third among States that qualify for assistance under section 8(e).

(ii) Two-thirds among States that qualify for assistance under section 8(e), to each such State in proportion to—

(I)   the number of dams in the State that are listed as State-regulated dams on the inventory of dams and low-head dams maintained under section 6; as compared to

(II)   the number of dams in all States that are listed as State-regulated dams on the inventory of dams and low-head dams maintained under section 6.

(B) MAXIMUM AMOUNT OF ALLOCATION.— The amount of funds allocated to a State under this paragraph for a fiscal year may not exceed the amount that is equal to 4 times the amount of funds committed by the State to implement dam safety activities for that fiscal year.

(C) DETERMINATION.— The Administrator and the Board shall determine the amount allocated to States.

(b) NATIONAL INVENTORY OF DAMS AND LOW-HEAD DAMS.— There is authorized to be appropriated to carry out section 6 $500,000 for each of fiscal years 2019 through 2028.

(c) PUBLIC AWARENESS.— There is authorized to be appropriated to carry out section 11 $1,000,000 for each of fiscal years 2019 through 2028.

(d) RESEARCH.— There is authorized to be appropriated to carry out section 9 $1,450,000 for each of fiscal years 2019 through 2028, to remain until expended.

(e) DAM SAFETY TRAINING.— There is authorized to be appropriated to carry out section 10 $750,000 for each of fiscal years 2019 through 2028.

(f) STAFF.— There is authorized to be appropriated to FEMA for the employment of such additional staff personnel as are necessary to carry out sections 8 through 10 $1,000,000 for each of fiscal years 2019 through 2028.

(g) LIMITATION ON USE OF AMOUNTS.— Amounts made available under this Act may not be used to construct or repair any Federal or non-Federal dam.

[33 U.S.C. 467j]

★

HAZARD-SPECIFIC LAWS
FIRES

FEDERAL FIRE PREVENTION AND CONTROL ACT OF 1974

PUBLIC LAW 93–498
AS AMENDED THROUGH PUB. L. 118–67

FEDERAL FIRE PREVENTION AND CONTROL ACT OF 1974

[Pub. L. 93–498; Approved Oct. 29, 1974; 88 Stat. 1535]

[As Amended Through P.L. 118–67, Enacted July 9, 2024]

AN ACT To reduce losses of life and property, through better fire prevention and control, and for other purposes.

Be it enacted by the Senate and House of Representatives of the United States of America in Congress assembled,

That this Act may be cited as the "Federal Fire Prevention and Control Act of 1974".

[15 U.S.C. 2201 note]

FINDINGS

SEC. 2. The Congress finds that—

(1) The National Commission on Fire Prevention and Control, established pursuant to Public Law 90–259, has made an exhaustive and comprehensive examination of the Nation's fire problem, has made detailed findings as to the extent of this problem in terms of human suffering and loss of life and property, and has made ninety thoughtful recommendations.

(2) The United States today has the highest per capita rate of death and property loss from fire of all the major industrialized nations in the world.

(3) Fire is an undue burden affecting all Americans, and fire also constitutes a public health and safety problem of great dimensions. Fire kills 12,000 and scars and injures 300,000 Americans each year, including 50,000 individuals who require extended hospitalization. Almost $3 billion worth of property is destroyed annually by fire, and the total economic cost of destructive fire in the United States is estimated conservatively to be $11,000,000,000 per year. Firefighting is the Nation's most hazardous profession.

(4) Such losses of life and property from fire are unacceptable to the Congress.

(5) While fire prevention and control is and should remain a State and local responsibility, the Federal Government must help if a significant reduction in fire losses is to be achieved.

(6) The fire service and the civil defense program in each locality would both

benefit from closer cooperation.

(7)   The Nation's fire problem is exacerbated by (A) the indifference with which some Americans confront the subject; (B) the Nation's failure to undertake enough research and development into fire and fire-related problems; (C) the scarcity of reliable data and information; (D) the fact that designers and purchasers of buildings and products generally give insufficient attention to fire safety; (E) the fact that many communities lack adequate building and fire prevention codes; and (F) the fact that local fire departments spend about 95 cents of every dollar appropriated to the fire services on efforts to extinguish fires and only about 5 cents on fire prevention.

(8)   There is a need for improved professional training and education oriented toward improving the effectiveness of the fire services, including an increased emphasis on preventing fires and on reducing injuries to firefighters.

(9)   A national system for the collection, analysis, and dissemination of fire data is needed to help local fire services establish research and action priorities.

(10)   The number of specialized medical centers which are properly equipped and staffed for the treatment of burns and the rehabilitation of victims of fires is inadequate.

(11)   The unacceptably high rates of death, injury, and property loss from fire can be reduced if the Federal Government establishes a coordinated program to support and reinforce the fire prevention and control activities of State and local governments.
[15 U.S.C. 2201]

PURPOSES

SEC. 3. It is declared to be the purpose of Congress in this Act to—

(1)   reduce the Nation's losses caused by fire through better fire prevention and control;

(2)   supplement existing programs of research, training, and education, and to encourage new and improved programs and activities by State and local governments;

(3)   establish the United States Fire Administration and the Fire Research Center within the Department of Commerce; and

(4)   establish an intensified program of research into the treatment of burn and smoke injuries and the rehabilitation of victims of fires within the National Institutes of Health.
[15 U.S.C. 2202]

DEFINITIONS

SEC. 4. As used in this Act, the term—

(1)   Academy means the National Academy for Fire Prevention and Control;

(2)   Administration means the United States Fire Administration established pursuant to section 5 of this Act;

(3)   Administrator means, except as otherwise provided, the Administrator of the United States Fire Administration, within the Federal Emergency Management

Agency;

(4) Administrator of FEMA means the Administrator of the Federal Emergency Management Agency;

(5) fire service means any organization in any State consisting of personnel, apparatus, and equipment which has as its purpose protecting property and maintaining the safety and welfare of the public from the dangers of fire, including a private firefighting brigade. The personnel of any such organization may be paid employees or unpaid volunteers or any combination thereof. The location of any such organization and its responsibility for extinguishment and suppression of fires may include, but need not be limited to, a Federal installation, a State, city, town, borough, parish, county, Indian tribe, fire district, fire protection district, rural fire district, or other special district. The terms fire prevention, firefighting, and `fire control" relate to activities conducted by a fire service;

(6) Indian tribe has the meaning given that term in section 4 of the Indian Self-Determination and Education Assistance Act (25 U.S.C. 450b) and tribal means of or pertaining to an Indian tribe;

(7) local means of or pertaining to any city, town, county, special purpose district, unincorporated territory, or other political subdivision of a State;

(8) place of public accommodation affecting commerce means any inn, hotel, or other establishment not owned by the Federal Government that provides lodging to transient guests, except that such term does not include an establishment treated as an apartment building for purposes of any State or local law or regulation or an establishment located within a building that contains not more than 5 rooms for rent or hire and that is actually occupied as a residence by the proprietor of such establishment;

(9) Secretary means, except as otherwise provided, the Secretary of Homeland Security;

(10) State has the meaning given the term in section 2 of the Homeland Security Act of 2002 (6 U.S.C. 101).

(11) wildland-urban interface has the meaning given such term in section 101 of the Healthy Forests Restoration Act of 2003 (16 U.S.C. 6511).

[15 U.S.C. 2203]

ESTABLISHMENT OF THE UNITED STATES FIRE ADMINISTRATION

SEC. 5. (a) ESTABLISHMENT OF ADMINISTRATION.— There is hereby established in the Department of Commerce an agency which shall be known as the United States Fire Administration.

(b) ADMINISTRATOR.— There shall be at the head of the Administration the Administrator of the United States Fire Administration. The Administrator shall be appointed by the President and shall be compensated at the rate now or hereafter provided for level IV of the Executive Schedule pay rates (5 U.S.C. 5315). The Administrator shall report and be responsible to the Administrator of FEMA.

(c) DEPUTY ADMINISTRATOR.—The Administrator may appoint a Deputy Administrator, who shall—

(1)   perform such functions as the Administrator shall from time to time assign or delegate; and

(2)   act as Administrator during the absence or disability of the Administrator or in the event of a vacancy in the office of Administrator.

[15 U.S.C. 2204]

PUBLIC EDUCATION

SEC. 6.   The Administrator is authorized to take such steps as the Administrator considers appropriate to educate the public and overcome public indifference as to fire, fire prevention, and individual preparedness. Such steps may include, but are not limited to, publications, audiovisual presentations, and demonstrations. Such public education efforts shall include programs to provide specialized information for those groups of individuals who are particularly vulnerable to fire hazards, such as the young and the elderly. The Administrator shall sponsor and encourage research, testing, and experimentation to determine the most effective means of such public education.

[15 U.S.C. 2205]

NATIONAL ACADEMY FOR FIRE PREVENTION AND CONTROL

SEC. 7. (a) ESTABLISHMENT.— The Administrator of FEMA shall establish, at the earliest practicable date, a National Academy for Fire Prevention and Control. The purpose of the Academy shall be to advance the professional development of fire service personnel and of other persons engaged in fire prevention and control activities.

(b) SUPERINTENDENT.— The Academy shall be headed by a Superintendent, who shall be appointed by the Administrator of FEMA. In exercising the powers and authority contained in this section the Superintendent shall be subject to the direction of the Administrator.

(c) POWERS OF SUPERINTENDENT.—The Superintendent is authorized to—

(1)   develop and revise curricula, standards for admission and performance, and criteria for the awarding of degrees and certifications;

(2)   appoint such teaching staff and other personnel as he determines to be necessary or appropriate;

(3)   conduct courses and programs of training and education, as defined in subsection (d) of this section;

(4)   appoint faculty members and consultants without regard to the provisions of title 5, United States Code, governing appointments in the competitive service, and, with respect to temporary and intermittent services, to make appointments to the same extent as is authorized by section 3109 of title 5, United States Code;

(5)   establish fees and other charges for attendance at, and subscription to, courses and programs offered by the Academy. Such fees may be modified or waived as determined by the Superintendent;

(6)   conduct short courses, seminars, workshops, conferences, and similar education and training activities in all parts and localities of the United States, including on-site training;

(7) enter into such contracts and take such other actions as may be necessary in carrying out the purposes of the Academy; and

(8) consult with officials of the fire services and other interested persons in the exercise of the foregoing powers.

(d) PROGRAM OF THE ACADEMY.—The Superintendent is authorized to—

(1) train fire service personnel in such skills and knowledge as may be useful to advance their ability to prevent and control fires, including, but not limited to—

(A) techniques of fire prevention, fire inspection, fire-fighting, and fire and arson investigation;

(B) tactics and command of firefighting for present and future fire chiefs and commanders;

(C) administration and management of fire services;

(D) tactical training in the specialized field of aircraft fire control and crash rescue;

(E) tactical training in the specialized field of fire control and rescue aboard waterborne vessels;

(F) strategies for building collapse rescue;

(G) the use of technology in response to fires, including terrorist incidents and other national emergencies;

(H) tactics and strategies for dealing with natural disasters, acts of terrorism, and other man-made disasters;

(I) tactics and strategies for fighting large-scale fires or multiple fires in a general area that cross jurisdictional boundaries;

(J) tactics and strategies for fighting fires occurring at the wildland-urban interface;

(K) tactics and strategies for fighting fires involving hazardous materials;

(L) advanced emergency medical services training;

(M) use of and familiarity with the Federal Response Plan;

(N) leadership and strategic skills, including integrated management systems operations and integrated response;

(O) applying new technology and developing strategies and tactics for fighting wildland fires;

(P) integrating the activities of terrorism response agencies into national terrorism incident response systems;

(Q) tactics and strategies for fighting fires at United States ports, including fires on the water and aboard vessels; and

(R) the training of present and future instructors in the aforementioned subjects;

(2) develop model curricula, training programs, and other educational materials

suitable for use at other educational institutions, and to make such materials available without charge;

(3) develop and administer a program of correspondence courses to advance the knowledge and skills of fire service personnel;

(4) develop and distribute to appropriate officials model questions suitable for use in conducting entrance and promotional examinations for fire service personnel; and

(5) encourage the inclusion of fire prevention and detection technology and practices in the education and professional practice of architects, builders, city planners, and others engaged in design and planning affected by fire safety problems.

(e) TECHNICAL ASSISTANCE.—The Administrator is authorized, to the extent that he determines it necessary to meet the needs of the Nation, to encourage new programs and to strengthen existing programs of education and training by local fire services, units and departments, State and local governments, and private institutions, by providing technical assistance and advice to—

(1) vocational training programs in techniques of fire prevention, fire inspection, firefighting, and fire and arson investigation;

(2) fire training courses and programs at junior colleges; and

(3) four-year degree programs in fire engineering at colleges and universities.

(f) ASSISTANCE.— The Administrator is authorized to provide assistance to State and local fire service training programs through grants, contracts, or otherwise. Such assistance shall not exceed 4 per centum[1] of the amount authorized to be appropriated in each fiscal year pursuant to section 17 of this Act.

---

[1]   Section 4(b)(2) of Public Law 110–376 provides that subsection (f) is amended by striking 4 percent and inserting 7.5 percent. The amendment cannot be executed because the term to be struck does not appear.

(g) SITE SELECTION.—The Academy shall be located on such site as the Administrator of FEMA selects, subject to the following provisions:

(1) The Administrator of FEMA is authorized to appoint a Site Selection Board consisting of the Academy Superintendent and two other members to survey the most suitable sites for the location of the Academy and to make recommendations to the Administrator of FEMA.

(2) The Site Selection Board in making its recommendations and the Administrator of FEMA in making his final selection, shall give consideration to the training and facility needs of the Academy, environmental effects, the possibility of using a surplus Government facility, and such other factors as are deemed important and relevant. The Administrator of FEMA shall make a final site selection not later than 2 years after the date of enactment of this Act.

(h) CONSTRUCTION COSTS.— Of the sums authorized to be appropriated for the purpose of implementing the programs of the Administration, not more than $9,000,000 shall be available for the construction of facilities of the Academy on the site selected under subsection (g) of this section. Such sums for such construction shall remain available until expended.

(i) EDUCATIONAL AND PROFESSIONAL ASSISTANCE.—The Administrator is authorized to—

(1) provide stipends to students attending Academy courses and programs in amounts up to 75 per centum of the expense of attendance, as established by the Superintendent;

(2) provide stipends to students attending courses and nondegree training programs approved by the Superintendent at universities, colleges, and junior colleges, in amounts up to 50 per centum of the cost of tuition;

(3) make or enter into contracts to make payments to institutions of higher education for loans, not to exceed $2,500 per academic year for any individual who is enrolled on a full-time basis in an undergraduate or graduate program of fire research or engineering which is certified by the Superintendent. Loans under this paragraph shall be made on such terms and subject to such conditions as the Superintendent and each institution involved may jointly determine; and

(4) establish and maintain a placement and promotion opportunities center in cooperation with the fire services, for fire-fighters who wish to learn and take advantage of different or better career opportunities. Such center shall not limit such assistance to students and graduates of the Academy, but shall undertake to assist all fire service personnel.

(j) BOARD OF VISITORS.— Upon establishment of the Academy, the Administrator of FEMA shall establish a procedure for the selection of professionals in the field of fire safety, fire prevention, fire control, research and development in fire protection, treatment and rehabilitation of fire victims, or local government services management to serve as members of a Board of Visitors for the Academy. Pursuant to such procedure, the Administrator of FEMA shall select eight such persons to serve as members of such Board of Visitors to serve such terms as the Administrator of FEMA may prescribe. The function of such Board shall be to review annually the program of the Academy and to make comments and recommendations to the Administrator of FEMA regarding the operation of the Academy and any improvements therein which such Board deems appropriate. Each member of such Board shall be reimbursed for any expenses actually incurred by him in the performance of his duties as a member of such Board.

(k) ACCREDITATION.— The Superintendent is authorized to establish a Committee on Fire Training and Education which shall inquire into and make recommendations regarding the desirability of establishing a mechanism for accreditation of fire training and education programs and courses, and the role which the Academy should play if such a mechanism is recommended. The Committee shall consist of the Superintendent as Chairman and eighteen other members appointed by the Administrator from among individuals and organizations possessing special knowledge and experience in the field of fire training and education or related fields. The Committee shall submit to the Administrator within two years after its appointment, a full and complete report of its findings and recommendations. Upon the submission of such report, the Committee shall cease to exist. Each appointed member of the Committee shall be reimbursed for expenses actually incurred in the performance of his duties as a member.

(l) ADMISSION.— The Superintendent is authorized to admit to the courses and programs of the Academy individuals who are members of the firefighting, rescue, and civil defense forces of the Nation and such other individuals, including candidates for membership in these forces, as he determines can benefit from attendance. Students shall be admitted from any State, with due regard to adequate representation in the student body of all geographic regions of the Nation. In selecting students, the Superintendent may seek nominations and advice from the fire services and other organizations which wish to send students to the Academy. The Superintendent shall offer, at the Academy and at other sites, courses and training assistance as necessary to accommodate all geographic regions and needs of career and volunteer firefighters.

(m) ON-SITE TRAINING.—

(1) IN GENERAL.— Except as provided in paragraph (2), the Administrator may enter into a contract with nationally recognized organizations that have established on-site training programs that comply with national voluntary consensus standards for fire service personnel to facilitate the delivery of the education and training programs outlined in subsection (d)(1) directly to fire service personnel.

(2) LIMITATION.—

(A) IN GENERAL.—The Administrator may not enter into a contract with an organization described in paragraph (1) unless such organization provides training that—

(i) leads to certification by a program that is accredited by a nationally recognized accreditation organization; or

(ii) the Administrator determines is of equivalent quality to a fire service training program described by clause (i).

(B) APPROVAL OF UNACCREDITED FIRE SERVICE TRAINING PROGRAMS.— The Administrator may consider the fact that an organization has provided a satisfactory fire service training program pursuant to a cooperative agreement with a Federal agency as evidence that such program is of equivalent quality to a fire service training program described by subparagraph (A)(i).

(3) RESTRICTION ON USE OF FUNDS.— The amounts expended by the Administrator to carry out this subsection in any fiscal year shall not exceed 7.5 per centum of the amount authorized to be appropriated in such fiscal year pursuant to section 17.

(n) TRIENNIAL REPORT.—In the first annual report filed pursuant to section 16 for which the deadline for filing is after the expiration of the 18-month period that begins on the date of the enactment of the United States Fire Administration Reauthorization Act of 2008, and in every third annual report thereafter, the Administrator shall include information about changes made to the National Fire Academy curriculum, including—

(1) the basis for such changes, including a review of the incorporation of lessons learned by emergency response personnel after significant emergency events and emergency preparedness exercises performed under the National Exercise Program; and

(2) the desired training outcome of all such changes.

[15 U.S.C. 2206]

FIRE TECHNOLOGY

SEC. 8. (a) TECHNOLOGY DEVELOPMENT PROGRAM.—The Administrator shall conduct a continuing program of development, testing, and evaluation of equipment for use by the Nation's fire, rescue, and civil defense services, with the aim of making available improved suppression, protective, auxiliary, and warning devices incorporating the latest technology. Attention shall be given to the standardization, compatibility, and interchangeability of such equipment. Such development, testing, and evaluation activities shall include, but need not be limited to—

(1) safer, less cumbersome articles of protective clothing, including helmets, boots, and coats;

(2) breathing apparatus with the necessary duration of service, reliability, low weight, and ease of operation for practical use;

(3) safe and reliable auxiliary equipment for use in fire prevention, detection, and control, such as fire location detectors, visual and audio communications equipment, and mobile equipment;

(4) special clothing and equipment needed for forest fires, brush fires, oil and gasoline fires, aircraft fires and crash rescue, fires occurring aboard waterborne vessels, and in other special firefighting situations;

(5) fire detectors and related equipment for residential use with high sensitivity and reliability, and which are sufficiently inexpensive to purchase, install, and maintain to insure wide acceptance and use;

(6) in-place fire prevention systems of low cost and of increased reliability and effectiveness;

(7) methods of testing fire alarms and fire protection devices and systems on a non-interference basis;

(8) the development of purchase specifications, standards, and acceptance and validation test procedures for all such equipment and devices; and

(9) operation tests, demonstration projects, and fire investigations in support of the activities set forth in this section.

(b) LIMITATION.— The Administration shall not engage in the manufacture or sale of any equipment or device developed pursuant to this section, except to the extent that it deems it necessary to adequately develop, test, or evaluate such equipment or device.

(c) MANAGEMENT STUDIES.—(1) The Administrator is authorized to conduct, directly or through contracts or grants, studies of the operations and management aspects of fire services, utilizing quantitative techniques, such as operations research, management economics, cost effectiveness studies, and such other techniques and methods as may be applicable and useful. Such studies shall include, but need not be limited to, the allocation of resources, the optimum location of fire stations, the optimum geographical area for an integrated fire service, the manner of responding to alarms, the operation of citywide and regional fire dispatch centers, firefighting under conditions of civil disturbance, and the effectiveness, frequency, and methods of building inspections.

(2) The Administrator is authorized to conduct, directly or through contracts

or grants, studies of the operations and management aspects of fire service-based emergency medical services and coordination between emergency medical services and fire services. Such studies may include the optimum protocols for on-scene care, the allocation of resources, and the training requirements for fire service-based emergency medical services.

(3) The Administrator is authorized to conduct, directly or through contracts or grants, research concerning the productivity and efficiency of fire service personnel, the job categories and skills required by fire services under varying conditions, the reduction of injuries to fire service personnel, the most effective fire prevention programs and activities, and techniques for accurately measuring and analyzing the foregoing.

(4) The Administrator is authorized to conduct, directly or through contracts, grants, or other forms of assistance, development, testing, and demonstration projects to the extent deemed necessary to introduce and to encourage the acceptance of new technology, standards, operating methods, command techniques, and management systems for utilization by the fire services.

(5) The Administrator is authorized to assist the Nation's fire services, directly or through contracts, grants, or other forms of assistance, to measure and evaluate, on a cost-benefit basis, the effectiveness of the programs and activities of each fire service and the predictable consequences on the applicable local fire services of coordination or combination, in whole or in part, in a regional, metropolitan, or statewide fire service.

(d) RURAL AND WILDLAND-URBAN INTERFACE ASSISTANCE.—The Administrator may, in coordination with the Secretary of Agriculture, the Secretary of the Interior, and the Wildland Fire Leadership Council, assist the fire services of the United States, directly or through contracts, grants, or other forms of assistance, in sponsoring and encouraging research into approaches, techniques, systems, equipment, and land-use policies to improve fire prevention and control in—

(1) the rural and remote areas of the United States; and

(2) the wildland-urban interface.

(e) ASSISTANCE TO OTHER FEDERAL AGENCIES.— At the request of other Federal agencies, including the Department of Agriculture and the Department of the Interior, the Administrator may provide assistance in fire prevention and control technologies, including methods of containing insect-infested forest fires and limiting dispersal of resultant fire particle smoke, and methods of measuring and tracking the dispersal of fine particle smoke resulting from fires of insect-infested fuel.

(f) TECHNOLOGY EVALUATION AND STANDARDS DEVELOPMENT.—

(1) IN GENERAL.—In addition to, or as part of, the program conducted under subsection (a), the Administrator, in consultation with the National Institute of Standards and Technology, the Inter-Agency Board for Equipment Standardization and Inter-Operability, the National Institute for Occupational Safety and Health, the Directorate of Science and Technology of the Department of Homeland Security, national voluntary consensus standards development organizations, interested Federal, State, and local agencies, and other interested parties, shall—

(A) develop new, and utilize existing, measurement techniques and testing methodologies for evaluating new firefighting technologies, including—

(i) personal protection equipment;

(ii) devices for advance warning of extreme hazard;

(iii) equipment for enhanced vision;

(iv) devices to locate victims, firefighters, and other rescue personnel in above-ground and below-ground structures;

(v) equipment and methods to provide information for incident command, including the monitoring and reporting of individual personnel welfare;

(vi) equipment and methods for training, especially for virtual reality training; and

(vii) robotics and other remote-controlled devices;

(B) evaluate the compatibility of new equipment and technology with existing firefighting technology; and

(C) support the development of new voluntary consensus standards through national voluntary consensus standards organizations for new firefighting technologies based on techniques and methodologies described in subparagraph (A).

(2) STANDARDS FOR NEW EQUIPMENT.—(A) The Administrator shall, by regulation, require that new equipment or systems purchased through the assistance program established by the first section 33 meet or exceed applicable voluntary consensus standards for such equipment or systems for which applicable voluntary consensus standards have been established. The Administrator may waive the requirement under this subparagraph with respect to specific standards.

(B) If an applicant for a grant under the first section 33 proposes to purchase, with assistance provided under the grant, new equipment or systems that do not meet or exceed applicable voluntary consensus standards, the applicant shall include in the application an explanation of why such equipment or systems will serve the needs of the applicant better than equipment or systems that do meet or exceed such standards.

(C) In making a determination whether or not to waive the requirement under subparagraph (A) with respect to a specific standard, the Administrator shall, to the greatest extent practicable—

(i) consult with grant applicants and other members of the fire services regarding the impact on fire departments of the requirement to meet or exceed the specific standard;

(ii) take into consideration the explanation provided by the applicant under subparagraph (B); and

(iii) seek to minimize the impact of the requirement to meet or exceed the specific standard on the applicant, particularly if meeting the standard would impose additional costs.

(D)   Applicants that apply for a grant under the terms of subparagraph (B) may include a second grant request in the application to be considered by the Administrator in the event that the Administrator does not approve the primary grant request on the grounds of the equipment not meeting applicable voluntary consensus standards.

(g) COORDINATION.— In establishing and conducting programs under this section, the Administrator shall take full advantage of applicable technological developments made by other departments and agencies of the Federal Government, by State and local governments, and by business, industry, and nonprofit associations.

(h) PUBLICATION OF RESEARCH RESULTS.—

(1) IN GENERAL.—For each fire-related research program funded by the Administration, the Administrator shall make available to the public on the Internet website of the Administration the following:

(A)   A description of such research program, including the scope, methodology, and goals thereof.

(B)   Information that identifies the individuals or institutions conducting the research program.

(C)   The amount of funding provided by the Administration for such program.

(D)   The results or findings of the research program.

(2) DEADLINES.—

(A) IN GENERAL.—Except as provided in subparagraph (B), the information required by paragraph (1) shall be published with respect to a research program as follows:

(i)   The information described in subparagraphs (A), (B), and (C) of paragraph (1) with respect to such research program shall be made available under paragraph (1) not later than 30 days after the Administrator has awarded the funding for such research program.

(ii)   The information described in subparagraph (D) of paragraph (1) with respect to a research program shall be made available under paragraph (1) not later than 60 days after the date such research program has been completed.

(B) EXCEPTION.— No information shall be required to be published under this subsection before the date that is 1 year after the date of the enactment of the United States Fire Administration Reauthorization Act of 2008.

[15 U.S.C. 2207]

NATIONAL FIRE DATA CENTER

SEC. 9. (a) GENERAL.—The Administrator shall operate, directly or through contracts or grants, an integrated, comprehensive National Fire Data Center for the selection, analysis, publication, and dissemination of information related to the prevention, occurrence, control, and results of fires of all types. The program of such Data Center shall be designed to (1) provide an accurate nationwide analysis of the fire problem,

(2) identify major problem areas, (3) assist in setting priorities, (4) determine possible solutions to problems, and (5) monitor the progress of programs to reduce fire losses. To carry out these functions, the Data Center shall gather and analyze—

(1) information on the frequency, causes, spread, and extinguishment of fires;

(2) information on the number of injuries and deaths resulting from fires, including the maximum available information on the specific causes and nature of such injuries and deaths, categorized by the type of fire, and information on property losses;

(3) information on the occupational hazards faced by firefighters, including the causes of deaths and injuries arising, directly and indirectly, from firefighting activities, including—

(A) all injuries sustained by a firefighter and treated by a doctor, categorized by the type of firefighter;

(B) all deaths sustained while undergoing a pack test or preparing for a work capacity;

(C) all injuries or deaths resulting from vehicle accidents; and

(D) all injuries or deaths resulting from aircraft crashes;

(4) information on all types of firefighting activities, including inspection practices;

(5) technical information related to building construction, fire properties of materials, and similar information;

(6) information on fire prevention and control laws, systems, methods, techniques, and administrative structures used in foreign nations;

(7) information on the causes, behavior, and best method of control of other types of fire, including, but not limited to, forest fires, brush fires, fire underground, oil blow-out fires, and waterborne fires; and

(8) such other information and data as is deemed useful and applicable.

(b) METHODS.—In carrying out the program of the Data Center, the Administrator is authorized to—

(1) develop standardized data reporting methods;

(2) encourage and assist Federal, State, local, and other agencies, public and private, in developing and reporting information; and

(3) make full use of existing data gathering and analysis organizations, both public and private, including the Center for Firefighter Injury Research and Safety Trends.

(c) DISSEMINATION.— The Administrator shall insure dissemination to the maximum extent possible of fire data collected and developed by the Data Center, and shall make sure data, information, and analysis available in appropriate form to Federal agencies, State and local governments, private organizations, industry, business, and other interested persons.

(d) NATIONAL FIRE INCIDENT REPORTING SYSTEM UPDATE.— The Administrator shall update the National Fire Incident Reporting System to ensure that the information in the system is available, and can be updated, through the Internet and in real time.

(e) MEDICAL PRIVACY OF FIREFIGHTERS.—The collection, storage, and transfer of any medical data collected under this section shall be conducted in accordance with—

(1) the privacy regulations promulgated under section 264(c) of the Health Insurance Portability and Accountability Act of 1996 (42 U.S.C. 1320d–2 note; Public Law 104–191); and

(2) other applicable regulations, including parts 160, 162, and 164 of title 45, Code of Federal Regulations (as in effect on the date of enactment of this subsection).

[15 U.S.C. 2208]

MASTER PLANS

SEC. 10. (a) GENERAL.— The establishment of master plans for fire prevention and control are the responsibility of the States and the political subdivisions thereof. The Administrator is authorized to encourage and assist such States and political subdivisions in such planning activities, consistent with his powers and duties under this Act.

(b) MUTUAL AID SYSTEMS.—

(1) IN GENERAL.—The Administrator shall provide technical assistance and training to State and local fire service officials to establish nationwide and State mutual aid systems for dealing with national emergencies that—

(A) include threat assessment and equipment deployment strategies;

(B) include means of collecting asset and resource information to provide accurate and timely data for regional deployment; and

(C) are consistent with the Federal Response Plan.

(2) MODEL MUTUAL AID PLANS.— The Administrator shall develop and make available to State and local fire service officials model mutual aid plans for both intrastate and interstate assistance.

(c) DEFINITION.— For the purposes of this section, a master plan is one which will result in the planning and implementation in the area involved of a general program of action for fire prevention and control. Such master plan is reasonably expected to include (1) a survey of the resources and personnel of existing fire services and an analysis of the effectiveness of the fire and building codes in such area; (2) an analysis of short and long term fire prevention and control needs in such area; (3) a plan to meet the fire prevention and control needs in such area; and (4) an estimate of cost and realistic plans for financing the implementation of the plan and operation on a continuing basis and a summary of problems that are anticipated in implementing such master plan.

[15 U.S.C. 2209]

REIMBURSEMENT FOR COSTS OF FIREFIGHTING ON FEDERAL PROPERTY

SEC. 11. (a) CLAIM.— Each fire service that engages in the fighting of a fire on property which is under the jurisdiction of the United States may file a claim with the Administrator for the amount of direct expenses and direct losses incurred by such fire service as a result of fighting such fire. The claim shall include such supporting information as the Administrator may prescribe.

(b) DETERMINATION.—Upon receipt of a claim filed under subsection (a) of this section, the Administrator shall determine—

(1) what payments, if any, to the fire service or its parent jurisdiction, including taxes or payments in lieu of taxes, the United States has made for the support of fire services on the property in question;

(2) the extent to which the fire service incurred additional firefighting costs, over and above its normal operating costs, in connection with the fire which is the subject of the claim; and

(3) the amount, if any, of the additional costs referred to in paragraph (2) of this subsection which were not adequately covered by the payments referred to in paragraph (1) of this subsection;

(c) PAYMENT.— The Administrator of FEMA shall forward the claim and a copy of the Administrator's determination under subsection (b)(3) of this section to the Secretary of the Treasury. The Secretary of the Treasury shall, upon receipt of the claim and determination, pay such fire service or its parent jurisdiction, from any moneys in the Treasury not otherwise appropriated but subject to reimbursement (from any appropriations which may be available or which may be made available for the purpose) by the Federal department or agency under whose jurisdiction the fire occurred, a sum no greater than the amount determined with respect to the claim under subsection (b)(3) of this section.

(d) ADJUDICATION.— In the case of a dispute arising in connection with a claim under this section, the United States Claims Court shall have jurisdiction to adjudicate the claim and enter judgment accordingly.

[15 U.S.C. 2210]

REVIEW OF CODES

SEC. 12.   The Administrator is authorized to review, evaluate, and suggest improvements in State and local fire prevention codes, building codes, and any relevant Federal or private codes and regulations. In evaluating any such code or codes, the Administrator shall consider the human impact of all code requirements, standards, or provisions in terms of comfort and habitability for residents or employees, as well as the fire prevention and control value or potential of each such requirement, standard, or provision.

[15 U.S.C. 2211]

FIRE SAFETY EFFECTIVENESS STATEMENTS

SEC. 13.   The Administrator is authorized to encourage owners and managers of residential multiple-unit, commercial, industrial, and transportation structures to prepare Fire Safety Effectiveness Statements, pursuant to standards, forms, rules, and regulations to be developed and issued by the Administrator.

[15 U.S.C. 2212]

ANNUAL CONFERENCE

SEC. 14.   The Administrator is authorized to organize, or to participate in organizing, an annual conference on fire prevention and control. He may pay, in whole or in part, the cost of such conference and the expenses of some or all of the participants. All of the Nation's fire services shall be eligible to send representatives to each such conference to discuss, exchange ideas on, and participate in educational programs on new techniques in fire prevention and control. Such conferences shall be open to the public.
[15 U.S.C. 2213]

PUBLIC SAFETY AWARDS

SEC. 15. (a) ESTABLISHMENT.— There is hereby established an honorary award for the recognition of outstanding and distinguished service by public safety officers to be known as the Administrator's Award For Distinguished Public Safety Service (Administrator's Award).

(b) DESCRIPTION.— The Administrator's Award shall be presented by the Administrator of FEMA or by the Attorney General to public safety officers for distinguished service in the field of public safety.

(c) AWARD.— Each Administrator's Award shall consist of an appropriate citation.

(d) REGULATIONS.— The Administrator of FEMA and the Attorney General are authorized and directed to issue jointly such regulations as may be necessary to carry out this section.

(e) DEFINITIONS.—As used in this section, the term public safety officer means a person serving a public agency, with or without compensation, as—

(1)   a firefighter;

(2)   a law enforcement officer, including a corrections or court officer; or

(3)   a civil defense officer.
[15 U.S.C. 2214]

ANNUAL REPORT

SEC. 16. The Administrator of FEMA shall report to the Congress and the President not later than ninety calendar days following the year ending September 30, 1980 and similarly each year thereafter on all activities relating to fire prevention and control, and all measures taken to implement and carry out this Act during the preceding calendar year. Such report shall include, but need not be limited to—

(a)   a thorough appraisal, including statistical analysis, estimates, and long-term projections of the human and economic losses due to fire;

(b)   a survey and summary, in such detail as is deemed advisable, of the research and technology program undertaken or sponsored pursuant to this Act;

(c) a summary of the activities of the Academy for the preceding 12 months, including, but not limited to—

(1)   an explanation of the curriculum of study;

(2)   a description of the standards of admission and performance;

334

(3)   the criteria for the awarding of degrees and certificates; and

(4)   a statistical compilation of the number of students attending the Academy and receiving degrees or certificates;

(d)   a summary of the activities undertaken to assist the Nation's fire services;

(e)   a summary of the public education programs undertaken;

(f)   an analysis of the extent of participation in preparing and submitting Fire Safety Effectiveness Statements;

(g)   a summary of outstanding problems confronting the administration of this Act, in order of priority;

(h)   such recommendations for additional legislation as are deemed necessary or appropriate; and

(i)   a summary of reviews, evaluations, and suggested improvements in State and local fire prevention and building codes, fire services, and any relevant Federal or private codes, regulations, and fire services.

[15 U.S.C. 2215]

AUTHORIZATION OF APPROPRIATIONS

SEC. 17. (a) There are authorized to be appropriated to carry out the foregoing provisions of this Act, except as otherwise specifically provided, with respect to the payment of claims, under section 11 of this Act, an amount not to exceed $25,210,000 for the fiscal year ending September 30, 1980, which amount includes—

(1) $4,781,000 for programs which are recommended in the report submitted to the Congress by the Administrator pursuant to section 24(b)(1);

(2) $9,430,000 for the National Academy for Fire Prevention and Control;

(3) $307,000 for adjustments required by law in salaries, pay, retirement, and employee benefits;

(4) $500,000 for additional rural firefighting technical assistance and information activities;

(5) $500,000 for the study required by section 26 of this Act; and

(6) $110,000 for the study required by section 27 of this Act.

(b)   There are authorized to be appropriated for the additional administrative expenses of the Federal Emergency Management Agency, which are related to this Act and which result from Reorganization Plan Numbered 3 of 1978 (submitted June 19, 1978) and related Executive orders, an amount not to exceed $600,000 for the fiscal year ending September 30, 1980.

(c) There are authorized to be appropriated to carry out this Act, except as otherwise specifically provided with respect to the payment of claims under section 11 this Act, an amount not to exceed $23,814,000 for the fiscal year ending September 30, 1981, which amount includes—

(1)   not less than $1,100,000 for the first year of a three-year concentrated demonstration program of fire prevention and control in two States with high fire death rates;

(2)   not less than $2,575,000 for rural fire prevention and control; and

(3)   not less than $4,255,000 for research and development for the activities under section 18 of this Act at the Fire Research Center of the National Bureau of Standards, of which not less than $250,000 shall be available for adjustments required by law in salaries, pay, retirement, and employee benefits.

The funds authorized in paragraph (3) shall be in addition to funds authorized in any other law for research and development at the Fire Research Center.

(d) Except as otherwise specifically provided with respect to the payment of claims under section 11 of this Act, to carry out the purposes of this Act, there are authorized to be appropriated—

(1) $20,815,000 for the fiscal year ending September 30, 1982, and $23,312,800 for the fiscal year ending September 30, 1983, which amount shall include—

(A)   such sums as may be necessary for the support of research and development at the Fire Research Center of the National Bureau of Standards under section 18 of this Act, which sums shall be in addition to those funds authorized to be appropriated under the National Bureau of Standards Authorization Act for fiscal years 1981 and 1982; and

(B) $654,000 for the fiscal year ending September 30, 1982, and $732,480 for the fiscal year ending September 30, 1983, for executive direction by the Federal Emergency Management Agency of program activities for which appropriations are authorized by this subsection; and

(2)   such further sums as may be necessary in each of the fiscal years ending September 30, 1982, and September 30, 1983, for adjustments required by law in salaries, pay, retirement, and employee benefits incurred in the conduct of activities for which funds are authorized by paragraph (1) of this subsection.

The funds authorized under section 18 shall be in addition to funds authorized in any other law for research and development at the Fire Research Center of the National Bureau of Standards.

(e) Except as otherwise specifically provided with respect to the payment of claims under section 11 of this Act, to carry out the purposes of this Act, there are authorized to be appropriated—

(1) $15,720,000 for the fiscal year ending September 30, 1984, and $20,983,000 for the fiscal year ending September 30, 1985; and

(2)   such further sums as may be necessary in each of the fiscal years ending September 30, 1984, and September 30, 1985, for adjustments required by law in salaries, pay, retirement, and employee benefits incurred in the conduct of activities for which funds are authorized by paragraph (1) of this subsection.

The funds authorized under this subsection shall be in addition to funds authorized in any other law for research and development at the Fire Research Center of the National Bureau of Standards.

(f)   Except as otherwise specifically provided with respect to the payment of claims under section 11 of this Act, to carry out the purposes of this Act, there are authorized to be appropriated $22,037,000 for the fiscal year ending September 30, 1986 and $18,300,000 for the fiscal year ending September 30, 1987.

(g)(1) Except as otherwise specifically provided with respect to the payment of claims under section 11 of this Act, there are authorized to be appropriated to carry out the purposes of this Act—

    (A) $63,000,000 for fiscal year 2005, of which $2,266,000 shall be used to carry out section 8(f);

    (B) $64,850,000 for fiscal year 2006, of which $2,334,000 shall be used to carry out section 8(f);

    (C) $66,796,000 for fiscal year 2007, of which $2,404,000 shall be used to carry out section 8(f);

    (D) $68,800,000 for fiscal year 2008, of which $2,476,000 shall be used to carry out section 8(f);

    (E) $70,000,000 for fiscal year 2009, of which $2,520,000 shall be used to carry out section 8(f);

    (F) $72,100,000 for fiscal year 2010, of which $2,595,600 shall be used to carry out section 8(f);

    (G) $74,263,000 for fiscal year 2011, of which $2,673,468 shall be used to carry out section 8(f);

    (H) $76,490,890 for fiscal year 2012, of which $2,753,672 shall be used to carry out section 8(f);

    (I) $76,490,890 for fiscal year 2013, of which $2,753,672 shall be used to carry out section 8(f);

    (J) $76,490,890 for fiscal year 2014, of which $2,753,672 shall be used to carry out section 8(f);

    (K) $76,490,890 for fiscal year 2015, of which $2,753,672 shall be used to carry out section 8(f);

    (L) $76,490,890 for fiscal year 2016, of which $2,753,672 shall be used to carry out section 8(f);

    (M) $76,490,890 for each of fiscal years 2017 through 2023, of which $2,753,672 for each such fiscal year shall be used to carry out section 8(f); and

    (N)[2] $95,000,000 for each of fiscal years 2024 through 2028, of which $3,420,000 for each such fiscal year shall be used to carry out section 8(f).

---

[2]   Margin so in law.

---

    (2) Of the amount referred to in paragraph (1), not more than $4,150,000 is authorized to be appropriated for each fiscal year for National Emergency Training Center site administration.

(h) In addition to any other amounts that are authorized to be appropriated to carry out this Act, there are authorized to be appropriated to carry out this Act—

    (1) $500,000 for fiscal year 1995 for basic research on the development of an advanced course on arson prevention;

    (2) $2,000,000 for fiscal year 1996 for the expansion of arson investigator

training programs at the Academy under section 24 and at the Federal Law Enforcement Training Center, or through regional delivery sites;

(3) $4,000,000 for each of fiscal years 1995 and 1996 for carrying out section 25, except for salaries and expenses for carrying out section 25; and

(4) $250,000 for each of the fiscal years 1995 and 1996 for salaries and expenses for carrying out section 25.

[15 U.S.C. 2216]

FIRE RESEARCH CENTER

SEC. 18.3

---

3 Section 18 amended the National Institute of Standards and Technology Act, which is shown elsewhere in this compilation.

VICTIMS OF FIRE

SEC. 19. (a) PROGRAM.—The Secretary of Health, Education, and Welfare shall establish, within the National Institutes of Health and in cooperation with the Administrator of FEMA, an expanded program of research on burns, treatment of burn injuries, and rehabilitation of victims of fires. The National Institutes of Health shall—

(1) sponsor and encourage the establishment throughout the Nation of twenty-five additional burn centers, which shall comprise separate hospital facilities providing specialized burn treatment and including research and teaching programs, and twenty-five additional burn units, which shall comprise specialized facilities in general hospitals used only for burn victims;

(2) provide training and continuing support of specialists to staff the new burn centers and burn units;

(3) sponsor and encourage the establishment of ninety burn programs in general hospitals which comprise staffs of burn injury specialists;

(4) provide special training in emergency care for burn victims;

(5) augment sponsorship of research on burns and burn treatment;

(6) administer and support a systematic program of research concerning smoke inhalation injuries; and

(7) sponsor and support other research and training programs in the treatment and rehabilitation of burn injury victims.

(b) AUTHORIZATION OF APPROPRIATION.— For purposes of this section, there are authorized to be appropriated not to exceed $5,000,000 for the fiscal year ending June 30, 1975 and not to exceed $8,000,000 for the fiscal year ending June 30, 1976.

[42 U.S.C. 290a]

PUBLIC ACCESS TO INFORMATION

SEC. 20. Copies of any document, report, statement, or information received or sent by the Administrator of FEMA or the Administrator shall be made available to the public pursuant to the provisions of section 552 of title 5, United States Code: *Provided,* That, notwithstanding the provisions of subsection (b) of such section and of section 1905 of title 18, United States Code, the Administrator of FEMA may disclose information which concerns or relates to a trade secret—

(1)   upon request, to other Federal Government departments and agencies for official use;

(2)   upon request, to any committee of Congress having jurisdiction over the subject matter to which the information relates;

(3)   in any judicial proceeding under a court order formulated to preserve the confidentiality of such information without impairing the proceedings; and

(4)   to the public when he determines such disclosure to be necessary in order to protect health and safety after notice and opportunity for comment in writing or for discussion in closed session within fifteen days by the party to which the information pertains (if the delay resulting from such notice and opportunity for comment would not be detrimental to health and safety).

[15 U.S.C. 2217]

ADMINISTRATIVE PROVISIONS

SEC. 21. (a) ASSISTANCE.— Each department, agency, and instrumentality of the executive branch of the Federal Government and each independent regulatory agency of the United States is authorized and directed to furnish to the Administrator, upon written request, on a reimbursable basis or otherwise, such assistance as the Administrator deems necessary to carry out his functions and duties pursuant to this Act, including, but not limited to, transfer of personnel with their consent and without prejudice to their position and ratings.

(b) POWERS.—With respect to this Act, the Administrator is authorized to—

(1)   enter into, without regard to section 3709 of the Revised Statutes, as amended (41 U.S.C. 5) such contracts, grants, leases, cooperative agreements, or other transactions as may be necessary to carry out the provisions of this Act;

(2)   accept gifts and voluntary and uncompensated services, notwithstanding the provisions of section 3679 of the Revised Statutes (31 U.S.C. 665(b));

(3)   purchase, lease, or otherwise acquire, own, hold, improve, use, or deal in and with any property (real, personal, or mixed, tangible or intangible), or interest in property, wherever situated; and sell, convey, mortgage, pledge, lease, exchange, or otherwise dispose of property and assets;

(4)   procure temporary and intermittent services to the same extent as is authorized under section 3109 of title 5, United States Code, but at rates not to exceed the daily equivalent of the maximum annual rate of basic pay then in effect for grade GS–15 of the General Schedule (5 U.S.C. 5332(a)) for qualified experts; and

(5)   establish such rules, regulations, and procedures as are necessary to carry out the provisions of this Act.

(c) AUDIT.— The Administrator of FEMA and the Comptroller General of the United States, or any of their duly authorized representatives, shall have access to any books, documents, papers, and records of the recipients of contracts, grants, or other forms of assistance that are pertinent to its activities under this Act for the purpose of audit or to determine if a proposed activity is in the public interest.

(d) INVENTIONS AND DISCOVERIES.— All property rights with respect to inventions and discoveries, which are made in the course of or under contract with any government agency pursuant to this Act, shall be subject to the basic policies set forth in the President's Statement of Government Patent Policy issued August 23, 1971, or such revisions of that statement of policy as may subsequently be promulgated and published in the Federal Register.

(e) COORDINATION.—

(1) IN GENERAL.— To the extent practicable, the Administrator shall use existing programs, data, information, and facilities already available in other Federal Government departments and agencies and, where appropriate, existing research organizations, centers, and universities.

(2) COORDINATION OF FIRE PREVENTION AND CONTROL PROGRAMS.— The Administrator shall provide liaison at an appropriate organizational level to assure coordination of the activities of the Administrator with Federal, State, and local government agencies and departments and nongovernmental organizations concerned with any matter related to programs of fire prevention and control.

(3) COORDINATION OF EMERGENCY MEDICAL SERVICES PROGRAMS.— The Administrator shall provide liaison at an appropriate organizational level to assure coordination of the activities of the Administrator related to emergency medical services provided by fire service-based systems with Federal, State, and local government agencies and departments and nongovernmental organizations so concerned, as well as those entities concerned with emergency medical services generally.

[15 U.S.C. 2218]

ASSISTANCE TO CONSUMER PRODUCT SAFETY COMMISSION

SEC. 22.   Upon request, the Administrator shall assist the Consumer Product Safety Commission in the development of fire safety standards or codes for consumer products, as defined in the Consumer Product Safety Act (15 U.S.C. 2051 et seq.).

[15 U.S.C. 2219]

* * * * * * *

FEDERAL PROGRAMS TO COMBAT ARSON

SEC. 24. The Administrator shall—

(1)   develop arson detection techniques to assist Federal agencies and States and local jurisdictions in improving arson prevention, detection, and control;

(2)   provide training and instructional materials in the skills and knowledge necessary to assist Federal, State, and local fire service and law enforcement personnel in arson prevention, detection, and control, with particular emphasis on the needs of volunteer firefighters for improved and more widely available arson training courses;

(3) formulate methods for collection of arson data which would be compatible with methods of collection used for the uniform crime statistics of the Federal Bureau of Investigation;

(4) develop and implement programs for improved collection of nationwide arson statistics within the National Fire Incident Reporting System at the National Fire Data Center;

(5) develop programs for public education on the extent, causes, and prevention of arson; and

(6) develop handbooks to assist Federal, State, and local fire service and law enforcement personnel in arson prevention and detention.
[15 U.S.C. 2220]

SEC. 25. ARSON PREVENTION GRANTS.

(a) DEFINITIONS.—As used in this section:

(1) ARSON.— The term arson includes all incendiary and suspicious fires.

(2) OFFICE.— The term Office means the Office of Fire Prevention and Arson Control of the United States Fire Administration.

(b) GRANTS.— The Administrator, acting through the Office, shall carry out a demonstration program under which not more than 10 grant awards shall be made to States, or consortia of States, for programs relating to arson research, prevention, and control.

(c) GOALS.—In carrying out this section, the Administrator shall award 2-year grants on a competitive, merit basis to States, or consortia of States, for projects that promote one or more of the following goals:

(1) To improve the training by States leading to professional certification of arson investigators, in accordance with nationally recognized certification standards.

(2) To provide resources for the formation of arson task forces or interagency organizational arrangements involving police and fire departments and other relevant local agencies, such as a State arson bureau and the office of a fire marshal of a State.

(3) To combat fraud as a cause of arson and to advance research at the State and local levels on the significance and prevention of fraud as a motive for setting fires.

(4) To provide for the management of arson squads, including—

(A) training courses for fire departments in arson case management, including standardization of investigative techniques and reporting methodology;

(B) the preparation of arson unit management guides; and

(C) the development and dissemination of new public education materials relating to the arson problem.

(5) To combat civil unrest as a cause of arson and to advance research at the State and local levels on the prevention and control of arson linked to urban

341

disorders.

(6) To combat juvenile arson, such as juvenile fire-setter counseling programs and similar intervention programs, and to advance research at the State and local levels on the prevention of juvenile arson.

(7) To combat drug-related arson and to advance research at the State and local levels on the causes and prevention of drug-related arson.

(8) To combat domestic violence as a cause of arson and to advance research at the State and local levels on the prevention of arson arising from domestic violence.

(9) To combat arson in rural areas and to improve the capability of firefighters to identify and prevent arson initiated fires in rural areas and public forests.

(10) To improve the capability of firefighters to identify and combat arson through expanded training programs, including—

(A) training courses at the State fire academies; and

(B) innovative courses developed with the Academy and made available to volunteer firefighters through regional delivery methods, including teleconferencing and satellite delivered television programs.

(d) STRUCTURING OF APPLICATIONS.— The Administrator shall assist grant applicants in structuring their applications so as to ensure that at least one grant is awarded for each goal described in subsection (c).

(e) STATE QUALIFICATION CRITERIA.—In order to qualify for a grant under this section, a State, or consortium of States, shall provide assurances adequate to the Administrator that the State or consortium—

(1) will obtain at least 25 percent of the cost of programs funded by the grant, in cash or in kind, from non-Federal sources;

(2) will not as a result of receiving the grant decrease the prior level of spending of funds of the State or consortium from non-Federal sources for arson research, prevention, and control programs;

(3) will use no more than 10 percent of funds provided under the grant for administrative costs of the programs; and

(4) is making efforts to ensure that all local jurisdictions will provide arson data to the National Fire Incident Reporting System or the Uniform Crime Reporting program.

(f) EXTENSION.— A grant awarded under this section may be extended for one or more additional periods, at the discretion of the Administrator, subject to the availability of appropriations.

(g) TECHNICAL ASSISTANCE.— The Administrator shall provide technical assistance to States in carrying out programs funded by grants under this section.

(h) CONSULTATION AND COOPERATION.— In carrying out this section, the Administrator shall consult and cooperate with other Federal agencies to enhance program effectiveness and avoid duplication of effort, including the conduct of regular meetings initiated by the Administrator with representatives of other Federal agencies concerned with arson and concerned with efforts to develop a more comprehensive profile of the magnitude of the national arson problem.

(i) ASSESSMENT.—Not later than 18 months after the date of enactment of this subsection, the Administrator shall submit a report to Congress that—

(1)   identifies grants made under this section;

(2)   specifies the identity of grantees;

(3)   states the goals of each grant; and

(4)   contains a preliminary assessment of the effectiveness of the grant program under this section.

(j) REGULATIONS.— Not later than 90 days after the date of enactment of this subsection, the Administrator shall issue regulations to implement this section, including procedures for grant applications.

(k) ADMINISTRATION.— The Administrator shall directly administer the grant program required by this section, and shall not enter into any contract under which the grant program or any portion of the program will be administered by another party.

(l) PURCHASE OF AMERICAN MADE EQUIPMENT AND PRODUCTS.—

(1) SENSE OF CONGRESS.— It is the sense of Congress that any recipient of a grant under this section should purchase, when available and cost-effective, American made equipment and products when expending grant monies.

(2) NOTICE TO RECIPIENTS OF ASSISTANCE.— In allocating grants under this section, the Administrator shall provide to each recipient a notice describing the statement made in paragraph (1) by the Congress.

[15 U.S.C. 2221]

[SEC. 26.   Repealed by section 110(a)(1)(B) of P.L. 106–503 (114 Stat. 2302).]

[SEC. 27.   Repealed by section 110(a)(1)(B) of P.L. 106–503 (114 Stat. 2302).]

LISTINGS OF PLACES OF PUBLIC ACCOMMODATION

SEC. 28. (a) SUBMISSIONS BY STATES.—(1)   Not later than 2 years after the date of enactment of this section, each State (acting through its Governor or the Governor's designee) shall, under procedures formulated by the Administrator of FEMA, submit to the Administrator of FEMA a list of those places of public accommodation affecting commerce located in the State which meet the requirements of the guidelines described in section 29.

(2)   The Administrator of FEMA shall formulate procedures under which each State (acting through its Governor or the Governor's designee) shall periodically update the list submitted pursuant to paragraph (1).

(b) COMPILATION AND DISTRIBUTION OF MASTER LIST.—(1)   Not later than 60 days after the expiration of the 2-year period referred to in subsection (a), the Administrator of FEMA shall compile and publish in the Federal Register a national master list of all of the places of public accommodation affecting commerce located in each State that meet the requirements of the guidelines described in section 29, and shall distribute such list to each agency of the Federal Government and take steps to make the employees of such agencies aware of its existence and contents.

(2)   The Administrator of FEMA shall periodically update the national master list compiled pursuant to paragraph (1) to reflect changes in the State lists submitted to the Administrator of FEMA pursuant to subsection (a), and shall periodically redistribute the updated master list to each agency of the Federal Government.

(3)   For purposes of this subsection, the term agency has the meaning given to it under section 5701(1) of title 5, United States Code.

[15 U.S.C. 2224]

FIRE PREVENTION AND CONTROL GUIDELINES FOR PLACES OF PUBLIC ACCOMMODATION

SEC. 29. (a) CONTENTS OF GUIDELINES.—The guidelines referred to in sections 28 and 30 consist of—

(1)   a requirement that hard-wired, single-station smoke detectors be installed in accordance with National Fire Protection Association Standard 74 or any successor standard to that standard in each guest room in each place of public accommodation affecting commerce; and

(2)   a requirement that an automatic sprinkler system be installed in accordance with National Fire Protection Association Standard 13 or 13–R, or any successor standard to that standard, whichever is appropriate, in each place of public accommodation affecting commerce except those places that are 3 stories or lower.

(b) EXCEPTIONS.—(1)   The requirement described in subsection (a)(2) shall not apply to a place of public accommodation affecting commerce with an automatic sprinkler system installed before October 25, 1992, if the automatic sprinkler system is installed in compliance with an applicable standard (adopted by the governmental authority having jurisdiction, and in effect, at the time of installation) that required the placement of a sprinkler head in the sleeping area of each guest room.

(2)   The requirement described in subsection (a)(2) shall not apply to a place of public accommodation affecting commerce to the extent that such place of public accommodation affecting commerce is subject to a standard that includes a requirement or prohibition that prevents compliance with a provision of National Fire Protection Association Standard 13 or 13–R, or any successor standard to that standard. In such a case, the place of public accommodation affecting commerce is exempt only from that specific provision.

(c) EFFECT ON STATE AND LOCAL LAW.— The provisions of this section shall not be construed to limit the power of any State or political subdivision thereof to implement or enforce any law, rule, regulation, or standard concerning fire prevention and control.

(d) DEFINITIONS.—For purposes of this section, the following definitions shall apply:

(1)   The term smoke detector means an alarm that is designed to respond to the presence of visible or invisible particles of combustion.

(2)   The term automatic sprinkler system means an electronically supervised, integrated system of piping to which sprinklers are attached in a systematic pattern, and which, when activated by heat from a fire, will protect human lives by discharging water over the fire area, and by providing appropriate warning signals

(to the extent such signals are required by Federal, State, or local laws or regulations) through the building's fire alarm system.

(3)   The term governmental authority having jurisdiction means the Federal, State, local, or other governmental entity with statutory or regulatory authority for the approval of fire safety systems, equipment, installations, or procedures within a specified locality.

[15 U.S.C. 2225]

DISSEMINATION OF FIRE PREVENTION AND CONTROL INFORMATION

SEC. 30.   The Administrator of FEMA, acting through the Administrator, is authorized to take steps to encourage the States to promote the use of automatic sprinkler systems and automatic smoke detection systems, and to disseminate to the maximum extent possible information on the life safety value and use of such systems. Such steps may include, but need not be limited to, providing copies of the guidelines described in section 29 and of the master list compiled under section 28(b) to Federal agencies, State and local governments, and fire services throughout the United States, and making copies of the master list compiled under section 28(b) available upon request to interested private organizations and individuals.

[15 U.S.C. 2226]

SEC. 31. FIRE SAFETY SYSTEMS IN FEDERALLY ASSISTED BUILDINGS.

(a) DEFINITIONS.—For purposes of this section, the following definitions apply:

(1)   The term affordable cost means the cost to a Federal agency of leasing office space in a building that is protected by an automatic sprinkler system or equivalent level of safety, which cost is no more than 10 percent greater than the cost of leasing available comparable office space in a building that is not so protected.

(2) The term automatic sprinkler system means an electronically supervised, integrated system of piping to which sprinklers are attached in a systematic pattern, and which, when activated by heat from a fire—

(A)   will protect human lives by discharging water over the fire area, in accordance with the National Fire Protection Association Standard 13, 13D, or 13R, whichever is appropriate for the type of building and occupancy being protected, or any successor standard thereto; and

(B)   includes an alarm signaling system with appropriate warning signals (to the extent such alarm systems and warning signals are required by Federal, State, or local laws or regulations) installed in accordance with the National Fire Protection Association Standard 72, or any successor standard thereto.

(3)   The term equivalent level of safety means an alternative design or system (which may include automatic sprinkler systems), based upon fire protection engineering analysis, which achieves a level of safety equal to or greater than that provided by automatic sprinkler systems.

(4)   The term Federal employee office building means any office building in the United States, whether owned or leased by the Federal Government, that is regularly occupied by more than 25 full-time Federal employees in the course of their employment.

(5) The term housing assistance—

(A)   means assistance provided by the Federal Government to be used in connection with the provision of housing, that is provided in the form of a grant, contract, loan, loan guarantee, cooperative agreement, interest subsidy, insurance, or direct appropriation; and

(B)   does not include assistance provided by the Secretary of Veterans Affairs; the Federal Emergency Management Agency; the Secretary of Housing and Urban Development under the single family mortgage insurance programs under the National Housing Act or the homeownership assistance program under section 235 of such Act; the National Homeownership Trust; the Federal Deposit Insurance Corporation under the affordable housing program under section 40 of the Federal Deposit Insurance Act; or the Resolution Trust Corporation under the affordable housing program under section 21A(c) of the Federal Home Loan Bank Act.

(6)   The term hazardous areas means those areas in a building referred to as hazardous areas in National Fire Protection Association Standard 101, known as the Life Safety Code, or any successor standard thereto.

(7) The term multifamily property means—

(A)   in the case of housing for Federal employees or their dependents, a residential building consisting of more than 2 residential units that are under one roof; and

(B)   in any other case, a residential building consisting of more than 4 residential units that are under one roof.

(8)   The term prefire plan means specific plans for fire fighting activities at a property or location.

(9)   The term rebuilding means the repairing or reconstructing of portions of a multifamily property where the cost of the alterations is 70 percent or more of the replacement cost of the completed multifamily property, not including the value of the land on which the multifamily property is located.

(10)   The term renovated means the repairing or reconstructing of 50 percent or more of the current value of a Federal employee office building, not including the value of the land on which the Federal employee office building is located.

(11)   The term smoke detectors means single or multiple station, self-contained alarm devices designed to respond to the presence of visible or invisible particles of combustion, installed in accordance with the National Fire Protection Association Standard 74 or any successor standard thereto.

(12)   The term United States means the States collectively.

(b) FEDERAL EMPLOYEE OFFICE BUILDINGS.—(1)(A)   No Federal funds may be used for the construction or purchase of a Federal employee office building of 6 or more stories unless during the period of occupancy by Federal employees the building is protected by an automatic sprinkler system or equivalent level of safety. No Federal funds may be used for the construction or purchase of any other Federal employee office building unless during the period of occupancy by Federal employees the hazardous areas of the building are protected by automatic sprinkler systems or an equivalent level of safety.

(B)(i)   Except as provided in clause (ii), no Federal funds may be used for the lease of a Federal employee office building of 6 or more stories, where at least some portion of the federally leased space is on the sixth floor or above and at least 35,000 square feet of space is federally occupied, unless during the period of occupancy by Federal employees the entire Federal employee office building is protected by an automatic sprinkler system or equivalent level of safety. No Federal funds may be used for the lease of any other Federal employee office building unless during the period of occupancy by Federal employees the hazardous areas of the entire Federal employee office building are protected by automatic sprinkler systems or an equivalent level of safety.

(ii)   The first sentence of clause (i) shall not apply to the lease of a building the construction of which is completed before the date of enactment of this section if the leasing agency certifies that no suitable building with automatic sprinkler systems or an equivalent level of safety is available at an affordable cost.

(2) Paragraph (1) shall not apply to—

(A)   a Federal employee office building that was owned by the Federal Government before the date of enactment of this section;

(B)   space leased in a Federal employee office building if the space was leased by the Federal Government before such date of enactment;

(C)   space leased on a temporary basis for not longer than 6 months;

(D)   a Federal employee office building that becomes a Federal employee office building pursuant to a commitment to move Federal employees into the building that is made prior to such date of enactment; or

(E)   a Federal employee office building that is owned or managed by the Resolution Trust Corporation.

Nothing in this subsection shall require the installation of an automatic sprinkler system or equivalent level of safety by reason of the leasing, after such date of enactment, of space below the sixth floor in a Federal employee office building.

(3)   No Federal funds may be used for the renovation of a Federal employee office building of 6 or more stories that is owned by the Federal Government unless after that renovation the Federal employee office building is protected by an automatic sprinkler system or equivalent level of safety. No Federal funds may be used for the renovation of any other Federal employee office building that is owned by the Federal Government unless after that renovation the hazardous areas of the Federal employee office building are protected by automatic sprinkler systems or an equivalent level of safety.

(4)   No Federal funds may be used for entering into or renewing a lease of a Federal employee office building of 6 or more stories that is renovated after the date of enactment of this section, where at least some portion of the federally leased space is on the sixth floor or above and at least 35,000 square feet of space is federally occupied, unless after that renovation the Federal employee office building

is protected by an automatic sprinkler system or equivalent level of safety. No Federal funds may be used for entering into or renewing a lease of any other Federal employee office building that is renovated after such date of enactment of this section, unless after that renovation the hazardous areas of the Federal employee office building are protected by automatic sprinkler systems or an equivalent level of safety.

(c) HOUSING.—(1)(A) Except as otherwise provided in this paragraph, no Federal funds may be used for the construction, purchase, lease, or operation by the Federal Government of housing in the United States for Federal employees or their dependents unless—

(i)   in the case of a multifamily property acquired or rebuilt by the Federal Government after the date of enactment of this section, the housing is protected, before occupancy by Federal employees or their dependents, by an automatic sprinkler system (or equivalent level of safety) and hard-wired smoke detectors; and

(ii) in the case of any other housing, the housing, before—

(I)   occupancy by the first Federal employees (or their dependents) who do not occupy such housing as of such date of enactment; or

(II)   the expiration of 3 years after such date of enactment, whichever occurs first, is protected by hard-wired smoke detectors.

(B)   Nothing in this paragraph shall be construed to supersede any guidelines or requirements applicable to housing for Federal employees that call for a higher level of fire safety protection than is required under this paragraph.

(C)   Housing covered by this paragraph that does not have an adequate and reliable electrical system shall not be subject to the requirement under subparagraph (A) for protection by hard-wired smoke detectors, but shall be protected by battery operated smoke detectors.

(D)   If funding has been programmed or designated for the demolition of housing covered by this paragraph, such housing shall not be subject to the fire protection requirements of subparagraph (A), but shall be protected by battery operated smoke detectors.

(2)(A)(i)   Housing assistance may not be used in connection with any newly constructed multifamily property, unless after the new construction the multifamily property is protected by an automatic sprinkler system and hard-wired smoke detectors.

(ii) For purposes of clause (i), the term newly constructed multifamily property means a multifamily property of 4 or more stories above ground level—

(I)   that is newly constructed after the date of enactment of this section; and

(II)   for which (a) housing assistance is used for such new construction, or (b) a binding commitment is made, before commencement of such construction, to provide housing assistance for the newly constructed property.

(iii)   Clause (i) shall not apply to any multifamily property for which, before such date of enactment, a binding commitment is made to provide housing assistance for the new construction of the property or for the newly constructed property.

(B)(i)   Except as provided in clause (ii), housing assistance may not be used in connection with any rebuilt multifamily property, unless after the rebuilding the multifamily property complies with the chapter on existing apartment buildings of National Fire Protection Association Standard 101 (known as the Life Safety Code) or any successor standard to that standard, as in effect at the earlier of (I) the time of any approval by the Department of Housing and Urban Development of the specific plan or budget for rebuilding, or (II) the time that a binding commitment is made to provide housing assistance for the rebuilt property.

(ii)   If any rebuilt multifamily property is subject to, and in compliance with, any provision of a State or local fire safety standard or code that prevents compliance with a specific provision of National Fire Protection Association Standard 101 or any successor standard to that standard, the requirement under clause (i) shall not apply with respect to such specific provision.

(iii) For purposes of this subparagraph, the term rebuilt multifamily property means a multifamily property of 4 or more stories above ground level—

(I)   that is rebuilt after the last day of the second fiscal year that ends after the date of enactment of this section; and

(II)   for which (a) housing assistance is used for such rebuilding, or (b) a binding commitment is made, before commencement of such rebuilding, to provide housing assistance for the rebuilt property.

(C)   After the expiration of the 180-day period beginning on the date of enactment of this section, housing assistance may not be used in connection with any other dwelling unit, unless the unit is protected by a hard-wired or battery-operated smoke detector. For purposes of this subparagraph, housing assistance shall be considered to be used in connection with a particular dwelling unit only if such assistance is provided (i) for the particular unit, in the case of assistance provided on a unit-by-unit basis, or (ii) for the multifamily property in which the unit is located, in the case of assistance provided on a structure-by-structure basis.

(d) REGULATIONS.—   The Administrator of General Services, in cooperation with the United States Fire Administration, the National Institute of Standards and Technology, and the Department of Defense, within 2 years after the date of enactment of this section, shall promulgate regulations to further define the term equivalent level of safety, and shall, to the extent practicable, base those regulations on nationally recognized codes.

(e) STATE AND LOCAL AUTHORITY NOT LIMITED.—   Nothing in this section shall be construed to limit the power of any State or political subdivision thereof to implement or enforce any law, rule, regulation, or standard that establishes requirements concerning fire prevention and control. Nothing in this section shall be construed to reduce fire resistance requirements which otherwise would have been required.

(f) PREFIRE PLAN.— The head of any Federal agency that owns, leases, or operates a building or housing unit with Federal funds shall invite the local agency or voluntary organization having responsibility for fire protection in the jurisdiction where the building or housing unit is located to prepare, and biennially review, a prefire plan for the building or housing unit.

(g) REPORTS TO CONGRESS.—(1)   Within 3 years after the date of enactment of this section, and every 3 years thereafter, the Administrator of General Services shall transmit to Congress a report on the level of fire safety in Federal employee office buildings subject to fire safety requirements under this section. Such report shall contain a description of such buildings for each Federal agency.

(2)   Within 10 years after the date of enactment of this section, each Federal agency providing housing to Federal employees or housing assistance shall submit a report to Congress on the progress of that agency in implementing subsection (c) and on plans for continuing such implementation.

(3)(A) The National Institute of Standards and Technology shall conduct a study and submit a report to Congress on the use, in combination, of fire detection systems, fire suppression systems, and compartmentation. Such study shall—

(i)   quantify performance and reliability for fire detection systems, fire suppression systems, and compartmentation, including a field assessment of performance and determination of conditions under which a reduction or elimination of 1 or more of those systems would result in an unacceptable risk of fire loss; and

(ii)   include a comparative analysis and compartmentation using fire resistive materials and compartmentation using noncombustible materials.

(B)   The National Institute of Standards and Technology shall obtain funding from non-Federal sources in an amount equal to 25 percent of the cost of the study required by subparagraph (A). Funding for the National Institute of Standards and Technology for carrying out such study shall be derived from amounts otherwise authorized to be appropriated, for the Building and Fire Research Center at the National Institute of Standards and Technology, not to exceed $750,000. The study shall commence until receipt of all matching funds from non-Federal sources. The scope and extent of the study shall be determined by the level of project funding. The Institute shall submit a report to Congress on the study within 30 months after the date of enactment of this section.

(h) RELATION TO OTHER REQUIREMENTS.— In the implementation of this section, the process for meeting space needs in urban areas shall continue to give first consideration to a centralized community business area and adjacent areas of similar character to the extent of any Federal requirement therefor.

[15 U.S.C. 2227]

SEC. 32. CPR TRAINING.

No funds shall be made available to a State or local government under section 25 unless such government has a policy to actively promote the training of its firefighters in cardiopulmonary resuscitation.

[15 U.S.C. 2228]

SEC. 33. FIREFIGHTER ASSISTANCE.

(a) DEFINITIONS.—In this section:

(1) ADMINISTRATOR OF FEMA.— The term Administrator of FEMA means the Administrator of FEMA, acting through the Administrator.

(2) AVAILABLE GRANT FUNDS.— The term available grant funds, with respect to a fiscal year, means those funds appropriated pursuant to the authorization of appropriations in subsection (q)(1) for such fiscal year less any funds used for administrative costs pursuant to subsection (q)(2) in such fiscal year.

(3) CAREER FIRE DEPARTMENT.— The term career fire department means a fire department that has an all-paid force of firefighting personnel other than paid-on-call firefighters.

(4) COMBINATION FIRE DEPARTMENT.—The term combination fire department means a fire department that has—

(A) paid firefighting personnel; and

(B) volunteer firefighting personnel.

(5) FIREFIGHTING PERSONNEL.— The term firefighting personnel means individuals, including volunteers, who are firefighters, officers of fire departments, or emergency medical service personnel of fire departments.

(6) INSTITUTION OF HIGHER EDUCATION.— The term institution of higher education has the meaning given such term in section 101 of the Higher Education Act of 1965 (20 U.S.C. 1001).

(7) NONAFFILIATED EMS ORGANIZATION.— The term nonaffiliated EMS organization means a public or private nonprofit emergency medical services organization that is not affiliated with a hospital and does not serve a geographic area in which the Administrator of FEMA finds that emergency medical services are adequately provided by a fire department.

(8) PAID-ON-CALL.— The term paid-on-call with respect to firefighting personnel means firefighting personnel who are paid a stipend for each event to which they respond.

(9) VOLUNTEER FIRE DEPARTMENT.— The term volunteer fire department means a fire department that has an all-volunteer force of firefighting personnel.

(b) ASSISTANCE PROGRAM.—

(1) AUTHORITY.—In accordance with this section, the Administrator of FEMA may award—

(A) assistance to firefighters grants under subsection (c); and

(B) fire prevention and safety grants and other assistance under subsection (d).

(2) ADMINISTRATIVE ASSISTANCE.—The Administrator of FEMA shall—

(A) establish specific criteria for the selection of grant recipients under this

351

section; and

(B)   provide assistance with application preparation to applicants for such grants.

(c) ASSISTANCE TO FIREFIGHTERS GRANTS.—

(1) IN GENERAL.—The Administrator of FEMA may, in consultation with the chief executives of the States in which the recipients are located, award grants on a competitive basis directly to—

(A)   fire departments, for the purpose of protecting the health and safety of the public and firefighting personnel throughout the United States against fire, fire-related, and other hazards;

(B)   nonaffiliated EMS organizations to support the provision of emergency medical services; and

(C)   State fire training academies for the purposes described in subparagraphs (G), (H), and (I) of paragraph (3).

(2) MAXIMUM GRANT AMOUNTS.—

(A) POPULATION.—The Administrator of FEMA may not award a grant under this subsection in excess of amounts as follows:

(i)   In the case of a recipient that serves a jurisdiction with 100,000 people or fewer, the amount of the grant awarded to such recipient shall not exceed $1,000,000 in any fiscal year.

(ii)   In the case of a recipient that serves a jurisdiction with more than 100,000 people but not more than 500,000 people, the amount of the grant awarded to such recipient shall not exceed $2,000,000 in any fiscal year.

(iii)   In the case of a recipient that serves a jurisdiction with more than 500,000 but not more than 1,000,000 people, the amount of the grant awarded to such recipient shall not exceed $3,000,000 in any fiscal year.

(iv)   In the case of a recipient that serves a jurisdiction with more than 1,000,000 people but not more than 2,500,000 people, the amount of the grant awarded to such recipient shall not exceed $6,000,000 for any fiscal year.

(v)   In the case of a recipient that serves a jurisdiction with more than 2,500,000 people, the amount of the grant awarded to such recipient shall not exceed $9,000,000 in any fiscal year.

(B) AGGREGATE.—

(i) IN GENERAL.— Notwithstanding subparagraphs (A) and (B) and except as provided under clause (ii), the Administrator of FEMA may not award a grant under this subsection in a fiscal year in an amount that exceeds the amount that is one percent of the available grant funds in such fiscal year.

(ii) EXCEPTION.— The Administrator of FEMA may waive the limitation in clause (i) with respect to a grant recipient if the Administrator of FEMA determines that such recipient has an extraordinary need for a grant in an amount that exceeds the limit under clause (i).

(3) USE OF GRANT FUNDS.—Each entity receiving a grant under this subsection shall use the grant for one or more of the following purposes:

(A) To train firefighting personnel in—

(i) firefighting;

(ii) emergency medical services and other emergency response (including response to natural disasters, acts of terrorism, and other man-made disasters);

(iii) arson prevention and detection;

(iv) maritime firefighting; or

(v) the handling of hazardous materials.

(B) To train firefighting personnel to provide any of the training described under subparagraph (A).

(C) To fund the creation of rapid intervention teams to protect firefighting personnel at the scenes of fires and other emergencies.

(D) To certify—

(i) fire inspectors; and

(ii) building inspectors—

(I) whose responsibilities include fire safety inspections; and

(II) who are employed by or serving as volunteers with a fire department.

(E) To establish wellness and fitness programs for firefighting personnel to ensure that the firefighting personnel are able to carry out their duties as firefighters, including programs dedicated to raising awareness of, and prevention of, job-related mental health issues.

(F) To fund emergency medical services provided by fire departments and nonaffiliated EMS organizations.

(G) To acquire additional firefighting vehicles, including fire trucks and other apparatus.

(H) To acquire additional firefighting equipment, including equipment for—

(i) fighting fires with foam in remote areas without access to water; and

(ii) communications, monitoring, and response to a natural disaster, act of terrorism, or other man-made disaster, including the use of a weapon of mass destruction.

(I) To acquire personal protective equipment, including personal protective equipment—

(i) prescribed for firefighting personnel by the Occupational Safety and Health Administration of the Department of Labor; or

(ii) for responding to a natural disaster or act of terrorism or other man-made disaster, including the use of a weapon of mass destruction.

(J)   To modify fire stations, fire training facilities, and other facilities to protect the health and safety of firefighting personnel.

(K)   To educate the public about arson prevention and detection.

(L)   To provide incentives for the recruitment and retention of volunteer firefighting personnel for volunteer firefighting departments and other firefighting departments that utilize volunteers.

(M)   To support such other activities, consistent with the purposes of this subsection, as the Administrator of FEMA determines appropriate.

(N)   To provide specialized training to firefighters, paramedics, emergency medical service workers, and other first responders to recognize individuals who have mental illness and how to properly intervene with individuals with mental illness, including strategies for verbal de-escalation of crisis.

(d) FIRE PREVENTION AND SAFETY GRANTS.—

(1) IN GENERAL.—For the purpose of assisting fire prevention programs and supporting firefighter health and safety research and development, the Administrator of FEMA may, on a competitive basis—

(A)   award grants to fire departments;

(B) award grants to, or enter into contracts or cooperative agreements with, national, State, local, tribal, or nonprofit organizations that are not fire departments and that are recognized for their experience and expertise with respect to fire prevention or fire safety programs and activities and firefighter research and development programs, for the purpose of carrying out—

(i)   fire prevention programs; and

(ii)   research to improve firefighter health and life safety; and

(C)   award grants to institutions of higher education, national fire service organizations, or national fire safety organizations to establish and operate fire safety research centers.

(2) MAXIMUM GRANT AMOUNT.—   A grant awarded under this subsection may not exceed $1,500,000 for a fiscal year.

(3) USE OF GRANT FUNDS.—Each entity receiving a grant under this subsection shall use the grant for one or more of the following purposes:

(A)   To enforce fire codes and promote compliance with fire safety standards.

(B)   To fund fire prevention programs, including programs that educate the public about arson prevention and detection.

(C)   To fund wildland fire prevention programs, including education, awareness, and mitigation programs that protect lives, property, and natural resources from fire in the wildland-urban interface.

(D)   In the case of a grant awarded under paragraph (1)(C), to fund the establishment or operation of a fire safety research center for the purpose of

354

significantly reducing the number of fire-related deaths and injuries among firefighters and the general public through research, development, and technology transfer activities.

(E)   To support such other activities, consistent with the purposes of this subsection, as the Administrator of FEMA determines appropriate.

(4) LIMITATION.— None of the funds made available under this subsection may be provided to the Association of Community Organizations for Reform Now (ACORN) or any of its affiliates, subsidiaries, or allied organizations.

(e) APPLICATIONS FOR GRANTS.—

(1) IN GENERAL.— An entity seeking a grant under this section shall submit to the Administrator of FEMA an application therefor in such form and in such manner as the Administrator of FEMA determines appropriate.

(2) ELEMENTS.—Each application submitted under paragraph (1) shall include the following:

(A)   A description of the financial need of the applicant for the grant.

(B)   An analysis of the costs and benefits, with respect to public safety, of the use for which a grant is requested.

(C)   An agreement to provide information to the national fire incident reporting system for the period covered by the grant.

(D) A list of other sources of funding received by the applicant—

(i)   for the same purpose for which the application for a grant under this section was submitted; or

(ii)   from the Federal Government for other fire-related purposes.

(E)   Such other information as the Administrator of FEMA determines appropriate.

(3) JOINT OR REGIONAL APPLICATIONS.—

(A) IN GENERAL.— Two or more entities may submit an application under paragraph (1) for a grant under this section to fund a joint program or initiative, including acquisition of shared equipment or vehicles.

(B) NONEXCLUSIVITY.— Applications under this paragraph may be submitted instead of or in addition to any other application submitted under paragraph (1).

(C) GUIDANCE.—The Administrator of FEMA shall—

(i)   publish guidance on applying for and administering grants awarded for joint programs and initiatives described in subparagraph (A); and

(ii)   encourage applicants to apply for grants for joint programs and initiatives described in subparagraph (A) as the Administrator of FEMA determines appropriate to achieve greater cost effectiveness and regional efficiency.

(f) PEER REVIEW OF GRANT APPLICATIONS.—

(1) IN GENERAL.— The Administrator of FEMA shall, after consultation with

national fire service and emergency medical services organizations, appoint fire service personnel to conduct peer reviews of applications received under subsection (e)(1).

(2) APPLICABILITY OF CHAPTER 10 OF TITLE 5, UNITED STATES CODE.— Chapter 10 of title 5, United States Code, shall not apply to activities carried out pursuant to this subsection.

(g) PRIORITIZATION OF GRANT AWARDS.—In awarding grants under this section, the Administrator of FEMA shall consider the following:

(1) The findings and recommendations of the peer reviews carried out under subsection (f).

(2) The degree to which an award will reduce deaths, injuries, and property damage by reducing the risks associated with fire-related and other hazards.

(3) The extent of the need of an applicant for a grant under this section and the need to protect the United States as a whole.

(4) The number of calls requesting or requiring a fire fighting or emergency medical response received by an applicant.

(h) ALLOCATION OF GRANT AWARDS.—In awarding grants under this section, the Administrator of FEMA shall ensure that of the available grant funds in each fiscal year—

(1) not less than 25 percent are awarded under subsection (c) to career fire departments;

(2) not less than 25 percent are awarded under subsection (c) to volunteer fire departments;

(3) not less than 25 percent are awarded under subsection (c) to combination fire departments and fire departments using paid-on-call firefighting personnel;

(4) not less than 10 percent are available for open competition among career fire departments, volunteer fire departments, combination fire departments, and fire departments using paid-on-call firefighting personnel for grants awarded under subsection (c);

(5) not less than 10 percent are awarded under subsection (d); and

(6) not more than 2 percent are awarded under this section to nonaffiliated EMS organizations described in subsection (c)(1)(B).

(i) ADDITIONAL REQUIREMENTS AND LIMITATIONS.—

(1) FUNDING FOR EMERGENCY MEDICAL SERVICES.— Not less than 3.5 percent of the available grant funds for a fiscal year shall be awarded under this section for purposes described in subsection (c)(3)(F).

(2) STATE FIRE TRAINING ACADEMIES.—

(A) MAXIMUM SHARE.— Not more than 3 percent of the available grant funds for a fiscal year may be awarded under subsection (c)(1)(C).

(B) MAXIMUM GRANT AMOUNT.— The Administrator of FEMA may not award a grant under subsection (c)(1)(C) to a State fire training academy in an amount that exceeds $1,000,000 in any fiscal year.

(3) AMOUNTS FOR PURCHASING FIREFIGHTING VEHICLES.— Not more than 25 percent of the available grant funds for a fiscal year may be used to assist grant recipients to purchase vehicles pursuant to subsection (c)(3)(G).

(j) FURTHER CONSIDERATIONS.—

(1) ASSISTANCE TO FIREFIGHTERS GRANTS TO FIRE DEPARTMENTS.—In considering applications for grants under subsection (c)(1)(A), the Administrator of FEMA shall consider—

(A) the extent to which the grant would enhance the daily operations of the applicant and the impact of such a grant on the protection of lives and property; and

(B) a broad range of factors important to the applicant's ability to respond to fires and related hazards, such as the following:

(i)   Population served.

(ii)   Geographic response area.

(iii)   Hazards vulnerability.

(iv)   Call volume.

(v)   Financial situation, including unemployment rate of the area being served.

(vi)   Need for training or equipment.

(2) APPLICATIONS FROM NONAFFILIATED EMS ORGANIZATIONS.— In the case of an application submitted under subsection (e)(1) by a nonaffiliated EMS organization, the Administrator of FEMA shall consider the extent to which other sources of Federal funding are available to the applicant to provide the assistance requested in such application.

(3) AWARDING FIRE PREVENTION AND SAFETY GRANTS TO CERTAIN ORGANIZATIONS THAT ARE NOT FIRE DEPARTMENTS.—In the case of applicants for grants under this section who are described in subsection (d)(1)(B), the Administrator of FEMA shall give priority to applicants who focus on—

(A)   prevention of injuries to high risk groups from fire; and

(B)   research programs that demonstrate a potential to improve firefighter safety.

(4) AWARDING GRANTS FOR FIRE SAFETY RESEARCH CENTERS.—

(A) CONSIDERATIONS.—In awarding grants under subsection (d)(1)(C), the Administrator of FEMA shall—

(i) select each grant recipient on—

(I)   the demonstrated research and extension resources available to the recipient to carry out the research, development, and technology transfer activities;

(II)   the capability of the recipient to provide leadership in making national contributions to fire safety;

(III)   the recipient's ability to disseminate the results of fire safety research; and

(IV)   the strategic plan the recipient proposes to carry out under the grant;

(ii) give special consideration in selecting recipients under subparagraph (A) to an applicant for a grant that consists of a partnership between—

(I)   a national fire service organization or a national fire safety organization; and

(II)   an institution of higher education, including a minority-serving institution (as described in section 371(a) of the Higher Education Act of 1965 (20 U.S.C. 1067q(a))); and

(iii)   consider the research needs identified and prioritized through the workshop required by subparagraph (B)(i).

(B) RESEARCH NEEDS.—

(i) IN GENERAL.— Not later than 90 days after the date of the enactment of the Fire Grants Reauthorization Act of 2012, the Administrator of FEMA shall convene a workshop of the fire safety research community, fire service organizations, and other appropriate stakeholders to identify and prioritize fire safety research needs.

(ii) PUBLICATION.— The Administrator of FEMA shall ensure that the results of the workshop are made available to the public.

(C) LIMITATIONS ON GRANTS FOR FIRE SAFETY RESEARCH CENTERS.—

(i) IN GENERAL.— The Administrator of FEMA may award grants under subsection (d) to establish not more than 3 fire safety research centers.

(ii) RECIPIENTS.— An institution of higher education, a national fire service organization, and a national fire safety organization may not directly receive a grant under subsection (d) for a fiscal year for more than 1 fire safety research center.

(5) AVOIDING DUPLICATION.— The Administrator of FEMA shall review lists submitted by applicants pursuant to subsection (e)(2)(D) and take such actions as the Administrator of FEMA considers necessary to prevent unnecessary duplication of grant awards.

(k) MATCHING AND MAINTENANCE OF EXPENDITURE REQUIREMENTS.—

(1) MATCHING REQUIREMENT FOR ASSISTANCE TO FIREFIGHTERS GRANTS.—

(A) IN GENERAL.— Except as provided in subparagraph (B), an applicant seeking a grant to carry out an activity under subsection (c) shall agree to make available non-Federal funds to carry out such activity in an amount equal to not less than 15 percent of the grant awarded to such applicant under such subsection.

(B) EXCEPTION FOR ENTITIES SERVING SMALL COMMUNITIES.—In the case that an applicant seeking a grant to carry out an activity under subsection (c) serves a jurisdiction of—

(i)   more than 20,000 residents but not more than 1,000,000 residents, the application shall agree to make available non-Federal funds in an amount equal to not less than 10 percent of the grant awarded to such applicant under such subsection; and

(ii)   20,000 residents or fewer, the applicant shall agree to make available non-Federal funds in an amount equal to not less than 5 percent of the grant awarded to such applicant under such subsection.

(2) MATCHING REQUIREMENT FOR FIRE PREVENTION AND SAFETY GRANTS.—

(A) IN GENERAL.—   An applicant seeking a grant to carry out an activity under subsection (d) shall agree to make available non-Federal funds to carry out such activity in an amount equal to not less than 5 percent of the grant awarded to such applicant under such subsection.

(B) MEANS OF MATCHING.—   An applicant for a grant under subsection (d) may meet the matching requirement under subparagraph (A) through direct funding, funding of complementary activities, or the provision of staff, facilities, services, material, or equipment.

(3) MAINTENANCE OF EXPENDITURES.—   An applicant seeking a grant under subsection (c) or (d) shall agree to maintain during the term of the grant the applicant's aggregate expenditures relating to the uses described in subsections (c)(3) and (d)(3) at not less than 80 percent of the average amount of such expenditures in the 2 fiscal years preceding the fiscal year in which the grant amounts are received.

(4) WAIVER.—

(A) IN GENERAL.—   Except as provided in subparagraph (C)(ii), the Administrator of FEMA may waive or reduce the requirements of paragraphs (1), (2), and (3) in cases of demonstrated economic hardship.

(B) GUIDELINES.—

(i) IN GENERAL.—   The Administrator of FEMA shall establish and publish guidelines for determining what constitutes economic hardship for purposes of this paragraph.

(ii) CONSULTATION.—In developing guidelines under clause (i), the Administrator of FEMA shall consult with individuals who are—

(I)   recognized for expertise in firefighting, emergency medical services provided by fire services, or the economic affairs of State and local governments; and

(II)   members of national fire service organizations or national organizations representing the interests of State and local governments.

(iii) CONSIDERATIONS.—In developing guidelines under clause (i), the Administrator of FEMA shall consider, with respect to relevant communities, the following:

(I)   Changes in rates of unemployment from previous years.

(II)   Whether the rates of unemployment of the relevant communities are currently and have consistently exceeded the annual national average rates of unemployment.

(III)   Changes in percentages of individuals eligible to receive food stamps from previous years.

(IV)   Such other factors as the Administrator of FEMA considers appropriate.

(C) CERTAIN APPLICANTS FOR FIRE PREVENTION AND SAFETY GRANTS.—The authority under subparagraph (A) shall not apply with respect to a nonprofit organization that—

(i)   is described in subsection (d)(1)(B); and

(ii)   is not a fire department or emergency medical services organization.

(l) GRANT GUIDELINES.—

(1) GUIDELINES.—For each fiscal year, prior to awarding any grants under this section, the Administrator of FEMA shall publish in the Federal Register—

(A) guidelines that describe—

(i)   the process for applying for grants under this section; and

(ii)   the criteria that will be used for selecting grant recipients; and

(B)   an explanation of any differences between such guidelines and the recommendations obtained under paragraph (2).

(2) ANNUAL MEETING TO OBTAIN RECOMMENDATIONS.—

(A) IN GENERAL.—For each fiscal year, the Administrator of FEMA shall convene a meeting of qualified members of national fire service organizations and, at the discretion of the Administrator of FEMA, qualified members of emergency medical service organizations to obtain recommendations regarding the following:

(i)   Criteria for the awarding of grants under this section.

(ii)   Administrative changes to the assistance program established under subsection (b).

(B) QUALIFIED MEMBERS.—For purposes of this paragraph, a qualified member of an organization is a member who—

(i)   is recognized for expertise in firefighting or emergency medical services;

(ii)   is not an employee of the Federal Government; and

(iii)   in the case of a member of an emergency medical service organization, is a member of an organization that represents—

(I)   providers of emergency medical services that are affiliated with fire departments; or

(II) nonaffiliated EMS providers.

(3) APPLICABILITY OF CHAPTER 10 OF TITLE 5, UNITED STATES CODE.— Chapter 10 of title 5, United States Code, shall not apply to activities carried out under this subsection.

(m) ACCOUNTING DETERMINATION.— Notwithstanding any other provision of law, for purposes of this section, equipment costs shall include all costs attributable to any design, purchase of components, assembly, manufacture, and transportation of equipment not otherwise commercially available.

(n) ELIGIBLE GRANTEE ON BEHALF OF ALASKA NATIVE VILLAGES.— The Alaska Village Initiatives, a non-profit organization incorporated in the State of Alaska, shall be eligible to apply for and receive a grant or other assistance under this section on behalf of Alaska Native villages.

(o) TRAINING STANDARDS.— If an applicant for a grant under this section is applying for such grant to purchase training that does not meet or exceed any applicable national voluntary consensus standards, including those developed under section 647 of the Post-Katrina Emergency Management Reform Act of 2006 (6 U.S.C. 747), the applicant shall submit to the Administrator of FEMA an explanation of the reasons that the training proposed to be purchased will serve the needs of the applicant better than training that meets or exceeds such standards.

(p) ENSURING EFFECTIVE USE OF GRANTS.—

(1) AUDITS.—The Administrator of FEMA may audit a recipient of a grant awarded under this section to ensure that—

(A) the grant amounts are expended for the intended purposes; and

(B) the grant recipient complies with the requirements of subsection (k).

(2) PERFORMANCE ASSESSMENT.—

(A) IN GENERAL.— The Administrator of FEMA shall develop and implement a performance assessment system, including quantifiable performance metrics, to evaluate the extent to which grants awarded under this section are furthering the purposes of this section, including protecting the health and safety of the public and firefighting personnel against fire and fire-related hazards.

(B) CONSULTATION.— The Administrator of FEMA shall consult with fire service representatives and with the Comptroller General of the United States in developing the assessment system required by subparagraph (A).

(3) ANNUAL REPORTS TO ADMINISTRATOR OF FEMA.— Not less frequently than once each year during the term of a grant awarded under this section, the recipient of the grant shall submit to the Administrator of FEMA an annual report describing how the recipient used the grant amounts.

(4) ANNUAL REPORTS TO CONGRESS.—

(A) IN GENERAL.—Not later than September 30, 2013, and each year thereafter through 2017, the Administrator of FEMA shall submit to the Committee on Homeland Security and Governmental Affairs of the Senate and the Committee on Science and Technology and the Committee on Transportation and

Infrastructure of the House of Representatives a report that provides—

 (i) information on the performance assessment system developed under paragraph (2); and

 (ii) using the performance metrics developed under such paragraph, an evaluation of the effectiveness of the grants awarded under this section.

 (B) ADDITIONAL INFORMATION.— The report due under subparagraph (A) on September 30, 2016, shall also include recommendations for legislative changes to improve grants under this section.

(q) AUTHORIZATION OF APPROPRIATIONS.—

 (1) IN GENERAL.— There is authorized to be appropriated to carry out this section $750,000,000 for each of fiscal years 2024 through 2028.

 (2) ADMINISTRATIVE EXPENSES.— Of the amounts appropriated pursuant to paragraph (1) for a fiscal year, the Administrator of FEMA may use not more than 5 percent of such amounts for salaries and expenses and other administrative costs incurred by the Administrator of FEMA in the course of awarding grants and providing assistance under this section.

 (3) CONGRESSIONALLY DIRECTED SPENDING.— Consistent with the requirements in subsections (c)(1) and (d)(1) that grants under those subsections be awarded on a competitive basis, none of the funds appropriated pursuant to this subsection may be used for any congressionally directed spending item (as defined under the rules of the Senate and the House of Representatives).

(r) SUNSET OF AUTHORITIES.— The authority to award assistance and grants under this section shall expire on September 30, 2030.

[15 U.S.C. 2229]

SEC. 34. STAFFING FOR ADEQUATE FIRE AND EMERGENCY RESPONSE.

(a) EXPANDED AUTHORITY TO MAKE GRANTS.—

 (1) HIRING GRANTS.—(A) The Administrator of FEMA shall make grants directly to career fire departments, combination fire departments, and volunteer fire departments, in consultation with the chief executive of the State in which the applicant is located, for the purpose of increasing the number of firefighters to help communities meet industry minimum standards and attain 24-hour staffing to provide adequate protection from fire and fire-related hazards, and to fulfill traditional missions of fire departments that antedate the creation of the Department of Homeland Security.

 (B) Grants made under this paragraph shall be for 3 years and be used for programs to hire new, additional firefighters or to change the status of part-time or paid-on-call (as defined in section 33(a)) firefighters to full-time firefighters.

 (C) In awarding grants under this subsection, the Administrator of FEMA may give preferential consideration to applications that involve a non-Federal contribution exceeding the minimums under subparagraph (E).

 (D) The Administrator of FEMA may provide technical assistance to States, units of local government, Indian tribal governments, and to other public entities, in furtherance of the purposes of this section.

(E) The portion of the costs of hiring firefighters provided by a grant under this paragraph may not exceed—

(i) 75 percent in the first year of the grant;

(ii) 75 percent in the second year of the grant; and

(iii) 35 percent in the third year of the grant.

(F) Notwithstanding any other provision of law, any firefighter hired with funds provided under this subsection shall not be discriminated against for, or be prohibited from, engaging in volunteer activities in another jurisdiction during off-duty hours.

(G) All grants made pursuant to this subsection shall be awarded on a competitive basis through a neutral peer review process.

(H) At the beginning of the fiscal year, the Administrator of FEMA shall set aside 10 percent of the funds appropriated for carrying out this paragraph for departments with majority volunteer or all volunteer personnel. After awards have been made, if less than 10 percent of the funds appropriated for carrying out this paragraph are not awarded to departments with majority volunteer or all volunteer personnel, the Administrator of FEMA shall transfer from funds appropriated for carrying out this paragraph to funds available for carrying out paragraph (2) an amount equal to the difference between the amount that is provided to such fire departments and 10 percent.

(2) RECRUITMENT AND RETENTION GRANTS.— In addition to any amounts transferred under paragraph (1)(H), the Administrator of FEMA shall direct at least 10 percent of the total amount of funds appropriated pursuant to this section annually to a competitive grant program for the recruitment and retention of volunteer firefighters who are involved with or trained in the operations of firefighting and emergency response. Eligible entities shall include volunteer or combination fire departments, and national, State, local, or tribal organizations that represent the interests of volunteer firefighters.

(b) APPLICATIONS.—(1) No grant may be made under this section unless an application has been submitted to, and approved by, the Administrator of FEMA.

(2) An application for a grant under this section shall be submitted in such form, and contain such information, as the Administrator of FEMA may prescribe.

(3) At a minimum, each application for a grant under this section shall—

(A) explain the applicant's inability to address the need without Federal assistance;

(B) in the case of a grant under subsection (a)(1), explain how the applicant plans to meet the requirements of subsection (a)(1)(F);

(C) specify long-term plans for retaining firefighters following the conclusion of Federal support provided under this section; and

(D) provide assurances that the applicant will, to the extent practicable, seek, recruit, and hire members of racial and ethnic minority groups and women in order to increase their ranks within firefighting.

(c) LIMITATION ON USE OF FUNDS.—(1) Funds made available under this section to fire departments for salaries and benefits to hire new, additional firefighters shall not be used to supplant State or local funds, or, in the case of Indian tribal governments, funds supplied by the Bureau of Indian Affairs, but shall be used to increase the amount of funds that would, in the absence of Federal funds received under this section, be made available from State or local sources, or in the case of Indian tribal governments, from funds supplied by the Bureau of Indian Affairs.

(2) No grant shall be awarded pursuant to this section to a municipality or other recipient whose annual budget at the time of the application for fire-related programs and emergency response has been reduced below 80 percent of the average funding level in the 3 years prior to the date of the application for the grant.

(3) Funds appropriated by the Congress for the activities of any agency of an Indian tribal government or the Bureau of Indian Affairs performing firefighting functions on any Indian lands may be used to provide the non-Federal share of the cost of programs or projects funded under this section.

(4) The amount of funding provided under this section to a recipient fire department for hiring a firefighter in any fiscal year may not exceed—

(A) in the first year of the grant, 75 percent of the usual annual cost of a first-year firefighter in that department at the time the grant application was submitted;

(B) in the second year of the grant, 75 percent of the usual annual cost of a first-year firefighter in that department at the time the grant application was submitted; and

(C) in the third year of the grant, 35 percent of the usual annual cost of a first-year firefighter in that department at the time the grant application was submitted.

(d) WAIVERS.—

(1) IN GENERAL.—In a case of demonstrated economic hardship, the Administrator of FEMA may—

(A) waive the requirements of subsection (c)(1); or

(B) waive or reduce the requirements in subsection (a)(1)(E), (c)(2), or (c)(4).

(2) GUIDELINES.—

(A) IN GENERAL.— The Administrator of FEMA shall establish and publish guidelines for determining what constitutes economic hardship for purposes of paragraph (1).

(B) CONSULTATION.—In developing guidelines under subparagraph (A), the Administrator of FEMA shall consult with individuals who are—

(i) recognized for expertise in firefighting, emergency medical services provided by fire services, or the economic affairs of State and local governments; and

(ii)   members of national fire service organizations or national organizations representing the interests of State and local governments.

(C) CONSIDERATIONS.—In developing guidelines under subparagraph (A), the Administrator of FEMA shall consider, with respect to relevant communities, the following:

(i)   Changes in rates of unemployment from previous years.

(ii)   Whether the rates of unemployment of the relevant communities are currently and have consistently exceeded the annual national average rates of unemployment.

(iii)   Changes in percentages of individuals eligible to receive food stamps from previous years.

(iv)   Such other factors as the Administrator of FEMA considers appropriate.

(e) PERFORMANCE EVALUATION.—

(1) IN GENERAL.— The Administrator of FEMA shall establish a performance assessment system, including quantifiable performance metrics, to evaluate the extent to which grants awarded under this section are furthering the purposes of this section.

(2) SUBMITTAL OF INFORMATION.— The Administrator of FEMA may require a grant recipient to submit any information the Administrator of FEMA considers reasonably necessary to evaluate the program.

(f) REPORT.— Not later than September 30, 2014, the Administrator of FEMA shall submit to the Committee on Homeland Security and Governmental Affairs of the Senate and the Committee on Science and Technology and the Committee on Transportation and Infrastructure of the House of Representatives a report on the experience with, and effectiveness of, such grants in meeting the objectives of this section. The report may include any recommendations the Administrator of FEMA may have for amendments to this section and related provisions of law.

(g) REVOCATION OR SUSPENSION OF FUNDING.— If the Administrator of FEMA determines that a grant recipient under this section is not in substantial compliance with the terms and requirements of an approved grant application submitted under this section, the Administrator of FEMA may revoke or suspend funding of that grant, in whole or in part.

(h) ACCESS TO DOCUMENTS.—(1)   The Administrator of FEMA shall have access for the purpose of audit and examination to any pertinent books, documents, papers, or records of a grant recipient under this section and to the pertinent books, documents, papers, or records of State and local governments, persons, businesses, and other entities that are involved in programs, projects, or activities for which assistance is provided under this section.

(2)   Paragraph (1) shall apply with respect to audits and examinations conducted by the Comptroller General of the United States or by an authorized representative of the Comptroller General.

(i) DEFINITIONS.—In this section:

(1)   The term firefighter has the meaning given the term employee in fire protection activities under section 3(y) of the Fair Labor Standards Act (29 U.S.C. 203(y)).

(2)   The terms Administrator of FEMA, career fire department, combination fire department, and volunteer fire department have the meanings given such terms in section 33(a).

(j) AUTHORIZATION OF APPROPRIATIONS.—

(1) IN GENERAL.—There are authorized to be appropriated for the purposes of carrying out this section—

(A) $1,000,000,000 for fiscal year 2004;

(B) $1,030,000,000 for fiscal year 2005;

(C) $1,061,000,000 for fiscal year 2006;

(D) $1,093,000,000 for fiscal year 2007;

(E) $1,126,000,000 for fiscal year 2008;

(F) $1,159,000,000 for fiscal year 2009;

(G) $1,194,000,000 for fiscal year 2010; and

(H) $750,000,000 for each of fiscal years 2024 through 2028.

(2) ADMINISTRATIVE EXPENSES.— Of the amounts appropriated pursuant to paragraph (1) for a fiscal year, the Administrator of FEMA may use not more than 5 percent of such amounts to cover salaries and expenses and other administrative costs incurred by the Administrator of FEMA to make grants and provide assistance under this section.

(3) CONGRESSIONALLY DIRECTED SPENDING.— Consistent with the requirement in subsection (a) that grants under this section be awarded on a competitive basis, none of the funds appropriated pursuant to this subsection may be used for any congressionally direct spending item (as defined under the rules of the Senate and the House of Representatives).

(k) SUNSET OF AUTHORITIES.— The authority to award assistance and grants under this section shall expire on September 30, 2030.

[15 U.S.C. 2229a]

SEC. 35. SURPLUS AND EXCESS FEDERAL EQUIPMENT.

The Administrator shall make publicly available, including through the Internet, information on procedures for acquiring surplus and excess equipment or property that may be useful to State and local fire, emergency, and hazardous material handling service providers.

[15 U.S.C. 2230]

SEC. 36. COOPERATIVE AGREEMENTS WITH FEDERAL FACILITIES.

The Administrator shall make publicly available, including through the Internet, information on procedures for establishing cooperative agreements between State and local fire and emergency services and Federal facilities in their region relating to the provision of fire and emergency services.

[15 U.S.C. 2231]

SEC. 37. ENCOURAGING ADOPTION OF STANDARDS FOR FIREFIGHTER HEALTH AND SAFETY.

The Administrator shall promote adoption by fire services of national voluntary consensus standards for firefighter health and safety, including such standards for firefighter operations, training, staffing, and fitness, by—

(1) educating fire services about such standards;

(2) encouraging the adoption at all levels of government of such standards; and

(3) making recommendations on other ways in which the Federal Government can promote the adoption of such standards by fire services.

[15 U.S.C. 2234]

SEC. 38. INVESTIGATION AUTHORITIES.

(a) IN GENERAL.— In the case of a major fire, the Administrator may send incident investigators, which may include safety specialists, fire protection engineers, codes and standards experts, researchers, and fire training specialists, to the site of the fire to conduct a fire safety investigation as described in subsection (b).

(b) INVESTIGATION REQUIRED.—A fire safety investigation conducted under this section—

(1) shall be conducted in coordination and cooperation with appropriate Federal, State, local, Tribal, and territorial authorities, including Federal agencies that are authorized to investigate any fire; and

(2) shall examine the previously determined cause and origin of the fire and assess broader systematic matters to include use of codes and standards, demographics, structural characteristics, smoke and fire dynamics (movement) during the event, and costs of associated injuries and deaths.

(c) REPORT.—

(1) IN GENERAL.—Subject to paragraph (2), upon concluding any fire safety investigation under this section, the Administrator shall—

(A) issue a public report to the appropriate Federal, State, local, Tribal, and territorial authorities on the findings of such investigation; or

(B) collaborate with another investigating Federal, State, local, Tribal, or territorial agency on the report of that agency.

(2) EXCEPTION.— If the Administrator, in consultation with appropriate Federal, State, local, Tribal, and territorial authorities determines that issuing a report under paragraph (1) would have a negative impact on a potential or ongoing criminal investigation, the Administrator is not required to issue such report.

(3) CONTENTS.—Each public report issued under paragraph (1) shall include recommendations on—

(A) any other buildings with similar characteristics that may bear similar fire risks;

(B) improving tactical response to similar fires;

(C) improving civilian safety practices;

(D) assessing the costs and benefits to the community of adding fire safety features; and

(E) how to mitigate the causes of the fire.

(d) DISCRETIONARY AUTHORITY.— In addition to a fire safety investigation conducted pursuant to subsection (a), provided doing so would not have a negative impact on a potential or ongoing criminal investigation, the Administrator may send fire investigators to conduct a fire safety investigation at the site of any fire with unusual or remarkable context that results in losses less severe than those occurring as a result of a major fire, in coordination and cooperation with the appropriate Federal, State, local, Tribal, and territorial authorities, including Federal agencies that are authorized to investigate the fire.

(e) CONSTRUCTION.—Nothing in this section shall be construed to—

(1) affect or otherwise diminish the authorities or the mandates vested in other Federal agencies;

(2) grant the Administrator authority to investigate a major fire for the purpose of an enforcement action or criminal prosecution; or

(3) require the Administrator to send investigators or issue a report for a major fire when the Administrator, in coordination and cooperation with the appropriate Federal, State, local, Tribal, and territorial authorities, determine that it may compromise a potential or ongoing criminal investigation.

(f) MAJOR FIRE DEFINED.— For purposes of this section, the term major fire shall have the meaning given such term under regulations to be issued by the Administrator.

[15 U.S.C. 2235]

★

UNITED STATES FIRE ADMINISTRATION, AFG, AND SAFER PROGRAM REAUTHORIZATION ACT OF 2017

PUBLIC LAW 115–98

UNITED STATES FIRE ADMINISTRATION, AFG, AND SAFER PROGRAM REAUTHORIZATION ACT OF 2017

[(Public Law 115–98)]

[This law has not been amended]

AN ACT To reauthorize the United States Fire Administration, the Assistance to Firefighters Grants program, the Fire Prevention and Safety Grants program, and the Staffing for Adequate Fire and Emergency Response grant program, and for other purposes.

Be it enacted by the Senate and House of Representatives of the United States of America in Congress assembled,

SECTION 1. [15 U.S.C. 2201 note] SHORT TITLE.

This Act may be cited as the "United States Fire Administration, AFG, and SAFER Program Reauthorization Act of 2017".

* * * * * * *

SEC. 5. [15 U.S.C. 2229 note] TRAINING ON ADMINISTRATION OF FIRE GRANT PROGRAMS.

(a) IN GENERAL.— The Administrator of the Federal Emergency Management Agency, acting through the Administrator of the United States Fire Administration, may develop and make widely available an electronic, online training course for members of the fire and emergency response community on matters relating to the administration of grants under sections 33 and 34 of the Federal Fire Prevention and Control Act of 1974 (15 U.S.C. 2229 and 2229a).

(b) REQUIREMENTS.—The Administrator of the Federal Emergency Management Agency shall ensure that any training developed and made available under subsection (a) is—

(1) tailored to the financial and time constraints of members of the fire and emergency response community; and

(2) accessible to all individuals in the career, combination, paid-on-call, and volunteer fire and emergency response community.

SEC. 6. [22 U.S.C. 2229 note] FRAMEWORK FOR OVERSIGHT AND MONITORING OF THE ASSISTANCE TO FIREFIGHTERS GRANTS PROGRAM, THE FIRE PREVENTION AND

SAFETY GRANTS PROGRAM, AND THE STAFFING FOR ADEQUATE FIRE AND EMERGENCY RESPONSE GRANT PROGRAM.

(a) FRAMEWORK.— Not later than 90 days after the date of enactment of this Act, the Administrator of the Federal Emergency Management Agency, acting through the Administrator of the United States Fire Administration, shall develop and implement a grant monitoring and oversight framework to mitigate and minimize risks of fraud, waste, abuse, and mismanagement relating to the grants programs under sections 33 and 34 of the Federal Fire Prevention and Control Act of 1974 (15 U.S.C. 2229 and 2229a).

(b) ELEMENTS.—The framework required under subsection (a) shall include the following:

(1) Developing standardized guidance and training for all participants in the grant programs described in subsection (a).

(2) Conducting regular risk assessments.

(3) Conducting desk reviews and site visits.

(4) Enforcement actions to recoup potential questionable costs of grant recipients.

(5) Such other oversight and monitoring tools as the Administrator of the Federal Emergency Management Agency considers necessary to mitigate and minimize fraud, waste, abuse, and mismanagement relating to the grant programs described in subsection (a).

★

HAZARD-SPECIFIC LAWS
EARTHQUAKES

SECTION 109 OF THE COMPREHENSIVE ENVIRONMENTAL RESPONSE, COMPENSATION, AND LIABILITY ACT OF 1980

PUBLIC LAW 96–510
AS AMENDED THROUGH PUB. L. 115–141

COMPREHENSIVE ENVIRONMENTAL RESPONSE, COMPENSATION, AND LIABILITY ACT OF 1980 (SUPERFUND)[1]

[As Amended Through P.L. 115–141, Enacted March 23, 2018]

AN ACT To provide for liability, compensation, cleanup, and emergency response for hazardous substances released into the environment and the cleanup of inactive hazardous waste disposal sites.

Be it enacted by the Senate and House of Representatives of the United States of America in Congress assembled,

That this Act may be cited as the "Comprehensive Environmental Response, Compensation, and Liability Act of 1980".

---

[1] The Comprehensive Environmental Response, Compensation, and Liability Act of 1980 (42 U.S.C. 9601–9675), commonly known as Superfund, consists of Public Law 96–510 (Dec. 11, 1980) and the amendments made by subsequent enactments.

TITLE I—HAZARDOUS SUBSTANCES RELEASES, LIABILITY, COMPENSATION

* * * * * * *

RESPONSE AUTHORITIES

SEC. 104. (a) (1) Whenever (A) any hazardous substance is released or there is a substantial threat of such a release into the environment, or (B) there is a release or substantial threat of release into the environment of any pollutant or contaminant which may present an imminent and substantial danger to the public health or welfare, the President is authorized to act, consistent with the national contingency plan, to remove or arrange for the removal of, and provide for remedial action relating to such hazardous substance, pollutant, or contaminant at any time (including its removal from any contaminated natural resource), or take any other response measure consistent with the national contingency plan which the President deems necessary to protect the public health or welfare or the environment. When the President determines that such action will be done properly and promptly by the owner or operator of the facility or vessel or by any other responsible party, the President may allow such person to carry out the action, conduct the remedial investigation, or conduct the feasibility study in accordance with section 122. No remedial investigation or feasibility study (RI/FS) shall be authorized except on a determination by the President that the party is qualified to conduct the RI/FS and only if the President contracts with or arranges for a qualified person to assist the President in overseeing and reviewing the conduct of such RI/FS and if the responsible party agrees to reimburse the Fund for any cost incurred by the President under, or in connection with, the oversight contract or arrangement. In no event shall a potentially responsible party be subject to a lesser standard of liability, receive preferential treatment, or in any other way, whether direct or indirect, benefit from any such arrangements as a response action contractor, or as a person hired or retained by such a response action contractor, with respect to the release or facility in question. The President shall give primary attention to those releases which the President deems may present a public health threat.

(2) REMOVAL ACTION.— Any removal action undertaken by the President under this subsection (or by any other person referred to in section 122) should, to the extent the President deems practicable, contribute to the efficient performance of any long term remedial action with respect to the release or threatened release concerned.

(3) LIMITATIONS ON RESPONSE.— The President shall not provide for a removal or remedial action under this section in response to a release or threat of release—

(A) of a naturally occurring substance in its unaltered form, or altered solely through naturally occurring processes or phenomena, from a location where it is naturally found;

(B) from products which are part of the structure of, and result in exposure within, residential buildings or business or community structures; or

(C) into public or private drinking water supplies due to deterioration of the system through ordinary use.

(4) EXCEPTION TO LIMITATIONS.— Notwithstanding paragraph (3) of this subsection, to the extent authorized by this section, the President may respond to any release or threat of release if in the President's discretion, it constitutes a public health or environmental emergency and no other person with the authority and capability to respond to the emergency will do so in a timely manner.

(b) (1) INFORMATION; STUDIES AND INVESTIGATIONS.— Whenever the President is authorized to act pursuant to subsection (a) of this section, or whenever the President has reason to believe that a release has occurred or is about to occur, or that illness, disease, or complaints thereof may be attributable to exposure to a hazardous substance, pollutant, or contaminant and that a release may have occurred or be occurring, he may undertake such investigations, monitoring, surveys, testing, and other information gathering as he may deem necessary or appropriate to identify the existence and extent of the release or threat thereof, the source and nature of the hazardous substances, pollutants or contaminants involved, and the extent of danger to the public health or welfare or to the environment. In addition, the President may undertake such planning, legal, fiscal, economic, engineering, architectural, and other studies or investigations as he may deem necessary or appropriate to plan and direct response actions, to recover the costs thereof, and to enforce the provisions of this Act.

(2) COORDINATION OF INVESTIGATIONS.— The President shall promptly notify

378

the appropriate Federal and State natural resource trustees of potential damages to natural resources resulting from releases under investigation pursuant to this section and shall seek to coordinate the assessments, investigations, and planning under this section with such Federal and State trustees.

(c) (1) Unless (A) the President finds that (i) continued response actions are immediately required to prevent, limit, or mitigate an emergency, (ii) there is an immediate risk to public health or welfare or the environment, and (iii) such assistance will not otherwise be provided on a timely basis, or (B) the President has determined the appropriate remedial actions pursuant to paragraph (2) of this subsection and the State or States in which the source of the release is located have complied with the requirements of paragraph (3) of this subsection, or (C) continued response action is otherwise appropriate and consistent with the remedial action to be taken[1] obligations from the Fund, other than those authorized by subsection (b) of this section, shall not continue after $2,000,000 has been obligated for response actions or 12 months has elapsed from the date of initial response to a release or threatened release of hazardous substances.

---

[1]

So in law. Probably should be followed by a comma.

---

(2) The President shall consult with the affected State or States before determining any appropriate remedial action to be taken pursuant to the authority granted under subsection (a) of this section.

(3) The President shall not provide any remedial actions pursuant to this section unless the State in which the release occurs first enters into a contract or cooperative agreement with the President providing assurances deemed adequate by the President that (A) the State will assure all future maintenance of the removal and remedial actions provided for the expected life of such actions as determined by the President; (B) the State will assure the availability of a hazardous waste disposal facility acceptable to the President and in compliance with the requirements of subtitle C of the Solid Waste Disposal Act for any necessary offsite storage, destruction, treatment, or secure disposition of the hazardous substances; and (C) the State will pay or assure payment of (i) 10 per centum of the costs of the remedial action, including all future maintenance, or (ii) 50 percent (or such greater amount as the President may determine appropriate, taking into account the degree of responsibility of the State or political subdivision for the release) of any sums expended in response to a release at a facility, that was operated by the State or a political subdivision thereof, either directly or through a contractual relationship or otherwise, at the time of any disposal of hazardous substances therein. For the purpose of clause (ii) of this subparagraph, the term facility does not include navigable waters or the beds underlying those waters. The President shall grant the State a credit against the share of the costs for which it is responsible under this paragraph for any documented direct out-of-pocket non-Federal funds expended or obligated by the State or a political subdivision thereof after January 1, 1978, and before the date of enactment of this Act for cost-eligible response actions and claims for damages compensable under section 111 of this title relating to the specific

release in question: *Provided, however,* That in no event shall the amount of the credit granted exceed the total response costs relating to the release. In the case of remedial action to be taken on land or water held by an Indian tribe, held by the United States in trust for Indians, held by a member of an Indian tribe (if such land or water is subject to a trust restriction on alienation), or otherwise within the borders of an Indian reservation, the requirements of this paragraph for assurances regarding future maintenance and cost-sharing shall not apply, and the President shall provide the assurance required by this paragraph regarding the availability of a hazardous waste disposal facility.

(4) SELECTION OF REMEDIAL ACTION.— The President shall select remedial actions to carry out this section in accordance with section 121 of this Act (relating to cleanup standards).

(5) STATE CREDITS.—

(A) GRANTING OF CREDIT.— The President shall grant a State a credit against the share of the costs, for which it is responsible under paragraph (3) with respect to a facility listed on the National Priorities List under the National Contingency Plan, for amounts expended by a State for remedial action at such facility pursuant to a contract or cooperative agreement with the President. The credit under this paragraph shall be limited to those State expenses which the President determines to be reasonable, documented, direct out-of-pocket expenditures of non-Federal funds.

(B) EXPENSES BEFORE LISTING OR AGREEMENT.— The credit under this paragraph shall include expenses for remedial action at a facility incurred before the listing of the facility on the National Priorities List or before a contract or cooperative agreement is entered into under subsection (d) for the facility if—

(i) after such expenses are incurred the facility is listed on such list and a contract or cooperative agreement is entered into for the facility, and

(ii) the President determines that such expenses would have been credited to the State under subparagraph (A) had the expenditures been made after listing of the facility on such list and after the date on which such contract or cooperative agreement is entered into.

(C) RESPONSE ACTIONS BETWEEN 1978 AND 1980.— The credit under this paragraph shall include funds expended or obligated by the State or a political subdivision thereof after January 1, 1978, and before December 11, 1980, for cost-eligible response actions and claims for damages compensable under section 111.

(D) STATE EXPENSES AFTER DECEMBER 11, 1980, IN EXCESS OF 10 PERCENT OF COSTS.— The credit under this paragraph shall include 90 percent of State expenses incurred at a facility owned, but not operated, by such State or by a political subdivision thereof. Such credit applies only to expenses incurred pursuant to a contract or cooperative agreement under subsection (d) and only to expenses incurred after December 11, 1980, but before the date of the enactment of this paragraph.

(E) ITEM-BY-ITEM APPROVAL.— In the case of expenditures made after the date of the enactment of this paragraph, the President may require prior approval of each item of expenditure as a condition of granting a credit under this paragraph.

(F) USE OF CREDITS.— Credits granted under this paragraph for funds expended with respect to a facility may be used by the State to reduce all or part of the share of costs otherwise required to be paid by the State under paragraph (3) in connection with remedial actions at such facility. If the amount of funds for which credit is allowed under this paragraph exceeds such share of costs for such facility, the State may use the amount of such excess to reduce all or part of the share of such costs at other facilities in that State. A credit shall not entitle the State to any direct payment.

(6) OPERATION AND MAINTENANCE.— For the purposes of paragraph (3) of this subsection, in the case of ground or surface water contamination, completed remedial action includes the completion of treatment or other measures, whether taken onsite or offsite, necessary to restore ground and surface water quality to a level that assures protection of human health and the environment. With respect to such measures, the operation of such measures for a period of up to 10 years after the construction or installation and commencement of operation shall be considered remedial action. Activities required to maintain the effectiveness of such measures following such period or the completion of remedial action, whichever is earlier, shall be considered operation or maintenance.

(7) LIMITATION ON SOURCE OF FUNDS FOR O&M.— During any period after the availability of funds received by the Hazardous Substance Superfund established under subchapter A of chapter 98 of the Internal Revenue Code of 1954 from tax revenues or appropriations from general revenues, the Federal share of the payment of the cost of operation or maintenance pursuant to paragraph (3)(C)(i) or paragraph (6) of this subsection (relating to operation and maintenance) shall be from funds received by the Hazardous Substance Superfund from amounts recovered on behalf of such fund under this Act.

(8) RECONTRACTING.— The President is authorized to undertake or continue whatever interim remedial actions the President determines to be appropriate to reduce risks to public health or the environment where the performance of a complete remedial action requires recontracting because of the discovery of sources, types, or quantities of hazardous substances not known at the time of entry into the original contract. The total cost of interim actions undertaken at a facility pursuant to this paragraph shall not exceed $2,000,000.

(9) SITING.— Effective 3 years after the enactment of the Superfund Amendments and Reauthorization Act of 1986, the President shall not provide any remedial actions pursuant to this section unless the State in which the release occurs first enters into a contract or cooperative agreement with the President providing assurances deemed adequate by the President that the State will assure the availability of hazardous waste treatment or disposal facilities which—

(A) have adequate capacity for the destruction, treatment, or secure disposition of all hazardous wastes that are reasonably expected to be generated within the State during the 20-year period following the date of such contract or cooperative agreement and to be disposed of, treated, or destroyed,

(B)   are within the State or outside the State in accordance with an interstate agreement or regional agreement or authority,

(C)   are acceptable to the President, and

(D)   are in compliance with the requirements of subtitle C of the Solid Waste Disposal Act.

(d) (1) COOPERATIVE AGREEMENTS.—

(A) STATE APPLICATIONS.— A State or political subdivision thereof or Indian tribe may apply to the President to carry out actions authorized in this section. If the President determines that the State or political subdivision or Indian tribe has the capability to carry out any or all of such actions in accordance with the criteria and priorities established pursuant to section 105(a)(8) and to carry out related enforcement actions, the President may enter into a contract or cooperative agreement with the State or political subdivision or Indian tribe to carry out such actions. The President shall make a determination regarding such an application within 90 days after the President receives the application.

(B) TERMS AND CONDITIONS.— A contract or cooperative agreement under this paragraph shall be subject to such terms and conditions as the President may prescribe. The contract or cooperative agreement may cover a specific facility or specific facilities.

(C) REIMBURSEMENTS.— Any State which expended funds during the period beginning September 30, 1985, and ending on the date of the enactment of this subparagraph for response actions at any site included on the National Priorities List and subject to a cooperative agreement under this Act shall be reimbursed for the share of costs of such actions for which the Federal Government is responsible under this Act.

(2)   If the President enters into a cost-sharing agreement pursuant to subsection (c) of this section or a contract or cooperative agreement pursuant to this subsection, and the State or political subdivision thereof fails to comply with any requirements of the contract, the President may, after providing sixty days notice, seek in the appropriate Federal district court to enforce the contract or to recover any funds advanced or any costs incurred because of the breach of the contract by the State or political subdivision.

(3)   Where a State or a political subdivision thereof is acting in behalf of the President, the President is authorized to provide technical and legal assistance in the administration and enforcement of any contract or subcontract in connection with response actions assisted under this title, and to intervene in any civil action involving the enforcement of such contract or subcontract.

(4)   Where two or more noncontiguous facilities are reasonably related on the basis of geography, or on the basis of the threat, or potential threat to the public health or welfare or the environment, the President may, in his discretion, treat these related facilities as one for purposes of this section.

(e) INFORMATION GATHERING AND ACCESS.—

(1) ACTION AUTHORIZED.— Any officer, employee, or representative of the President, duly designated by the President, is authorized to take action under paragraph (2), (3), or (4) (or any combination thereof) at a vessel, facility, establishment, place, property, or location or, in the case of paragraph (3) or (4), at any vessel, facility, establishment, place, property, or location which is adjacent to the vessel, facility, establishment, place, property, or location referred to in such paragraph (3) or (4). Any duly designated officer, employee, or representative of a State or political subdivision under a contract or cooperative agreement under subsection (d)(1) is also authorized to take such action. The authority of paragraphs (3) and (4) may be exercised only if there is a reasonable basis to believe there may be a release or threat of release of a hazardous substance or pollutant or contaminant. The authority of this subsection may be exercised only for the purposes of determining the need for response, or choosing or taking any response action under this title, or otherwise enforcing the provisions of this title.

(2) ACCESS TO INFORMATION.— Any officer, employee, or representative described in paragraph (1) may require any person who has or may have information relevant to any of the following to furnish, upon reasonable notice, information or documents relating to such matter:

(A)   The identification, nature, and quantity of materials which have been or are generated, treated, stored, or disposed of at a vessel or facility or transported to a vessel or facility.

(B)   The nature or extent of a release or threatened release of a hazardous substance or pollutant or contaminant at or from a vessel or facility.

(C)   Information relating to the ability of a person to pay for or to perform a cleanup.

In addition, upon reasonable notice, such person either (i) shall grant any such officer, employee, or representative access at all reasonable times to any vessel, facility, establishment, place, property, or location to inspect and copy all documents or records relating to such matters or (ii) shall copy and furnish to the officer, employee, or representative all such documents or records, at the option and expense of such person.

(3) ENTRY.— Any officer, employee, or representative described in paragraph (1) is authorized to enter at reasonable times any of the following:

(A)   Any vessel, facility, establishment, or other place or property where any hazardous substance or pollutant or contaminant may be or has been generated, stored, treated, disposed of, or transported from.

(B)   Any vessel, facility, establishment, or other place or property from which or to which a hazardous substance or pollutant or contaminant has been or may have been released.

(C)   Any vessel, facility, establishment, or other place or property where such release is or may be threatened.

(D)   Any vessel, facility, establishment, or other place or property where entry is needed to determine the need for response or the appropriate response or to effectuate a response action under this title.

(4) INSPECTION AND SAMPLES.—

(A) AUTHORITY.— Any officer, employee or representative described in paragraph (1) is authorized to inspect and obtain samples from any vessel, facility, establishment, or other place or property referred to in paragraph (3) or from any location of any suspected hazardous substance or pollutant or contaminant. Any such officer, employee, or representative is authorized to inspect and obtain samples of any containers or labeling for suspected hazardous substances or pollutants or contaminants. Each such inspection shall be completed with reasonable promptness.

(B) SAMPLES.— If the officer, employee, or representative obtains any samples, before leaving the premises he shall give to the owner, operator, tenant, or other person in charge of the place from which the samples were obtained a receipt describing the sample obtained and, if requested, a portion of each such sample. A copy of the results of any analysis made of such samples shall be furnished promptly to the owner, operator, tenant, or other person in charge, if such person can be located.

(5) COMPLIANCE ORDERS.—

(A) ISSUANCE.— If consent is not granted regarding any request made by an officer, employee, or representative under paragraph (2), (3), or (4), the President may issue an order directing compliance with the request. The order may be issued after such notice and opportunity for consultation as is reasonably appropriate under the circumstances.

(B) COMPLIANCE.— The President may ask the Attorney General to commence a civil action to compel compliance with a request or order referred to in subparagraph (A). Where there is a reasonable basis to believe there may be a release or threat of a release of a hazardous substance or pollutant or contaminant, the court shall take the following actions:

(i) In the case of interference with entry or inspection, the court shall enjoin such interference or direct compliance with orders to prohibit interference with entry or inspection unless under the circumstances of the case the demand for entry or inspection is arbitrary and capricious, an abuse of discretion, or otherwise not in accordance with law.

(ii) In the case of information or document requests or orders, the court shall enjoin interference with such information or document requests or orders or direct compliance with the requests or orders to provide such information or documents unless under the circumstances of the case the demand for information or documents is arbitrary and capricious, an abuse of discretion, or otherwise not in accordance with law.

The court may assess a civil penalty not to exceed $25,000 for each day of noncompliance against any person who unreasonably fails to comply with the provisions of paragraph (2), (3), or (4) or an order issued pursuant to subparagraph (A) of this paragraph.

(6) OTHER AUTHORITY.— Nothing in this subsection shall preclude the President from securing access or obtaining information in any other lawful manner.

(7) CONFIDENTIALITY OF INFORMATION.— (A)   Any records, reports, or information obtained from any person under this section (including records, reports, or information obtained by representatives of the President) shall be available to the public, except that upon a showing satisfactory to the President (or the State, as the case may be) by any person that records, reports, or information, or particular part thereof (other than health or safety effects data), to which the President (or the State, as the case may be) or any officer, employee, or representative has access under this section if made public would divulge information entitled to protection under section 1905 of title 18 of the United States Code, such information or particular portion thereof shall be considered confidential in accordance with the purposes of that section, except that such record, report, document or information may be disclosed to other officers, employees, or authorized representatives of the United States concerned with carrying out this Act, or when relevant in any proceeding under this Act.

(B)   Any person not subject to the provisions of section 1905 of title 18 of the United States Code who knowingly and willfully divulges or discloses any information entitled to protection under this subsection shall, upon conviction, be subject to a fine of not more than $5,000 or to imprisonment not to exceed one year, or both.

(C)   In submitting data under this Act, a person required to provide such data may (i) designate the data which such person believes is entitled to protection under this subsection and (ii) submit such designated data separately from other data submitted under this Act. A designation under this paragraph shall be made in writing and in such manner as the President may prescribe by regulation.

(D)   Notwithstanding any limitation contained in this section or any other provision of law, all information reported to or otherwise obtained by the President (or any representative of the President) under this Act shall be made available, upon written request of any duly authorized committee of the Congress, to such committee.

(E) No person required to provide information under this Act may claim that the information is entitled to protection under this paragraph unless such person shows each of the following:

(i)   Such person has not disclosed the information to any other person, other than a member of a local emergency planning committee established under title III of the Amendments and Reauthorization Act of 1986[2], an officer or employee of the United States or a State or local government, an employee of such person, or a person who is bound by a confidentiality agreement, and such person has taken reasonable measures to protect the confidentiality of such information and intends to continue to take such measures.

---

[2]

So in law. Probably means title III of the Superfund Amendments and Reauthorization Act of 1986 (P.L. 99–499; 100 Stat. 1728).

(ii)   The information is not required to be disclosed, or otherwise made available, to the public under any other Federal or State law.

(iii)   Disclosure of the information is likely to cause substantial harm to the competitive position of such person.

(iv)   The specific chemical identity, if sought to be protected, is not readily discoverable through reverse engineering.

(F) The following information with respect to any hazardous substance at the facility or vessel shall not be entitled to protection under this paragraph:

(i)   The trade name, common name, or generic class or category of the hazardous substance.

(ii)   The physical properties of the substance, including its boiling point, melting point, flash point, specific gravity, vapor density, solubility in water, and vapor pressure at 20 degrees celsius.

(iii)   The hazards to health and the environment posed by the substance, including physical hazards (such as explosion) and potential acute and chronic health hazards.

(iv)   The potential routes of human exposure to the substance at the facility, establishment, place, or property being investigated, entered, or inspected under this subsection.

(v)   The location of disposal of any waste stream.

(vi)   Any monitoring data or analysis of monitoring data pertaining to disposal activities.

(vii)   Any hydrogeologic or geologic data.

(viii)   Any groundwater monitoring data.

(f)   In awarding contracts to any person engaged in response actions, the President or the State, in any case where it is awarding contracts pursuant to a contract entered into under subsection (d) of this section, shall require compliance with Federal health and safety standards established under section 301(f) of this Act by contractors and subcontractors as a condition of such contracts.

(g) (1)   All laborers and mechanics employed by contractors or subcontractors in the performance of construction, repair, or alteration work funded in whole or in part under this section or section 128(a)(1)(B)(ii)(III) shall be paid wages at rates not less than those prevailing on projects of a character similar in the locality as determined by the Secretary of Labor in accordance with the Davis-Bacon Act. The President shall not approve any such funding without first obtaining adequate assurance that required labor standards will be maintained upon the construction work.

(2)   The Secretary of Labor shall have, with respect to the labor standards specified in paragraph (1), the authority and functions set forth in Reorganization Plan Numbered 14 of 1950 (15 F.R. 3176; 64 Stat. 1267) and section 276c of title 40 of the United States Code.

(h)   Notwithstanding any other provision of law, subject to the provisions of section 111 of this Act, the President may authorize the use of such emergency procurement powers as he deems necessary to effect the purpose of this Act. Upon determination that such procedures are necessary, the President shall promulgate regulations prescribing the circumstances under which such authority shall be used and the procedures governing the use of such authority.

(i) (1) There is hereby established within the Public Health Service an agency, to be known as the Agency for Toxic Substances and Disease Registry, which shall report directly to the Surgeon General of the United States. The Administrator of said Agency shall, with the cooperation of the Administrator of the Environmental Protection Agency, the Commissioner of the Food and Drug Administration, the Directors of the National Institute of Medicine, National Institute of Environmental Health Sciences, National Institute of Occupational Safety and Health, Centers for Disease Control and Prevention, the Administrator of the Occupational Safety and Health Administration, the Administrator of the Social Security Administration, the Secretary of Transportation, and appropriate State and local health officials, effectuate and implement the health related authorities of this Act. In addition, said Administrator shall—

(A) in cooperation with the States, establish and maintain a national registry of serious diseases and illnesses and a national registry of persons exposed to toxic substances;

(B) establish and maintain inventory of literature, research, and studies on the health effects of toxic substances;

(C) in cooperation with the States, and other agencies of the Federal Government, establish and maintain a complete listing of areas closed to the public or otherwise restricted in use because of toxic substance contamination;

(D) in cases of public health emergencies caused or believed to be caused by exposure to toxic substances, provide medical care and testing to exposed individuals, including but not limited to tissue sampling, chromosomal testing where appropriate, epidemiological studies, or any other assistance appropriate under the circumstances; and

(E) either independently or as part of other health status survey, conduct periodic survey and screening programs to determine relationships between exposure to toxic substances and illness. In cases of public health emergencies, exposed persons shall be eligible for admission to hospitals and other facilities and services operated or provided by the Public Health Service.

(2) (A) Within 6 months after the enactment of the Superfund Amendments and Reauthorization Act of 1986, the Administrator of the Agency for Toxic Substances and Disease Registry (ATSDR) and the Administrator of the Environmental Protection Agency (EPA) shall prepare a list, in order of priority, of at least 100 hazardous substances which are most commonly found at facilities on the National Priorities List and which, in their sole discretion, they determine are posing the most significant potential threat to human health due to their known or suspected toxicity to humans and the potential for human exposure to such substances at facilities on the National Priorities List or at facilities to which a response to a release or a threatened release under this section is under consideration.

(B) Within 24 months after the enactment of the Superfund Amendments and Reauthorization Act of 1986, the Administrator of ATSDR and the

Administrator of EPA shall revise the list prepared under subparagraph (A). Such revision shall include, in order of priority, the addition of 100 or more such hazardous substances. In each of the 3 consecutive 12-month periods that follow, the Administrator of ATSDR and the Administrator of EPA shall revise, in the same manner as provided in the 2 preceding sentences, such list to include not fewer than 25 additional hazardous substances per revision. The Administrator of ATSDR and the Administrator of EPA shall not less often than once every year thereafter revise such list to include additional hazardous substances in accordance with the criteria in subparagraph (A).

(3) Based on all available information, including information maintained under paragraph (1)(B) and data developed and collected on the health effects of hazardous substances under this paragraph, the Administrator of ATSDR shall prepare toxicological profiles of each of the substances listed pursuant to paragraph (2). The toxicological profiles shall be prepared in accordance with guidelines developed by the Administrator of ATSDR and the Administrator of EPA. Such profiles shall include, but not be limited to each of the following:

(A)   An examination, summary, and interpretation of available toxicological information and epidemiologic evaluations on a hazardous substance in order to ascertain the levels of significant human exposure for the substance and the associated acute, subacute, and chronic health effects.

(B)   A determination of whether adequate information on the health effects of each substance is available or in the process of development to determine levels of exposure which present a significant risk to human health of acute, subacute, and chronic health effects.

(C)   Where appropriate, an identification of toxicological testing needed to identify the types or levels of exposure that may present significant risk of adverse health effects in humans.

Any toxicological profile or revision thereof shall reflect the Administrator of ATSDR's assessment of all relevant toxicological testing which has been peer reviewed. The profiles required to be prepared under this paragraph for those hazardous substances listed under subparagraph (A) of paragraph (2) shall be completed, at a rate of no fewer than 25 per year, within 4 years after the enactment of the Superfund Amendments and Reauthorization Act of 1986. A profile required on a substance listed pursuant to subparagraph (B) of paragraph (2) shall be completed within 3 years after addition to the list. The profiles prepared under this paragraph shall be of those substances highest on the list of priorities under paragraph (2) for which profiles have not previously been prepared. Profiles required under this paragraph shall be revised and republished as necessary, but no less often than once every 3 years. Such profiles shall be provided to the States and made available to other interested parties.

(4)   The Administrator of the ATSDR shall provide consultations upon request on health issues relating to exposure to hazardous or toxic substances, on the basis of available information, to the Administrator of EPA, State officials, and local officials. Such consultations to individuals may be provided by States under cooperative agreements established under this Act.

(5) (A) For each hazardous substance listed pursuant to paragraph (2), the Administrator of ATSDR (in consultation with the Administrator of EPA and other agencies and programs of the Public Health Service) shall assess whether adequate information on the health effects of such substance is available. For any such substance for which adequate information is not available (or under development), the Administrator of ATSDR, in cooperation with the Director of the National Toxicology Program, shall assure the initiation of a program of research designed to determine the health effects (and techniques for development of methods to determine such health effects) of such substance. Where feasible, such program shall seek to develop methods to determine the health effects of such substance in combination with other substances with which it is commonly found. Before assuring the initiation of such program, the Administrator of ATSDR shall consider recommendations of the Interagency Testing Committee established under section 4(e) of the Toxic Substances Control Act on the types of research that should be done. Such program shall include, to the extent necessary to supplement existing information, but shall not be limited to—

(i) laboratory and other studies to determine short, intermediate, and long-term health effects;

(ii) laboratory and other studies to determine organ-specific, site-specific, and system-specific acute and chronic toxicity;

(iii) laboratory and other studies to determine the manner in which such substances are metabolized or to otherwise develop an understanding of the biokinetics of such substances; and

(iv) where there is a possibility of obtaining human data, the collection of such information.

(B) In assessing the need to perform laboratory and other studies, as required by subparagraph (A), the Administrator of ATSDR shall consider—

(i) the availability and quality of existing test data concerning the substance on the suspected health effect in question;

(ii) the extent to which testing already in progress will, in a timely fashion, provide data that will be adequate to support the preparation of toxicological profiles as required by paragraph (3); and

(iii) such other scientific and technical factors as the Administrator of ATSDR may determine are necessary for the effective implementation of this subsection.

(C) In the development and implementation of any research program under this paragraph, the Administrator of ATSDR and the Administrator of EPA shall coordinate such research program implemented under this paragraph with the National Toxicology Program and with programs of toxicological testing established under the Toxic Substances Control Act and the Federal Insecticide, Fungicide and Rodenticide Act. The purpose of such coordination shall be to avoid duplication of effort and to assure that the hazardous substances listed pursuant to this subsection are tested thoroughly at the earliest practicable date. Where appropriate, consistent with such purpose, a research program under this paragraph may be carried out using such programs of toxicological testing.

(D)   It is the sense of the Congress that the costs of research programs under this paragraph be borne by the manufacturers and processors of the hazardous substance in question, as required in programs of toxicological testing under the Toxic Substances Control Act. Within 1 year after the enactment of the Superfund Amendments and Reauthorization Act of 1986, the Administrator of EPA shall promulgate regulations which provide, where appropriate, for payment of such costs by manufacturers and processors under the Toxic Substances Control Act, and registrants under the Federal Insecticide, Fungicide, and Rodenticide Act, and recovery of such costs from responsible parties under this Act.

(6) (A)   The Administrator of ATSDR shall perform a health assessment for each facility on the National Priorities List established under section 105. Such health assessment shall be completed not later than December 10, 1988, for each facility proposed for inclusion on such list prior to the date of the enactment of the Superfund Amendments and Reauthorization Act of 1986 or not later than one year after the date of proposal for inclusion on such list for each facility proposed for inclusion on such list after such date of enactment.

(B)   The Administrator of ATSDR may perform health assessments for releases or facilities where individual persons or licensed physicians provide information that individuals have been exposed to a hazardous substance, for which the probable source of such exposure is a release. In addition to other methods (formal or informal) of providing such information, such individual persons or licensed physicians may submit a petition to the Administrator of ATSDR providing such information and requesting a health assessment. If such a petition is submitted and the Administrator of ATSDR does not initiate a health assessment, the Administrator of ATSDR shall provide a written explanation of why a health assessment is not appropriate.

(C)   In determining the priority in which to conduct health assessments under this subsection, the Administrator of ATSDR, in consultation with the Administrator of EPA, shall give priority to those facilities at which there is documented evidence of the release of hazardous substances, at which the potential risk to human health appears highest, and for which in the judgment of the Administrator of ATSDR existing health assessment data are inadequate to assess the potential risk to human health as provided in subparagraph (F). In determining the priorities for conducting health assessments under this subsection, the Administrator of ATSDR shall consider the National Priorities List schedules and the needs of the Environmental Protection Agency and other Federal agencies pursuant to schedules for remedial investigation and feasibility studies.

(D)   Where a health assessment is done at a site on the National Priorities List, the Administrator of ATSDR shall complete such assessment promptly and, to the maximum extent practicable, before the completion of the remedial investigation and feasibility study at the facility concerned.

(E)   Any State or political subdivision carrying out a health assessment for a facility shall report the results of the assessment to the Administrator of ATSDR and the Administrator of EPA and shall include recommendations with respect to further activities which need to be carried out under this section. The Administrator of ATSDR shall state such recommendation in any report on the results of any assessment carried out directly by the Administrator of ATSDR for such facility and shall issue periodic reports which include the results of all the assessments carried out under this subsection.

(F)   For the purposes of this subsection and section 111(c)(4), the term health assessments shall include preliminary assessments of the potential risk to human health posed by individual sites and facilities, based on such factors as the nature and extent of contamination, the existence of potential pathways of human exposure (including ground or surface water contamination, air emissions, and food chain contamination), the size and potential susceptibility of the community within the likely pathways of exposure, the comparison of expected human exposure levels to the short-term and long-term health effects associated with identified hazardous substances and any available recommended exposure or tolerance limits for such hazardous substances, and the comparison of existing morbidity and mortality data on diseases that may be associated with the observed levels of exposure. The Administrator of ATSDR shall use appropriate data, risk assessments, risk evaluations and studies available from the Administrator of EPA.

(G)   The purpose of health assessments under this subsection shall be to assist in determining whether actions under paragraph (11) of this subsection should be taken to reduce human exposure to hazardous substances from a facility and whether additional information on human exposure and associated health risks is needed and should be acquired by conducting epidemiological studies under paragraph (7), establishing a registry under paragraph (8), establishing a health surveillance program under paragraph (9), or through other means. In using the results of health assessments for determining additional actions to be taken under this section, the Administrator of ATSDR may consider additional information on the risks to the potentially affected population from all sources of such hazardous substances including known point or nonpoint sources other than those from the facility in question.

(H)   At the completion of each health assessment, the Administrator of ATSDR shall provide the Administrator of EPA and each affected State with the results of such assessment, together with any recommendations for further actions under this subsection or otherwise under this Act. In addition, if the health assessment indicates that the release or threatened release concerned may pose a serious threat to human health or the environment, the Administrator of ATSDR shall so notify the Administrator of EPA who shall promptly evaluate such release or threatened release in accordance with the hazard ranking system referred to in section 105(a)(8)(A) to determine whether the site shall be placed on the National Priorities List or, if the site is already on the list, the Administrator of ATSDR may recommend to the Administrator of EPA that the site be accorded a higher priority.

(7) (A)   Whenever in the judgment of the Administrator of ATSDR it is

appropriate on the basis of the results of a health assessment, the Administrator of ATSDR shall conduct a pilot study of health effects for selected groups of exposed individuals in order to determine the desirability of conducting full scale epidemiological or other health studies of the entire exposed population.

(B)   Whenever in the judgment of the Administrator of ATSDR it is appropriate on the basis of the results of such pilot study or other study or health assessment, the Administrator of ATSDR shall conduct such full scale epidemiological or other health studies as may be necessary to determine the health effects on the population exposed to hazardous substances from a release or threatened release. If a significant excess of disease in a population is identified, the letter of transmittal of such study shall include an assessment of other risk factors, other than a release, that may, in the judgment of the peer review group, be associated with such disease, if such risk factors were not taken into account in the design or conduct of the study.

(8)   In any case in which the results of a health assessment indicate a potential significant risk to human health, the Administrator of ATSDR shall consider whether the establishment of a registry of exposed persons would contribute to accomplishing the purposes of this subsection, taking into account circumstances bearing on the usefulness of such a registry, including the seriousness or unique character of identified diseases or the likelihood of population migration from the affected area.

(9) Where the Administrator of ATSDR has determined that there is a significant increased risk of adverse health effects in humans from exposure to hazardous substances based on the results of a health assessment conducted under paragraph (6), an epidemiologic study conducted under paragraph (7), or an exposure registry that has been established under paragraph (8), and the Administrator of ATSDR has determined that such exposure is the result of a release from a facility, the Administrator of ATSDR shall initiate a health surveillance program for such population. This program shall include but not be limited to—

(A)   periodic medical testing where appropriate of population subgroups to screen for diseases for which the population or subgroup is at significant increased risk; and

(B)   a mechanism to refer for treatment those individuals within such population who are screened positive for such diseases.

(10) Two years after the date of the enactment of the Superfund Amendments and Reauthorization Act of 1986, and every 2 years thereafter, the Administrator of ATSDR shall prepare and submit to the Administrator of EPA and to the Congress a report on the results of the activities of ATSDR regarding—

(A)   health assessments and pilot health effects studies conducted;

(B)   epidemiologic studies conducted;

(C)   hazardous substances which have been listed under paragraph (2), toxicological profiles which have been developed, and toxicologic testing which has been conducted or which is being conducted under this subsection;

(D)   registries established under paragraph (8); and

(E)   an overall assessment, based on the results of activities conducted by the Administrator of ATSDR of the linkage between human exposure to individual or combinations of hazardous substances due to releases from facilities covered by this Act or the Solid Waste Disposal Act and any increased incidence or prevalence of adverse health effects in humans.

(11) If a health assessment or other study carried out under this subsection contains a finding that the exposure concerned presents a significant risk to human health, the President shall take such steps as may be necessary to reduce such exposure and eliminate or substantially mitigate the significant risk to human health. Such steps may include the use of any authority under this Act, including, but not limited to—

(A)   provision of alternative water supplies, and

(B)   permanent or temporary relocation of individuals.

In any case in which information is insufficient, in the judgment of the Administrator of ATSDR or the President to determine a significant human exposure level with respect to a hazardous substance, the President may take such steps as may be necessary to reduce the exposure of any person to such hazardous substance to such level as the President deems necessary to protect human health.

(12)   In any case which is the subject of a petition, a health assessment or study, or a research program under this subsection, nothing in this subsection shall be construed to delay or otherwise affect or impair the authority of the President, the Administrator of ATSDR or the Administrator of EPA to exercise any authority vested in the President, the Administrator of ATSDR or the Administrator of EPA under any other provision of law (including, but not limited to, the imminent hazard authority of section 7003 of the Solid Waste Disposal Act) or the response and abatement authorities of this Act.

(13)   All studies and results of research conducted under this subsection (other than health assessments) shall be reported or adopted only after appropriate peer review. Such peer review shall be completed, to the maximum extent practicable, within a period of 60 days. In the case of research conducted under the National Toxicology Program, such peer review may be conducted by the Board of Scientific Counselors. In the case of other research, such peer review shall be conducted by panels consisting of no less than three nor more than seven members, who shall be disinterested scientific experts selected for such purpose by the Administrator of ATSDR or the Administrator of EPA, as appropriate, on the basis of their reputation for scientific objectivity and the lack of institutional ties with any person involved in the conduct of the study or research under review. Support services for such panels shall be provided by the Agency for Toxic Substances and Disease Registry, or by the Environmental Protection Agency, as appropriate.

(14)   In the implementation of this subsection and other health-related authorities of this Act, the Administrator of ATSDR shall assemble, develop as necessary, and distribute to the States, and upon request to medical colleges, physicians, and other health professionals, appropriate educational materials (including short courses) on the medical surveillance, screening, and methods of diagnosis and treatment of injury or disease related to exposure to hazardous substances (giving priority to

those listed in paragraph (2)), through such means as the Administrator of ATSDR deems appropriate.

(15) The activities of the Administrator of ATSDR described in this subsection and section 111(c)(4) shall be carried out by the Administrator of ATSDR, either directly or through cooperative agreements with States (or political subdivisions thereof) which the Administrator of ATSDR determines are capable of carrying out such activities. Such activities shall include provision of consultations on health information, the conduct of health assessments, including those required under section 3019(b) of the Solid Waste Disposal Act, health studies, registries, and health surveillance.

(16) The President shall provide adequate personnel for ATSDR, which shall not be fewer than 100 employees. For purposes of determining the number of employees under this subsection, an employee employed by ATSDR on a part-time career employment basis shall be counted as a fraction which is determined by dividing 40 hours into the average number of hours of such employee's regularly scheduled workweek.

(17) In accordance with section 120 (relating to Federal facilities), the Administrator of ATSDR shall have the same authorities under this section with respect to facilities owned or operated by a department, agency, or instrumentality of the United States as the Administrator of ATSDR has with respect to any nongovernmental entity.

(18) If the Administrator of ATSDR determines that it is appropriate for purposes of this section to treat a pollutant or contaminant as a hazardous substance, such pollutant or contaminant shall be treated as a hazardous substance for such purpose.

(j) ACQUISITION OF PROPERTY.—

(1) AUTHORITY.— The President is authorized to acquire, by purchase, lease, condemnation, donation, or otherwise, any real property or any interest in real property that the President in his discretion determines is needed to conduct a remedial action under this Act. There shall be no cause of action to compel the President to acquire any interest in real property under this Act.

(2) STATE ASSURANCE.— The President may use the authority of paragraph (1) for a remedial action only if, before an interest in real estate is acquired under this subsection, the State in which the interest to be acquired is located assures the President, through a contract or cooperative agreement or otherwise, that the State will accept transfer of the interest following completion of the remedial action.

(3) EXEMPTION.— No Federal, State, or local government agency shall be liable under this Act solely as a result of acquiring an interest in real estate under this subsection.

(k) BROWNFIELDS REVITALIZATION FUNDING.—

(1) DEFINITION OF ELIGIBLE ENTITY.— In this subsection, the term eligible entity means—

(A) a general purpose unit of local government;

(B) a land clearance authority or other quasi-governmental entity that operates under the supervision and control of or as an agent of a general purpose unit of local government;

(C) a government entity created by a State legislature;

(D) a regional council or group of general purpose units of local government;

(E) a redevelopment agency that is chartered or otherwise sanctioned by a State;

(F) a State;

(G) an Indian Tribe other than in Alaska;

(H) an Alaska Native Regional Corporation and an Alaska Native Village Corporation as those terms are defined in the Alaska Native Claims Settlement Act (43 U.S.C. 1601 and following) and the Metlakatla Indian community;

(I) an organization described in section 501(c)(3) of the Internal Revenue Code of 1986 and exempt from taxation under section 501(a) of that Code;

(J) a limited liability corporation in which all managing members are organizations described in subparagraph (I) or limited liability corporations whose sole members are organizations described in subparagraph (I);

(K) a limited partnership in which all general partners are organizations described in subparagraph (I) or limited liability corporations whose sole members are organizations described in subparagraph (I); or

(L) a qualified community development entity (as defined in section 45D(c)(1) of the Internal Revenue Code of 1986).

(2) BROWNFIELD SITE CHARACTERIZATION AND ASSESSMENT GRANT PROGRAM.—

(A) ESTABLISHMENT OF PROGRAM.— The Administrator shall establish a program to—

(i) provide grants to inventory, characterize, assess, and conduct planning related to brownfield sites under subparagraph (B); and

(ii) perform targeted site assessments at brownfield sites.

(B) ASSISTANCE FOR SITE CHARACTERIZATION AND ASSESSMENT.—

(i) IN GENERAL.— On approval of an application made by an eligible entity, the Administrator may make a grant to the eligible entity to be used for programs to inventory, characterize, assess, and conduct planning related to one or more brownfield sites.

(ii) SITE CHARACTERIZATION AND ASSESSMENT.— A site characterization and assessment carried out with the use of a grant under clause (i) shall be performed in accordance with section 101(35)(B).

(C) EXEMPTION FOR CERTAIN PUBLICLY OWNED BROWNFIELD SITES.— Notwithstanding paragraph (5)(B)(iii), an eligible entity described in any of subparagraphs (A) through (H) of paragraph (1) may receive a grant under this paragraph for property acquired by that eligible entity prior to January 11, 2002, even if the eligible entity does not qualify as a bona fide prospective purchaser, so long as the eligible entity has not caused or contributed to a release or threatened release of a hazardous substance at the property.

(3) GRANTS AND LOANS FOR BROWNFIELD REMEDIATION.—

(A) GRANTS PROVIDED BY THE PRESIDENT.— Subject to paragraphs (5) and (6), the President shall establish a program to provide grants to—

(i)   eligible entities, to be used for capitalization of revolving loan funds; and

(ii)   eligible entities or nonprofit organizations, where warranted, as determined by the President based on considerations under subparagraph (C), to be used directly for remediation of one or more brownfield sites owned by the entity or organization that receives the grant and in amounts not to exceed $500,000 for each site to be remediated, which limit may be waived by the Administrator, but not to exceed a total of $650,000 for each site, based on the anticipated level of contamination, size, or ownership status of the site.

(B) LOANS AND GRANTS PROVIDED BY ELIGIBLE ENTITIES.— An eligible entity that receives a grant under subparagraph (A)(i) shall use the grant funds to provide assistance for the remediation of brownfield sites in the form of—

(i)   one or more loans to an eligible entity, a site owner, a site developer, or another person; or

(ii)   one or more grants to an eligible entity or other nonprofit organization, where warranted, as determined by the eligible entity that is providing the assistance, based on considerations under subparagraph (C), to remediate sites owned by the eligible entity or nonprofit organization that receives the grant.

(C) CONSIDERATIONS.— In determining whether a grant under subparagraph (A)(ii) or (B)(ii) is warranted, the President or the eligible entity, as the case may be, shall take into consideration—

(i)   the extent to which a grant will facilitate the creation of, preservation of, or addition to a park, a greenway, undeveloped property, recreational property, or other property used for nonprofit purposes;

(ii)   the extent to which a grant will meet the needs of a community that has an inability to draw on other sources of funding for environmental remediation and subsequent redevelopment of the area in which a brownfield site is located because of the small population or low income of the community;

(iii)   the extent to which a grant will facilitate the use or reuse of existing infrastructure;

(iv)   the benefit of promoting the long-term availability of funds from a revolving loan fund for brownfield remediation; and

(v)   such other similar factors as the Administrator considers appropriate to consider for the purposes of this subsection.

(D) TRANSITION.— Revolving loan funds that have been established before the date of the enactment of this subsection may be used in accordance with this paragraph.

(E) EXEMPTION FOR CERTAIN PUBLICLY OWNED BROWNFIELD SITES.— Notwithstanding paragraph (5)(B)(iii), an eligible entity described in any of subparagraphs (A) through (H) of paragraph (1) may receive a grant or loan under this paragraph for property acquired by that eligible entity prior to January 11, 2002, even if the eligible entity does not qualify as a bona fide prospective purchaser, so long as the eligible entity has not caused or contributed to a release or threatened release of a hazardous substance at the property.

(4) MULTIPURPOSE BROWNFIELDS GRANTS.—

(A) IN GENERAL.— Subject to subparagraph (D) and paragraphs (5) and (6), the Administrator shall establish a program to provide multipurpose grants to an eligible entity based on the criteria under subparagraph (C) and the considerations under paragraph (3)(C), to carry out inventory, characterization, assessment, planning, or remediation activities at 1 or more brownfield sites in an area proposed by the eligible entity.

(B) GRANT AMOUNTS.—

(i) INDIVIDUAL GRANT AMOUNTS.— Each grant awarded under this paragraph shall not exceed $1,000,000.

(ii) CUMULATIVE GRANT AMOUNTS.— The total amount of grants awarded for each fiscal year under this paragraph may not exceed 15 percent of the funds made available for the fiscal year to carry out this subsection.

(C) CRITERIA.— In awarding a grant under this paragraph, the Administrator shall consider the extent to which the eligible entity is able—

(i) to provide an overall plan for revitalization of the 1 or more brownfield sites in the proposed area in which the multipurpose grant will be used;

(ii) to demonstrate a capacity to conduct the range of eligible activities that will be funded by the multipurpose grant; and

(iii) to demonstrate that a multipurpose grant will meet the needs of the 1 or more brownfield sites in the proposed area.

(D) CONDITION.— As a condition of receiving a grant under this paragraph, each eligible entity shall expend the full amount of the grant by not later than the date that is 5 years after the date on which the grant is awarded to the eligible entity, unless the Administrator provides an extension.

(E) OWNERSHIP.— An eligible entity that receives a grant under this paragraph may not expend any of the grant funds for the remediation of a brownfield site unless the eligible entity owns the brownfield site.

(5) GENERAL PROVISIONS.—

(A) MAXIMUM GRANT AMOUNT.—

(i) BROWNFIELD SITE CHARACTERIZATION AND ASSESSMENT.—

(I) In GENERAL.— A grant under paragraph (2) may be awarded to an eligible entity on a community-wide or site-by-site basis, and shall not exceed, for any individual brownfield site covered by the grant, $200,000.

(II) WAIVER.— The Administrator may waive the $200,000 limitation under subclause (I) to permit the brownfield site to receive a grant of not to exceed $350,000, based on the anticipated level of contamination, size, or status of ownership of the site.

(ii) BROWNFIELD REMEDIATION.— A grant under paragraph (3)(A)(i) may be awarded to an eligible entity on a community-wide or site-by-site basis, not to exceed $1,000,000 per eligible entity. The Administrator may make an additional grant to an eligible entity described in the previous sentence for any year after the year for which the initial grant is made, taking into consideration—

(I) the number of sites and number of communities that are addressed by the revolving loan fund;

(II) the demand for funding by eligible entities that have not previously received a grant under this subsection;

(III) the demonstrated ability of the eligible entity to use the revolving loan fund to enhance remediation and provide funds on a continuing basis; and

(IV) such other similar factors as the Administrator considers appropriate to carry out this subsection.

(B) PROHIBITION.— No part of a grant or loan under this subsection may be used for the payment of—

(i) a penalty or fine;

(ii) a Federal cost-share requirement;

(iii) a response cost at a brownfield site for which the recipient of the grant or loan is potentially liable under section 107; or

(iv) a cost of compliance with any Federal law (including a Federal law specified in section 101(39)(B)), excluding the cost of compliance with laws applicable to the cleanup.

(C) ASSISTANCE FOR DEVELOPMENT OF LOCAL GOVERNMENT SITE REMEDIATION PROGRAMS.— A local government that receives a grant under this subsection may use not to exceed 10 percent of the grant funds to develop and implement a brownfields program that may include—

(i) monitoring the health of populations exposed to one or more hazardous substances from a brownfield site; and

(ii) monitoring and enforcement of any institutional control used to prevent human exposure to any hazardous substance from a brownfield site.

(D) INSURANCE.— A recipient of a grant or loan awarded under paragraph

(2), (3), or (4) that performs a characterization, assessment, or remediation of a brownfield site may use a portion of the grant or loan to purchase insurance for the characterization, assessment, or remediation of that site.

(E) ADMINISTRATIVE COSTS.—

(i) IN GENERAL.— An eligible entity may use up to 5 percent of the amounts made available under a grant or loan under this subsection for administrative costs.

(ii) RESTRICTION.— For purposes of clause (i), the term administrative costs does not include—

(I)   investigation and identification of the extent of contamination of a brownfield site;

(II)   design and performance of a response action; or

(III)   monitoring of a natural resource.

(6) GRANT APPLICATIONS.—

(A) SUBMISSION.—

(i) IN GENERAL.—

(I) APPLICATION.— An eligible entity may submit to the Administrator, through a regional office of the Environmental Protection Agency and in such form as the Administrator may require, an application for a grant under this subsection for one or more brownfield sites (including information on the criteria used by the Administrator to rank applications under subparagraph (C), to the extent that the information is available).

(II) NCP REQUIREMENTS.— The Administrator may include in any requirement for submission of an application under subclause (I) a requirement of the National Contingency Plan only to the extent that the requirement is relevant and appropriate to the program under this subsection.

(ii) COORDINATION.— The Administrator shall coordinate with other Federal agencies to assist in making eligible entities aware of other available Federal resources.

(iii) GUIDANCE.— The Administrator shall publish guidance to assist eligible entities in applying for grants under this subsection.

(B) APPROVAL.—The Administrator shall—

(i)   at least annually, complete a review of applications for grants that are received from eligible entities under this subsection; and

(ii)   award grants under this subsection to eligible entities that the Administrator determines have the highest rankings under the ranking criteria established under subparagraph (C).

(C) RANKING CRITERIA.—The Administrator shall establish a system for ranking grant applications received under this paragraph that includes the following criteria:

(i)   The extent to which a grant will stimulate the availability of other funds for environmental assessment or remediation, and subsequent reuse, of an area in which one or more brownfield sites are located.

(ii)   The potential of the proposed project or the development plan for an area in which one or more brownfield sites are located to stimulate economic development of the area on completion of the cleanup.

(iii)   The extent to which a grant would address or facilitate the identification and reduction of threats to human health and the environment, including threats in areas in which there is a greater-than-normal incidence of diseases or conditions (including cancer, asthma, or birth defects) that may be associated with exposure to hazardous substances, pollutants, or contaminants.

(iv)   The extent to which a grant would facilitate the use or reuse of existing infrastructure.

(v)   The extent to which a grant would facilitate the creation of, preservation of, or addition to a park, a greenway, undeveloped property, recreational property, or other property used for nonprofit purposes.

(vi)   The extent to which a grant would meet the needs of a community that has an inability to draw on other sources of funding for environmental remediation and subsequent redevelopment of the area in which a brownfield site is located because of the small population or low income of the community.

(vii)   The extent to which the applicant is eligible for funding from other sources.

(viii)   The extent to which a grant will further the fair distribution of funding between urban and nonurban areas.

(ix)   The extent to which the grant provides for involvement of the local community in the process of making decisions relating to cleanup and future use of a brownfield site.

(x)   The extent to which a grant would address or facilitate the identification and reduction of threats to the health or welfare of children, pregnant women, minority or low-income communities, or other sensitive populations.

(xi)   The extent to which a grant would address a site adjacent to a body of water or a federally designated flood plain.

(xii) The extent to which a grant would facilitate—

(I)   the location at a brownfield site of a facility that generates renewable electricity from wind, solar, or geothermal energy; or

(II)   any energy efficiency improvement project at a brownfield site, including a project for a combined heat and power system or a district energy system.

(D) REPORT ON RANKING CRITERIA.— Not later than September 30, 2022, the Administrator shall submit to Congress a report regarding the Administrator's use of the ranking criteria described in subparagraph (C) in awarding grants under this subsection.

(7) IMPLEMENTATION OF BROWNFIELDS PROGRAMS.—

(A) ESTABLISHMENT OF PROGRAM.— The Administrator may provide, or fund eligible entities or nonprofit organizations to provide, training, research, and technical assistance to individuals and organizations, as appropriate, to facilitate the inventory of brownfield sites, site assessments, remediation of brownfield sites, community involvement, or site preparation.

(B) FUNDING RESTRICTIONS.— The total Federal funds to be expended by the Administrator under this paragraph shall not exceed 15 percent of the total amount appropriated to carry out this subsection in any fiscal year.

(8) AUDITS.—

(A) IN GENERAL.— The Inspector General of the Environmental Protection Agency shall conduct such reviews or audits of grants and loans under this subsection as the Inspector General considers necessary to carry out this subsection.

(B) PROCEDURE.— An audit under this subparagraph shall be conducted in accordance with the auditing procedures of the General Accounting Office, including chapter 75 of title 31, United States Code.

(C) VIOLATIONS.—If the Administrator determines that a person that receives a grant or loan under this subsection has violated or is in violation of a condition of the grant, loan, or applicable Federal law, the Administrator may—

(i)   terminate the grant or loan;

(ii)   require the person to repay any funds received; and

(iii)   seek any other legal remedies available to the Administrator.

(D) REPORT TO CONGRESS.— Not later than September 30, 2022, the Inspector General of the Environmental Protection Agency shall submit to Congress a report that provides a description of the management of the program (including a description of the allocation of funds under this subsection).

(9) LEVERAGING.— An eligible entity that receives a grant under this subsection may use the grant funds for a portion of a project at a brownfield site for which funding is received from other sources if the grant funds are used only for the purposes described in paragraph (2), (3), or (4).

(10) AGREEMENTS.—Each grant or loan made under this subsection shall—

(A)   include a requirement of the National Contingency Plan only to the extent that the requirement is relevant and appropriate to the program under this subsection, as determined by the Administrator; and

(B) be subject to an agreement that—

(i) requires the recipient to—

(I)   comply with all applicable Federal and State laws; and

(II)   ensure that the cleanup protects human health and the environment;

(ii)   requires that the recipient use the grant or loan exclusively for purposes specified in paragraph (2), (3), or (4), as applicable;

(iii)   in the case of an application by an eligible entity under paragraph (3)(A), requires the eligible entity to pay a matching share (which may be in the form of a contribution of labor, material, or services) of at least 20 percent, from non-Federal sources of funding, unless the Administrator determines that the matching share would place an undue hardship on the eligible entity; and

(iv)   contains such other terms and conditions as the Administrator determines to be necessary to carry out this subsection.

(11) FACILITY OTHER THAN BROWNFIELD SITE.— The fact that a facility may not be a brownfield site within the meaning of section 101(39)(A) has no effect on the eligibility of the facility for assistance under any other provision of Federal law.

(12) EFFECT ON FEDERAL LAWS.—Nothing in this subsection affects any liability or response authority under any Federal law, including—

(A)   this Act (including the last sentence of section 101(14));

(B)   the Solid Waste Disposal Act (42 U.S.C. 6901 et seq.);

(C)   the Federal Water Pollution Control Act (33 U.S.C. 1251 et seq.);

(D)   the Toxic Substances Control Act (15 U.S.C. 2601 et seq.); and

(E)   the Safe Drinking Water Act (42 U.S.C. 300f et seq.).

(13) AUTHORIZATION OF APPROPRIATIONS.— There is authorized to be appropriated to carry out this subsection $200,000,000 for each of fiscal years 2019 through 2023.

[42 U.S.C. 9604]

★

SECTION 303 OF THE EMERGENCY PLANNING AND COMMUNITY RIGHT-TO-KNOW ACT OF 1986

PUBLIC LAW 99–499
AS AMENDED THROUGH PUB. L. 116–92

EMERGENCY PLANNING AND COMMUNITY RIGHT-TO-KNOW

(Title II of the Superfund Amendments and Reauthorization Act of 1986)

[P.L. 99–499]

[As Amended Through P.L. 116–92, Enacted December 20, 2019]

* * * * * * *

TITLE III—EMERGENCY PLANNING AND COMMUNITY RIGHT-TO-KNOW

SEC. 300. SHORT TITLE; TABLE OF CONTENTS.

(a) SHORT TITLE.— This title may be cited as the "Emergency Planning and Community Right-To-Know Act of 1986".

* * * * * * *

SUBTITLE A—EMERGENCY PLANNING AND NOTIFICATION

* * * * * * *

SEC. 303. COMPREHENSIVE EMERGENCY RESPONSE PLANS.

(a) PLAN REQUIRED.— Each local emergency planning committee shall complete preparation of an emergency plan in accordance with this section not later than two years after the date of the enactment of this title. The committee shall review such plan once a year, or more frequently as changed circumstances in the community or at any facility may require.

(b) RESOURCES.— Each local emergency planning committee shall evaluate the need for resources necessary to develop, implement, and exercise the emergency plan, and shall make recommendations with respect to additional resources that may be required and the means for providing such additional resources.

(c) PLAN PROVISIONS.—Each emergency plan shall include (but is not limited to) each of the following:

(1) Identification of facilities subject to the requirements of this subtitle that are within the emergency planning district, identification of routes likely to be used for the transportation of substances on the list of extremely hazardous substances

405

referred to in section 302(a), and identification of additional facilities contributing or subjected to additional risk due to their proximity to facilities subject to the requirements of this subtitle, such as hospitals or natural gas facilities.

(2)   Methods and procedures to be followed by facility owners and operators and local emergency and medical personnel to respond to any release of such substances.

(3)   Designation of a community emergency coordinator and facility emergency coordinators, who shall make determinations necessary to implement the plan.

(4)   Procedures providing reliable, effective, and timely notification by the facility emergency coordinators and the community emergency coordinator to persons designated in the emergency plan, and to the public, that a release has occurred (consistent with the emergency notification requirements of section 304).

(5)   Methods for determining the occurrence of a release, and the area or population likely to be affected by such release.

(6)   A description of emergency equipment and facilities in the community and at each facility in the community subject to the requirements of this subtitle, and an identification of the persons responsible for such equipment and facilities.

(7)   Evacuation plans, including provisions for a precautionary evacuation and alternative traffic routes.

(8)   Training programs, including schedules for training of local emergency response and medical personnel.

(9)   Methods and schedules for exercising the emergency plan.

(d) PROVIDING OF INFORMATION.—For each facility subject to the requirements of this subtitle:

(1)   Within 30 days after establishment of a local emergency planning committee for the emergency planning district in which such facility is located, or within 11 months after the date of the enactment of this title, whichever is earlier, the owner or operator of the facility shall notify the emergency planning committee (or the Governor if there is no committee) of a facility representative who will participate in the emergency planning process as a facility emergency coordinator.

(2)   The owner or operator of the facility shall promptly inform the emergency planning committee of any relevant changes occurring at such facility as such changes occur or are expected to occur.

(3)   Upon request from the emergency planning committee, the owner or operator of the facility shall promptly provide information to such committee necessary for developing and implementing the emergency plan.

(e) REVIEW BY THE STATE EMERGENCY RESPONSE COMMISSION.— After completion of an emergency plan under subsection (a) for an emergency planning district, the local emergency planning committee shall submit a copy of the plan to the State emergency response commission of each State in which such district is located. The commission shall review the plan and make recommendations to the committee on revisions of the plan that may be necessary to ensure coordination of such plan with emergency response plans of other emergency planning districts. To the maximum extent practicable, such review shall not delay implementation of such plan.

(f) GUIDANCE DOCUMENTS.— The national response team, as established pursuant to the National Contingency Plan as established under section 105 of the Comprehensive Environmental Response, Compensation, and Liability Act of 1980 (42 U.S.C. 9601 et seq.), shall publish guidance documents for preparation and implementation of emergency plans. Such documents shall be published not later than five months after the date of the enactment of this title.

(g) REVIEW OF PLANS BY REGIONAL RESPONSE TEAMS.— The regional response teams, as established pursuant to the National Contingency Plan as established under section 105 of the Comprehensive Environmental Response, Compensation, and Liability Act of 1980 (42 U.S.C. 9601 et seq.), may review and comment upon an emergency plan or other issues related to preparation, implementation, or exercise of such a plan upon request of a local emergency planning committee. Such review shall not delay implementation of the plan.

[42 U.S.C. 11003]

* * * * * * *

★

CHEMICAL STOCKPILE EMERGENCY PREPAREDNESS PROGRAM PROVISIONS DEPARTMENT OF DEFENSE AUTHORIZATION ACT, 1986

PUBLIC LAW 99–145
AS AMENDED THROUGH PUB. L. 118–159

DEPARTMENT OF DEFENSE AUTHORIZATION ACT, 1986

[(Public Law 99–145; approved Nov. 8, 1985)]

[As Amended Through P.L. 118–159, Enacted December 23, 2024]

* * * * * * *

SEC. 1412. [50 U.S.C. 1521] DESTRUCTION OF EXISTING STOCKPILE OF LETHAL CHEMICAL AGENTS AND MUNITIONS.

(a) In General.— The Secretary of Defense shall, in accordance with the provisions of this section, carry out the destruction of the United States' stockpile of lethal chemical agents and munitions that exists on November 8, 1985.

(b) Date for Completion.—(1) The destruction of such stockpile shall be completed by the stockpile elimination deadline.

(2) If the Secretary of Defense determines at any time that there will be a delay in meeting the requirement in paragraph (1) for the completion of the destruction of chemical weapons by the stockpile elimination deadline, the Secretary shall immediately notify the Committee on Armed Services of the Senate and the Committee on Armed Services of the House of Representatives of that projected delay.

(3) For purposes of this section, the term stockpile elimination deadline means the deadline established by the Chemical Weapons Convention, but not later than December 31, 2023.

(c) Initiation of Demilitarization Operations.—The Secretary of Defense may not initiate destruction of the chemical munitions stockpile stored at a site until the following support measures are in place:

(1) Support measures that are required by Department of Defense and Army chemical surety and security program regulations.

(2) Support measures that are required by the general and site chemical munitions demilitarization plans specific to that installation.

(3) Support measures that are required by the permits required by the Solid Waste Disposal Act (42 U.S.C. 6901 et seq.) and the Clean Air Act (42 U.S.C. 7401 et seq.) for chemical munitions demilitarization operations at that installation, as approved by the appropriate State regulatory agencies.

(d) Environmental Protection and Use of Facilities.—(1) In carrying out the requirement of subsection (a), the Secretary of Defense shall provide for—

(A)   maximum protection for the environment, the general public, and the personnel who are involved in the destruction of the lethal chemical agents and munitions referred to in subsection (a), including but not limited to the use of technologies and procedures that will minimize risk to the public at each site; and

(B)   adequate and safe facilities designed solely for the destruction of lethal chemical agents and munitions.

(2)   Facilities constructed to carry out this section shall, when no longer needed for the purposes for which they were constructed, be disposed of in accordance with applicable laws and regulations and mutual agreements between the Secretary of the Army and the Governor of the State in which the facility is located.

(3)(A)   Facilities constructed to carry out this section may not be used for a purpose other than the destruction of the stockpile of lethal chemical agents and munitions that exists on November 8, 1985.

(B)   The prohibition in subparagraph (A) shall not apply with respect to items designated by the Secretary of Defense as lethal chemical agents, munitions, or related materials after November 8, 1985, if the State in which a destruction facility is located issues the appropriate permit or permits for the destruction of such items at the facility.

(e)   GRANTS AND COOPERATIVE AGREEMENTS.—(1)(A)   In order to carry out subsection (d)(1)(A), the Secretary of Defense may make grants to State and local governments and to tribal organizations (either directly or through the Federal Emergency Management Agency) to assist those governments and tribal organizations in carrying out functions relating to emergency preparedness and response in connection with the disposal of the lethal chemical agents and munitions referred to in subsection (a). Funds available to the Department of Defense for the purpose of carrying out this section may be used for such grants.

(B)   Additionally, the Secretary may provide funds through cooperative agreements with State and local governments, and with tribal organizations, for the purpose of assisting them in processing, approving, and overseeing permits and licenses necessary for the construction and operation of facilities to carry out this section. The Secretary shall ensure that funds provided through such a cooperative agreement are used only for the purpose set forth in the preceding sentence.

(C)   In this paragraph, the term tribal organization has the meaning given that term in section 4(l) of the Indian Self-Determination and Education Assistance Act (25 U.S.C. 450b(l)).

(2)(A)   In coordination with the Secretary of the Army and in accordance with agreements between the Secretary of the Army and the Administrator of the Federal Emergency Management Agency, the Administrator shall carry out a program to provide assistance to State and local governments in developing capabilities to respond to emergencies involving risks to the public health or safety within their jurisdictions that are identified by the Secretary as being risks resulting from—

(i)   the storage of lethal chemical agents and munitions referred to in subsection (a) at military installations in the continental United States; or

(ii)   the destruction of such agents and munitions at facilities referred to in subsection (d)(1)(B).

(B) Assistance may be provided under this paragraph for capabilities to respond to emergencies involving an installation or facility as described in subparagraph (A) until the earlier of the following:

(i) The date of the completion of all grants and cooperative agreements with respect to the installation or facility for purposes of this paragraph between the Federal Emergency Management Agency and the State and local governments concerned.

(ii) The date that is 180 days after the date of the completion of the destruction of lethal chemical agents and munitions at the installation or facility.

(C) Not later than December 15 of each year, the Administrator shall transmit a report to Congress on the activities carried out under this paragraph during the fiscal year preceding the fiscal year in which the report is submitted.

(f) REQUIREMENT FOR STRATEGIC PLAN.—(1) The[1] Under Secretary of Defense for Acquisition and Sustainment and the Secretary of the Army shall jointly prepare, and from time to time shall update as appropriate, a strategic plan for future activities for destruction of the United States' stockpile of lethal chemical agents and munitions.

---

[1] Section 902(91) of division A of Public Law 116-92 amends subsections (f)(1) and (g)(2) of section 1412 of Public Law 99-145 by striking Under Secretary of Defense for Acquisition, Technology, and Logistics and inserting Under Secretary of Defense for Acquisition and Sustainment. However section 902(91) incorrectly references this Act as the National Defense Authorization Act, 1986 but the amendments were carried out to reflect the probable intent of Congress.

---

(2) The plan shall include, at a minimum, the following considerations:

(A) Realistic budgeting for stockpile destruction and related support programs.

(B) Contingency planning for foreseeable or anticipated problems.

(C) A management approach and associated actions that address compliance with the obligations of the United States under the Chemical Weapons Convention and that take full advantage of opportunities to accelerate destruction of the stockpile.

(3) The Secretary of Defense shall each year submit to the Committee on the Armed Services of the Senate and the Committee on Armed Services of the House of Representatives the strategic plan as most recently prepared and updated under paragraph (1). Such submission shall be made each year at the time of the submission to the Congress that year of the President's budget for the next fiscal year.

(g) MANAGEMENT ORGANIZATION.—(1) In carrying out this section, the Secretary of Defense shall provide for a management organization within the Department of the Army. The Secretary of the Army shall be responsible for management of the destruction of agents and munitions at all sites except Blue Grass Army Depot, Kentucky, and Pueblo Chemical Depot, Colorado

(2) The program manager for the Assembled Chemical Weapons Alternative

Program shall be responsible for management of the construction, operation, and closure, and any contracting relating thereto, of chemical demilitarization activities at Blue Grass Army Depot, Kentucky, and Pueblo Army Depot, Colorado, including management of the pilot-scale facility phase of the alternative technology selected for the destruction of lethal chemical munitions. In performing such management, the program manager shall act independently of the Army program manager for Chemical Demilitarization and shall report to the [1]Under Secretary of Defense for Acquisition and Sustainment[2]

---

[2]   So in original. Probably should be followed by a period.

---

(3) The Secretary of Defense shall designate a general officer or civilian equivalent as the director of the management organization established under paragraph (1). Such officer shall have—

(A)   experience in the acquisition, storage, and destruction of chemical agents and munitions; and

(B)   outstanding qualifications regarding safety in handling chemical agents and munitions.

(h) IDENTIFICATION OF FUNDS.—(1)   Funds for carrying out this section, including funds for military construction projects necessary to carry out this section, shall be set forth in the budget of the Department of Defense for any fiscal year as a separate account. Such funds shall not be included in the budget accounts for any military department.

(2)   Amounts appropriated to the Secretary of Defense for the purpose of carrying out subsection (e) shall be promptly made available to the Administrator of the Federal Emergency Management Agency.

(i) ANNUAL REPORTS.—(1)   Except as provided by paragraph (3), the Secretary of Defense shall transmit, by December 15 each year, a report to Congress on the activities carried out under this section during the fiscal year ending on September 30 of the calendar year in which the report is to be made.

(2) Each annual report shall include the following:

(A)   A site-by-site description of the construction, equipment, operation, and dismantling of facilities (during the fiscal year for which the report is made) used to carry out the destruction of agents and munitions under this section, including any accidents or other unplanned occurrences associated with such construction and operation.

(B)   A site-by-site description of actions taken to assist State and local governments (either directly or through the Federal Emergency Management Agency) in carrying out functions relating to emergency preparedness and response in accordance with subsection (e).

(C) An accounting of all funds expended (during such fiscal year) for activities carried out under this section, with a separate accounting for amounts expended for—

(i)   the construction of and equipment for facilities used for the destruction of agents and munitions;

(ii) the operation of such facilities;

(iii) the dismantling or other closure of such facilities;

(iv) research and development;

(v) program management;

(vi) travel and associated travel costs for Citizens' Advisory Commissioners under subsection (m)(7); and

(vii) grants to State and local governments to assist those governments in carrying out functions relating to emergency preparedness and response in accordance with subsection (e).

(D) An assessment of the safety status and the integrity of the stockpile of lethal chemical agents and munitions subject to this section, including—

(i) an estimate on how much longer that stockpile can continue to be stored safely;

(ii) a site-by-site assessment of the safety of those agents and munitions; and

(iii) a description of the steps taken (to the date of the report) to monitor the safety status of the stockpile and to mitigate any further deterioration of that status.

(E) A description of any supplemental chemical agent and munitions destruction technologies used at Pueblo Chemical Depot, Colorado, and Blue Grass Army Depot, Kentucky, during the period covered by the report, including explosive destruction technologies and any technologies developed for the treatment and disposal of energetic or agent hydrolystates.

(3) The Secretary shall transmit the final report under paragraph (1) not later than 120 days following the completion of activities under this section.

(j) QUARTERLY BRIEFING.—[1] (1) Not later than 90 days after the date of the enactment of the National Defense Authorization Act for Fiscal Year 2019, and every 90 days thereafter until the United States completes the destruction of its entire stockpile of chemical weapons under the terms of the Chemical Weapons Convention, the Secretary of Defense shall brief the members and committees of Congress referred to in paragraph (3) on the progress made by the United States toward fulfilling its chemical weapons destruction obligations under the Chemical Weapons Convention.

---

[1] Section 1424(1) of division A of Public Law 115–232 provides for an amendment to the heading. The matter proposed to be struck did not appear in the proper casing for subsections, however, such amendment was carried out to reflect the probable intent of Congress.

---

(2)[2] Each briefing under paragraph (1) shall include a description of contractor costs and performance relative to schedule, the progress to date toward the complete destruction of the stockpile, and any other information the Secretary determines to be relevant.

415

---

² Margin for paragraph (2) is so in law.

---

(3) The members and committees of Congress referred to in this paragraph are—

(A) the majority leader and the minority leader of the Senate and the Committee on Armed Services and the Committee on Appropriations of the Senate; and

(B) the Speaker of the House of Representatives, the majority leader and the minority leader of the House of Representatives, and the Committee on Armed Services and the Committee on Appropriations of the House of Representatives.

(k) AUTHORIZED USE OF TOXIC CHEMICALS.— Consistent with United States obligations under the Chemical Weapons Convention, the Secretary of Defense may develop, produce, otherwise acquire, retain, transfer, and use toxic chemicals and their precursors for purposes not prohibited by the Chemical Weapons Convention if the types and quantities of such chemicals and precursors are consistent with such purposes, including for protective purposes such as protection against toxic chemicals and protection against chemical weapons.

(l) SURVEILLANCE AND ASSESSMENT PROGRAM.—The Secretary of Defense shall conduct an ongoing comprehensive program of—

(1) surveillance of the existing United States stockpile of chemical weapons; and

(2) assessment of the condition of the stockpile.

(m) CHEMICAL DEMILITARIZATION CITIZENS' ADVISORY COMMISSIONS.—(1)(A) The Secretary of the Army shall establish a citizens' commission for each State in which there is a chemical demilitarization facility under Army management.

(B) The Assistant Secretary of Defense for Nuclear Deterrence, Chemical, and Biological Defense Policy and Programs shall establish a chemical demilitarization citizens' commission in Colorado and in Kentucky.

(C) Each commission under this subsection shall be known as the Chemical Demilitarization Citizens' Advisory Commission for the State concerned.

(2)(A) The Secretary of the Army, or the Department of Defense with respect to Colorado and Kentucky, shall provide for a representative to meet with each commission established under this subsection to receive citizen and State concerns regarding the ongoing program for the disposal of the lethal chemical agents and munitions in the stockpile referred to in subsection (a) at each of the sites with respect to which a commission is established pursuant to paragraph (1).

(B) The Secretary of the Army shall provide for a representative from the Office of the Assistant Secretary of the Army (Acquisition, Logistics, and Technology) to meet with each commission under Army management.

(C) The Department of Defense shall provide for a representative from the Office of the Assistant Secretary of Defense for Nuclear Deterrence, Chemical, and Biological Defense Policy and Programs to meet with the commissions in Colorado and Kentucky.

(3)(A) Each commission under this subsection shall be composed of nine members appointed by the Governor of the State. Seven of such members shall be citizens from the local affected areas in the State. The other two shall be representatives of State government who have direct responsibilities related to the chemical demilitarization program.

(B) For purposes of this paragraph, affected areas are those areas located within a 50-mile radius of a chemical weapons storage site.

(4) For a period of five years after the termination of any commission under this subsection, no corporation, partnership, or other organization in which a member of that commission, a spouse of a member of that commission, or a natural or adopted child of a member of that commission has an ownership interest may be awarded—

(A) a contract related to the disposal of lethal chemical agents or munitions in the stockpile referred to in subsection (a); or

(B) a subcontract under such a contract.

(5) The members of each commission under this subsection shall designate the chair of such commission from among the members of such commission.

(6) Each commission under this subsection shall meet with a representative from the Army, or the Office of the Assistant Secretary of Defense for Nuclear Deterrence, Chemical, and Biological Defense Policy and Programs with respect to the commissions in Colorado and Kentucky, upon joint agreement between the chair of such commission and that representative. The two parties shall meet not less often than twice a year and may meet more often at their discretion.

(7) Members of each commission under this subsection shall receive no pay for their involvement in the activities of their commissions. Funds appropriated for the Chemical Stockpile Demilitarization Program may be used for travel and associated travel costs for commissioners of commissions under this subsection when such travel is conducted at the invitation of the Assistant Secretary of the Army (Acquisition, Logistics, and Technology) or the invitation of the Assistant Secretary of Defense for Nuclear Deterrence, Chemical, and Biological Defense Policy and Programs for the commissions in Colorado and Kentucky.

(8) Each commission under this subsection shall be terminated after the closure activities required pursuant to regulations prescribed by the Administrator of the Environmental Protection Agency pursuant to the Solid Waste Disposal Act (42 U.S.C. 6901 et seq.) have been completed for the chemical agent destruction facility in such commission's State, or upon the request of the Governor of such commission's State, whichever occurs first.

(n) INCENTIVE CLAUSES IN CHEMICAL DEMILITARIZATION CONTRACTS.—(1)(A) The Secretary of Defense may, for the purpose specified in paragraph (B), authorize the inclusion of an incentives clause in any contract for the destruction of the United States stockpile of lethal chemical agents and munitions carried out pursuant to subsection (a).

(B) The purpose of a clause referred to in subparagraph (A) is to provide the contractor for a chemical demilitarization facility an incentive to accelerate the safe elimination of the United States chemical weapons stockpile and to reduce the total cost of the Chemical Demilitarization Program by providing incentive payments for the early completion of destruction operations and the closure of such facility.

(2)(A) An incentives clause under this subsection shall permit the contractor for the chemical demilitarization facility concerned the opportunity to earn incentive payments for the completion of destruction operations and facility closure activities within target incentive ranges specified in such clause.

(B) The maximum incentive payment under an incentives clause with respect to a chemical demilitarization facility may not exceed the following amounts:

(i) In the case of an incentive payment for the completion of destruction operations within the target incentive range specified in such clause, $110,000,000.

(ii) In the case of an incentive payment for the completion of facility closure activities within the target incentive range specified in such clause, $55,000,000.

(C) An incentives clause in a contract under this section shall specify the target incentive ranges of costs for completion of destruction operations and facility closure activities, respectively, as jointly agreed upon by the contracting officer and the contractor concerned. An incentives clause shall require a proportionate reduction in the maximum incentive payment amounts in the event that the contractor exceeds an agreed-upon target cost if such excess costs are the responsibility of the contractor.

(D) The amount of the incentive payment earned by a contractor for a chemical demilitarization facility under an incentives clause under this subsection shall be based upon a determination by the Secretary on how early in the target incentive range specified in such clause destruction operations or facility closure activities, as the case may be, are completed.

(E) The provisions of any incentives clause under this subsection shall be consistent with the obligation of the Secretary of Defense under subsection (d)(1)(A), to provide for maximum protection for the environment, the general public, and the personnel who are involved in the destruction of the lethal chemical agents and munitions.

(F) In negotiating the inclusion of an incentives clause in a contract under this subsection, the Secretary may include in such clause such additional terms and conditions as the Secretary considers appropriate.

(3)(A) No payment may be made under an incentives clause under this subsection unless the Secretary determines that the contractor concerned has satisfactorily performed its duties under such incentives clause.

(B) An incentives clause under this subsection shall specify that the obligation of the Government to make payment under such incentives clause is subject to the availability of appropriations for that purpose. Amounts appropriated for Chemical Agents and Munitions Destruction, Defense, shall be available for payments under incentives clauses under this subsection.

(o) SUPPLEMENTAL DESTRUCTION TECHNOLOGIES.—In determining the technologies to supplement the neutralization destruction of the stockpile of lethal chemical agents and munitions at Pueblo Chemical Depot, Colorado, and Blue Grass Army Depot, Kentucky, the Secretary of Defense may consider the following:

(1) Explosive Destruction Technologies.

(2) Any technologies developed for the treatment and disposal of energetic or agent hydrolysates, if problems with the current on-site treatment of hydrolysates are encountered.

(p) DEFINITIONS.—In this section:

(1) The term chemical agent and munition means an agent or munition that, through its chemical properties, produces lethal or other damaging effects on human beings, except that such term does not include riot control agents, chemical herbicides, smoke and other obscuration materials.

(2) The term Chemical Weapons Convention means the Convention on the Prohibition of Development, Production, Stockpiling and Use of Chemical Weapons and on Their Destruction, with annexes, done at Paris, January 13, 1993, and entered into force April 29, 1997 (T. Doc. 103–21).

(3) The term lethal chemical agent and munition means a chemical agent or munition that is designed to cause death, through its chemical properties, to human beings in field concentrations.

(4) The term destruction means, with respect to chemical munitions or agents—

(A) the demolishment of such munitions or agents by incineration or by any other means; or

(B) the dismantling or other disposal of such munitions or agents so as to make them useless for military purposes and harmless to human beings under normal circumstances.

★

RADIOLOGICAL EMERGENCY PREPAREDNESS FUND

42 U.S.C. §5196E
AS AMENDED THROUGH PUB. L. 117–81

TITLE 42—THE PUBLIC HEALTH AND WELFARE

* * * * * * *

CHAPTER 68—DISASTER RELIEF

* * * * * * *

SUBCHAPTER IV–B—EMERGENCY PREPAREDNESS

* * * * * * *

Part A—Powers and Duties

* * * * * * *

§5196e. Radiological Emergency Preparedness Fund

There is hereby established in the Treasury a Radiological Emergency Preparedness Fund, which shall be available under the Atomic Energy Act of 1954 [42 U.S.C. 2011 et seq.], as amended, and Executive Order 12657, for offsite radiological emergency planning, preparedness, and response. Beginning in fiscal year 1999 and thereafter, the Administrator of the Federal Emergency Management Agency (FEMA) shall promulgate through rulemaking fees to be assessed and collected, applicable to persons subject to FEMA's radiological emergency preparedness regulations. The aggregate charges assessed pursuant to this section during fiscal year 1999 shall not be less than 100 percent of the amounts anticipated by FEMA necessary for its radiological emergency preparedness program for such fiscal year. The methodology for assessment and collection of fees shall be fair and equitable; and shall reflect costs of providing such services, including administrative costs of collecting such fees. Fees received pursuant to this section shall be deposited in the Fund as offsetting collections and will become available for authorized purposes on October 1, 1999, and remain available until expended.

(Pub. L. 105–276, title III, Oct. 21, 1998, 112 Stat. 2502; Pub. L. 109–295, title VI, §612(c), Oct. 4, 2006, 120 Stat. 1410.)

STATUTORY NOTES AND RELATED SUBSIDIARIES

CHANGE OF NAME

"Administrator of the Federal Emergency Management Agency" substituted for "Director of the Federal Emergency Management Agency" on authority of section 612(c) of Pub. L. 109–295, set out as a note under section 313 of Title 6, Domestic Security. Any reference to the Administrator of the Federal Emergency Management Agency in title VI of Pub. L. 109–295 or an amendment by title VI to be considered to refer and apply to the Director of the Federal Emergency Management Agency until Mar. 31, 2007, see section 612(f)(2) of Pub. L. 109–295, set out as a note under section 313 of Title 6.

TRANSFER OF FUNCTIONS

For transfer of all functions, personnel, assets, components, authorities, grant programs, and liabilities of the Federal Emergency Management Agency, including the functions of the Under Secretary for Federal Emergency Management relating thereto, to the Federal Emergency Management Agency, see section 315(a)(1) of Title 6, Domestic Security.

For transfer of functions, personnel, assets, and liabilities of the Federal Emergency Management Agency, including the functions of the Director of the Federal Emergency Management Agency relating thereto, to the Secretary of Homeland Security, and for treatment of related references, see former section 313(1) and sections 551(d), 552(d), and 557 of Title 6, Domestic Security, and the Department of Homeland Security Reorganization Plan of November 25, 2002, as modified, set out as a note under section 542 of Title 6.

49 U.S.C. §5115 AND §5116

49 U.S.C. §5115 AND §5116
AS AMENDED THROUGH PUB. L. 117–158

TITLE 49—TRANSPORTATION

This title was enacted by Pub. L. 95–473, §1, Oct. 17, 1978, 92 Stat. 1337; Pub. L. 97–449, §1, Jan. 12, 1983, 96 Stat. 2413; Pub. L. 103–272, July 5, 1994, 108 Stat. 745

* * * * * * *

SUBTITLE III—GENERAL AND INTERMODAL PROGRAMS

* * * * * * *

CHAPTER 51—TRANSPORTATION OF HAZARDOUS MATERIAL

* * * * * * *

§5115. Training curriculum for the public sector

(a) IN GENERAL.—In coordination with the Administrator of the Federal Emergency Management Agency, the Chairman of the Nuclear Regulatory Commission, the Administrator of the Environmental Protection Agency, the Secretaries of Labor, Energy, and Health and Human Services, and the Director of the National Institute of Environmental Health Sciences, and using existing coordinating mechanisms of the National Response Team and, for radioactive material, the Federal Radiological Preparedness Coordinating Committee, the Secretary of Transportation shall maintain, and update periodically, a current curriculum of courses, including online curriculum as appropriate, necessary to train public sector emergency response and preparedness teams in matters relating to the transportation of hazardous material. Only in developing the curriculum, the Secretary of Transportation shall consult with regional response teams established under the national contingency plan established under section 105 of the Comprehensive Environmental Response, Compensation, and Liability Act of 1980 (42 U.S.C. 9605), representatives of commissions established under section 301 of the Emergency Planning and Community Right-To-Know Act of 1986 (42 U.S.C. 11001), persons (including governmental entities) that provide training for responding to accidents and incidents involving the transportation of hazardous material, and representatives of persons that respond to those accidents and incidents.

(b) REQUIREMENTS.—The curriculum maintained and updated under subsection (a) of this section—

(1) shall include—

(A) a recommended course of study to train public sector employees to respond to an accident or incident involving the transportation of hazardous material and to plan for those responses;

(B) recommended courses and minimum number of hours of instruction necessary for public sector employees to be able to respond safely and efficiently to an accident or incident involving the transportation of hazardous material and to plan those responses; and

(C) appropriate emergency response training and planning programs for public sector employees developed with Federal financial assistance, including programs developed with grants made under section 126(g) of the Superfund Amendments and Reauthorization Act of 1986 (42 U.S.C. 9660a); and

(2) may include recommendations on material appropriate for use in a recommended course described in clause (1)(B) of this subsection.

(c) TRAINING ON COMPLYING WITH LEGAL REQUIREMENTS.—A recommended course described in subsection (b)(1)(B) of this section shall provide the training necessary for public sector employees to comply with—

(1) regulations related to hazardous waste operations and emergency response contained in part 1910 of title 29, Code of Federal Regulations, prescribed by the Secretary of Labor;

(2) regulations related to worker protection standards for hazardous waste operations contained in part 311 of title 40, Code of Federal Regulations, prescribed by the Administrator; and

(3) standards related to emergency response training prescribed by the National Fire Protection Association and such other voluntary consensus standard-setting organizations as the Secretary of Transportation determines appropriate.

(d) DISTRIBUTION AND PUBLICATION.—With the National Response Team—

(1) the Secretary shall distribute the curriculum and any updates to the curriculum to the regional response teams and all committees and commissions established under section 301 of the Emergency Planning and Community Right-To-Know Act of 1986 (42 U.S.C. 11001); and

(2) the Secretary may publish and distribute a list of programs and courses maintained and updated under this section and of any programs utilizing such courses.

(Pub. L. 103–272, §1(d), July 5, 1994, 108 Stat. 772; Pub. L. 103–429, §6(5), Oct. 31, 1994, 108 Stat. 4378; Pub. L. 109–59, title VII, §§7113, 7126, Aug. 10, 2005, 119 Stat. 1899, 1909; Pub. L. 109–295, title VI, §612(c), Oct. 4, 2006, 120 Stat. 1410; Pub. L. 112–141, div. C, title III, §33004(a), July 6, 2012, 126 Stat. 832; Pub. L. 114–94, div. A, title VI, §6013, Dec. 4, 2015, 129 Stat. 1570.)

§5116. PLANNING AND TRAINING GRANTS, MONITORING, AND REVIEW

(a) PLANNING AND TRAINING GRANTS.—(1) The Secretary shall make grants to States and Indian tribes—

(A) to develop, improve, and carry out emergency plans under the Emergency Planning and Community Right-To-Know Act of 1986 (42 U.S.C. 11001 et seq.), including ascertaining flow patterns of hazardous material on lands under the jurisdiction of a State or Indian tribe, and between lands under the jurisdiction of a State or Indian tribe and lands of another State or Indian tribe;

(B) to decide on the need for regional hazardous material emergency response teams; and

(C) to train public sector employees to respond to accidents and incidents involving hazardous material.

(2) To the extent that a grant is used to train emergency responders under paragraph (1)(C), the State or Indian tribe shall provide written certification to the Secretary that the emergency responders who receive training under the grant will have the ability to protect nearby persons, property, and the environment from the effects of accidents or incidents involving the transportation of hazardous material in accordance with existing regulations or National Fire Protection Association standards for competence of responders to accidents and incidents involving hazardous materials.

(3) The Secretary may make a grant to a State or Indian tribe under paragraph (1) of this subsection only if—

(A) the State or Indian tribe certifies that the total amount the State or Indian tribe expends (except amounts of the Federal Government) for the purpose of the grant will at least equal the average level of expenditure for the last 5 years; and

(B) any emergency response training provided under the grant shall consist of—

(i) a course developed or identified under section 5115 of this title; or

(ii) any other course the Secretary determines is consistent with the objectives of this section.

(4) A State or Indian tribe receiving a grant under this subsection shall ensure that planning and emergency response training under the grant is coordinated with adjacent States and Indian tribes.

(5) A training grant under paragraph (1)(C) may be used—

(A) to pay—

(i) the tuition costs of public sector employees being trained;

(ii) travel expenses of those employees to and from the training facility;

(iii) room and board of those employees when at the training facility; and

(iv) travel expenses of individuals providing the training;

(B) by the State, political subdivision, or Indian tribe to provide the training; and

(C) to make an agreement with a person (including an authority of a State, a political subdivision of a State or Indian tribe, or a local jurisdiction), subject to approval by the Secretary, to provide the training if—

(i) the agreement allows the Secretary and the State or Indian tribe to conduct random examinations, inspections, and audits of the training without prior notice;

(ii) the person agrees to have an auditable accounting system; and

(iii) the State or Indian tribe conducts at least one on-site observation of the training each year.

(6) The Secretary shall allocate amounts made available for grants under this subsection among eligible States and Indian tribes based on the needs of the States and Indian tribes for emergency response planning and training. In making a decision about those needs, the Secretary shall consider—

(A) the number of hazardous material facilities in the State or on land under the jurisdiction of the Indian tribe;

(B) the types and amounts of hazardous material transported in the State or on such land;

(C) whether the State or Indian tribe imposes and collects a fee for transporting hazardous material;

(D) whether such fee is used only to carry out a purpose related to transporting hazardous material;

(E) the past record of the State or Indian tribe in effectively managing planning and training grants; and

(F) any other factors the Secretary determines are appropriate to carry out this subsection.

(b) COMPLIANCE WITH CERTAIN LAW.—The Secretary may make a grant to a State under this section in a fiscal year only if the State certifies that the State complies with sections 301 and 303 of the Emergency Planning and Community Right-To-Know Act of 1986 (42 U.S.C. 11001, 11003).

(c) APPLICATIONS.—A State or Indian tribe interested in receiving a grant under this section shall submit an application to the Secretary. The application must be submitted at the time, and contain information, the Secretary requires by regulation to carry out the objectives of this section.

(d) GOVERNMENT'S SHARE OF COSTS.—A grant under this section is for 80 percent of the cost the State or Indian tribe incurs in the fiscal year to carry out the activity for which the grant is made. Amounts of the State or tribe under subsection (a)(3)(A) of this section are not part of the non-Government share under this subsection.

(e) MONITORING AND TECHNICAL ASSISTANCE.—In coordination with the Secretaries of Transportation and Energy, Administrator of the Environmental Protection Agency, and Director of the National Institute of Environmental Health Sciences, the Administrator of the Federal Emergency Management Agency shall monitor public sector emergency response planning and training for an accident or incident involving hazardous material. Considering the results of the monitoring, the Secretaries, Administrators, and Director each shall provide technical assistance to a State, political subdivision of a State, or Indian tribe for carrying out emergency response training and planning for an accident or incident involving hazardous material and shall coordinate the assistance using the existing coordinating mechanisms of the National Response Team and, for radioactive material, the Federal Radiological Preparedness Coordinating Committee.

(f) DELEGATION OF AUTHORITY.—To minimize administrative costs and to coordinate Federal financial assistance for emergency response training and planning, the Secretary may delegate to the Administrator of the Federal Emergency Management Agency, Director of the National Institute of Environmental Health Sciences, Chairman of the Nuclear Regulatory Commission, Administrator of the Environmental Protection Agency, and Secretaries of Labor and Energy any of the following:

(1) authority to receive applications for grants under this section.

(2) authority to review applications for technical compliance with this section.

(3) authority to review applications to recommend approval or disapproval.

(4) any other ministerial duty associated with grants under this section.

(g) MINIMIZING DUPLICATION OF EFFORT AND EXPENSES.—The Secretaries of Transportation, Labor, and Energy, Administrator of the Federal Emergency Management Agency, Director of the National Institute of Environmental Health Sciences, Chairman of the Nuclear Regulatory Commission, and Administrator of the Environmental Protection Agency shall review periodically, with the head of each department, agency, or instrumentality of the Government, all emergency response and preparedness training programs of that department, agency, or instrumentality to minimize duplication of effort and expense of the department, agency, or instrumentality in carrying out the programs and shall take necessary action to minimize duplication.

(h) ANNUAL REGISTRATION FEE ACCOUNT AND ITS USES.—The Secretary of the Treasury shall establish an account in the Treasury (to be known as the "Hazardous Materials Emergency Preparedness Fund") into which the Secretary of the Treasury shall deposit amounts the Secretary of Transportation transfers to the Secretary of the Treasury under section 5108(g)(2)(C) of this title. Without further appropriation, amounts in the account are available—

(1) to make grants under this section and section 5107(e);

(2) to monitor and provide technical assistance under subsection (e) of this section;

(3) to publish and distribute an emergency response guide; and

(4) to pay administrative costs of carrying out this section and sections 5107(e) and 5108(g)(2) of this title, except that not more than 2 percent of the amounts made available from the account in a fiscal year may be used to pay those costs.

(i) SUPPLEMENTAL TRAINING GRANTS.—

(1) In order to further the purposes of subsection (a), the Secretary shall, subject to the availability of funds and through a competitive process, make a grant or make grants to national nonprofit fire service organizations for the purpose of training instructors to conduct hazardous materials response training programs for individuals with statutory responsibility to respond to hazardous materials accidents and incidents.

(2) For the purposes of this subsection the Secretary, after consultation with interested organizations, shall—

(A) identify regions or locations in which fire departments or other organizations which provide emergency response to hazardous materials transportation accidents and incidents are in need of hazardous materials training; and

(B) prioritize such needs and develop a means for identifying additional specific training needs.

(3) Funds granted to an organization under this subsection shall only be used—

(A) to provide training, including portable training, for instructors to conduct hazardous materials response training programs;

(B) to purchase training equipment used exclusively to train instructors to conduct such training programs; and

(C) to disseminate such information and materials as are necessary for the conduct of such training programs.

(4) The Secretary may only make a grant to an organization under this subsection in a fiscal year if the organization enters into an agreement with the Secretary to provide

training, including portable training, for instructors to conduct hazardous materials response training programs in such fiscal year that will use—

(A) a course or courses developed or identified under section 5115 of this title; or

(B) other courses which the Secretary determines are consistent with the objectives of this subsection;

for training individuals with statutory responsibility to respond to accidents and incidents involving hazardous materials. Such agreement also shall provide that training courses shall comply with Federal regulations and national consensus standards for hazardous materials response and be open to all such individuals on a nondiscriminatory basis.

(5) The Secretary may not award a grant to an organization under this subsection unless the organization ensures that emergency responders who receive training under the grant will have the ability to protect nearby persons, property, and the environment from the effects of accidents or incidents involving the transportation of hazardous material in accordance with existing regulations or National Fire Protection Association standards for competence of responders to accidents and incidents involving hazardous materials.

(6) Notwithstanding paragraphs (1) and (3), to the extent determined appropriate by the Secretary, a grant awarded by the Secretary to an organization under this subsection to conduct hazardous material response training programs may be used to train individuals with responsibility to respond to accidents and incidents involving hazardous material.

(7) For the purposes of this subsection, the term "portable training" means live, instructor-led training provided by certified fire service instructors that can be offered in any suitable setting, rather than specific designated facilities. Under this training delivery model, instructors travel to locations convenient to students and utilize local facilities and resources.

(8) The Secretary may impose such additional terms and conditions on grants to be made under this subsection as the Secretary determines are necessary to protect the interests of the United States and to carry out the objectives of this subsection.

(j) ALERT GRANT PROGRAM.—

(1) ASSISTANCE FOR LOCAL EMERGENCY RESPONSE TRAINING.—The Secretary shall establish a grant program to make grants to eligible entities described in paragraph (2)—

(A) to develop a hazardous materials response training curriculum for emergency responders, including response activities for the transportation of crude oil, ethanol, and other flammable liquids by rail, consistent with the standards of the National Fire Protection Association; and

(B) to make the training described in subparagraph (A) available in an electronic format.

(2) ELIGIBLE ENTITIES.—An eligible entity referred to in paragraph (1) is a nonprofit organization that—

(A) represents first responders or public officials responsible for coordinating disaster response; and

(B) is able to provide direct or web-based training to individuals responsible for responding to accidents and incidents involving hazardous materials.

(3) FUNDING.—

(A) IN GENERAL.—To carry out the grant program under paragraph (1), the Secretary may use, for each fiscal year, any amounts recovered during such fiscal year from grants awarded under this section during a prior fiscal year.

(B) OTHER HAZARDOUS MATERIAL TRAINING ACTIVITIES.—For each fiscal year, after providing grants under paragraph (1), if funds remain available, the Secretary may use the amounts described in subparagraph (A)—

(i) to make grants under—

(I) subsection (a)(1)(C);

(II) subsection (i); and

(III) section 5107(e);

(ii) to conduct monitoring and provide technical assistance under subsection (e);

(iii) to publish and distribute the emergency response guide referred to in subsection (h)(3); and

(iv) to pay administrative costs in accordance with subsection (h)(4).

(C) OBLIGATION LIMITATION.—Notwithstanding any other provision of law, for each fiscal year, amounts described in subparagraph (A) shall not be included in the obligation limitation for the Hazardous Materials Emergency Preparedness grant program for that fiscal year.

(k) REPORTS.—The Secretary shall submit an annual report to the Committee on Transportation and Infrastructure of the House of Representatives and the Committee on Commerce, Science, and Transportation of the Senate and make available the report to the public. The report submitted under this subsection shall include information on the allocation and uses of the planning and training grants under subsection (a) and grants under subsections (i) and (j) of this section and under subsections (e) and (i) of section 5107. The report submitted under this subsection shall identify the ultimate recipients of such grants and include—

(1) a detailed accounting and description of each grant expenditure by each grant recipient, including the amount of, and purpose for, each expenditure;

(2) the number of persons trained under the grant program, by training level;

(3) an evaluation of the efficacy of such planning and training programs; and

(4) any recommendations the Secretary may have for improving such grant programs.

(Pub. L. 103–272, §1(d), July 5, 1994, 108 Stat. 773; Pub. L. 103–311, title I, §§105, 119(a), (d)(2), (3), Aug. 26, 1994, 108 Stat. 1673, 1679, 1680; Pub. L. 103–429, §7(c), Oct. 31, 1994, 108 Stat. 4389; Pub. L. 104–287, §§5(8), 6(b), Oct. 11, 1996, 110 Stat. 3389, 3398; Pub. L. 109–59, title VII, §§7114(a)–(d)(2), (e), 7126, Aug. 10, 2005, 119 Stat. 1900, 1909; Pub. L. 109–295, title VI, §612(c), Oct. 4, 2006, 120 Stat. 1410; Pub. L. 112–141, div. C, title III, §33004(b), July 6, 2012, 126 Stat. 832; Pub. L. 114–94, div. A, title VII, §7203(a), (b)(2), Dec. 4, 2015, 129 Stat. 1589, 1591; Pub. L. 117–58, div. B, title VI, §26002, Nov. 15, 2021, 135 Stat. 882.)

INFRASTRUCTURE AND TRANSPORTATION RESILIENCE

SELECTED PROVISIONS OF THE FAA REAUTHORIZATION ACT OF 2018

PUBLIC LAW 115–254
AS AMENDED THROUGH PUB. L. 118–63

Disaster Recovery Reform Act of 2018

(Division D of the FAA Reauthorization Act of 2018

[(Public Law 115–254)]

[As Amended Through P.L. 118–63, Enacted May 16, 2024]

AN ACT To provide protections for certain sports medicine professionals, to reauthorize Federal aviation programs, to improve aircraft safety certification processes, and for other purposes.

Be it enacted by the Senate and House of Representatives of the United States of America in Congress assembled,

DIVISION D—DISASTER RECOVERY REFORM

SEC. 1201. [42 U.S.C. 5121 note] SHORT TITLE.
This division may be cited as the "Disaster Recovery Reform Act of 2018".

SEC. 1202. [42 U.S.C. 5121 note] APPLICABILITY.

(a) APPLICABILITY FOR STAFFORD ACT.— Except as otherwise expressly provided, the amendments in this division to the Robert T. Stafford Disaster Relief and Emergency Assistance Act (42 U.S.C. 5121 et seq.) apply to each major disaster and emergency declared by the President on or after August 1, 2017, under the Robert T. Stafford Disaster Relief and Emergency Assistance Act.

(b) DIVISION APPLICABILITY.— Except as otherwise expressly provided, the authorities provided under this division apply to each major disaster and emergency declared by the President under the Robert T. Stafford Disaster Relief and Emergency Assistance Act on or after January 1, 2016.

SEC. 1203. [42 U.S.C. 5122 note] DEFINITIONS.
In this division:

(1) ADMINISTRATOR.— The term Administrator means the Administrator of the Federal Emergency Management Agency.

(2) AGENCY.— The term Agency means the Federal Emergency Management Agency.

(3) STATE.— The term State has the meaning given that term in section 102 of the Robert T. Stafford Disaster Relief and Emergency Assistance Act (42 U.S.C.

5122).

SEC. 1204. WILDFIRE PREVENTION.

* * * * * * *

(c) [42 U.S.C. 5187 note] REPORTING REQUIREMENT.— Not later than 1 year after the date of enactment of this Act and annually thereafter, the Administrator shall submit to the Committee on Homeland Security and Governmental Affairs of the Senate, the Committee on Transportation and Infrastructure of the House of Representatives, and the Committees on Appropriations of the Senate and the House of Representatives a report containing a summary of any projects carried out, and any funding provided to those projects, under subsection (d) of section 420 of the Robert T. Stafford Disaster Relief and Emergency Assistance Act (42 U.S.C. 5187) (as amended by this section).

* * * * * * *

SEC. 1208. [6 U.S.C. 748a] PRIORITIZATION OF FACILITIES.

Not later than 180 days after the date of enactment of this Act, the Administrator shall provide guidance and training on an annual basis to State, local, and Indian tribal governments, first responders, and utility companies on—

(1) the need to prioritize assistance to hospitals, nursing homes, and other long-term care facilities to ensure that such health care facilities remain functioning or return to functioning as soon as practicable during power outages caused by natural hazards, including severe weather events;

(2) how hospitals, nursing homes and other long-term care facilities should adequately prepare for power outages during a major disaster or emergency, as those terms are defined in section 102 of the Robert T. Stafford Disaster Relief and Emergency Assistance Act (42 U.S.C. 5122); and

(3) how State, local, and Indian tribal governments, first responders, utility companies, hospitals, nursing homes, and other long-term care facilities should develop a strategy to coordinate emergency response plans, including the activation of emergency response plans, in anticipation of a major disaster, including severe weather events.

SEC. 1209. [6 U.S.C. 721 note] GUIDANCE ON EVACUATION ROUTES.

(a) IN GENERAL.—

(1) IDENTIFICATION.— The Administrator, in coordination with the Administrator of the Federal Highway Administration, shall develop and issue guidance for State, local, and Indian tribal governments regarding the identification of evacuation routes.

(2) GUIDANCE.— The Administrator of the Federal Highway Administration, in coordination with the Administrator, shall revise existing guidance or issue new guidance as appropriate for State, local, and Indian tribal governments regarding the design, construction, maintenance, and repair of evacuation routes.

(b) CONSIDERATIONS.—

SEC. 1209. [6 U.S.C. 721 note] GUIDANCE ON EVACUATION ROUTES.

Disaster Recovery Reform Act of 2018

(1) IDENTIFICATION.—In developing the guidance under subsection (a)(1), the Administrator shall consider—

(A) whether evacuation routes have resisted impacts and recovered quickly from disasters, regardless of cause;

(B) the need to evacuate special needs populations, including—

(i) individuals with a physical or mental disability;

(ii) individuals in schools, daycare centers, mobile home parks, prisons, nursing homes and other long-term care facilities, and detention centers;

(iii) individuals with limited-English proficiency;

(iv) the elderly; and

(v) individuals who are tourists, seasonal workers, or homeless;

(C) the sharing of information and other public communications with evacuees during evacuations;

(D) the sheltering of evacuees, including the care, protection, and sheltering of animals;

(E) the return of evacuees to their homes; and

(F) such other items the Administrator considers appropriate.

(2) DESIGN, CONSTRUCTION, MAINTENANCE, AND REPAIR.—In revising or issuing guidance under subsection (a)(2), the Administrator of the Federal Highway Administration shall consider—

(A) methods that assist evacuation routes to—

(i) withstand likely risks to viability, including flammability and hydrostatic forces;

(ii) improve durability, strength (including the ability to withstand tensile stresses and compressive stresses), and sustainability; and

(iii) provide for long-term cost savings;

(B) the ability of evacuation routes to effectively manage contraflow operations;

(C) for evacuation routes on public lands, the viewpoints of the applicable Federal land management agency regarding emergency operations, sustainability, and resource protection; and

(D) such other items the Administrator of the Federal Highway Administration considers appropriate.

(c) STUDY.—The Administrator, in coordination with the Administrator of the Federal Highway Administration and State, local, territorial, and Indian tribal governments, may—

(1) conduct a study of the adequacy of available evacuation routes to accommodate the flow of evacuees; and

(2) submit recommendations on how to help with anticipated evacuation route

flow, based on the study conducted under paragraph (1), to—

(A)   the Federal Highway Administration;

(B)   the Agency;

(C)   State, local, territorial, and Indian tribal governments; and

(D)   Congress.

SEC. 1210. DUPLICATION OF BENEFITS.

(a) IN GENERAL.—

(1) AUTHORITY.— Section 312(b) of the Robert T. Stafford Disaster Relief and Emergency Assistance Act (42 U.S.C. 5155(b)) is amended by adding at the end the following:

"(4) WAIVER OF GENERAL PROHIBITION.—

"(A) IN GENERAL.—The President may waive the general prohibition provided in subsection (a) upon request of a Governor on behalf of the State or on behalf of a person, business concern, or any other entity suffering losses as a result of a major disaster or emergency, if the President finds such waiver is in the public interest and will not result in waste, fraud, or abuse. In making this decision, the President may consider the following:

"(i)   The recommendations of the Administrator of the Federal Emergency Management Agency made in consultation with the Federal agency or agencies administering the duplicative program.

"(ii)   If a waiver is granted, the assistance to be funded is cost effective.

"(iii)   Equity and good conscience.

"(iv)   Other matters of public policy considered appropriate by the President.

"(B) GRANT OR DENIAL OF WAIVER.— A request under subparagraph (A) shall be granted or denied not later than 45 days after submission of such request.

"(C) PROHIBITION ON DETERMINATION THAT LOAN IS A DUPLICATION.— Notwithstanding subsection (c), in carrying out subparagraph (A), the President may not determine that a loan is a duplication of assistance, provided that all Federal assistance is used toward a loss suffered as a result of the major disaster or emergency.".

(2) [42 U.S.C. 5155 note] LIMITATION.— This subsection, including the amendment made by paragraph (1), shall not be construed to apply to section 406 or 408 of the Robert T. Stafford Disaster Relief and Emergency Assistance Act (42 U.S.C. 5172, 5174).

(3) [42 U.S.C. 5155 note] APPLICABILITY.— The amendment made by paragraph (1) shall apply to any major disaster or emergency declared by the President under section 401 or 501, respectively, of the Robert T. Stafford Disaster Relief and Emergency Assistance Act (42 U.S.C. 5170, 5191) between January 1, 2016, and

December 31, 2021.

(4) [42 U.S.C. 5155 note] SUNSET.— On the date that is 5 years after the date of enactment of this Act, section 312(b) of the Robert T. Stafford Disaster Relief and Emergency Assistance Act (42 U.S.C. 5155(b)) is amended by striking paragraph (4), as added by subsection (a)(1) of this section.

(5) REPORT.—

(A) IN GENERAL.— Not later than 1 year after the date of enactment of this Act, the Administrator, in coordination with other relevant Federal agencies, shall submit to the congressional committees of jurisdiction a report conducted by all relevant Federal agencies to improve the comprehensive delivery of disaster assistance to individuals following a major disaster or emergency declaration under the Robert T. Stafford Disaster Relief and Emergency Assistance Act.

(B) CONTENTS.—The report required under subparagraph (A) shall include both administrative actions taken, or planned to be taken, by the agencies as well as legislative proposals, where appropriate, of the following:

(i) Efforts to improve coordination between the Agency and other relevant Federal agencies when delivering disaster assistance to individuals.

(ii) Clarify the sequence of delivery of disaster assistance to individuals from the Agency, and other relevant Federal agencies.

(iii) Clarify the interpretation and implementation of section 312 of the Robert T. Stafford Disaster Relief and Emergency Assistance Act (42 U.S.C. 5155) when providing disaster assistance to individuals, including providing a common interpretation across the Agency, and other relevant Federal agencies, of the definitions and requirements under such section 312.

(iv) Increase the effectiveness of communication to applicants for assistance programs for individuals after a disaster declaration, including the breadth of programs available and the potential impacts of utilizing one program versus another.

(C) REPORT UPDATE.— Not later than 4 years after the date of enactment of this subsection, the Administrator, in coordination with other relevant Federal agencies, shall submit to the congressional committees of jurisdiction an update to the report required under subparagraph (A).

(b) [42 U.S.C. 5170c note] FUNDING OF A FEDERALLY AUTHORIZED WATER RESOURCES DEVELOPMENT PROJECT.—

(1) ELIGIBLE ACTIVITIES.— Notwithstanding section 312 of the Robert T. Stafford Disaster Relief and Emergency Assistance Act (42 U.S.C. 5155) and its implementing regulations, assistance provided pursuant to section 404 of such Act may be used to fund activities authorized for construction within the scope of a federally authorized water resources development project of the Army Corps of Engineers if such activities are also eligible activities under such section.

(2) FEDERAL FUNDING.— All Federal funding provided under section 404 pursuant to this section shall be applied toward the Federal share of such project.

(3) NON-FEDERAL MATCH.— All non-Federal matching funds required under section 404 pursuant to this section shall be applied toward the non-Federal share of such project.

(4) TOTAL FEDERAL SHARE.— Funding provided under section 404 pursuant to this section may not exceed the total Federal share for such project.

(5) NO EFFECT.—Nothing in this section shall—

(A) affect the cost-share requirement of a hazard mitigation measure under section 404;

(B) affect the eligibility criteria for a hazard mitigation measure under section 404;

(C) affect the cost share requirements of a federally authorized water resources development project; and

(D) affect the responsibilities of a non-Federal interest with respect to the project, including those related to the provision of lands, easements, rights-of-way, dredge material disposal areas, and necessary relocations.

(6) LIMITATION.— If a federally authorized water resources development project of the Army Corps of Engineers is constructed with funding provided under section 404 pursuant to this subsection, no further Federal funding shall be provided for construction of such project.

SEC. 1211. STATE ADMINISTRATION OF ASSISTANCE FOR DIRECT TEMPORARY HOUSING AND PERMANENT HOUSING CONSTRUCTION.

* * * * * * *

(b) [42 U.S.C. 5174 note] REIMBURSEMENT.—The Federal Emergency Management Agency (FEMA) shall reimburse State and local units of government (for requests received within a period of 3 years after the declaration of a major disaster under section 401 of the Robert T. Stafford Disaster Relief and Emergency Assistance Act (42 U.S.C. 5170)) upon determination that a locally implemented housing solution, implemented by State or local units of government—

(1) costs 50 percent of comparable FEMA solution or whatever the locally implemented solution costs, whichever is lower;

(2) complies with local housing regulations and ordinances; and

(3) the housing solution was implemented within 90 days of the disaster.

* * * * * * *

SEC. 1213. MULTIFAMILY LEASE AND REPAIR ASSISTANCE.

* * * * * * *

(c) INSPECTOR GENERAL REPORT.—Not later than 2 years after the date of the enactment of this Act, the inspector general of the Department of Homeland Security shall—

  (1) assess the use of the authority provided under section 408(c)(1)(B) of the Robert T. Stafford Disaster Relief and Emergency Assistance Act (42 U.S.C. 5174(c)(1)(B)), as amended by this division, including the adequacy of any benefit-cost analysis done to justify the use of this alternative; and

  (2) submit a report on the results of the assessment conducted under paragraph (1) to the appropriate committees of Congress.

* * * * * * *

SEC. 1216. [42 U.S.C. 5174a] FLEXIBILITY.

 (a) WAIVER AUTHORITY.—

  (1) DEFINITION.—In this subsection, the term covered assistance means assistance provided—

   (A) under section 408 of the Robert T. Stafford Disaster Relief and Emergency Assistance Act (42 U.S.C. 5174); and

   (B) in relation to a major disaster or emergency declared by the President under section 401 or 501, respectively, of the Robert T. Stafford Disaster Relief and Emergency Assistance Act (42 U.S.C. 5170, 5191) on or after October 28, 2012.

  (2) AUTHORITY.—Notwithstanding section 3716(e) of title 31, United States Code, the Administrator—

   (A) except as provided in subparagraph (B), shall—

    (i) waive a debt owed to the United States related to covered assistance provided to an individual or household if the covered assistance was distributed based on an error by the Agency and such debt shall be construed as a hardship; and

    (ii) waive a debt owed to the United States related to covered assistance provided to an individual or household if such assistance is subject to a claim or legal action, including in accordance with section of the Robert T. Stafford Disaster Relief and Emergency Assistance Act (42 U.S.C. 5160); and

   (B) may not waive a debt under subparagraph (A) if the debt involves fraud, the presentation of a false claim, or misrepresentation by the debtor or any party having an interest in the claim.

  (3) MONITORING OF COVERED ASSISTANCE DISTRIBUTED BASED ON ERROR.—

   (A) IN GENERAL.— The Inspector General of the Department of Homeland Security shall monitor the distribution of covered assistance to individuals and households to determine the percentage of such assistance distributed based on an error.

   (B) REPORT ON[8] WAIVER AUTHORITY BASED ON EXCESSIVE ERROR RATE.—If the Inspector General of the Department of Homeland Security determines, with respect to any 12-month period, that the amount of covered assistance distributed based on an error by the Agency exceeds 4 percent of the total amount of covered assistance distributed—

(i) the Inspector General shall notify the Administrator and publish the determination in the Federal Register; and

---

[8] Section 5602(a)(2)(A) of division E of Public Law 117–263 amends paragraph (3)(B) by striking Removal of and inserting Report on. The amendment was carried out to the heading of subparagraph (B) even though it wasn't formatted in header or casing style.

(ii) with respect to any major disaster or emergency declared by the President under section 401 or section 501, respectively, of the Robert T. Stafford Disaster Relief and Emergency Assistance Act (42 U.S.C. 5170; 42 U.S.C. 5191) after the date on which the determination is published under subparagraph (A), the Administrator shall report to the Committee on Transportation and Infrastructure of the House of Representatives and the Committee on Homeland Security and Governmental Affairs of the Senate actions that the Administrator will take to reduce the error rate.

(b) RECOUPMENT OF CERTAIN ASSISTANCE PROHIBITED.—

(1) IN GENERAL.— Notwithstanding section 3716(e) of title 31, United States Code, and unless there is evidence of civil or criminal fraud, the Agency may not take any action to recoup covered assistance from the recipient of such assistance if the receipt of such assistance occurred on a date that is more than 3 years before the date on which the Agency first provides to the recipient written notification of an intent to recoup.

(2) COVERED ASSISTANCE DEFINED.—In this subsection, the term covered assistance means assistance provided—

(A) under section 408 of the Robert T. Stafford Disaster Relief and Emergency Assistance Act (42 U.S.C. 5174); and

(B) in relation to a major disaster or emergency declared by the President under section 401 or 501, respectively, of such Act (42 U.S.C. 5170; 42 U.S.C. 5191) on or after January 1, 2012.

(c) STATUTE OF LIMITATIONS.—

* * * * * * *

(2) APPLICABILITY.—

(A) IN GENERAL.—With respect to disaster or emergency assistance provided to a State or local government on or after January 1, 2004—

(i) no administrative action may be taken to recover a payment of such assistance after the date of enactment of this Act if the action is prohibited under section 705(a)(1) of the Robert T. Stafford Disaster Relief and Emergency Assistance Act (42 U.S.C. 5205(a)(1)), as amended by paragraph (1); and

(ii) any administrative action to recover a payment of such assistance that is pending on such date of enactment shall be terminated if the action is prohibited under section 705(a)(1) of that Act, as amended by paragraph

(1).

(B) LIMITATION.— This section, including the amendments made by this section, may not be construed to invalidate or otherwise affect any administration action completed before the date of enactment of this Act.

* * * * * * *

SEC. 1218. [42 U.S.C. 5165g] NATIONAL VETERINARY EMERGENCY TEAMS.

(a) IN GENERAL.— The Administrator of the Federal Emergency Management Agency may establish one or more national veterinary emergency teams at accredited colleges of veterinary medicine.

(b) RESPONSIBILITIES.—A national veterinary emergency team shall—

(1) deploy with a team of the National Urban Search and Rescue Response System to assist with—

(A) veterinary care of canine search teams;

(B) locating and treating companion animals, service animals, livestock, and other animals; and

(C) surveillance and treatment of zoonotic diseases;

(2) recruit, train, and certify veterinary professionals, including veterinary students, in accordance with an established set of plans and standard operating guidelines to carry out the duties associated with planning for and responding to major disasters and emergencies as described in paragraph (1);

(3) assist State governments, Indian tribal governments, local governments, and nonprofit organizations in developing emergency management and evacuation plans that account for the care and rescue of animals and in improving local readiness for providing veterinary medical response during an emergency or major disaster; and

(4) coordinate with the Department of Homeland Security, the Department of Health and Human Services, the Department of Agriculture, State, local, and Indian tribal governments (including departments of animal and human health), veterinary and health care professionals, and volunteers.

* * * * * * *

SEC. 1220. [42 U.S.C. 5189g note] UNIFIED FEDERAL ENVIRONMENTAL AND HISTORIC PRESERVATION REVIEW.

(a) REVIEW AND ANALYSIS.—Not later than 180 days after the date of enactment of this Act, the Administrator shall review the Unified Federal Environmental and Historic Preservation review process established pursuant to section 429 of the Robert T. Stafford Disaster Relief and Emergency Assistance Act (42 U.S.C. 5189g), and submit a report to the Committee on Transportation and Infrastructure of the House of Representatives and the Committee on Homeland Security and Governmental Affairs of the Senate that includes the following:

(1) An analysis of whether and how the unified process has expedited the interagency review process to ensure compliance with the environmental and

historic requirements under Federal law relating to disaster recovery projects.

(2)   A survey and analysis of categorical exclusions used by other Federal agencies that may be applicable to any activity related to a major disaster or emergency declared by the President under section 401 or 501, respectively, of the Robert T. Stafford Disaster Relief and Emergency Assistance Act (42 U.S.C. 5170, 5191).

(3)   Recommendations on any further actions, including any legislative proposals, needed to expedite and streamline the review process.

(b) REGULATIONS.— After completing the review, survey, and analyses under subsection (a), but not later than 2 years after the date of enactment of this Act, and after providing notice and opportunity for public comment, the Administrator shall issue regulations to implement any regulatory recommendations, including any categorical exclusions identified under subsection (a), to the extent that the categorical exclusions meet the criteria for a categorical exclusion under section 1508.4 of title 40, Code of Federal Regulations, and section II of DHS Instruction Manual 023-01-001-01.

SEC. 1221. CLOSEOUT INCENTIVES.

(a) FACILITATING CLOSEOUT.— Section 705 of the Robert T. Stafford Disaster Relief and Emergency Assistance Act (42 U.S.C. 5205) is amended by adding at the end the following:

"(d) FACILITATING CLOSEOUT.—

"(1)   INCENTIVES.— The Administrator of the Federal Emergency Management Agency may develop incentives and penalties that encourage State, local, or Indian tribal governments to close out expenditures and activities on a timely basis related to disaster or emergency assistance.

"(2)   AGENCY REQUIREMENTS.— The Federal Emergency Management Agency shall, consistent with applicable regulations and required procedures, meet its responsibilities to improve closeout practices and reduce the time to close disaster program awards.".

(b) [42 U.S.C. 5205 note] REGULATIONS.— The Administrator shall issue regulations to implement the amendment made by this section.

* * * * * * *

SEC. 1223. STUDY TO STREAMLINE AND CONSOLIDATE INFORMATION COLLECTION.

Not later than 1 year after the date of enactment of this Act, the Administrator—

(1)   in coordination with the Small Business Administration, the Department of Housing and Urban Development, the Disaster Assistance Working Group of the Council of the Inspectors General on Integrity and Efficiency, and other appropriate agencies, conduct a study and develop a plan, consistent with law, under which the collection of information from disaster assistance applicants and grantees will be modified, streamlined, expedited, efficient, flexible, consolidated, and simplified to be less burdensome, duplicative, and time consuming for applicants and grantees;

(2)   in coordination with the Small Business Administration, the Department of Housing and Urban Development, the Disaster Assistance Working Group of the

Council of the Inspectors General on Integrity and Efficiency, and other appropriate agencies, develop a plan for the regular collection and reporting of information on Federal disaster assistance awarded, including the establishment and maintenance of a website for presenting the information to the public; and

(3)   submit the plans developed under paragraphs (1) and (2) to the Committee on Transportation and Infrastructure of the House of Representatives and the Committee on Homeland Security and Governmental Affairs of the Senate.

* * * * * * *

SEC. 1225. [42 U.S.C. 5161a] AUDIT OF CONTRACTS.

Notwithstanding any other provision of law, the Administrator of the Federal Emergency Management Agency shall not reimburse a State or local government, an Indian tribal government (as defined in section 102 of the Robert T. Stafford Disaster Relief and Emergency Assistance Act (42 U.S.C. 5122), or the owner or operator of a private nonprofit facility (as defined in section 102 of the Robert T. Stafford Disaster Relief and Emergency Assistance Act (42 U.S.C. 5122) for any activities made pursuant to a contract entered into after August 1, 2017, that prohibits the Administrator or the Comptroller General of the United States from auditing or otherwise reviewing all aspects relating to the contract.

SEC. 1226. INSPECTOR GENERAL AUDIT OF FEMA CONTRACTS FOR TARPS AND PLASTIC SHEETING.

(a) IN GENERAL.— Not later than 30 days after the date of enactment of this Act, the Inspector General of the Department of Homeland Security shall initiate an audit of the contracts awarded by the Agency for tarps and plastic sheeting for the Commonwealth of Puerto Rico and the United States Virgin Islands in response to Hurricane Irma and Hurricane Maria.

(b) CONSIDERATIONS.—In carrying out the audit under subsection (a), the inspector general shall review—

(1)   the contracting process used by the Agency to evaluate offerors and award the relevant contracts to contractors;

(2)   the assessment conducted by the Agency of the past performance of the contractors, including any historical information showing that the contractors had supported large-scale delivery quantities in the past;

(3)   the assessment conducted by the Agency of the capacity of the contractors to carry out the relevant contracts, including with respect to inventory, production, and financial capabilities;

(4)   how the Agency ensured that the contractors met the terms of the relevant contracts; and

(5)   whether the failure of the contractors to meet the terms of the relevant contracts and the subsequent cancellation by the Agency of the relevant contracts affected the provision of tarps and plastic sheeting to the Commonwealth of Puerto Rico and the United States Virgin Islands.

(c) REPORT.— Not later than 270 days after the date of initiation of the audit under subsection (a), the inspector general shall submit to the Committee on Transportation and Infrastructure of the House of Representatives and the Committee on Homeland Security and Governmental Affairs of the Senate a report on the results of the audit, including findings and recommendations.

* * * * * * *

SEC. 1228. [42 U.S.C. 5172 note] GUIDANCE ON INUNDATED AND SUBMERGED ROADS.

The Administrator of the Federal Emergency Management Agency, in coordination with the Administrator of the Federal Highway Administration, shall develop and issue guidance for State, local, and Indian tribal governments regarding repair, restoration, and replacement of inundated and submerged roads damaged or destroyed by a major disaster, and for associated expenses incurred by the Government, with respect to roads eligible for assistance under section 406 of the Robert T. Stafford Disaster Relief and Emergency Assistance Act (42 U.S.C. 5172).

SEC. 1229. EXTENSION OF ASSISTANCE.

(a) IN GENERAL.— Notwithstanding any other provision of law, in the case of an individual eligible to receive unemployment assistance under section 410(a) of the Robert T. Stafford Disaster Relief and Emergency Assistance Act (42 U.S.C. 5177(a)) as a result of a disaster declaration made for Hurricane Irma and Hurricane Maria in the Commonwealth of Puerto Rico and the United States Virgin Islands, the President shall make such assistance available for 52 weeks after the date of the disaster declaration effective as if enacted at the time of the disaster declaration.

(b) NO ADDITIONAL FUNDS AUTHORIZED.— No additional funds are authorized to carry out the requirements of this section.

SEC. 1230. [42 U.S.C. 5172 note] GUIDANCE AND RECOMMENDATIONS.

(a) GUIDANCE.— The Administrator shall provide guidance to a common interest community that provides essential services of a governmental nature on actions that a common interest community may take in order to be eligible to receive reimbursement from a grantee that receives funds from the Agency for certain activities performed after an event that results in a major disaster declared by the President under section 401 of the Robert T. Stafford Disaster Relief and Emergency Assistance Act (42 U.S.C. 5170).

(b) RECOMMENDATIONS.— Not later than 90 days after the date of enactment of this Act, the Administrator shall provide to the Committee on Transportation and Infrastructure of the House of Representatives and the Committee on Homeland Security and Governmental Affairs of the Senate a legislative proposal on how to provide eligibility for disaster assistance with respect to common areas of condominiums and housing cooperatives.

(c) EFFECTIVE DATE.— This section shall be effective on the date of enactment of this Act.

SEC. 1231. [42 U.S.C. 5172 note] GUIDANCE ON HAZARD MITIGATION ASSISTANCE.

(a) IN GENERAL.—Not later than 180 days after the date of enactment of this Act, the

Administrator shall issue guidance regarding the acquisition of property for open space as a mitigation measure under section 404 of the Robert T. Stafford Disaster Relief and Emergency Assistance Act (42 U.S.C. 5170c) that includes—

(1) a process by which the State hazard mitigation officer appointed for such an acquisition shall, not later than 60 days after the applicant for assistance enters into an agreement with the Administrator regarding the acquisition, provide written notification to each affected unit of local government for such acquisition that includes—

(A) the location of the acquisition;

(B) the State-local assistance agreement for the hazard mitigation grant program;

(C) a description of the acquisition; and

(D) a copy of the deed restriction; and

(2) recommendations for entering into and implementing a memorandum of understanding between units of local government and covered entities that includes provisions to allow an affected unit of local government notified under paragraph (1) to—

(A) use and maintain the open space created by such a project, consistent with section 404 (including related regulations, standards, and guidance) and consistent with all adjoining property, subject to the notification of the adjoining property, so long as the cost of the maintenance is borne by the local government; and

(B) maintain the open space pursuant to standards exceeding any local government standards defined in the agreement with the Administrator described under paragraph (1).

(b) DEFINITIONS.—In this section:

(1) AFFECTED UNIT OF LOCAL GOVERNMENT.— The term affected unit of local government means any entity covered by the definition of local government in section 102 of the Robert T. Stafford Disaster Relief and Emergency Assistance Act (42 U.S.C. 5122), that has jurisdiction over the property subject to the acquisition described in subsection (a).

(2) COVERED ENTITY.—The term covered entity means—

(A) the grantee or subgrantee receiving assistance for an open space project described in subsection (a);

(B) the State in which such project is located; and

(C) the applicable Regional Administrator of the Agency.

SEC. 1232. [42 U.S.C. 5170 note] LOCAL IMPACT.

(a) IN GENERAL.— In making recommendations to the President regarding a major disaster declaration, the Administrator of the Federal Emergency Management Agency shall give greater consideration to severe local impact or recent multiple disasters. Further, the Administrator shall make corresponding adjustments to the Agency's policies and regulations regarding such consideration. Not later than 1 year after the date of enactment of this section, the Administrator shall report to the Committee on Transportation and Infrastructure of the House of Representatives and the Committee on Homeland Security and Governmental Affairs of the Senate on the changes made to regulations and policies and the number of declarations that have been declared based on the new criteria.

(b) EFFECTIVE DATE.— This section shall be effective on the date of enactment of this Act.

* * * * * * *

SEC. 1234. NATIONAL PUBLIC INFRASTRUCTURE PREDISASTER HAZARD MITIGATION.

* * * * * * *

(b) [42 U.S.C. 5133 note] APPLICABILITY.— The amendments made to section 203 of the Robert T. Stafford Disaster Relief and Emergency Assistance Act (42 U.S.C. 5133) by paragraphs (3) and (5) of subsection (a) shall apply to funds appropriated on or after the date of enactment of this Act.

(c) SENSE OF CONGRESS.—It is the sense of Congress that—

(1) all funding expended from the National Public Infrastructure Predisaster Mitigation Assistance created by Section 203(i)(1) of the Robert T. Stafford Disaster Relief and Emergency Assistance Act (42 U.S.C. 5133), as added by this section, shall not be considered part of FEMA's regular appropriations for non-Stafford activities, also known as the Federal Emergency Management Agency's Disaster Relief Fund base; and

(2) the President should have the funds related to the National Public Infrastructure Predisaster Mitigation Assistance created by Section 203(i)(1) of the Robert T. Stafford Disaster Relief and Emergency Assistance Act (42 U.S.C. 5133), as added by this section, identified in and allocated from the Federal Emergency Management Agency's Disaster Relief Fund for major disasters declared pursuant to the Robert T. Stafford Disaster Relief and Emergency Assistance Act (42 U.S.C. 5121 et seq.).

(d) [42 U.S.C. 5133 note] SUNSET.— On the date that is 5 years after the date of enactment of this Act, section 203 of the Robert T. Stafford Disaster Relief and Emergency Assistance Act (42 U.S.C. 5133) is amended by striking subsection (m), as added by subsection (a)(8) of this section.

* * * * * * *

SEC. 1236. [42 U.S.C. 5196g] GUIDANCE AND TRAINING BY FEMA ON COORDINATION OF EMERGENCY RESPONSE PLANS.

(a) TRAINING REQUIREMENT.—The Administrator, in coordination with other relevant agencies, shall provide guidance and training on an annual basis to State, local, and Indian tribal governments, first responders, and facilities that store hazardous materials on coordination of emergency response plans in the event of a major disaster or emergency, including severe weather events. The guidance and training shall include the following:

(1)   Providing a list of equipment required in the event a hazardous substance is released into the environment.

(2)   Outlining the health risks associated with exposure to hazardous substances to improve treatment response.

(3)   Publishing best practices for mitigating further danger to communities from hazardous substances.

(b) IMPLEMENTATION.— The requirement of subsection (a) shall be implemented not later than 180 days after the date of enactment of this Act.

SEC. 1237. [42 U.S.C. 5205a] CERTAIN RECOUPMENT PROHIBITED.

(a) IN GENERAL.— Notwithstanding any other provision of law, the Agency shall deem any covered disaster assistance to have been properly procured, provided, and utilized, and shall restore any funding of covered disaster assistance previously provided but subsequently withdrawn or deobligated.

(b) COVERED DISASTER ASSISTANCE DEFINED.—In this section, the term covered disaster assistance means assistance—

(1)   provided to a local government pursuant to section 403, 406, or 407 of the Robert T. Stafford Disaster Relief and Emergency Assistance Act (42 U.S.C. 5170b, 5172, or 5173); and

(2)   with respect to which the inspector general of the Department of Homeland Security has determined, after an audit, that—

(A)   the Agency deployed to the local government a Technical Assistance Contractor to review field operations, provide eligibility advice, and assist with day-to-day decisions;

(B)   the Technical Assistance Contractor provided inaccurate information to the local government; and

(C)   the local government relied on the inaccurate information to determine that relevant contracts were eligible, reasonable, and reimbursable.

(c) EFFECTIVE DATE.— This section shall be effective on the date of enactment of this Act.

SEC. 1238. FEDERAL ASSISTANCE TO INDIVIDUALS AND HOUSEHOLDS AND NONPROFIT FACILITIES.

(a) [42 U.S.C. 5174b] CRITICAL DOCUMENT FEE WAIVER.—

(1) IN GENERAL.—Notwithstanding section 1 of the Passport Act of June 4, 1920 (22 U.S.C. 214) or any other provision of law, the President, in consultation with the Governor of a State, may provide a waiver under this subsection to an individual or household described in section 408(e)(1) of the Robert T. Stafford Disaster Relief and Emergency Assistance Act (42 U.S.C. 5174(e)(1)) for the following document replacement fees:

(A)   The passport application fee for individuals who lost their United States passport in a major disaster within the preceding three calendar years.

(B)   The file search fee for a United States passport.

(C)   The Application for Waiver of Passport and/or Visa form (Form I-193) fee.

(D)   The Permanent Resident Card replacement form (Form I-90) filing fee.

(E)   The Declaration of Intention form (Form N-300) filing fee.

(F)   The Naturalization/Citizenship Document replacement form (Form N-565) filing fee.

(G)   The Employment Authorization form (Form I-765) filing fee.

(H)   The biometric service fee.

(2) EXEMPTION FROM FORM REQUIREMENT.— The authority of the President to waive fees under subparagraphs (C) through (H) of paragraph (1) applies regardless of whether the individual or household qualifies for a Form I-912 Request for Fee Waiver, or any successor thereto.

(3) EXEMPTION FROM ASSISTANCE MAXIMUM.— The assistance limit in section 408(h) of the Robert T. Stafford Disaster Relief and Emergency Assistance Act (42 U.S.C. 5174(h)) shall not apply to any fee waived under this subsection.

(4) REPORT.— Not later than 365 days after the date of enactment of this subsection, the Administrator and the head of any other agency given critical document fee waiver authority under this subsection shall submit a report to the Committee on Homeland Security and Governmental Affairs of the Senate and the Committee on Transportation and Infrastructure of the House of Representatives on the costs associated with providing critical document fee waivers as described in paragraph (1).

(b) FEDERAL ASSISTANCE TO PRIVATE NONPROFIT CHILDCARE FACILITIES.—Section 102(11)(A) of the Robert T. Stafford Disaster Relief and Emergency Assistance Act (42 U.S.C. 5122(11)(A)) is amended—

(1)   in the second subparagraph (A) (as added by Public Law 115-123), by inserting center-based childcare, after facility),; and

(2)   in the first subparagraph (A), by striking (a) in general.—The term 'private nonprofit facility' means private nonprofit educational, utility and all that follows through President..

(c) [42 U.S.C. 5122 note] APPLICABILITY.— The amendment made by subsection (b)(1) shall apply to any major disaster or emergency declared by the President under section 401 or 501, respectively, of the Robert T. Stafford Disaster Relief and Emergency Assistance Act (42 U.S.C. 5170, 5191) on or after the date of enactment of this Act.

SEC. 1239. [42 U.S.C. 5170 note] COST OF ASSISTANCE ESTIMATES.

(a) IN GENERAL.— Not later than 270 days after the date of enactment of this Act, the Administrator shall review the factors considered when evaluating a request for a major disaster declaration under the Robert T. Stafford Disaster Relief and Emergency Assistance Act (42 U.S.C. 5121 et seq.), specifically the estimated cost of the assistance, and provide a report and briefing to the Committee on Homeland Security and Governmental Affairs of the Senate and the Committee on Transportation and

Infrastructure of the House of Representatives.

(b) RULEMAKING.— Not later than 2 years after the date of enactment of this Act, the Administrator shall review and initiate a rulemaking to update the factors considered when evaluating a Governor's request for a major disaster declaration, including reviewing how the Agency estimates the cost of major disaster assistance, and consider other impacts on the capacity of a jurisdiction to respond to disasters. In determining the capacity of a jurisdiction to respond to disasters, and prior to the issuance of such a rule, the Administrator shall engage in meaningful consultation with relevant representatives of State, regional, local, and Indian tribal government stakeholders.

SEC. 1240. REPORT ON INSURANCE SHORTFALLS.

Not later than 2 years after the date of enactment of this section, and each year thereafter until 2023, the Administrator of the Federal Emergency Management Agency shall submit a report to Congress on the number of instances and the estimated amounts involved, by State, for cases in which self-insurance amounts have been insufficient to address flood damages.

SEC. 1241. [42 U.S.C. 5172 note] POST DISASTER BUILDING SAFETY ASSESSMENT.

(a) BUILDING SAFETY ASSESSMENT TEAM.—

(1) IN GENERAL.— The Administrator shall coordinate with State and local governments and organizations representing design professionals, such as architects and engineers, to develop guidance, including best practices, for post-disaster assessment of buildings by licensed architects and engineers to ensure the design professionals properly analyze the structural integrity and livability of buildings and structures.

(2) PUBLICATION.— The Administrator shall publish the guidance required to be developed under paragraph (1) not later than 1 year after the date of enactment of this Act.

(b) NATIONAL INCIDENT MANAGEMENT SYSTEM.— The Administrator shall revise or issue guidance as required to the National Incident Management System Resource Management component to ensure the functions of post-disaster building safety assessment, such as those functions performed by design professionals are accurately resource typed within the National Incident Management System.

(c) EFFECTIVE DATE.— This section shall be effective on the date of enactment of this Act.

SEC. 1242. FEMA UPDATES ON NATIONAL PREPAREDNESS ASSESSMENT.

Not later than 6 months after the date of enactment of this Act, and every 6 months thereafter until completion, the Administrator shall submit to the Committee on Homeland Security and Governmental Affairs of the Senate and the Committees on Transportation and Infrastructure and Homeland Security of the House of Representatives an update on the progress of the Agency in completing action 6 with respect to the report published by the Government Accountability Office entitled 2012 Annual Report: Opportunities to Reduce Duplication, Overlap and Fragmentation, Achieve Savings, and Enhance Revenue (February 28, 2012), which recommends the Agency to—

(1)   complete a national preparedness assessment of capability gaps at each level based on tiered, capability-specific performance objectives to enable prioritization of grant funding; and

(2)   identify the potential costs for establishing and maintaining those capabilities at each level and determine what capabilities Federal agencies should provide.

SEC. 1243. FEMA REPORT ON DUPLICATION IN NON-NATURAL DISASTER PREPAREDNESS GRANT PROGRAMS.

Not later than 180 days after the date of enactment of this Act, the Administrator shall submit to the Committees on Homeland Security and Governmental Affairs of the Senate and the Committees on Transportation and Infrastructure and Homeland Security of the House of Representatives a report on the results of the efforts of the Agency to identify and prevent unnecessary duplication within and across the non-natural disaster preparedness grant programs of the Agency, as recommended in the report published by the Government Accountability Office entitled 2012 Annual Report: Opportunities to Reduce Duplication, Overlap and Fragmentation, Achieve Savings, and Enhance Revenue (February 28, 2012), including with respect to—

(1)   the Urban Area Security Initiative established under section 2003 of the Homeland Security Act of 2002 (6 U.S.C. 604);

(2)   the Port Security Grant Program authorized under section 70107 of title 46, United States Code;

(3)   the State Homeland Security Grant Program established under section 2004 of the Homeland Security Act of 2002 (6 U.S.C. 605); and

(4)   the Transit Security Grant Program authorized under titles XIV and XV of the Implementing Recommendations of the 9/11 Commission Act of 2007 (6 U.S.C. 1131 et seq.).

SEC. 1244. STUDY AND REPORT.

(a) IN GENERAL.— Not later than 90 days after the date of enactment of this Act, the Administrator shall enter into a contract with the National Academy of Medicine to conduct a study and prepare a report as described in subsection (b).

(b) STUDY AND REPORT.—

(1) STUDY.—

(A) IN GENERAL.— The study described in this subsection shall be a study of matters concerning best practices in mortality counts as a result of a major disaster (as defined in section 102 of the Robert T. Stafford Disaster Relief and Emergency Assistance Act (42 U.S.C. 5122)).

(B) CONTENTS.—The study described in this subsection shall address approaches to quantifying mortality and significant morbidity among populations affected by major disasters, which shall include best practices and policy recommendations for—

(i)   equitable and timely attribution, in order to facilitate access to available benefits, among other things;

(ii) timely prospective tracking of population levels of mortality and significant morbidity, and their causes, in order to continuously inform response efforts; and

(iii) a retrospective study of disaster-related mortality and significant morbidity to inform after-action analysis and improve subsequent preparedness efforts.

(2) REPORT.— Not later than 2 years after the date on which the contract described in subsection (a) is entered into, the National Academy of Medicine shall complete and transmit to the Administrator a report on the study described in paragraph (1).

(c) NO ADDITIONAL FUNDS AUTHORIZED.— No additional funds are authorized to carry out the requirements of this section.

SEC. 1245. [42 U.S.C. 5172 note] REVIEW OF ASSISTANCE FOR DAMAGED UNDERGROUND WATER INFRASTRUCTURE.

(a) DEFINITION OF PUBLIC ASSISTANCE GRANT PROGRAM.— The term public assistance grant program means the public assistance grant program authorized under sections 403, 406, 407, 428, and 502(a) of the Robert T. Stafford Disaster Relief and Emergency Assistance Act (42 U.S.C. 5170b, 5172, 5173, 5192(a)).

(b) REVIEW AND BRIEFING.—Not later than 60 days after the date of enactment of this Act, the Administrator shall—

(1) conduct a review of the assessment and eligibility process under the public assistance grant program with respect to assistance provided for damaged underground water infrastructure as a result of a major disaster declared under section 401 of such Act (42 U.S.C. 5170), including wildfires, and shall include the extent to which local technical memoranda, prepared by a local unit of government in consultation with the relevant State or Federal agencies, identified damaged underground water infrastructure that should be eligible for the public assistance grant program; and

(2) provide to the Committee on Homeland Security and Governmental Affairs of the Senate and the Committee on Transportation and Infrastructure of the House of Representatives a briefing on the review conducted under paragraph (1).

(c) REPORT AND RECOMMENDATIONS.—The Administrator shall—

(1) not later than 180 days after the date of enactment of this Act, issue a report on the review conducted under subsection (b)(1); and

(2) not later than 180 days after the date on which the Administrator issues the report required under paragraph (1), initiate a rulemaking, if appropriate, to address any recommendations contained in the report.

SEC. 1246. EXTENSION.

The Administrator shall extend the deadlines to implement the reasonable and prudent alternative outlined in the jeopardy biological opinion dated April 14, 2016, by up to 3 years from the date of enactment of this Act. Within 18 months from the date of enactment of this Act, the Administrator shall submit to the Committee on

Homeland Security and Governmental Affairs, the Committee on Banking, Housing, and Urban Affairs, and the Committee on Environment and Public Works of the Senate; and the Committee on Homeland Security, the Committee on Natural Resources, and the Committee on Transportation and Infrastructure of the House of Representatives a report on the status of implementing these reasonable and prudent alternatives.

★

SECTION 20017(B) OF MAP–21

PUBLIC LAW 112–141
AS AMENDED THROUGH PUB. L. 117–81

Moving Ahead for Progress in the 21st Century Act

(MAP-21)

[(Public Law 112–141)]

[As Amended Through P.L. 117–58, Enacted November 15, 2021]

AN ACT Moving Ahead for Progress in the 21st Century Act

Be it enacted by the Senate and House of Representatives of the United States of America in Congress assembled,

SECTION 1. SHORT TITLE; ORGANIZATION OF ACT INTO DIVISIONS; TABLE OF CONTENTS.

(a) [23 U.S.C. 101 note] SHORT TITLE.— This Act may be cited as the "Moving Ahead for Progress in the 21st Century Act" or the "MAP-21".

* * * * * * *

DIVISION B—PUBLIC TRANSPORTATION

* * * * * * *

SEC. 20017. PUBLIC TRANSPORTATION EMERGENCY RELIEF PROGRAM.

* * * * * * *

(b) [49 U.S.C. 5324 note] MEMORANDUM OF AGREEMENT.—

(1) PURPOSES.—The purposes of this subsection are—

(A) to improve coordination between the Department of Transportation and the Department of Homeland Security; and

(B) to expedite the provision of Federal assistance for public transportation systems for activities relating to a major disaster or emergency declared by the President under the Robert T. Stafford Disaster Relief and Emergency Assistance Act (42 U.S.C. 5121 et seq.) (referred to in this subsection as a major disaster or emergency).

(2) AGREEMENT.— Not later than 180 days after the date of enactment of this Act, the Secretary of Transportation and the Secretary of Homeland Security shall enter into a memorandum of agreement to coordinate the roles and responsibilities

of the Department of Transportation and the Department of Homeland Security in providing assistance for public transportation, including the provision of public transportation services and the repair and restoration of public transportation systems in areas for which the President has declared a major disaster or emergency.

(3) CONTENTS OF AGREEMENT.—The memorandum of agreement required under paragraph (2) shall—

(A)   provide for improved coordination and expeditious use of public transportation, as appropriate, in response to and recovery from a major disaster or emergency;

(B) establish procedures to address—

(i)   issues that have contributed to delays in the reimbursement of eligible transportation-related expenses relating to a major disaster or emergency;

(ii)   any challenges identified in the review under paragraph (4); and

(iii)   the coordination of assistance for public transportation provided under the Robert T. Stafford Disaster Relief and Emergency Assistance Act and section 5324 of title 49, United States Code, as amended by this Act, as appropriate; and

(C) provide for the development and distribution of clear guidelines for State, local, and tribal governments, including public transportation systems, relating to—

(i) assistance available for public transportation systems for activities relating to a major disaster or emergency—

(I)   under the Robert T. Stafford Disaster Relief and Emergency Assistance Act;

(II)   under section 5324 of title 49, United States Code, as amended by this Act; and

(III)   from other sources, including other Federal agencies; and

(ii) reimbursement procedures that speed the process of—

(I)   applying for assistance under the Robert T. Stafford Disaster Relief and Emergency Assistance Act and section 5324 of title 49, United States Code, as amended by this Act; and

(II)   distributing assistance for public transportation systems under the Robert T. Stafford Disaster Relief and Emergency Assistance Act and section 5324 of title 49, United States Code, as amended by this Act.

(4) AFTER ACTION REVIEW.—   Before entering into a memorandum of agreement under paragraph (2), the Secretary of Transportation and the Secretary of Homeland Security (acting through the Administrator of the Federal Emergency Management Agency), in consultation with State, local, and tribal governments (including public transportation systems) that have experienced a major disaster or emergency, shall review after action reports relating to major disasters, emergencies, and exercises, to identify areas where coordination between the Department of Transportation and

the Department of Homeland Security and the provision of public transportation services should be improved.

(5) FACTORS FOR DECLARATIONS OF MAJOR DISASTERS AND EMERGENCIES.— The Administrator of the Federal Emergency Management Agency shall make available to State, local, and tribal governments, including public transportation systems, a description of the factors that the President considers in declaring a major disaster or emergency, including any pre-disaster emergency declaration policies.

(6) BRIEFINGS.—

(A) INITIAL BRIEFING.— Not later than 180 days after the date of enactment of this Act, the Secretary of Transportation and the Secretary of Homeland Security shall jointly brief the Committee on Banking, Housing, and Urban Affairs and the Committee on Homeland Security and Governmental Affairs of the Senate on the memorandum of agreement required under paragraph (2).

(B) QUARTERLY BRIEFINGS.— Each quarter of the 1-year period beginning on the date on which the Secretary of Transportation and the Secretary of Homeland Security enter into the memorandum of agreement required under paragraph (2), the Secretary of Transportation and the Secretary of Homeland Security shall jointly brief the Committee on Banking, Housing, and Urban Affairs and the Committee on Homeland Security and Governmental Affairs of the Senate on the implementation of the memorandum of agreement.

★

23 U.S.C. §125–EMERGENCY RELIEF

AS AMENDED THROUGH PUB. L. 117–58

TITLE 23—HIGHWAYS

This title was enacted by Pub. L. 85–767, §1, Aug. 27, 1958, 72 Stat. 885

* * * * * * *

CHAPTER 1—FEDERAL-AID HIGHWAYS

* * * * * * *

§125. EMERGENCY RELIEF

(a) IN GENERAL.—Subject to this section and section 120, an emergency fund is authorized for expenditure by the Secretary for the repair or reconstruction of highways, roads, and trails, in any area of the United States, including Indian reservations, that the Secretary finds have suffered serious damage as a result of—

(1) a natural disaster over a wide area, such as by a flood, hurricane, tidal wave, earthquake, severe storm, wildfire, or landslide; or

(2) catastrophic failure from any external cause.

(b) RESTRICTION ON ELIGIBILITY.—Funds under this section shall not be used for the repair or reconstruction of a bridge that has been permanently closed to all vehicular traffic by the State or responsible local official because of imminent danger of collapse due to a structural deficiency or physical deterioration.

(c) FUNDING.—

(1) IN GENERAL.—Subject to the limitations described in paragraph (2), there are authorized to be appropriated from the Highway Trust Fund (other than the Mass Transit Account) such sums as are necessary to establish the fund authorized by this section and to replenish that fund on an annual basis.

(2) LIMITATIONS.—The limitations referred to in paragraph (1) are that—

(A) not more than $100,000,000 is authorized to be obligated in any 1 fiscal year commencing after September 30, 1980, to carry out this section, except that, if for any fiscal year the total of all obligations under this section is less than the amount authorized to be obligated for the fiscal year, the unobligated balance of that amount shall—

(i) remain available until expended; and

(ii) be in addition to amounts otherwise available to carry out this section for each year; and

(B)(i) pending such appropriation or replenishment, the Secretary may obligate from any funds appropriated at any time for obligation in accordance with this title, including existing Federal-aid appropriations, such sums as are necessary for the immediate prosecution of the work herein authorized; and

(ii) funds obligated under this subparagraph shall be reimbursed from the appropriation or replenishment.

(d) ELIGIBILITY.—

(1) IN GENERAL.—The Secretary may expend funds from the emergency fund authorized by this section only for the repair or reconstruction of highways on Federal-aid highways in accordance with this chapter, except that—

(A) no funds shall be so expended unless an emergency has been declared by the Governor of the State with concurrence by the Secretary, unless the President has declared the emergency to be a major disaster for the purposes of the Robert T. Stafford Disaster Relief and Emergency Assistance Act (42 U.S.C. 5121 et seq.) for which concurrence of the Secretary is not required; and

(B) the Secretary has received an application from the State transportation department that includes a comprehensive list of all eligible project sites and repair costs by not later than 2 years after the natural disaster or catastrophic failure.

(2) COST LIMITATION.—

(A) DEFINITION OF COMPARABLE FACILITY.—In this paragraph, the term "comparable facility" means a facility that—

(i) meets the current geometric and construction standards required for the types and volume of traffic that the facility will carry over its design life; and

(ii) incorporates economically justifiable improvements that will mitigate the risk of recurring damage from extreme weather, flooding, and other natural disasters.

(B) LIMITATION.—The total cost of a project funded under this section may not exceed the cost of repair or reconstruction of a comparable facility.

(3) PROTECTIVE FEATURES.—

(A) IN GENERAL.—The cost of an improvement that is part of a project under this section shall be an eligible expense under this section if the improvement is a protective feature that will mitigate the risk of recurring damage or the cost of future repair from extreme weather, flooding, and other natural disasters.

(B) PROTECTIVE FEATURES DESCRIBED.—A protective feature referred to in subparagraph (A) includes—

(i) raising roadway grades;

(ii) relocating roadways in a floodplain to higher ground above projected flood elevation levels or away from slide prone areas;

(iii) stabilizing slide areas;

(iv) stabilizing slopes;

(v) lengthening or raising bridges to increase waterway openings;

(vi) increasing the size or number of drainage structures;

(vii) replacing culverts with bridges or upsizing culverts;

(viii) installing seismic retrofits on bridges;

(ix) adding scour protection at bridges, installing riprap, or adding other scour, stream stability, coastal, or other hydraulic countermeasures, including spur dikes; and

(x) the use of natural infrastructure to mitigate the risk of recurring damage or the cost of future repair from extreme weather, flooding, and other natural disasters.

(4) DEBRIS REMOVAL.—The costs of debris removal shall be an eligible expense under this section only for—

(A) an event not declared a major disaster or emergency by the President under the Robert T. Stafford Disaster Relief and Emergency Assistance Act (42 U.S.C. 5121 et seq.);

(B) an event declared a major disaster or emergency by the President under that Act if the debris removal is not eligible for assistance under section 403, 407, or 502 of that Act (42 U.S.C. 5170b, 5173, 5192); or

(C) projects eligible for assistance under this section located on tribal transportation facilities, Federal lands transportation facilities, or other federally owned roads that are open to public travel (as defined in subsection (e)(1)).

(5) SUBSTITUTE TRAFFIC.—Notwithstanding any other provision of this section, actual and necessary costs of maintenance and operation of ferryboats or additional transit service providing temporary substitute highway traffic service, less the amount of fares charged for comparable service, may be expended from the emergency fund authorized by this section for Federal-aid highways.

(e) TRIBAL TRANSPORTATION FACILITIES, FEDERAL LANDS TRANSPORTATION FACILITIES, AND PUBLIC ROADS ON FEDERAL LANDS.—

(1) DEFINITIONS.—In this subsection, the following definitions apply:

(A) OPEN TO PUBLIC TRAVEL.—The term "open to public travel" means, with respect to a road, that, except during scheduled periods, extreme weather conditions, or emergencies, the road—

(i) is maintained;

(ii) is open to the general public; and

(iii) can accommodate travel by a standard passenger vehicle, without restrictive gates or prohibitive signs or regulations, other than for general traffic control or restrictions based on size, weight, or class of registration.

(B) STANDARD PASSENGER VEHICLE.—The term "standard passenger vehicle" means a vehicle with 6 inches of clearance from the lowest point of the frame, body, suspension, or differential to the ground.

(2) EXPENDITURE OF FUNDS.—Notwithstanding subsection (d)(1), the Secretary may expend funds from the emergency fund authorized by this section, independently or in cooperation with any other branch of the Federal Government, a State agency, a tribal government, an organization, or a person, for the repair or reconstruction of tribal transportation facilities, Federal lands transportation facilities, and other federally owned roads that are open to public travel, whether or not those facilities are Federal-aid highways.

(3) REIMBURSEMENT.—

(A) IN GENERAL.—The Secretary may reimburse Federal and State agencies (including political subdivisions) for expenditures made for projects determined eligible under this section, including expenditures for emergency repairs made before a determination of eligibility.

(B) TRANSFERS.—With respect to reimbursements described in subparagraph (A)—

(i) those reimbursements to Federal agencies and Indian tribal governments shall be transferred to the account from which the expenditure was made, or to a similar account that remains available for obligation; and

(ii) the budget authority associated with the expenditure shall be restored to the agency from which the authority was derived and shall be available for obligation until the end of the fiscal year following the year in which the transfer occurs.

(f) TREATMENT OF TERRITORIES.—For purposes of this section, the Virgin Islands, Guam, American Samoa, and the Commonwealth of the Northern Mariana Islands shall be considered to be States and parts of the United States, and the chief executive officer of each such territory shall be considered to be a Governor of a State.

(g) PROTECTING PUBLIC SAFETY AND MAINTAINING ROADWAYS.—The Secretary may use not more than 5 percent of amounts from the emergency fund authorized by this section to carry out projects that the Secretary determines are necessary to protect the public safety or to maintain or protect roadways that are included within the scope of an emergency declaration by the Governor of the State or by the President, in accordance with this section, and the Governor deems to be an ongoing concern in order to maintain vehicular traffic on the roadway.

(Pub. L. 85–767, Aug. 27, 1958, 72 Stat. 901; Pub. L. 86–342, title I, §107(a), Sept. 21, 1959, 73 Stat. 612; Pub. L. 89–574, §9(b), (c), Sept. 13, 1966, 80 Stat. 769; Pub. L. 90–495, §27(a), Aug. 23, 1968, 82 Stat. 829; Pub. L. 91–605, title I, §109(a), Dec. 31, 1970, 84 Stat. 1718; Pub. L. 92–361, Aug. 3, 1972, 86 Stat. 503; Pub. L. 94–280, title I, §119, May 5, 1976, 90 Stat. 437; Pub. L. 95–599, title I, §119, Nov. 6, 1978, 92 Stat. 2700; Pub. L. 96–106, §19, Nov. 9, 1979, 93 Stat. 799; Pub. L. 97–424, title I, §153(a), (c), (d), (h), Jan. 6, 1983, 96 Stat. 2132, 2133; Pub. L. 99–190, §101(e) [title III, §334], Dec. 19, 1985, 99 Stat. 1267, 1290; Pub. L. 99–272, title IV, §4103, Apr. 7, 1986, 100 Stat. 114; Pub. L. 100–17, title I, §§118(a)(1), (b)(1), (2), 133(b)(9), Apr. 2, 1987, 101 Stat. 156, 171; Pub. L. 100–707, §109(k), Nov. 23, 1988, 102 Stat. 4709; Pub. L. 102–240, title I, §1022(b), Dec. 18, 1991, 105 Stat. 1951; Pub. L. 102–302, §101, June 22, 1992, 106 Stat. 252; Pub. L. 105–178, title I, §§1113(b), 1212(a)(2)(A)(i), June 9, 1998, 112 Stat. 151, 193; Pub. L. 112–141, div. A, title I, §1107, July 6, 2012, 126 Stat. 437; Pub. L. 114–94, div. A, title I, §1107, Dec. 4, 2015, 129 Stat. 1337; Pub. L. 116–94, div. H, title I, §127, Dec. 20, 2019, 133 Stat. 2953; Pub. L. 117–58, div. A, title I, §11106, Nov. 15, 2021, 135 Stat. 458.)

PUBLIC TRANSPORTATION EMERGENCY RELIEF PROGRAM PROVISIONS

49 U.S.C. §5324
AS AMENDED THROUGH PUB. L. 117–158

TITLE 49—TRANSPORTATION

This title was enacted by Pub. L. 95–473, §1, Oct. 17, 1978, 92 Stat. 1337; Pub. L. 97–449, §1, Jan. 12, 1983, 96 Stat. 2413; Pub. L. 103–272, July 5, 1994, 108 Stat. 745

* * * * * * *

SUBTITLE III—GENERAL AND INTERMODAL PROGRAMS

* * * * * * *

CHAPTER 53—PUBLIC TRANSPORTATION

* * * * * * *

§5324. PUBLIC TRANSPORTATION EMERGENCY RELIEF PROGRAM

(a) DEFINITION.—In this section the following definitions shall apply:

(1) ELIGIBLE OPERATING COSTS.—The term "eligible operating costs" means costs relating to—

(A) evacuation services;

(B) rescue operations;

(C) temporary public transportation service; or

(D) reestablishing, expanding, or relocating public transportation route service before, during, or after an emergency.

(2) EMERGENCY.—The term "emergency" means a natural disaster affecting a wide area (such as a flood, hurricane, tidal wave, earthquake, severe storm, or landslide) or a catastrophic failure from any external cause, as a result of which—

(A) the Governor of a State has declared an emergency and the Secretary has concurred; or

(B) the President has declared a major disaster under section 401 of the Robert T. Stafford Disaster Relief and Emergency Assistance Act (42 U.S.C. 5170).

(b) GENERAL AUTHORITY.—The Secretary may make grants and enter into contracts and other agreements (including agreements with departments, agencies, and instrumentalities of the Government) for—

(1) capital projects to protect, repair, reconstruct, or replace equipment and

facilities of a public transportation system operating in the United States or on an Indian reservation that the Secretary determines is in danger of suffering serious damage, or has suffered serious damage, as a result of an emergency; and

(2) eligible operating costs of public transportation equipment and facilities in an area directly affected by an emergency during—

    (A) the 1-year period beginning on the date of a declaration described in subsection (a)(2); or

    (B) if the Secretary determines there is a compelling need, the 2-year period beginning on the date of a declaration described in subsection (a)(2).

(c) COORDINATION OF EMERGENCY FUNDS.—

    (1) USE OF FUNDS.—Funds appropriated to carry out this section shall be in addition to any other funds available under this chapter.

    (2) NO EFFECT ON OTHER GOVERNMENT ACTIVITY.—The provision of funds under this section shall not affect the ability of any other agency of the Government, including the Federal Emergency Management Agency, or a State agency, a local governmental entity, organization, or person, to provide any other funds otherwise authorized by law.

    (3) NOTIFICATION.—The Secretary shall notify the Secretary of Homeland Security of the purpose and amount of any grant made or contract or other agreement entered into under this section.

(d) GRANT REQUIREMENTS.—A grant awarded under this section or under section 5307 or 5311 that is made to address an emergency defined under subsection (a)(2) shall be—

    (1) subject to the terms and conditions the Secretary determines are necessary; and

    (2) made only for expenses that are not reimbursed under the Robert T. Stafford Disaster Relief and Emergency Assistance Act (42 U.S.C. 5121 et seq.).

(e) GOVERNMENT SHARE OF COSTS.—

    (1) CAPITAL PROJECTS AND OPERATING ASSISTANCE.—A grant, contract, or other agreement for a capital project or eligible operating costs under this section shall be, at the option of the recipient, for not more than 80 percent of the net project cost, as determined by the Secretary.

    (2) NON-FEDERAL SHARE.—The remainder of the net project cost may be provided from an undistributed cash surplus, a replacement or depreciation cash fund or reserve, or new capital.

    (3) WAIVER.—The Secretary may waive, in whole or part, the non-Federal share required under—

        (A) paragraph (2); or

        (B) section 5307 or 5311, in the case of a grant made available under section 5307 or 5311, respectively, to address an emergency.

(f) INSURANCE.—Before receiving a grant under this section following an emergency, an applicant shall—

    (1) submit to the Secretary documentation demonstrating proof of insurance required under Federal law for all structures related to the grant application; and

    (2) certify to the Secretary that the applicant has insurance required under State law for all structures related to the grant application.

(Pub. L. 103–272, §1(d), July 5, 1994, 108 Stat. 824; Pub. L. 109–59, title III, §3024(a), Aug. 10, 2005, 119 Stat. 1619; Pub. L. 112–141, div. B, §20017(a), July 6, 2012, 126 Stat. 703; Pub. L. 117–58, div. C, §30011, Nov. 15, 2021, 135 Stat. 904.)

NATIONAL SECURITY AND DEFENSE AUTHORITIES

THE DEFENSE PRODUCTION ACT OF 1950

ACT OF SEPTEMBER 8, 1950
AS AMENDED THROUGH PUB. L. 118–31

THE DEFENSE PRODUCTION ACT OF 1950[1]

[Chapter 922; 64 Stat. 798; 50 U.S.C. 4501 et seq.]

[As Amended Through P.L. 118–31, Enacted December 22, 2023]

AN ACT To establish a system of priorities and allocations for materials and facilities, authorize the requisitioning thereof, provide financial assistance for expansion of productive capacity and supply, provide for price and wage stabilization, provide for the settlement of labor disputes, strengthen controls over credit, and by these measures facilitate the production of goods and services necessary for the national security, and for other purposes.

Be it enacted by the Senate and House of Representatives of the United States of America in Congress assembled,

That this Act, divided into titles, may be cited as "the Defense Production Act of 1950."

TABLE OF CONTENTS

---

[2] Authority to condemn added July 31, 1951; title terminated at the close of June 30, 1953. Section 2(a)(2) of Public Law 111–67 repeals title II without striking such item in the table of contents.

---

[3] Authority terminated at the close of April 30, 1953. Section 2(a)(2) of Public Law 111–67 repeals titles IV and V without striking such item in the table of contents.

---

[4] Control of consumer credit terminated June 30, 1952. Control of real estate credit terminated at the close of June 30, 1953. Section 2(a)(2) of Public Law 111–67 repeals title VI without striking such item in the table of contents.

Title VII. General provisions.

---

¹ The Defense Production Act of 1950 was originally enacted by Public Law 774, 81st Cong., 64 Stat. 798, Sept. 8, 1950, 50 U.S.C. App. Secs. 2061–2166.

[50 U.S.C. 4501]

SEC. 2. DECLARATION OF POLICY.

(a) FINDINGS.—Congress finds that—

(1) the security of the United States is dependent on the ability of the domestic industrial base to supply materials and services for the national defense and to prepare for and respond to military conflicts, natural or man-caused disasters, or acts of terrorism within the United States;

(2) to ensure the vitality of the domestic industrial base, actions are needed—

(A) to promote industrial resources preparedness in the event of domestic or foreign threats to the security of the United States;

(B) to support continuing improvements in industrial efficiency and responsiveness;

(C) to provide for the protection and restoration of domestic critical infrastructure operations under emergency conditions; and

(D) to respond to actions taken outside of the United States that could result in reduced supplies of strategic and critical materials, including energy, necessary for national defense and the general economic well-being of the United States;

(3) in order to provide for the national security, the national defense preparedness effort of the United States Government requires—

(A) preparedness programs to respond to both domestic emergencies and international threats to national defense;

(B) measures to improve the domestic industrial base for national defense;

(C) the development of domestic productive capacity to meet—

(i) essential national defense needs that can result from emergency conditions; and

(ii) unique technological requirements; and

(D) the diversion of certain materials and facilities from ordinary use to national defense purposes, when national defense needs cannot otherwise be satisfied in a timely fashion;

(4) to meet the requirements referred to in this subsection, this Act provides the President with an array of authorities to shape national defense preparedness programs and to take appropriate steps to maintain and enhance the domestic industrial base;

(5) in order to ensure national defense preparedness, it is necessary and appropriate to assure the availability of domestic energy supplies for national

defense needs;

(6) to further assure the adequate maintenance of the domestic industrial base, to the maximum extent possible, domestic energy supplies should be augmented through reliance on renewable energy sources (including solar, geothermal, wind, and biomass sources), more efficient energy storage and distribution technologies, and energy conservation measures;

(7) much of the industrial capacity that is relied upon by the United States Government for military production and other national defense purposes is deeply and directly influenced by—

(A) the overall competitiveness of the industrial economy of the United States; and

(B) the ability of industries in the United States, in general, to produce internationally competitive products and operate profitably while maintaining adequate research and development to preserve competitiveness with respect to military and civilian production; and

(8) the inability of industries in the United States, especially smaller subcontractors and suppliers, to provide vital parts and components and other materials would impair the ability to sustain the Armed Forces of the United States in combat for longer than a short period.

(b) STATEMENT OF POLICY.—It is the policy of the United States that—

(1) to ensure the adequacy of productive capacity and supply, Federal departments and agencies that are responsible for national defense acquisition should continuously assess the capability of the domestic industrial base to satisfy production requirements under both peacetime and emergency conditions, specifically evaluating the availability of adequate production sources, including subcontractors and suppliers, materials, skilled labor, and professional and technical personnel;

(2) every effort should be made to foster cooperation between the defense and commercial sectors for research and development and for acquisition of materials, components, and equipment;

(3) plans and programs to carry out the purposes of this Act should be undertaken with due consideration for promoting efficiency and competition;

(4) in providing United States Government financial assistance under this Act to correct a domestic industrial base shortfall, the President should give consideration to the creation or maintenance of production sources that will remain economically viable after such assistance has ended;

(5) authorities under this Act should be used to reduce the vulnerability of the United States to terrorist attacks, and to minimize the damage and assist in the recovery from terrorist attacks that occur in the United States;

(6) in order to ensure productive capacity in the event of an attack on the United States, the United States Government should encourage the geographic dispersal of industrial facilities in the United States to discourage the concentration of such productive facilities within limited geographic areas that are vulnerable to attack by

an enemy of the United States;

(7)   to ensure that essential national defense requirements are met, consideration should be given to stockpiling strategic materials, to the extent that such stockpiling is economical and feasible; and

(8)   in the construction of any industrial facility owned by the United States Government, in the rendition of any financial assistance by the United States Government for the construction, expansion, or improvement of any industrial facility, and in the production of goods and services, under this Act or any other provision of law, each department and agency of the United States Government should apply, under the coordination of the Federal Emergency Management Agency, when practicable and consistent with existing law and the desirability for maintaining a sound economy, the principle of geographic dispersal of such facilities in the interest of national defense.

[50 U.S.C. 4502]

TITLE I—PRIORITIES AND ALLOCATIONS

Sec. 101. (a)   The President is hereby authorized (1) to require that performance under contracts or orders (other than contracts of employment) which he deems necessary or appropriate to promote the national defense shall take priority over performance under any other contract or order, and, for the purpose of assuring such priority, to require acceptance and performance of such contracts or orders in preference to other contracts or orders by any person he finds to be capable of their performance, and (2) to allocate materials, services, and facilities in such manner, upon such conditions, and to such extent as he shall deem necessary or appropriate to promote the national defense.

(b)   The powers granted in this section shall not be used to control the general distribution of any material in the civilian market unless the President finds (1) that such material is a scarce and critical material essential to the national defense, and (2) that the requirements of the national defense for such material cannot otherwise be met without creating a significant dislocation of the normal distribution of such material in the civilian market to such a degree as to create appreciable hardship.

(c)[5](1)   Notwithstanding any other provision of this Act, the President may, by rule or order, require the allocation of, or the priority performance under contracts or orders (other than contracts of employment) relating to, materials, equipment, and services in order to maximize domestic energy supplies if he makes the findings required by paragraph (3) of this subsection.

---

[5]

Subsection (c) of sec. 101 was added by Public Law 94–163, the Energy Policy and Conservation Act of Dec. 22, 1975, sec. 104(a), 89 Stat. 878. Sec. 104(b) of Public Law 94–163 (50 U.S.C. 4511 note) provides as follows:

"(b) The expiration of the Defense Production Act of 1950 or any amendment of such Act after the date of enactment of this Act shall not affect the authority of the President under section 101(c) of such Act, as amended by subsection (a) of this section and in effect on the date of enactment of this Act, unless Congress by law expressly provides to the contrary.".

---

(2)[6] The authority granted by this subsection may not be used to require priority performance of contracts or orders, or to control the distribution of any supplies of materials, services, and facilities in the marketplace, unless the President finds that—

---

[6] Section 6(3) of P.L. 102–99 amended section 101 by striking paragraphs (2) and (3) and inserting a new paragraph (2). The amendment probably should have been made to subsection (c) of section 101.

(A) such materials, services, and facilities are scarce, critical, and essential—

(i) to maintain or expand exploration, production, refining, transportation;

(ii) to conserve energy supplies; or

(iii) to construct or maintain energy facilities; and

(B) maintenance or expansion of exploration, production, refining, transportation, or conservation of energy supplies or the construction and maintenance of energy facilities cannot reasonably be accomplished without exercising the authority specified in paragraph (1) of this subsection.

(3)[7] During any period when the authority conferred by this subsection is being exercised, the President shall take such action as may be appropriate to assure that such authority is being exercised in a manner which assures the coordinated administration of such authority with any priorities or allocations established under subsection (a) of this section and in effect during the same period.

---

[7] Section 6(4) of P.L. 102–99 amended section 101 by redesignating paragraph (4) as (3). The amendment probably should have been made to subsection (c) of section 101.

(d) The head of each Federal agency to which the President delegates authority under this section shall—

(1) issue, and annually review and update whenever appropriate, final rules, in accordance with section 553 of title 5, United States Code, that establish standards and procedures by which the priorities and allocations authority under this section is used to promote the national defense, under both emergency and nonemergency conditions; and

(2) as appropriate and to the extent practicable, consult with the heads of other Federal agencies to develop a consistent and unified Federal priorities and allocations system.

[50 U.S.C. 4511]

Sec. 102.

In order to prevent hoarding, no person shall accumulate (1) in excess of the reasonable demands of business, personal, or home consumption, or (2) for the purpose of resale at prices in excess of prevailing market prices, materials which have been designated by the President as scarce materials or materials the supply of which would be threatened by such accumulation. The President shall order published in the Federal Register, and in such other manner as he may deem appropriate, every designation of materials the accumulation of which is unlawful and any withdrawal of such designation. In making such designations the President

485

may prescribe such conditions with respect to the accumulation of materials in excess of the reasonable demands of business, personal, or home consumption as he deems necessary to carry out the objectives of this Act. This section shall not be construed to limit the authority contained in sections 101 and 704 of this Act.

[50 U.S.C. 4512]

Sec. 103.

Any person who willfully performs any act prohibited, or willfully fails to perform any act required, by the provisions of this title or any rule, regulation, or order thereunder, shall, upon conviction, be fined not more than $10,000 or imprisoned for not more than one year, or both.

[50 U.S.C. 4513]

SEC. 104. LIMITATION ON ACTIONS WITHOUT CONGRESSIONAL AUTHORIZATION.

(a) WAGE OR PRICE CONTROLS.— No provision of this Act shall be interpreted as providing for the imposition of wage or price controls without the prior authorization of such action by a joint resolution of Congress.

(b) CHEMICAL OR BIOLOGICAL WEAPONS.— No provision of title I of this Act shall be exercised or interpreted to require action or compliance by any private person to assist in any way in the production of or other involvement in chemical or biological warfare capabilities, unless authorized by the President (or the President's designee who is serving in a position at level I of the Executive Schedule in accordance with section 5312 of title 5, United States Code) without further redelegation.

[50 U.S.C. 4514]

Sec. 105.

Nothing in this Act shall be construed to authorize the President to institute, without the approval of the Congress, a program for the rationing of gasoline among classes of end-users.

[50 U.S.C. 4515]

Sec. 106.

For purposes of this Act, energy shall be designated as a strategic and critical material after the date of the enactment of this section: Provided, That no provision of this Act shall, by virtue of such designation grant any new direct or indirect authority to the President for the mandatory allocation or pricing of any fuel or feedstock (including, but not limited to, crude oil, residual fuel oil, any refined petroleum product, natural gas, or coal) or electricity or any other form of energy.

[50 U.S.C. 4516]

SEC. 107. STRENGTHENING DOMESTIC CAPABILITY.

(a) IN GENERAL.— Utilizing the authority of title III of this Act or any other provision of law, the President may provide appropriate incentives to develop, maintain, modernize, restore, and expand the productive capacities of domestic sources for critical components, critical technology items, materials, and industrial resources essential for the execution of the national security strategy of the United States.

(b) CRITICAL COMPONENTS AND CRITICAL TECHNOLOGY ITEMS.—

(1) MAINTENANCE OF RELIABLE SOURCES OF SUPPLY.— The President shall take appropriate actions to assure that critical components, critical technology items, essential materials, and industrial resources are available from reliable sources when needed to meet defense requirements during peacetime, graduated mobilization, and national emergency.

(2) APPROPRIATE ACTION.—For purposes of this subsection, appropriate action may include—

(A)   restricting contract solicitations to reliable sources;

(B) restricting contract solicitations to domestic sources pursuant to—

(i)[8]   section 3203(a)(1)(B) or 3204(a)(3) of title 10, United States Code;

(ii)[8]   section 3303(a)(1)(B) or 3304(a)(3) of title 41, United States Code; or

---

[8]   Section 1702(k)(4) of division A of Public Law 117-81 provides for an amendment to strike clauses (i) and (ii) and insert new clauses (i) and (ii). Such amendment incorrectly references the Defense Production Act instead of The Defense Production Act of 1950, however, it was carried out above to reflect the probable intent of Congress.

(iii)   other statutory authority;

(C)   stockpiling critical components; and

(D)   developing substitutes for a critical component or a critical technology item.

[50 U.S.C. 4517]

SEC. 108. MODERNIZATION OF SMALL BUSINESS SUPPLIERS.

(a) IN GENERAL.— In providing any assistance under this Act, the President shall accord a strong preference for small business concerns which are subcontractors or suppliers, and, to the maximum extent practicable, to such small business concerns located in areas of high unemployment or areas that have demonstrated a continuing pattern of economic decline, as identified by the Secretary of Labor.

(b) MODERNIZATION OF EQUIPMENT.—

(1) IN GENERAL.— Funds authorized under title III may be used to guarantee the purchase or lease of advance manufacturing equipment, and any related services with respect to any such equipment for purposes of this Act.

(2) SMALL BUSINESS SUPPLIERS.—In considering proposals for title III projects under paragraph (1), the President shall provide a strong preference for proposals submitted by a small business supplier or subcontractor whose proposal—

(A)   has the support of the department or agency which will provide the guarantee;

(B)   reflects that the small business concern has made arrangements to obtain qualified outside assistance to support the effective utilization of the advanced manufacturing equipment being proposed for installation; and

(C)   meets the requirements of section 301, 302, or 303.

[50 U.S.C. 4518]

TITLE II—AUTHORITY TO REQUISITION AND
CONDEMN [The authority to condemn was added by section 102 of the Defense Production Act Amendments of 1951, 65 Stat. 132–133, July 31, 1951. The title was terminated at the close of June 30, 1953, by section 11 of the Defense Production Act Amendments of 1953, 67 Stat. 131, June 30, 1953. Title II repealed by section 2(a)(2) of Public Law 111–67.]

TITLE III—EXPANSION OF PRODUCTIVE CAPACITY AND SUPPLY

SEC. 301. PRESIDENTIAL AUTHORIZATION FOR THE NATIONAL DEFENSE.

(a) EXPEDITING PRODUCTION AND DELIVERIES OR SERVICES.—

(1) AUTHORIZED ACTIVITIES.— To reduce current or projected shortfalls of industrial resources, critical technology items, or essential materials needed for national defense purposes, subject to such regulations as the President may prescribe, the President may authorize a guaranteeing agency to provide guarantees of loans by private institutions for the purpose of financing any contractor, subcontractor, provider of critical infrastructure, or other person in support of production capabilities or supplies that are deemed by the guaranteeing agency to be necessary to create, maintain, expedite, expand, protect, or restore production and deliveries or services essential to the national defense.

(2) PRESIDENTIAL DETERMINATIONS REQUIRED.—Except during a period of national emergency declared by Congress or the President, a loan guarantee may be entered into under this section only if the President determines that—

(A) the loan guarantee is for an activity that supports the production or supply of an industrial resource, critical technology item, or material that is essential for national defense purposes;

(B) without a loan guarantee, credit is not available to the loan applicant under reasonable terms or conditions sufficient to finance the activity;

(C) the loan guarantee is the most cost effective, expedient, and practical alternative for meeting the needs of the Federal Government;

(D) the prospective earning power of the loan applicant and the character and value of the security pledged provide a reasonable assurance of repayment of the loan to be guaranteed;

(E) the loan to be guaranteed bears interest at a rate determined by the Secretary of the Treasury to be reasonable, taking into account the then-current average yield on outstanding obligations of the United States with remaining periods of maturity comparable to the maturity of the loan;

(F) the loan agreement for the loan to be guaranteed provides that no provision of the loan agreement may be amended or waived without the consent of the fiscal agent of the United States for the guarantee; and

(G) the loan applicant has provided or will provide—

(i)   an assurance of repayment, as determined by the President; and

(ii) security—

(I)   in the form of a performance bond, insurance, collateral, or other means acceptable to the fiscal agent of the United States; and

(II)   in an amount equal to not less than 20 percent of the amount of the loan.

(3) LIMITATIONS ON LOANS.—Loans under this section may be—

(A) made or guaranteed under the authority of this section only to the extent that an appropriations Act—

(i)   provides, in advance, budget authority for the cost of such guarantees, as defined in section 502 of the Federal Credit Reform Act of 1990 (2 U.S.C. 661a); and

(ii)   establishes a limitation on the total loan principal that may be guaranteed; and

(B)   made without regard to the limitations of existing law, other than section 1341 of title 31, United States Code.

(b) FISCAL AGENTS OF THE UNITED STATES.—

(1) IN GENERAL.— Any Federal agency or any Federal reserve bank, when designated by the President, is hereby authorized to act, on behalf of any guaranteeing agency, as fiscal agent of the United States in the making of such contracts of guarantee and in otherwise carrying out the purposes of this section.

(2) FUNDS.— All such funds as may be necessary to enable any fiscal agent described in paragraph (1) to carry out any guarantee made by it on behalf of any guaranteeing agency shall be supplied and disbursed by or under authority from such guaranteeing agency.

(3) LIMIT ON LIABILITY.— No fiscal agent described in paragraph (1) shall have any responsibility or accountability, except as agent in taking any action pursuant to or under authority of this section.

(4) REIMBURSEMENTS.— Each fiscal agent described in paragraph (1) shall be reimbursed by each guaranteeing agency for all expenses and losses incurred by such fiscal agent in acting as agent on behalf of such guaranteeing agency, including, notwithstanding any other provision of law, attorneys' fees and expenses of litigation.

(c) OVERSIGHT.—

(1) IN GENERAL.— All actions and operations of fiscal agents under authority of or pursuant to this section shall be subject to the supervision of the President, and to such regulations as the President may prescribe.

(2) OTHER AUTHORITY.—The President is authorized to prescribe—

(A)   either specifically or by maximum limits or otherwise, rates of interest, guarantee and commitment fees, and other charges which may be made in connection with loans, discounts, advances, or commitments guaranteed by the guaranteeing agencies through fiscal agents under this section; and

(B)   regulations governing the forms and procedures (which shall be uniform to the extent practicable) to be utilized in connection with such guarantees.

(d) AGGREGATE GUARANTEE AMOUNTS.—

(1) INDUSTRIAL RESOURCE AND CRITICAL TECHNOLOGY SHORTFALLS.—

(A) IN GENERAL.—If the making of any guarantee or obligation of the Federal Government under this title relating to a domestic industrial base shortfall would cause the aggregate outstanding amount of all guarantees for such shortfall to exceed $50,000,000, any such guarantee may be made only—

(i)   if the President has notified the Committee on Banking, Housing, and Urban Affairs of the Senate and the Committee on Financial Services of the House of Representatives in writing of the proposed guarantee; and

(ii)   after the 30-day period following the date on which notice under clause (i) is provided.

(B) WAIVERS AUTHORIZED.—The requirements of subparagraph (A) may be waived—

(i)   during a period of national emergency declared by Congress or the President; or

(ii)   upon a determination by the President, on a nondelegable basis, that a specific guarantee is necessary to avert an industrial resource or critical technology item shortfall that would severely impair national defense capability.

(2) OTHER LIMITATIONS.—The authority conferred by this section shall not be used primarily to prevent the financial insolvency or bankruptcy of any person, unless—

(A)   the President certifies that the insolvency or bankruptcy would have a direct and substantially adverse effect upon national defense production; and

(B)   a copy of the certification under subparagraph (A), together with a detailed justification thereof, is transmitted to the Committee on Banking, Housing, and Urban Affairs of the Senate and the Committee on Financial Services of the House of Representatives not later than 10 days prior to the exercise of that authority for such use.

[50 U.S.C. 4531]

SEC. 302. LOANS TO PRIVATE BUSINESS ENTERPRISES.

(a) LOAN AUTHORITY.— To reduce current or projected shortfalls of industrial resources, critical technology items, or materials essential for the national defense, the President may make provision for loans to private business enterprises (including nonprofit research corporations and providers of critical infrastructure) for the creation, maintenance, expansion, protection, or restoration of capacity, the development of technological processes, or the production of essential materials, including the exploration, development, and mining of strategic and critical metals and minerals.

(b) CONDITIONS OF LOANS.—Loans may be made under this section on such terms and conditions as the President deems necessary, except that—

(1) financial assistance may be extended only to the extent that it is not otherwise available from private sources on reasonable terms; and

(2) during periods of national emergency declared by the Congress or the President, no such loan may be made unless the President determines that—

(A) the loan is for an activity that supports the production or supply of an industrial resource, critical technology item, or material that is essential to the national defense;

(B) without the loan, United States industry cannot reasonably be expected to provide the needed capacity, technological processes, or materials in a timely manner;

(C) the loan is the most cost-effective, expedient, and practical alternative method for meeting the need;

(D) the prospective earning power of the loan applicant and the character and value of the security pledged provide a reasonable assurance of repayment of the loan in accordance with the terms of the loan, as determined by the President; and

(E) the loan bears interest at a rate determined by the Secretary of the Treasury to be reasonable, taking into account the then-current average yield on outstanding obligations of the United States with remaining periods of maturity comparable to the maturity of the loan.

(c) LIMITATIONS ON LOANS.—Loans under this section may be—

(1) made or guaranteed under the authority of this section only to the extent that an appropriations Act—

(A) provides, in advance, budget authority for the cost of such guarantees, as defined in section 502 of the Federal Credit Reform Act of 1990 (2 U.S.C. 661a); and

(B) establishes a limitation on the total loan principal that may be guaranteed; and

(2) made without regard to the limitations of existing law, other than section 1341 of title 31, United States Code.

(d) AGGREGATE LOAN AMOUNTS.—

(1) IN GENERAL.—If the making of any loan under this section to correct a shortfall would cause the aggregate outstanding amount of all obligations of the Federal Government under this title relating to such shortfall to exceed $50,000,000, such loan may be made only—

(A) if the President has notified the Committee on Banking, Housing, and Urban Affairs of the Senate and the Committee on Financial Services of the House of Representatives, in writing, of the proposed loan; and

(B) after the 30-day period following the date on which notice under subparagraph (A) is provided.

(2) WAIVERS AUTHORIZED.—The requirements of paragraph (1) may be waived—

(A) during a period of national emergency declared by the Congress or the President; and

(B) upon a determination by the President, on a nondelegable basis, that a specific loan is necessary to avert an industrial resource or critical technology shortfall that would severely impair national defense capability.

[50 U.S.C. 4532]

SEC. 303. OTHER PRESIDENTIAL ACTION AUTHORIZED.

(a) IN GENERAL.—

(1) IN GENERAL.—To create, maintain, protect, expand, or restore domestic industrial base capabilities essential for the national defense, the President may make provision—

(A) for purchases of or commitments to purchase an industrial resource or a critical technology item, for Government use or resale;

(B) for the encouragement of exploration, development, and mining of critical and strategic materials, and other materials;

(C) for the development of production capabilities; and

(D) for the increased use of emerging technologies in security program applications and the rapid transition of emerging technologies—

(i) from Government-sponsored research and development to commercial applications; and

(ii) from commercial research and development to national defense applications.

(2) TREATMENT OF CERTAIN AGRICULTURAL COMMODITIES.— A purchase for resale under this subsection shall not include that part of the supply of an agricultural commodity which is domestically produced, except to the extent that such domestically produced supply may be purchased for resale for industrial use or stockpiling.

(3) TERMS OF SALES.—No commodity purchased under this subsection shall be sold at less than—

(A) the established ceiling price for such commodity, except that minerals, metals, and materials shall not be sold at less than the established ceiling price, or the current domestic market price, whichever is lower; or

(B) if no ceiling price has been established, the higher of—

(i) the current domestic market price for such commodity; or

(ii) the minimum sale price established for agricultural commodities owned or controlled by the Commodity Credit Corporation, as provided in section 407 of the Agricultural Act of 1949 (7 U.S.C. 1427).

(4) DELIVERY DATES.— No purchase or commitment to purchase any imported agricultural commodity shall specify a delivery date which is more than 1 year after

the date of termination of this section.

(5) PRESIDENTIAL DETERMINATIONS.—Except as provided in paragraph (7), the President may not execute a contract under this subsection unless the President , on a non-delegable basis, determines, with appropriate explanatory material and in writing, that—

(A) the industrial resource, material, or critical technology item is essential to the national defense;

(B) without Presidential action under this section, United States industry cannot reasonably be expected to provide the capability for the needed industrial resource, material, or critical technology item in a timely manner; and

(C) purchases, purchase commitments, or other action pursuant to this section are the most cost effective, expedient, and practical alternative method for meeting the need.

(6) NOTIFICATION TO CONGRESS OF SHORTFALL.—

(A) IN GENERAL.— Except as provided in paragraph (7), the President shall provide written notice to the Committee on Banking, Housing, and Urban Affairs of the Senate and the Committee on Financial Services of the House of Representatives of a domestic industrial base shortfall prior to taking action under this subsection to remedy the shortfall. The notice shall include the determinations made by the President under paragraph (5).

(B) AGGREGATE AMOUNTS.— If the taking of any action under this subsection to correct a domestic industrial base shortfall would cause the aggregate outstanding amount of all such actions for such shortfall to exceed $50,000,000, the action or actions may be taken only after the 30-day period following the date on which the Committee on Banking, Housing, and Urban Affairs of the Senate and the Committee on Financial Services of the House of Representatives have been notified in writing of the proposed action.

(C) LIMITATION.— If the taking of any action or actions under this section to correct an industrial resource shortfall would cause the aggregate outstanding amount of all such actions for such industrial resource shortfall to exceed $50,000,000, no such action or actions may be taken, unless such action or actions are authorized to exceed such amount by an Act of Congress.

(7) WAIVERS AUTHORIZED.—The requirements of paragraphs (1) through (6) may be waived—

(A) during a period of national emergency declared by the Congress or the President; or

(B) upon a determination by the President, on a nondelegable basis, that action is necessary to avert an industrial resource or critical technology item shortfall that would severely impair national defense capability.

(b) EXEMPTION FOR CERTAIN LIMITATIONS.— Subject to the limitations in subsection (a), purchases and commitments to purchase and sales under subsection (a) may be made without regard to the limitations of existing law (other than section 1341 of title 31, United States Code), for such quantities, and on such terms and conditions, including advance payments, and for such periods, but not extending beyond a date that is not more than 10 years from the date on which such purchase, purchase commitment, or sale was initially made, as the President deems necessary, except that purchases or commitments to purchase involving higher than established ceiling prices (or if no such established ceiling prices exist, currently prevailing market prices) or anticipated loss on resale shall not be made, unless it is determined that supply of the materials could not be effectively increased at lower prices or on terms more favorable to the Government, or that such purchases are necessary to assure the availability to the United States of overseas supplies.

(c) PRESIDENTIAL FINDINGS.—

(1) IN GENERAL.—The President may take the actions described in paragraph (2), if the President finds that—

(A) under generally fair and equitable ceiling prices, for any raw or nonprocessed material, there will result a decrease in supplies from high-cost sources of such material, and that the continuation of such supplies is necessary to carry out the objectives of this title; or

(B) an increase in cost of transportation is temporary in character and threatens to impair maximum production or supply in any area at stable prices of any materials.

(2) SUBSIDY PAYMENTS AUTHORIZED.— Upon a finding under paragraph (1), the President may make provision for subsidy payments on any such domestically produced material, other than an agricultural commodity, in such amounts and in such manner (including purchases of such material and its resale at a loss), and on such terms and conditions, as the President determines to be necessary to ensure that supplies from such high-cost sources are continued, or that maximum production or supply in such area at stable prices of such materials is maintained, as the case may be.

(d) INCIDENTAL AUTHORITY.— The procurement power granted to the President by this section shall include the power to transport and store and have processed and refined any materials procured under this section.

(e) INSTALLATION OF EQUIPMENT IN INDUSTRIAL FACILITIES.—

(1) INSTALLATION AUTHORIZED.—If the President determines that such action will aid the national defense, the President is authorized—

(A) to procure and install additional equipment, facilities, processes or improvements to plants, factories, and other industrial facilities owned by the Federal Government;

(B) to procure and install equipment owned by the Federal Government in plants, factories, and other industrial facilities owned by private persons;

(C) to provide for the modification or expansion of privately owned facilities, including the modification or improvement of production processes, when taking actions under section 301, 302, or this section; and

(D) to sell or otherwise transfer equipment owned by the Federal Government and installed under this subsection to the owners of such plants, factories, or other industrial facilities.

(2) INDEMNIFICATION.—The owner of any plant, factory, or other industrial facility that receives equipment owned by the Federal Government under this section shall agree—

(A)   to waive any claim against the United States under section 107 or 113 of the Comprehensive Environmental Response, Compensation, and Liability Act of 1980 (42 U.S.C. 9607 and 9613); and

(B)   to indemnify the United States against any claim described in paragraph (1) made by a third party that arises out of the presence or use of equipment owned by the Federal Government.

(f) EXCESS METALS, MINERALS, AND MATERIALS.—

(1) IN GENERAL.— Notwithstanding any other provision of law to the contrary, metals, minerals, and materials acquired pursuant to this section which, in the judgment of the President, are excess to the needs of programs under this Act, shall be transferred to the National Defense Stockpile established by the Strategic and Critical Materials Stock Piling Act (50 U.S.C. 98 et seq.), when the President deems such action to be in the public interest.

(2) TRANSFERS AT NO CHARGE.— Transfers made pursuant to this subsection shall be made without charge against or reimbursement from funds appropriated for the purposes of the Strategic and Critical Materials Stock Piling Act (50 U.S.C. 98 et seq.), except that costs incident to such transfer, other than acquisition costs, shall be paid or reimbursed from such funds.

(g) SUBSTITUTES.— When, in the judgement of the President, it will aid the national defense, the President may make provision for the development of substitutes for strategic and critical materials, critical components, critical technology items, and other industrial resources.

[50 U.S.C. 4533]

SEC. 304. DEFENSE PRODUCTION ACT FUND.

(a) ESTABLISHMENT OF FUND.— There is established in the Treasury of the United States a separate fund to be known as the Defense Production Act Fund (in this section referred to as the Fund).

(b) MONEYS IN FUND.—There shall be credited to the Fund—

(1)   all moneys appropriated for the Fund, as authorized by section 711; and

(2)   all moneys received by the Fund on transactions entered into pursuant to section 303.

(c) USE OF FUND.— The Fund shall be available to carry out the provisions and purposes of this title, subject to the limitations set forth in this Act and in appropriations Acts.

(d) DURATION OF FUND.— Moneys in the Fund shall remain available until expended.

(e) FUND BALANCE.— The Fund balance at the close of each fiscal year shall not exceed $750,000,000, excluding any moneys appropriated to the Fund during that fiscal year or obligated funds. If, at the close of any fiscal year, the Fund balance exceeds $750,000,000, the amount in excess of $750,000,000 shall be paid into the general fund of the Treasury.

(f) FUND MANAGER.—The President shall designate a Fund manager. The duties of the Fund manager shall include—

(1) determining the liability of the Fund in accordance with subsection (g);

(2) ensuring the visibility and accountability of transactions engaged in through the Fund; and

(3) reporting to the Congress each year regarding activities of the Fund during the previous fiscal year.

(g) LIABILITIES AGAINST FUND.— When any agreement entered into pursuant to this title after December 31, 1991, imposes any contingent liability upon the United States, such liability shall be considered an obligation against the Fund.

[50 U.S.C. 4534]

SEC. 305. REPORTS ON EXERCISE OF AUTHORITIES.

(a) IN GENERAL.—The President, or the head of an agency to which the President has delegated authorities under this title, shall submit a report and provide a briefing to the appropriate congressional committees with respect to any action taken pursuant to such authorities—

(1) except as provided by paragraph (2), not later than 30 days after taking the action; and

(2) in the case of an action that involves a business concern in the United Kingdom or Australia, not later than 30 days before taking the action.

(b) ELEMENTS.—

(1) IN GENERAL.—Each report and briefing required by subsection (a) with respect to an action described in that subsection shall include—

(A) a justification of the necessity of the use of authorities under this title; and

(B) a description of the financial terms of any related financial transaction.

(2) ADDITIONAL ELEMENTS RELATING TO BUSINESS CONCERNS IN THE UNITED KINGDOM OR AUSTRALIA.—Each report and briefing required by subsection (a) with respect to an action described in paragraph (2) of that subsection shall include, in addition to the elements under paragraph (1)—

(A) a certification that business concerns in the United States or Canada were not available with respect to the action; and

(B) an analysis of why such business concerns were not available.

(c) APPROPRIATE CONGRESSIONAL COMMITTEES DEFINED.—In this section, the term appropriate congressional committees means—

(1) the Committee on Banking, Housing, and Urban Affairs of the Senate and the Committee on Financial Services of the House of Representatives; and

(2)   in the case of an action described in subsection (a) involving materials critical to national security (as defined in section 702(7)(B)(ii)(II)(bb)), the Committee on Energy and Natural Resources of the Senate and the Committee on Natural Resources of the House of Representatives.

[50 U.S.C. 4535]

[Titles IV through VI repealed by section 2(a)(2) of Public Law 111–67.]

TITLE VII—GENERAL PROVISIONS

SEC. 701. SMALL BUSINESS.

(a) PARTICIPATION.— Small business concerns shall be given the maximum practicable opportunity to participate as contractors, and subcontractors at various tiers, in all programs to maintain and strengthen the Nation's industrial base and technology base undertaken pursuant to this Act.

(b) ADMINISTRATION OF ACT.— In administering the programs, implementing regulations, policies, and procedures under this Act, requests, applications, or appeals from small business concerns shall, to the maximum extent practicable, be expeditiously handled.

(c) ADVISORY COMMITTEE PARTICIPATION.— Representatives of small business concerns shall be afforded the maximum opportunity to participate in such advisory committees as may be established pursuant to this Act.

(d) INFORMATION.— Information about this Act and activities undertaken in accordance with this Act shall be made available to small business concerns.

(e) ALLOCATIONS UNDER SECTION 101.— Whenever the President makes a determination to exercise any authority to allocate any material pursuant to section 101, small business concerns shall be accorded, to the extent practicable, a fair share of such material, in proportion to the share received by such business concerns under normal conditions, giving such special consideration as may be possible to emerging small business concerns.

[50 U.S.C. 4551]

SEC. 702. DEFINITIONS.

For purposes of this Act, the following definitions shall apply:

(1) CRITICAL COMPONENT.— The term critical component includes such components, subsystems, systems, and related special tooling and test equipment essential to the production, repair, maintenance, or operation of weapon systems or other items of equipment identified by the President as being essential to the execution of the national security strategy of the United States. Components identified as critical by a National Security Assessment conducted pursuant to section 113(i) of title 10, United States Code, or by a Presidential determination as a result of a petition filed under section 232 of the Trade Expansion Act of 1962 shall be designated as critical components for purposes of this Act, unless the President determines that the designation is unwarranted.

(2) CRITICAL INFRASTRUCTURE.— The term critical infrastructure means any systems and assets, whether physical or cyber-based, so vital to the United States

497

that the degradation or destruction of such systems and assets would have a debilitating impact on national security, including, but not limited to, national economic security and national public health or safety.

(3) CRITICAL TECHNOLOGY.— The term critical technology includes any technology designated by the President to be essential to the national defense.

(4) CRITICAL TECHNOLOGY ITEM.— The term critical technology item means materials directly employing, derived from, or utilizing a critical technology.

(5) DEFENSE CONTRACTOR.—The term defense contractor means any person who enters into a contract with the United States—

(A)   to furnish materials, industrial resources, or a critical technology for the national defense; or

(B)   to perform services for the national defense.

(6) DOMESTIC INDUSTRIAL BASE.— The term domestic industrial base means domestic sources which are providing, or which would be reasonably expected to provide, materials or services to meet national defense requirements during peacetime, national emergency, or war.

(7) DOMESTIC SOURCE.—

(A) IN GENERAL.—Except as provided in subparagraph (B), the termdomestic source means a business concern—

(i)   that performs in the United States or Canada substantially all of the research and development, engineering, manufacturing, and production activities required of such business concern under a contract with the United States relating to a critical component or a critical technology item; and

(ii)   that procures from business concerns described in clause (i) substantially all of any components and assemblies required under a contract with the United States relating to a critical component or critical technology item.

(B) DOMESTIC SOURCE FOR TITLE III.—

(i) IN GENERAL.—For purposes of title III, the term domestic source means a business concern that—

(I)   performs substantially all of the research and development, engineering, manufacturing, and production activities required of such business concern under a contract with the United States relating to a critical component or a critical technology item in—

(aa)   the United States or Canada; or

(bb)   subject to clause (ii), Australia or the United Kingdom; and

(II)   procures from business concerns described in subclause (I) substantially all of any components or assemblies required under a contract with the United States relating to a critical component or critical technology item.

(ii) LIMITATIONS ON USE OF BUSINESS CONCERNS IN AUSTRALIA AND UNITED

KINGDOM.—

(I) IN GENERAL.— A business concern described in clause (i)(I)(bb) may be treated as a domestic source only for purposes of the exercise of authorities under title III relating to national defense matters that cannot be fully addressed with business concerns described in clause (i)(I)(aa).

(II) NATIONAL DEFENSE MATTER DEFINED.—For purposes of subclause (I), the term national defense matter is a matter relating to the development or production of—

(aa) a defense article, as defined in section 301 of title 10, United States Code; or

(bb) materials critical to national security, as defined in section 10(f) of the Strategic and Critical Materials Stock Piling Act (50 U.S.C. 98h–1(f)).

(8) FACILITIES.— The term facilities includes all types of buildings, structures, or other improvements to real property (but excluding farms, churches or other places of worship, and private dwelling houses), and services relating to the use of any such building, structure, or other improvement.

(9) FOREIGN SOURCE.— The term foreign source means a business entity other than a domestic source.

(10) GUARANTEEING AGENCY.— The term guaranteeing agency means a department or agency of the United States engaged in procurement for the national defense.

(11) HOMELAND SECURITY.—The term homeland security includes efforts—

(A) to prevent terrorist attacks within the United States;

(B) to reduce the vulnerability of the United States to terrorism;

(C) to minimize damage from a terrorist attack in the United States; and

(D) to recover from a terrorist attack in the United States.

(12) INDUSTRIAL RESOURCES.— The term industrial resources means materials, services, processes, or manufacturing equipment (including the processes, technologies, and ancillary services for the use of such equipment) needed to establish or maintain an efficient and modern national defense industrial base.

(13) MATERIALS.—The term materials includes—

(A) any raw materials (including minerals, metals, and advanced processed materials), commodities, articles, components (including critical components), products, and items of supply; and

(B) any technical information or services ancillary to the use of any such materials, commodities, articles, components, products, or items.

(14) NATIONAL DEFENSE.— The term national defense means programs for military and energy production or construction, military or critical infrastructure assistance to any foreign nation, homeland security, stockpiling, space, and any directly related activity. Such term includes emergency preparedness activities

499

conducted pursuant to title VI of The Robert T. Stafford Disaster Relief and Emergency Assistance Act and critical infrastructure protection and restoration.

(15) PERSON.— The term person includes an individual, corporation, partnership, association, or any other organized group of persons, or legal successor or representative thereof, or any State or local government or agency thereof.

(16) SERVICES.—The term services includes any effort that is needed for or incidental to—

(A) the development, production, processing, distribution, delivery, or use of an industrial resource or a critical technology item;

(B) the construction of facilities;

(C) the movement of individuals and property by all modes of civil transportation; or

(D) other national defense programs and activities.

(17) SMALL BUSINESS CONCERN.— The term small business concern means a business concern that meets the requirements of section 3(a) of the Small Business Act and the regulations promulgated pursuant to that section, and includes such business concerns owned and controlled by socially and economically disadvantaged individuals or by women.

[50 U.S.C. 4552]

SEC. 703. CIVILIAN PERSONNEL.

Any officer or agency head may—

(1) appoint civilian personnel without regard to section 5331(b) of title 5, United States Code, and without regard to the provisions of title 5, United States Code, governing appointments in the competitive service; and

(2) fix the rate of basic pay for such personnel without regard to the provisions of chapter 51 and subchapter III of chapter 53 of title 5, United States Code, relating to classification and General Schedule pay rates,

except that no individual so appointed may receive pay in excess of the annual rate of basic pay payable for GS–18 of the General Schedule, as the President deems appropriate to carry out this Act.

[50 U.S.C. 4553]

SEC. 704. REGULATIONS AND ORDERS.

(a) IN GENERAL.— Subject to section 709 and subsection (b), the President may prescribe such regulations and issue such orders as the President may determine to be appropriate to carry out this Act.

(b) PROCUREMENT REGULATIONS.— Any procurement regulation, procedure, or form issued pursuant to subsection (a) shall be issued pursuant to section 25 of the Office of Federal Procurement Policy Act, and shall conform to any governmentwide procurement policy or regulation issued pursuant to section 6 or 25 of that Act.

[50 U.S.C. 4554]

Sec. 705. (a) The President shall be entitled, while this Act is in effect and for a period of two years thereafter, by regulation, subpoena, or otherwise, to obtain such information from, require such reports and the keeping of such records by, make such inspection of the books, records, and other writings, premises or property of, and take the sworn testimony of, and administer oaths and affirmations to, any person as may be necessary or appropriate, in his discretion, to the enforcement or the administration of this Act and the regulations or orders issued thereunder. The authority of the President under this section includes the authority to obtain information in order to perform industry studies assessing the capabilities of the United States industrial base to support the national defense. The President shall issue regulations insuring that the authority of this subsection will be utilized only after the scope and purpose of the investigation, inspection, or inquiry to be made have been defined by competent authority, and it is assured that no adequate and authoritative data are available from any Federal or other responsible agency. In case of contumacy by, or refusal to obey a subpoena served upon, any person referred to in this subsection, the district court of the United States for any district in which such person is found or resides or transacts business, upon application by the President, shall have jurisdiction to issue an order requiring such person to appear and give testimony or to appear and produce documents, or both; and any failure to obey such order of the court may be punished by such court as a contempt thereof.

(b)   The production of a person's books, records, or other documentary evidence shall not be required at any place other than the place where such person usually keeps them, if prior to the return date specified in the regulations, subpoena, or other document issued with respect thereto, such person furnishes the President with a true copy of such books, records, or other documentary evidence (certified by such person under oath to be a true and correct copy) or enters into a stipulation with the President as to the information contained in such books, records, or other documentary evidence. Witnesses shall be paid the same fees and mileage that are paid witnesses in the courts of the United States.

(c)   Any person who willfully performs any act prohibited or willfully fails to perform any act required by the above provisions of this section, or any rule, regulation, or order thereunder, shall upon conviction be fined not more than $10,000 or imprisoned for not more than one year or both.

(d)   Information obtained under this section which the President deems confidential or with reference to which a request for confidential treatment is made by the person furnishing such information shall not be published or disclosed unless the President determines that the withholding thereof is contrary to the interest of the national defense, and any person willfully violating this provision shall, upon conviction, be fined not more than $10,000, or imprisoned for not more than one year, or both.

(e)   Any person subpoenaed under this section shall have the right to make a record of his testimony and to be represented by counsel.

[50 U.S.C. 4555]

Sec. 706. (a)   Whenever in the judgment of the President any person has engaged or is about to engage in any acts or practices which constitute or will constitute a violation of any provision of this Act, he may make application to the appropriate court for an order enjoining such acts or practices, or for an order enforcing compliance with such provision, and upon a showing by the President that such person has engaged or is

501

about to engage in any such acts or practices a permanent or temporary injunction, restraining order, or other order, with or without such injunction or restraining order, shall be granted without bond.

(b)   The district courts of the United States and the United States courts of any Territory or other place subject to the jurisdiction of the United States shall have jurisdiction of violations of this Act or any rule, regulation, order, or subpena thereunder, and of all civil actions under this Act to enforce any liability or duty created by, or to enjoin any violation of, this Act or any rule, regulation, order, or subpena thereunder. Any criminal proceeding on account of any such violation may be brought in any district in which any act, failure to act, or transaction constituting the violation occurred. Any such civil action may be brought in any such district or in the district in which the defendant resides or transacts business. Process in such cases, criminal or civil, may be served in any district wherein the defendant resides or transacts business or wherever the defendant may be found; the subpena for witnesses who are required to attend a court in any district in such case may run into any other district. The termination of the authority granted in any title or section of this Act, or of any rule, regulation, or order issued thereunder, shall not operate to defeat any suit, action, or prosecution, whether theretofore or thereafter commenced, with respect to any right, liability, or offense incurred or committed prior to the termination date of such title or of such rule, regulation, or order. No costs shall be assessed against the United States in any proceeding under this Act. All litigation arising under this Act or the regulations promulgated thereunder shall be under the supervision and control of the Attorney General.

[50 U.S.C. 4556]

Sec. 707.

No person shall be held liable for damages or penalties for any act or failure to act resulting directly or indirectly from compliance with a rule, regulation, or order issued pursuant to this Act notwithstanding that any such rule, regulation, or order shall thereafter be declared by judicial or other competent authority to be invalid. No person shall discriminate against orders or contracts to which priority is assigned or for which materials or facilities are allocated under title I of this Act or under any rule, regulation, or order issued thereunder, by charging higher prices or by imposing different terms and conditions for such orders or contracts than for other generally comparable orders or contracts, on in any other manner.

[50 U.S.C. 4557]

Sec. 708.[9] (a)   Except as specifically provided in subsection (j) of this section, no provision of this Act shall be deemed to convey to any person any immunity from civil or criminal liability, or to create defenses to actions, under the antitrust laws.

---

[9]

Law 94–152, Dec. 16, 1975, sec. 3, 89 Stat. 810, revised sec. 708 and added sec. 708A effective on the one hundred and twentieth day beginning after Dec. 16, 1975 (Public Law 94–152, sec. 9, 89 Stat. 821), Sec. 4 of Public Law 94–152 (89 Stat. 820) provided further:

''(a) Any voluntary agreement—

''(1) entered into under section 708 of the Defense Production Act of 1950 prior to the effective date of this Act, and

"(2) in effect immediately prior to such date

may continue in effect (except as otherwise provided in section 708A(o) of the Defense Production Act of 1950, as amended by this Act) and shall be carried out in accordance with such section 708, as amended by this Act, and such section 708A.

"(b) No provision of the Defense Production Act of 1950, as amended by this Act, shall be construed as granting immunity for, nor as limiting or in any way affecting any remedy or penalty which may result from any legal action or proceeding arising from, any acts or practices which occurred (1) prior to the date of enactment of this Act, (2) outside the scope and purpose or not in compliance with the terms and conditions of the Defense Production Act of 1950, or (3) subsequent to the expiration or repeal of the Defense Production Act of 1950.

"(c) Effective on the date of enactment of this Act, the immunity conferred by section 708 or 708A of the Defense Production Act of 1950, as amended by this Act, shall not apply to any action taken or authorized to be taken by or under the Emergency Petroleum Allocation Act of 1973".

(b) DEFINITIONS.—For purposes of this Act—

(1) ANTITRUST LAWS.— The term antitrust laws has the meaning given to such term in subsection (a) of the first section of the Clayton Act, except that such term includes section 5 of the Federal Trade Commission Act to the extent that such section 5 applies to unfair methods of competition.

(2) PLAN OF ACTION.— The term plan of action means any of 1 or more documented methods adopted by participants in an existing voluntary agreement implement that agreement.

(c)(1) Upon finding that conditions exist which may pose a direct threat to the national defense or its preparedness programs, the President may consult with representatives of industry, business, financing, agriculture, labor, and other interests in order to provide for the making by such persons, with the approval of the President, of voluntary agreements and plans of action to help provide for the national defense.

(2) The authority granted to the President in paragraph (1) and subsection (d) may be delegated by him (A) to individuals who are appointed by and with the advice and consent of the Senate, or are holding offices to which they have been appointed by and with the advice and consent of the Senate, (B) upon the condition that such individuals consult with the Attorney General and with the Federal Trade Commission not less than ten days before consulting with any persons under paragraph (1), and (C) upon the condition that such individuals obtain the prior approval of the Attorney General, after consultation by the Attorney General with the Federal Trade Commission, to consult under paragraph (1).

(3) Upon a determination by the President, on a nondelegable basis, that a specific voluntary agreement or plan of action is necessary to meet national defense requirements resulting from an event that degrades or destroys critical infrastructure—

(A) an individual that has been delegated authority under paragraph (1) with respect to such agreement or plan shall not be required to consult with the Attorney General or the Federal Trade Commission under paragraph (2)(B); and

(B)   the President shall publish a rule in accordance with subsection (e)(2)(B) and publish notice in accordance with subsection (e)(3)(B) with respect to such agreement or plan as soon as is practicable under the circumstances.

(d)(1)   To achieve the objectives of subsection (c)(1) of this section, the President or any individual designated pursuant to subsection (c)(2) may provide for the establishment of such advisory committees as he determines are necessary. In addition to the requirement specified in this section and except as provided in subsection (n), any such advisory committee shall be subject to the provisions of chapter 10 of title 5, United States Code, whether or not such chapter or any of its provisions expire or terminate during the term of this Act or of such committees, and in all cases such advisory committees shall be chaired by a Federal employee (other than an individual employed pursuant to section 3109 of title 5, United States Code) and shall include representatives of the public. The Attorney General and the Federal Trade Commission shall have adequate advance notice of any meeting and may have an official representative attend and participate in any such meeting.

(2)   A full and complete verbatim transcript shall be kept of such advisory committee meetings, and shall be taken and deposited, together with any agreement resulting therefrom, with the Attorney General and the Federal Trade Commission. Such transcript and agreement shall be made available for public inspection and copying, subject to the provisions of paragraphs (1), (3), and (4) of section 552(b) of title 5, United States Code.

(e)(1)   The individual or individuals referred to in subsection (c)(2) shall, after approval of the Attorney General, after consultation by the Attorney General with the Chairman of the Federal Trade Commission, promulgate rules, in accordance with section 553 of title 5, United States Code, incorporating standards and procedures by which voluntary agreements and plans of action may be developed and carried out.

(2) In addition to the requirements of section 553 of title 5, United States Code—

(A) general notice of the proposed rulemaking referred to in paragraph (1) shall be published in the Federal Register, and such notice shall include—

(i)   a statement of the time, place, and nature of the proposed rulemaking proceedings;

(ii)   reference to the legal authority under which the rule is being proposed; and

(iii)   either the terms of substance of the proposed rule or a description of the subjects and issues involved;

(B)   the required publication of a rule shall be made not less than thirty days before its effective date; and

(C)   the individual or individuals referred to in paragraph (1) shall give interested persons the right to petition for the issuance, amendment, or repeal of a rule.

(3) The rules promulgated pursuant to this subsection incorporating standards and procedures by which voluntary agreements may be developed shall provide, among other things, that—

(A) such agreements shall be developed at meetings which include—

    (i) the Attorney General or his delegate,

    (ii) the Chairman of the Federal Trade Commission or his delegate, and

    (iii) an individual designated by the President in subsection (c)(2) or his delegate,

and which are chaired by the individual referred to in clause (iii);

(B) at least seven days prior to any such meeting, notice of the time, place, and nature of the meeting shall be published in the Federal Register;

(C) interested persons may submit written data and views concerning the proposed voluntary agreement, with or without opportunity for oral presentation;

(D) interested persons may attend any such meeting unless the individual designated by the President in subsection (c)(2) finds that the matter or matters to be discussed at such meeting falls within the purview of matters described in section 552b(c) of title 5, United States Code;

(E) a full and verbatim transcript shall be made of any such meeting and shall be transmitted by the chairman of the meeting to the Attorney General and to the Chairman of the Federal Trade Commission;

(F) any voluntary agreement resulting from the meetings shall be transmitted by the chairman of the meetings to the Attorney General, the Chairman of the Federal Trade Commission, and the Congress; and

(G) any transcript referred to in subparagraph (E) and any voluntary agreement referred to in subparagraph (F) shall be available for public inspection and copying, subject to paragraphs (1), (3), and (4) of section 552(b) of title 5, United States Code.

(f)(1) A voluntary agreement or plan of action may not become effective unless and until—

(A) the individual referred to in subsection (c)(2) who is to administer the agreement or plan approves it and certifies, in writing, that the agreement or plan is necessary to carry out the purposes of subsection (c)(1) and submits a copy of such agreement or plan to the Congress; and

(B) the Attorney General (after consultation with the Chairman of the Federal Trade Commission) finds, in writing, that such purpose may not reasonably be achieved through a voluntary agreement or plan of action having less anticompetitive effects or without any voluntary agreement or plan of action and publishes such finding in the Federal Register.

(2) Each voluntary agreement or plan of action which becomes effective under paragraph (1) shall expire 5 years after the date it becomes effective (and at 5-year intervals thereafter, as the case may be), unless (immediately prior to such expiration date) the individual referred to in subsection (c)(2) who administers the agreement or plan and the Attorney General (after consultation with the Chairman of the Federal Trade Commission) make the certification or finding, as the case may be, described in paragraph (1) with respect to such voluntary agreement or plan of action and

publishes such certification or finding in the Federal Register, in which case, the voluntary agreement or plan of action may be extended for an additional period of 5 years.

(g) The Attorney General and the Chairman of the Federal Trade Commission shall monitor the carrying out of any voluntary agreement or plan of action to assure—

(1)   that the agreement or plan is carrying out the purposes of subsection (c)(1);

(2)   that the agreement or plan is being carried out under rules promulgated pursuant to subsection (e);

(3)   that the participants are acting in accordance with the terms of the agreement or plan; and

(4)   the protection and fostering of competition and the prevention of anticompetitive practices and effects.

(h) The rules promulgated under subsection (e) with respect to the carrying out of voluntary agreements and plans of action shall provide—

(1)   for the maintenance, by participants in any voluntary agreement or plan of action, of documents, minutes of meetings, transcripts, records, and other data related to the carrying out of any voluntary agreement or plan of action;

(2)   that participants in any voluntary agreement or plan of action agree, in writing, to make available to the individual designated by the President in subsection (c)(2) to administer the voluntary agreement or plan of action, the Attorney General and the Chairman of the Federal Trade Commission for inspection and copying at reasonable times and upon reasonable notice any item maintained pursuant to paragraph (1);

(3)   that any item made available to the individual designated by the President in subsection (c)(2) to administer the voluntary agreement or plan of action, the Attorney General, or the Chairman of the Federal Trade Commission pursuant to paragraph (2) shall be available from such individual, the Attorney General, or the Chairman of the Federal Trade Commission, as the case may be, for public inspection and copying, subject to paragraph (1), (3), or (4) of section 552(b) of title 5, United States Code;

(4)   that the individual designated by the President in subsection (c)(2) to administer the voluntary agreement or plan of action, the Attorney General, and the Chairman of the Federal Trade Commission, or their delegates, may attend meetings to carry out any voluntary agreement or plan of action;

(5)   that a Federal employee (other than an individual employed pursuant to section 3109 of title 5 of the United States Code) shall attend meetings to carry out any voluntary agreement or plan of action;

(6)   that participants in any voluntary agreement or plan of action provide the individual designated by the President in subsection (c)(2) to administer the voluntary agreement or plan of action, the Attorney General, and the Chairman of the Federal Trade Commission with adequate prior notice of the time, place, and nature of any meeting to be held to carry out the voluntary agreement or plan of action;

(7) for the attendance by interested persons of any meeting held to carry out any voluntary agreement or plan of action, unless the individual designated by the President in subsection (c)(2) to administer the voluntary agreement or plan of action finds that the matter or matters to be discussed at such meeting falls within the purview of matters described in section 552b(c) of title 5, United States Code;

(8) that the individual designated by the President in subsection (c)(2) to administer the voluntary agreement or plan of action has published in the Federal Register prior notification of the time, place, and nature of any meeting held to carry out any voluntary agreement or plan of action, unless he finds that the matter or matters to be discussed at such meeting falls within the purview of matters described in section 552b(c) of title 5, United States Code, in which case, notification of the time, place, and nature of such meeting shall be published in the Federal Register within ten days of the date of such meeting;

(9) that—

(A) the Attorney General (after consultation with the Chairman of the Federal Trade Commission and the individual designated by the President in subsection (c)(2) to administer a voluntary agreement or plan of action), or

(B) the individual designated by the President in subsection (c)(2) to administer a voluntary agreement or plan of action (after consultation with the Attorney General and the Chairman of the Federal Trade Commission),

may terminate or modify, in writing, the voluntary agreement or plan of action at any time, and that effective, immediately upon such termination or modification, any antitrust immunity conferred upon the participants in the voluntary agreement or plan of action by subsection (j) shall not apply to any act or omission occurring after the time of such termination or modification;

(10) that participants in any voluntary agreement or plan of action be reasonably representative of the appropriate industry or segment of such industry; and

(11) that the individual designated by the President in subsection (c)(2) to administer the voluntary agreement or plan of action shall provide prior written notification of the time, place, and nature of any meeting to carry out a voluntary agreement or plan of action to the Attorney General, the Chairman of the Federal Trade Commission and the Congress.

(i) The Attorney General and the Chairman of the Federal Trade Commission shall each promulgate such rules as each deems necessary or appropriate to carry out his responsibility under this section.

(j) DEFENSES.—

(1) IN GENERAL.—Subject to paragraph (4), there shall be available as a defense for any person to any civil or criminal action brought under the antitrust laws (or any similar law of any State) with respect to any action taken to develop or carry out any voluntary agreement or plan of action under this section that—

(A) such action was taken—

(i) in the course of developing a voluntary agreement initiated by the President or a plan of action adopted under any such agreement; or

(ii)   to carry out a voluntary agreement initiated by the President and approved in accordance with this section or a plan of action adopted under any such agreement, and

(B) such person—

(i)   complied with the requirements of this section and any regulation prescribed under this section; and

(ii)   acted in accordance with the terms of the voluntary agreement or plan of action.

(2) SCOPE OF DEFENSE.— Except in the case of actions taken to develop a voluntary agreement or plan of action, the defense established in paragraph (1) shall be available only if and to the extent that the person asserting the defense demonstrates that the action was specified in, or was within the scope of, an approved voluntary agreement initiated by the President and approved in accordance with this section or a plan of action adopted under any such agreement and approved in accordance with this section. The defense established in paragraph (1) shall not be available unless the President or the President's designee has authorized and actively supervised the voluntary agreement or plan of action.

(3) BURDEN OF PERSUASION.— Any person raising the defense established in paragraph (1) shall have the burden of proof to establish the elements of the defense.

(4) EXCEPTION FOR ACTIONS TAKEN TO VIOLATE THE ANTITRUST LAWS.— The defense established in paragraph (1) shall not be available if the person against whom the defense is asserted shows that the action was taken for the purpose of violating the antitrust laws.

(k)   The Attorney General and the Federal Trade Commission shall each make surveys for the purpose of determining any factors which may tend to eliminate competition, create or strengthen monopolies, injure small business, or otherwise promote undue concentration of economic power in the course of the administration of this section. Such surveys shall include studies of the voluntary agreements and plans of action authorized by this section. The Attorney General shall (after consultation with the Federal Trade Commission) submit to the Congress and the President at least once every year reports setting forth the results of such studies of voluntary agreements and plans of action.

(l)   The individual or individuals designated by the President in subsection (c)(2) shall submit to the Congress and the President at least once every year reports describing each voluntary agreement or plan of action in effect and its contribution to achievement of the purpose of subsection (c)(1).

(m)   On complaint, the United States District Court for the District of Columbia shall have jurisdiction to enjoin any exemption or suspension pursuant to subsections (d)(2), (e)(3) (D) and (G), and (h) (3), (7), and (8), and to order the production of transcripts, agreements, items, or other records maintained pursuant to this section by the Attorney General, the Federal Trade Commission or any individual designated under subsection (c)(2), where the court determines that such transcripts, agreements, items, or other records have been improperly withheld from the complainant. In such a case the court shall determine the matter de novo, and may examine the contents of such transcripts, agreements, items, or other records in camera to determine whether such transcripts, agreements, items, or other records or any parts thereof shall be withheld under any of the exemption or suspension provisions referred to in this subsection, and the burden is on the Attorney General, the Federal Trade Commission, or such designated individual, as the case may be, to sustain its action.

(n)[10] EXEMPTION FROM CHAPTER 10 OF TITLE 5, UNITED STATES CODE,.—Notwithstanding any other provision of law, chapter 10 of title 5, United States Code, and any other provision of Federal law relating to advisory committees shall not apply to—

(1) the consultations referred to in subsection (c)(1); or

(2) any activity conducted under a voluntary agreement or plan of action approved pursuant to this section that complies with the requirements of this section.

---

[10] The comma before .– in the subsection heading is so in law. See amendment made by section 4(a)(322)(A) of Public Law 117–283.

(o) PREEMPTION OF CONTRACT LAW IN EMERGENCIES.— In any action in any Federal or State court for breach of contract, there shall be available as a defense that the alleged breach of contract was caused predominantly by action taken during an emergency to carry out a voluntary agreement or plan of action authorized and approved in accordance with this section. Such defense shall not release the party asserting it from any obligation under applicable law to mitigate damages to the greatest extent possible.

[50 U.S.C. 4558]

SEC. 709. PUBLIC PARTICIPATION IN RULEMAKING.

(a) EXEMPTION FROM THE ADMINISTRATIVE PROCEDURE ACT.— Any regulation issued under this Act shall not be subject to sections 551 through 559 of title 5, United States Code.

(b) OPPORTUNITY FOR NOTICE AND COMMENT.—

(1) IN GENERAL.— Except as provided in subsection (c), any regulation issued under this Act shall be published in the Federal Register and opportunity for public comment shall be provided for not less than 30 days, consistent with the requirements of section 553(b) of title 5, United States Code.

(2) WAIVER FOR TEMPORARY PROVISIONS.—The requirements of paragraph (1) may be waived, if—

(A) the officer authorized to issue the regulation finds that urgent and compelling circumstances make compliance with such requirements impracticable;

(B) the regulation is issued on a temporary basis; and

(C) the publication of such temporary regulation is accompanied by the finding made under subparagraph (A) (and a brief statement of the reasons for such finding) and an opportunity for public comment is provided for not less than 30 days before any regulation becomes final.

Sec. 710. [Subsec. (a) was repealed by section
12(c)(1) of the Federal Employees Salary

The Defense Production Act of 195

(3) CONSIDERATION OF PUBLIC COMMENTS.— All comments received during the public comment period specified pursuant to paragraph (1) or (2) shall be considered and the publication of the final regulation shall contain written responses to such comments.

(c) PUBLIC COMMENT ON PROCUREMENT REGULATIONS.— Any procurement policy, regulation, procedure, or form (including any amendment or modification of any such policy, regulation, procedure, or form) issued under this Act shall be subject to section 22 of the Office of Federal Procurement Policy Act.

[50 U.S.C. 4559]

Sec. 710. (a) [Subsec. (a) was repealed by section 12(c)(1) of the Federal Employees Salary Increase Act of 1955, 69 Stat. 180, June 28, 1955.]

(b)(1)   The President is further authorized, to the extent he deems it necessary and appropriate in order to carry out the provisions of this Act and subject to such regulations as he may issue, to employ persons of outstanding experience and ability without compensation;

(2) The President shall be guided in the exercise of the authority provided in this subsection by the following policies:

(i)   So far as possible, operations under the Act shall be carried on by full-time salaried employees of the Government, and appointments under this authority shall be to advisory or consultative positions only.

(ii)   Appointments to positions other than advisory or consultative may be made under this authority only when the requirements of the positions are such that the incumbent must personally possess outstanding experience and ability not obtainable on a full-time, salaried basis.

(3)   Appointees under this subsection (b) shall when policy matters are involved, be limited to advising appropriate full-time salaried Government officials who are responsible for making policy decisions.

(4) Appointments under this subsection (b) shall be supported by written certification by the head of the employing department or agency—

(i)   that the appointment is necessary and appropriate in order to carry out the provisions of the Act;

(ii)   that the duties of the position to which the appointment is being made require outstanding experience and ability;

(iii)   that the appointee has the outstanding experience and ability required by the position; and

(iv)   that the department or agency head has been unable to obtain a person with the qualifications necessary for the position on a full-time, salaried basis.

(5) NOTICE AND FINANCIAL DISCLOSURE REQUIREMENTS.—

(A) PUBLIC NOTICE OF APPOINTMENT.— The head of any department or agency who appoints any individual under this subsection shall publish a notice of such appointment in the Federal Register, including the name of the appointee,

ec. 710. [Subsec. (a) was repealed by section 2(c)(1) of the Federal Employees Salary

The Defense Production Act of 1950

the employing department or agency, the title of the appointee's position, and the name of the appointee's private employer.

(B) FINANCIAL DISCLOSURE.— Any individual appointed under this subsection who is not required to file a financial disclosure report pursuant to section 13103 of title 5, United States Code, shall file a confidential financial disclosure report pursuant to section 13109 of title 5, United States Code, with the appointing department or agency.

(6) The Director of the Office of Personnel Management shall carry out a biennial survey of appointments made under this subsection and shall report his or her findings to the President and make such recommendations as he or she may deem proper.

(7) Persons appointed under the authority of this subsection may be allowed reimbursement for travel, subsistence, and other necessary expenses incurred by them in carrying out the functions for which they were appointed in the same manner as persons employed intermittently in the Federal Government are allowed expenses under section 5703 of title 5, United States Code.

(c) The President is authorized, to the extent he deems it necessary and appropriate in order to carry out the provisions of this Act, to employ experts and consultants or organizations thereof, as authorized by section 55a of title 5 of the United States Code. Individuals so employed may be compensated at rates not in excess of $50 per diem and while away from their homes or regular places of business they may be allowed transportation and not to exceed $15 per diem in lieu of subsistence and other expenses while so employed.

(d) The President may utilize the services of Federal, State, and local agencies and may utilize and establish such regional, local, or other agencies and, utilize such voluntary and uncompensated services, as may from time to time be needed.

(e) The President is further authorized to provide for the establishment and training of a nucleus executive reserve for employment in executive positions in Government during periods of national defense emergency, as determined by the President. Members of this executive reserve who are not full-time Government employees may be allowed transportation and per diem in lieu of subsistence, in accordance with title 5 of the United States Code (with respect to individuals serving without pay, while away from their homes or regular places of business), for the purpose of participating in the executive reserve training program.

(f) Whoever, being an officer or employee of the United States or any department or agency thereof (including any Member of the Senate or House of Representatives), receives, by virtue of his office or employment, confidential information, and (1) uses such information in speculating directly or indirectly on any commodity exchange, or (2) discloses such information for the purpose of aiding any other person so to speculate, shall be fined not more than $10,000 or imprisoned not more than one year, or both. As used in this section, the term speculate shall not include a legitimate hedging transaction, or a purchase or sale which is accompanied by actual delivery of the commodity.

(g) The President, when he deems such action necessary, may make provision for the printing and distribution of reports, in such number and in such manner as he deems appropriate, concerning the actions taken to carry out the objectives of this Act.

[50 U.S.C. 4560]

Sec. 711.

There is authorized to be appropriated $133,000,000 for fiscal year 2015 and each fiscal year thereafter for the carrying out of the provisions and purposes of this Act by the President and such agencies as he may designate or create. In addition to the appropriations authorized by the previous sentence, there is authorized to be appropriated $117,000,000 for each of fiscal years 2020 through 2024 to carry out title III.

[50 U.S.C. 4561]

[Section 712 repealed by section 153 of P.L. 102–558 (106 Stat. 4219).]

Sec. 713.

The provisions of this Act shall be applicable to the United States, its Territories and possessions, and the District of Columbia.

[50 U.S.C. 4562]

Sec. 714. [The Small Defense Plants Administration created by this section, added by the Defense Production Act amendments of 1951, was terminated at the close of July 31, 1953, and was succeeded by the Small Business Administration created under the Small business Act of 1953. For purposes of section 301(a) of this Act, section 714(a)(1) defined a small-business concern as follows:

* * *

a small-business concern shall be deemed to be one which is independently owned and operated and which is not dominant in its field of operation, and provided that, The Administration, in making a detailed definition, may use these criteria, among others: independency of ownership and operation, number of employees, dollar volume of business, and nondominance in its field.]

Sec. 715.

If any provision of this Act or the application of such provision to any person or circumstances shall be held invalid, the remainder of the Act, and the application of such provision to persons or circumstances other than those as to which it is held invalid, shall not be affected thereby.

[50 U.S.C. 4563]

[Section 716 repealed by section 154 of P.L. 102–558 (106 Stat. 4219).]

Sec. 717. (a)   Title I (except section 104), title III, and title VII (except sections 707, 708[11], and 721) shall terminate on September 30, 2025, except that all authority extended under title III shall be effective for any fiscal year only to such extent or in such amounts as are provided in advance in appropriations Acts.

---

[11]   Authority of the President to approve certain voluntary agreements made permanent, May 18, 1971, by 85 Stat. 38.

(b)   Notwithstanding subsection (a), any agency created under a provision of law that is terminated under subsection (a) may continue in existence, for purposes of liquidation, for a period not to exceed 6 months, beginning on the date of termination of the provision authorizing the creation of such agency under subsection (a).

(c)   The termination of any section of this Act, or of any agency or corporation utilized under this Act, shall not affect the disbursement of funds under, or the carrying out of, any contract, guarantee, commitment or other obligation entered into pursuant to this Act prior to the date of such termination, or the taking of any action necessary to preserve or protect the interests of the United States in any amounts advanced or paid out in carrying on operations under this Act, or the taking of any action (including the making of new guarantees) deemed by a guaranteeing agency to be necessary to accomplish the orderly liquidation, adjustment or settlement of any loans guaranteed under this Act, including actions deemed necessary to avoid undue hardship to borrowers in reconverting to normal civilian production; and all of the authority granted to the President, guaranteeing agencies, and fiscal agents, under section 301 of this Act shall be applicable to actions taken pursuant to the authority contained in this subsection.

(d)   No action for the recovery of any cooperative payment made to a cooperative association by a Market Administrator under an invalid provision of a milk marketing order issued by the Secretary of Agriculture pursuant to the Agricultural Marketing Agreement Act of 1937 shall be maintained unless such action is brought by producers specifically named as party plaintiffs to recover their respective share of such payments within ninety days after the date of enactment of the Defense Production Act Amendments of 1952 with respect to any cause of action heretofore accrued and not otherwise barred, or within ninety days after accrual with respect to future payments, and unless each claimant shall allege and prove (1) that he objected at the hearing to the provisions of the order under which such payments were made and (2) that he either refused to accept payments computed with such deduction or accepted them under protest to either the Secretary or the Administrator. The district courts of the United States shall have exclusive original jurisdiction of all such actions regardless of the amount involved. This subsection shall not apply to funds held in escrow pursuant to court order. Notwithstanding any other provision of this Act, no termination date shall be applicable to this subsection.

[50 U.S.C. 4564]

[Section 718 repealed by section 155 of P.L. 102–558 (106 Stat. 4219).] [Section 719 repealed by section 5(b) of P.L. 100–679 (102 Stat. 4063).] [Section 720 repealed by section 156 of P.L. 102–558 (106 Stat. 4219).]

AUTHORITY TO REVIEW CERTAIN MERGERS, ACQUISITIONS, AND TAKEOVERS

Sec. 721. (a) DEFINITIONS.—For purposes of this section, the following definitions shall apply:

(1) CLARIFICATION.— The term national security shall be construed so as to include those issues relating to homeland security, including its application to critical infrastructure.

(2) COMMITTEE; CHAIRPERSON.— The terms Committee and chairperson mean the Committee on Foreign Investment in the United States and the chairperson thereof, respectively.

(3) CONTROL.— The term control means the power, direct or indirect, whether

exercised or not exercised, to determine, direct, or decide important matters affecting an entity, subject to regulations prescribed by the Committee.

(4) COVERED TRANSACTION.—

(A) IN GENERAL.—Except as otherwise provided, the term covered transaction means—

(i) any transaction described in subparagraph (B)(i); and

(ii) any transaction described in clauses (ii) through (v) of subparagraph (B) that is proposed, pending, or completed on or after the effective date set forth in section 1727 of the Foreign Investment Risk Review Modernization Act of 2018.

(B) TRANSACTIONS DESCRIBED.—A transaction described in this subparagraph is any of the following:

(i) Any merger, acquisition, or takeover that is proposed or pending after August 23, 1988, by or with any foreign person that could result in foreign control of any United States business, including such a merger, acquisition, or takeover carried out through a joint venture.

(ii) Subject to subparagraphs (C) and (E), the purchase or lease by, or a concession to, a foreign person of private or public real estate that—

(I) is located in the United States;

(II)(aa) is, is located within, or will function as part of, an air or maritime port; or

(bb)(AA) is in close proximity to a United States military installation or another facility or property of the United States Government that is sensitive for reasons relating to national security;

(BB) could reasonably provide the foreign person the ability to collect intelligence on activities being conducted at such an installation, facility, or property; or

(CC) could otherwise expose national security activities at such an installation, facility, or property to the risk of foreign surveillance; and

(III) meets such other criteria as the Committee prescribes by regulation, except that such criteria may not expand the categories of real estate to which this clause applies beyond the categories described in subclause (II).

(iii) Any other investment, subject to regulations prescribed under subparagraphs (D) and (E), by a foreign person in any unaffiliated United States business that—

(I) owns, operates, manufactures, supplies, or services critical infrastructure;

(II) produces, designs, tests, manufactures, fabricates, or develops one or more critical technologies; or

(III)   maintains or collects sensitive personal data of United States citizens that may be exploited in a manner that threatens national security.

(iv) Any change in the rights that a foreign person has with respect to a United States business in which the foreign person has an investment, if that change could result in—

(I)   foreign control of the United States business; or

(II)   an investment described in clause (iii).

(v)   Any other transaction, transfer, agreement, or arrangement, the structure of which is designed or intended to evade or circumvent the application of this section, subject to regulations prescribed by the Committee.

(C) REAL ESTATE TRANSACTIONS.—

(i) EXCEPTION FOR CERTAIN REAL ESTATE TRANSACTIONS.—A real estate purchase, lease, or concession described in subparagraph (B)(ii) does not include a purchase, lease, or concession of—

(I)   a single housing unit, as defined by the Census Bureau; or

(II)   real estate in urbanized areas, as defined by the Census Bureau in the most recent census, except as otherwise prescribed by the Committee in regulations in consultation with the Secretary of Defense.

(ii) DEFINITION OF CLOSE PROXIMITY.— With respect to a real estate purchase, lease, or concession described in subparagraph (B)(ii)(II)(bb)(AA), the Committee shall prescribe regulations to ensure that the term close proximity refers only to a distance or distances within which the purchase, lease, or concession of real estate could pose a national security risk in connection with a United States military installation or another facility or property of the United States Government described in that subparagraph.

(D) OTHER INVESTMENTS.—

(i) OTHER INVESTMENT DEFINED.—For purposes of subparagraph (B)(iii), the term other investment means an investment, direct or indirect, by a foreign person in a United States business described in that subparagraph that is not an investment described in subparagraph (B)(i) and that affords the foreign person—

(I)   access to any material nonpublic technical information in the possession of the United States business;

(II)   membership or observer rights on the board of directors or equivalent governing body of the United States business or the right to nominate an individual to a position on the board of directors or equivalent governing body; or

(III)   any involvement, other than through voting of shares, in substantive decisionmaking of the United States business regarding—

(aa) the use, development, acquisition, safekeeping, or release of sensitive personal data of United States citizens maintained or collected by the United States business;

(bb) the use, development acquisition, or release of critical technologies; or

(cc) the management, operation, manufacture, or supply of critical infrastructure.

(ii) MATERIAL NONPUBLIC TECHNICAL INFORMATION DEFINED.—

(I) IN GENERAL.—For purposes of clause (i)(I), and subject to regulations prescribed by the Committee, the term material nonpublic technical information means information that—

(aa) provides knowledge, know-how, or understanding, not available in the public domain, of the design, location, or operation of critical infrastructure; or

(bb) is not available in the public domain, and is necessary to design, fabricate, develop, test, produce, or manufacture critical technologies, including processes, techniques, or methods.

(II) EXEMPTION FOR FINANCIAL INFORMATION.— Notwithstanding subclause (I), for purposes of this subparagraph, the term material nonpublic technical information does not include financial information regarding the performance of a United States business.

(iii) REGULATIONS.—

(I) IN GENERAL.— The Committee shall prescribe regulations providing guidance on the types of transactions that the Committee considers to be other investment for purposes of subparagraph (B)(iii).

(II) UNITED STATES BUSINESSES THAT OWN, OPERATE, MANUFACTURE, SUPPLY, OR SERVICE CRITICAL INFRASTRUCTURE.—The regulations prescribed by the Committee with respect to an investment described in subparagraph (B)(iii)(I) shall—

(aa) specify the critical infrastructure subject to that subparagraph based on criteria intended to limit application of that subparagraph to the subset of critical infrastructure that is likely to be of importance to the national security of the United States; and

(bb) enumerate specific types and examples of such critical infrastructure.

(iv) SPECIFIC CLARIFICATION FOR INVESTMENT FUNDS.—

(I) TREATMENT OF CERTAIN INVESTMENT FUND INVESTMENTS.—Notwithstanding clause (i)(II) and subject to regulations prescribed by the Committee, an indirect investment by a foreign person in a United States business described in subparagraph (B)(iii) through an investment fund that affords the foreign person (or a designee of the foreign person) membership as a limited partner or equivalent on an advisory board or a committee of the fund shall not be considered an other investment for purposes of subparagraph (B)(iii) if—

(aa)　the fund is managed exclusively by a general partner, a managing member, or an equivalent;

(bb)　the general partner, managing member, or equivalent is not a foreign person;

(cc) the advisory board or committee does not have the ability to approve, disapprove, or otherwise control—

(AA)　investment decisions of the fund; or

(BB)　decisions made by the general partner, managing member, or equivalent related to entities in which the fund is invested;

(dd) the foreign person does not otherwise have the ability to control the fund, including the authority—

(AA)　to approve, disapprove, or otherwise control investment decisions of the fund;

(BB)　to approve, disapprove, or otherwise control decisions made by the general partner, managing member, or equivalent related to entities in which the fund is invested; or

(CC)　to unilaterally dismiss, prevent the dismissal of, select, or determine the compensation of the general partner, managing member, or equivalent;

(ee)　the foreign person does not have access to material nonpublic technical information as a result of its participation on the advisory board or committee; and

(ff)　the investment otherwise meets the requirements of this subparagraph.

(II) TREATMENT OF CERTAIN WAIVERS.—

(aa) IN GENERAL.— For the purposes of items (cc) and (dd) of subclause (I) and except as provided in item (bb), a waiver of a potential conflict of interest, a waiver of an allocation limitation, or a similar activity, applicable to a transaction pursuant to the terms of an agreement governing an investment fund shall not be considered to constitute control of investment decisions of the fund or decisions relating to entities in which the fund is invested.

(bb) EXCEPTION.— The Committee may prescribe regulations providing for exceptions to item (aa) for extraordinary circumstances.

(v) EXCEPTION FOR AIR CARRIERS.— For purposes of subparagraph (B)(iii), the term other investment does not include an investment involving an air carrier, as defined in section 40102(a)(2) of title 49, United States Code, that holds a certificate issued under section 41102 of that title.

517

(vi) RULE OF CONSTRUCTION.— Any definition of critical infrastructure established under any provision of law other than this section shall not be determinative for purposes of this section.

(E) COUNTRY SPECIFICATION.— The Committee shall prescribe regulations that further define the term foreign person for purposes of clauses (ii) and (iii) of subparagraph (B). In prescribing such regulations, the Committee shall specify criteria to limit the application of such clauses to the investments of certain categories of foreign persons. Such criteria shall take into consideration how a foreign person is connected to a foreign country or foreign government, and whether the connection may affect the national security of the United States.

(F) TRANSFERS OF CERTAIN ASSETS PURSUANT TO BANKRUPTCY PROCEEDINGS OR OTHER DEFAULTS.— The Committee shall prescribe regulations to clarify that the term covered transaction includes any transaction described in subparagraph (B) that arises pursuant to a bankruptcy proceeding or other form of default on debt.

(5) CRITICAL INFRASTRUCTURE.— The term critical infrastructure means, subject to regulations prescribed by the Committee, systems and assets, whether physical or virtual, so vital to the United States that the incapacity or destruction of such systems or assets would have a debilitating impact on national security.

(6) CRITICAL TECHNOLOGIES.—

(A) IN GENERAL.—The term critical technologies means the following:

(i) Defense articles or defense services included on the United States Munitions List set forth in the International Traffic in Arms Regulations under subchapter M of chapter I of title 22, Code of Federal Regulations.

(ii) Items included on the Commerce Control List set forth in Supplement No. 1 to part 774 of the Export Administration Regulations under subchapter C of chapter VII of title 15, Code of Federal Regulations, and controlled—

(I) pursuant to multilateral regimes, including for reasons relating to national security, chemical and biological weapons proliferation, nuclear nonproliferation, or missile technology; or

(II) for reasons relating to regional stability or surreptitious listening.

(iii) Specially designed and prepared nuclear equipment, parts and components, materials, software, and technology covered by part 810 of title 10, Code of Federal Regulations (relating to assistance to foreign atomic energy activities).

(iv) Nuclear facilities, equipment, and material covered by part 110 of title 10, Code of Federal Regulations (relating to export and import of nuclear equipment and material).

(v) Select agents and toxins covered by part 331 of title 7, Code of Federal Regulations, part 121 of title 9 of such Code, or part 73 of title 42 of such Code.

(vi) Emerging and foundational technologies controlled pursuant to section 1758 of the Export Control Reform Act of 2018.

(B) RECOMMENDATIONS.—

(i) IN GENERAL.— The chairperson may recommend technologies for identification under the interagency process set forth in section 1758(a) of the Export Control Reform Act of 2018.

(ii) MATTERS INFORMING RECOMMENDATIONS.— Recommendations by the chairperson under clause (i) shall draw upon information arising from reviews and investigations conducted under subsection (b), notices submitted under subsection (b)(1)(C)(i), declarations filed under subsection (b)(1)(C)(v), and non-notified and non-declared transactions identified under subsection (b)(1)(H).

(7) FOREIGN GOVERNMENT-CONTROLLED TRANSACTION.— The term foreign government-controlled transaction means any covered transaction that could result in the control of any United States business by a foreign government or an entity controlled by or acting on behalf of a foreign government.

(8) INTELLIGENCE COMMUNITY.— The term intelligence community has the meaning given that term in section 3(4) of the National Security Act of 1947 (50 U.S.C. 3003(4)).

(9) INVESTMENT.— The term investment means the acquisition of equity interest, including contingent equity interest, as further defined in regulations prescribed by the Committee.

(10) LEAD AGENCY.— The term lead agency means the agency or agencies designated as the lead agency or agencies pursuant to subsection (k)(5).

(11) PARTY.— The term party has the meaning given that term in regulations prescribed by the Committee.

(12) UNITED STATES.— The term United States means the several States, the District of Columbia, and any territory or possession of the United States.

(13) UNITED STATES BUSINESS.— The term United States business means a person engaged in interstate commerce in the United States.

(b) NATIONAL SECURITY REVIEWS AND INVESTIGATIONS.—

(1) NATIONAL SECURITY REVIEWS.—

(A) IN GENERAL.—Upon receiving written notification under subparagraph (C) of any covered transaction, or pursuant to a unilateral notification initiated under subparagraph (D) with respect to any covered transaction, the President, acting through the Committee—

(i)   shall review the covered transaction to determine the effects of the transaction on the national security of the United States; and

(ii)   shall consider the factors specified in subsection (f) for such purpose, as appropriate.

(B) CONTROL BY FOREIGN GOVERNMENT.— If the Committee determines that the covered transaction is a foreign government-controlled transaction, the Committee shall conduct an investigation of the transaction under paragraph

(2).

(C) WRITTEN NOTICE.—

(i) IN GENERAL.—

(I) IN GENERAL.— Any party or parties to any covered transaction may initiate a review of the transaction under this paragraph by submitting a written notice of the transaction to the Chairperson of the Committee.

(II) COMMENTS AND ACCEPTANCE.—

(aa) IN GENERAL.— Subject to item (cc), the Committee shall provide comments on a draft or formal written notice or accept a formal written notice submitted under subclause (I) with respect to a covered transaction not later than the date that is 10 business days after the date of submission of the draft or formal written notice.

(bb) COMPLETENESS.— If the Committee determines that a draft or formal written notice described in item (aa) is not complete, the Committee shall notify the party or parties to the transaction in writing that the notice is not complete and provide an explanation of all material respects in which the notice is incomplete.

(cc) STIPULATIONS REQUIRED.— The timing requirement under item (aa) shall apply only in a case in which the parties stipulate under clause (vi) that the transaction is a covered transaction.

(ii) WITHDRAWAL OF NOTICE.— No covered transaction for which a notice was submitted under clause (i) may be withdrawn from review, unless a written request for such withdrawal is submitted to the Committee by any party to the transaction and approved by the Committee.

(iii) CONTINUING DISCUSSIONS.— A request for withdrawal under clause (ii) shall not be construed to preclude any party to the covered transaction from continuing informal discussions with the Committee or any member thereof regarding possible resubmission for review pursuant to this paragraph.

(iv) INCLUSION OF PARTNERSHIP AND SIDE AGREEMENTS.— The Committee may require a written notice submitted under clause (i) to include a copy of any partnership agreements, integration agreements, or other side agreements relating to the transaction, as specified in regulations prescribed by the Committee.

(v) DECLARATIONS FOR CERTAIN COVERED TRANSACTIONS.—

(I) IN GENERAL.— A party to any covered transaction may submit to the Committee a declaration with basic information regarding the transaction instead of a written notice under clause (i).

(II) REGULATIONS.— The Committee shall prescribe regulations establishing requirements for declarations submitted under this clause. In prescribing such regulations, the Committee shall ensure that such declarations are submitted as abbreviated notifications that would not generally exceed 5 pages in length.

(III) COMMITTEE RESPONSE TO DECLARATION.—

(aa) IN GENERAL.—Upon receiving a declaration under this clause with respect to a covered transaction, the Committee may, at the discretion of the Committee—

(AA) request that the parties to the transaction file a written notice under clause (i);

(BB) inform the parties to the transaction that the Committee is not able to complete action under this section with respect to the transaction on the basis of the declaration and that the parties may file a written notice under clause (i) to seek written notification from the Committee that the Committee has completed all action under this section with respect to the transaction;

(CC) initiate a unilateral review of the transaction under subparagraph (D); or

(DD) notify the parties in writing that the Committee has completed all action under this section with respect to the transaction.

(bb) TIMING.— The Committee shall take action under item (aa) not later than 30 days after receiving a declaration under this clause.

(cc) RULE OF CONSTRUCTION.— Nothing in this subclause (other than item (aa)(CC)) shall be construed to affect the authority of the President or the Committee to take any action authorized by this section with respect to a covered transaction.

(IV) MANDATORY DECLARATIONS.—

(aa) REGULATIONS.— The Committee shall prescribe regulations specifying the types of covered transactions for which the Committee requires a declaration under this subclause.

(bb) CERTAIN COVERED TRANSACTIONS WITH FOREIGN GOVERNMENT INTERESTS.—

(AA) IN GENERAL.— Except as provided in subitem (BB), the parties to a covered transaction shall submit a declaration described in subclause (I) with respect to the transaction if the transaction involves an investment that results in the acquisition, directly or indirectly, of a substantial interest in a United States business described in subsection (a)(4)(B)(iii) by a foreign person in which a foreign government has, directly or indirectly, a substantial interest.

(BB) SUBSTANTIAL INTEREST DEFINED.— In this item, the term substantial interest has the meaning given that term in regulations which the Committee shall prescribe. In developing those regulations, the Committee shall consider the means by which

521

a foreign government could influence the actions of a foreign person, including through board membership, ownership interest, or shareholder rights. An interest that is excluded under subparagraph (D) of subsection (a)(4) from the term other investment as used in subparagraph (B)(iii) of that subsection or that is less than a 10 percent voting interest shall not be considered a substantial interest.

(CC) WAIVER.— The Committee may waive, with respect to a foreign person, the requirement under subitem (AA) for the submission of a declaration described in subclause (I) if the Committee determines that the foreign person demonstrates that the investments of the foreign person are not directed by a foreign government and the foreign person has a history of cooperation with the Committee.

(cc) OTHER DECLARATIONS REQUIRED BY COMMITTEE.— The Committee may require the submission of a declaration described in subclause (I) with respect to any covered transaction identified under regulations prescribed by the Committee for purposes of this item, at the discretion of the Committee, that involves a United States business described in subsection (a)(4)(B)(iii)(II).

(dd) EXCEPTION.—The submission of a declaration described in subclause (I) shall not be required pursuant to this subclause with respect to an investment by an investment fund if—

(AA) the fund is managed exclusively by a general partner, a managing member, or an equivalent;

(BB) the general partner, managing member, or equivalent is not a foreign person; and

(CC) the investment fund satisfies, with respect to any foreign person with membership as a limited partner on an advisory board or a committee of the fund, the criteria specified in items (cc) and (dd) of subsection (a)(4)(D)(iv).

(ee) SUBMISSION OF WRITTEN NOTICE AS AN ALTERNATIVE.— Parties to a covered transaction for which a declaration is required under this subclause may instead elect to submit a written notice under clause (i).

(ff) TIMING AND REFILING OF SUBMISSION.—

(AA) IN GENERAL.— In the regulations prescribed under item (aa), the Committee may not require a declaration to be submitted under this subclause with respect to a covered transaction more than 45 days before the completion of the transaction.

(BB) REFILING OF DECLARATION.— The Committee may not request or recommend that a declaration submitted under this subclause be withdrawn and refiled, except to permit parties to a covered transaction to correct material errors or omissions in the declaration submitted with respect to that transaction.

(gg) PENALTIES.— The Committee may impose a penalty pursuant to subsection (h)(3) with respect to a party that fails to comply with this subclause.

(vi) STIPULATIONS REGARDING TRANSACTIONS.—

(I) IN GENERAL.—In a written notice submitted under clause (i) or a declaration submitted under clause (v) with respect to a transaction, a party to the transaction may—

(aa) stipulate that the transaction is a covered transaction; and

(bb) if the party stipulates that the transaction is a covered transaction under item (aa), stipulate that the transaction is a foreign government-controlled transaction.

(II) BASIS FOR STIPULATION.— A written notice submitted under clause (i) or a declaration submitted under clause (v) that includes a stipulation under subclause (I) shall include a description of the basis for the stipulation.

(D) UNILATERAL INITIATION OF REVIEW.—Subject to subparagraph (G), the President or the Committee may initiate a review under subparagraph (A) of—

(i) any covered transaction (other than a covered transaction described in subparagraph (E));

(ii) any covered transaction described in subparagraph (E), if any party to the transaction submitted false or misleading material information to the Committee in connection with the Committee's consideration of the transaction or omitted material information, including material documents, from information submitted to the Committee; or

(iii) any covered transaction described in subparagraph (E), if—

(I) any party to the transaction or the entity resulting from consummation of the transaction materially breaches a mitigation agreement or condition described in subsection (l)(3)(A);

(II) such breach is certified to the Committee by the lead department or agency monitoring and enforcing such agreement or condition as a material breach; and

(III) the Committee determines that there are no other adequate and appropriate remedies or enforcement tools available to address such breach.

(E) COVERED TRANSACTIONS DESCRIBED.—A covered transaction is described in this subparagraph if—

(i) the Committee has informed the parties to the transaction in writing that the Committee has completed all action under this section with respect to the transaction; or

(ii) the President has announced a decision not to exercise the President's authority under subsection (d) with respect to the transaction.

(F) TIMING.— Any review under this paragraph shall be completed before the end of the 45-day period beginning on the date of the acceptance of written notice under subparagraph (C) by the chairperson, or beginning on the date of the initiation of the review in accordance with subparagraph (D), as applicable.

(G) LIMIT ON DELEGATION OF CERTAIN AUTHORITY.— The authority of the Committee to initiate a review under subparagraph (D) may not be delegated to any person, other than the Deputy Secretary or an appropriate Under Secretary of the department or agency represented on the Committee.

(H) IDENTIFICATION OF NON-NOTIFIED AND NON-DECLARED TRANSACTIONS.—The Committee shall establish a process to identify covered transactions for which—

(i) a notice under clause (i) of subparagraph (C) or a declaration under clause (v) of that subparagraph is not submitted to the Committee; and

(ii) information is reasonably available.

(2) NATIONAL SECURITY INVESTIGATIONS.—

(A) IN GENERAL.— In each case described in subparagraph (B), the Committee shall immediately conduct an investigation of the effects of a covered transaction on the national security of the United States, and take any necessary actions in connection with the transaction to protect the national security of the United States.

(B) APPLICABILITY.—Subparagraph (A) shall apply in each case in which—

(i) a review of a covered transaction under paragraph (1) results in a determination that—

(I) the transaction threatens to impair the national security of the United States and the risk has not been mitigated during or prior to the review of a covered transaction under paragraph (1);

(II) the transaction is a foreign government-controlled transaction; or

(III) the transaction would result in control of any critical infrastructure of or within the United States by or on behalf of any foreign person, if the Committee determines that the transaction could impair national security, and that such impairment to national security has not been mitigated by assurances provided or renewed with the approval of the Committee, as described in subsection (l), during the review period under paragraph (1); or

(ii) the lead agency recommends, and the Committee concurs, that an investigation be undertaken.

(C) TIMING.—

(i) IN GENERAL.— Except as provided in clause (ii), any investigation under subparagraph (A) shall be completed before the end of the 45-day period beginning on the date on which the investigation commenced.

(ii) EXTENSION FOR EXTRAORDINARY CIRCUMSTANCES.—

(I) In GENERAL.— In extraordinary circumstances (as defined by the Committee in regulations), the chairperson may, at the request of the head of the lead agency, extend an investigation under subparagraph (A) for one 15-day period.

(II) NONDELEGATION.— The authority of the chairperson and the head of the lead agency referred to in subclause (I) may not be delegated to any person other than the Deputy Secretary of the Treasury or the deputy head (or equivalent thereof) of the lead agency, as the case may be.

(III) NOTIFICATION TO PARTIES.— If the Committee extends the deadline under subclause (I) with respect to a covered transaction, the Committee shall notify the parties to the transaction of the extension.

(D) EXCEPTION.—

(i) In GENERAL.— Notwithstanding subparagraph (B)(i), an investigation of a foreign government-controlled transaction described in subclause (II) of subparagraph (B)(i) or a transaction involving critical infrastructure described in subclause (III) of subparagraph (B)(i) shall not be required under this paragraph, if the Secretary of the Treasury and the head of the lead agency jointly determine, on the basis of the review of the transaction under paragraph (1), that the transaction will not impair the national security of the United States.

(ii) NONDELEGATION.— The authority of the Secretary or the head of an agency referred to in clause (i) may not be delegated to any person, other than the Deputy Secretary of the Treasury or the deputy head (or the equivalent thereof) of the lead agency, respectively.

(E) GUIDANCE ON CERTAIN TRANSACTIONS WITH NATIONAL SECURITY IMPLICATIONS.— The Chairperson shall, not later than 180 days after the effective date of the Foreign Investment and National Security Act of 2007, publish in the Federal Register guidance on the types of transactions that the Committee has reviewed and that have presented national security considerations, including transactions that may constitute covered transactions that would result in control of critical infrastructure relating to United States national security by a foreign government or an entity controlled by or acting on behalf of a foreign government.

(3) CERTIFICATIONS TO CONGRESS.—

(A) CERTIFIED NOTICE AT COMPLETION OF REVIEW OR ASSESSMENT.— Upon completion of a review under this subsection that concludes action under this section, or upon the Committee making a notification under paragraph (1)(C)(v)(III)(aa)(DD), the chairperson and the head of the lead agency shall transmit a certified notice to the members of Congress specified in subparagraph (C)(iii).

(B) CERTIFIED REPORT AT COMPLETION OF INVESTIGATION.— As soon as is practicable after completion of an investigation under subsection (b) that concludes action under this section, the chairperson and the head of the lead agency shall transmit to the members of Congress specified in subparagraph

525

(C)(iii) a certified written report (consistent with the requirements of subsection (c)) on the results of the investigation, unless the matter under investigation has been sent to the President for decision.

(C) CERTIFICATION PROCEDURES.—

(i) IN GENERAL.—Each certified notice and report required under subparagraphs (A) and (B), respectively, shall be submitted to the members of Congress specified in clause (iii), and shall include—

(I) a description of the actions taken by the Committee with respect to the transaction;

(II) a certification that all relevant national security factors have received full consideration; and

(III) whether the transaction is described under clause (i), (ii), (iii), (iv), or (v) of subsection (a)(4)(B).

(ii) CONTENT OF CERTIFICATION.— Each certified notice and report required under subparagraphs (A) and (B), respectively, shall be signed by the chairperson and the head of the lead agency, and shall state that, in the determination of the Committee, there are no unresolved national security concerns with the transaction that is the subject of the notice or report.

(iii) MEMBERS OF CONGRESS.—Each certified notice and report required under subparagraphs (A) and (B), respectively, shall be transmitted—

(I) to the Majority Leader and the Minority Leader of the Senate;

(II) to the chair and ranking member of the Committee on Banking, Housing, and Urban Affairs of the Senate and of any committee of the Senate having oversight over the lead agency;

(III) to the Speaker and the Minority Leader of the House of Representatives;

(IV) to the chair and ranking member of the Committee on Financial Services of the House of Representatives and of any committee of the House of Representatives having oversight over the lead agency; and

(V) with respect to covered transactions involving critical infrastructure, to the members of the Senate from the State in which the principal place of business of the acquired United States person is located, and the member from the Congressional District in which such principal place of business is located.

(iv) SIGNATURES; LIMIT ON DELEGATION.—

(I) IN GENERAL.— Each certified notice and report required under subparagraphs (A) and (B), respectively, shall be signed by the chairperson and the head of the lead agency, which signature requirement may only be delegated in accordance with subclause (II).

(II) DELEGATION OF CERTIFICATIONS.—

(aa) IN GENERAL.— Subject to item (bb), the chairperson, in consultation with the Committee, may determine the level of official to whom the signature requirement under subclause (I) for the chairperson and the head of the lead agency may be delegated. The level of official to whom the signature requirement may be delegated may differ based on any factor relating to a transaction that the chairperson, in consultation with the Committee, deems appropriate, including the type or value of the transaction.

(bb) LIMITATION ON DELEGATION WITH RESPECT TO CERTAIN TRANSACTIONS.— The signature requirement under subclause (I) may be delegated not below the level of the Assistant Secretary of the Treasury or an equivalent official of the lead agency.

(v) AUTHORITY TO CONSOLIDATE DOCUMENTS.— Instead of transmitting a separate certified notice or certified report under subparagraph (A) or (B) with respect to each covered transaction, the Committee may, on a monthly basis, transmit such notices and reports in a consolidated document to the Members of Congress specified in clause (iii).

(4) ANALYSIS BY DIRECTOR OF NATIONAL INTELLIGENCE.—

(A) ANALYSIS REQUIRED.—

(i) IN GENERAL.— Except as provided in subparagraph (B), the Director of National Intelligence shall expeditiously carry out a thorough analysis of any threat to the national security of the United States posed by any covered transaction, which shall include the identification of any recognized gaps in the collection of intelligence relevant to the analysis.

(ii) VIEWS OF INTELLIGENCE COMMUNITY.— The Director shall seek and incorporate into the analysis required by clause (i) the views of all affected or appropriate agencies of the intelligence community with respect to the transaction.

(iii) UPDATES.— At the request of the lead agency, the Director shall update the analysis conducted under clause (i) with respect to a covered transaction with respect to which an agreement was entered into under subsection (l)(3)(A).

(iv) INDEPENDENCE AND OBJECTIVITY.— The Committee shall ensure that its processes under this section preserve the ability of the Director to conduct analysis under clause (i) that is independent, objective, and consistent with all applicable directives, policies, and analytic tradecraft standards of the intelligence community.

(B) BASIC THREAT INFORMATION.—

(i) IN GENERAL.— The Director of National Intelligence may provide the Committee with basic information regarding any threat to the national security of the United States posed by a covered transaction described in clause (ii) instead of conducting the analysis required by subparagraph (A).

(ii) COVERED TRANSACTION DESCRIBED.—A covered transaction is described in this clause if—

(I) the transaction is described in subsection (a)(4)(B)(ii);

(II)   the Director of National Intelligence has completed an analysis pursuant to subparagraph (A) involving each foreign person that is a party to the transaction during the 12 months preceding the review or investigation of the transaction under this section; or

(III)   the transaction otherwise meets criteria agreed upon by the Committee and the Director for purposes of this subparagraph.

(C) TIMING.— The analysis required under subparagraph (A) shall be provided by the Director of National Intelligence to the Committee not later than 30 days after the date on which notice of the transaction is accepted by the Committee under paragraph (1)(C), but such analysis may be supplemented or amended, as the Director considers necessary or appropriate, or upon a request for additional information by the Committee. The Director may begin the analysis at any time prior to acceptance of the notice, in accordance with otherwise applicable law.

(D) INTERACTION WITH INTELLIGENCE COMMUNITY.— The Director of National Intelligence shall ensure that the intelligence community remains engaged in the collection, analysis, and dissemination to the Committee of any additional relevant information that may become available during the course of any investigation conducted under subsection (b) with respect to a transaction.

(E) INDEPENDENT ROLE OF DIRECTOR.— The Director of National Intelligence shall be a nonvoting, ex officio member of the Committee, and shall be provided with all notices received by the Committee under paragraph (1)(C) regarding covered transactions, but shall serve no policy role on the Committee, other than to provide analysis under subparagraphs (A) and (C) in connection with a covered transaction.

(F) ASSESSMENT OF OPERATIONAL IMPACT.— The Director may provide to the Committee an assessment, separate from the analyses under subparagraphs (A) and (B), of any operational impact of a covered transaction on the intelligence community and a description of any actions that have been or will be taken to mitigate any such impact.

(G) SUBMISSION TO CONGRESS.— The Committee shall submit the analysis required by subparagraph (A) with respect to a covered transaction to the Select Committee on Intelligence of the Senate and the Permanent Select Committee on Intelligence of the House of Representatives upon the conclusion of action under this section (other than compliance plans under subsection (l)(6)) with respect to the transaction.

(5) SUBMISSION OF ADDITIONAL INFORMATION.— No provision of this subsection shall be construed as prohibiting any party to a covered transaction from submitting additional information concerning the transaction, including any proposed restructuring of the transaction or any modifications to any agreements in connection with the transaction, while any review or investigation of the transaction is ongoing.

(6) NOTICE OF RESULTS TO PARTIES.— The Committee shall notify the parties to a covered transaction of the results of a review or investigation under this section,

promptly upon completion of all action under this section.

(7) REGULATIONS.—Regulations prescribed under this section shall include standard procedures for—

(A) submitting any notice of a covered transaction to the Committee;

(B) submitting a request to withdraw a covered transaction from review;

(C) resubmitting a notice of a covered transaction that was previously withdrawn from review; and

(D) providing notice of the results of a review or investigation to the parties to the covered transaction, upon completion of all action under this section.

(8) TOLLING OF DEADLINES DURING LAPSE IN APPROPRIATIONS.— Any deadline or time limitation under this subsection shall be tolled during a lapse in appropriations.

(c) CONFIDENTIALITY OF INFORMATION.—

(1) IN GENERAL.— Except as provided in paragraph (2), any information or documentary material filed with the President or the President's designee pursuant to this section shall be exempt from disclosure under section 552 of title 5, United States Code, and no such information or documentary material may be made public.

(2) EXCEPTIONS.—Paragraph (1) shall not prohibit the disclosure of the following:

(A) Information relevant to any administrative or judicial action or proceeding.

(B) Information to Congress or any duly authorized committee or subcommittee of Congress.

(C) Information important to the national security analysis or actions of the Committee to any domestic governmental entity, or to any foreign governmental entity of a United States ally or partner, under the exclusive direction and authorization of the chairperson, only to the extent necessary for national security purposes, and subject to appropriate confidentiality and classification requirements.

(D) Information that the parties have consented to be disclosed to third parties.

(3) COOPERATION WITH ALLIES AND PARTNERS.—

(A) IN GENERAL.— The chairperson, in consultation with other members of the Committee, should establish a formal process for the exchange of information under paragraph (2)(C) with governments of countries that are allies or partners of the United States, in the discretion of the chairperson, to protect the national security of the United States and those countries.

(B) REQUIREMENTS.—The process established under subparagraph (A) should, in the discretion of the chairperson—

(i) be designed to facilitate the harmonization of action with respect to trends in investment and technology that could pose risks to the national

529

security of the United States and countries that are allies or partners of the United States;

(ii)   provide for the sharing of information with respect to specific technologies and entities acquiring such technologies as appropriate to ensure national security; and

(iii)   include consultations and meetings with representatives of the governments of such countries on a recurring basis.

(d) ACTION BY THE PRESIDENT.—

(1) IN GENERAL.— Subject to paragraph (4), the President may take such action for such time as the President considers appropriate to suspend or prohibit any covered transaction that threatens to impair the national security of the United States.

(2) ANNOUNCEMENT BY THE PRESIDENT.—The President shall announce the decision on whether or not to take action pursuant to paragraph (1) with respect to a covered transaction not later than 15 days after the earlier of—

(A)   the date on which the investigation of the transaction under subsection (b) is completed; or

(B)   the date on which the Committee otherwise refers the transaction to the President under subsection (l)(2).

(3) ENFORCEMENT.— The President may direct the Attorney General of the United States to seek appropriate relief, including divestment relief, in the district courts of the United States, in order to implement and enforce this subsection.

(4) FINDINGS OF THE PRESIDENT.—The President may exercise the authority conferred by paragraph (1), only if the President finds that—

(A)   there is credible evidence that leads the President to believe that a foreign person that would acquire an interest in a United States business or its assets as a result of the covered transaction might take action that threatens to impair the national security; and

(B)   provisions of law, other than this section and the International Emergency Economic Powers Act, do not, in the judgment of the President, provide adequate and appropriate authority for the President to protect the national security in the matter before the President.

(5) FACTORS TO BE CONSIDERED.— For purposes of determining whether to take action under paragraph (1), the President shall consider, among other factors each of the factors described in subsection (f), as appropriate.

(e) ACTIONS AND FINDINGS NONREVIEWABLE.—

(1) IN GENERAL.— The actions of the President under paragraph (1) of subsection (d) and the findings of the President under paragraph (4) of subsection (d) shall not be subject to judicial review.

(2) CIVIL ACTIONS.— A civil action challenging an action or finding under this section may be brought only in the United States Court of Appeals for the District of Columbia Circuit.

(3) PROCEDURES FOR REVIEW OF PRIVILEGED INFORMATION.— If a civil action challenging an action or finding under this section is brought, and the court determines that protected information in the administrative record, including classified or other information subject to privilege or protections under any provision of law, is necessary to resolve the challenge, that information shall be submitted ex parte and in camera to the court and the court shall maintain that information under seal.

(4) APPLICABILITY OF USE OF INFORMATION PROVISIONS.— The use of information provisions of sections 106, 305, 405, and 706 of the Foreign Intelligence Surveillance Act of 1978 (50 U.S.C. 1806, 1825, 1845, and 1881e) shall not apply in a civil action brought under this subsection.

(f) FACTORS TO BE CONSIDERED.—For purposes of this section, the President or the President's designee may, taking into account the requirements of national security, consider—

(1) domestic production needed for projected national defense requirements,

(2) the capability and capacity of domestic industries to meet national defense requirements, including the availability of human resources, products, technology, materials, and other supplies and services,

(3) the control of domestic industries and commercial activity by foreign citizens as it affects the capability and capacity of the United States to meet the requirements of national security,

(4) the potential effects of the proposed or pending transaction on sales of military goods, equipment, or technology to any country—

(A) identified by the Secretary of State—

(i) under section 6(j) of the Export Administration Act of 1979, as a country that supports terrorism;

(ii) under section 6(l) of the Export Administration Act of 1979, as a country of concern regarding missile proliferation; or

(iii) under section 6(m) of the Export Administration Act of 1979, as a country of concern regarding the proliferation of chemical and biological weapons;

(B) identified by the Secretary of Defense as posing a potential regional military threat to the interests of the United States; or

(C) listed under section 309(c) of the Nuclear Non-Proliferation Act of 1978 on the Nuclear Non-Proliferation-Special Country List (15 C.F.R. Part 778, Supplement No. 4) or any successor list;

(5) the potential effects of the proposed or pending transaction on United States international technological leadership in areas affecting United States national security;

(6) the potential national security-related effects on United States critical infrastructure, including major energy assets;

(7) the potential national security-related effects on United States critical

technologies;

(8) whether the covered transaction is a foreign government-controlled transaction, as determined under subsection (b)(1)(B);

(9) as appropriate, and particularly with respect to transactions requiring an investigation under subsection (b)(1)(B), a review of the current assessment of—

(A) the adherence of the subject country to nonproliferation control regimes, including treaties and multilateral supply guidelines, which shall draw on, but not be limited to, the annual report on Adherence to and Compliance with Arms Control, Nonproliferation and Disarmament Agreements and Commitments required by section 403 of the Arms Control and Disarmament Act;

(B) the relationship of such country with the United States, specifically on its record on cooperating in counter-terrorism efforts, which shall draw on, but not be limited to, the report of the President to Congress under section 7120 of the Intelligence Reform and Terrorism Prevention Act of 2004; and

(C) the potential for transshipment or diversion of technologies with military applications, including an analysis of national export control laws and regulations;

(10) the long-term projection of United States requirements for sources of energy and other critical resources and material; and

(11) such other factors as the President or the Committee may determine to be appropriate, generally or in connection with a specific review or investigation.

(g) ADDITIONAL INFORMATION TO CONGRESS; CONFIDENTIALITY.—

(1) BRIEFING REQUIREMENT ON REQUEST.— The Committee shall, upon request from any Member of Congress specified in subsection (b)(3)(C)(iii), promptly provide briefings on a covered transaction for which all action has concluded under this section, or on compliance with a mitigation agreement or condition imposed with respect to such transaction, on a classified basis, if deemed necessary by the sensitivity of the information. Briefings under this paragraph may be provided to the congressional staff of such a Member of Congress having appropriate security clearance.

(2) APPLICATION OF CONFIDENTIALITY PROVISIONS.—

(A) IN GENERAL.— The disclosure of information under this subsection shall be consistent with the requirements of subsection (c). Members of Congress and staff of either House of Congress or any committee of Congress, shall be subject to the same limitations on disclosure of information as are applicable under subsection (c).

(B) PROPRIETARY INFORMATION.— Proprietary information which can be associated with a particular party to a covered transaction shall be furnished in accordance with subparagraph (A) only to a committee of Congress, and only when the committee provides assurances of confidentiality, unless such party otherwise consents in writing to such disclosure.

(h) REGULATIONS.—

(1) IN GENERAL.— The President shall direct, subject to notice and comment, the issuance of regulations to carry out this section.

(2) CONTENT.—Regulations issued under this subsection shall—

(A) provide for the imposition of civil penalties for any violation of this section, including any mitigation agreement entered into, conditions imposed, or order issued pursuant to this section;

(B) to the extent possible—

(i) minimize paperwork burdens; and

(ii) coordinate reporting requirements under this section with reporting requirements under any other provision of Federal law;

(C) provide for an appropriate role for the Secretary of Labor with respect to mitigation agreements; and

(D) provide that, in any review or investigation of a covered transaction conducted by the Committee under subsection (b), the Committee should—

(i) consider the factors specified in subsection (f); and

(ii) as appropriate, require parties to provide to the Committee the information necessary to consider such factors.

(i) EFFECT ON OTHER LAW.— No provision of this section shall be construed as altering or affecting any other authority, process, regulation, investigation, enforcement measure, or review provided by or established under any other provision of Federal law, including the International Emergency Economic Powers Act, or any other authority of the President or the Congress under the Constitution of the United States.

(j) TECHNOLOGY RISK ASSESSMENTS.— In any case in which an assessment of the risk of diversion of defense critical technology is performed by a designee of the President, a copy of such assessment shall be provided to any other designee of the President responsible for reviewing or investigating a transaction under this section.

(k) COMMITTEE ON FOREIGN INVESTMENT IN THE UNITED STATES.—

(1) ESTABLISHMENT.— The Committee on Foreign Investment in the United States, established pursuant to Executive Order No. 11858, shall be a multi agency committee to carry out this section and such other assignments as the President may designate.

(2) MEMBERSHIP.—The Committee shall be comprised of the following members or the designee of any such member:

(A) The Secretary of the Treasury.

(B) The Secretary of Homeland Security.

(C) The Secretary of Commerce.

(D) The Secretary of Defense.

(E) The Secretary of State.

(F) The Attorney General of the United States.

(G) The Secretary of Energy.

(H)   The Secretary of Labor (nonvoting, ex officio).

(I)   The Director of National Intelligence (nonvoting, ex officio).

(J)   The heads of any other executive department, agency, or office, as the President determines appropriate, generally or on a case-by-case basis.

(3) CHAIRPERSON.— The Secretary of the Treasury shall serve as the chairperson of the Committee.

(4) HIRING AUTHORITY.—

(A) SENIOR OFFICIALS.—

(i) IN GENERAL.— Each member of the Committee shall designate an Assistant Secretary, or an equivalent official, who is appointed by the President, by and with the advice and consent of the Senate, to carry out such duties related to the Committee as the member of the Committee may delegate.

(ii) DEPARTMENT OF THE TREASURY.—

(I) IN GENERAL.— There shall be established in the Office of International Affairs at the Department of the Treasury 2 additional positions of Assistant Secretary of the Treasury, who shall be appointed by the President, by and with the advice and consent of the Senate, to carry out such duties related to the Committee as the Secretary of the Treasury may delegate, consistent with this section.

(II) ASSISTANT SECRETARY FOR INVESTMENT SECURITY.— One of the positions of Assistant Secretary of the Treasury authorized under subclause (I) shall be the Assistant Secretary for Investment Security, whose duties shall be principally related to the Committee, as delegated by the Secretary of the Treasury under this section.

(B) SPECIAL HIRING AUTHORITY.— The heads of the departments and agencies represented on the Committee may appoint, without regard to the provisions of sections 3309 through 3318 of title 5, United States Code, candidates directly to positions in the competitive service (as defined in section 2102 of that title) in their respective departments and agencies. The primary responsibility of positions authorized under the preceding sentence shall be to administer this section.

(5) DESIGNATION OF LEAD AGENCY.—The Secretary of the Treasury shall designate, as appropriate, a member or members of the Committee to be the lead agency or agencies on behalf of the Committee—

(A)   for each covered transaction, and for negotiating any mitigation agreements or other conditions necessary to protect national security; and

(B)   for all matters related to the monitoring of the completed transaction, to ensure compliance with such agreements or conditions and with this section.

(6) OTHER MEMBERS.— The chairperson shall consult with the heads of such other Federal departments, agencies, and independent establishments in any review or investigation under subsection (a), as the chairperson determines to be

appropriate, on the basis of the facts and circumstances of the covered transaction under review or investigation (or the designee of any such department or agency head).

(7) MEETINGS.— The Committee shall meet upon the direction of the President or upon the call of the chairperson, without regard to section 552b of title 5, United States Code (if otherwise applicable).

(l) ACTIONS BY THE COMMITTEE TO ADDRESS NATIONAL SECURITY RISKS.—

(1) SUSPENSION OF TRANSACTIONS.— The Committee, acting through the chairperson, may suspend a proposed or pending covered transaction that may pose a risk to the national security of the United States for such time as the covered transaction is under review or investigation under subsection (b).

(2) REFERRAL TO PRESIDENT.— The Committee may, at any time during the review or investigation of a covered transaction under subsection (b), complete the action of the Committee with respect to the transaction and refer the transaction to the President for action pursuant to subsection (d).

(3) MITIGATION.—

(A) AGREEMENTS AND CONDITIONS.—

(i) IN GENERAL.— The Committee or a lead agency may, on behalf of the Committee, negotiate, enter into or impose, and enforce any agreement or condition with any party to the covered transaction in order to mitigate any risk to the national security of the United States that arises as a result of the covered transaction.

(ii) ABANDONMENT OF TRANSACTIONS.— If a party to a covered transaction has voluntarily chosen to abandon the transaction, the Committee or lead agency, as the case may be, may negotiate, enter into or impose, and enforce any agreement or condition with any party to the covered transaction for purposes of effectuating such abandonment and mitigating any risk to the national security of the United States that arises as a result of the covered transaction.

(iii) AGREEMENTS AND CONDITIONS RELATING TO COMPLETED TRANSACTIONS.— The Committee or lead agency, as the case may be, may negotiate, enter into or impose, and enforce any agreement or condition with any party to a completed covered transaction in order to mitigate any interim risk to the national security of the United States that may arise as a result of the covered transaction until such time that the Committee has completed action pursuant to subsection (b) or the President has taken action pursuant to subsection (d) with respect to the transaction.

(B) TREATMENT OF OUTDATED AGREEMENTS OR CONDITIONS.— The chairperson and the head of the lead agency shall periodically review the appropriateness of an agreement or condition imposed under subparagraph (A) and terminate, phase out, or otherwise amend the agreement or condition if a threat no longer requires mitigation through the agreement or condition.

(C) LIMITATIONS.—An agreement may not be entered into or condition imposed under subparagraph (A) with respect to a covered transaction unless the Committee determines that the agreement or condition resolves the national security concerns posed by the transaction, taking into consideration whether the agreement or condition is reasonably calculated to—

(i) be effective;

(ii) allow for compliance with the terms of the agreement or condition in an appropriately verifiable way; and

(iii) enable effective monitoring of compliance with and enforcement of the terms of the agreement or condition.

(D) JURISDICTION.— The provisions of section 706(b) shall apply to any mitigation agreement entered into or condition imposed under subparagraph (A).

(4) RISK-BASED ANALYSIS REQUIRED.—

(A) IN GENERAL.— Any determination of the Committee to suspend a covered transaction under paragraph (1), to refer a covered transaction to the President under paragraph (2), or to negotiate, enter into or impose, or enforce any agreement or condition under paragraph (3)(A) with respect to a covered transaction, shall be based on a risk-based analysis, conducted by the Committee, of the effects on the national security of the United States of the covered transaction, which shall include an assessment of the threat, vulnerabilities, and consequences to national security related to the transaction.

(B) ACTIONS OF MEMBERS OF THE COMMITTEE.—

(i) IN GENERAL.— Any member of the Committee who concludes that a covered transaction poses an unresolved national security concern shall recommend to the Committee that the Committee suspend the transaction under paragraph (1), refer the transaction to the President under paragraph (2), or negotiate, enter into or impose, or enforce any agreement or condition under paragraph (3)(A) with respect to the transaction. In making that recommendation, the member shall propose or contribute to the risk-based analysis required by subparagraph (A).

(ii) FAILURE TO REACH CONSENSUS.—If the Committee fails to reach consensus with respect to a recommendation under clause (i) regarding a covered transaction, the members of the Committee who support an alternative recommendation shall produce—

(I) a written statement justifying the alternative recommendation; and

(II) as appropriate, a risk-based analysis that supports the alternative recommendation.

(C) DEFINITIONS.— For purposes of subparagraph (A), the terms threat, vulnerabilities, and consequences to national security shall have the meanings given those terms by the Committee by regulation.

(5) TRACKING AUTHORITY FOR WITHDRAWN NOTICES.—

(A) IN GENERAL.—If any written notice of a covered transaction that was submitted to the Committee under this section is withdrawn before any review or investigation by the Committee under subsection (b) is completed, the Committee shall establish, as appropriate—

(i) interim protections to address specific concerns with such transaction that have been raised in connection with any such review or investigation pending any resubmission of any written notice under this section with respect to such transaction and further action by the President under this section;

(ii) specific time frames for resubmitting any such written notice; and

(iii) a process for tracking any actions that may be taken by any party to the transaction, in connection with the transaction, before the notice referred to in clause (ii) is resubmitted.

(B) DESIGNATION OF AGENCY.— The lead agency, other than any entity of the intelligence community, shall, on behalf of the Committee, ensure that the requirements of subparagraph (A) with respect to any covered transaction that is subject to such subparagraph are met.

(6) NEGOTIATION, MODIFICATION, MONITORING, AND ENFORCEMENT.—

(A) DESIGNATION OF LEAD AGENCY.— The lead agency shall negotiate, modify, monitor, and enforce, on behalf of the Committee, any agreement entered into or condition imposed under paragraph (3) with respect to a covered transaction, based on the expertise with and knowledge of the issues related to such transaction on the part of the designated department or agency. The lead agency may, at its discretion, seek and receive the assistance of other departments or agencies in carrying out the purposes of this paragraph.

(B) REPORTING BY DESIGNATED AGENCY.—The lead agency in connection with any agreement entered into or condition imposed with respect to a covered transaction shall—

(i) provide periodic reports to the Committee on any material modification to any such agreement or condition imposed with respect to the transaction; and

(ii) ensure that any material modification to any such agreement or condition is reported to the Director of National Intelligence, the Attorney General of the United States, and any other Federal department or agency that may have a material interest in such modification.

(C) COMPLIANCE PLANS.—

(i) IN GENERAL.— In the case of a covered transaction with respect to which an agreement is entered into under paragraph (3)(A), the Committee or lead agency, as the case may be, shall formulate, adhere to, and keep updated a plan for monitoring compliance with the agreement.

(ii) ELEMENTS.—Each plan required by clause (i) with respect to an agreement entered into under paragraph (3)(A) shall include an explanation of—

(I)   which member of the Committee will have primary responsibility for monitoring compliance with the agreement;

(II)   how compliance with the agreement will be monitored;

(III)   how frequently compliance reviews will be conducted;

(IV)   whether an independent entity will be utilized under subparagraph (E) to conduct compliance reviews; and

(V)   what actions will be taken if the parties fail to cooperate regarding monitoring compliance with the agreement.

(D) EFFECT OF LACK OF COMPLIANCE.—If, at any time after a mitigation agreement or condition is entered into or imposed under paragraph (3)(A), the Committee or lead agency, as the case may be, determines that a party or parties to the agreement or condition are not in compliance with the terms of the agreement or condition, the Committee or lead agency may, in addition to the authority of the Committee to impose penalties pursuant to subsection (h)(3) and to unilaterally initiate a review of any covered transaction under subsection (b)(1)(D)(iii)—

(i)   negotiate a plan of action for the party or parties to remediate the lack of compliance, with failure to abide by the plan or otherwise remediate the lack of compliance serving as the basis for the Committee to find a material breach of the agreement or condition;

(ii)   require that the party or parties submit a written notice under clause (i) of subsection (b)(1)(C) or a declaration under clause (v) of that subsection with respect to a covered transaction initiated after the date of the determination of noncompliance and before the date that is 5 years after the date of the determination to the Committee to initiate a review of the transaction under subsection (b); or

(iii)   seek injunctive relief.

(E) USE OF INDEPENDENT ENTITIES TO MONITOR COMPLIANCE.— If the parties to an agreement entered into under paragraph (3)(A) enter into a contract with an independent entity from outside the United States Government for the purpose of monitoring compliance with the agreement, the Committee shall take such action as is necessary to prevent a conflict of interest from arising by ensuring that the independent entity owes no fiduciary duty to the parties.

(F) SUCCESSORS AND ASSIGNS.— Any agreement or condition entered into or imposed under paragraph (3)(A) shall be considered binding on all successors and assigns unless and until the agreement or condition terminates on its own terms or is otherwise terminated by the Committee in its sole discretion.

(G) ADDITIONAL COMPLIANCE MEASURES.— Subject to subparagraphs (A) through (F), the Committee shall develop and agree upon methods for evaluating compliance with any agreement entered into or condition imposed with respect to a covered transaction that will allow the Committee to adequately ensure compliance without unnecessarily diverting Committee resources from assessing any new covered transaction for which a written notice under clause (i) of subsection (b)(1)(C) or declaration under clause (v) of that subsection has been filed, and if necessary, reaching a mitigation agreement with or imposing a condition on a party to such covered transaction or any covered transaction for which a review has been reopened for any reason.

(m) ANNUAL REPORT TO CONGRESS.—

(1) IN GENERAL.— The chairperson shall transmit a report to the chairman and ranking member of the committee of jurisdiction in the Senate and the House of Representatives, before July 31 of each year on all of the reviews and investigations of covered transactions completed under subsection (b) during the 12-month period covered by the report.

(2) CONTENTS OF REPORT RELATING TO COVERED TRANSACTIONS.—The annual report under paragraph (1) shall contain the following information, with respect to each covered transaction, for the reporting period:

(A) A list of all notices filed and all reviews or investigations of covered transactions completed during the period, with—

(i) a description of the outcome of each review or investigation, including whether an agreement was entered into or condition was imposed under subsection (l)(3)(A) with respect to the transaction being reviewed or investigated, and whether the President took any action under this section with respect to that transaction;

(ii) basic information on each party to each such transaction;

(iii) the nature of the business activities or products of the United States business with which the transaction was entered into or intended to be entered into; and

(iv) information about any withdrawal from the process.

(B) Specific, cumulative, and, as appropriate, trend information on the numbers of filings, investigations, withdrawals, and decisions or actions by the President under this section.

(C) Cumulative and, as appropriate, trend information on the business sectors involved in the filings which have been made, and the countries from which the investments have originated.

(D) Information on whether companies that withdrew notices to the Committee in accordance with subsection (b)(1)(C)(ii) have later refiled such notices, or, alternatively, abandoned the transaction.

(E) The types of security arrangements and conditions the Committee has used to mitigate national security concerns about a transaction, including a discussion of the methods that the Committee and any lead agency are using to determine compliance with such arrangements or conditions.

(F) A detailed discussion of all perceived adverse effects of covered transactions on the national security or critical infrastructure of the United States that the Committee will take into account in its deliberations during the period before delivery of the next report, to the extent possible.

(G)   Statistics on compliance plans conducted and actions taken by the Committee under subsection (l)(6), including subparagraph (D) of that subsection, during that period, a general assessment of the compliance of parties with agreements entered into and conditions imposed under subsection (l)(3)(A) that are in effect during that period, including a description of any actions taken by the Committee to impose penalties or initiate a unilateral review pursuant to subsection (b)(1)(D)(iii), and any recommendations for improving the enforcement of such agreements and conditions.

(H)   Cumulative and, as appropriate, trend information on the number of declarations filed under subsection (b)(1)(C)(v), the actions taken by the Committee in response to those declarations, the business sectors involved in those declarations, and the countries involved in those declarations.

(I) A description of—

(i)   the methods used by the Committee to identify non-notified and non-declared transactions under subsection (b)(1)(H);

(ii)   potential methods to improve such identification and the resources required to do so; and

(iii)   the number of transactions identified through the process established under that subsection during the reporting period and the number of such transactions flagged for further review.

(J)   A summary of the hiring practices and policies of the Committee pursuant to subsection (k)(4).

(K)   A list of the waivers granted by the Committee under subsection (b)(1)(C)(v)(IV)(bb)(CC).

(3) CONTENTS OF REPORT RELATING TO CRITICAL TECHNOLOGIES.—In order to assist Congress in its oversight responsibilities with respect to this section, the President and such agencies as the President shall designate shall include in the annual report submitted under paragraph (1)—

(A)   an evaluation of whether there is credible evidence of a coordinated strategy by 1 or more countries or companies to acquire United States companies involved in research, development, or production of critical technologies for which the United States is a leading producer;

(B)   an evaluation of whether there are industrial espionage activities directed or directly assisted by foreign governments against private United States companies aimed at obtaining commercial secrets related to critical technologies; and

(C)   a description of the technologies recommended by the chairperson under subsection (a)(6)(B) for identification under the interagency process set forth in section 1758(a) of the Export Control Reform Act of 2018.

(4) FORM OF REPORT.—

(A) IN GENERAL.— All appropriate portions of the annual report under paragraph (1) may be classified. An unclassified version of the report, as appropriate, consistent with safeguarding national security and privacy, shall be made available to the public.

(B) INCLUSION IN CLASSIFIED VERSION.— If the Committee recommends that the President suspend or prohibit a covered transaction because the transaction threatens to impair the national security of the United States, the Committee shall, in the classified version of the report required under paragraph (1), notify Congress of the recommendation and, upon request, provide a classified briefing on the recommendation.

(C) INCLUSIONS IN UNCLASSIFIED VERSION.—The unclassified version of the report required under paragraph (1) shall include, with respect to covered transactions for the reporting period—

   (i)   the number of notices submitted under subsection (b)(1)(C)(i);

   (ii)   the number of declarations submitted under subsection (b)(1)(C)(v) and the number of such declarations that were required under subclause (IV) of that subsection;

   (iii)   the number of declarations submitted under subsection (b)(1)(C)(v) for which the Committee required resubmission as notices under subsection (b)(1)(C)(i);

   (iv)   the average number of days that elapsed between submission of a declaration under subsection (b)(1)(C)(v) and the acceptance of the declaration by the Committee;

   (v)   the median and average number of days that elapsed between acceptance of a declaration by the Committee and a response described in subsection (b)(1)(C)(v)(III);

   (vi) information on the time it took the Committee to provide comments on, or to accept, notices submitted under subsection (b)(1)(C)(i), including—

      (I)   the average number of business days that elapsed between the date of submission of a draft notice and the date on which the Committee provided written comments on the draft notice;

      (II)   the average number of business days that elapsed between the date of submission of a formal written notice and the date on which the Committee accepted or provided written comments on the formal written notice; and

      (III) if the average number of business days for a response by the Committee reported under subclause (I) or (II) exceeded 10 business days—

         (aa)   an explanation of the causes of such delays, including whether such delays are caused by resource shortages, unusual fluctuations in the volume of notices, transaction characteristics, or other factors; and

         (bb)   an explanation of the steps that the Committee anticipates taking to mitigate the causes of such delays and otherwise to improve the ability of the Committee to provide comments on, or to accept, notices within 10 business days;

(vii)   the number of reviews or investigations conducted under subsection (b);

(viii)   the number of investigations that were subject to an extension under subsection (b)(2)(C)(ii);

(ix)   information on the duration of those reviews and investigations, including the median and average number of days required to complete those reviews and investigations;

(x)   the number of notices submitted under subsection (b)(1)(C)(i) and declarations submitted under subsection (b)(1)(C)(v) that were rejected by the Committee;

(xi)   the number of such notices and declarations that were withdrawn by a party to the covered transaction;

(xii)   the number of such withdrawals that were followed by the submission of a subsequent such notice or declaration relating to a substantially similar covered transaction; and

(xiii)   such other specific, cumulative, or trend information that the Committee determines is advisable to provide for an assessment of the time required for reviews and investigations of covered transactions under this section.

(n) CERTIFICATION OF NOTICES AND ASSURANCES.—

(1) IN GENERAL.—Each notice, and any followup information, submitted under this section and regulations prescribed under this section to the President or the Committee by a party to a covered transaction, and any information submitted by any such party in connection with any action for which a report is required pursuant to paragraph (6)(B) of subsection (l), with respect to the implementation of any mitigation agreement or condition described in paragraph (3)(A) of subsection (l), or any material change in circumstances, shall be accompanied by a written statement by the chief executive officer or the designee of the person required to submit such notice or information certifying that, to the best of the knowledge and belief of that person—

(A)   the notice or information submitted fully complies with the requirements of this section or such regulation, agreement, or condition; and

(B)   the notice or information is accurate and complete in all material respects.

(2) EFFECT OF FAILURE TO SUBMIT.—The Committee may not complete a review under this section of a covered transaction and may recommend to the President that the President suspend or prohibit the transaction under subsection (d) if the Committee determines that a party to the transaction has—

(A)   failed to submit a statement required by paragraph (1); or

(B)   included false or misleading information in a notice or information described in paragraph (1) or omitted material information from such notice or information.

(3) APPLICABILITY OF LAW ON FRAUD AND FALSE STATEMENTS.— The Committee shall prescribe regulations expressly providing for the application of section 1001 of title 18, United States Code, to all information provided to the Committee under this section by any party to a covered transaction.

(o) TESTIMONY.—

(1) IN GENERAL.—Not later than March 31 of each year, the chairperson, or the designee of the chairperson, shall appear before the Committee on Financial Services of the House of Representatives and the Committee on Banking, Housing, and Urban Affairs of the Senate to present testimony on—

(A)   anticipated resources necessary for operations of the Committee in the following fiscal year at each of the departments or agencies represented on the Committee;

(B) the adequacy of appropriations for the Committee in the current and the previous fiscal year to—

(i)   ensure that thorough reviews and investigations are completed as expeditiously as possible;

(ii)   monitor and enforce mitigation agreements; and

(iii)   identify covered transactions for which a notice under clause (i) of subsection (b)(1)(C) or a declaration under clause (v) of that subsection was not submitted to the Committee;

(C)   management efforts to strengthen the ability of the Committee to meet the requirements of this section; and

(D) activities of the Committee undertaken in order to—

(i)   educate the business community, with a particular focus on the technology sector and other sectors of importance to national security, on the goals and operations of the Committee;

(ii) disseminate to the governments of countries that are allies or partners of the United States best practices of the Committee that—

(I)   strengthen national security reviews of relevant investment transactions; and

(II)   expedite such reviews when appropriate; and

(iii)   promote openness to foreign investment, consistent with national security considerations.

(2) SUNSET.— This subsection shall have no force or effect on or after the date that is 7 years after the date of the enactment of the Foreign Investment Risk Review Modernization Act of 2018.

(p) FUNDING.—

(1) ESTABLISHMENT OF FUND.— There is established in the Treasury of the United States a fund, to be known as the Committee on Foreign Investment in the United States Fund (in this subsection referred to as the Fund), to be administered by the chairperson.

(2) AUTHORIZATION OF APPROPRIATIONS FOR THE COMMITTEE.— There are authorized to be appropriated to the Fund for each of fiscal years 2019 through 2023 $20,000,000 to perform the functions of the Committee.

(3) FILING FEES.—

(A) IN GENERAL.— The Committee may assess and collect a fee in an amount determined by the Committee in regulations, to the extent provided in advance in appropriations Acts, without regard to section 9701 of title 31, United States Code, and subject to subparagraph (B), with respect to each covered transaction for which a written notice is submitted to the Committee under subsection (b)(1)(C)(i). The total amount of fees collected under this paragraph may not exceed the costs of administering this section.

(B) DETERMINATION OF AMOUNT OF FEE.—

(i) IN GENERAL.—The amount of the fee to be assessed under subparagraph (A) with respect to a covered transaction—

(I) may not exceed an amount equal to the lesser of—

(aa) 1 percent of the value of the transaction; or

(bb) $300,000, adjusted annually for inflation pursuant to regulations prescribed by the Committee; and

(II) shall be based on the value of the transaction, taking into account—

(aa) the effect of the fee on small business concerns (as defined in section 3 of the Small Business Act (15 U.S.C. 632));

(bb) the expenses of the Committee associated with conducting activities under this section;

(cc) the effect of the fee on foreign investment; and

(dd) such other matters as the Committee considers appropriate.

(ii) UPDATES.— The Committee shall periodically reconsider and adjust the amount of the fee to be assessed under subparagraph (A) with respect to a covered transaction to ensure that the amount of the fee does not exceed the costs of administering this section and otherwise remains appropriate.

(C) DEPOSIT AND AVAILABILITY OF FEES.—Notwithstanding section 3302 of title 31, United States Code, fees collected under subparagraph (A) shall—

(i) be deposited into the Fund solely for use in carrying out activities under this section;

(ii) to the extent and in the amounts provided in advance in appropriations Acts, be available to the chairperson;

(iii) remain available until expended; and

(iv) be in addition to any appropriations made available to the members of the Committee.

(D) STUDY ON PRIORITIZATION FEE.—

(i) IN GENERAL.— Not later than 270 days after the date of the enactment of the Foreign Investment Risk Review Modernization Act of 2018, the chairperson, in consultation with the Committee, shall complete a study of the feasibility and merits of establishing a fee or fee scale to prioritize the timing of the response of the Committee to a draft or formal written notice during the period before the Committee accepts the formal written notice under subsection (b)(1)(C)(i), in the event that the Committee is unable to respond during the time required by subclause (II) of that subsection because of an unusually large influx of notices, or for other reasons.

(ii) SUBMISSION TO CONGRESS.— After completing the study required by clause (i), the chairperson, or a designee of the chairperson, shall submit to the Committee on Banking, Housing, and Urban Affairs of the Senate and the Committee on Financial Services of the House of Representatives a report on the findings of the study.

(4) TRANSFER OF FUNDS.— To the extent provided in advance in appropriations Acts, the chairperson may transfer any amounts in the Fund to any other department or agency represented on the Committee for the purpose of addressing emerging needs in carrying out activities under this section. Amounts so transferred shall be in addition to any other amounts available to that department or agency for that purpose.

(q) CENTRALIZATION OF CERTAIN COMMITTEE FUNCTIONS.—

(1) IN GENERAL.— The chairperson, in consultation with the Committee, may centralize certain functions of the Committee within the Department of the Treasury for the purpose of enhancing interagency coordination and collaboration in carrying out the functions of the Committee under this section.

(2) FUNCTIONS.— Functions that may be centralized under paragraph (1) include identifying non-notified and non-declared transactions pursuant to subsection (b)(1)(H), and other functions as determined by the chairperson and the Committee.

(3) RULE OF CONSTRUCTION.— Nothing in this section shall be construed as limiting the authority of any department or agency represented on the Committee to represent its own interests before the Committee.

[50 U.S.C. 4565]

SEC. 722. DEFENSE PRODUCTION ACT COMMITTEE.

(a) COMMITTEE ESTABLISHED.— There is established the Defense Production Act Committee (in this section referred to as the Committee), which shall coordinate and plan for on the effective use of the priorities and allocations authorities under this Act by the departments, agencies, and independent establishments of the Federal Government to which the President has delegated authority under this Act.

(b) MEMBERSHIP.—

(1) IN GENERAL.—The members of the Committee shall be—

(A) the head of each Federal agency to which the President has delegated authority under this Act; and

(B)   the Chairperson of the Council of Economic Advisors.

(2)   The Chairperson of the Committee shall be the head of the agency to which the President has delegated primary responsibility for government-wide coordination of the authorities in this Act.

(c) COORDINATION OF COMMITTEE ACTIVITIES.—The Chairperson shall appoint one person to coordinate all of the activities of the Committee, and such person shall—

(1)   be a full-time employee of the Federal Government;

(2)   report to the Chairperson; and

(3)   carry out such activities relating to the Committee as the Chairperson may determine appropriate.

(d) REPORT.—The Committee shall issue a report each year by March 31 to the Committee on Banking, Housing, and Urban Affairs of the Senate and the Committee on Financial Services of the House of Representatives a report signed by the Chairperson that contains—

(1)   a description of the contingency planning by each department, agency, or independent establishment of the Federal Government to which the President has delegated authority under this Act for events that might require the use of the priorities and allocations authorities;

(2)   recommendations for the effective use of the priorities and allocations authorities in this Act in a manner consistent with the statement of policy under section 2(b);

(3)   recommendations for legislation actions, as appropriate, to support the effective use of the priorities and allocations authorities in this Act;

(4)   recommendations for improving information sharing between departments, agencies, and independent establishments of the Federal Government relating to the use of the priorities and allocations authorities in this Act;

(5)   up-to-date copies of the rules described under section 101(d)(1); and

(6)   short attestations signed by each member of the Committee stating their concurrence in the report.

(e) CHAPTER 10 OF TITLE 5, UNITED STATES CODE.— The provisions of chapter 10 of title 5, United States Code, shall not apply to the Committee.
[50 U.S.C. 4567]

SEC. 723. ANNUAL REPORT ON IMPACT OF OFFSETS.

(a) REPORT REQUIRED.—

(1) IN GENERAL.— The President shall submit to the Committee on Banking, Housing, and Urban Affairs of the Senate and the Committee on Financial Services of the House of Representatives, a detailed annual report on the impact of offsets on the defense preparedness, industrial competitiveness, employment, and trade of the United States.

(2) DUTIES OF THE SECRETARY OF COMMERCE.—The Secretary of Commerce (hereafter in this subsection referred to as the Secretary) shall—

(A) prepare the report required by paragraph (1);

(B) consult with the Secretary of Defense, the Secretary of the Treasury, the Secretary of State, and the United States Trade Representative in connection with the preparation of such report; and

(C) function as the President's Executive Agent for carrying out this section.

(b) INTERAGENCY STUDIES AND RELATED DATA.—

(1) PURPOSE OF REPORT.—Each report required under subsection (a) shall identify the cumulative effects of offset agreements on—

(A) the full range of domestic defense productive capability (with special attention paid to the firms serving as lower-tier subcontractors or suppliers); and

(B) the domestic defense technology base as a consequence of the technology transfers associated with such offset agreements.

(2) USE OF DATA.— Data developed or compiled by any agency while conducting any interagency study or other independent study or analysis shall be made available to the Secretary to facilitate the execution of the Secretary's responsibilities with respect to trade offset and countertrade policy development.

(c) NOTICE OF OFFSET AGREEMENTS.—

(1) IN GENERAL.— If a United States firm enters into a contract for the sale of a weapon system or defense-related item to a foreign country or foreign firm and such contract is subject to an offset agreement exceeding $5,000,000 in value, such firm shall furnish to the official designated in the regulations promulgated pursuant to paragraph (2) information concerning such sale.

(2) REGULATIONS.— The information to be furnished under paragraph (1) shall be prescribed in regulations promulgated by the Secretary. Such regulations shall provide protection from public disclosure for such information, unless public disclosure is subsequently specifically authorized by the firm furnishing the information.

(d) CONTENTS OF REPORT.—

(1) IN GENERAL.—Each report under subsection (a) shall include—

(A) a net assessment of the elements of the industrial base and technology base covered by the report;

(B) recommendations for appropriate remedial action under the authority of this Act, or other law or regulations;

(C) a summary of the findings and recommendations of any interagency studies conducted during the reporting period under subsection (b);

(D) a summary of offset arrangements concluded during the reporting period for which information has been furnished pursuant to subsection (c); and

(E) a summary and analysis of any bilateral and multilateral negotiations relating to the use of offsets completed during the reporting period.

(2) ALTERNATIVE FINDINGS OR RECOMMENDATIONS.— Each report required under this section shall include any alternative findings or recommendations offered by any departmental Secretary, agency head, or the United States Trade Representative to the Secretary.

(e) UTILIZATION OF ANNUAL REPORT IN NEGOTIATIONS.— The findings and recommendations of the reports required by subsection (a), and any interagency reports and analyses shall be considered by representatives of the United States during bilateral and multilateral negotiations to minimize the adverse effects of offsets.

[50 U.S.C. 4568]

★

NATIONAL SECURITY ACT OF 1947 §303

61 STAT. 496
AS AMENDED THROUGH PUB. L. 118–159

[Chapter 343; 61 Stat. 496; approved July 26, 1947]

[As Amended Through P.L. 118–159, Enacted December 23, 2024]

AN ACT To promote the national security by providing for a Secretary of Defense; for a National Military Establishment; for a Department of the Army, a Department of the Navy, and a Department of the Air Force; and for the coordination of the activities of the National Military Establishment with other departments and agencies of the Government concerned with the national security.

Be it enacted by the Senate and House of Representatives of the United States of America in Congress assembled,

SHORT TITLE

That [50 U.S.C. 3001] this Act may be cited as the "National Security Act of 1947".

* * * * * * *

TITLE III—MISCELLANEOUS

* * * * * * *

ADVISORY COMMITTEES AND PERSONNEL

SEC. 303. [50 U.S.C. 3073] (a)   The Director of the Office of Defense Mobilization, the Director of National Intelligence, and the National Security Council, acting through its Executive Secretary, are authorized to appoint such advisory committees and to employ, consistent with other provisions of this Act, such part-time advisory personnel as they may deem necessary in carrying out their respective functions and the functions of agencies under their control. Persons holding other offices or positions under the United States for which they receive compensation, while serving as members of such committees, shall receive no additional compensation for such service. Retired members of the uniformed services employed by the Director of National Intelligence who hold no other office or position under the United States for which they receive compensation, other members of such committees and other part-time advisory personnel so employed may serve without compensation or may receive compensation at a daily rate not to exceed the daily equivalent of the rate of pay in effect for grade GS–18 of the General Schedule established by section 5332 of title 5, United States Code, as determined by the appointing authority.

(b)   Service of an individual as a member of any such advisory committee, or in any other part-time capacity for a department or agency hereunder, shall not be considered as service bringing such individual within the provisions of section 203, 205, or 207, of title 18, United States Code, unless the act of such individual, which by such section is made unlawful when performed by an individual referred to in such section, is with respect to any particular matter which directly involves a department or agency which such person is advising or in which such department or agency is directly interested.

★

NATIONAL EMERGENCIES ACT

PUBLIC LAW 94–412
AS AMENDED THROUGH PUB. L. 117–81

[(Public Law 94–412; 90 Stat. 1255; approved September 14, 1976)]

[As Amended Through P.L. 117–81, Enacted December 27, 2021]

AN ACT To terminate certain authorities with respect to national emergencies still in effect, and to provide for orderly implementation and termination of future national emergencies.

Be it enacted by the Senate and House of Representatives of the United States of America in Congress assembled,

That this Act may be cited as the "National Emergencies Act".

TITLE I—TERMINATING EXISTING DECLARED EMERGENCIES

SEC. 101. [50 U.S.C. 1601] (a) All powers and authorities possessed by the President, any other officer or employee of the Federal Government, or any executive agency, as defined in section 105 of title 5, United States Code, as a result of the existence of any declaration of national emergency in effect on the date of enactment of this Act are terminated two years from the date of such enactment. Such termination shall not affect—

(1) any action taken or proceeding pending not finally concluded or determined on such date;

(2) any action or proceeding based on any act committed prior to such date; or

(3) any rights or duties that matured or penalties that were incurred prior to such date.

(b) For the purpose of this section, the words any national emergency in effect means a general declaration of emergency made by the President.

TITLE II—DECLARATIONS OF FUTURE NATIONAL EMERGENCIES

SEC. 201. [50 U.S.C. 1621] (a) With respect to Acts of Congress authorizing the exercise, during the period of a national emergency, of any special or extraordinary power, the

President is authorized to declare such national emergency. Such proclamation shall immediately be transmitted to the Congress and published in the Federal Register.

(b)   Any provisions of law conferring powers and authorities to be exercised during a national emergency shall be effective and remain in effect (1) only when the President (in accordance with subsection (a) of this section), specifically declares a national emergency, and (2) only in accordance with this Act. No law enacted after the date of enactment of this Act shall supersede this title unless it does so in specific terms, referring to this title, and declaring that the new law supersedes the provisions of this title.

SEC. 202. [50 U.S.C. 1622] (a) Any national emergency declared by the President in accordance with this title shall terminate if—

(1)   there is enacted into law a joint resolution terminating the emergency; or

(2)   the President issues a proclamation terminating the emergency.

Any national emergency declared by the President shall be terminated on the date specified in any joint resolution referred to in clause (1) or on the date specified in a proclamation by the President terminating the emergency as provided in clause (2) of this subsection, whichever date is earlier, and any powers or authorities exercised by reason of said emergency shall cease to be exercised after such specified date, except that such termination shall not affect—

(A)   any action taken or proceeding pending not finally concluded or determined on such date;

(B)   any action or proceeding based on any act committed prior to such date; or

(C)   any rights or duties that matured or penalties that were incurred prior to such date.

(b)   Not later than six months after a national emergency is declared, and not later than the end of each six-month period thereafter that such emergency continues, each House of Congress shall meet to consider a vote on a joint resolution to determine whether that emergency shall be terminated.

(c)(1)   A joint resolution to terminate a national emergency declared by the President shall be referred to the appropriate committee of the House of Representatives or the Senate, as the case may be. One such joint resolution shall be reported out by such committee together with its recommendations within fifteen calendar days after the day on which such resolution is referred to such committee, unless such House shall otherwise determine by the yeas and nays.

(2)   Any joint resolution so reported shall become the pending business of the House in question (in the case of the Senate the time for debate shall be equally divided between the proponents and the opponents) and shall be voted on within three calendar days after the day on which such resolution is reported, unless such House shall otherwise determine by yeas and nays.

(3)   Such a joint resolution passed by one House shall be referred to the appropriate committee of the other House and shall be reported out by such committee together with its recommendations within fifteen calendar days after the

day on which such resolution is referred to such committee and shall thereupon become the pending business of such House and shall be voted upon within three calendar days after the day on which such resolution is reported, unless such House shall otherwise determine by yeas and nays.

(4)   In the case of any disagreement between the two Houses of Congress with respect to a joint resolution passed by both Houses, conferees shall be promptly appointed and the committee of conference shall make and file a report with respect to such joint resolution within six calendar days after the day on which managers on the part of the Senate and the House have been appointed. Notwithstanding any rule in either House concerning the printing of conference reports or concerning any delay in the consideration of such reports, such report shall be acted on by both Houses not later than six calendar days after the conference report is filed in the House in which such report is filed first. In the event the conferees are unable to agree within forty-eight hours, they shall report back to their respective Houses in disagreement.

(5) Paragraphs (1)–(4) of this subsection, subsection (b) of this section, and section 502(b) of this Act are enacted by Congress—

(A)   as an exercise of the rulemaking power of the Senate and the House of Representatives, respectively, and as such they are deemed a part of the rules of each House, respectively, but applicable only with respect to the procedure to be followed in the House in the case of resolutions described by this subsection; and they supersede other rules only to the extent that they are inconsistent therewith; and

(B)   with full recognition of the constitutional right of either House to change the rules (so far as relating to the procedure of that House) at any time, in the same manner, and to the same extent as in the case of any other rule of that House.

(d)   Any national emergency declared by the President in accordance with this title, and not otherwise previously terminated, shall terminate on the anniversary of the declaration of that emergency if, within the ninety-day period prior to each anniversary date, the President does not publish in the Federal Register and transmit to the Congress a notice stating that such emergency is to continue in effect after such anniversary.

TITLE III—EXERCISE OF EMERGENCY POWERS AND AUTHORITIES

SEC. 301. [50 U.S.C. 1631]   When the President declares a national emergency, no powers or authorities made available by statute for use in the event of an emergency shall be exercised unless and until the President specifies the provisions of law under which he proposes that he, or other officers will act. Such specification may be made either in the declaration of a national emergency, or by one or more contemporaneous or subsequent Executive orders published in the Federal Register and transmitted to the Congress.

TITLE IV—ACCOUNTABILITY AND REPORTING

REQUIREMENTS OF THE PRESIDENT

SEC. 401. [50 U.S.C. 1641] (a)   When the President declares a national emergency, or Congress declares war, the President shall be responsible for maintaining a file and index of all significant orders of the President, including Executive orders and proclamations, and each Executive agency shall maintain a file and index of all rules and regulations, issued during such emergency or war issued pursuant to such declarations.

(b)   All such significant orders of the President, including Executive orders, and such rules and regulations shall be transmitted to the Congress promptly under means to assure confidentiality where appropriate.

(c)   When the President declares a national emergency or Congress declares war, the President shall transmit to Congress, within ninety days after the end of each six-month period after such declarations, a report on the total expenditures incurred by the United States Government during such six-month period which are directly attributable to the exercise of powers and authorities conferred by such declaration. Not later than ninety days after the termination of each such emergency or war, the President shall transmit a final report on all such expenditures.

TITLE V—REPEAL AND CONTINUATION OF CERTAIN EMERGENCY POWER AND OTHER STATUTES

SEC. 501. [50 U.S.C. 1651] (a) [Section 501(a) amended section 349 of the Immigration and Nationality Act (8 U.S.C. 1481).]

(b) [Section 501(b) amended section 2667 of title 10, United States Code.]

(c) [Section 501(c) repealed the joint resolution entitled Joint resolution to authorize the temporary continuation of regulation of consumer credit(12 U.S.C. 249).]

(d) [Section 501(d) repealed section 5(m) the Tennessee Valley Authority Act of 1933 as amended (16 U.S.C. 831d(m)).]

(e) [Section 501(e) repealed section 1383 of title 18, United States Code.]

(f) [Section 501(f) amended section 6 of the Act entitled An Act to amend the Public Health Service Act in regard to certain matters of personnel and administration, and for other purposes.]

(g) [Section 501(g) repealed Section 9 of the Merchant Ship Sales Act of 1946 (50 U.S.C. App. 1742).]

(h) This section shall not affect—

(1)   any action taken or proceeding pending not finally concluded or determined at the time of repeal;

(2)   any action or proceeding based on any act committed prior to repeal; or

(3)   any rights or duties that matured or penalties that were incurred prior to repeal;

SEC. 502. [50 U.S.C. 1651] (a) The provisions of this Act shall not apply to the following provisions of law, the powers and authorities conferred thereby, and actions taken thereunder:

(1)   Chapters 1 to 11 of title 40, United States Code, and division C (except sections 3302, 3307(e), 3501(b), 3509, 3906, 4710, and 4711) of subtitle I of title 41, United States Code.

(2)   Section 3727(a)–(e)(1) of title 31, United States Code.

(3)   Section 6305 of title 41, United States Code.

(4)   Public Law 85–804 (Act of Aug. 28, 1958, 72 Stat. 972; 50 U.S.C. 1431 et seq.).

(5)   Section 3201(a) of title 10, United States Code.

(b)   Each committee of the House of Representatives and the Senate having jurisdiction with respect to any provision of law referred to in subsection (a) of this section shall make a complete study and investigation concerning that provision of law and make a report, including any recommendations and proposed revisions such committee may have, to its respective House of Congress within two hundred and seventy days after the date of enactment of this Act.

★

SECTION 5 OF THE ACT OF AUGUST 18, 1941

ACT OF AUGUST 18, 1941
AS AMENDED THROUGH PUB. L. 118–272

SECTION 5 OF THE ACT OF AUGUST 18, 1941

(As listed in Section 701n of Chapter 15, 33 U.S.C.)

(Aug. 18, 1941, ch. 377, §2, 55 Stat. 638.)

§701N. EMERGENCY RESPONSE TO NATURAL DISASTERS

(A) EMERGENCY FUND

(1) There is authorized an emergency fund to be expended in preparation for emergency response to any natural disaster, in flood fighting and rescue operations, or in the repair or restoration of any flood control work threatened or destroyed by flood, including the strengthening, raising, extending, realigning, or other modification thereof as may be necessary in the discretion of the Chief of Engineers for the adequate functioning of the work for flood control and subject to the condition that the Chief of Engineers may include modifications to the structure or project, or in implementation of nonstructural alternatives to the repair or restoration of such flood control work if requested by the non-Federal sponsor; in the emergency protection of federally authorized hurricane or shore protection being threatened when in the discretion of the Chief of Engineers such protection is warranted to protect against imminent and substantial loss to life and property; in the repair and restoration of any federally authorized hurricane or shore protective structure or project damaged or destroyed by wind, wave, or water action of other than an ordinary nature to the pre-storm level of protection, to the design level of protection, or, notwithstanding the authorized dimensions of the structure or project, to a level sufficient to meet the authorized purpose of such structure or project, whichever provides greater protection, when, in the discretion of the Chief of Engineers, such repair and restoration is warranted for the adequate functioning of the structure or project for hurricane or shore protection, including to ensure the structure or project is functioning adequately to protect against projected changes in wave action or height or storm surge (including changes that result from relative sea level change over the useful life of the structure or project), subject to the condition that the Chief of Engineers may, if requested by the non-Federal sponsor, include modifications to the structure or project (including the addition of new project features) to address major deficiencies, increase resilience, increase benefits from the reduction of damages from inundation, wave action, or erosion, or implement nonstructural alternatives to the repair or restoration of the structure. The emergency fund may also be expended for emergency dredging for restoration of authorized project depths for Federal navigable channels and waterways made necessary by flood, drought,

earthquake, or other natural disasters. In any case in which the Chief of Engineers is otherwise performing work under this section in an area for which the Governor of the affected State has requested a determination that an emergency exists or a declaration that a major disaster exists under the Disaster Relief and Emergency Assistance Act [42 U.S.C. 5121 et seq.], the Chief of Engineers is further authorized to perform on public and private lands and waters for a period of ten days following the Governor's request any emergency work made necessary by such emergency or disaster which is essential for the preservation of life and property, including, but not limited to, channel clearance, emergency shore protection, clearance and removal of debris and wreckage endangering public health and safety, and temporary restoration of essential public facilities and services. The Chief of Engineers, in the exercise of his discretion, is further authorized to provide emergency supplies of clean water, on such terms as he determines to be advisable, to any locality which he finds is confronted with a source of contaminated water causing or likely to cause a substantial threat to the public health and welfare of the inhabitants of the locality. The appropriation of such moneys for the initial establishment of this fund and for its replenishment on an annual basis, is authorized: *Provided*, That pending the appropriation of sums to such emergency fund, the Secretary of the Army may allot, from existing flood-control appropriations, such sums as may be necessary for the immediate prosecution of the work herein authorized, such appropriations to be reimbursed from the appropriation herein authorized when made. The Chief of Engineers is authorized, in the prosecution of work in connection with rescue operations, or in conducting other flood emergency work, to acquire on a rental basis such motor vehicles, including passenger cars and buses, as in his discretion are deemed necessary.

(2) COST AND BENEFIT FEASIBILITY ASSESSMENT.—

(A) CONSIDERATION OF BENEFITS.—In preparing a cost and benefit feasibility assessment for any emergency project described in paragraph (1), the Chief of Engineers shall consider the benefits to be gained by such project for the protection of—

(i) residential establishments;

(ii) commercial establishments, including the protection of inventory; and

(iii) agricultural establishments, including the protection of crops.

(B) SPECIAL CONDITIONS.—

(i) AUTHORITY TO CARRY OUT WORK.—The Chief of Engineers may carry out repair or restoration work described in paragraph (1) that does not produce benefits greater than the cost if—

(I) the non-Federal sponsor agrees to pay, or provide contributions equal to, an amount sufficient to make the remaining costs of the project equal to the estimated value of the benefits of the repair or restoration work; and

(II) the Secretary determines that

(aa) the damage to the structure was not a result of negligent operation or maintenance; and

(bb) repair of the project could benefit another Corps project.

(ii) TREATMENT OF PAYMENTS AND CONTRIBUTIONS.—Non-Federal payments or contributions pursuant to clause (i) shall be in addition to any non-Federal payments or contributions required by the Chief of Engineers that are applicable to the remaining costs of the repair or restoration work.

(3) EXTENDED ASSISTANCE.—Upon request by a locality receiving assistance under the fourth sentence of paragraph (1), the Secretary shall, subject to the availability of appropriations, enter into an agreement with the locality to provide such assistance beyond the time period otherwise provided for by the Secretary under such sentence.

(4) NONSTRUCTURAL ALTERNATIVES DEFINED.—In this subsection, the term "nonstructural alternatives" includes efforts to restore or protect natural resources, including streams, rivers, floodplains, wetlands, or coasts, if those efforts will reduce flood risk.

(5) FEASIBILITY STUDY.—

(A) DETERMINATION.—Not later than 180 days after receiving, from a non-Federal sponsor of a project to repair or rehabilitate a flood control work described in paragraph (1), a request to initiate a feasibility study to further modify the relevant flood control work to provide for an increased level of protection, the Secretary shall provide to the non-Federal sponsor a written decision on whether the Secretary has the authority under section 549a of this title to undertake the requested feasibility study.

(B) RECOMMENDATION.—If the Secretary determines under subparagraph (B) that the Secretary does not have the authority to undertake the requested feasibility study, the Secretary shall include the request for a feasibility study in the annual report submitted under section 2282d of this title.

(B) EMERGENCY SUPPLIES OF DRINKING WATER; DROUGHT; WELL CONSTRUCTION AND WATER TRANSPORTATION

(1) The Secretary, upon a written request for assistance under this paragraph made by any farmer, rancher, or political subdivision within a distressed area, and after a determination by the Secretary that (A) as a result of the drought such farmer, rancher, or political subdivision has an inadequate supply of water, (B) an adequate supply of water can be made available to such farmer, rancher, or political subdivision through the construction of a well, and (C) as a result of the drought such well could not be constructed by a private business, the Secretary, subject to paragraph (3) of this subsection, may enter into an agreement with such farmer, rancher, or political subdivision for the construction of such well.

(2) The Secretary, upon a written request for assistance under this paragraph made by any farmer, rancher, or political subdivision within a distressed area, and after a determination by the Secretary that as a result of the drought such farmer, rancher, or political subdivision has an inadequate supply of water and water cannot be obtained by such farmer, rancher, or political subdivision, the Secretary may transport water to such farmer, rancher, or political subdivision by methods which include, but are not limited to, small-diameter emergency water lines and tank trucks, until such time as the Secretary determines that an adequate supply of water is available to such farmer, rancher, or political subdivision.

(3)(A) Any agreement entered into by the Secretary pursuant to paragraph (1) of this subsection shall require the farmer, rancher, or political subdivision for whom the well is constructed to pay to the United States the reasonable cost of such construction, with interest, over such number of years, not to exceed thirty, as the Secretary deems appropriate. The rate of interest shall be that rate which the Secretary determines would apply if the amount to be repaid was a loan made pursuant to section 636(b)(2) of title 15.

(B) The Secretary shall not construct any well pursuant to this subsection unless the farmer, rancher, or political subdivision for whom the well is being constructed has obtained, prior to construction, all necessary State and local permits.

(4) The Federal share for the transportation of water pursuant to paragraph (2) of this subsection shall be 100 per centum.

(5) For purposes of this subsection—

(A) the term "construction" includes construction, reconstruction, or repair;

(B) the term "distressed area" means an area which the Secretary determines due to drought conditions has an inadequate water supply which is causing, or is likely to cause, a substantial threat to the health and welfare of the inhabitants of the area including threat of damage or loss of property;

(C) the term "political subdivision" means a city, town, borough, county, parish, district, association, or other public body created by or pursuant to State law and having jurisdiction over the water supply of such public body;

(D) the term "reasonable cost" means the lesser of (i) the cost to the Secretary of constructing a well pursuant to this subsection exclusive of the cost of transporting equipment used in the construction of wells, or (ii) the cost to a private business of constructing such well;

(E) the term "Secretary" means the Secretary of the Army, acting through the Chief of Engineers; and

(F) the term "State" means a State, the District of Columbia, the Commonwealth of Puerto Rico, the Virgin Islands, Guam, American Samoa, and the Trust Territory of the Pacific Islands.

(C) ELIGIBILITY

(1) LEVEE OWNER'S MANUAL

Not later than 1 year after October 12, 1996, in accordance with chapter 5 of title 5, the Secretary of the Army shall prepare a manual describing the maintenance and upkeep responsibilities that the Corps of Engineers requires of a non-Federal interest in order for the non-Federal interest to receive Federal assistance under this section. The Secretary shall provide a copy of the manual at no cost to each non-Federal interest that is eligible to receive Federal assistance under this section.

(2) SYSTEMWIDE IMPROVEMENT PLAN

(A) IN GENERAL

Notwithstanding the status of compliance of a non-Federal interest with the requirements of a levee owner's manual described in paragraph (1), or any other eligibility requirement established by the Secretary related to the maintenance and upkeep responsibilities of the non-Federal interest, the Secretary shall consider the non-Federal interest to be eligible for repair and rehabilitation assistance under this section if—

(i) in coordination with the Secretary, the non-Federal interest develops a systemwide improvement plan, prior to the natural disaster, that—

(I) identifies any items of deferred or inadequate maintenance and upkeep, including any such items identified by the Secretary or through periodic inspection of the flood control work;

(II) identifies any additional measures, including repair and rehabilitation work, that the Secretary determines necessary to ensure that the flood control work performs as designed and intended;

(III) includes specific timelines for addressing such items and measures;

(IV) requires the non-Federal interest to be responsible for the cost of addressing the items and measures identified under subclauses (I) and (II); and

(ii) the Secretary—

(I) determines that the systemwide improvement plan meets the requirements of clause (i) and the Secretary, acting through the District Commander, approves such plan; and

(II) determines that the non-Federal interest makes satisfactory progress in meeting the timelines described in subclause (III) of that clause.

(B) GRANDFATHERED ENCROACHMENTS

At the request of the non-Federal interest, the Secretary—

(i) shall review documentation developed by the non-Federal interest showing a covered encroachment does not negatively impact the integrity of the flood control work;

(ii) shall make a written determination with respect to whether removal or modification of such covered encroachment is necessary to ensure the encroachment does not negatively impact the integrity of the flood control work; and

(iii) may not determine that a covered encroachment is a deficiency requiring corrective action unless such action is necessary to ensure the encroachment does not negatively impact the integrity of the flood control work.

(3) AUTHORIZATION OF APPROPRIATIONS

There is authorized to be appropriated $1,000,000 to carry out paragraph (1).

(4) DEFINITIONS

In this subsection, the following definitions apply:

(A) COVERED ENCROACHMENT

The term "covered encroachment" means a permanent nonproject structure that—

(i) is located inside the boundaries of a flood control work;

(ii) is depicted on construction drawings or operation and maintenance plans for the flood control work that are signed by an engineer of record; and

(iii) is determined by the Secretary to be an encroachment of such flood control work.

(B) Maintenance and upkeep

The term "maintenance and upkeep" means all maintenance and general upkeep of a levee performed on a regular and consistent basis that is not repair and rehabilitation.

(C) Repair and rehabilitation

The term "repair and rehabilitation"—
(i) means the repair or rebuilding of a levee or other flood control structure, after the structure has been damaged by a flood, to the level of protection provided by the structure before the flood; but
(ii) does not include—
(I) any improvement to the structure; or
(II) repair or rebuilding described in clause (i) if, in the normal course of usage, the structure becomes structurally unsound and is no longer fit to provide the level of protection for which the structure was designed.

(D) Increased level of protection

In conducting repair or restoration work under subsection (a), at the request of the non-Federal sponsor, the Chief of Engineers may increase the level of protection above the level to which the system was designed, or, if the repair or restoration includes repair or restoration of a pumping station, increase the capacity of a pump, if—
(1) the Chief of Engineers determines the improvements are in the public interest, including consideration of whether—
(A) the authority under this section has been used more than once at the same location;
(B) there is an opportunity to decrease significantly the risk of loss of life and property damage; or
(C) there is an opportunity to decrease total life cycle rehabilitation costs for the project; and
(2) the non-Federal sponsor agrees to pay the difference between the cost of repair or restoration to the original design level or original capacity and the cost of achieving the higher level of protection or capacity sought by the non-Federal sponsor.

(E) Notice

The Secretary shall notify and consult with the non-Federal sponsor regarding the opportunity to request implementation of nonstructural alternatives to the repair or restoration of a flood control work under subsection (a).

(Aug. 18, 1941, ch. 377, §5, 55 Stat. 650; July 24, 1946, ch. 596, §12, 60 Stat. 652; July 26, 1947, ch. 343, title II, §205(a), 61 Stat. 501; June 30, 1948, ch. 771, title II, §206, 62 Stat. 1182; May 17, 1950, ch. 188, title II, §210, 64 Stat. 183; June 28, 1955, ch. 194, 69 Stat. 186; Pub. L. 87–874, title II, §206, Oct. 23, 1962, 76 Stat. 1194; Pub. L. 93–251, title I, §82, Mar. 7, 1974, 88 Stat. 34; Pub. L. 95–51, §2, June 20, 1977, 91 Stat. 233; Pub. L. 99–662, title IX, §917, Nov. 17, 1986, 100 Stat. 4192; Pub. L. 100–45, §9, May 27, 1987, 101 Stat. 323; Pub. L. 100–707, title I, §109(m), Nov. 23, 1988, 102 Stat. 4709; Pub. L. 101–640, title III, §302, Nov. 28, 1990, 104 Stat. 4633; Pub. L. 104–303, title II, §202(e), (f), Oct. 12, 1996, 110 Stat. 3675; Pub. L. 113–121, title III, §3029(a), June 10, 2014, 128 Stat. 1305; Pub. L. 114–322, title I, §1176, Dec. 16, 2016, 130 Stat. 1673; Pub. L. 115–270, title I, §§1160, 1161(a), 1162, Oct. 23, 2018, 132 Stat. 3795, 3796; Pub. L. 116–260, div. AA, title I, §120, Dec. 27, 2020, 134 Stat.

2633; Pub. L. 117–263, div. H, title LXXXI, §8102(a), Dec. 23, 2022, 136 Stat. 3695; Pub. L. 118–272, div. A, title I, §1146(a), Jan. 4, 2025, 138 Stat. 3036.)

SECTION 706 OF THE COMMUNICATIONS ACT OF 1934

ACT OF JUNE 19, 1934
AS AMENDED THROUGH PUB. L. 117–338

COMMUNICATIONS ACT OF 1934

[As Amended Through P.L. 117–338, Enacted January 5, 2023]

AN ACT To provide for the regulation of interstate and foreign communication by wire or radio, and for other purposes.

Be it enacted by the Senate and House of Representatives of the United States of America in Congress assembled,

* * * * * * *

TITLE VII—MISCELLANEOUS PROVISIONS

* * * * * * *

SEC. 706. [47 U.S.C. 606] WAR EMERGENCY—POWERS OF PRESIDENT.

(a)   During the continuance of a war in which the United States is engaged, the President is authorized, if he finds it necessary for the national defense and security, to direct that such communications as in his judgment may be essential to the national defense and security shall have preference or priority with any carrier subject to this Act. He may give these directions at and for such times as he may determine, and may modify, change, suspend, or annul them and for any such purpose he is hereby authorized to issue orders directly, or through such person or persons as he designates for the purpose, or through the Commission. Any carrier complying with any such order or direction or preference or priority herein authorized shall be exempt from any and all provisions in existing law imposing civil or criminal penalties, obligations, or liabilities upon carriers by reason of giving preference or priority in compliance with such order or direction.

(b)   It shall be unlawful for any person during any war in which the United States is engaged to knowingly or willfully, by physical force or intimidation by threats of physical force, obstruct or retard or aid in obstructing or retarding interstate or foreign communication by radio or wire. The President is hereby authorized, whenever in his judgment the public interest requires, to employ the armed forces of the United States to prevent any such obstruction or retardation of communication: *Provided,* That nothing in this section shall be construed to repeal, modify, or affect either section 6 or section 20 of the Act entitled An Act to supplement existing laws against unlawful restraints and monopolies, and for other purposes, approved October 15, 1914.

SEC. 706. [47 U.S.C. 606] WAR
EMERGENCY—POWERS OF PRESIDENT.

Communications Act of 193

(c) Upon proclamation by the President that there exists war or a threat of war, or a state of public peril or disaster or other national emergency, or in order to preserve the neutrality of the United States, the President, if he deems it necessary in the interest of national security or defense, may suspend or amend, for such time as he may see fit, the rules and regulations applicable to any or all stations or devices capable of emitting electromagnetic radiations within the jurisdiction of the United States as prescribed by the Commission, and may cause the closing of any station for radio communication, or any device capable of emitting electromagnetic radiations between 10 kilocycles and 100,000 megacycles, which is suitable for use as a navigational aid beyond five miles, and the removal therefrom of its apparatus and equipment, or he may authorize the use or control of any such station or device and/or its apparatus and equipment, by any department of the Government under such regulations as he may prescribe upon just compensation to the owners. The authority granted to the President, under this subsection, to cause the closing of any station or device and the removal therefrom of its apparatus and equipment, or to authorize the use or control of any station or device and/ or its apparatus and equipment, may be exercised in the Canal Zone.

(d) Upon proclamation by the President that there exists a state or threat of war involving the United States, the President, if he deems it necessary in the interest of the national security and defense, may, during a period ending not later than six months after the termination of such state or threat of war and not later than such earlier date as the Congress by concurrent resolution may designate, (1) suspend or amend the rules and regulations applicable to any or all facilities or stations for wire communication within the jurisdiction of the United States as prescribed by the Commission, (2) cause the closing of any facility or station for wire communication and the removal therefrom of its apparatus and equipment, or (3) authorize the use or control of any such facility or station and its apparatus and equipment by any department of the Government under such regulations as he may prescribe, upon just compensation to the owners.

(e) The President shall ascertain the just compensation for such use or control and certify the amount ascertained to Congress for appropriation and payment to the person entitled thereto. If the amount so certified is unsatisfactory to the person entitled thereto, such person shall be paid only 75 per centum of the amount and shall be entitled to sue the United States to recover such further sums as added to such payment of 75 per centum will make such amount as will be just compensation for the use and control. Such suit shall be brought in the manner provided by paragraph 20 of section 24, or by section 145, of the Judicial Code, as amended.

(f) Nothing in subsection (c) or (d) shall be construed to amend, repeal, impair, or effect existing laws or powers of the States in relation to taxation or the lawful police regulations of the several States, except wherein such laws, powers, or regulations may affect the transmission of Government communications, or the issue of stocks and bonds by any communication system or systems.

(g) Nothing in subsection (c) or (d) shall be construed to authorize the President to make any amendment to the rules and regulations of the Commission which the Commission would not be authorized by law to make; and nothing in subsection (d) shall be construed to authorize the President to take any action the force and effect of which shall continue beyond the date after which taking of such action would not have been authorized.

(h)   Any person who willfully does or causes or suffers to be done any act prohibited pursuant to the exercise of the President's authority under this section, or who willfully fails to do any act which he is required to do pursuant to the exercise of the President's authority under this section, or who willfully causes or suffers such failure, shall, upon conviction thereof, be punished for such offense by a fine of not more than $1,000 or by imprisonment for not more than one year, or both, and, if a firm, partnership, association, or corporation, by fine of not more than $5,000, except that any person who commits such an offense with intent to injure the United States, or with intent to secure an advantage to any foreign nation, shall, upon conviction thereof, be punished by a fine of not more than $20,000 or by imprisonment for not more than 20 years, or both.

★

HOMELAND SECURITY AND FEMA PROVISIONS

DEPARTMENT OF HOMELAND SECURITY APPROPRIATIONS ACT, 2015

PUBLIC LAW 114-4
AS AMENDED THROUGH PUB. L. 117-328

DEPARTMENT OF HOMELAND SECURITY APPROPRIATIONS ACT, 2015

[(Public Law 114–4)]

[As Amended Through P.L. 117–328, Enacted December 29, 2022]

AN ACT Making appropriations for the Department of Homeland Security for the fiscal year ending September 30, 2015, and for other purposes.

Be it enacted by the Senate and House of Representatives of the United States of America in Congress assembled,

That the following sums are appropriated, out of any money in the Treasury not otherwise appropriated, for the Department of Homeland Security for the fiscal year ending September 30, 2015, and for other purposes, namely:

* * * * * * *

FEDERAL EMERGENCY MANAGEMENT AGENCY

* * * * * * *

DISASTER RELIEF FUND(INCLUDING TRANSFER OF FUNDS)

* * * * * * *

Provided further, That the Administrator shall publish on the Agency's Web site not later than 5 days after an award of a public assistance grant under section 406 of the Robert T. Stafford Disaster Relief and Emergency Assistance Act (42 U.S.C. 5172) the specifics of the grant award: Provided further, That for any mission assignment or mission assignment task order to another Federal department or agency regarding a major disaster, not later than 5 days after the issuance of the mission assignment or task order, the Administrator shall publish on the Agency's website the following: the name of the impacted State and the disaster declaration for such State, the assigned agency, the assistance requested, a description of the disaster, the total cost estimate, and the amount obligated: Provided further, That not later than 10 days after the last day of each month until the mission assignment or task order is completed and closed out, the Administrator shall update any changes to the total cost estimate and the amount obligated:

★

FEMA ACCOUNTABILITY, MODERNIZATION AND TRANSPARENCY ACT OF 2017

PUBLIC LAW 115–87

FEMA ACCOUNTABILITY, MODERNIZATION AND TRANSPARENCY ACT OF 2017

[(Public Law 115–87)]

[This law has not been amended]

AN ACT To ensure that the Federal Emergency Management Agency's current efforts to modernize its grant management system includes applicant accessibility and transparency, and for other purposes.

Be it enacted by the Senate and House of Representatives of the United States of America in Congress assembled,

SECTION 1. [42 U.S.C. 5121 note] SHORT TITLE.

This Act may be cited as the "FEMA Accountability, Modernization and Transparency Act of 2017".

SEC. 2. REQUIREMENTS.

(a) IN GENERAL.—The Administrator of the Federal Emergency Management Agency shall ensure the ongoing modernization of the grant systems for the administration of assistance under the Robert T. Stafford Disaster Relief and Emergency Assistance Act (42 U.S.C. 5121 et seq.) includes the following:

(1) An online interface, including online assistance, for applicants to complete application forms, submit materials, and access the status of applications.

(2) Mechanisms to eliminate duplication of benefits.

(3) If appropriate, enable the sharing of information among agencies and with State, local, and tribal governments, to eliminate the need to file multiple applications and speed disaster recovery.

(4) Any additional tools the Administrator determines will improve the implementation of this section.

(b) IMPLEMENTATION.— To the extent practicable, the Administrator shall deliver the system capabilities described in subsection (a) in increments or iterations as working components for applicant use.

SEC. 3. NO ADDITIONAL FUNDS AUTHORIZED.

No additional funds are authorized to carry out the requirements of this Act. Such requirements shall be carried out using amounts otherwise authorized.

★

INTEGRATED PUBLIC ALERT AND WARNING SYSTEM MODERNIZATION ACT OF 2015

PUBLIC LAW 114–143

INTEGRATED PUBLIC ALERT AND WARNING SYSTEM MODERNIZATION ACT OF 2015

[(Public Law 114–143)]

[This law has not been amended]

AN ACT To amend the Homeland Security Act of 2002 to direct the Administrator of the Federal Emergency Management Agency to modernize the integrated public alert and warning system of the United States, and for other purposes.

Be it enacted by the Senate and House of Representatives of the United States of America in Congress assembled,

SECTION 1. [6 U.S.C. 101 note] SHORT TITLE.

This Act may be cited as the "Integrated Public Alert and Warning System Modernization Act of 2015".

SEC. 2. INTEGRATED PUBLIC ALERT AND WARNING SYSTEM MODERNIZATION.

* * * * * * *

(b) INTEGRATED PUBLIC ALERT AND WARNING SYSTEM SUBCOMMITTEE.—

(1) ESTABLISHMENT.— Not later than 90 days after the date of enactment of this Act, the Administrator of the Federal Emergency Management Agency (in this subsection referred to as the Administrator) shall establish a subcommittee to the National Advisory Council established under section 508 of the Homeland Security Act of 2002 (6 U.S.C. 318) to be known as the Integrated Public Alert and Warning System Subcommittee (in this subsection referred to as the Subcommittee).

(2) MEMBERSHIP.—Notwithstanding section 508(c) of the Homeland Security Act of 2002 (6 U.S.C. 318(c)), the Subcommittee shall be composed of the following members (or their designees):

(A) The Deputy Administrator for Protection and National Preparedness of the Federal Emergency Management Agency.

(B) The Chairman of the Federal Communications Commission.

(C) The Administrator of the National Oceanic and Atmospheric Administration of the Department of Commerce.

(D)   The Assistant Secretary for Communications and Information of the Department of Commerce.

(E)   The Under Secretary for Science and Technology of the Department of Homeland Security.

(F)   The Under Secretary for the National Protection and Programs Directorate.

(G)   The Director of Disability Integration and Coordination of the Federal Emergency Management Agency.

(H)   The Chairperson of the National Council on Disability.

(I) Qualified individuals appointed by the Administrator as soon as practicable after the date of enactment of this Act from among the following:

(i)   Representatives of State and local governments, representatives of emergency management agencies, and representatives of emergency response providers.

(ii)   Representatives from federally recognized Indian tribes and national Indian organizations.

(iii) Individuals who have the requisite technical knowledge and expertise to serve on the Subcommittee, including representatives of—

(I)   communications service providers;

(II)   vendors, developers, and manufacturers of systems, facilities, equipment, and capabilities for the provision of communications services;

(III)   third-party service bureaus;

(IV)   the broadcasting industry, including public broadcasting;

(V)   the commercial mobile radio service industry;

(VI)   the cable industry;

(VII)   the satellite industry;

(VIII)   national organizations representing individuals with disabilities, the blind, deaf, and hearing-loss communities, individuals with access and functional needs, and the elderly;

(IX)   consumer or privacy advocates; and

(X)   organizations representing individuals with limited-English proficiency.

(iv)   Qualified representatives of such other stakeholders and interested and affected parties as the Administrator considers appropriate.

(3) CHAIRPERSON.— The Deputy Administrator for Protection and National Preparedness of the Federal Emergency Management Agency shall serve as the Chairperson of the Subcommittee.

(4) MEETINGS.—

(A) INITIAL MEETING.— The initial meeting of the Subcommittee shall take place not later than 120 days after the date of enactment of this Act.

(B) OTHER MEETINGS.— After the initial meeting, the Subcommittee shall meet, at least annually, at the call of the Chairperson.

(5) CONSULTATION WITH NONMEMBERS.—The Subcommittee and the program offices for the integrated public alert and warning system for the United States shall consult with individuals and entities that are not represented on the Subcommittee to consider new and developing technologies that may be beneficial to the public alert and warning system, including—

(A)   the Defense Advanced Research Projects Agency;

(B)   entities engaged in federally funded research; and

(C)   academic institutions engaged in relevant work and research.

(6) RECOMMENDATIONS.—The Subcommittee shall—

(A)   develop recommendations for an integrated public alert and warning system; and

(B) in developing the recommendations under subparagraph (A), consider—

(i)   recommendations for common alerting and warning protocols, standards, terminology, and operating procedures for the public alert and warning system; and

(ii) recommendations to provide for a public alert and warning system that—

(I)   has the capability to adapt the distribution and content of communications on the basis of geographic location, risks, or personal user preferences, as appropriate;

(II)   has the capability to alert and warn individuals with disabilities and individuals with limited-English proficiency;

(III)   to the extent appropriate, incorporates multiple communications technologies;

(IV)   is designed to adapt to, and incorporate, future technologies for communicating directly with the public;

(V)   is designed to provide alerts to the largest portion of the affected population feasible, including nonresident visitors and tourists, and improve the ability of remote areas to receive alerts;

(VI)   promotes local and regional public and private partnerships to enhance community preparedness and response; and

(VII)   provides redundant alert mechanisms, if practicable, to reach the greatest number of people regardless of whether they have access to, or use, any specific medium of communication or any particular device.

(7) REPORT.—

(A) SUBCOMMITTEE SUBMISSION.— Not later than 1 year after the date of enactment of this Act, the Subcommittee shall submit to the National Advisory Council a report containing any recommendations required to be developed under paragraph (6) for approval by the National Advisory Council.

(B) SUBMISSION BY NATIONAL ADVISORY COUNCIL.—If the National Advisory Council approves the recommendations contained in the report submitted under subparagraph (A), the National Advisory Council shall submit the report to—

(i) the head of each agency represented on the Subcommittee;

(ii) the Committee on Homeland Security and Governmental Affairs and the Committee on Commerce, Science, and Transportation of the Senate; and

(iii) the Committee on Homeland Security and the Committee on Transportation and Infrastructure of the House of Representatives.

(8) TERMINATION.— The Subcommittee shall terminate not later than 3 years after the date of enactment of this Act.

(c) AUTHORIZATION OF APPROPRIATIONS.— There are authorized to be appropriated to carry out this Act and the amendments made by this Act such sums as may be necessary for each of fiscal years 2016, 2017, and 2018.

(d) [6 U.S.C. 3210 note] LIMITATIONS ON STATUTORY CONSTRUCTION.—

(1) DEFINITION.— In this subsection, the term participating commercial mobile service provider has the meaning given that term under section 10.10(f) of title 47, Code of Federal Regulations, as in effect on the date of enactment of this Act.

(2) LIMITATIONS.—Nothing in this Act, including an amendment made by this Act, shall be construed—

(A) to affect any authority—

(i) of the Department of Commerce;

(ii) of the Federal Communications Commission; or

(iii) provided under the Robert T. Stafford Disaster Relief and Emergency Assistance Act (42 U.S.C. 5121 et seq.);

(B) to provide the Secretary of Homeland Security with authority to require any action by the Department of Commerce, the Federal Communications Commission, or any nongovernmental entity;

(C) to apply to, or to provide the Administrator of the Federal Emergency Management Agency with authority over, any participating commercial mobile service provider;

(D) to alter in any way the wireless emergency alerts service established under the Warning, Alert, and Response Network Act (47 U.S.C. 1201 et seq.) or any related orders issued by the Federal Communications Commission after October 13, 2006; or

(E) to provide the Federal Emergency Management Agency with authority to require a State or local jurisdiction to use the integrated public alert and warning system of the United States.

★

CYBERSECURITY AND INFRASTRUCTURE
SECURITY AGENCY ACT OF 2018

PUBLIC LAW 115–278

CYBERSECURITY AND INFRASTRUCTURE SECURITY AGENCY ACT OF 2018

[(Public Law 115–278)]

[This law has not been amended]

AN ACT To amend the Homeland Security Act of 2002 to authorize the Cybersecurity and Infrastructure Security Agency of the Department of Homeland Security, and for other purposes.

Be it enacted by the Senate and House of Representatives of the United States of America in Congress assembled,

SECTION 1. [6 U.S.C. 101 note] SHORT TITLE.

This Act may be cited as the "Cybersecurity and Infrastructure Security Agency Act of 2018".

SEC. 2. CYBERSECURITY AND INFRASTRUCTURE SECURITY AGENCY.

* * * * * * *

(b) TREATMENT OF CERTAIN POSITIONS.—

(1) [6 U.S.C. 652 note] UNDER SECRETARY.— The individual serving as the Under Secretary appointed pursuant to section 103(a)(1)(H) of the Homeland Security Act of 2002 (6 U.S.C. 113(a)(1)(H)) of the Department of Homeland Security on the day before the date of enactment of this Act may continue to serve as the Director of Cybersecurity and Infrastructure Security of the Department on and after such date.

(2) [6 U.S.C. 571 note] DIRECTOR FOR EMERGENCY COMMUNICATIONS.— The individual serving as the Director for Emergency Communications of the Department of Homeland Security on the day before the date of enactment of this Act may continue to serve as the Assistant Director for Emergency Communications of the Department on and after such date.

(3) [6 U.S.C. 653 note] ASSISTANT SECRETARY FOR CYBERSECURITY AND COMMUNICATIONS.— The individual serving as the Assistant Secretary for Cybersecurity and Communications on the day before the date of enactment of this Act may continue to serve as the Assistant Director for Cybersecurity on and after such date.

(4) [6 U.S.C. 654 note] ASSISTANT SECRETARY FOR INFRASTRUCTURE

PROTECTION.— The individual serving as the Assistant Secretary for Infrastructure Protection on the day before the date of enactment of this Act may continue to serve as the Assistant Director for Infrastructure Security on and after such date.

(c) [6 U.S.C. 571 note] REFERENCE.—Any reference to—

(1) the Office of Emergency Communications in any law, regulation, map, document, record, or other paper of the United States shall be deemed to be a reference to the Emergency Communications Division; and

(2) the Director for Emergency Communications in any law, regulation, map, document, record, or other paper of the United States shall be deemed to be a reference to the Assistant Director for Emergency Communications.

(d) OVERSIGHT.—The Director of Cybersecurity and Infrastructure Security of the Department of Homeland Security shall provide to Congress, in accordance with the deadlines specified in paragraphs (1) through (6), information on the following:

(1) Not later than 60 days after the date of enactment of this Act, a briefing on the activities of the Agency relating to the development and use of the mechanisms required pursuant to section 2202(c)(6) of the Homeland Security Act of 2002 (as added by subsection (a)).

(2) Not later than 1 year after the date of the enactment of this Act, a briefing on the activities of the Agency relating to the use and improvement by the Agency of the mechanisms required pursuant to section 2202(c)(6) of the Homeland Security Act of 2002 and how such activities have impacted coordination, situational awareness, and communications with Sector-Specific Agencies.

(3) Not later than 90 days after the date of the enactment of this Act, information on the mechanisms of the Agency for regular and ongoing consultation and collaboration, as required pursuant to section 2202(c)(7) of the Homeland Security Act of 2002 (as added by subsection (a)).

(4) Not later than 1 year after the date of the enactment of this Act, information on the activities of the consultation and collaboration mechanisms of the Agency as required pursuant to section 2202(c)(7) of the Homeland Security Act of 2002, and how such mechanisms have impacted operational coordination, situational awareness, and integration across the Agency.

(5) Not later than 180 days after the date of enactment of this Act, information, which shall be made publicly available and updated as appropriate, on the mechanisms and structures of the Agency responsible for stakeholder outreach and engagement, as required under section 2202(c)(10) of the Homeland Security Act of 2002 (as added by subsection (a)).

(e) CYBER WORKFORCE.— Not later than 90 days after the date of enactment of this Act, the Director of the Cybersecurity and Infrastructure Security Agency of the Department of Homeland Security, in coordination with the Director of the Office of Personnel Management, shall submit to Congress a report detailing how the Agency is meeting legislative requirements under the Cybersecurity Workforce Assessment Act (Public Law 113-246; 128 Stat. 2880) and the Homeland Security Cybersecurity Workforce Assessment Act (enacted as section 4 of the Border Patrol Agent Pay Reform Act of 2014; Public Law 113-277) to address cyber workforce needs.

(f) FACILITY.— Not later than 180 days after the date of enactment of this Act, the Director of the Cybersecurity and Infrastructure Security Agency of the Department of Homeland Security shall report to Congress on the most efficient and effective methods of consolidating Agency facilities, personnel, and programs to most effectively carry out the Agency's mission.

* * * * * * *

SEC. 3. [6 U.S.C. 452 note] TRANSFER OF OTHER ENTITIES.

(a) OFFICE OF BIOMETRIC IDENTITY MANAGEMENT.— The Office of Biometric Identity Management of the Department of Homeland Security located in the National Protection and Programs Directorate of the Department of Homeland Security on the day before the date of enactment of this Act is hereby transferred to the Management Directorate of the Department.

(b) FEDERAL PROTECTIVE SERVICE.—

(1) IN GENERAL.— Not later than 90 days after the completion of the Government Accountability Office review of the organizational placement of the Federal Protective Service (authorized under section 1315 of title 40, United States Code), the Secretary of Homeland Security shall determine the appropriate placement of the Service within the Department of Homeland Security and commence the transfer of the Service to such component, directorate, or other office of the Department that the Secretary so determines appropriate.

(2) EXCEPTION.—If the Secretary of Homeland Security determines pursuant to paragraph (1) that no component, directorate, or other office of the Department of Homeland Security is an appropriate placement for the Federal Protective Service, the Secretary shall—

(A) provide to the Committee on Homeland Security and the Committee on Transportation and Infrastructure of the House of Representatives and the Committee on Homeland Security and Governmental Affairs of the Senate and the Office of Management and Budget a detailed explanation, in writing, of the reason for such determination that includes—

(i) information on how the Department considered the Government Accountability Office review described in such paragraph;

(ii) a list of the components, directorates, or other offices of the Department that were considered for such placement; and

(iii) information on why each such component, directorate, or other office of the Department was determined to not be an appropriate placement for the Service;

(B) not later than 120 days after the completion of the Government Accountability Office review described in such paragraph, develop and submit to the committees specified in subparagraph (A) and the Office of Management and Budget a plan to coordinate with other appropriate Federal agencies, including the General Services Administration, to determine a more appropriate placement for the Service; and

(C)   not later than 180 days after the completion of such Government Accountability Office review, submit to such committees and the Office of Management and Budget a recommendation regarding the appropriate placement of the Service within the executive branch of the Federal Government.

SEC. 4. DHS REPORT ON CLOUD-BASED CYBERSECURITY.

(a) DEFINITION.— In this section, the term Department means the Department of Homeland Security.

(b) REPORT.—Not later than 120 days after the date of enactment of this Act, the Secretary of Homeland Security, in coordination with the Director of the Office of Management and Budget and the Administrator of General Services, shall submit to the Committee on Homeland Security and Governmental Affairs of the Senate and the Committee on Oversight and Government Reform and the Committee on Homeland Security of the House of Representatives a report on the leadership role of the Department in cloud-based cybersecurity deployments for civilian Federal departments and agencies, which shall include—

(1)   information on the plan of the Department for ensuring access to a security operations center as a service capability in accordance with the December 19, 2017 Report to the President on Federal IT Modernization issued by the American Technology Council;

(2) information on what service capabilities under paragraph (1) the Department will prioritize, including—

(A)   criteria the Department will use to evaluate capabilities offered by the private sector; and

(B)   how Federal government- and private sector-provided capabilities will be integrated to enable visibility and consistency of such capabilities across all cloud and on premise environments, as called for in the report described in paragraph (1); and

(3)   information on how the Department will adapt the current capabilities of, and future enhancements to, the intrusion detection and prevention system of the Department and the Continuous Diagnostics and Mitigation Program of the Department to secure civilian Federal government networks in a cloud environment.

SEC. 5. [6 U.S.C. 651 note] RULE OF CONSTRUCTION.

Nothing in this Act or an amendment made by this Act may be construed as—

(1)   conferring new authorities to the Secretary of Homeland Security, including programmatic, regulatory, or enforcement authorities, outside of the authorities in existence on the day before the date of enactment of this Act;

(2)   reducing or limiting the programmatic, regulatory, or enforcement authority vested in any other Federal agency by statute; or

(3)   affecting in any manner the authority, existing on the day before the date of enactment of this Act, of any other Federal agency or component of the Department

of Homeland Security.

SEC. 6. PROHIBITION ON ADDITIONAL FUNDING.

No additional funds are authorized to be appropriated to carry out this Act or the amendments made by this Act. This Act and the amendments made by this Act shall be carried out using amounts otherwise authorized.

★

COMMUNITY SUPPORT PROGRAMS

EMERGENCY FOOD AND SHELTER PROGRAM PROVISIONS MCKINNEY-VENTO HOMELESS ASSISTANCE ACT

PUBLIC LAW 100–77
AS AMENDED THROUGH PUB. L. 117–263

McKINNEY-VENTO HOMELESS ASSISTANCE ACT

[Public Law 100–77, 101 Stat. 482; 42 U.S.C. 11301 et seq.]

[As Amended Through P.L. 117–263, Enacted December 23, 2022]

* * * * * * *

TITLE III—FEDERAL EMERGENCY MANAGEMENT FOOD AND SHELTER PROGRAM

SUBTITLE A—ADMINISTRATIVE PROVISIONS

SEC. 301. [42 U.S.C. 11331] EMERGENCY FOOD AND SHELTER PROGRAM NATIONAL BOARD.

(a) ESTABLISHMENT.— There is established to carry out the provisions of this title the Emergency Food and Shelter Program National Board. The Director of the Federal Emergency Management Agency[10] shall constitute the National Board in accordance with subsection (b) in administering the program under this title.

---

[10] Section 611 of Public Law 111–295 provides for the transfer of duties for this entity under the Department of Homeland Security. Section 612(c) of such Public Law provides: [a]ny reference to the Director of the Federal Emergency Management Agency, in any law, rule, regulation, certificate, directive, instruction, or other official paper shall be considered to refer and apply to the Administrator of the Federal Emergency Management Agency..

(b) MEMBERS.—The National Board shall consist of the Director and 6 members appointed by the Director. The initial members of the National Board shall be appointed by the Director not later than 30 days after the date of the enactment of this Act.[11] Each such member shall be appointed from among individuals nominated by 1 of the following organizations:

---

[11] The date of enactment was July 22, 1987.

---

(1) The United Way of America.

(2) The Salvation Army.

(3) The National Council of Churches of Christ in the U.S.A.

(4) Catholic Charities U.S.A.

(5)   The Council of Jewish Federations, Inc.

(6)   The American Red Cross.

(c) CHAIRPERSON.— The Director shall be the Chairperson of the National Board.

(d) OTHER ACTIVITIES.— Except as otherwise specifically provided in this title, the National Board shall establish its own procedures and policies for the conduct of its affairs.

(e) TRANSFERS FROM PREVIOUS NATIONAL BOARD.—Upon the appointment of members to the National Board under subsec- tion (b)—

(1)   the national board constituted under the emergency food and shelter program established pursuant to section 101(g) of Public Law 99–500 or Public Law 99–591 shall cease to exist; and

(2)   the personnel, property, records, and undistributed program funds of such national board shall be transferred to the National Board.

SEC. 302. [42 U.S.C. 11332] LOCAL BOARDS.

(a) ESTABLISHMENT.— Each locality designated by the National Board shall constitute a local board for the purpose of determining how program funds allotted to the locality will be distributed. The local board shall consist, to the extent practicable, of representatives of the same organizations as the National Board, except that the mayor or other appropriate heads of government will replace the Federal members, and except that each local board administering program funds for a locality within which is located a reservation (as such term is defined in section 3(d) of the Indian Financing Act of 1974 (25 U.S.C. 1452(d)), or a portion thereof, shall include a board member who is a member of an Indian tribe (as such term is defined in section 102(a)(17) of the Housing and Community Development Act of 1974 (42 U.S.C. 5302(a)(17)). The chairperson of the local board shall be elected by a majority of the members of the local board. Local boards are encouraged to expand participation of other private nonprofit organizations on the local board.

(b) RESPONSIBILITIES.—Each local board shall—

(1)   determine which private nonprofit organizations or public organizations of the local government in the individual locality shall receive grants to act as service providers;

(2)   monitor recipient service providers for program com- pliance;

(3)   reallocate funds among service providers;

(4)   ensure proper reporting; and

(5)   coordinate with other Federal, State, and local government assistance programs available in the locality.

SEC. 303. [42 U.S.C. 11333] ROLE OF FEDERAL EMERGENCY MANAGEMENT AGENCY.

(a) IN GENERAL.— The Director shall provide the National Board with administrative support and act as Federal liaison to the National Board.

(b) SPECIFIC SUPPORT ACTIVITIES.—The Director shall—

(1)   make available to the National Board, upon request, the services of the legal

counsel and Inspector General of the Federal Emergency Management Agency;

(2) assign clerical personnel to the National Board on a temporary basis; and

(3) conduct audits of the National Board annually and at such other times as may be appropriate.

SEC. 304. [42 U.S.C. 11334] RECORDS AND AUDIT OF NATIONAL BOARD AND RECIPIENTS OF ASSISTANCE.

(a) ANNUAL INDEPENDENT AUDIT OF NATIONAL BOARD.—

(1) The accounts of the National Board shall be audited annually in accordance with generally accepted auditing standards by independent certified public accountants or independent licensed public accountants certified or licensed by a regulatory authority of a State or other political subdivision of the United States. The audits shall be conducted at the place or places where the accounts of the National Board are normally kept. All books, accounts, financial records, reports, files, and all other papers, things, or property belonging to or in use by the National Board and necessary to facilitate the audits shall be made available to the person or persons conducting the audits, and full facilities for verifying transactions with any assets held by depositories, fiscal agents, and custodians shall be afforded to such person or persons.

(2) The report of each such independent audit shall be included in the annual report required in section 305. Such report shall set forth the scope of the audit and include such statements as are necessary to present fairly the assets and liabilities of the National Board, surplus or deficit, with an analysis of the changes during the year, supplemented in reasonable detail by a statement of the income and expenses of the National Board during the year, and a statement of the application of funds, together with the opinion of the independent auditor of such statements.

(b) ACCESS TO RECORDS OF RECIPIENTS OF ASSISTANCE.—

(1) Each recipient of assistance under this title shall keep such records as may be reasonably necessary to fully disclose the amount and the disposition by such recipient of the proceeds of such assistance, the total cost of the project or undertaking in connection with which such assistance is given or used, and the amount and nature of that portion of the cost of the project or undertaking supplied by other sources, and such other records as will facilitate an effective audit.

(2) The National Board, or any of its duly authorized representatives, shall have access for the purpose of audit and examination to any books, documents, papers, and records of the recipient that are pertinent to assistance received under this title.

(c) AUTHORITY OF COMPTROLLER GENERAL.— The Comptroller General of the United States, or any of the duly authorized representatives of the Comptroller General, shall also have access to any books, documents, papers, and records of the National Board and recipients for such purpose.

SEC. 305. [42 U.S.C. 11335] ANNUAL REPORT.

The National Board shall transmit to the Congress an annual report covering each year in which it conducts activities with funds made available under this title.

SUBTITLE B—EMERGENCY FOOD AND SHELTER GRANTS

SEC. 311. [42 U.S.C. 11341] GRANTS BY THE DIRECTOR.

Not later than 30 days following the date on which appropriations become available to carry out this subtitle, the Director shall award a grant for the full amount that the Congress appropriates for the program under this subtitle to the National Board for the purpose of providing emergency food and shelter to needy individuals through private nonprofit organizations and local governments in accordance with section 313.

SEC. 312. [42 U.S.C. 11342] RETENTION OF INTEREST EARNED.

Interest accrued on the balance of any grant to the National Board shall be available to the National Board for reallocation, and total administrative costs shall be determined based on total amount of funds available, including interest and any private contributions that are made to the National Board.

SEC. 313. [42 U.S.C. 11343] PURPOSES OF GRANTS.

(a) ELIGIBLE ACTIVITIES.—Grants to the National Board may be used—

(1) to supplement and expand ongoing efforts to provide shelter, food, and supportive services for homeless individuals with sensitivity to the transition from temporary shelter to permanent homes, and attention to the special needs of homeless individuals with mental and physical disabilities and illnesses, and to facilitate access for homeless individuals to other sources of services and benefits;

(2) to strengthen efforts to create more effective and innovative local programs by providing funding for them; and

(3) to conduct minimum rehabilitation of existing mass shelter or mass feeding facilities, but only to the extent necessary to make facilities safe, sanitary, and bring them into compliance with local building codes.

(b) LIMITATIONS ON ACTIVITIES.—

(1) The National Board may only provide funding provided under this subtitle for—

(A) programs undertaken by private nonprofit organizations and local governments; and

(B) programs that are consistent with the purposes of this title.

(2) The National Board may not carry out programs directly.

SEC. 314. [42 U.S.C. 11344] LIMITATION ON CERTAIN COSTS.

Not more than 5 percent of the total amount appropriated for the emergency food and shelter program for each fiscal year may be expended for the costs of administration.

SEC. 315. [42 U.S.C. 11345] DISBURSEMENT OF FUNDS.

Any amount made available by appropriation Acts under this title shall be disbursed by the National Board before the expiration of the 3-month period beginning on the date on which such amount becomes available.

SEC. 316. [42 U.S.C. 11346] PROGRAM GUIDELINES.

(a) GUIDELINES.—The National Board shall establish written guidelines for carrying out the program under this subtitle, including—

(1) methods for identifying localities with the highest need for emergency food and shelter assistance;

(2) methods for determining the amount and distribution to such localities;

(3) eligible program costs, including maximum flexibility in meeting currently existing needs;

(4) guidelines specifying the responsibilities and reporting requirements of the National Board, its recipients, and service providers;

(5) guidelines requiring each private nonprofit organization and local government carrying out a local emergency food and shelter program with amounts provided under this subtitle, to the maximum extent practicable, to involve homeless individuals and families, through employment, volunteer services, or otherwise, in providing emergency food and shelter and in otherwise carrying out the local program; and

(6) guidelines requiring each private nonprofit organization and local government carrying out a local emergency food and shelter program with amounts provided under this subtitle to provide for the participation of not less than 1 homeless individual or former homeless individual on the board of directors or other equivalent policy making entity of the organization or governmental agency to the extent that such entity considers and makes policies and decisions regarding the local program of the organization or locality; except that such guidelines may grant waivers to applicants unable to meet such requirement if the organization or government agrees to otherwise consult with homeless or formerly homeless individuals in considering and making such policies and decisions.

(b) PUBLICATION.— Guidelines established under subsection (a) shall be published annually, and whenever modified, in the Federal Register. The National Board shall not be subject to the procedural rulemaking requirements of subchapter II of chapter 5 of title 5, United States Code.

SUBTITLE C—GENERAL PROVISIONS

SEC. 321. [42 U.S.C. 11351] DEFINITIONS.

For purposes of this title:

(1) The term Director means the Director of the Federal Emergency Management Agency[12].

---

[12] Section 611 of Public Law 111–295 provides for the transfer of duties for this entity under the Department of Homeland Security. Section 612(c) of such Public Law provides: [a]ny reference to the Director of the Federal Emergency Management Agency, in any law, rule, regulation, certificate, directive, instruction, or other official paper shall be considered to refer and apply to the Administrator of the Federal Emergency Management Agency..

---

(2) The term emergency shelter means a facility all or a part of which is used or

designed to be used to provide temporary housing.

(3)   The term local government means a unit of general purpose local government.

(4)   The term locality means the geographical area within the jurisdiction of a local government.

(5)   The term National Board means the Emergency Food and Shelter Program National Board.

(6) The term private nonprofit organization means an organization—

(A)   no part of the net earnings of which inures to the benefit of any member, founder, contributor, or individual;

(B)   that has a voluntary board;

(C)   that has an accounting system, or has designated a fiscal agent in accordance with requirements established by the Director; and

(D)   that practices nondiscrimination in the provision of assistance.

(7)   The term State means each of the several States, the District of Columbia, the Commonwealth of Puerto Rico, the Virgin Islands, Guam, American Samoa, the Northern Mariana Islands, the Trust Territory of the Pacific Islands, and any other territory or possession of the United States.

SEC. 322. [42 U.S.C. 11352] AUTHORIZATION OF APPROPRIATIONS.

There are authorized to be appropriated to carry out this title $180,000,000 for fiscal year 1993 and $187,560,000 for fiscal year 1994.

★

DIRECTING DOLLARS TO DISASTER RELIEF
ACT OF 2015

PUBLIC LAW 114–132

DIRECTING DOLLARS TO DISASTER RELIEF ACT OF 2015

[(Public Law 114–132)]

[This law has not been amended]

AN ACT To direct the Administrator of the Federal Emergency Management Agency to develop an integrated plan to reduce administrative costs under the Robert T. Stafford Disaster Relief and Emergency Assistance Act, and for other purposes.

Be it enacted by the Senate and House of Representatives of the United States of America in Congress assembled,

SECTION 1. [42 U.S.C. 5121 note] SHORT TITLE.

This Act may be cited as the "Directing Dollars to Disaster Relief Act of 2015".

SEC. 2. [42 U.S.C. 5165e note] DEFINITIONS.

In this Act—

(1) the term administrative cost—

(A) means a cost incurred by the Agency in support of the delivery of disaster assistance for a major disaster; and

(B) does not include a cost incurred by a grantee or subgrantee;

(2) the term Administrator means the Administrator of the Agency;

(3) the term Agency means the Federal Emergency Management Agency;

(4) the term direct administrative cost means a cost incurred by a grantee or subgrantee of a program authorized by the Robert T. Stafford Disaster Relief and Emergency Assistance Act (42 U.S.C. 5121 et seq.) that can be identified separately and assigned to a specific project;

(5) the term hazard mitigation program means the hazard mitigation grant program authorized under section 404 of the Robert T. Stafford Disaster Relief and Emergency Assistance Act (42 U.S.C. 5170c);

(6) the term individual assistance program means the individual assistance grant program authorized under sections 408, 410, 415, 416, 426, and 502(a) of the Robert T. Stafford Disaster Relief and Emergency Assistance Act (42 U.S.C. 5174, 5177, 5182, 5183, 5189d, and 5192(a));

(7)   the term major disaster means a major disaster declared by the President under section 401 of the Robert T. Stafford Disaster Relief and Emergency Assistance Act (42 U.S.C. 5170);

(8)   the term mission assignment has the meaning given the term in section 641 of the Post-Katrina Emergency Management Reform Act of 2006 (6 U.S.C. 741); and

(9)   the term public assistance program means the public assistance grant program authorized under sections 403(a)(3), 406, 418, 419, 428, and 502(a) of the Robert T. Stafford Disaster Relief and Emergency Assistance Act (42 U.S.C. 5170b(a)(3), 5172, 5185, 5186, 5189f, and 5192(a)).

SEC. 3. [42 U.S.C. 5165e] INTEGRATED PLAN FOR ADMINISTRATIVE COST REDUCTION.

(a) IN GENERAL.—Not later than 365 days after the date of enactment of this Act, the Administrator shall—

(1) develop and implement an integrated plan to control and reduce administrative costs for major disasters, which shall include—

(A)   steps the Agency will take to reduce administrative costs;

(B)   milestones needed for accomplishing the reduction of administrative costs;

(C)   strategic goals for the average annual percentage of administrative costs of major disasters for each fiscal year;

(D)   the assignment of clear roles and responsibilities, including the designation of officials responsible for monitoring and measuring performance; and

(E)   a timetable for implementation;

(2)   compare the costs and benefits of tracking the administrative cost data for major disasters by the public assistance, individual assistance, hazard mitigation, and mission assignment programs, and if feasible, track this information; and

(3)   clarify Agency guidance and minimum documentation requirements for a direct administrative cost claimed by a grantee or subgrantee of a public assistance grant program.

(b) CONGRESSIONAL UPDATE.— Not later than 90 days after the date of enactment of this Act, the Administrator shall brief the Committee on Homeland Security and Governmental Affairs of the Senate and the Committee on Transportation and Infrastructure of the House of Representatives on the plan required to be developed under subsection (a)(1).

(c) UPDATES.— If the Administrator modifies the plan or the timetable under subsection (a), the Administrator shall submit to the Committee on Homeland Security and Governmental Affairs of the Senate and the Committee on Transportation and Infrastructure of the House of Representatives a report notifying Congress of the modification, which shall include the details of the modification.

SEC. 4. [42 U.S.C. 5165e note] REPORTING REQUIREMENT.

(a) ANNUAL REPORT.— Not later than November 30 of each year for 7 years beginning on the date of enactment of this Act, the Administrator shall submit to Committee on Homeland Security and Governmental Affairs of the Senate and the Committee on Transportation and Infrastructure of the House of Representatives a report on the development and implementation of the integrated plan required under section 3 for the previous fiscal year.

(b) REPORT UPDATES.—

(1) THREE YEAR UPDATE.— Not later than 3 years after the date on which the Administrator submits a report under subsection (a), the Administrator shall submit an updated report for the previous 3-fiscal-year period.

(2) FIVE YEAR UPDATE.— Not later than 5 years after the date on which the Administrator submits a report under subsection (a), the Administrator shall submit an updated report for the previous 5-fiscal-year period.

(c) CONTENTS OF REPORTS.—Each report required under subsections (a) and (b) shall contain, at a minimum—

(1)   the total amount spent on administrative costs for the fiscal year period for which the report is being submitted;

(2)   the average annual percentage of administrative costs for the fiscal year period for which the report is being submitted;

(3)   an assessment of the effectiveness of the plan developed under section 3(a)(1);

(4) an analysis of—

(A)   whether the Agency is achieving the strategic goals established under section 3(a)(1)(C); and

(B)   in the case of the Agency not achieving such strategic goals, what is preventing the Agency from doing so;

(5)   any actions the Agency has identified as useful in improving upon and reaching the goals for administrative costs established under section 3(a)(1)(C); and

(6)   any data described in section 3(a)(2), if the Agency determines it is feasible to track such data.

(d) PUBLIC AVAILABILITY.— Not later than 30 days after the date on which the Administrator submits a report to Congress under this section, the Administrator shall make the report publicly available on the website of the Agency.

★

RESEARCH, FORECASTING, AND INNOVATION

WEATHER RESEARCH AND FORECASTING
INNOVATION ACT OF 2017

PUBLIC LAW 115–24
AS AMENDED THROUGH PUB. L. 117–316

WEATHER RESEARCH AND FORECASTING INNOVATION ACT OF 2017

[(Public Law 115–25; Approved April 18, 2017)]

[As Amended Through P.L. 117–316, Enacted December 27, 2022]

AN ACT To improve the National Oceanic and Atmospheric Administration's weather research through a focused program of investment on affordable and attainable advances in observational, computing, and modeling capabilities to support substantial improvement in weather forecasting and prediction of high impact weather events, to expand commercial opportunities for the provision of weather data, and for other purposes.

Be it enacted by the Senate and House of Representatives of the United States of America in Congress assembled,

SECTION 1. SHORT TITLE; TABLE OF CONTENTS.

(a) [15 U.S.C. 8501 note] SHORT TITLE.— This Act may be cited as the "Weather Research and Forecasting Innovation Act of 2017".

(b) TABLE OF CONTENTS.— The table of contents for this Act is as follows:

TITLE III—WEATHER SATELLITE AND DATA INNOVATION

TITLE IV—FEDERAL WEATHER COORDINATION

TITLE V—TSUNAMI WARNING, EDUCATION, AND RESEARCH ACT OF 2017

* * * * * * *

* * * * * * *

* * * * * * *

TITLE VI—IMPROVING FEDERAL PRECIPITATION INFORMATION

SEC. 2. [15 U.S.C. 8501] DEFINITIONS.

In this Act:

(1) SEASONAL.— The term seasonal means the time range between 3 months and 2 years.

(2) STATE.— The term State means a State, a territory, or possession of the United States, including a Commonwealth, or the District of Columbia.

(3) SUBSEASONAL.— The term subseasonal means the time range between 2 weeks and 3 months.

(4) UNDER SECRETARY.— The term Under Secretary means the Under Secretary of Commerce for Oceans and Atmosphere.

(5) WEATHER INDUSTRY AND WEATHER ENTERPRISE.— The terms weather industry and weather enterprise are interchangeable in this Act, and include individuals and organizations from public, private, and academic sectors that contribute to the research, development, and production of weather forecast products, and primary consumers of these weather forecast products.

TITLE I—UNITED STATES WEATHER RESEARCH AND FORECASTING IMPROVEMENT

SEC. 101. [15 U.S.C. 8511] PUBLIC SAFETY PRIORITY.

In conducting research, the Under Secretary shall prioritize improving weather data, modeling, computing, forecasting, and warnings for the protection of life and property and for the enhancement of the national economy.

SEC. 102. [15 U.S.C. 8512] WEATHER RESEARCH AND FORECASTING INNOVATION.

(a) PROGRAM.— The Assistant Administrator for the Office of Oceanic and Atmospheric Research shall conduct a program to develop improved understanding of and forecast capabilities for atmospheric events and their impacts, placing priority on developing more accurate, timely, and effective warnings and forecasts of high impact weather events that endanger life and property.

(b) PROGRAM ELEMENTS.—The program described in subsection (a) shall focus on the following activities:

(1) Improving the fundamental understanding of weather consistent with section 101, including the boundary layer and other processes affecting high impact weather events.

(2) Improving the understanding of how the public receives, interprets, and responds to warnings and forecasts of high impact weather events that endanger life and property.

(3) Research and development, and transfer of knowledge, technologies, and applications to the National Weather Service and other appropriate agencies and entities, including the United States weather industry and academic partners, related to—

(A) advanced radar, radar networking technologies, and other ground-based technologies, including those emphasizing rapid, fine-scale sensing of the boundary layer and lower troposphere, and the use of innovative, dual-polarization, phased-array technologies;

(B)   aerial weather observing systems;

(C)   high performance computing and information technology and wireless communication networks;

(D) advanced numerical weather prediction systems and forecasting tools and techniques that improve the forecasting of timing, track, intensity, and severity of high impact weather, including through—

(i)   the development of more effective mesoscale models;

(ii)   more effective use of existing, and the development of new, regional and national cloud-resolving models;

(iii)   enhanced global weather models; and

(iv)   integrated assessment models;

(E)   quantitative assessment tools for measuring the impact and value of data and observing systems, including Observing System Simulation Experiments (as described in section 107), Observing System Experiments, and Analyses of Alternatives;

(F)   atmospheric chemistry and interactions essential to accurately characterizing atmospheric composition and predicting meteorological processes, including cloud microphysical, precipitation, and atmospheric electrification processes, to more effectively understand their role in severe weather; and

(G)   additional sources of weather data and information, including commercial observing systems.

(4)   A technology transfer initiative, carried out jointly and in coordination with the Director of the National Weather Service, and in cooperation with the United States weather industry and academic partners, to ensure continuous development and transition of the latest scientific and technological advances into operations of the National Weather Service and to establish a process to sunset outdated and expensive operational methods and tools to enable cost-effective transfer of new methods and tools into operations.

(5) Advancing weather modeling skill, reclaiming and maintaining international leadership in the area of numerical weather prediction, and improving the transition of research into operations by—

(A)   leveraging the weather enterprise to provide expertise on removing barriers to improving numerical weather prediction;

(B)   enabling scientists and engineers to effectively collaborate in areas important for improving operational global numerical weather prediction skill, including model development, data assimilation techniques, systems architecture integration, and computational efficiencies;

(C)   strengthening the National Oceanic and Atmospheric Administration's ability to undertake research projects in pursuit of substantial advancements in weather forecast skill;

(D) utilizing and leverage existing resources across the National Oceanic and Atmospheric Administration enterprise; and

(E) creating a community global weather research modeling system that—

(i) is accessible by the public;

(ii) meets basic end-user requirements for running on public computers and networks located outside of secure National Oceanic and Atmospheric Administration information and technology systems; and

(iii) utilizes, whenever appropriate and cost-effective, innovative strategies and methods, including cloud-based computing capabilities, for hosting and management of part or all of the system described in this subsection.

(c) EXTRAMURAL RESEARCH.—

(1) IN GENERAL.— In carrying out the program under this section, the Assistant Administrator for Oceanic and Atmospheric Research shall collaborate with and support the non-Federal weather research community, which includes institutions of higher education, private entities, and nongovernmental organizations, by making funds available through competitive grants, contracts, and cooperative agreements.

(2) SENSE OF CONGRESS.— It is the sense of Congress that not less than 30 percent of the funds for weather research and development at the Office of Oceanic and Atmospheric Research should be made available for the purpose described in paragraph (1).

(d) ANNUAL REPORT.— Each year, concurrent with the annual budget request submitted by the President to Congress under section 1105 of title 31, United States Code, for the National Oceanic and Atmospheric Administration, the Under Secretary shall submit to Congress a description of current and planned activities under this section.

SEC. 103. [15 U.S.C. 8513] TORNADO WARNING IMPROVEMENT AND EXTENSION PROGRAM.

(a) IN GENERAL.— The Under Secretary, in collaboration with the United States weather industry and academic partners, shall establish a tornado warning improvement and extension program.

(b) GOAL.— The goal of such program shall be to reduce the loss of life and economic losses from tornadoes through the development and extension of accurate, effective, and timely tornado forecasts, predictions, and warnings, including the prediction of tornadoes beyond 1 hour in advance.

(c) INNOVATIVE OBSERVATIONS.— The Under Secretary shall ensure that the program periodically examines the value of incorporating innovative observations, such as acoustic or infrasonic measurements, observations from phased array radars, and observations from mesonets, with respect to the improvement of tornado forecasts, predictions, and warnings.

SEC. 104. [15 U.S.C. 8514] HURRICANE
FORECAST IMPROVEMENT PROGRAM.

Weather Research and Forecasting Innovation
Act of 2017

(d) PROGRAM PLAN.— Not later than 180 days after the date of the enactment of this Act, the Assistant Administrator for Oceanic and Atmospheric Research, in coordination with the Director of the National Weather Service, shall develop a program plan that details the specific research, development, and technology transfer activities, as well as corresponding resources and timelines, necessary to achieve the program goal.

(e) ANNUAL BUDGET FOR PLAN SUBMITTAL.— Following completion of the plan, the Under Secretary, acting through the Assistant Administrator for Oceanic and Atmospheric Research and in coordination with the Director of the National Weather Service, shall, not less frequently than once each year, submit to Congress a proposed budget corresponding with the activities identified in the plan.

SEC. 104. [15 U.S.C. 8514] HURRICANE FORECAST IMPROVEMENT PROGRAM.

(a) IN GENERAL.— The Under Secretary, in collaboration with the United States weather industry and such academic entities as the Administrator considers appropriate, shall maintain a project to improve hurricane forecasting.

(b) GOAL.—The goal of the project maintained under subsection (a) shall be to develop and extend accurate hurricane forecasts and warnings in order to reduce loss of life, injury, and damage to the economy, with a focus on—

(1) improving the prediction of rapid intensification and track of hurricanes;

(2) improving the forecast and communication of storm surges from hurricanes;

(3) incorporating risk communication research to create more effective watch and warning products; and

(4) evaluating and incorporating, as appropriate, innovative observations, including acoustic or infrasonic measurements.

(c) PROJECT PLAN.— Not later than 1 year after the date of the enactment of this Act, the Under Secretary, acting through the Assistant Administrator for Oceanic and Atmospheric Research and in consultation with the Director of the National Weather Service, shall develop a plan for the project maintained under subsection (a) that details the specific research, development, and technology transfer activities, as well as corresponding resources and timelines, necessary to achieve the goal set forth in subsection (b).

SEC. 105. [15 U.S.C. 8515] WEATHER RESEARCH AND DEVELOPMENT PLANNING.

Not later than 1 year after the date of the enactment of this Act, and not less frequently than once each year thereafter, the Under Secretary, acting through the Assistant Administrator for Oceanic and Atmospheric Research and in coordination with the Director of the National Weather Service and the Assistant Administrator for Satellite and Information Services, shall issue a research and development and research to operations plan to restore and maintain United States leadership in numerical weather prediction and forecasting that—

(1) describes the forecasting skill and technology goals, objectives, and progress of the National Oceanic and Atmospheric Administration in carrying out the program conducted under section 102;

(2)   identifies and prioritizes specific research and development activities, and performance metrics, weighted to meet the operational weather and flood-event mission of the National Weather Service to achieve a weather-ready Nation;

(3)   describes how the program will collaborate with stakeholders, including the United States weather industry and academic partners; and

(4)   identifies, through consultation with the National Science Foundation, the United States weather industry, and academic partners, research necessary to enhance the integration of social science knowledge into weather forecast and warning processes, including to improve the communication of threat information necessary to enable improved severe weather planning and decisionmaking on the part of individuals and communities.

SEC. 106. [15 U.S.C. 8516] OBSERVING SYSTEM PLANNING.

The Under Secretary shall—

(1)   develop and maintain a prioritized list of observation data requirements necessary to ensure weather forecasting capabilities to protect life and property to the maximum extent practicable;

(2)   consistent with section 107, utilize Observing System Simulation Experiments, Observing System Experiments, Analyses of Alternatives, and other appropriate assessment tools to ensure continuous systemic evaluations of the observing systems, data, and information needed to meet the requirements of paragraph (1), including options to maximize observational capabilities and their cost-effectiveness;

(3)   identify current and potential future data gaps in observing capabilities related to the requirements listed under paragraph (1); and

(4)   determine a range of options to address gaps identified under paragraph (3).

SEC. 107. [15 U.S.C. 8517] OBSERVING SYSTEM SIMULATION EXPERIMENTS.

(a) IN GENERAL.—In support of the requirements of section 106, the Assistant Administrator for Oceanic and Atmospheric Research shall undertake Observing System Simulation Experiments, or such other quantitative assessments as the Assistant Administrator considers appropriate, to quantitatively assess the relative value and benefits of observing capabilities and systems. Technical and scientific Observing System Simulation Experiment evaluations—

(1) may include assessments of the impact of observing capabilities on—

(A)   global weather prediction;

(B)   hurricane track and intensity forecasting;

(C)   tornado warning lead times and accuracy;

(D)   prediction of mid-latitude severe local storm outbreaks; and

(E)   prediction of storms that have the potential to cause extreme precipitation and flooding lasting from 6 hours to 1 week; and

(2)   shall be conducted in cooperation with other appropriate entities within the National Oceanic and Atmospheric Administration, other Federal agencies, the

United States weather industry, and academic partners to ensure the technical and scientific merit of results from Observing System Simulation Experiments or other appropriate quantitative assessment methodologies.

(b) REQUIREMENTS.—Observing System Simulation Experiments shall quantitatively—

(1) determine the potential impact of proposed space-based, suborbital, and in situ observing systems on analyses and forecasts, including potential impacts on extreme weather events across all parts of the Nation;

(2) evaluate and compare observing system design options; and

(3) assess the relative capabilities and costs of various observing systems and combinations of observing systems in providing data necessary to protect life and property.

(c) IMPLEMENTATION.—Observing System Simulation Experiments—

(1) shall be conducted prior to the acquisition of major Government-owned or Government-leased operational observing systems, including polar-orbiting and geostationary satellite systems, with a lifecycle cost of more than $500,000,000; and

(2) shall be conducted prior to the purchase of any major new commercially provided data with a lifecycle cost of more than $500,000,000.

(d) PRIORITY OBSERVING SYSTEM SIMULATION EXPERIMENTS.—

(1) GLOBAL NAVIGATION SATELLITE SYSTEM RADIO OCCULTATION.— Not later than 30 days after the date of the enactment of this Act, the Assistant Administrator for Oceanic and Atmospheric Research shall complete an Observing System Simulation Experiment to assess the value of data from Global Navigation Satellite System Radio Occultation.

(2) GEOSTATIONARY HYPERSPECTRAL SOUNDER GLOBAL CONSTELLATION.— Not later than 120 days after the date of the enactment of this Act, the Assistant Administrator for Oceanic and Atmospheric Research shall complete an Observing System Simulation Experiment to assess the value of data from a geostationary hyperspectral sounder global constellation.

(e) RESULTS.— Upon completion of all Observing System Simulation Experiments, the Assistant Administrator shall make available to the public the results an assessment of related private and public sector weather data sourcing options, including their availability, affordability, and cost-effectiveness. Such assessments shall be developed in accordance with section 50503 of title 51, United States Code.

SEC. 108. [15 U.S.C. 8518] COMPUTING RESOURCE EFFICIENCY IMPROVEMENT AND ANNUAL REPORT.

(a) COMPUTING RESOURCES.—

(1) IN GENERAL.— In acquiring computing capabilities, including high performance computing technologies and supercomputing technologies, that enable the National Oceanic and Atmospheric Administration to meet its mission requirements, the Under Secretary shall, when appropriate and cost-effective, assess

and prioritize options for entering into multi-year lease agreements for computing capabilities over options for purchasing computing hardware outright.

(2) ACQUISITION.—In carrying out the requirements of paragraph (1), the Under Secretary shall structure multi-year lease agreements in such a manner that the expiration of the lease is set for a date on or around—

(A) the expected degradation point of the computing resources; or

(B) the point at which significantly increased computing capabilities are expected to be available for lease.

(3) PILOT PROGRAMS.—

(A) IN GENERAL.— In order to more efficiently and effectively meet the mission requirements of the National Oceanic and Atmospheric Administration, the Under Secretary may create 1 or more pilot programs for assessing new or innovative information and technology capabilities and services.

(B) PROGRAM REQUIREMENTS.—Any program created under paragraph (3) shall assess only those capabilities and services that—

(i) meet or exceed the standards and requirements of the National Oceanic and Atmospheric Administration, including for processing speed, cybersecurity, and overall reliability; or

(ii) meet or exceed, or are expected to meet or exceed, the performance of similar, in-house information and technology capabilities and services that are owned and operated by the National Oceanic and Atmospheric Administration prior to the establishment of the pilot program.

(C) AUTHORIZATION OF APPROPRIATIONS.— There is authorized to be appropriated, out of funds appropriated to the National Environmental Satellite, Data, and Information Service, to carry out this paragraph $5,000,000 for fiscal year 2019, $10,000,000 for fiscal year 2020, and $5,000,000 for each of fiscal years 2021 through 2023, to remain available until expended.

(b) REPORTS.—Not later than 1 year after the date of enactment of the National Integrated Drought Information System Reauthorization Act of 2018, and triennially thereafter until the date that is 6 years after the date on which the first report is submitted, the Under Secretary, acting through the Chief Information Officer of the National Oceanic and Atmospheric Administration and in coordination with the Assistant Administrator for Oceanic and Atmospheric Research and the Director of the National Weather Service, shall produce and make publicly available a report that explains how the Under Secretary intends—

(1) to continually support upgrades to pursue the fastest, most powerful, and cost-effective high performance computing technologies in support of its weather prediction mission;

(2) to ensure a balance between the research to operations requirements to develop the next generation of regional and global models as well as highly reliable operational models;

(3) to take advantage of advanced development concepts to, as appropriate, make next generation weather prediction models available in beta-test mode to

operational forecasters, the United States weather industry, and partners in academic and Government research;

(4) to use existing computing resources to improve advanced research and operational weather prediction;

(5) to utilize non-Federal contracts to obtain the necessary expertise for advanced weather computing, if appropriate;

(6) to utilize cloud computing; and

(7) to create a long-term strategy to transition the programming language of weather model code to current and broadly-used coding language.

* * * * * * *

SEC. 110. [15 U.S.C. 8519] AUTHORIZATION OF APPROPRIATIONS.

(a) IN GENERAL.—There are authorized to be appropriated to the Office of Oceanic and Atmospheric Research to carry out this title—

(1) $136,516,000 for fiscal year 2019, of which—

(A) $85,758,000 is authorized for weather laboratories and cooperative institutes;

(B) $30,758,000 is authorized for weather and air chemistry research programs; and

(C) $20,000,000 is authorized for the joint technology transfer initiative described in section 102(b)(4);

(2) $148,154,000 for fiscal year 2020, of which—

(A) $87,258,000 is authorized for weather laboratories and cooperative institutes;

(B) $40,896,000 is authorized for weather and air chemistry research programs; and

(C) $20,000,000 is authorized for the joint technology transfer initiative described in section 102(b)(4);

(3) $150,154,000 for fiscal year 2021, of which—

(A) $88,758,000 is authorized for weather laboratories and cooperative institutes;

(B) $41,396,000 is authorized for weather and air chemistry research programs; and

(C) $20,000,000 is authorized for the joint technology transfer initiative described in section 102(b)(4);

(4) $152,154,000 for fiscal year 2022, of which—

(A) $90,258,000 is authorized for weather laboratories and cooperative institutes;

(B) $41,896,000 is authorized for weather and air chemistry research programs; and

(C) $20,000,000 is authorized for the joint technology transfer initiative described in section 102(b)(4); and

(5) $154,154,000 for fiscal year 2023, of which—

(A) $91,758,000 is authorized for weather laboratories and cooperative institutes;

(B) $42,396,000 is authorized for weather and air chemistry research programs; and

(C) $20,000,000 is authorized for the joint technology transfer initiative described in section 102(b)(4).

(b) LIMITATION.— No additional funds are authorized to carry out this title and the amendments made by this title.

* * * * * * *

TITLE III—WEATHER SATELLITE AND DATA INNOVATION

SEC. 301. [15 U.S.C. 8531] NATIONAL OCEANIC AND ATMOSPHERIC ADMINISTRATION SATELLITE AND DATA MANAGEMENT.

(a) SHORT-TERM MANAGEMENT OF ENVIRONMENTAL OBSERVATIONS.—

(1) MICROSATELLITE CONSTELLATIONS.—

(A) IN GENERAL.—The Under Secretary shall complete and operationalize the Constellation Observing System for Meteorology, Ionosphere, and Climate-1 and Climate-2 (COSMIC) in effect on the day before the date of the enactment of this Act—

(i) by deploying constellations of microsatellites in both the equatorial and polar orbits;

(ii) by integrating the resulting data and research into all national operational and research weather forecast models; and

(iii) by ensuring that the resulting data of National Oceanic and Atmospheric Administration's COSMIC-1 and COSMIC-2 programs are free and open to all communities.

(B) ANNUAL REPORTS.— Not less frequently than once each year until the Under Secretary has completed and operationalized the program described in subparagraph (A) pursuant to such subparagraph, the Under Secretary shall submit to Congress a report on the status of the efforts of the Under Secretary to carry out such subparagraph.

(2) INTEGRATION OF OCEAN AND COASTAL DATA FROM THE INTEGRATED OCEAN OBSERVING SYSTEM.—In National Weather Service Regions where the Director of the National Weather Service determines that ocean and coastal data would improve forecasts, the Director, in consultation with the Assistant Administrator for Oceanic

and Atmospheric Research and the Assistant Administrator of the National Ocean Service, shall—

(A) integrate additional coastal and ocean observations, and other data and research, from the Integrated Ocean Observing System (IOOS) into regional weather forecasts to improve weather forecasts and forecasting decision support systems;

(B) support the development of real-time data sharing products and forecast products in collaboration with the regional associations of such system, including contributions from the private sector, academia, and research institutions to ensure timely and accurate use of ocean and coastal data in regional forecasts; and

(C) support increasing use of autonomous, mobile surface, sub-surface, and submarine vehicle ocean and fresh water sensor systems and the infrastructure necessary to share and analyze these data in real-time and feed them into predictive early warning systems.

(3) EXISTING MONITORING AND OBSERVATION-CAPABILITY.— The Under Secretary shall identify degradation of existing monitoring and observation capabilities that could lead to a reduction in forecast quality.

(4) SPECIFICATIONS FOR NEW SATELLITE SYSTEMS OR DATA DETERMINED BY OPERATIONAL NEEDS.— In developing specifications for any satellite systems or data to follow the Joint Polar Satellite System, Geostationary Operational Environmental Satellites, and any other satellites, in effect on the day before the date of enactment of this Act, the Under Secretary shall ensure the specifications are determined to the extent practicable by the recommendations of the reports under subsection (b) of this section.

(b) INDEPENDENT STUDY ON FUTURE OF NATIONAL OCEANIC AND ATMOSPHERIC ADMINISTRATION SATELLITE SYSTEMS AND DATA.—

(1) AGREEMENT.—

(A) IN GENERAL.— The Under Secretary shall seek to enter into an agreement with the National Academy of Sciences to perform the services covered by this subsection.

(B) TIMING.— The Under Secretary shall seek to enter into the agreement described in subparagraph (A) before September 30, 2018.

(2) STUDY.—

(A) IN GENERAL.— Under an agreement between the Under Secretary and the National Academy of Sciences under this subsection, the National Academy of Sciences shall conduct a study on matters concerning future satellite data needs.

(B) ELEMENTS.—In conducting the study under subparagraph (A), the National Academy of Sciences shall—

(i) develop recommendations on how to make the data portfolio of the Administration more robust and cost-effective;

(ii) assess the costs and benefits of moving toward a constellation of many small satellites, standardizing satellite bus design, relying more on the purchasing of data, or acquiring data from other sources or methods;

(iii) identify the environmental observations that are essential to the performance of weather models, based on an assessment of Federal, academic, and private sector weather research, and the cost of obtaining the environmental data;

(iv) identify environmental observations that improve the quality of operational and research weather models in effect on the day before the date of enactment of this Act;

(v) identify and prioritize new environmental observations that could contribute to existing and future weather models; and

(vi) develop recommendations on a portfolio of environmental observations that balances essential, quality-improving, and new data, private and nonprivate sources, and space-based and Earth-based sources.

(C) DEADLINE AND REPORT.— In carrying out the study under subparagraph (A), the National Academy of Sciences shall complete and transmit to the Under Secretary a report containing the findings of the National Academy of Sciences with respect to the study not later than 2 years after the date on which the Administrator enters into an agreement with the National Academy of Sciences under paragraph (1)(A).

(3) ALTERNATE ORGANIZATION.—

(A) IN GENERAL.—If the Under Secretary is unable within the period prescribed in subparagraph (B) of paragraph (1) to enter into an agreement described in subparagraph (A) of such paragraph with the National Academy of Sciences on terms acceptable to the Under Secretary, the Under Secretary shall seek to enter into such an agreement with another appropriate organization that—

(i) is not part of the Federal Government;

(ii) operates as a not-for-profit entity; and

(iii) has expertise and objectivity comparable to that of the National Academy of Sciences.

(B) TREATMENT.— If the Under Secretary enters into an agreement with another organization as described in subparagraph (A), any reference in this subsection to the National Academy of Sciences shall be treated as a reference to the other organization.

(4) AUTHORIZATION OF APPROPRIATIONS.— There are authorized to be appropriated, out of funds appropriated to National Environmental Satellite, Data, and Information Service, to carry out this subsection $1,000,000 for the period encompassing fiscal years 2018 through 2019.

(c) NEXT GENERATION SATELLITE ARCHITECTURE.—

(1) IN GENERAL.—The Under Secretary shall analyze, test, and plan the

procurement of future data sources and satellite architectures, including respective ground system elements, identified in the National Oceanic and Atmospheric Administration's Satellite Observing System Architecture Study that—

(A)   lower the cost of observations used to meet the National Oceanic and Atmospheric Administration's mission requirements;

(B)   disaggregate current satellite systems, where appropriate;

(C)   include new, value-adding technological advancements; and

(D) improve—

(i)   weather and climate forecasting and predictions; and

(ii)   the understanding, management, and exploration of the ocean.

(2) QUANTITATIVE ASSESSMENTS AND PARTNERSHIP AUTHORITY.—In meeting the requirements described in paragraph (1), the Under Secretary—

(A)   may partner with the commercial and academic sectors, non-governmental and not-for-profit organizations, and other Federal agencies; and

(B)   shall, consistent with section 107 of this Act, undertake quantitative assessments for objective analyses, as the Under Secretary considers appropriate, to evaluate relative value and benefits of future data sources and satellite architectures described in paragraph (1).

(d) ADDITIONAL FORMS OF TRANSACTION AUTHORIZED.—

(1) IN GENERAL.—Subject to paragraph (2), in order to enhance the effectiveness of data, satellite, and other observing systems used by the National Oceanic and Atmospheric Administration to meet its missions, the Under Secretary may enter into and perform such transaction agreements on such terms as the Under Secretary considers appropriate to carry out—

(A)   basic, applied, and advanced research projects and ocean exploration missions to meet the objectives described in subparagraphs (A) through (D) of subsection (c)(1); or

(B)   any other type of project to meet other mission objectives, as determined by the Under Secretary.

(2) METHOD AND SCOPE.—

(A) IN GENERAL.— A transaction agreement under paragraph (1) shall be limited to research and development activities.

(B) PERMISSIBLE USES.—A transaction agreement under paragraph (1) may be used—

(i)   for the construction, use, operation, or procurement of new, improved, innovative, or value-adding systems, including satellites, instrumentation, ground stations, data, and data processing;

(ii)   to make determinations on how to best use existing or planned data, systems, and assets of the National Oceanic and Atmospheric Administration; and

(iii)   only when the objectives of the National Oceanic and Atmospheric

Administration cannot be met using a cooperative research and development agreement, grants procurement contract, or cooperative agreement.

(3) TERMINATION OF EFFECTIVENESS.— The authority provided in this subsection terminates effective September 30, 2030.

(e) TRANSPARENCY.— Not later than 60 days after the date that a transaction agreement is made under subsection (d), the Under Secretary shall make publicly available, in a searchable format, on the website of the National Oceanic and Atmospheric Administration all uses of the authority under subsection (d), including an estimate of committed National Oceanic and Atmospheric Administration resources and the expected benefits to National Oceanic and Atmospheric Administration objectives for the transaction agreement, with appropriate redactions for proprietary, sensitive, or classified information.

(f) REPORTS.—

(1) IN GENERAL.— Not later than 90 days after September 30 of each fiscal year through September 30, 2023, the Under Secretary shall submit to the Committee on Commerce, Science, and Transportation of the Senate and the Committee on Science, Space, and Technology of the House of Representatives a report on the use of additional transaction authority by the National Oceanic and Atmospheric Administration during the previous fiscal year.

(2) CONTENTS.—Each report shall include—

(A) for each transaction agreement in effect during the fiscal year covered by the report—

(i) an indication of whether the transaction agreement is a reimbursable, non-reimbursable, or funded agreement;

(ii) a description of—

(I) the subject and terms;

(II) the parties;

(III) the responsible National Oceanic and Atmospheric Administration line office;

(IV) the value;

(V) the extent of the cost sharing among Federal Government and non-Federal sources;

(VI) the duration or schedule; and

(VII) all milestones;

(iii) an indication of whether the transaction agreement was renewed during the previous fiscal year;

(iv) the technology areas in which research projects were conducted under that agreement;

(v) the extent to which the use of that agreement—

(I) has contributed to a broadening of the technology and industrial base available for meeting National Oceanic and Atmospheric

Administration needs; and

(II) has fostered within the technology and industrial base new relationships and practices that support the United States; and

(vi) the total value received by the Federal Government under that agreement for that fiscal year; and

(B) a list of all anticipated reimbursable, non-reimbursable, and funded transaction agreements for the upcoming fiscal year.

(g) RULE OF CONSTRUCTION.— Nothing in this section may be construed as limiting the authority of the National Oceanic and Atmospheric Administration to use cooperative research and development agreements, grants, procurement contracts, or cooperative agreements.

SEC. 302. [15 U.S.C. 8532] COMMERCIAL WEATHER DATA.

(a) DATA AND HOSTED SATELLITE PAYLOADS.—Notwithstanding any other provision of law, the Secretary of Commerce may enter into agreements for—

(1) the purchase of weather data through contracts with commercial providers; and

(2) the placement of weather satellite instruments on cohosted government or private payloads.

(b) STRATEGY.—

(1) IN GENERAL.— Not later than 180 days after the date of the enactment of this Act, the Secretary of Commerce, in consultation with the Under Secretary, shall submit to the Committee on Commerce, Science, and Transportation of the Senate and the Committee on Science, Space, and Technology of the House of Representatives a strategy to enable the procurement of quality commercial weather data. The strategy shall assess the range of commercial opportunities, including public-private partnerships, for obtaining surface-based, aviation-based, and space-based weather observations. The strategy shall include the expected cost-effectiveness of these opportunities as well as provide a plan for procuring data, including an expected implementation timeline, from these nongovernmental sources, as appropriate.

(2) REQUIREMENTS.—The strategy shall include—

(A) an analysis of financial or other benefits to, and risks associated with, acquiring commercial weather data or services, including through multiyear acquisition approaches;

(B) an identification of methods to address planning, programming, budgeting, and execution challenges to such approaches, including—

(i) how standards will be set to ensure that data is reliable and effective;

(ii) how data may be acquired through commercial experimental or innovative techniques and then evaluated for integration into operational use;

(iii) how to guarantee public access to all forecast-critical data to ensure that the United States weather industry and the public continue to have access to information critical to their work; and

    (iv) in accordance with section 50503 of title 51, United States Code, methods to address potential termination liability or cancellation costs associated with weather data or service contracts; and

  (C) an identification of any changes needed in the requirements development and approval processes of the Department of Commerce to facilitate effective and efficient implementation of such strategy.

(3) AUTHORITY FOR AGREEMENTS.— The Assistant Administrator for National Environmental Satellite, Data, and Information Service may enter into multiyear agreements necessary to carry out the strategy developed under this subsection.

(c) PILOT PROGRAM.—

(1) CRITERIA.— Not later than 30 days after the date of the enactment of this Act, the Under Secretary shall publish data and metadata standards and specifications for space-based commercial weather data, including radio occultation data, and, as soon as possible, geostationary hyperspectral sounder data.

(2) PILOT CONTRACTS.—

  (A) CONTRACTS.— Not later than 90 days after the date of enactment of this Act, the Under Secretary shall, through an open competition, enter into at least one pilot contract with one or more private sector entities capable of providing data that meet the standards and specifications set by the Under Secretary for providing commercial weather data in a manner that allows the Under Secretary to calibrate and evaluate the data for its use in National Oceanic and Atmospheric Administration meteorological models.

  (B) ASSESSMENT OF DATA VIABILITY.—Not later than the date that is 3 years after the date on which the Under Secretary enters into a contract under subparagraph (A), the Under Secretary shall assess and submit to the Committee on Commerce, Science, and Transportation of the Senate and the Committee on Science, Space, and Technology of the House of Representatives the results of a determination of the extent to which data provided under the contract entered into under subparagraph (A) meet the criteria published under paragraph (1) and the extent to which the pilot program has demonstrated—

    (i) the viability of assimilating the commercially provided data into National Oceanic and Atmospheric Administration meteorological models;

    (ii) whether, and by how much, the data add value to weather forecasts; and

    (iii) the accuracy, quality, timeliness, validity, reliability, usability, information technology security, and cost-effectiveness of obtaining commercial weather data from private sector providers.

(3) AUTHORIZATION OF APPROPRIATIONS.— For each of fiscal years 2019 through 2023, there are authorized to be appropriated for procurement, acquisition, and construction at the National Environmental Satellite, Data, and Information Service, $6,000,000 to carry out this subsection.

(d) OBTAINING FUTURE DATA.—If an assessment under subsection (c)(2)(B) demonstrates the ability of commercial weather data to meet data and metadata standards and specifications published under subsection (c)(1), the Under Secretary shall—

(1)   where appropriate, cost-effective, and feasible, obtain commercial weather data from private sector providers;

(2)   as early as possible in the acquisition process for any future National Oceanic and Atmospheric Administration meteorological space system, consider whether there is a suitable, cost-effective, commercial capability available or that will be available to meet any or all of the observational requirements by the planned operational date of the system;

(3)   if a suitable, cost-effective, commercial capability is or will be available as described in paragraph (2), determine whether it is in the national interest to develop a governmental meteorological space system; and

(4)   submit to the Committee on Commerce, Science, and Transportation of the Senate and the Committee on Science, Space, and Technology of the House of Representatives a report detailing any determination made under paragraphs (2) and (3).

(e) DATA SHARING PRACTICES.— The Under Secretary shall continue to meet the international meteorological agreements into which the Under Secretary has entered, including practices set forth through World Meteorological Organization Resolution 40.

SEC. 303. [15 U.S.C. 8533] UNNECESSARY DUPLICATION.

In meeting the requirements under this title, the Under Secretary shall avoid unnecessary duplication between public and private sources of data and the corresponding expenditure of funds and employment of personnel.

TITLE IV—FEDERAL WEATHER COORDINATION

SEC. 401. [15 U.S.C. 8541] ENVIRONMENTAL INFORMATION SERVICES WORKING GROUP.

(a) ESTABLISHMENT.—The National Oceanic and Atmospheric Administration Science Advisory Board shall continue to maintain a standing working group named the Environmental Information Services Working Group (in this section referred to as the Working Group)—

(1)   to provide advice for prioritizing weather research initiatives at the National Oceanic and Atmospheric Administration to produce real improvement in weather forecasting;

(2)   to provide advice on existing or emerging technologies or techniques that can be found in private industry or the research community that could be incorporated into forecasting at the National Weather Service to improve forecasting skill;

(3) to identify opportunities to improve—

(A)   communications between weather forecasters, Federal, State, local, tribal, and other emergency management personnel, and the public; and

(B) communications and partnerships among the National Oceanic and Atmospheric Administration and the private and academic sectors; and

(4) to address such other matters as the Science Advisory Board requests of the Working Group.

(b) COMPOSITION.—

(1) IN GENERAL.— The Working Group shall be composed of leading experts and innovators from all relevant fields of science and engineering including atmospheric chemistry, atmospheric physics, meteorology, hydrology, social science, risk communications, electrical engineering, and computer sciences. In carrying out this section, the Working Group may organize into subpanels.

(2) NUMBER.— The Working Group shall be composed of no fewer than 15 members. Nominees for the Working Group may be forwarded by the Working Group for approval by the Science Advisory Board. Members of the Working Group may choose a chair (or co-chairs) from among their number with approval by the Science Advisory Board.

(c) ANNUAL REPORT.— Not less frequently than once each year, the Working Group shall transmit to the Science Advisory Board for submission to the Under Secretary a report on progress made by National Oceanic and Atmospheric Administration in adopting the Working Group's recommendations. The Science Advisory Board shall transmit this report to the Under Secretary. Within 30 days of receipt of such report, the Under Secretary shall submit to the Committee on Commerce, Science, and Transportation of the Senate and the Committee on Science, Space, and Technology of the House of Representatives a copy of such report.

SEC. 402. [15 U.S.C. 8542] INTERAGENCY WEATHER RESEARCH AND FORECAST INNOVATION COORDINATION.

(a) ESTABLISHMENT.—The Director of the Office of Science and Technology Policy shall establish an Interagency Committee for Advancing Weather Services to improve coordination of relevant weather research and forecast innovation activities across the Federal Government. The Interagency Committee shall—

(1) include participation by the National Aeronautics and Space Administration, the Federal Aviation Administration, National Oceanic and Atmospheric Administration and its constituent elements, the National Science Foundation, and such other agencies involved in weather forecasting research as the President determines are appropriate;

(2) identify and prioritize top forecast needs and coordinate those needs against budget requests and program initiatives across participating offices and agencies; and

(3) share information regarding operational needs and forecasting improvements across relevant agencies.

(b) CO-CHAIR.— The Federal Coordinator for Meteorology shall serve as a co-chair of this panel.

(c) FURTHER COORDINATION.— The Director of the Office of Science and Technology Policy shall take such other steps as are necessary to coordinate the activities of the Federal Government with those of the United States weather industry, State governments, emergency managers, and academic researchers.

SEC. 403. [15 U.S.C. 8543] OFFICE OF OCEANIC AND ATMOSPHERIC RESEARCH AND NATIONAL WEATHER SERVICE EXCHANGE PROGRAM.

(a) IN GENERAL.— The Assistant Administrator for Oceanic and Atmospheric Research and the Director of National Weather Service may establish a program to detail Office of Oceanic and Atmospheric Research personnel to the National Weather Service and National Weather Service personnel to the Office of Oceanic and Atmospheric Research.

(b) GOAL.— The goal of this program is to enhance forecasting innovation through regular, direct interaction between the Office of Oceanic and Atmospheric Research's world-class scientists and the National Weather Service's operational staff.

(c) ELEMENTS.— The program shall allow up to 10 Office of Oceanic and Atmospheric Research staff and National Weather Service staff to spend up to 1 year on detail. Candidates shall be jointly selected by the Assistant Administrator for Oceanic and Atmospheric Research and the Director of the National Weather Service.

(d) ANNUAL REPORT.— Not less frequently than once each year, the Under Secretary shall submit to the Committee on Commerce, Science, and Transportation of the Senate and the Committee on Science, Space, and Technology of the House of Representatives a report on participation in such program and shall highlight any innovations that come from this interaction.

SEC. 404. [15 U.S.C. 8544] VISITING FELLOWS AT NATIONAL WEATHER SERVICE.

(a) IN GENERAL.— The Director of the National Weather Service may establish a program to host postdoctoral fellows and academic researchers at any of the National Centers for Environmental Prediction.

(b) GOAL.— This program shall be designed to provide direct interaction between forecasters and talented academic and private sector researchers in an effort to bring innovation to forecasting tools and techniques to the National Weather Service.

(c) SELECTION AND APPOINTMENT.— Such fellows shall be competitively selected and appointed for a term not to exceed 1 year.

SEC. 405. [15 U.S.C. 8545] WARNING COORDINATION METEOROLOGISTS AT WEATHER FORECAST OFFICES OF NATIONAL WEATHER SERVICE.

(a) DESIGNATION OF WARNING COORDINATION METEOROLOGISTS.—

(1) IN GENERAL.— The Director of the National Weather Service shall designate at least one warning coordination meteorologist at each weather forecast office of the National Weather Service.

(2) NO ADDITIONAL EMPLOYEES AUTHORIZED.— Nothing in this section shall be construed to authorize or require a change in the authorized number of full time equivalent employees in the National Weather Service or otherwise result in the employment of any additional employees.

(3) PERFORMANCE BY OTHER EMPLOYEES.— Performance of the responsibilities outlined in this section is not limited to the warning coordination meteorologist

position.

(b) PRIMARY ROLE OF WARNING COORDINATION METEOROLOGISTS.— The primary role of the warning coordination meteorologist shall be to carry out the responsibilities required by this section.

(c) RESPONSIBILITIES.—

(1) IN GENERAL.—Subject to paragraph (2), consistent with the analysis described in section 409, and in order to increase impact-based decision support services, each warning coordination meteorologist designated under subsection (a) shall—

(A) be responsible for providing service to the geographic area of responsibility covered by the weather forecast office at which the warning coordination meteorologist is employed to help ensure that users of products of the National Weather Service can respond effectively to improve outcomes from weather events;

(B) liaise with users of products and services of the National Weather Service, such as the public, media outlets, users in the aviation, marine, and agricultural communities, and forestry, land, and water management interests, to evaluate the adequacy and usefulness of the products and services of the National Weather Service;

(C) collaborate with such weather forecast offices and State, local, and tribal government agencies as the Director considers appropriate in developing, proposing, and implementing plans to develop, modify, or tailor products and services of the National Weather Service to improve the usefulness of such products and services;

(D) ensure the maintenance and accuracy of severe weather call lists, appropriate office severe weather policy or procedures, and other severe weather or dissemination methodologies or strategies; and

(E) work closely with State, local, and tribal emergency management agencies, and other agencies related to disaster management, to ensure a planned, coordinated, and effective preparedness and response effort.

(2) OTHER STAFF.— The Director may assign a responsibility set forth in paragraph (1) to such other staff as the Director considers appropriate to carry out such responsibility.

(d) ADDITIONAL RESPONSIBILITIES.—

(1) IN GENERAL.—Subject to paragraph (2), a warning coordination meteorologist designated under subsection (a) may—

(A) work with a State agency to develop plans for promoting more effective use of products and services of the National Weather Service throughout the State;

(B) identify priority community preparedness objectives;

(C) develop plans to meet the objectives identified under paragraph (2); and

(D) conduct severe weather event preparedness planning and citizen education efforts with and through various State, local, and tribal government agencies and other disaster management-related organizations.

(2) OTHER STAFF.— The Director may assign a responsibility set forth in paragraph (1) to such other staff as the Director considers appropriate to carry out such responsibility.

(e) PLACEMENT WITH STATE AND LOCAL EMERGENCY MANAGERS.—

(1) IN GENERAL.— In carrying out this section, the Director of the National Weather Service may place a warning coordination meteorologist designated under subsection (a) with a State or local emergency manager if the Director considers doing so is necessary or convenient to carry out this section.

(2) TREATMENT.— If the Director determines that the placement of a warning coordination meteorologist placed with a State or local emergency manager under paragraph (1) is near a weather forecast office of the National Weather Service, such placement shall be treated as designation of the warning coordination meteorologist at such weather forecast office for purposes of subsection (a).

SEC. 406. IMPROVING NATIONAL OCEANIC AND ATMOSPHERIC ADMINISTRATION COMMUNICATION OF HAZARDOUS WEATHER AND WATER EVENTS.

(a) PURPOSE OF SYSTEM.— For purposes of the assessment required by subsection (b)(1)(A), the purpose of National Oceanic and Atmospheric Administration system for issuing watches and warnings regarding hazardous weather and water events shall be risk communication to the general public that informs action to prevent loss of life and property.

(b) ASSESSMENT OF SYSTEM.—

(1) IN GENERAL.—Not later than 2 years after the date of the enactment of this Act, the Under Secretary shall—

(A)   assess the National Oceanic and Atmospheric Administration system for issuing watches and warnings regarding hazardous weather and water events; and

(B)   submit to Congress a report on the findings of the Under Secretary with respect to the assessment conducted under subparagraph (A).

(2) ELEMENTS.—The assessment required by paragraph (1)(A) shall include the following:

(A)   An evaluation of whether the National Oceanic and Atmospheric Administration system for issuing watches and warnings regarding hazardous weather and water events meets the purpose described in subsection (a).

(B) Development of recommendations for—

(i)   legislative and administrative action to improve the system described in paragraph (1)(A); and

(ii)   such research as the Under Secretary considers necessary to address the focus areas described in paragraph (3).

(3) FOCUS AREAS.—The assessment required by paragraph (1)(A) shall focus on

the following:

(A)   Ways to communicate the risks posed by hazardous weather or water events to the public that are most likely to result in action to mitigate the risk.

(B)   Ways to communicate the risks posed by hazardous weather or water events to the public as broadly and rapidly as practicable.

(C)   Ways to preserve the benefits of the existing watches and warnings system.

(D)   Ways to maintain the utility of the watches and warnings system for Government and commercial users of the system.

(4) CONSULTATION.—In conducting the assessment required by paragraph (1)(A), the Under Secretary shall—

(A)   consult with such line offices within the National Oceanic and Atmospheric Administration as the Under Secretary considers relevant, including the National Ocean Service, the National Weather Service, and the Office of Oceanic and Atmospheric Research;

(B)   consult with individuals in the academic sector, including individuals in the field of social and behavioral sciences, and other weather services;

(C)   consult with media outlets that will be distributing the watches and warnings;

(D)   consult with non-Federal forecasters that produce alternate severe weather risk communication products;

(E)   consult with emergency planners and responders, including State and local emergency management agencies, and other government users of the watches and warnings system, including the Federal Emergency Management Agency, the Office of Personnel Management, the Coast Guard, and such other Federal agencies as the Under Secretary determines rely on watches and warnings for operational decisions; and

(F)   make use of the services of the National Academy of Sciences, as the Under Secretary considers necessary and practicable, including contracting with the National Research Council to review the scientific and technical soundness of the assessment required by paragraph (1)(A), including the recommendations developed under paragraph (2)(B).

(5) METHODOLOGIES.— In conducting the assessment required by paragraph (1)(A), the Under Secretary shall use such methodologies as the Under Secretary considers are generally accepted by the weather enterprise, including social and behavioral sciences.

(c) IMPROVEMENTS TO SYSTEM.—

(1) IN GENERAL.—The Under Secretary shall, based on the assessment required by subsection (b)(1)(A), make such recommendations to Congress to improve the system as the Under Secretary considers necessary—

(A)   to improve the system for issuing watches and warnings regarding hazardous weather and water events; and

(B) to support efforts to satisfy research needs to enable future improvements to such system.

(2) REQUIREMENTS REGARDING RECOMMENDATIONS.—In carrying out paragraph (1)(A), the Under Secretary shall ensure that any recommendation that the Under Secretary considers a major change—

(A) is validated by social and behavioral science using a generalizable sample;

(B) accounts for the needs of various demographics, vulnerable populations, and geographic regions;

(C) accounts for the differences between types of weather and water hazards;

(D) responds to the needs of Federal, State, and local government partners and media partners; and

(E) accounts for necessary changes to Federally operated watch and warning propagation and dissemination infrastructure and protocols.

(d) WATCHES AND WARNINGS DEFINED.—

(1) IN GENERAL.— Except as provided in paragraph (2), in this section, the terms watch and warning, with respect to a hazardous weather and water event, mean products issued by the Administration, intended for consumption by the general public, to alert the general public to the potential for or presence of the event and to inform action to prevent loss of life and property.

(2) EXCEPTION.— In this section, the terms watch and warning do not include technical or specialized meteorological and hydrological forecasts, outlooks, or model guidance products.

SEC. 407. [15 U.S.C. 8546] NATIONAL OCEANIC AND ATMOSPHERIC ADMINISTRATION WEATHER READY ALL HAZARDS AWARD PROGRAM.

(a) PROGRAM.— The Director of the National Weather Service is authorized to establish the National Oceanic and Atmospheric Administration Weather Ready All Hazards Award Program. This award program shall provide annual awards to honor individuals or organizations that use or provide National Oceanic and Atmospheric Administration Weather Radio All Hazards receivers or transmitters to save lives and protect property. Individuals or organizations that utilize other early warning tools or applications also qualify for this award.

(b) GOAL.— This award program draws attention to the life-saving work of the National Oceanic and Atmospheric Administration Weather Ready All Hazards Program, as well as emerging tools and applications, that provide real-time warning to individuals and communities of severe weather or other hazardous conditions.

(c) PROGRAM ELEMENTS.—

(1) NOMINATIONS.— Nominations for this award shall be made annually by the Weather Field Offices to the Director of the National Weather Service. Broadcast meteorologists, weather radio manufacturers and weather warning tool and application developers, emergency managers, and public safety officials may

nominate individuals or organizations to their local Weather Field Offices, but the final list of award nominees must come from the Weather Field Offices.

(2) SELECTION OF AWARDEES.— Annually, the Director of the National Weather Service shall choose winners of this award whose timely actions, based on National Oceanic and Atmospheric Administration Weather Radio All Hazards receivers or transmitters or other early warning tools and applications, saved lives or property, or demonstrated public service in support of weather or all hazard warnings.

(3) AWARD CEREMONY.— The Director of the National Weather Service shall establish a means of making these awards to provide maximum public awareness of the importance of National Oceanic and Atmospheric Administration Weather Radio, and such other warning tools and applications as are represented in the awards.

SEC. 408. DEPARTMENT OF DEFENSE WEATHER FORECASTING ACTIVITIES.

Not later than 60 days after the date of the enactment of this Act, the Under Secretary shall submit to the Committee on Commerce, Science, and Transportation of the Senate and the Committee on Science, Space, and Technology of the House of Representatives a report analyzing the impacts of the proposed Air Force divestiture in the United States Weather Research and Forecasting Model, including—

(1) the impact on—

 (A) the United States weather forecasting capabilities;

 (B) the accuracy of civilian regional forecasts;

 (C) the civilian readiness for traditional weather and extreme weather events in the United States; and

 (D) the research necessary to develop the United States Weather Research and Forecasting Model; and

(2) such other analysis relating to the divestiture as the Under Secretary considers appropriate.

SEC. 409. NATIONAL WEATHER SERVICE; OPERATIONS AND WORKFORCE ANALYSIS.

The Under Secretary shall contract or continue to partner with an external organization to conduct a baseline analysis of National Weather Service operations and workforce.

SEC. 410. [15 U.S.C. 8547] REPORT ON CONTRACT POSITIONS AT NATIONAL WEATHER SERVICE.

(a) REPORT REQUIRED.— Not later than 180 days after the date of the enactment of this Act, the Under Secretary shall submit to Congress a report on the use of contractors at the National Weather Service for the most recently completed fiscal year.

(b) CONTENTS.—The report required by subsection (a) shall include, with respect to the most recently completed fiscal year, the following:

 (1) The total number of full-time equivalent employees at the National Weather Service, disaggregated by each equivalent level of the General Schedule.

 (2) The total number of full-time equivalent contractors at the National Weather

Service, disaggregated by each equivalent level of the General Schedule that most closely approximates their duties.

(3) The total number of vacant positions at the National Weather Service on the day before the date of enactment of this Act, disaggregated by each equivalent level of the General Schedule.

(4) The five most common positions filled by full-time equivalent contractors at the National Weather Service and the equivalent level of the General Schedule that most closely approximates the duties of such positions.

(5) Of the positions identified under paragraph (4), the percentage of full-time equivalent contractors in those positions that have held a prior position at the National Weather Service or another entity in National Oceanic and Atmospheric Administration.

(6) The average full-time equivalent salary for Federal employees at the National Weather Service for each equivalent level of the General Schedule.

(7) The average salary for full-time equivalent contractors performing at each equivalent level of the General Schedule at the National Weather Service.

(8) A description of any actions taken by the Under Secretary to respond to the issues raised by the Inspector General of the Department of Commerce regarding the hiring of former National Oceanic and Atmospheric Administration employees as contractors at the National Weather Service such as the issues raised in the Investigative Report dated June 2, 2015 (OIG-12-0447).

(c) ANNUAL PUBLICATION.— For each fiscal year after the fiscal year covered by the report required by subsection (a), the Under Secretary shall, not later than 180 days after the completion of the fiscal year, publish on a publicly accessible Internet website the information described in paragraphs (1) through (8) of subsection (b) for such fiscal year.

SEC. 411. WEATHER IMPACTS TO COMMUNITIES AND INFRASTRUCTURE.

(a) REVIEW.—

(1) IN GENERAL.— The Director of the National Weather Service shall review existing research, products, and services that meet the specific needs of the urban environment, given its unique physical characteristics and forecasting challenges.

(2) ELEMENTS.— The review required by paragraph (1) shall include research, products, and services with the potential to improve modeling and forecasting capabilities, taking into account factors including varying building heights, impermeable surfaces, lack of tree canopy, traffic, pollution, and inter-building wind effects.

(b) REPORT AND ASSESSMENT.— Upon completion of the review required by subsection (a), the Under Secretary shall submit to Congress a report on the research, products, and services of the National Weather Service, including an assessment of such research, products, and services that is based on the review, public comment, and recent publications by the National Academy of Sciences.

SEC. 412. [15 U.S.C. 8548] WEATHER ENTERPRISE OUTREACH.

(a) IN GENERAL.—The Under Secretary may establish mechanisms for outreach to the weather enterprise—

(1)   to assess the weather forecasts and forecast products provided by the National Oceanic and Atmospheric Administration; and

(2)   to determine the highest priority weather forecast needs of the community described in subsection (b).

(b) OUTREACH COMMUNITY.—In conducting outreach under subsection (a), the Under Secretary shall contact leading experts and innovators from relevant stakeholders, including the representatives from the following:

(1)   State or local emergency management agencies.

(2)   State agriculture agencies.

(3)   Indian tribes (as defined in section 4 of the Indian Self-Determination and Education Assistance Act (25 U.S.C. 5304)) and Native Hawaiians (as defined in section 6207 of the Elementary and Secondary Education Act of 1965 (20 U.S.C. 7517)).

(4)   The private aerospace industry.

(5)   The private earth observing industry.

(6)   The operational forecasting community.

(7)   The academic community.

(8)   Professional societies that focus on meteorology.

(9)   Such other stakeholder groups as the Under Secretary considers appropriate.

SEC. 413. [15 U.S.C. 8549] HURRICANE HUNTER AIRCRAFT.

(a) BACKUP CAPABILITY.— The Under Secretary shall acquire backup for the capabilities of the WP-3D Orion and G-IV hurricane aircraft of the National Oceanic and Atmospheric Administration that is sufficient to prevent a single point of failure.

(b) AUTHORITY TO ENTER AGREEMENTS.— In order to carry out subsection (a), the Under Secretary shall negotiate and enter into 1 or more agreements or contracts, to the extent practicable and necessary, with governmental and non-governmental entities.

(c) FUTURE TECHNOLOGY.— The Under Secretary shall continue the development of Airborne Phased Array Radar under the United States Weather Research Program.

(d) AUTHORIZATION OF APPROPRIATIONS.— For each of fiscal years 2017 through 2020, support for implementing subsections (a) and (b) is authorized out of funds appropriated to the Office of Marine and Aviation Operations.

SEC. 414. STUDY ON GAPS IN NEXRAD COVERAGE AND RECOMMENDATIONS TO ADDRESS SUCH GAPS.

(a) STUDY ON GAPS IN NEXRAD COVERAGE.—

(1) IN GENERAL.— Not later than 180 days after the date of the enactment of this Act, the Secretary of Commerce shall complete a study on gaps in the coverage of the Next Generation Weather Radar of the National Weather Service (NEXRAD).

(2) ELEMENTS.—In conducting the study required under paragraph (1), the Secretary shall—

(A) identify areas in the United States where limited or no NEXRAD coverage has resulted in—

(i) instances in which no or insufficient warnings were given for hazardous weather events, including tornadoes; or

(ii) degraded forecasts for hazardous weather events that resulted in fatalities, significant injuries, or substantial property damage; and

(B) for the areas identified under subparagraph (A)—

(i) identify the key weather effects for which prediction would improve with improved radar detection;

(ii) identify additional sources of observations for high impact weather that were available and operational for such areas on the day before the date of the enactment of this Act, including dense networks of x-band radars, Terminal Doppler Weather Radar (commonly known as TDWR), air surveillance radars of the Federal Aviation Administration, and cooperative network observers;

(iii) assess the feasibility and advisability of efforts to integrate and upgrade Federal radar capabilities that are not owned or controlled by the National Oceanic and Atmospheric Administration, including radar capabilities of the Federal Aviation Administration and the Department of Defense;

(iv) assess the feasibility and advisability of incorporating State-operated and other non-Federal radars into the operations of the National Weather Service;

(v) identify options to improve hazardous weather detection and forecasting coverage; and

(vi) provide the estimated cost of, and timeline for, each of the options identified under clause (v).

(3) REPORT.— Upon the completion of the study required under paragraph (1), the Secretary shall submit to the Committee on Commerce, Science, and Transportation of the Senate and the Committee on Science, Space, and Technology of the House of Representatives a report that includes the findings of the Secretary with respect to the study.

(b) RECOMMENDATIONS TO IMPROVE RADAR COVERAGE.— Not later than 90 days after the completion of the study under subsection (a)(1), the Secretary of Commerce shall submit to the congressional committees referred to in subsection (a)(3) recommendations for improving hazardous weather detection and forecasting coverage in the areas identified under subsection (a)(2)(A) by integrating additional observation solutions to the extent practicable and meteorologically justified and necessary to protect public safety.

(c) THIRD-PARTY CONSULTATION REGARDING RECOMMENDATIONS TO IMPROVE RADAR COVERAGE.— The Secretary of Commerce may seek reviews by, or consult with, appropriate third parties regarding the scientific methodology relating to, and the feasibility and advisability of implementing, the recommendations submitted under subsection (b), including the extent to which warning and forecast services of the National Weather Service would be improved by additional observations.

TITLE V—TSUNAMI WARNING, EDUCATION, AND RESEARCH ACT OF 2017

SEC. 501. [33 U.S.C. 3201 note] SHORT TITLE.

This title may be cited as the "Tsunami Warning, Education, and Research Act of 2017".

SEC. 502. REFERENCES TO THE TSUNAMI WARNING AND EDUCATION ACT.

Except as otherwise expressly provided, whenever in this title an amendment or repeal is expressed in terms of an amendment to, or repeal of, a section or other provision, the reference shall be considered to be made to a section or other provision of the Tsunami Warning and Education Act enacted as title VIII of the Magnuson-Stevens Fishery Conservation and Management Reauthorization Act of 2006 (Public Law 109-479; 33 U.S.C. 3201 et seq.).

* * * * * * *

SEC. 505. MODIFICATION OF NATIONAL TSUNAMI HAZARD MITIGATION PROGRAM.

(a) IN GENERAL.— Section 805(a) (33 U.S.C. 3204(a)) is amended to read as follows:

"(a) PROGRAM REQUIRED.— The Administrator, in coordination with the Administrator of the Federal Emergency Management Agency and the heads of such other agencies as the Administrator considers relevant, shall conduct a community-based tsunami hazard mitigation program to improve tsunami preparedness and resiliency of at-risk areas in the United States and the territories of the United States.".

(b) NATIONAL TSUNAMI HAZARD MITIGATION PROGRAM.— Section 805 (33 U.S.C. 3204) is amended by striking subsections (c) and (d) and inserting the following:

"(c) PROGRAM COMPONENTS.—The Program conducted under subsection (a) shall include the following:

"(1) Technical and financial assistance to coastal States, territories, tribes, and local governments to develop and implement activities under this section.

"(2) Integration of tsunami preparedness and mitigation programs into ongoing State-based hazard warning, resilience planning, and risk management activities, including predisaster planning, emergency response, evacuation planning, disaster recovery, hazard mitigation, and community development and redevelopment planning programs in affected areas.

"(3) Coordination with other Federal preparedness and mitigation programs to leverage Federal investment, avoid duplication, and maximize effort.

"(4) Activities to promote the adoption of tsunami resilience, preparedness, warning, and mitigation measures by Federal, State, territorial, tribal, and local governments and nongovernmental entities, including educational and risk communication programs to discourage development in high-risk areas.

"(5) Activities to support the development of regional tsunami hazard and risk assessments. Such regional risk assessments may include the following:

"(A)   The sources, sizes, and other relevant historical data of tsunami in the region, including paleotsunami data.

"(B)   Inundation models and maps of critical infrastructure and socioeconomic vulnerability in areas subject to tsunami inundation.

"(C)   Maps of evacuation areas and evacuation routes, including, when appropriate, traffic studies that evaluate the viability of evacuation routes.

"(D)   Evaluations of the size of populations that will require evacuation, including populations with special evacuation needs.

"(E)   Evaluations and technical assistance for vertical evacuation structure planning for communities where models indicate limited or no ability for timely evacuation, especially in areas at risk of near shore generated tsunami.

"(F)   Evaluation of at-risk ports and harbors.

"(G)   Evaluation of the effect of tsunami currents on the foundations of closely-spaced, coastal high-rise structures.

"(6) Activities to promote preparedness in at-risk ports and harbors, including the following:

"(A)   Evaluation and recommendation of procedures for ports and harbors in the event of a distant or near-field tsunami.

"(B)   A review of readiness, response, and communication strategies to ensure coordination and data sharing with the Coast Guard.

"(7) Activities to support the development of community-based outreach and education programs to ensure community readiness and resilience, including the following:

"(A)   The development, implementation, and assessment of technical training and public education programs, including education programs that address unique characteristics of distant and near-field tsunami.

"(B)   The development of decision support tools.

"(C)   The incorporation of social science research into community readiness and resilience efforts.

"(D)   The development of evidence-based education guidelines.

"(8) Dissemination of guidelines and standards for community planning, education, and training products, programs, and tools, including—

"(A) standards for—

"(i)   mapping products;

"(ii)   inundation models; and

"(iii)   effective emergency exercises; and

"(B)   recommended guidance for at-risk port and harbor tsunami warning, evacuation, and response procedures in coordination with the Coast Guard and the Federal Emergency Management Agency.

"(d) AUTHORIZED ACTIVITIES.—In addition to activities conducted under subsection (c), the program conducted under subsection (a) may include the following:

"(1)   Multidisciplinary vulnerability assessment research, education, and training to help integrate risk management and resilience objectives with community development planning and policies.

"(2)   Risk management training for local officials and community organizations to enhance understanding and preparedness.

"(3)   In coordination with the Federal Emergency Management Agency, interagency, Federal, State, tribal, and territorial intergovernmental tsunami response exercise planning and implementation in high risk areas.

"(4)   Development of practical applications for existing or emerging technologies, such as modeling, remote sensing, geospatial technology, engineering, and observing systems, including the integration of tsunami sensors into Federal and commercial submarine telecommunication cables if practicable.

"(5) Risk management, risk assessment, and resilience data and information services, including—

"(A)   access to data and products derived from observing and detection systems; and

"(B)   development and maintenance of new integrated data products to support risk management, risk assessment, and resilience programs.

"(6)   Risk notification systems that coordinate with and build upon existing systems and actively engage decisionmakers, State, local, tribal, and territorial governments and agencies, business communities, nongovernmental organizations, and the media.

"(e) NO PREEMPTION WITH RESPECT TO DESIGNATION OF AT-RISK AREAS.— The establishment of national standards for inundation models under this section shall not prevent States, territories, tribes, and local governments from designating additional areas as being at risk based on knowledge of local conditions.

"(f) NO NEW REGULATORY AUTHORITY.— Nothing in this Act may be construed as establishing new regulatory authority for any Federal agency.".

(c) REPORT ON ACCREDITATION OF TSUNAMIREADY PROGRAM.— Not later than 180 days after the date of enactment of this Act, the Administrator of the National Oceanic and Atmospheric Administration shall submit to the Committee on Commerce, Science, and Transportation of the Senate and the Committee on Science, Space, and Technology of the House of Representatives a report on which authorities and activities would be needed to have the TsunamiReady program of the National Weather Service accredited by the Emergency Management Accreditation Program.

* * * * * * *

SEC. 509. REPORTS.

(a) REPORT ON IMPLEMENTATION OF TSUNAMI WARNING AND EDUCATION ACT.—

(1) IN GENERAL.— Not later than 1 year after the date of the enactment of this Act, the Administrator of the National Oceanic and Atmospheric Administration shall submit to Congress a report on the implementation of the Tsunami Warning and Education Act enacted as title VIII of the Magnuson- Stevens Fishery Conservation and Management Reauthorization Act of 2006 (Public Law 109-479; 33 U.S.C. 3201 et seq.), as amended by this Act.

(2) ELEMENTS.—The report required by paragraph (1) shall include the following:

(A) A detailed description of the progress made in implementing sections 804(d)(6), 805(b), and 806(b)(4) of the Tsunami Warning and Education Act the Magnuson-Stevens Fishery Conservation and Management Reauthorization Act of 2006 (Public Law 109-479; 33 U.S.C. 3201 et seq.).

(B) A description of the ways that tsunami warnings and warning products issued by the Tsunami Forecasting and Warning Program established under section 804 of the Tsunami Warning and Education Act (33 U.S.C. 3203), as amended by this Act, may be standardized and streamlined with warnings and warning products for hurricanes, coastal storms, and other coastal flooding events.

(b) REPORT ON NATIONAL EFFORTS THAT SUPPORT RAPID RESPONSE FOLLOWING NEAR-SHORE TSUNAMI EVENTS.—

(1) IN GENERAL.— Not later than 1 year after the date of the enactment of this Act, the Administrator and the Secretary of Homeland Security shall jointly, in coordination with the Director of the United States Geological Survey, Administrator of the Federal Emergency Management Agency, the Chief of the National Guard Bureau, and the heads of such other Federal agencies as the Administrator considers appropriate, submit to the appropriate committees of Congress a report on the national efforts in effect on the day before the date of the enactment of this Act that support and facilitate rapid emergency response following a domestic near-shore tsunami event to better understand domestic effects of earthquake derived tsunami on people, infrastructure, and communities in the United States.

(2) ELEMENTS.—The report required by paragraph (1) shall include the following:

(A) A description of scientific or other measurements collected on the day before the date of the enactment of this Act to quickly identify and quantify lost or degraded infrastructure or terrestrial formations.

(B)   A description of scientific or other measurements that would be necessary to collect to quickly identify and quantify lost or degraded infrastructure or terrestrial formations.

(C)   Identification and evaluation of Federal, State, local, tribal, territorial, and military first responder and search and rescue operation centers, bases, and other facilities as well as other critical response assets and infrastructure, including search and rescue aircraft, located within near-shore and distant tsunami inundation areas on the day before the date of the enactment of this Act.

(D)   An evaluation of near-shore tsunami response plans in areas described in subparagraph (C) in effect on the day before the date of the enactment of this Act, and how those response plans would be affected by the loss of search and rescue and first responder infrastructure described in such subparagraph.

(E)   A description of redevelopment plans and reports in effect on the day before the date of the enactment of this Act for communities in areas that are at high-risk for near-shore tsunami, as well identification of States or communities that do not have redevelopment plans.

(F)   Recommendations to enhance near-shore tsunami preparedness and response plans, including recommended responder exercises, predisaster planning, and mitigation needs.

(G)   Such other data and analysis information as the Administrator and the Secretary of Homeland Security consider appropriate.

(3)   APPROPRIATE COMMITTEES OF CONGRESS.—In this subsection, the term appropriate committees of Congress means—

(A)   the Committee on Commerce, Science, and Transportation and the Committee on Homeland Security and Governmental Affairs of the Senate; and

(B)   the Committee on Science, Space, and Technology, the Committee on Homeland Security, and the Committee on Transportation and Infrastructure of the House of Representatives.

* * * * * * *

SEC. 511. [33 U.S.C. 3208] OUTREACH RESPONSIBILITIES.

The Administrator of the National Oceanic and Atmospheric Administration, in coordination with State and local emergency managers, shall develop and carry out formal outreach activities to improve tsunami education and awareness and foster the development of resilient communities. Outreach activities may include—

(1)   the development of outreach plans to ensure the close integration of tsunami warning centers supported or maintained under section 804(d) of the Tsunami Warning and Education Act (33 U.S.C. 3203(d)), as amended by this Act, with local Weather Forecast Offices of the National Weather Service and emergency managers;

(2)   working with appropriate local Weather Forecast Offices to ensure they have

the technical knowledge and capability to disseminate tsunami warnings to the communities they serve; and

(3) evaluating the effectiveness of warnings and of coordination with local Weather Forecast Offices after significant tsunami events.

SEC. 512. REPEAL OF DUPLICATE PROVISIONS OF LAW.

(a) [33 U.S.C. 3201] REPEAL.— The Tsunami Warning and Education Act enacted by Public Law 109-424 (120 Stat. 2902) is repealed.

(b) [33 U.S.C. 3201 note] CONSTRUCTION.— Nothing in this section may be construed to repeal, or affect in any way, the Tsunami Warning and Education Act enacted as title VIII of the Magnuson-Stevens Fishery Conservation and Management Reauthorization Act of 2006 (Public Law 109-479; 33 U.S.C. 3201 et seq.).

★

Foundational Emergency Management Laws

Robert T. Stafford Disaster Relief and Emergency Assistance Act

42 U.S.C. Ch. 68–Disaster Relief

Disaster Mitigation Act of 2000

Post-Katrina Emergency Management Reform Act of 2006

Sandy Recovery Improvement Act of 2013

Consolidated and Further Continuing Appropriations Act, 2013

Consolidated Appropriations Act, 2016

Additional Supplemental Appropriations for Disaster Relief Requirements Act of 2017

Hazard-Specific Laws–Floods

National Flood Insurance Act of 1968

Biggert-Waters Flood Insurance Reform Act of 2012

Homeowner Flood Insurance Affordability Act of 2014

Hazard-Specific Laws –Earthquakes

Earthquake Hazards Reduction Act of 1977

National Earthquake Hazards Reduction Program Reauthorization Act of 2018

Hazard-Specific Laws –Dams

National Dam Safety Program Act

Hazard-Specific Laws –Fires

Federal Fire Prevention and Control Act of 1974

United States Fire Administration, AFG, and SAFER Program Reauthorization Act of 2017

Hazard-Specific Laws –Hazardous Materials / Chemical / Radiological

Comprehensive Environmental Response, Compensation, and Liability Act of 1980 §109

Emergency Planning and Community Right-To-Know Act of 1986 §303

Department of Defense Authorization Act, 1986

Radiological Emergency Preparedness Fund

49 U.S.C. §5115 and §5116

Infrastructure and Transportation Resilience

FAA Reauthorization Act of 2018

MAP–21 §20017(b)

23 U.S.C. §125–Emergency Relief

49 U.S.C. §5324 Public Transportation Emergency Relief Program Provisions

National Security and Defense Authorities

The Defense Production Act of 1950

National Security Act of 1947 §303

National Emergencies Act

Act of August 18, 1941 §5

Communications Act of 1934

Homeland Security and FEMA Provisions

Department of Homeland Security Appropriations Act, 2015

FEMA Accountability, Modernization and Transparency Act of 2017

Integrated Public Alert and Warning System Modernization Act of 2015

Cybersecurity and Infrastructure Security Agency Act of 2018

Community Support Programs

McKinney-Vento Homeless Assistance Act

Directing Dollars to Disaster Relief Act of 2015

Research, Forecasting, and Innovation

Weather Research and Forecasting Innovation Act of 2017

www.ingramcontent.com/pod-product-compliance
Lightning Source LLC
Chambersburg PA
CBHW070046030426
42335CB00016B/1809